# ALTERNATIVE INVESTMENTS, RISK MANAGEMENT, AND THE APPLICATION OF DERIVATIVES

CFA® PROGRAM CURRICULUM
2013 • Level III • Volume 5

D1295499

WILEY
John Wiley & Sons, Inc.

ISBN 978-1-937537-16-6 (paper)
ISBN 978-1-937537-37-1 (ebk)

10  9  8  7  6  5  4  3  2  1

Please visit our website at
www.WileyGlobalFinance.com.

# Contents

indicates an optional segment

◙ indicates an optional segment

◙ indicates an optional segment

# How to Use the CFA Program Curriculum

Congratulations on passing Level II of the Chartered Financial Analyst (CFA®) Program. This exciting and rewarding program of study reflects your desire to become a serious investment professional. You are embarking on a program noted for its high ethical standards and the breadth of knowledge, skills, and abilities it develops. Your commitment to the CFA Program should be educationally and professionally rewarding.

The credential you seek is respected around the world as a mark of accomplishment and dedication. Each level of the program represents a distinct achievement in professional development. Successful completion of the program is rewarded with membership in a prestigious global community of investment professionals. CFA charterholders are dedicated to life-long learning and maintaining currency with the ever-changing dynamics of a challenging profession. The CFA Program represents the first step towards a career-long commitment to professional education.

The CFA examination measures your mastery of the core skills required to succeed as an investment professional. These core skills are the basis for the Candidate Body of Knowledge (CBOK™). The CBOK consists of four components:

- A broad topic outline that lists the major top-level topic areas (CBOK Topic Outline)
- Topic area weights that indicate the relative exam weightings of the top-level topic areas
- Learning outcome statements (LOS) that advise candidates about the specific knowledge, skills, and abilities they should acquire from readings covering a topic area (LOS are provided in candidate study sessions and at the beginning of each reading)
- The CFA Program curriculum, readings, and end-of-reading questions, which candidates receive upon exam registration

Therefore, the keys to your success on the CFA exam is studying and understanding the CBOK™. The following sections provide background on the CBOK, the organization of the curriculum, and tips for developing an effective study program.

## CURRICULUM DEVELOPMENT PROCESS

The CFA Program is grounded in the practice of the investment profession. Using the Global Body of Investment Knowledge (GBIK) collaborative website, CFA Institute performs a continuous practice analysis with investment professionals around the world to determine the knowledge, skills, and abilities (competencies) that are relevant to the profession. Regional expert panels and targeted surveys are conducted annually to verify and reinforce the continuous feedback from the GBIK collaborative website. The practice analysis process ultimately defines the CBOK. The CBOK contains the competencies that are generally accepted and applied by investment professionals. These competencies are used in practice in a generalist context and are expected to be demonstrated by a recently qualified CFA charterholder.

A committee consisting of practicing charterholders, in conjunction with CFA Institute staff, designs the CFA Program curriculum in order to deliver the CBOK to candidates. The examinations, also written by practicing charterholders, are designed to allow you to demonstrate your mastery of the CBOK as set forth in the CFA Program curriculum. As you structure your personal study program, you should emphasize mastery of the CBOK and the practical application of that knowledge. For more information on the practice analysis, CBOK, and development of the CFA Program curriculum, please visit www.cfainstitute.org.

## ORGANIZATION OF THE CURRICULUM

The Level III CFA Program curriculum is organized into 10 topic areas. Each topic area begins with a brief statement of the material and the depth of knowledge expected.

Each topic area is then divided into one or more study sessions. These study sessions—18 sessions in the Level III curriculum—should form the basic structure of your reading and preparation.

Each study session includes a statement of its structure and objective, and is further divided into specific reading assignments. An outline illustrating the organization of these 18 study sessions can be found at the front of each volume.

*The reading assignments are the basis for all examination questions, and are selected or developed specifically to teach the knowledge, skills, and abilities reflected in the CBOK.* These readings are drawn from CFA Institute-commissioned content, textbook chapters, professional journal articles, research analyst reports, and cases. All readings include problems and solutions to help you understand and master the topic areas.

Reading-specific Learning Outcome Statements (LOS) are listed at the beginning of each reading. These LOS indicate what you should be able to accomplish after studying the reading. The LOS, the reading, and the end-of-reading questions are dependent on each other, with the reading and questions providing context for understanding the scope of the LOS.

You should use the LOS to guide and focus your study, as each examination question is based on an assigned reading and one or more LOS. The readings provide context for the LOS and enable you to apply a principle or concept in a variety of scenarios. The candidate is responsible for the entirety of all of the required material in a study session, the assigned readings as well as the end-of-reading questions and problems.

We encourage you to review the material on LOS (http://www.cfainstitute.org/cfaprogram/courseofstudy/Pages/cfa_los.aspx), including the descriptions of LOS "command words," (www.cfainstitute.org/Documents/cfa_and_cipm_los_command_words.pdf).

## FEATURES OF THE CURRICULUM

OPTIONAL
SEGMENT

- **Required vs. Optional Segments** - You should read all of an assigned reading. In some cases, however, we have reprinted an entire chapter or article and marked certain parts of the reading as "optional." The CFA examination is based only on the required segments, and the optional segments are included only when they might help you to better understand the required segments (by seeing the required material in its full context). When an optional segment begins, you will see text and a dashed vertical bar in the outside margin that will continue until the optional segment ends, accompanied by another icon. *Unless the material is specifically marked as optional, you should assume it is required.* You should rely on the required segments and the reading-specific LOS in preparing for the examination.

END OPTIONAL
SEGMENT

- **Problems/Solutions** - *All questions and problems in the readings as well as their solutions (which are provided directly following the problems) are part of the curriculum and are required material for the exam.* When appropriate, we have included problems within and after the readings to demonstrate practical application and reinforce your understanding of the concepts presented. The questions and problems are designed to help you learn these concepts and may serve as a basis for exam questions. Many of these questions are adapted from past CFA examinations.

- **Margins** - The wide margins in each volume provide space for your note-taking.

- **Six-Volume Structure** - For portability of the curriculum, the material is spread over six volumes.

- **Glossary and Index** - For your convenience, we have printed a comprehensive glossary and index in each volume. Throughout the curriculum, a **bolded blue** word in a reading denotes a term defined in the glossary.

- **Source Material** - The authorship, publisher, and copyright owners are given for each reading for your reference. We recommend that you use this CFA Institute curriculum rather than the original source materials because the curriculum may include only selected pages from outside readings, updated sections within the readings, and contains problems and solutions tailored to the CFA Program.

- **LOS Self-Check** - We have inserted checkboxes next to each LOS that you can use to track your progress in mastering the concepts in each reading.

# DESIGNING YOUR PERSONAL STUDY PROGRAM

**Create a Schedule** - An orderly, systematic approach to examination preparation is critical. You should dedicate a consistent block of time every week to reading and studying. Complete all reading assignments and the associated problems and solutions in each study session. Review the LOS both before and after you study each reading to ensure that you have mastered the applicable content and can demonstrate the knowledge, skill, or ability described by the LOS and the assigned reading. Use the LOS self-check to track your progress and highlight areas of weakness for later review.

As you prepare for your exam, we will e-mail you important exam updates, testing policies, and study tips. Be sure to read these carefully. Curriculum errata are periodically updated and posted on the study session page at www.cfainstitute.org. You may also sign up for an RSS feed to alert you to the latest errata update.

Successful candidates report an average of over 300 hours preparing for each exam. Your preparation time will vary based on your prior education and experience. For each level of the curriculum, there are 18 study sessions, so a good plan is to devote 15–20 hours per week, for 18 weeks, to studying the material. Use the final four to six weeks before the exam to review what you've learned and practice with sample and mock exams. This recommendation, however, may underestimate the hours needed for appropriate examination preparation depending on your individual circumstances, relevant experience, and academic background. You will undoubtedly adjust your study time to conform to your own strengths and weaknesses, and your educational and professional background.

You will probably spend more time on some study sessions than on others, but on average you should plan on devoting 15-20 hours per study session. You should allow ample time for both in-depth study of all topic areas and additional concentration on those topic areas for which you feel least prepared.

**Online Sample Examinations** - CFA Institute online sample examinations are intended to assess your exam preparation as you progress toward the end of your study. After each question, you will receive immediate feedback noting the correct response and indicating the relevant assigned reading, so you will be able to identify areas of weakness for further study. The 120-minute sample examinations reflect the question formats, topics, and level of difficulty of the actual CFA examinations. Aggregate data indicate that the CFA examination pass rate was higher among candidates who took one or more online sample examinations than among candidates who did not take the online sample examinations. For more information on the online sample examinations, please visit www.cfainstitute.org.

**Online Mock Examinations** - In response to candidate requests, CFA Institute has developed mock examinations that mimic the actual CFA examinations not only in question format and level of difficulty, but also in length and topic weight. The three-hour online mock exams simulate the morning and afternoon sessions of the actual CFA exam, and are intended to be taken after you complete your study of the full curriculum, so you can test your understanding of the CBOK and your readiness for the exam. The mock exams are available in a printable PDF format with feedback provided at the end of the exam, rather than after each question as with the sample exams. CFA Institute recommends that you take these mock exams at the final stage of your preparation toward the actual CFA examination. For more information on the online mock examinations, please visit www.cfainstitute.org.

**Preparatory Providers** - After you enroll in the CFA Program, you may receive numerous solicitations for preparatory courses and review materials. When considering a prep course make sure the provider is in compliance with the CFA Institute Prep Provider Guidelines Program (www.cfainstitute.org/partners/examprep/Pages/cfa_prep_provider_guidelines.aspx). Just remember, there are no shortcuts to success on the CFA examinations; reading and studying the CFA curriculum is the key to success on the examination. The CFA examinations reference only the CFA Institute assigned curriculum—no preparatory course or review course materials are consulted or referenced.

## SUMMARY

Every question on the CFA examination is based on the content contained in the required readings and on one or more LOS. Frequently, an examination question is based on a specific example highlighted within a reading or on a specific end-of-reading question and/or problem and its solution. To make effective use of the CFA Program curriculum, please remember these key points:

1. All pages printed in the curriculum are required reading for the examination except for occasional sections marked as optional. You may read optional pages as background, but you will not be tested on them.

2. All questions, problems, and their solutions - printed at the end of readings - are part of the curriculum and are required study material for the examination.

3. You should make appropriate use of the online sample/mock examinations and other resources available at www.cfainstitute.org.

4. You should schedule and commit sufficient study time to cover the 18 study sessions, review the materials, and take sample/mock examinations.

5. **Note:** Some of the concepts in the study sessions may be superseded by updated rulings and/or pronouncements issued after a reading was published. Candidates are expected to be familiar with the overall analytical framework contained in the assigned readings. Candidates are not responsible for changes that occur after the material was written.

## FEEDBACK

At CFA Institute, we are committed to delivering a comprehensive and rigorous curriculum for the development of competent, ethically grounded investment professionals. We rely on candidate and member feedback as we work to incorporate content, design, and packaging improvements. You can be assured that we will continue to listen to your suggestions. Please send any comments or feedback to curriculum@cfainstitute.org. Ongoing improvements in the curriculum will help you prepare for success on the upcoming examinations, and for a lifetime of learning as a serious investment professional.

# Portfolio Management

## STUDY SESSIONS

This volume includes Study Sessions 13–15.

## TOPIC LEVEL LEARNING OUTCOME

The candidate should be able to prepare an appropriate investment policy statement and asset allocation; formulate strategies for managing, monitoring, and rebalancing investment portfolios; evaluate portfolio performance; and analyze a presentation of investment returns for consistency with Global Investment Performance Standards (GIPS®).

# 13

# Alternative Investments for Portfolio Management

**A**lternative investments comprise groups of investments with risk and return characteristics that differ markedly from those of traditional stock and bond investments. Common features of alternative investments include:

1. relative illiquidity, which tends to be associated with a return premium as compensation;

2. diversifying potential relative to a portfolio of stocks and bonds;

3. high due diligence costs; and

4. performance appraisal that is unusually difficult, due in part to the complexity of establishing valid benchmarks.

Many institutional and high-net-worth individuals make portfolio allocations to alternative investments that are comparable in size to those they make to the traditional asset classes of stocks and bonds. In doing so, such investors may be seeking risk diversification and/or greater opportunities to apply active management skills and capture alpha. Portfolio managers who take advantage of the opportunities presented by alternative investments may have a substantial advantage over those who do not.

The first reading presents an overview of the investment classes generally considered alternative investments. The balance of the study session examines the role of swaps, forwards, and futures in managing certain alternative investments.

## READING ASSIGNMENTS

**Reading 31** *Alternative Investments Portfolio Management*

> *Managing Investment Portfolios: A Dynamic Process*, Third Edition, John L. Maginn, CFA, Donald L. Tuttle, CFA, Jerald E. Pinto, CFA, and Dennis W. McLeavey, CFA, editors

# 31

# Alternative Investments Portfolio Management

*by Jot K. Yau, CFA, Thomas Schneeweis, Thomas R. Robinson, CFA, and Lisa R. Weiss, CFA*

## LEARNING OUTCOMES

| Mastery | The candidate should be able to: |
|---|---|
| ☐ | **a** describe common features of alternative investments and their markets and how alternative investments may be grouped by the role they typically play in a portfolio; |
| ☐ | **b** explain and justify the major due diligence checkpoints involved in selecting active managers of alternative investments; |
| ☐ | **c** explain the special issues that alternative investments raise for investment advisers of private wealth clients; |
| ☐ | **d** distinguish among the principal classes of alternative investments, including real estate, private equity, commodity investments, hedge funds, managed futures, buyout funds, infrastructure funds, and distressed securities; |
| ☐ | **e** discuss the construction and interpretation of benchmarks and the problem of benchmark bias in alternative investment groups; |
| ☐ | **f** evaluate the return enhancement and/or risk diversification effects of adding an alternative investment to a reference portfolio (for example, a portfolio invested solely in common equity and bonds); |
| ☐ | **g** describe the advantages and disadvantages of direct equity investments in real estate; |
| ☐ | **h** discuss the major issuers and suppliers of venture capital, the stages through which private companies pass (seed stage through exit), the characteristic sources of financing at each stage, and the purpose of such financing; |
| ☐ | **i** compare venture capital funds and buyout funds; |
| ☐ | **j** discuss the use of convertible preferred stock in direct venture capital investment; |
| ☐ | **k** explain the typical structure of a private equity fund, including the compensation to the fund's sponsor (general partner) and typical timelines; |

*Managing Investment Portfolios: A Dynamic Process,* Third Edition, John L. Maginn, CFA, Donald L. Tuttle, CFA, Jerald E. Pinto, CFA, and Dennis W. McLeavey, CFA, editors. Copyright © 2007 by CFA Institute.

| Mastery | The candidate should be able to: |
|---------|----------------------------------|
| ☐ | l discuss the issues that must be addressed in formulating a private equity investment strategy; |
| ☐ | m compare indirect and direct commodity investment; |
| ☐ | n explain the three components of return for a commodity futures contract and the effect that an upward- or downward-sloping term structure of futures prices will have on roll yield; |
| ☐ | o describe the principle roles suggested for commodities in a portfolio and explain why some commodity classes may provide a better hedge against inflation than others; |
| ☐ | p identify and explain the style classification of a hedge fund, given a description of its investment strategy; |
| ☐ | q discuss the typical structure of a hedge fund, including the fee structure, and explain the rationale for high-water mark provisions; |
| ☐ | r describe the purpose and characteristics of fund-of-funds hedge funds; |
| ☐ | s critique the conventions and discuss the issues involved in hedge fund performance evaluation, including the use of hedge fund indices and the Sharpe ratio; |
| ☐ | t describe trading strategies of managed futures programs and the role of managed futures in a portfolio; |
| ☐ | u describe strategies and risks associated with investing in distressed securities; |
| ☐ | v explain event risk, market liquidity risk, market risk, and "J-factor risk" in relation to investing in distressed securities. |

# 1     INTRODUCTION

Today, many defined-benefit pension funds, endowments, foundations, and high-net-worth individuals allocate money to alternative investments in proportions comparable to those given to traditional assets, such as bonds and common equities. In doing so, such investors may be seeking risk diversification, greater opportunities to apply active management skills, or both. Portfolio managers who understand alternative investments have a substantial advantage over those who do not.

This reading presents six groups of alternative investments: real estate, private equity, commodities, hedge funds, managed futures, and distressed securities. These six diverse asset groups cover a wide spectrum of risk and return characteristics and are the major alternative asset classes in the portfolios of most institutional and individual investors.

This reading focuses on the distinguishing investment characteristics of alternative investments and their potential contributions in a portfolio context. Among the questions we will address in this reading are the following:

■ What types of investments are available in each market, and what are their most important differences for an investor?

■ What benchmarks are available to evaluate the performance of alternative investment managers, and what are their limitations?

- What investment strategies and portfolio roles are characteristic of each alternative investment?

- What should due diligence cover? (**Due diligence** is the investigation into the details of a potential investment, including the scrutiny of operations and management and the verification of material facts.)

The reading is organized as follows: Section 2 introduces and presents an overview of the field of alternative investments. In Sections 3 through 8, we present the six alternative asset groups. For each group, we discuss the market for the investments; benchmarks and historical performance, with a focus on the group's record as a stand-alone investment; the portfolio role of the investments and specific strategies; and issues in performance evaluation and reporting. The final section summarizes the reading.

## ALTERNATIVE INVESTMENTS: DEFINITIONS, SIMILARITIES, AND CONTRASTS

**2**

**Alternative investments** comprise groups of investments with risk and return characteristics that differ markedly from those of traditional stock and bond investments. Common features of alternative investments include:

- relative illiquidity, which tends to be associated with a return premium as compensation;

- diversifying potential relative to a portfolio of stocks and bonds;

- high due diligence costs for the following reasons: investment structures and strategies may be complex; evaluation may draw heavily on asset-class, business-specific, or other expertise; reporting often lacks transparency; and

- unusually difficult performance appraisal because of the complexity of establishing valid benchmarks.

In addition, many professional investors believe that alternative investment markets are informationally less efficient than the world's major equity and bond markets and offer greater scope for adding value through skill and superior information.

Historically, **real estate** (ownership interests in land or structures attached to land), **private equity** (ownership interests in non-publicly-traded companies), and **commodities** (articles of commerce such as agricultural goods, metals, and petroleum) have been viewed as the primary alternatives to traditional stock and bond investments. However, in recent years, additional investments—**hedge funds** (relatively loosely regulated, pooled investment vehicles) and **managed futures** (pooled investment vehicles in futures and options on futures, frequently structured as limited partnerships)—have increasingly been considered "modern alternatives," not only to traditional investments but also to traditional *alternative* investments. The modern alternative investments are more akin to investment or trading strategies than to asset classes. Exhibit 1 shows alternative investments grouped according to these distinctions. In some instances, placement of an alternative investment in more than one category can be justified. For example, we discuss **distressed securities** investing separately as a distinct type of alternative investment, but it could be classified differently.[1]

---

**1** Distressed securities/bankruptcy investing can be classified 1) within private equity if private debt is considered to be private equity, 2) as a subcategory of event-driven strategies under hedge funds as an alternative investment strategy, or 3) as a separate alternative investment strategy. In this reading, we introduce it as an event-driven substrategy of hedge funds, but we discuss it separately in Section 8.

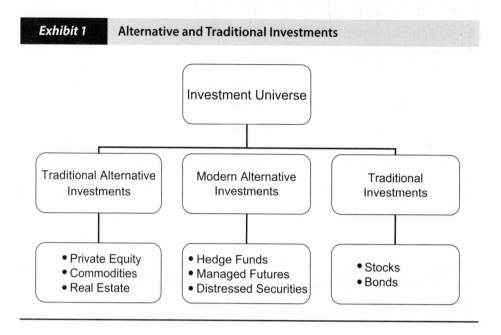

| Exhibit 1 | Alternative and Traditional Investments |

The list of alternative investments discussed in this reading is representative but by no means exhaustive. For example, some investors invest in timberland or intangibles (such as fine art), and benchmarks and professional advisory services for these and some other alternative investments have long been available.

In addition to the traditional-or-modern distinction, we can place alternative investments in three groups by the primary role they usually play in portfolios:

■ Investments that primarily provide exposure to risk factors not easily accessible through traditional stock and bond investments. Real estate and (long-only) commodities might be included in this group.

■ Investments that provide exposure to specialized investment strategies run by an outside manager. Hedge funds and managed futures might be placed in this category. Any value added by such investment is typically heavily dependent on the skills of the manager.

■ Investments that combine features of the prior two groups. Private equity funds and distressed securities might be included in this group.

However we group them, success in the field of alternative investments requires discipline. The portfolio management process still applies. In addition, familiarity with quantitative approaches to the management of risks in alternative investing, in particular risk budgeting, and with nontraditional measures of risk can be helpful. Thus, the reading on risk management is useful collateral reading.

### Example 1

## Alternative Investments in a Low-Return Environment

Interest in alternative investments from institutional investors soared after the severe equity bear markets of the first years of the 21st century. The resulting investment environment for traditional investments was seen as "low return." Return expectations for equities were widely ratcheted down from pre-bear-market and long-term historical levels. In that environment, using the revised capital market expectations and established strategic asset allocations, many investors foresaw built-in shortfalls relative to return requirements. The problem was particularly acute for defined-benefit pension funds in countries such as Canada and the United States, where such funds have traditionally had a strong equity orientation. With declining interest rates increasing the present value of liabilities, many defined-benefit plans faced severe pressures.

The experience led a number of industry leaders to question prior investment practices in areas such as strategic asset allocation and to reexamine the role of alternative investments in meeting return objectives and, to a lesser degree perhaps, in controlling risk. Many institutional investors made new and/or higher allocations to alternative investments. Vehicles such as hedge funds proliferated to meet the demand. This trend raised issues of capacity—that is, given the market opportunities, the ability of alternative investment managers to meet performance expectations with more assets.[2] In the private wealth marketplace, alternative investments also began to be packaged and marketed to new segments, such as the "mass affluent," raising issues of suitability and appropriate due diligence processes for such investors.[3]

Who are the major investors in alternative investments? The list includes both high-net-worth individuals (who were among the pioneer investors in hedge funds) and institutional investors, although banks and insurers may face regulatory restrictions and the investment policy statements of other investors may have self-imposed limitations. The themes already mentioned play varying roles for different investors. The potential risk-diversification benefits of alternative investments have broad appeal across investor types. The possibility of enhancing returns also draws many investors to seriously consider alternative investments. Illiquidity is a limiting factor in the size of the allocation to alternative investments for investors with short investment horizons. In contrast, investors with long investment horizons, such as endowments and some defined-benefit pension funds, may be competitively well placed to earn illiquidity premiums and to make large allocations.

The costs of due diligence in alternative investments may be a limiting factor for smaller portfolios. Deutsche Bank's Equity Prime Services Group 2004 Institutional Alternative Investment Survey, with a range of respondents serving the institutional and private markets, was revealing. In the case of hedge funds, the survey found that one major investor segment, pension funds, evaluates 40 managers, on average, to make only one to three allocations per year. Another major segment, endowments, researches 90 managers, on average, to make four to six placements per year. Sixty percent of respondents took three months to complete due diligence on a hedge fund.[4] In alternative investments as in traditional investments, expenses—whether management fees or trading or operational expenses—require justification and management.

For both traditional and alternative investments, selecting active managers is a process of attempting to identify superiorly skilled or informed managers. As Example 2 illustrates, the set of questions the investor needs to raise in selecting active managers in any investment field has a compellingly simple logic.

---

**2** See Christopher Wright, "Ripe for the Picking," *CFA Magazine*, September/October 2005 (pp. 27–35). The article's title refers to the question it colorfully posed: Does alpha grow on trees, and if so, is it being overharvested?

**3 Mass affluent** is an industry term for a segment of the private wealth marketplace that is not sufficiently wealthy to command certain individualized services (such as separately managed accounts) at many investment counseling firms. In the United States as of this writing, individuals with investable assets between US$100,000 and US$1 million would fall in this group.

**4** As reported by Jones (2005).

**Example 2**

## How One University Endowment Evaluates Alternative Investments

The University of Virginia Investment Management Company (UVIMCO) was responsible for the investment of more than US$2.5 billion in assets as of the end of 2005. With a policy portfolio at that time giving more than a 50 percent target weighting to hedge funds, private equity, and real assets as a group, UVIMCO has accumulated considerable experience in alternative investments portfolio management. Notably, the framework of questions to which UVIMCO seeks answers applies not only to alternative investments but also to active managers in general, reflecting the unity of the investment process.[5] The chief investment officer (CIO) of UVIMCO, Christopher J. Brightman, CFA, summarized the chief points of UVIMCO's active manager selection process as follows:[6]

1. *Market Opportunity*   What is the opportunity and why is it there? We start by studying capital markets and the types of managers operating within those markets. We identify market inefficiencies and try to understand their causes, such as regulatory structures or behavioral biases. We can rule out many broad groups of managers and strategies by simply determining that the degree of market inefficiency necessary to support a strategy is implausible. Importantly, we consider a past history of active returns meaningless unless we understand why markets will allow those active returns to continue into the future.

2. *Investment Process*   Who does this best and what's their edge? We identify groups of managers that seek to exploit these inefficiencies. Few, if any, important opportunities are exploited by a single manager. We study investment process and identify best practice and competitive advantages among similar managers.

3. *Organization*   Are all the pieces in place? Is the firm well organized and stable? Are research, trading, risk management, and operations properly staffed given the investment process and scale? Is compensation fair? Has there been turnover? What is the succession plan?

4. *People*   Do we trust the people? We speak at length to the principals face to face. We look for experience, intelligence, candor, and integrity. Then, we do reference checks; we speak to former bosses, colleagues, and business partners as well as current and past clients. We have real conversations with people who know the managers well and are willing to speak openly and at length. We also perform general Google and LexisNexis searches.

5. *Terms and Structure*   Are the terms fair? Are interests aligned? Is the fund or account structured appropriately to the opportunity? How much money can or should be invested in the space? Details here vary by market, asset class, and strategy.

---

**5** UVIMCO has a focus on active management (www.virginia.edu/uvimco/IPS.htm). For investors with passive and active investment components, the first major heading in "market opportunity" might be expanded to strategy/product/market opportunity to cover, in addition to market portfolio, questions such as "Is the product what it claims to be?" that a passive investor would explore.
**6** Based on a communication of 19 December 2005.

6. *Service Providers* Who supports them? We verify lawyers, auditors, prime brokers, lenders, etc. We investigate those with whom we are not familiar.

7. *Documents* Read the documents! We read the prospectus or private placement memorandum. If we do not understand everything in the documents, we hire lawyers who do. We also read the audits.

8. *Write-Up* Prior to making a manager selection decision, we produce a formal manager recommendation discussing the above steps. The write-up ensures organized thought, informs others, and formally documents the process.

Some questions in due diligence and alternative investment selection are unique, or more acute, for advisors of private wealth clients than for institutional investors. These include:

- *Tax issues.* This is a pervasive issue in investing for individuals. In contrast to equities and bonds, with alternative investments, the advisor will frequently be dealing with partnerships and other structures that have distinct tax issues.

- *Determining suitability.* This is often more complex for an advisor to an individual client or family than for an institutional investor. The advisor often addresses multistage time horizons and liquidity needs. Client-relevant facts— for example, the time horizon—may change more suddenly than for, say, a pension fund with thousands of participants. The private client advisor also may be faced with questions of emotional as well as financial needs.

- *Communication with client.* When the advisor explores the suitability of an alternative investment with a client as part of his or her fiduciary responsibilities, the advisor will often discuss suitability with the client. The advisor then faces the difficult problem of communicating and discussing the possible role in the portfolio (and risk) of an often complex investment with a nonprofessional investor.

- *Decision risk.* As used by one authority on investing for private wealth clients, **decision risk** is the risk of changing strategies at the point of maximum loss.[7] Many advisors to private wealth clients are familiar with the issue of clients who are acutely sensitive to positions of loss at stages prior to an investment policy statement's stated time horizon(s). Of course, advisors need to do continuing evaluation of investments, but the point is that the advisor needs to evaluate whether an alternative investment not only promises to be rewarding over a given time horizon but is also acceptable at all intermediate points in time.[8] In effect, the issue relates to downside risk at all points within a time horizon and investors' reactions to it. Many alternative investments— for example, many hedge fund strategies—have complex risk characteristics. Decision risk is increased by strategies that by their nature have:

  - frequent small positive returns but, when a large return occurs, it is more likely to be a large negative return than a large positive one[9], or

---

**7** See Brunel (2004).

**8** Brunel (2003).

**9** Technically, such a strategy would be said to have *negatively skewed returns*.

- extreme returns (relative to the mean return) with some unusual degree of frequency.[10]

■ *Concentrated equity position of the client in a closely held company.* For some clients, ownership in a closely held company may represent a substantial part of wealth. The advisor needs to be particularly sensitive to an investment's effect on the client's risk and liquidity position. For example, is a private equity fund suitable for the investor? The issues of concentrated risk and illiquidity also arise for concentrated positions in public equities with built-in capital gains, although hedging and monetization strategies are available. (These strategies are discussed in the reading on monitoring and rebalancing.) Although a client's residences are often viewed separately from the client's investable portfolio, a similar issue arises in real estate investment vis-à-vis wealth represented by residences. Problems of this type form an interface of suitability, tax, and asset allocation issues.

In discussing individual alternative investments, we will sometimes provide a perspective on what effect an alternative investment would have on the risk and expected return characteristics of a stock/bond portfolio in which some of the money is shifted to the alternative investment. In some cases, we can also refer to evidence on the effects of the addition of the new alternative investment to a portfolio that already includes stocks, bonds, and a different major alternative investment. This approach reflects the situation faced by many investors and is a type of exercise that can be informative.

In many cases, we give evidence based on data relating to the period 1990–2004.[11] *Here a caution is appropriate*: In any forward-looking exercise, the investor needs to evaluate the differences between current or forecasted economic fundamentals and those of any selected historical period used in the analysis. In addition, the results for any relatively short period can be affected by short-term dislocations, such as currency crises.

Overall, the 1990–2004 period was a time of historically low and stable or declining interest rates and inflation in the United States and many developed markets. The beginning year was recessionary in the United States. A long expansion followed in the United States and many developed countries (with the notable exception of Japan), but at least three dislocations with worldwide effects occurred.[12] In the United States and some other major markets, an exceptionally long equity bull market (1991–1999 inclusive) was followed by an extended bear market.[13] The year 2001 was recessionary in the United States, whereas 2002–2004 were recovery years. The period 1990 to 2004 covers one full business cycle for the United States and many developed markets.

---

10 Technically, such a strategy would be said to have *high kurtosis*. To summarize using the language of statistics, many investors are presumed to want *positive* skewness and *moderate or low kurtosis* (the standard for moderate is the kurtosis of a normal distribution). For more details on these statistical concepts, see Ch. 3 of DeFusco (2004). In discussions of alternative investments in trade publications as well as in outlets such as the *Financial Analysts Journal* and the *Journal of Wealth Management*, the practitioner will encounter these statistical terms which are covered in the CFA Institute curriculum, and we will use them occasionally in this reading.

11 Hedge funds have reliable data going back only to 1990. We chose to be consistent on the starting point for the sake of comparability across investment types.

12 The dislocations were the Mexican currency crisis of 1994, the Asian financial crisis of 1997, and the Russian debt crisis of 1998.

13 U.S. equities experienced a record nine-year string of positive-return years (1991–1999), including six years (1991 and 1995–1999) of plus 20 percent returns. This period was followed by a post-1941 record string of three negative-return years (2000–2002).

**Example 3**

### Alternative Investments and Core–Satellite Investing

A way of thinking about allocating money known as **core–satellite** seeks to define each investment's place in the portfolio in relation to specific investment goals or roles. A traditional core–satellite perspective places competitively priced assets, such as government bonds and/or large-capitalization stocks, in the core. Because alpha is hard to obtain with such assets, the core may be managed in a passive or risk-controlled active manner. (Informally, *alpha* is the return to skill.) In the satellite ring would go investments designed to play special roles, such as to add alpha or to diminish portfolio volatility via low correlation with the core. Alternative investments would be in the satellite ring for most investors.[14]

In a 2005 paper, Leibowitz and Bova championed an alternative position that would place alternative investments in an "alpha core" at their maximum allowable percentages and then add stocks and bonds as "swing assets" to get a portfolio that best reflected the desired balance between return and risk.[15] The traditional viewpoint takes traditional assets as the centerpiece, whereas the Leibowitz–Bova position builds the portfolio around alternative investments. The Leibowitz–Bova perspective is an example of the ferment in investment thinking mentioned in Example 1.

Having provided a bird's-eye view of the field of alternative investments, we use the following sections to analyze each in detail, beginning with real estate.

## REAL ESTATE

**3**

As one of the earliest of the traditional alternative investments, real estate plays an important role in institutional and individual investor portfolios internationally. The focus of our discussion is *equity investments* in real estate (covered in the definition given earlier). Investing in such instruments as mortgages, securitizations of mortgages, or hybrid debt/equity interests (e.g., mortgages in which the lender's interest includes participation in any appreciation of the underlying real estate) are not covered here.

### 3.1 The Real Estate Market

Both individual and institutional investors have had long-standing involvement in the real estate market. For centuries, individual investors have owned interests in real estate, primarily in the form of residential and agricultural properties. In the United States, institutional investors ventured into real estate in the late 1970s and early 1980s as they sought to diversify their portfolios and hedge against inflation. By the late 1980s, the performance of real estate had become lackluster as a result of volatile changes in U.S. tax policies, deregulation in the savings and loan industry, and the onset of risk-based capital regulations. These events culminated in the real

---

**14** See Singleton (2005).

**15** In the Leibowitz–Bova approach, the term *alpha* in *alpha core* strictly refers not to a return to skill or risk-adjusted excess return, as in standard finance theory, but to a type of return–risk enhancement that may be available relative to a more traditional asset allocation approach.

estate crash of the late 1980s and early 1990s. Outside the United States, real estate investment has always been an important part of institutional as well as individual portfolios. At the beginning of the 21st century, individual and institutional investors continue to focus on the potential return enhancement and risk-diversification benefits of real estate investments in a portfolio of stocks, bonds, and frequently, other alternative investments.

### 3.1.1 *Types of Real Estate Investments*

Investors may participate in real estate directly and indirectly (which is sometimes called "financial ownership"). Direct ownership includes investment in residences, business (commercial) real estate, and agricultural land.

Indirect investment includes investing in:

- companies engaged in real estate ownership, development, or management, such as homebuilders and real estate operating companies (which are in the business of owning such real estate assets as office buildings); such companies would be in the Global Industrial Classification System's (GICS) and FTSE Industry Classification Benchmark's real estate management and development subsector;

- **real estate investment trusts (REITs)**, which are publicly traded equities representing pools of money invested in real estate properties and/or real estate debt;

- **commingled real estate funds (CREFs)**, which are professionally managed vehicles for substantial commingled (i.e., pooled) investment in real estate properties;

- separately managed accounts, which are often offered by the same real estate advisors sponsoring CREFs; and

- **infrastructure funds**, which in cooperation with governmental authorities, make private investment in public infrastructure projects—such as roads, tunnels, schools, hospitals, and airports—in return for rights to specified revenue streams over a contracted period.

Investments in real estate management and development subsector shares and in REITS are both made through the public stock markets. REITs, however, unlike real estate management and development shares, essentially function as conduits to investors for the cash flows from the underlying real estate holdings. The list of markets in which REITs are available includes Australia, Belgium, Canada, China, France, Hong Kong, Japan, the Netherlands, Singapore, South Korea, and the United States.

Equity REITs own and manage such properties as office buildings, apartment buildings, and shopping centers. Shareholders receive rental income and income from capital appreciation if the property is sold for a gain. Mortgage REITs own portfolios in which more than 75 percent of the assets are mortgages. Mortgage REITs lend money to builders and make loan collections; shareholders receive interest income and capital appreciation income from improvement in the prices of loans. Hybrid REITs operate by buying real estate and by acquiring mortgages on both commercial and residential real estate.

REITs securitize illiquid real estate assets; their shares are listed on stock exchanges and over the counter. REITs permit smaller investors to gain real estate exposure. Exchange-traded funds, mutual funds, and traded closed-end investment companies allow investors to obtain a professionally managed diversified portfolio of real estate securities with a relatively small outlay.

CREFs include open-end funds and closed-end funds (i.e., funds that are closed to new investment after an initial period). Institutional and wealthy individual investors use these private real estate funds to access the real estate expertise of a professional real estate fund manager in selecting, developing, and realizing the value of real estate properties. In contrast to open-end funds, closed-end funds are usually leveraged and have higher return objectives; they operate by opportunistically acquiring, repositioning, and disposing of properties. Individually managed separate accounts are also an important alternative for investors.

In an infrastructure investment, a private company—or, more frequently, a consortium of private companies—designs, finances, and builds the new project (e.g., a road or hospital) for public use. The consortium maintains the physical infrastructure over a period that often ranges from 25 to 30 years. The public sector (via the government) leases the infrastructure and pays the consortium an annual fee for the use of the completed project over the contracted period. Thus, the public sector avoids the need to issue debt or raise taxes to finance infrastructure development. The public sector staffs the infrastructure and ensures safety. The projects are financed through bond issuance by the consortium as well as by an equity investment. The consortium will often want to pull its equity capital out of a project for reinvestment in other projects. It can do this by selling its interest to investors through a variety of investment structures. Public/private infrastructure investment has been classified under real estate, under private equity, and also as a distinct alternative investment class. Infrastructure investment was pioneered in the United Kingdom in 1992 (as the Private Financing Initiative) and is a rapidly growing alternative investment segment in North America, Western Europe, and Asia. One estimate as of early 2006 is that in the United Kingdom alone, there are more than 700 public/private infrastructure projects totaling US$100 billion in value.[16]

### 3.1.2 Size of the Real Estate Market

Estimates have been made that real estate represents one-third to one-half of the world's wealth, although figures are hard to document. In the United States, as of the end of 2005, real estate owned by households was valued at US$19.8 trillion and represented approximately one-third of total assets (tangible and financial) of U.S. households.

According to one report, U.S. real estate held in U.S. investment portfolios is estimated to be worth US$4.5 trillion.[17] According to the National Association of Real Estate Investment Trusts (NAREIT), the market capitalization of all publicly traded REITs in the United States was more than US$300 billion in 2004 and the market capitalization of REITs traded in Canada was about US$13 billion in the same year.

## 3.2 Benchmarks and Historical Performance

In this section, we discuss the performance measurement of real estate investments by using publicly available information. Performance of private equity in real estate may vary and does not necessarily correlate closely with the benchmarks discussed here. More importantly, it has been observed that the real estate market lags behind publicly traded real estate securities.

### 3.2.1 Benchmarks

Exhibit 2 shows some of the popular real estate indices for selected countries. The principal benchmark used to measure the performance of direct real estate investment in the United States is the National Council of Real Estate Investment Fiduciaries (NCREIF) Property Index. The NCREIF Index is a quarterly benchmark for real

---

**16** Jacobius (2006a).
**17** See Broad (2005).

estate covering a sample of commercial properties owned by large U.S. institutions. The NCREIF Index is essentially value weighted and includes subindices grouped by real estate sector (apartment, industrial, office, and retail) and geographical region. Property appraisals largely determine the values in the NCREIF Index because real estate properties change ownership relatively infrequently. Property appraisals are also conducted infrequently (typically once a year), so appraisal-based property values exhibit remarkable inertia. Therefore, returns calculated solely on percentage changes in the index suffer from a number of deficiencies, including the tendency to underestimate volatility in underlying values.[18] However, methods have been developed to "unsmooth" or correct for this bias.[19] Recently, a transaction-based index has been developed based on NCREIF data and the use of econometrics to address the issue of infrequent market transactions.

| Exhibit 2 | Selected Real Estate Benchmarks | | | |
|-----------|---------------------------------|---|---|---|
| **Country** | **Name** | **Type** | **Begin Date** | **Frequency** |
| Australia | Property Council of Australia index (PCA) | Appraisal based | 1984 | Quarterly |
| Canada | Institute of Canadian Real Estate Investment Managers (ICREIM)/ IPD Canadian Property Index | Appraisal based | 1985 | Quarterly |
| France | Investment Property Databank (IPD) | Appraisal based | 1998 | Quarterly and monthly |
| United Kingdom | IPD | Appraisal based | 1980 | Quarterly and monthly |
| United States | NCREIF Property Index | Individual properties; appraisal based | 1978 | Quarterly |
| | Transaction-Based Index (TBI) for Institutional Commercial Property Performance (MIT Center for Real Estate) | Individual properties; based on transaction prices of properties sold from the NCREIF Index database | 1984 | Quarterly |
| | S&P REIT Composite Index | REITs | 1997 | Daily |
| | NAREIT Index | REITs | 1972 | Real time |
| | Morgan Stanley REITs Index | REITs | 1996 | Real time |
| | Wilshire real estate indices | REITs and real estate operating companies | 1978 | Daily |
| | Dow Jones REIT indices | REITs | 1998 | Real time |
| World | FTSE EPRA/NAREIT Global Real Estate Index | REITs and real estate operating companies | 1989 | Daily |

*Sources*: CISDM (2005a) and Hoesli, Lekander, and Witkiewicz (2003), http://web.mit.edu/cre, www.ftse.com/indices.

The principal benchmark used to represent indirect investment in real estate is the index compiled by the NAREIT. Begun in 1972, the NAREIT Index is a real-time, market-cap-weighted index of all REITs actively traded on the New York Stock

---

[18] For details of the deficiencies, see Geltner (2000) and Geltner and Ling (2001).

[19] The approach used to unsmooth the NCREIF Index is based on the assumption that real estate returns follow a first-order autoregressive process as described in CISDM (2005a).

Exchange and American Stock Exchange. NAREIT also computes a monthly index based on month-end share prices of REITs that own and manage real estate assets, or equity REITs. NAREIT publishes several other indices, including a monthly index of REITs that specialize in acquiring various types of mortgage loans on many types of properties (mortgage REITs) and a monthly index based on share prices of hybrid REITs, which operate by buying real estate and by acquiring mortgages on both commercial and residential real estate. REIT indices are also published by various institutions, such as Standard & Poor's, Dow Jones, Wilshire Associates, and Morgan Stanley. The FTSE EPRA/NAREIT Global Real Estate Index listed in Exhibit 2 is an example of a global index of securitized real estate investment.

Both direct and indirect investments have significant measurement issues associated with them.

### 3.2.2 *Historical Performance*

In the United States, direct and indirect real estate investments as represented by the major indices produced better risk-adjusted performance over the 1990–2004 period than did general stocks and commodities, as shown in Exhibit 3. In Exhibit 3, the "hedged" REIT return series has been purged of its overall equity market return component, as represented by the S&P 500 Index. Such an adjustment is meaningful only for equity REITs because mortgage and hybrid REITs have different risk characteristics. However, equity REITs represent close to 95 percent of the composition of the index.[20] GSCI is the Goldman Sachs Commodity Index, discussed further in the section on commodities.

| Exhibit 3 | Real Estate Performance 1990–2004 |

| Measure | NAREIT Index | NAREIT Index Hedged | NCREIF Index | NCREIF Index Unsmoothed | S&P 500 Index | Lehman Aggregate Bond Index* | GSCI |
|---|---|---|---|---|---|---|---|
| Annualized return | 12.71% | 8.96% | 6.14% | 7.27% | 10.94% | 7.70% | 7.08% |
| Annualized std. dev. | 12.74% | 11.93% | 3.37% | 8.95% | 14.65% | 3.91% | 19.26% |
| Sharpe ratio | 0.66 | 0.39 | 0.55 | 0.33 | 0.45 | 0.87 | 0.15 |
| Minimum quarterly return | −14.19% | −10.16% | −5.33% | −18.55% | −17.28% | −2.87% | −17.73% |
| Correlation w/NAREIT | 1.00 | 0.94 | 0.00 | 0.21 | 0.35 | 0.18 | −0.04 |
| Correlation w/NAREIT hedged | 0.94 | 1.00 | 0.00 | 0.24 | 0.00 | 0.14 | −0.01 |
| Correlation w/NCREIF | 0.00 | 0.00 | 1.00 | 0.71 | 0.01 | −0.18 | 0.06 |
| Correlation w/NCREIF unsmoothed | 0.21 | 0.24 | 0.71 | 1.00 | −0.01 | −0.27 | 0.13 |

*Note*: Based on quarterly returns for stock, bond, commodity, and real estate indices; a quarterly risk-free rate based on the U.S. Treasury 30-day bill was used to compute Sharpe ratios.

* Barclays has acquired Lehman Brothers and will maintain the family of Lehman Brothers indices and the associated index calculation, publication, and analytical infrastructure and tools.

*Source*: CISDM (2005a).

---

**20** The data and methodology are described in CISDM (2005).

Note that the NCREIF Index represents nonleveraged investment only. In contrast, debt often represents 50 percent or more of the capital structure of REITs, so REITs are a levered exposure to real estate. This contrast is important for understanding the higher standard deviation of REITs compared with the unsmoothed NCREIF Index. The NCREIF Index is most representative of the performance of private real estate funds because these funds are the major contributors of data to NCREIF.

The performance properties of direct and securitized real estate investment differ significantly. REITs exhibit a relatively high return (12.71 percent) and high standard deviation (12.74 percent), whereas appraisal-based real estate returns are low (6.14 percent) with low volatility (3.37 percent). The extremely low standard deviation of NCREIF Index returns is indicative of the volatility dampening associated with smoothing because of stale valuations. After the correction for smoothing, the NCREIF Index's volatility more than doubles to 8.95 percent. However, the average return increases from 6.14 percent for the NCREIF Index to 7.27 percent for the unsmoothed NCREIF Index. The correlation between these two indices is 0.71. The correlations between the unhedged NAREIT Index and the NCREIF Index and the unsmoothed NCREIF Index are both low (0.00 and 0.21, respectively), suggesting that securitized real estate investment is a poor substitute for direct investment.

The volatility of the hedged NAREIT Index, 11.93 percent, is higher than that of the NCREIF Index unsmoothed, 8.95 percent. This suggests the presence of a residual equity component in the hedged NAREIT Index that could be related to small-cap stocks, be simply unique to REITs, or be both. Even though the hedging correction is imperfect, the hedged NAREIT Index is a more realistic representation of the underlying real estate market, with a higher correlation with the unsmoothed NCREIF Index (0.24) than without the correction.

### 3.2.3 *Interpretation Issues*

When NAREIT and NCREIF indices are used as benchmarks for real estate investments or in asset allocation studies, the problems associated with the construction of the indices mentioned previously must be taken into account.[21] Importantly for performance appraisal, the NCREIF Index is not an investable index.

## 3.3 Real Estate: Investment Characteristics and Roles

Real estate accounts for a major portion of many individuals' wealth. For example, equity in the residential property represented close to 30 percent of the net worth in the United Kingdom in 1999.[22] For all homeowners in the United States, home equity represented 43 percent of their net worth in 2001 and is expected to be much greater today because real estate values have risen substantially since then.[23] Because of the role of residential real estate for individuals as the place in which they live, however, most advisors to private clients do not include the clients' residences as "marketable" in the sense of assets that the advisor includes in a strategic asset allocation.

### 3.3.1 *Investment Characteristics*

In contrast to such alternative investments as hedge funds, which are essentially investment strategies and are similar to direct investment in commodities, real estate is an asset in itself, with some intrinsic value based on the benefits it may supply to

---

**21** For details see Geltner (2000) and Geltner and Ling (2001).
**22** See *Social Trends*, Issue 30, February 2000.
**23** See *Survey of Consumer Finances*, Federal Reserve Board, 2001.

individuals or businesses. Furthermore, investment in commercial real estate properties includes a substantial income component through rental income, which increases the stability of its returns.

A variety of investment characteristics affect the returns to real estate. The physical real estate market is characterized by relative lack of liquidity, large lot sizes, relatively high transaction costs, heterogeneity, immobility (with the asset fixed at a location), and relatively low information transparency (so the seller often knows more than the buyer). Physical real estate has rarely been traded on a centralized exchange. These characteristics can create the market opportunity for relatively high risk-adjusted returns for investors who can obtain cost-efficient, high-quality information.

The lack of reliable, high-frequency transaction data for properties necessitates the use of appraisal-based valuations. Later, we will discuss the checkpoints that a quantitative analysis of the returns to real estate must cover when evaluating real estate return data resulting from the use of appraisals.

Various market and economic factors affect real estate. For instance, interest rates directly or indirectly affect a multitude of factors associated with the demand and supply for real estate, such as business financing costs, employment levels, savings habits, and the demand and supply for mortgage financing. Worldwide, the returns to real estate are positively correlated with changes in gross national product.[24] Population growth is, in the long term, a positive factor for real estate returns, but the real estate investor needs to research the demographics affecting the particular investment (such as migration into or out of the area and changes in the wealth profile of the locality).

Investigators have come to mixed conclusions on the inflation-hedging capabilities of real estate investment. Bond and Seiler (1998) found that U.S. residential real estate provided a significant inflation hedge in the 1969–94 period. Hoesli et al. (1997) found that U.K. real estate provided a better short-term inflation hedge than bonds but a worse hedge than stocks. Stevenson and Murray (1999) did not find evidence that Irish real estate provided a significant inflation hedge. Liu et al. (1997) found that real estate provided a worse hedge than stocks in some countries but a comparable hedge in others. Analyzing U.S. REITs specifically, Chatrath and Liang (1998) found some long-run but no short-run inflation-hedging ability.

Real estate values are affected by idiosyncratic variables, such as location. There appear to be strong continent-specific factors in real estate returns for Europe and North America.[25] The implication is that complete diversification in real estate can be achieved only by investing internationally. Nearly optimal diversification can be achieved by targeting one country from each continent.

The following is a list of the general advantages and disadvantages of direct equity real estate investing.[26] Most of the advantages and disadvantages apply to both individual and institutional investors.

### Advantages

- To the extent that the law allows mortgage interest, property taxes, and other expenses to be tax deductible, taxable owners of real estate may benefit from tax subsidies.

- Mortgage loans permit most real estate borrowers to use more financial leverage than is available in most securities investing.

---

24 See Case, Goetzmann, and Rouwenhorst (2000).
25 See Eichholtz et al. (1998) and Eichholtz et al. (1999).
26 In part, this list reflects Francis and Ibbotson (2001).

- Real estate investors have direct control over their property and may take action, such as expanding or modernizing, to increase the market value of the property. In contrast, an investor who owns a small position in the equity of a publicly traded company has virtually no voice in the management of the company.

- Geographical diversification can be effective in reducing exposure to catastrophic risks (e.g., the risk of hurricanes or floods). The values of real estate investments in different locations can have low correlations; substantial geographical distance is often not necessary to achieve risk-reduction benefits.

- Real estate returns, on average, have relatively low volatility in comparison with returns to public equities—even after correcting for the downward bias that results from the smoothing process associated with real estate appraisals. We discuss this bias later.

**Disadvantages**

- Most parcels of real estate are not easy to divide into smaller pieces. As a result, when such properties are a relatively large part of an investor's total portfolio, real estate investing may involve large idiosyncratic risks for investors. Owners of single-family residences and large institutional investors that buy shopping centers may both experience this problem.

- The cost of acquiring information is high because each piece of real estate is unique.

- Real estate brokers charge high commissions relative to securities transaction fees.

- Real estate involves substantial operating and maintenance costs (e.g., for administration, leasing, repairs, and replacements) and hands-on management expertise, which are expenses or requirements not incurred by securities investors.

- Real estate investors are exposed to the risk of neighborhood deterioration, and the conditions that may lead to that are beyond the investor's control.

- Any income tax deductions that a taxable investor in real estate may benefit from are subject to political risk—they may be discontinued.

### 3.3.2  Roles in the Portfolio

According to the *2005–2006 Russell Survey on Alternative Investing*, strategic allocations to real estate average 3.4 percent of total assets in Japan, 6.7 percent in North America, 9.8 percent in Europe, and 10.4 percent in Australia. This survey forecasted increased allocations to real estate in all these countries except Australia. Almost two-thirds of European capital and about half of North American and Australian capital is reportedly committed to direct investment in land and buildings.[27] Japan has much less capital committed to direct investment in real estate. The survey also indicates a strong home bias is revealed in real estate investments. The range of allocations is broadly consistent with what a quantitative approach to asset allocation would suggest.[28]

Because real estate may follow many economic fundamentals, real estate markets follow economic cycles. From a tactical asset allocation point of view, good forecasting of economic cycles should thus result in improved dynamic strategies for reallocating among different assets on the basis of expected stages of their respective cycles.

---

**27** The survey points out that these data may be biased by the kind of respondents—namely, the larger institutions, which tend to use direct investments.
**28** For example, Kallberg and Liu (1996), using a mean–variance-optimization framework, found that a 9 percent allocation to real estate is optimal in a portfolio that includes stocks, bonds, and cash.

Among the variables to focus on as systematic determinants of real estate returns are growth in consumption, real interest rates, the term structure of interest rates, and unexpected inflation.[29]

**The Role of Real Estate as a Diversifier**   In addition to its potential to add value through active management, real estate has historically been viewed as an important diversifier. Real estate as an asset class typically responds differently from the way either stocks or bonds do. The reason is that, in the past, directly owned real estate was not highly correlated with the performance of other assets. For example, it was a good risk diversifier in the traditional stock and bond portfolio. Also, historically, real estate investment has experienced lower volatility than other asset classes because it is typically less affected by short-term economic conditions. Income-producing commercial real estate can be a relatively stable investment with income derived from tenants' lease payments. Thus, real estate can also be a good income enhancer.[30]

To illustrate the potential diversification benefit of real estate investments in a portfolio context, Exhibit 4 presents performance results using an approach that is also used in subsequent parts of this reading and elsewhere.[31] The exhibit shows statistics for a 50 percent/50 percent U.S. stock/U.S. bond portfolio (Portfolio I), which is a simple baseline portfolio. Then the allocations to U.S. stocks and bonds are each reduced by 10 percentage points and reassigned in various ways to other asset classes; the resulting portfolios include a portfolio containing the alternative investment under discussion, in this case real estate. This method of presentation provides information on the effect of holding the alternative investment under discussion in conjunction with various other asset classes that the investor might hold. A particular investor may have a different baseline portfolio, but the investor can adapt the approach shown here to his or her needs. In Section 2, we supplied the additional cautions the reader should be aware of in evaluating an analysis based on a given historical sample. In real estate, data series extend much further back than 1990, which we have selected for the reasons of comparability discussed in Section 2.

| Exhibit 4 | Real Estate Performance in Portfolios 1990–2004 | | | | | |
|---|---|---|---|---|---|---|
| **Measure** | **Portfolio I** | **Portfolio II** | **Portfolio III** | **Portfolio IV** | **Portfolio V** | **Portfolio VI** |
| Annualized return | 9.60% | 9.95% | 10.34% | 10.16% | 9.33% | 9.72% |
| Annualized std. dev. | 7.87% | 6.81% | 7.62% | 7.05% | 6.59% | 6.43% |
| Sharpe ratio | 0.67 | 0.83 | 0.79 | 0.83 | 0.77 | 0.85 |
| Minimum quarterly return | −6.45% | −5.18% | −7.99% | −5.47% | −5.35% | −4.67% |
| Correlation w/NAREIT Index | 0.37 | 0.36 | 0.64 | 0.52 | 0.51 | 0.50 |
| Correlation w/NAREIT Index hedged | 0.03 | 0.04 | 0.34 | 0.20 | 0.21 | 0.20 |
| Correlation w/NCREIF Index | −0.03 | −0.03 | −0.03 | −0.03 | 0.16 | 0.06 |
| Correlation w/NCREIF Index unsmoothed | −0.08 | −0.04 | 0.01 | −0.01 | 0.19 | 0.08 |

*(continued)*

---

29  See Ling and Naranjo (1997).
30  See Downs et al. (2003).
31  See Schneeweis and Spurgin (1997a) and Ankrim and Hensel (1993). The Hedge Fund Composite Index (HFCI) is created by CISDM of the University of Massachusetts as follows: Between 1990 and 1993, it is an equally weighted portfolio of EACM 100 and HFR; since 1994, it has been an equally weighted portfolio of EACM 100, HFR, and Credit Suisse/Tremont.

| Exhibit 4 | Continued |
|-----------|-----------|

*Notes*: In the following listing, HFCI is the Hedge Funds Composite Index published by CISDM (Center for International Securities and Derivatives Markets) of the University of Massachusetts. It is created as follows: For the period between 1990 and 1993, it is an equally weighted portfolio of the EACM 100 and Hedge Fund Research (HFR) indices; since 1994, it has been an equally weighted portfolio of EACM 100, HFR, and Credit Suisse/Tremont hedge fund indices.

Portfolio I: 50% S&P 500 and 50% Lehman Aggregate Bond Index.

Portfolio II: 40% S&P 500, 40% Lehman Aggregate, 10% HFCI, and 10% GSCI.

Portfolio III: 40% S&P 500, 40% Lehman Aggregate, and 20% NAREIT.

Portfolio IV: 40% S&P 500, 40% Lehman Aggregate, 5% HFCI, 5% GSCI, and 10% NAREIT.

Portfolio V: 40% S&P 500, 40% Lehman Aggregate, and 20% NCREIF unsmoothed.

Portfolio VI: 40% S&P 500, 40% Lehman Aggregate, 5% HFCI, 5% GSCI, and 10% NCREIF unsmoothed.

*Source*: CISDM (2005a).

Comparing Portfolio III (REITs, U.S. equities, and U.S. bonds) with Portfolio I (only U.S. equities and U.S bonds), one can see that the addition of REITs increases the Sharpe ratio from 0.67 to 0.79. The reason for this improvement is the high Sharpe ratio of REIT returns in the sample period coupled with their moderate correlation with S&P 500 Index returns (0.35, Exhibit 3). When REITs are added to a more diversified portfolio made up of assets included in Portfolio II to produce Portfolio IV, different results are observed: The Sharpe ratio is actually the same for Portfolios II and IV.

Overall, for the sample period, REITs provided some diversification benefits relative to a stock/bond portfolio, but it was relatively less effective in that role than hedge funds and commodities and did not have diversification benefits in a stock/bond portfolio to which hedge fund and commodity exposures had been added.

Direct investment in real estate as represented by unsmoothed NCREIF returns, however, provided more diversification benefit. Adding the unsmoothed NCREIF Index (20 percent) to a portfolio of stocks and bonds raised the Sharpe ratio of the portfolio from 0.67 (Portfolio I) to 0.77 (Portfolio V). This result would be expected because of the small negative correlation between unsmoothed NCREIF Index returns and the S&P 500 returns (−0.01, Exhibit 3) and the negative correlation between unsmoothed NCREIF Index returns and Lehman Aggregate returns (−0.27, Exhibit 3). As the results for Portfolio VI show, adding the unsmoothed NCREIF Index to a portfolio including hedge funds and commodities results in a slightly larger Sharpe ratio than that of Portfolio II, although adding NAREIT to such a portfolio results in the same Sharpe ratio as Portfolio II. These results may indicate that real estate is an *ex post* redundant asset in the presence of hedge funds and commodities.

These results are consistent with evidence indicating that direct real estate investment may provide some diversification benefits to stocks and bonds[32] but benefits may disappear when hedge funds and commodities are added to the portfolio.[33]

**Diversification within Real Estate Itself**     Investors also seek diversification by type and geography within real estate investing. Investments in different real estate sectors differ in regard to risk and return. The property types that have higher levels of embedded risk, such as large office assets, have generated lower risk-adjusted returns than other sectors and are likely to have more pronounced market cycles. Conversely, those sectors that offer higher risk-adjusted returns, such as apartments, appear to be less volatile and offer more defensive characteristics. As Exhibit 5 shows,

---

**32** See Kallberg and Liu (1996), Grauer and Hakansson (1995), and Chandrashekaran (1999).

**33** See also results in Section 4 (Commodity Investment), which are consistent with Froot (1995).

apartments offered the highest risk-adjusted returns, and office assets showed low returns (4.59 percent) and high volatility (10.63 percent) in the 1990–2004 period. This suggests that targeting the apartment sector of the commercial real estate market over the last decade would have yielded better results than simply diversifying across all sectors. The higher returns of apartment real estate can be partially explained by a low correlation with inflation. In addition, to the degree that inflation results in a slowdown in the real economy, the apartment sector would be negatively correlated with inflation. Thus, the office, retail, and industrial sectors, whose returns seem to include an inflation component, have been at a relative disadvantage in the 1990s.

| Exhibit 5 | Unsmoothed Performance of Direct Real Estate Indices 1990–2004 | | | | |
|---|---|---|---|---|---|
| **Measure** | **NCREIF Unsmoothed** | **Apartment** | **Industrial** | **Office** | **Retail** |
| Annualized return | 7.27% | 9.39% | 7.85% | 4.59% | 8.17% |
| Annualized std. dev. | 8.95% | 5.76% | 10.68% | 10.63% | 9.65% |
| Sharpe ratio | 0.33 | 0.89 | 0.33 | 0.03 | 0.40 |
| Minimum quarterly return | −18.55% | −10.45% | −16.15% | −20.91% | 14.25% |

*Source*: CISDM (2005a).

Overall, direct real estate investment may be able to provide an inflation hedge to some degree.

Exhibit 6 shows the correlation matrix of total returns for the four geographical NCREIF (unsmoothed) indices and the combined index. The correlations are high for all pairs of geographical subindices. This suggests that successful geographical diversification should take into account finer subdivisions, such as metropolitan areas or cities.

| Exhibit 6 | Correlation of Direct Real Estate Returns by U.S. Geographical Region | | | | |
|---|---|---|---|---|---|
| | **Index** | **East** | **Midwest** | **South** | **West** |
| Index | 1.00 | | | | |
| East | 0.95 | 1.00 | | | |
| Midwest | 0.91 | 0.88 | 1.00 | | |
| South | 0.91 | 0.85 | 0.86 | 1.00 | |
| West | 0.93 | 0.81 | 0.75 | 0.77 | 1.00 |

*Source*: CISDM (2005a).

The properties of real estate return distributions are important for the portfolio manager because they provide key inputs into the asset allocation process. Many return observations in indices of direct investment tend to be close to zero as a result of the illiquid market. Equity real estate returns generally have been found not to follow a normal distribution, in U.S. markets and elsewhere, for both the direct investments[34] and indirect investments.[35] Furthermore, the direct market exhibits a high degree of persistence in returns (positive following positive and negative following negative), whereas the indirect market does not show such persistence. The explanation for these facts is a matter of continuing investigation.[36]

**Investment in Real Estate Worldwide**   The benefit of real estate investment internationally has been researched. Overall, the evidence indicates that investors may benefit from including domestic and nondomestic investments in real estate in their portfolios.

Real estate has been found to be an effective portfolio diversifier for seven countries (Australia, France, the Netherlands, Sweden, Switzerland, the United Kingdom, and the United States) on three continents, based on data from 1987–2001, and including both domestic and international real estate assets increases the benefits.[37] Case, Goetzmann, and Wachter (1997) concluded that international real estate diversification would have been beneficial to a U.S. investor. The correlation between property share (real estate company) returns and other common stock returns appears to have declined in both the United States and the United Kingdom, indicating the possibility of increased diversification potential for property shares.[38] Research has also suggested that U.S. REITs may be an attractive addition to domestic stocks and bonds for investors from Canada and the United Kingdom.[39] Example 4 shows the application of some of the facts and methods discussed in the text.

---

**Example 4**

## Adding Real Estate to the Strategic Asset Allocation

As CIO of The Annette Hansen Charitable Foundation (TAHCF), a U.S.-based foundation supporting medical research, Maryann Dunn will present to the trustees a recommendation that they revise the foundation's strategic asset allocation to include direct investment in real estate.

- The Foundation's current portfolio and strategic asset allocation is allocated 50 percent common stocks/50 percent bonds. Twelve percent of the common stock allocation (six percent of the total portfolio) is invested in REITs.

- The risk-free rate of interest is 3.5 percent.

- The forecasted inflation rate is 3 percent.

- TAHCF's overall investment objective is to preserve the real (inflation-adjusted) value of assets after spending. Its spending rate is 5 percent of 12-month average asset value.

- TAHCF's cost of earning investment returns is 20 basis points per year.

Exhibit 7 shows Dunn's expectations for the current and proposed asset allocations. Dunn's expectations for direct investment are based on unsmoothed NCREIF historical data adjusted for her current economic outlook.

---

34 See Young and Graff (1995), Miles and McCue (1984), and Hartzell, Hekman, and Miles (1986).
35 See Lizieri and Satchell (1997), Sieler, Webb, and Myer (1999), Mei and Hu (2000), and Lizieri and Ward (2000) for a review.
36 See Lizieri and Ward (2000).
37 See Hoesli, Lekander, and Witkiewiez (2003).
38 See Brounen and Eichholtz (2003).
39 See Mull and Soenen (1997), who studied the 1985–94 period.

| | | 45/45/10 Stocks/Bonds/ U.S. Direct Real Estate Investment (%) |
|---|---|---|
| **Exhibit 7** | **Forecast Data** | |
| Measure | 50/50 Stocks/Bonds (%) | 45/45/10 Stocks/Bonds/ U.S. Direct Real Estate Investment (%) |
| Expected return | 5.5 | 5.9 |
| Std. dev. of return | 11.8 | 10.8 |

Dunn expects opposition to her proposal to come from a trustee, Bob Enicar. Enicar has stated at a prior board meeting: "TAHCF's allocation to equity includes substantial investment in REITs. REITs typically provide risk diversification comparable to that of direct equity investments for a balanced portfolio of stocks and bonds while offering substantially more liquidity."

1. State and explain two financial justifications that Dunn could present for revising TAHCF's asset allocation to 45/45/10 stocks/bonds/U.S. direct real estate investment.

2. State and explain one disadvantage of the proposed revised strategic asset allocation.

3. Contrast unsmoothed and smoothed NCREIF indices and justify Dunn's choice of the unsmoothed NCREIF Index in formulating expectations for direct real estate investment.

4. Draft a response to Enicar's critique.

## Solution to 1:

The financial justifications for adding direct real estate investment to the strategic asset allocation include the following:

- The Sharpe ratio of the 45/45/10 stock/bonds/U.S. direct real estate investment portfolio at (5.9% − 3.5%)/10.8 = 0.222 is greater than that of the current 50/50 stocks/bonds allocation at (5.5% − 3.5%)/11.8 = 0.169.

- Direct real estate investment's inflation-hedging qualities are consonant with TAHCF's stated concern for preserving the real purchasing power of funds.

- The revised strategic asset allocation is expected to come closer to satisfying TAHCF's investment objective than does the existing strategic asset allocation.

## Solution to 2:

The proposed strategic asset allocation's expected return of 5.9 percent falls well short of the (1.05)(1.03)(1.0020) − 1.0 = 8.37 percent return objective implicit in the description of the problem.

## Solution to 3:

The NCREIF Index is based on property appraisals rather than market values. Appraised values tend to be less volatile than market values, an effect known as smoothing. As a result of smoothing, volatility and correlations with other assets will tend to be understated, which means an overstatement of the benefits of real estate in the portfolio. Using the unsmoothed NCREIF index gives a more accurate picture of the benefits of real estate investment.

**Solution to 4:**

Enicar is correct that securitized real estate is more liquid than direct real estate investment. However, direct real estate's correlations with U.S. equities and U.S. bonds are lower than REITs' correlations, making direct real estate a stronger diversifier when added to a portfolio of stocks and bonds.

In Example 4, a strategic asset allocation involving direct real estate investment was reviewed that, in expectation, did not promise to fulfill the investor's return requirement. Section 4 discusses an alternative asset class that has become a popular vehicle for investors seeking high returns.

### 3.3.3  *Other Issues*

Due diligence in active direct real estate investment should cover the checkpoints outlined in Example 2: market opportunity, investment process, organization, people, terms and structure, service providers, documents, and write-up. Within each of these headings, some checkpoints will involve investment-specific points, such as valuation methods, financing, real estate legal issues (e.g., zoning, a title check), and for taxable investors especially, tax issues.

In the next section, we discuss another major type of alternative investment, private equity.

## 4  PRIVATE EQUITY/VENTURE CAPITAL

Private equity is an ownership interest in a private (non-publicly-traded) company. The term "private equity" refers to any security by which equity capital is raised via a private placement rather than through a public offering. As private placements, private equity securities are not registered with a regulatory body. To qualify as private placements, securities are generally offered for sale to either institutions or high-net-worth individuals (accredited investors). Private equity investments can be made face-to-face with the company needing financing or indirectly through private equity funds.

A variety of investment activities can take place in the investment structures known as **private equity funds**—the pooled investment vehicles through which many investors make (indirect) investments in generally highly illiquid assets. These investment activities range from financing private businesses, to leveraged buyouts of public companies, to distressed debt investing, to the public financing of public infrastructure projects. Thus, a host of investing activities requiring distinct expertise is often gathered under the rubric of private equity. In this section, the focus is on the two historically most important fields of private equity activity: the equity financing of new or growing private companies, an activity often called **venture capital**, and the buyout of established companies via private equity funds known as buyout funds.[40] In

---

[40] "Venture capital" is widely used to refer to early-stage financing of companies. Yet, practitioners also talk of late-stage venture capital, referring to the portion prior to exiting from the investment. According to Lerner (2000), p. 522, outside the United States, the term "venture capital" is often used as a synonym for "private equity." Confusingly, practitioners sometimes use "private equity" to refer to investment buyout funds rather than venture capital funds. In short, terminology varies, but the reader can understand the meaning from the context.

venture capital, a company that starts out as private may eventually become publicly owned. The converse process—taking a publicly owned company private in a buyout of publicly held interests and the private purchase of a division of a public corporation, as well as buyouts of established private companies—constitutes the chief sphere of activity of buyout funds.

---

**Example 5**

## Private Investment in Public Entity (PIPE)

The range of activities conducted via the structure of a private equity fund evolves and grows. An example is the PIPE—private investment in public entity. If the share price of a publicly traded company has dropped significantly from its value at the time of going public, the company may seek new sources of capital via a PIPE. Through a PIPE, an investor makes a relatively large investment in a company, usually at a price less than the current market value.

On 16 January 2004, Novatel Wireless, Inc., a publicly traded company, sold 1,142,855 shares of newly issued common stock to a group of private investment firms (a PIPE). The shares included warrants entitling the investors to purchase an additional 228,565 shares at a price of US$8.833 per share. Novatel raised net capital of US$7,525,000 in the initial transaction. On 13 February 2004, Novatel filed a registration statement with the U.S. SEC that would entitle these private investors to sell their shares on the open market. At the time of the original transaction, Novatel's shares were trading for US$9. At the time the registration statement was filed, the shares were trading for US$16.48.

*Sources: Business Week,* 10 May 2004, pp. 118–120, and Novatel Wireless, Inc., SEC Form S-3 filed 13 February 2004.

---

Private equity represents an important asset class that has received increasing interest from pension plans, endowments, foundations, and corporations, and from family offices and other advisors to the private wealth market. In some countries, such as the United Kingdom, exposure to this investment type is also available through exchange-traded vehicles.

In a number of countries, including the United States, private equity is one type of alternative investment that practitioners often point to as facing serious capacity issues. The high failure rate of young businesses is an indication that the combination of winning ideas for products/services and the entrepreneurial and/or managerial skill, experience, and commitment to realize them is in limited supply at any given point in time. The venture or business that is in a position of strength with respect to those qualities will be scrutinizing the potential investor for qualities needed in a partner/collaborator as closely as the investor will go over the investment checkpoints.

Most professional investors have wide experience and knowledge of public equity markets. Although public and private equity investments have common elements, private equity investment involves distinct knowledge and experience. The contrast is greatest in the case of direct private equity investment, which often calls on the investor's skills as a businessperson, as Exhibit 8 shows.

| Exhibit 8 | Investment Processes of (Direct) Private Equity Investment and Investment in Publicly Traded Equities |
|---|---|

| Private Equity Investments | Publicly Traded Securities |
|---|---|
| *Structure and Valuation* | |
| Deal structure and price are negotiated between the investor and company management. | Price is set in the context of the market. Deal structure is standardized. Variations typically require approval from securities regulators. |
| *Access to Information for Investment Selection* | |
| Investor can request access to all information, including internal projections. | Analysts can use only publicly available information to assess investment potential. |
| *Post-Investment Activity* | |
| Investors typically remain heavily involved in the company after the transaction by participating at the board level and through regular contact with management. | Investors typically do not sit on corporate boards or make ongoing assessments based on publicly available information and have limited access to management. |

*Source*: Prepared by Andrew Abouchar, CFA, of Tech Capital Partners.

The following section discusses some prominent characteristics of the private equity marketplace and private equity funds.

## 4.1 The Private Equity Market

The first question to address is why the market opportunities for private equity arise. Take the case of venture capital investment first: A closely held business is characterized by a small number of owners and is not publicly traded. Often, the owners of a closely held business are family members, but closely held businesses can also have unrelated owners. Such businesses may seek outside investors for a variety of reasons. For example, the original owners may not have adequate capital for growth or even to fund current operations. Entrepreneurs frequently lack the professional managerial skills and experience to manage the enterprise they started after it reaches a certain size. Venture capital firms may be able to supply valuable assistance in the transition to professional management.[41] The original owners may also want to diversify their wealth. For an individual investor, a closely held business can represent a significant portion of his or her overall wealth. The liquidity afforded by markets for publicly traded shares allows such investors to diversify their portfolios at lower costs. Venture capitalists also can assist in the initial public offering (IPO) of shares, which permits the original owners to eventually realize public market valuations for their holdings.[42]

Formative-stage companies usually raise money through marketing an effective business plan to potentially interested parties. The business plan describes the intended products and/or services, the market that will be served, the business strategy, the dates of expected financial milestones (such as profitability to be achieved), the expected cash "burn rate," the additional rounds of financing that the company expects to need, and other relevant information.

---

[41] As discussed in more detail shortly, **venture capital firms** represent dedicated pools of capital providing equity or equity-linked financing to privately held companies.

[42] An **initial public offering** is the initial issuance of common stock registered for public trading by a formerly private corporation.

In the case of funds raised through an agent, a document called a **private placement memorandum** may be used. This document should discuss a myriad of factors affecting the company. It should describe the company's business and competitive factors and discuss how it intends to use the proceeds from the offering. It should also contain financial statements and projections, although not necessarily audited financial statements.

**The Demand for Venture Capital**    Issuers of venture capital include the following:

- *Formative-stage companies.* This group ranges from newly formed companies, to young companies beginning product development ("start-ups"), to companies that are just beginning to sell a product. Worldwide, probably more than a million new businesses are formed every year, but venture capitalists frequently are not interested in companies at that earliest stage. In the United States, venture capitalists that do invest in formative-stage companies might be looking for companies with, for example, projected revenues in the US$10 million to US$50 million range within a five year horizon.[43]

- *Expansion-stage companies.* This group ranges from young companies that need financing for expanding sales, to established companies with significant revenues (middle-market companies), to companies that are preparing for an IPO of stock.

The financing stages through which many private companies pass include the following:[44]

*Early-Stage Financing*

- Seed—generally, seed money is a relatively small amount of money provided to the entrepreneur to form a company and prove that an idea has a reasonable chance of commercial success.

- Start-up—at this stage, the company has been formed and an idea has been proven but the company needs money to bring the product or idea to commercialization. This is a pre-revenue stage.

- First stage—if the company has exhausted its seed and start-up financing, the company may seek additional funds. Obviously, the company must have made progress from earlier stages to warrant an investment at this stage.

*Later-Stage Financing:*   This is the financing of promising companies that need funds for expanding sales.

**The Exit**   Because private equity is by definition not publicly traded, the exit (the liquidation or divestment of a private equity investment) is often difficult and is a major item of strategy. The investor can realize the value of the holding in several ways:

- merger with another company;

- acquisition by another company (including a private equity fund specializing in this); or

- an IPO by which the company becomes publicly traded.

---

**43** This comment supplies an idea of the stage at which venture capitalists become active; the numbers can be expected to change over time and may be different elsewhere.

**44** There is some variation in terminology. For example, after the seed and start-up stages, some practitioners distinguish Series A from Series B in reference to the series of preferred shares being issued in the transaction.

Of course, it is also possible that the venture will not succeed and the business will be closed without any recovery of the original investment by the equityholder. Exhibit 9 summarizes the venture capital timeline.

| Exhibit 9 | Venture Capital Timeline |
| --- | --- |

| | Formative-Stage Companies | | | Expansion-Stage Companies | | |
| --- | --- | --- | --- | --- | --- | --- |
| | Early Stage | | | Later Stage | | Pre-IPO |
| | Seed | Start-Up | First Stage | Second Stage | Third Stage | Mezzanine |
| Stage characteristics | Idea incorporation, first personnel hired, prototype development | Moving into operation, initial revenues | | Revenue growth | | Preparation for IPO |
| Stage financing (buyers of private equity) | Founders, FF&F,[a] angels, venture capital | Angels, venture capital | | Venture capital, strategic partners | | |
| Purpose of financing | Supports market research and establishment of business | **Start-up financing** supports product development and initial marketing **First-stage financing** supports such activities as initial manufacturing and sales | | **Second-stage financing** supports the initial expansion of a company already producing and selling a product **Third-stage financing** provides capital for major expansion **Mezzanine** (bridge) **financing** provides capital to prepare for the IPO—often a mix of debt and equity | | |

[a]FF&F = founder's friends and family. The sources of financing are listed in typical order of importance.

**The Supply of Venture Capital**    Suppliers of venture capital include the following:

- *Angel investors.* An **angel investor** is an accredited individual investing chiefly in seed and early-stage companies, sometimes after the resources of the founder's friends and family have been exhausted. Angel investors are often the first outside investors in a company, even before a company is organized or there is a real product. The size of the investments made by angels is relatively small. However, because they are generally invested at the earliest point, such investments are among the riskiest.

- *Venture capital.* **Venture capital** (VC) refers broadly to the pools of capital managed by specialists known as **venture capitalists** who seek to identify companies that have great business opportunities but need financial, managerial, and strategic support. Venture capitalists invest alongside company managers; they often take representation on the board of directors of the company and provide significant expertise in addition to capital. An individual pool is a **venture capital fund** (VC fund). An industry of investment firms sponsors series of such funds and sometimes a variety of similarly structured vehicles taking advantage of different opportunities. These firms may be private partnerships, closely held corporations, or sometimes, publicly traded corporations. In the United Kingdom, **venture capital trusts** (VCTs), which are exchange-traded, closed-end vehicles, provide an example of other opportunities that are available.

■ *Large companies.* A variety of major companies invest their own money via corporate private equity in promising young companies in the same or a related industry. The activity is known as **corporate venturing**, and the investors are often referred to as "strategic partners." Corporate venturing funds are not available to the public.

---

**Example 6**

## The IPO of Google

The IPO of Google, Inc., illustrates the timeline for private equity. Google was incorporated in 1998 with an initial investment of US$1,000,000 by family, friends, and angel investors. In early 1999, Google received US$25 million in venture capital funds. The two venture capital firms that provided capital in 1999 each own about 10.2 percent of the company. In April 2004, Google filed for an IPO. The IPO date was 19 August 2004, with Morgan Stanley and Credit Suisse First Boston as the lead underwriters in an unusual (for equities) Dutch auction–style auction, which affords more access to shares by smaller investors. The offering was for approximately 19.6 million shares of Class A common stock. Of that number, approximately 4.5 million shares were from selling shareholders realizing part of the cash value of their shareholdings, including company founders Larry Page and Sergey Brin. The offering was at US$85 per share and raised about US$1.2 billion for Google and US$464 million for the selling shareholders. After the offering, about 33.6 million Class A shares and about 237.6 million privately held Class B shares were outstanding. The Class B shares, held by the founders and other executives and investors, had 10 votes per share (versus 1 vote per share for the Class A shareholders). This dual-stock structure was viewed as unusual in technology IPOs, but it had been used by media companies, such as the *New York Times.* It permitted insiders to maintain voting control over Google and, according to Google executives, protected the company from pressures felt by public companies to produce short-term performance. At the same time, the Class B shares were convertible to the registered Class A shares, so the investing group could access public markets to realize the cash values of their holdings in the future. The August 2004 IPO was oversubscribed, and the shares (NASDAQ: GOOG) rose about 18 percent in initial trading. On 14 September 2005, Google made a follow-on offering of about 14.2 million shares at US$295 per share that raised US$4.18 billion. On 31 March 2006, Google was added to the S&P 500.

*Sources:* Reuters, "Key Dates in the History of Google" and "Update: Brin, Page Lead List of Google Shareholders," both on 29 April 2004 at www.google-ipo.com.

---

Most investors participate in private equity through private equity funds. Among these funds, buyout funds constitute a larger segment than VC funds, as measured by assets under management or the size of capital commitments. The capital commitments to buyout funds in many years have been two to three times the size of those to VC funds.

Buyout funds may be separated into two major groups, mega-cap buyout funds and middle-market buyout funds. **Mega-cap buy-out funds** take public companies private. **Middle-market buy-out funds** purchase private companies whose revenues and profits are too small to access capital from the public equity markets. Middle-market buyout funds typically purchase established businesses, such as small privately held companies (including those that may have received venture capital support) and divisions spun off from larger companies. The buyout fund manager seeks to add value by:

- restructuring operations and improving management;

- opportunistically identifying and executing the purchase of companies at a discount to intrinsic value; and

- capturing any gains from the addition of debt or restructuring of existing debt.

To further their ability to add value through restructuring operations and improving management, large buyout organizations maintain a pool of experienced operating and financial executives who can be inserted into the companies if necessary or appropriate. These organizations look to cut costs and increase revenues. As the owner/managers of companies, buyout organizations have well-developed processes for installing incentive compensation systems and management reporting systems. They have experience restructuring supply chains and distribution channels. Buyout firms may explain the market opportunity as the potential to add value by substitution of a highly focused private governance model, in which expert owners have complete control, for a public governance model with dispersed ownership, conflicts of interest, and high regulatory compliance costs.

Buyout funds can realize value gains through a sale of the acquired company, an IPO, or a dividend recapitalization. A **dividend recapitalization** involves the issuance of debt to finance a special dividend to owners (sometimes refinancing existing debt in the process). Dividend recapitalizations have at times allowed buyout funds to recoup all or most of the cash used to acquire a company within two to four years of the buyout while still retaining ownership and control of the company. However, dividend recapitalization has the potential to weaken the company as a going concern by overleveraging it.

The major investors in private equity funds are public pension funds, corporate defined-benefit pension plans, endowments, foundations, and family offices. In the United States, public pension plans are currently the most important players as measured by the amount of dollars committed; they are followed by the other investors in the order listed. Endowments and foundations have among the largest allocations in their policy portfolios. Family offices are a growing influence.[45]

### 4.1.1 *Types of Private Equity Investment*

Both direct and indirect investors in private equity need to understand the basics of direct private equity investment in order to have an informed grasp of its return and risk characteristics.

Direct venture capital investment is structured as convertible preferred stock rather than common stock. The terms of the preferred stock require that the corporation pay cash equal to some multiple (e.g., 2×) of preferred shareholders' original investment before any cash can be paid on the common stock, which is the equity investment of the founders. Preferred stock is senior to common stock also in its claims on liquidation value. This financing structure mitigates the risk that the company will take on the venture capital investment and distribute it to the owners/founders. It also provides an incentive to the company to meet the return goals of the outside investors.

Investors in subsequent rounds usually have rights to cash flows that are senior to preferred stock issued in previous financing rounds. All else being equal, therefore, shares issued in later rounds are more valuable than shares issued in earlier rounds, which in turn, are more valuable than the founders' common shares. Nevertheless, the differences in value may be slight and are frequently ignored in valuation. For convertible preferred shares issued in any round, an event such as a buyout or an acquisition of the common equity at a favorable price will trigger conversion of the preferred into the common shares of the company.

---

[45] See Boyer (2005).

Indirect investment is primarily through private equity funds, including VC funds and buyout funds. Private equity funds are usually structured as limited partnerships or limited liability companies (LLCs) with an expected life of 7–10 years with an option to extend the life for another 1–5 years.[46] The fund manager's objective is to realize the value of all portfolio investments by the fund's liquidation date. There is typically an offering period in which capital commitments are solicited.

The limited partnership and LLC forms are attractive because income and capital gains flow through to the limited partners (for the LLC, the shareholders) for tax purposes, thus avoiding the possible double taxation that can occur in the corporate form. The limited partners or shareholders do not bear any liability beyond the amount of their investments. The limited partners or shareholders commit to a specific investment amount that the general partner (in an LLC, the managing director) "takes down" over time in a series of capital calls to make specific investments or to pay expenses; private equity funds usually do not maintain a pool of uninvested capital. The general partner (or the managing director) is the venture capitalist, the party selecting and advising investments. The general partner, who may be an individual or another entity (such as a corporation or partnership), also commits its own capital. In this way, the interests of the outside investors and the fund manager/general partner/managing director are closely aligned.

The LLC form, available in the United States and some other countries under different names and with different requirements, is a hybrid of the corporate and partnership forms. It provides investors with more influence on the fund's operations than does a limited partnership interest—in particular, more control over the raising of additional committed capital. The LLC is often the preferred form when raising funds from a relatively small group of substantial and knowledgeable investors who may want to be proactive investors.

Private equity funds of funds are also available. Such funds invest in other private equity funds. Management fees of funds-of-funds vehicles range from 0.5 percent to 2 percent of the net assets managed; these fees are on top of fees charged by the underlying funds.

In contrast to the structure of private equity funds, in venture capital, the company receiving support is organized in a corporate form because one desirable exit is a successful initial offering of shares to the public. Examples of the corporate form of publicly traded companies include the U.K. public limited company (PLC), the corporation in the United States, the *kabushiki kaisha* (K.K.) in Japan, the *sociedad anónima* in Spain, the *société anonyme* in France, and the *Aktiengesellschaft* (AG) in Germany. The European Union has developed a new structure, the European company or *societas Europeae* (SE), that will permit companies in the EU to operate throughout the EU under one set of rules and with a uniform management system.

The compensation to the fund manager of a private equity fund consists of a management fee plus an incentive fee. The management fee is usually a percentage of limited partner *commitments* to the fund. (If the investor has made a capital commitment of US$50 million but actually invested only US$10 million, the investor generally pays a management fee on the US$50 million committed.) Management fees are often in the 1.5–2.5 percent range and often scale down in the later years of a partnership to reflect a lower work load.

The fund manager's incentive fee, the **carried interest**, is the share of the private equity fund's profits that the fund manager is due once the fund has returned the outside investors' capital (which may be specified as the capital committed or the capital invested). Carried interest is usually expressed as a percentage of the total profits of the fund. A common value is 20 percent. In such a structure, the fund manager will thus receive 20 percent of the profits and distribute the remaining 80 percent of the

---

**46** Anson (2002a), p. 273.

profits to investors. In some funds, the carried interest is computed on only those profits that represent a return in excess of a hurdle rate (the hurdle rate is also known as the **preferred return**). A hurdle rate of 6 percent means that only the private equity fund's profits in excess of an annualized return of 6 percent are subject to the 20 percent carried interest. Because early investments by the fund may achieve high rates of return but later investments do poorly, private equity funds sometimes have a **claw-back provision** that specifies that money from the fund manager be returned to investors if at the end of a fund's life investors have not received back their capital contributions and contractual share of profits.

In distributing cash flows to investors and the fund manager, a private equity fund first distributes to investors their invested capital and preferred return (if any is specified). Sometimes, the fund manager is allowed to take a small percentage of early distributions. Typically, following the period in which all or most distributions go to investors, there is a catch-up period in which the fund manager receives all or the major share of profits. After the fund manager has caught up to its specified share of profits according to the contract, subsequent profits are distributed according to the carried interest percentage—for example, 80 percent to investors and 20 percent to the fund manager. Some of the manager's profits may be put in an escrow account to satisfy any claw-back liability.

The investor in a private equity fund expects to receive the benefits of the general manager's ability to select worthy investments and maintain active involvement in the investments. The fund manager and the manager's team should be able to shore up weaknesses in the companies' management and assist in planning and executing a successful exit strategy that realizes the value of the investments.

### 4.1.2 Size of the Private Equity Market

A reliable estimate of direct private equity investment worldwide is hard to obtain, but as of early 2006, approximately US$200 billion was invested in private equity VC and buyout funds worldwide via approximately 1,000 private equity vehicles.[47] In the United States, a quarterly study of venture capital activity is performed through a joint effort of PricewaterhouseCoopers, Thomson Venture Economics, and the National Venture Capital Association (NVCA). Exhibit 10 presents a summary of the annual results through 2004.

| Exhibit 10 | U.S. Venture Capital Activity: MoneyTree™ Survey | |
|---|---|---|
| **Year** | **Investment Amount (US$)** | **Number of Deals** |
| 1995 | 7,627,158,000 | 1,874 |
| 1996 | 11,521,998,000 | 2,612 |
| 1997 | 14,799,528,000 | 3,185 |
| 1998 | 21,258,792,000 | 3,695 |
| 1999 | 54,525,275,000 | 5,608 |
| 2000 | 105,859,076,000 | 8,082 |
| 2001 | 40,582,005,000 | 4,600 |
| 2002 | 21,409,439,000 | 3,035 |
| 2003 | 18,186,857,000 | 2,715 |
| 2004 | 21,341,540,000 | 2,910 |

*Source*: www.pwcmoneytree.com.

---

**47** Goodman (2006).

PricewaterhouseCoopers, Thomson Venture Economics, and the European Private Equity and Venture Capital Association collaborate on similar surveys of private equity activity across continental Europe and the United Kingdom. Exhibit 11 summarizes recent investment activity of VC and buyout funds. As in the United States, 2000 marked a high point of activity.

| **Exhibit 11** | **Pan-European Private Equity Activity (in € Billions)** | | |
| --- | --- | --- | --- |
| Year | Venture Capital Fund Investment | Buyout Fund Investment | Total |
| 2000 | 19.6 | 15.3 | 34.9 |
| 2001 | 13.3 | 11.0 | 24.3 |
| 2002 | 10.7 | 16.9 | 27.6 |
| 2003 | 10.7 | 18.4 | 29.1 |
| 2004 | 11.2 | 25.7 | 36.9 |

*Note*: Numbers for venture capital rounded to make venture capital activity and buyout activity sum to the reported totals.
*Source*: www.evca.com.

## 4.2 Benchmarks and Historical Performance

As for many other alternative investment types, events that indicate the market value of a private equity investment generally occur infrequently. Typical market price–revealing events include the raising of new financing, the acquisition of the company by another company, the IPO, or failure of the business. Infrequent market pricing poses a major challenge to index construction. How can returns be calculated without market transactions?

When measuring the performance of a private equity investment, investors typically calculate an internal rate of return based on cash flows since inception of the investment and the ending valuation of the investment (the net asset value or residual value). Similarly, major venture capital benchmarks, such as Thomson Venture Economics, provide IRR estimates for private equity funds that are based on fund cash flows and valuations.

### 4.2.1 Benchmarks

Major benchmarks for U.S. and European private equity are those provided by Cambridge Associates and Thomson Venture Economics, who present an overall private equity index representing two major segments: VC funds and buyout funds. Custom benchmarks are also frequently used by private equity investors.

### 4.2.2 Historical Performance

Exhibit 12 gives U.S. private equity's annualized IRRs as compiled by the National Venture Capital Association and Thomson Venture Economics as of 2005. In Exhibit 12, "balanced VC funds" are funds that make both early-stage and late-stage investments.

| | **Venture Capital Funds** | | | | **Buyout** | | |
| Period | Seed/Early | Balanced | Late Stage | All | Funds | NASDAQ | S&P 500 |
|--------|-----------|----------|-----------|-----|--------|--------|---------|
| 3 Year | 0.4 | 9.3 | 6.1 | 4.9 | 14.7 | 22.4 | 14.7 |
| 5 Year | −13.2 | −5.6 | −7.7 | −9.3 | 3.1 | −10.1 | −3.1 |
| 10 Year | 46.8 | 20.8 | 13.0 | 26.5 | 8.7 | 7.5 | 7.7 |
| 20 Year | 20.2 | 14.6 | 13.7 | 16.5 | 13.3 | 12.3 | 11.2 |

**Exhibit 12**  U.S. Private Equity Returns as of 30 September 2005 (in Percent)

*Source*: NVCA and Thomson Venture Economics, 4 February 2004, news release, www.nvca.org.

Private equity returns have exhibited a low correlation with publicly traded securities, making them an attractive addition to a portfolio. However, because of a lack of observable market prices for private equity, short-term return and correlation data may be a result of stale prices. Emery (2003) showed that the correlation between venture capital and NASDAQ returns increased substantially when annual or biannual (i.e., calculated every two years) data were used rather than quarterly data.[48] Emery showed that venture capital returns demonstrated a 0.69 correlation with NASDAQ returns and a 0.40 correlation with S&P 500 returns based on quarterly data. When biannual data were used, the correlation was 0.93 with the NASDAQ and 0.64 with the S&P 500.

### 4.2.3 Interpretation Issues

The private equity investor thinks of returns in terms of IRR calculations based, generally, on estimates of the values of the investor's interest. However, the fund manager's appraisals (usually supplied on a quarterly basis) supply estimates, not a market price. Appraised values are often slow to adjust to new circumstances (use stale data) and focus only on company-specific events, so the returns may be erroneous. Furthermore, there is no generally accepted standard for appraisals.

In evaluating past records of returns of private equity funds, investors often make comparisons with funds closed in the same year (the funds' **vintage year**). This helps assure the funds are compared with other funds at a similar stage in their life cycle. The effects of vintage year on returns are known as "**vintage year effects**," and include, in addition to the effects of life-cycle stage, the influence that economic conditions and market opportunities associated with a given vintage year may have on various funds' probabilities of success.

## 4.3 Private Equity: Investment Characteristics and Roles

Like public equity investment, but to a greater degree, private equity plays a growth role in investment portfolios. On the one hand, at the company level, the highest earnings growth rates are usually achievable early, when the markets for the company's products may be largely untapped and competition may be slight. When a promising private company comes to market, its prospective growth may be capitalized at an above-market-average multiple. On the other hand, investment in established companies via buyout funds generally involves less risk and earlier returns. The private equity investor hopes to gauge and control the risk through appropriate due diligence processes. The following section provides more details on investment characteristics.

---

**48** See Emery (2003), pp. 43–50.

### 4.3.1 *Investment Characteristics*

The general investment characteristics of private equity investments include the following:

- *Illiquidity.* Private equity investments are generally highly illiquid. Convertible preferred stock investments do not trade in a secondary market. Private equity fund investors have more restricted opportunities to withdraw investments from the fund than do hedge fund investors. This is natural, because the underlying investments are not liquid.

- *Long-term commitments required.* Private equity investment generally requires long-term commitments. For direct VC investments, the time horizon also can be quite uncertain.

- *Higher risk than seasoned public equity investment.* The returns to private equity investments, on average, show greater dispersion than seasoned public equity investments, although they may be roughly comparable to those of publicly traded microcap shares.[49] The risk of complete loss of investment is also higher. The failure rate of new and young businesses is high.

- *High expected IRR required.* Private equity investors target high rates of returns as compensation for the risk and illiquidity of such investments.

For venture capital investments, the following also holds:

- *Limited information.* Because new ventures operate in product or service markets that may break new ground in some way, projections concerning cash flows are often based on limited information or make many assumptions. Although this is a risk factor, it is also related to the potential for unusual profits, however, of successful ventures.

Venture capitalists often target rates of return of 25–30 percent or more in individual investments. Dramatic success stories of venture capital include companies such as Apple Computers, Intel Corporation, Microsoft, and Google. Many investments do not work out. For bearing the additional risks of private equity compared with public equity, the private equity fund investor targets earning a substantial premium over expected public equity returns.

The illiquidity of private equity affects the value, of course, of an investor's interest. The value that is determined by using models such as the venture capital method or discounted cash flow method may be used as the estimate of the value for a marketable controlling interest.[50] If the owner has a minority interest and the equity interest does not have a ready market, then discounts are applied to reflect the value for a minority-interest holder with a nonmarketable interest. The discount for a minority interest reflects the lack of control that the investor has over the business and distributions. Studies have indicated that minority-interest discounts can range from 20 percent to 30 percent.[51] The discount for lack of marketability (for short, marketability discount) takes account of the lack of liquidity in the investment and depends on a number of factors, such as the size of the interest and the level of dividends paid. Studies of marketability discounts have shown mean discounts in the 28–36 percent range.[52] If the interest to be valued is a controlling interest, only the marketability discount needs to be considered. For a majority interest, the discount for lack of marketability might reflect both the cost of going public and a discount for owning a large block

---

**49** See Cochrane (2004).
**50** The venture capital method of valuation involves discounting at a high interest rate a projected future value of the company, where the projected future value assumes the company is successful.
**51** CCH Business Valuation Guide, paragraph 2105.
**52** Ibid, paragraph 2111.

of shares. Example 7 illustrates one possibility for the valuation of a nonmarketable minority interest. A cautionary note is that the valuation of a nonmarketable minority interest can figure in the value of an estate and the estate taxes due for deceased private wealth clients. The calculation shown is not intended as a guide to estate planning in any given jurisdiction.

---

**Example 7**

## A Nonmarketable Minority Interest

Brent Smith has determined that his company will make a small investment in a private company, Clark Computing. The investment will be a nonmarketable minority interest. Smith's investment banker estimates that the value of Clark equity, if it were publicly traded, would be £500 million. Smith's company's interest in Clark will be 10 percent of Clark's equity. Smith's investment banker determines that a minority interest discount of 20 percent and a marketability discount of 25 percent are appropriate. What is the value of the nonmarketable minority interest?

**Solution:**

The money amounts shown are in millions of pounds sterling.

> Marketable controlling interest value: (10% × 500) = 50.
>
> Minority interest discount: (20% × 50) = −10.
>
> Marketable minority interest: (50 − 10) = 40.
>
> Marketability discount: (25% × 40) = −10.
>
> Nonmarketable minority interest: (40 − 10) = 30.

Smith's investment banker values the investment at £30 million.

---

VC funds and buyout funds have some expected differences in return characteristics.[53]

- *Buyout funds are usually highly leveraged.* The capital raised by the fund may be 25–40 percent of capital used to purchase the equity of the target company, with the balance coming from debt collateralized by the target company's assets. The operating cash flows of the target company, typically an established company, are used to service the debt payments. In contrast, VC funds use no debt in obtaining their equity interests.

- *The cash flows to buyout fund investors come earlier and are often steadier than those to VC fund investors.* Because buyout funds purchase established companies, buyout fund investors usually realize returns earlier than VC fund investors, for which fund investments may still be in the cash-burning stage. The expected pattern of interim returns over the life of a successful venture capital fund has sometimes been described as a *J*-curve, in which early returns (e.g., over the first five or six years) are negative as the portfolio of companies burns cash but later returns accelerate as companies are exited. In general, the earlier the stage in which a fund invests in companies, the greater the risk and the potential.

- *The returns to VC fund investors are subject to greater error in measurement.* The interim return calculations of private equity funds depend not only on cash flow transactions with the fund but also on the valuations of the portfolio companies. These valuations are subject to much less uncertainty for buyout funds investing in established companies.

---

**53** Emery (2003).

Thus, venture capital investing may be expected to involve more frequent losses than buyouts in return for higher upside potential when investments are successful.

---

**Example 8**

## An Investment in Private Equity

The Lee Foundation was established 10 years ago to provide grants to minority- and female-owned enterprises. A well-diversified asset allocation has resulted in successful growth in the value of the foundation's investments. The trustees have thus decided to allocate US$5 million to private equity. Their objectives are to earn significantly high returns on a high-growth investment and to take an active and dominant role in control of the company in which they decide to invest. They understand that such an investment requires a high level of risk tolerance and a multi-year time horizon.

1. Evaluate the suitability of the following three potential investments, with specific reference to short- and long-term returns, sources of risk, and degree of investor control:

    **A.** Seed investment in a new medical device recently developed by three doctors.

    **B.** Venture capital trust that invests exclusively in 15–20 start-up companies at any given time.

    **C.** Second-stage (follow-on) investment in a company that successfully patented a new medical device two years ago and seeks to expand its manufacturing facilities.

2. Recommend and justify the investment that is most likely to satisfy the goals of the foundation's proposed US$5 million investment.

### Solution to 1:

**A.** The seed investment is an investment in an early-stage company with no proven "track record" or history of revenues. Therefore, there are not likely to be any immediate or short-term returns because the next stage is marketing and manufacturing this new device. If the sales of this unique device are successful, however, future long-term returns could be significant. Sources of risk include the failure of the device, future competition from other similar companies, lack of follow-on funds for marketing and manufacturing, and the possibility that the device may not receive a patent. Consequently, the level of risk is high. Because the foundation is likely to be the first outside investor, the possibility of taking an active role in the company, possibly as outside board members, is high.

**B.** The venture capital trust is diversified over many start-up companies and is thus probably providing some current return, with the potential for additional return in the future. Although there is considerable risk associated with start-up companies, the trust is well diversified over many companies, which mitigates the impact of risk of the failure of one or two of the start-ups. There is no outside investor control available because the trust makes all the decisions and is traded on a public exchange.

**C.** The second-stage investment is most likely already showing positive cash flow and net income because it is seeking financing to expand an existing manufacturing facility. Therefore, short-term returns may be attractive and projections probably indicate potential for additional long-term returns, although the level of these returns may be muted in comparison with a seed or start-up because some of the early money has already been made. Investors at the second stage may be able to negotiate some active control, although the founders and seed/start-up investors are probably directly involved in company decisions also.

### Solution to 2:

The seed company is most consistent with the foundation's objectives of earning a significant return in a high-growth opportunity and having the ability to take an active role in the company. Additionally, the foundation is willing to accept a high degree of risk and a longer-term perspective for future returns.

### 4.3.2 *Roles in the Portfolio*

The moderately high average correlation of private equity returns with publicly traded share returns that has been documented has an economic explanation that is at least plausible: All types of businesses have some exposure to economic and industry conditions, so correlations of public and private equity returns may be expected to be positive. Furthermore, venture capital has public equity markets as one main exit route, so returns to VC fund investors would be expected to be higher when public equity market values are advancing. Private equity bears more idiosyncratic or company-specific risk than the average seasoned public company, however, so any correlation should not be extremely high.

Private equity probably can play a moderate role as a risk diversifier. However, many investors look to private equity investment for long-term return enhancement.

Given the capacity issues already mentioned and private equity's generally high illiquidity, target allocations of 5 percent or less are commonplace. For example, in 2004, based on money already committed, Canadian public sector pension plans averaged allocations of 3.6 percent and corporate pension plans averaged 1.3 percent.[54]

Among the issues that must be addressed in formulating a strategy for private equity investment are the following:[55]

- *Ability to achieve sufficient diversification.* Suppose an investor's allocation to private equity is 5 percent. Given that institutional partnership commitments are typically not smaller than US$5 million, a reasonably diversified portfolio (5–10 investments) means commitments totaling 5 × US$5 million = US$25 million to 10 × US$5 million = US$50 million. These amounts imply that the assets of the institutions investing in this kind of investment typically need to exceed US$500 million (= US$25 million ÷ 5%). For smaller investors, a private equity fund of funds is a possible diversification choice, although it involves a second layer of fees.

- *Liquidity of the position.* Direct private equity investments are inherently illiquid. Consequently, private equity funds are also illiquid. Investors in funds must be prepared to have the capital tied up for 7–10 years. Although a limited secondary market for private equity commitments exists, the investments trade at highly discounted prices, which makes selling the positions an unattractive proposition.

---

**54** Based on Frank Russell Company data.
**55** Andrew Abouchar, CFA, contributed to this section.

■ *Provision for capital commitment.* An investor in a private equity fund makes a commitment of capital. The cash is advanced over a period of time known as the **commitment period**, which is typically five years. Therefore, the investor needs to make provisions to have cash available for future capital calls.

■ *Appropriate diversification strategy.* An investor contemplating an exposure to private equity should be clear on the stand-alone risk factors of an investment and also the effect on the overall risk of the portfolio. Each private equity fund will have a different investment focus, which when combined with other funds in the portfolio, modifies the overall risk. Diversification may be across industry sectors, by stage of company development, and by location:

- industry sector (information technology, biotechnology, alternative energy, etc.);

- stage (early stage, expansion, buyout, etc.);

- geography (locally focused, internationally focused, etc.).

The element shared by all private equity investment is the identification of promising private businesses with committed and talented owner/managers.

For the many private equity investors making indirect investment, the search is for fund managers who are expert in evaluating and managing private equity investments. Indirect investment can include investment not only in newly formed private equity funds but also in secondary-market private equity fund purchases from limited partners seeking liquidity.

### 4.3.3 Other Issues

Among the major requirements for private equity investing is careful due diligence. The framework discussed in Example 2 applies, of course; in particular, due diligence items for private equity can usually be placed into one of the following three bins:

1. Evaluation of prospects for market success.

2. Operational review, focusing on internal processes, such as sales management, employment contracts, internal financial controls, product engineering and development, and intellectual property management.

3. Financial/legal review, including the examination of internal financial statements, audited financial statements, auditor's management letters, prior-year budgets, documentation of past board of directors meetings, board minutes, corporate minute books, and assessment of all legal proceedings, intellectual property positions, contracts and contingent liabilities.

Some practical details and comments are as follows:

1. Evaluation of Prospects for Market Success

- *Markets, competition, and sales prospects.* The private equity investor needs to form a judgment about the prospects for success of the company in the targeted product/service market. This review includes an evaluation of markets, competition, and sales prospects. The information in the business plan is a starting point in making such an appraisal.

- *Management experience and capabilities.* Quality of management is often considered the single biggest factor in the success of a venture. Due diligence includes a background check on the managers and other key personnel. This should include not only references provided by the company but also independently gathered information from the investor's own sources. The investor should use all available information in assessing the management team's acumen. Moreover, the assessment of management does not stop when the initial investment is made; it is ongoing.

- *Management's commitment.* Much of the success of a private equity company depends on its managers. Therefore, a potential investor will want to gauge how committed the managers are to the company. There are several factors to use in assessing this:

  - Percentage ownership. How much of the company is owned by the management team? Ownership of a large portion of the company is an indication of high commitment to the company.

  - Compensation incentives. If management is key to the company's success, an investor will want to ensure that the current managers' interests align with those of the shareholders through the company compensation arrangements.

- *Cash invested.* How much cash or "skin" has management invested in the company? Investors generally regard the fact that the managers have invested a large portion of their net worth in the company as a particularly good indicator of a highly committed management team. Conversely, if the managers have invested little of their own cash in the company, the presumption is that they are less than wholly committed to the company's success.

- *Opinion of customers.* When the company is already marketing a product or service, the investor should attempt to learn customer opinions of the company and its product or services.

- *Identity of current investors.* Current investors can give an indication of the company's future success. For example, if a company's product is a medical device dealing with the heart, it is meaningful if several leading cardiologists have already invested in the company.

2. Operational Review

- *Expert validation of technology.* If the company intends to market a new technology, the investor needs to obtain expert validation that the technology is valid and represents an advance.

- *Employment contracts.* Do key employees have contracts to ensure that they stay with the company? Do non-key employees have contracts with severance clauses that could burden the company's finances?

- *Intellectual property.* In many companies, the ability to succeed hinges on proprietary information (formulas, processes, designs). An investor should determine whether the company holds relevant patents in such cases (or at least has applied for such patents). These patents could be a design for a machine, a new application of an existing technology, a drug, a medical device, or so on. Potential investors should have reasonable assurance that the company has the ability to conduct business without another company's infringement. Often in this area, an investor will want to consult with patent experts.

3. Financial/Legal Review

- *Potential for dilution of interest.* Potential investors also want to investigate the stock options that have been issued to managers and other potential means by which investor interests may be diluted and to ensure contractually that their investment will not be significantly diluted.

- *Examination of financial statements.* Early-stage companies, in particular, may not have audited financial statements to show. Thus, investors may want to ask for tax returns or conduct their own audits of financial records.

Due diligence for private equity funds includes the managers' experience, capabilities, and commitment, the compensation arrangements, and compliance of the fund with Global Investment Performance Standards® in reporting performance. Fund selection is largely an exercise in evaluating the capabilities of the general manager's management team. Factors that should be considered include the following:

- historical returns generated on prior funds;

- consistency of returns. Has the team had one successful fund or many?

- roles and capabilities of specific individuals at the fund. The investor will want to evaluate whether the fund manager has the needed human resources to effectively select and guide private equity investment;

- stability of the team. Did the current senior personnel generate the track record of the fund manager, or has there been significant personnel turnover?

As the discussion of due diligence makes clear, many characteristics of people, structure, and costs can differentiate a set of private equity investments focused on a similar market opportunity. In contrast, different examples of a commodity, such as natural gas, have highly similar characteristics. Commodity investments are the subject of the next section.

# COMMODITY INVESTMENTS

## 5

A **commodity** is a tangible asset that is typically relatively homogeneous in nature. Because of their relative homogeneity, commodities lend themselves to being the subject of contracts to buy and sell that have standardized terms (as in futures market contracts).[56] Commodity investments are direct or indirect investments in commodities.

The question of whether commodities represent a separate asset class has been extensively debated in both the academic and practitioner literature.[57] Practically, the question is not whether commodity investment is an asset class but whether commodity investment is appropriate for a given investor. If it is, what is the best approach to implement the investment and the appropriate allocation? In some statements of strategic asset allocations, commodities may be included under a heading of "real assets" or "real assets: resources," in which case, they may not be separately distinguished from such real investments as timberland.

Historically, commodity-linked businesses have been the major players in the cash and futures commodity markets. Individual investors in many countries have long been active in the cash markets for precious metals. In some markets, **commodity trading advisors** (CTAs, registered advisors to managed futures funds) are another active group. Historically and currently, institutional investors have been more active in financial futures markets than in commodity futures markets. Investment in publicly traded equities of commodity-linked businesses has probably been the most common approach for both individual and institutional investors to obtain exposure, albeit indirectly, to commodities. Only investment in commodities via cash and the derivatives markets constitutes alternative investing. Those markets are the focus of this treatment.

---

**56** The relative homogeneity of commodities distinguishes them from tangible assets, such as fine art and other collectibles.
**57** See Huberman (1995), Strongin and Petsch (1995), Greer (1994), Froot (1995), Schneeweis and Spurgin (1997b), Geman (2005), and Erb and Harvey (2006).

## 5.1 The Commodity Market

Investors can gain direct exposure to commodities in spot (cash) markets or in markets for deferred delivery, such as futures and forwards markets. Spot commodity trading can be traced back thousands of years, and commodity futures trading is at least as old as the rice futures trading in Japan several hundred years ago.

Commodity futures markets developed as a response to an economic need by suppliers and users of various agricultural and nonagricultural goods to transfer risk. Moreover, commodity futures markets tend to improve the functioning of the spot and forward markets. For instance, commodity futures may permit greater commodity production and trade because the use of futures hedges reduces the risk of holding spot inventories. By facilitating risk management and trading, commodity futures have grown to become an essential part of the production and marketing of agricultural and nonagricultural goods. Other types of commodity derivatives include options on commodity futures and swap markets.

Commodities futures are traded on agricultural products, metals, and energy resources. A commodity futures transaction may involve possible physical delivery (i.e., actual delivery of the underlying commodity) or may be "cash-settled," which means that no delivery takes place but a settlement in cash occurs at maturity equal to the gain that a delivery transaction would entail. Although physical delivery is possible for some futures contracts, in practice most positions in futures contracts are offset prior to maturity.

### 5.1.1 Types of Commodity Investments

There are two broad approaches to investing in commodities: direct and indirect. **Direct commodity investment** entails cash market purchase of physical commodities—agricultural products, metals, and crude oil—or exposure to changes in spot market values via derivatives, such as futures. Cash market purchases involve actual possession and storage of the physical commodities and incur carrying costs and storage costs. Thus, investors have generally preferred to use derivatives or indirect commodity investment.

**Indirect commodity investment** involves the acquisition of indirect claims on commodities, such as equity in companies specializing in commodity production. As mentioned previously, indirect commodity investment was historically the principal means that most investors used to obtain exposure to commodities. There is increasing evidence, however, that indirect commodity investment—in particular, equity instruments in commodity-linked companies—does not provide effective exposure to commodity price changes.[58] To the degree that companies hedge a major portion of their commodity risk, even commodity-linked companies may not be exposed to the risk of commodity price movement.[59] This fact has been a spur to the creation of investable commodity indices and a current preference for gaining exposure to commodities through derivative markets. In some markets, such as the United States, even small investors can access the commodity markets via mutual funds or exchange-traded funds.

### 5.1.2 Size of the Commodity Market

With billions of dollars worth of commodities recorded by so many countries in international trade over a given year, spot commodity markets are enormous in scope and value. In the United States alone, the notional value of open interest

---

**58** See Schneeweis and Spurgin (1997a).
**59** See Chung (2000).

in commodity futures was estimated at US$350 billion as of the fourth quarter of 2005, with energy futures (natural gas, crude oil, heating oil, and gasoline) the dominant segment.[60]

## 5.2 Benchmarks and Historical Performance[61]

Although the physical markets for commodities are not centralized, information about commodity prices is transmitted around the world through commodity-based financial products. Thus, performance of commodity investments can be evaluated by using commodity indices that form the basis for many products. The development of active markets for indexed commodity investments has been a major force in broadening investor interest in commodity investment.

### 5.2.1 *Benchmarks*

A variety of indices based on futures prices can be used as benchmarks for the performance of futures-based commodity investments. These include the Reuters Jefferies/ Commodity Research Bureau (RJ/CRB) Index, the Goldman Sachs Commodity Index (GSCI), the Dow Jones–AIG Commodity Index (DJ-AIGCI), and the S&P Commodity Index (S&PCI).

Commodity indices attempt to replicate the returns available to holding long positions in commodities. The DJ-AIGCI, the RJ/CRB Index, the GSCI, and the S&PCI provide returns comparable to passive long positions in listed futures contracts. Because the cost-of-carry model ensures that the return on a fully margined position in a futures contract mimics the return on an underlying spot deliverable, futures contract returns are often used as a surrogate for cash market performance. (The cost-of-carry model relates the futures price to the current spot price and the cost of holding the spot commodity.) All of these indices are considered investable.

The major indices contain different groups of underlying assets. For example, the RJ/CRB Index and the GSCI include energy (oil and gas), metals (industrial and precious), grains (corn, soybeans, and wheat), and soft commodities (cocoa, coffee, cotton, and sugar). Beyond these basic groupings, commodity indices differ widely in composition, weighting scheme, and purpose.

The commodity indices also differ in the relative emphasis placed on various commodities and the procedure used to determine the weightings in the index. A market-cap weighting scheme, so common for equity and bond market indices, cannot be carried over to indices of commodity futures. Because every long futures position has a corresponding short futures position, the market capitalization of a futures contract is always zero. The RJ/CRB Index, for example, groups commodities into four sectors and gives unequal fixed weights to a sector to reflect its perceived relative importance. The GSCI uses world-production weighting. The weights assigned to individual commodities in the GSCI are based on a five-year moving average of world production. Weights are determined each July and are made effective the following January.

Commodity index providers use either arithmetic or geometric averaging to calculate the index return from the component returns. For example, the RJ/CRB Index is based on arithmetic averaging of the monthly component returns; the GSCI is an arithmetic measure of the performance of actively traded, dollar-denominated nearby commodity futures contracts. All contracts are rolled on the fifth business day of the month prior to the expiration month of the contract. Investors attempting to replicate the GSCI must rebalance their portfolios monthly to maintain constant dollar weights.

---

**60** See Barclays Capital's *The Commodity Refiner* (Fourth Quarter 2005), p. 24.
**61** This section draws on CISDM (2005b).

Subindices of the GSCI are calculated for agricultural, energy, industrial, livestock, and precious metals contracts. Two versions of the indices are available: a total-return version, which assumes that capital sufficient to purchase the basket of commodities is invested at the risk-free rate, and a spot version, which tracks movements in only the futures prices.

### 5.2.2 *Historical Performance*

Exhibit 13 presents the monthly return, the annualized return, standard deviation of returns, Sharpe ratio, minimum monthly return, and correlations of the GSCI, S&PCI, and DJ-AIGCI with a sample of stock, bond, and hedge fund indices for the period January 1990 through December 2004. The results for the S&PCI and DJ-AIGCI differ meaningfully from the results for the GSCI, with the DJ-AIGCI showing comparable mean returns but lower volatility and the S&PCI evidencing both lower mean returns and the volatility.

| Exhibit 13 | Commodity Index Performance 1990–2004 |
|---|---|

| Measure | GSCI | S&PCI | DJ-AIGCI | S&P 500 | Lehman Gov./Corp. Bond | MSCI World | Lehman Global Bond |
|---|---|---|---|---|---|---|---|
| Annualized mean return | 7.08% | 4.78% | 6.89% | 10.94% | 7.77% | 7.08% | 8.08% |
| Annualized std. dev. | 19.26% | 12.85% | 11.85% | 14.65% | 4.46% | 14.62% | 5.23% |
| Sharpe ratio | 0.15 | 0.04 | 0.22 | 0.45 | 0.78 | 0.19 | 0.72 |
| Minimum monthly return | −14.41% | −8.97% | −7.54% | −14.46% | −4.19% | −13.32% | −3.66% |
| Correlation with GSCI | 1.00 | 0.84 | 0.89 | −0.08 | 0.03 | −0.06 | 0.06 |
| Correlation with S&PCI | 0.84 | 1.00 | 0.91 | 0.03 | 0.02 | 0.05 | 0.07 |
| Correlation with DJ-AIGCI | 0.89 | 0.91 | 1.00 | 0.08 | 0.03 | 0.15 | 0.12 |

*Note*: MSCI World is the MSCI World equity index.
*Source*: CISDM (2005b).

The differences can be explained, at least in part, by differences in the components of the indices and different approaches to determining the weights of individual commodity futures contracts in each index. For example, the performance of energy has played the dominant role in results for the GSCI because its portfolio weights are based on the value of worldwide production for each included commodity. Based on that criterion, the weight of energy-related futures has exceeded two-thirds.[62] Energy was a good performer over the period examined. The DJ-AIGCI's weights reflect primarily futures contract liquidity data as supplemented by production data, and the influence of energy on the DJ-AIGCI's results, although important, is less than for the GSCI.[63] Each index represents a somewhat distinct view of the world commodity marketplace.

On a stand-alone basis, as judged by the Sharpe ratio, commodities have underperformed U.S. and world bonds and equities (except for the DJ-AIGCI versus the MSCI World Index). In terms of the minimum monthly return, the GSCI registered −14.41 percent, which is not significantly different from the S&P 500's −14.46 percent but is higher than the minimum monthly return of either U.S. or global bonds.

---

**62** According to Erb and Harvey (2006), Table 1, the weight of energy-related futures in the GSCI exceeded two-thirds as of May 2004.
**63** Erb and Harvey, ibid., Table 3, show a weight of energy for the DJ-AIGCI of less than 40 percent as of May 2004.

The correlations of the three commodity indices with the traditional asset classes are of a similar order of magnitude and close to zero, indicating potential as risk diversifiers.

Exhibit 14, which presents the performance statistics for the six GSCI sector subindices, shows considerable difference in stand-alone risk and return among them (particularly between the GSCI Energy Index and the other subindices). Energy plays a major role in the positive Sharpe ratio and the high volatility of the GSCI shown in Exhibit 13.

---

**Exhibit 14**     Performance of GSCI Subindices 1990–2004

| Subindex | Annualized Return (%) | Annualized Std. Dev. (%) | Sharpe Ratio | Minimum Monthly Return (%) |
|---|---|---|---|---|
| GSCI Agricultural | −2.49 | 13.99 | −0.49 | −10.57 |
| GSCI Energy | 9.77 | 32.48 | 0.17 | −22.14 |
| GSCI Industrial Metals | 5.42 | 16.98 | 0.07 | −12.89 |
| GSCI Livestock | 3.58 | 13.75 | −0.05 | −12.76 |
| GSCI Nonenergy | 1.21 | 9.04 | −0.34 | −6.27 |
| GSCI Precious Metals | 1.66 | 12.68 | −0.21 | −11.03 |

*Source*: CISDM (2005b).

---

Another message of Exhibit 14 is that one cannot think of commodities as a homogeneous market of similar investments. In data not reported, the average correlation of GSCI commodity sector returns is low.

*Recent Performance (2000–2004)* Exhibit 15 shows that during this recent period, all commodity indices outperformed U.S. and world equities but not bonds. The stand-alone comparisons with traditional asset classes appear to be time-period dependent. The consistent feature in the evidence is correlation. Although the commodities' correlations with bonds have gone up in comparison with the longer (1990–2004) period, the generally low correlations among commodities and traditional asset classes in Exhibit 15 are consistent with the evidence for the longer time period.

---

**Exhibit 15**     Recent Commodity Index Performance 2000–2004

| Measure | GSCI | S&PCI | DJ-AIGCI | S&P 500 | Lehman Gov./Corp. Bond | MSCI World | Lehman Global Bond |
|---|---|---|---|---|---|---|---|
| Annualized mean return | 13.77% | 10.27% | 12.63% | −2.30% | 8.00% | −2.05% | 8.47% |
| Annualized std. dev. | 22.10% | 16.62% | 13.85% | 16.35% | 4.76% | 15.62% | 6.02% |
| Sharpe ratio | 0.50 | 0.06 | 0.72 | −0.31 | 1.11 | −0.30 | 0.96 |
| Minimum monthly return | −14.41% | −8.71% | −7.54% | −10.87% | −4.19% | −10.98% | −3.66% |
| Correlation with GSCI | 1.00 | 0.89 | 0.89 | −0.05 | 0.05 | 0.00 | 0.10 |
| Correlation with S&PCI | 0.89 | 1.00 | 0.94 | 0.03 | 0.07 | 0.08 | 0.18 |
| Correlation with DJ-AIGCI | 0.89 | 0.94 | 1.00 | 0.09 | 0.05 | 0.14 | 0.20 |

*Source*: CISDM (2005b).

*Commodity Index Return Components*  In general, the return on a commodity futures contract is not the same as the return on the underlying spot commodity. A commodity futures investor needs to understand, in particular, how the returns on a futures contract-based commodity index are calculated. The returns have three components: the spot return, the collateral return, and the roll return.

The **spot return** or **price return** is calculated as the change in the spot price of the underlying commodity over the specified time period. The spot return measures the change in commodity futures prices that should result from changes in the underlying spot prices, according to the cost of carry model.[64] Because of the cost of owning and storing spot commodities, when the spot price goes up (down), so does the futures price, which gives rise to a positive (negative) return to a long futures position. The change in spot prices should be reflected in the change in the price of the futures price with the shortest time to maturity (the nearby futures contract) over the time period. Anson (2002a) noted that most of the shocks with respect to physical commodities tend to be events that reduce the current supply and cause prices to rise; thus, physical commodities have positive event risk.

**Collateral return** or collateral yield comes from the assumption that the full value of the underlying futures contract is invested to earn the risk-free interest rate—that is, that an investor long a futures contract posts 100 percent margin in the form of T-bills (in such a case the futures position is said to be fully collateralized). The implied yield is the collateral return.

**Roll return** or roll yield arises from rolling long futures positions forward through time. The concept is best explained through an example. Consider the data given in Exhibit 16, which shows a downward-sloping term structure of futures prices (i.e., the more distant the contract maturity, the lower the futures price), a situation known as **backwardation**.

| Exhibit 16 | Calculation of Roll Return (in US$) | | | |

| (1) | (2) | (3) | (4) | (5) = (2) – (3) – (4) |
|---|---|---|---|---|
| Contract Maturity | Futures Price as of May 200X | Futures Price as of April 200X | Change in Spot Price | Roll Return/ Yield |
| June 200X | 40.58 | 39.10 | 0.40 | 1.08 |
| Sept. 200X | 39.67 | 38.70 | 0.40 | 0.57 |
| Dec. 200X | 38.45 | 37.65 | 0.40 | 0.40 |

A monthly roll return is computed as the change in the futures contract price over the month minus the change in the spot price over the month. Suppose an investor establishes a position in the June 200X contract in April 200X when the futures price is US$39.10. Between April 200X and May 200X, the futures price increases to US$40.58, for a gain of US$1.48, of which US$0.40 is attributable to a US$0.40 increase in the spot price (perhaps because the supply has been reduced as a result of bad weather). Note that the closer the futures contract is to maturity, the greater the roll return/ yield is. In this example, the roll return on the June contract (US$1.08) is greater than the next position, the September contract (US$0.57), which is, in turn, greater than that of the December contract (US$0.40).

---

**64** Recall that the cost-of-carry model is $F = Se^{(r + c - y)(T - t)}$, where $F$ is the futures price, $S$ is the current spot price of the underlying commodity, $r$ is the risk-free rate of return, $c$ is the cost of storage, $y$ is the convenience yield, and $T - t$ is the time to maturity of the contract. For more details, see Chance (2003).

When the futures markets are in backwardation, a positive return will be earned from a simple buy-and-hold strategy. The positive return is earned because as the futures contract gets closer to maturity, its price must converge to that of the spot price of the commodity. Because in backwardation the spot price is greater than the futures price, the futures price must increase in value. (The opposite is true with an upward-sloping term structure of futures prices, or **contango**.) All else being equal, an increase in a commodity's convenience yield (the nonmonetary benefit from owning the spot commodity) should lead to futures market conditions offering higher roll returns; the converse holds for a decline in convenience yields. (Convenience yields are discussed later.) Over the 1990–2004 period, there was an overall positive relationship between the mean monthly roll return and intramonth spot price volatility in the GSCI Energy and Industrial Metals subindices; because of the importance for the GSCI of the sectors associated with these subindices, the relationship held for the GSCI overall.[65] In general, the effect is more pronounced for nonperishable, storable commodities, whose convenience yield rises in periods of increased volatility because of demand and supply shocks.

| Exhibit 17 | Calculation of Commodity Index Total Return | | | |
| --- | --- | --- | --- | --- |
| Year | GSCI Total Annual Return | GSCI Collateral Yield | GSCI Roll Return/ Yield | GSCI Spot Annual Return |
| 1970 | 15.1% | 7.3% | 2.9% | 4.9% |
| : | : | : | : | : |
| 2000 | 49.7% | 8.6% | 14.2% | 26.9% |
| Average | 15.3% | 7.6% | 3.0% | 4.7% |

*Source*: Anson (2002a).

Using the data in Exhibit 17, we can illustrate the calculation of the total return for the GSCI.

The total return on a commodity index = Collateral return + Roll return + Spot return. Thus, for 2000, the total return on the GSCI = 8.6% + 14.2% + 26.9% = 49.7%.

### 5.2.3 Interpretation Issues

The use of the commodity indices as benchmarks assumes that commodities are approved in the investor's investment policy statement as a distinct asset class in which the investor may invest. If commodities do not receive separate treatment but are included within some broader asset class, such as real assets, evaluation of performance should be based on a customized benchmark that reflects the other assets included in the asset class.

In interpreting historical results, such as those presented here, the investor should also be sensitive to differences in economic conditions between the historical period and current and forecasted future period.

## 5.3 Commodities: Investment Characteristics and Roles

Some experts are now advising investors to afford commodity investment a larger allocation in their portfolios than they have heretofore given it. (Allocations to commodities in most institutional and individual portfolios have typically been well under 5 percent.) In the following sections, we discuss the characteristics of commodities as investments.

---

**65** See CISDM (2005b). The findings relate to the 1990–2004 period.

For the reasons discussed earlier, direct investment in commodities for most investors will be via the futures markets. For investors seeking passive exposure to commodities, the liquidity of the market for futures contracts on a given commodity index will be a major consideration. The three most widely used futures contracts are those based on the GSCI, the DJ-AIGCI, and the RJ/CRB Index, with the GSCI representing approximately 85 percent of the combined open interest of these contracts as of the time of this writing.

### 5.3.1 *Investment Characteristics*

The discussion of the historical performance of commodities highlighted the need for active investors to understand the investment characteristics of commodities on a sector- or individual-commodity level. However, there are some common themes. The chief two relate to characteristics that affect use of commodities in managing portfolio risk and serving as an inflation hedge.

**Special Risk Characteristics**   With some consistency, commodities have tended to have correlations with equities and bonds that are unusually low even in the realm of alternative investments. But the risk characteristics of commodities are more nuanced than simple correlation statistics can reveal and indicate several attractive features of commodities. In periods of financial and economic distress, commodity prices tend to rise, potentially providing valuable diversification services in such times. Long-term growth in world demand for certain commodities in limited supply, such as petroleum-related commodities, may be a factor in their long-term trend growth.

Nevertheless, commodities are generally business-cycle sensitive. The reason commodities behave differently under different economic conditions has to do with the sources of their returns. The determinants of commodity returns include the following:

1. *Business cycle-related supply and demand.* Commodity prices are determined by the supply and demand of the underlying commodities. Because the supply and demand conditions are determined by different economic fundamentals from those affecting stocks and bonds, commodity prices are expected to be sensitive to the business cycle but have little or even negative correlation with stocks and bonds. For example, the variation in spot and futures prices of industrial metals has a strong business-cycle component.[66] Anson (2002a) suggested three reasons commodity returns have been weakly correlated with stock and bond returns. First, commodities correlate positively with inflation whereas stocks and bonds are negatively correlated with inflation. Second, commodity prices and stock/bond prices react differently in different phases of the business cycle. Commodity future prices are more affected by short-term expectations, whereas stock and bond prices are affected by long-term expectations. Finally, commodity prices tend to decline during times of a weak economy.

2. *Convenience yield.* The theory of storage splits the difference between the futures price and the spot price into three components: the forgone interest from purchasing and storing the commodity, storage costs, and the commodity's convenience yield.[67] Convenience yield reflects an embedded consumption-timing option in holding a storable commodity. Furthermore, the theory predicts an inverse relationship between the level of inventories and convenience yield: At low inventory levels, convenience yields are high, and vice versa. A related implication is that the term structure of forward price volatility generally declines with **time to expiration** of the futures contract—the

---

66 See Fama and French (1988), Schneeweis, Spurgin (1997b), and CISDM (2005b).
67 See Kaldor (1939), Working (1948, 1949), and Telser (1958).

so-called Samuelson effect. This is caused by the expectation that, although at shorter horizons mismatched supply and demand forces for the underlying commodity increase the volatility of cash prices, these forces will fall into equilibrium at longer horizons.

3. *Real options under uncertainty.* Oil futures markets are often backwardated; in these markets, futures prices are often below the current spot price. This may be caused by the existence of real options under uncertainty.[68] A **real option** is an option involving decisions related to tangible assets or processes. In other words, producers are holding valuable real options—options to produce or not to produce—and will not exercise them unless the spot prices start to climb up. Production occurs only if discounted futures prices are below spot prices, and backwardation results if the risk of future prices is sufficiently high. A major consequence of a downward-sloping term structure of futures prices is the opportunity to capture a positive roll return as investment in expiring contracts is moved to cheaper new outstanding contracts.

The role of commodities in regard to protecting portfolio value against unexpected inflation has been a continuing theme of comments on the characteristics of commodities as investments. Among the reasons for including commodities in a portfolio are that they are:[69]

- "natural" sources of return (i.e., related to economic fundamentals) over the long term, as discussed above, and

- providers of protection for a portfolio against unexpected inflation.

The premise that investments in physical commodities may hedge inflation is natural. The prices of some commodities, such as crude oil, may have significant links to the component costs of official price indices, and certain commodities, such as gold, have been traditionally demanded as stores of value by investors during inflationary times.

---

**Example 9**

## An Investment in Energy Commodities

Nancy Lopez, CIO of a university endowment fund, is reviewing investment data with the university's treasurer, Sergio Garcia. They are discussing performance of the fund's investment in oil futures. Garcia refers to Exhibit 18 and states: "I thought prices for futures contracts maturing in more distant months were usually higher than prices for nearer-month contracts, but this exhibit shows the opposite case. Spot prices are even higher than the futures. What is this situation called, and what is causing it?"

| Exhibit 18 | Futures Data | | | |
|---|---|---|---|---|
| Contract Maturity | Futures Price as of July 200X | Futures Price as of June 200X | Change in Spot Price | Roll Return |
| Aug. 200X | US$28.90 | US$27.90 | US$0.35 | US$ ? |
| Sep. 200X | US$28.55 | US$27.65 | US$0.35 | US$ ? |
| Oct. 200X | US$27.88 | US$27.01 | US$0.35 | US$ ? |

---

68 See Litzenberger and Rabinowitz (1995).
69 See Strongin and Petsch (1995), who also include pricing inefficiencies (opportunities for active management), a feature that is particularly relevant to managed futures investing, which is discussed later.

1. Compute the roll return from the information above.
2. Characterize the term structure of futures prices.
3. Discuss one reason the situation shown above might exist.

Garcia then asks, "In this situation, it seems our investment in energy commodities can only show negative returns. Is this true? Given the recent hurricane activity, I thought our investments would be making money."

4. Recommend a futures strategy that will provide a positive return in this scenario. Justify your recommendation with reference to the roll return calculated in Part 1, and formulate your response by explaining the benefit of this strategy in an environment of a declining term structure of futures prices.

### Solution to 1:

The roll returns are as follows:
August contract = US$28.9 – US$27.9 – US$0.35 = US$0.65
September contract = US$28.55 – US$27.65 – US$0.35 = US$0.55
October contract = US$27.88 – US$27.01 – US$0.35 = US$0.52

### Solution to 2:

The term structure of futures prices is downward sloping. The oil futures market is in backwardation.

### Solution to 3:

Oil producers hold valuable real options to produce or not to produce. They may not exercise this option unless spot prices begin to rise. Production may occur only if futures prices are below the current spot price, which is associated with a downward-sloping term structure of futures prices.

### Solution to 4:

When futures markets are in backwardation, a positive return will be earned from a simple buy-and-hold strategy. This occurs because as the futures contract gets closer to maturity, its price will rise to converge with the higher spot price. This increase in value produces a positive roll return, as calculated in the solution to 1.

**Commodities as an Inflation Hedge**[70]     The premise that commodities are an inflation hedge can be tested by calculating the correlation of spot GSCI returns, as well as stock, bond, and hedge fund returns, with a proxy for unexpected inflation.[71] The proxy we have used is the monthly change in the rate of inflation. For the 1990–2004 period, correlations were calculated by using data in months in which the change in the rate of inflation was beyond 1 standard deviation from the average change. The results are presented in the last column of Exhibit 19.

---

**70** There is extensive research on commodities as an inflation hedge covering a variety of time periods and markets; overall, it supports the proposition that at least some commodities or commodity index investments have value as inflation hedges. See Becker and Finnerty (2000) and references therein.
**71** Inflation was measured by changes in the U.S. Consumer Price Index.

| Exhibit 19 | | | Factor Correlations 1990–2004 | | | | |
|---|---|---|---|---|---|---|---|

| Index | S&P | Lehman Gov./Corp. | Change in Credit Spread (Baa-Aaa) | Change in Term Spread | Change in Bond Volume | Change in Stock Volume | Unexpected Inflation |
|---|---|---|---|---|---|---|---|
| GSCI | −0.08 | 0.03 | −0.09 | −0.03 | −0.05 | −0.13 | 0.44 |
| GSCI Agric. | 0.18 | −0.03 | −0.01 | 0.02 | 0.01 | 0.00 | −0.27 |
| GSCI Energy | −0.11 | 0.03 | −0.08 | −0.03 | −0.03 | −0.09 | 0.46 |
| GSCI Industrial Metals | 0.21 | −0.14 | −0.22 | 0.19 | 0.07 | −0.13 | 0.11 |
| GSCI Livestock | 0.01 | 0.01 | −0.02 | −0.01 | −0.03 | −0.03 | −0.12 |
| GSCI Nonenergy | 0.20 | −0.03 | −0.09 | 0.05 | −0.01 | −0.08 | −0.23 |
| GSCI Precious Metals | −0.08 | 0.04 | 0.09 | −0.02 | −0.02 | −0.06 | 0.15 |
| S&P 500 | 1.00 | 0.13 | −0.14 | −0.05 | 0.00 | −0.29 | −0.23 |
| Lehman Gov./Corp. | 0.13 | 1.00 | 0.00 | −0.96 | −0.11 | −0.02 | −0.06 |
| HFCI | 0.59 | 0.17 | −0.24 | −0.08 | −0.17 | −0.35 | 0.19 |

*Notes*: Monthly changes in inflation beyond 1 standard deviation of the average were used to proxy for unexpected inflation. The HFCI is the Hedge Fund Composite Index computed by CISDM.
*Source*: CISDM (2005b).

Stocks and bonds in Exhibit 19 exhibit a negative correlation with unexpected inflation (−0.23 and −0.06, respectively), as do some commodity classes (e.g., agriculture, livestock, and nonenergy). However, storable commodities directly related to the intensity of economic activity exhibit positive correlation with unexpected inflation (0.15 for precious metals and 0.46 for energy). Similarly, industrial metals have a correlation of 0.11. These results suggest that direct investment in energy—and, to a lesser degree, industrial and precious metals—may provide a significant inflation hedge.

As shown in Exhibit 19, the returns to the GSCI reflect the inflation-hedging properties of its dominant sector, energy. The broad conclusion from the time period examined, 1990–2004, is that commodity sectors differ in inflation-hedging properties, with storable commodities (such as energy) that are directly linked to the intensity of economic activity having superior inflation-hedging properties.

### 5.3.2 *Roles in the Portfolio*

The principal roles that have been suggested for commodities in the portfolio are as:

- a potent portfolio risk diversifier, and
- an inflation hedge, providing an expected offset to the losses to such assets as conventional debt instruments, which typically lose value during periods of unexpected inflation.[72]

There is support both in the historical record and economics for these roles. Research also indicates a link between the two roles, which suggests that most investable commodity indices provide diversification advantages to stock and bond investment primarily during periods of unexpected changes in inflation.[73] To the degree that inflation is already incorporated into the yield structure of bonds and the cash flow of companies—that is, inflation is fully anticipated—the economy may have periods of high commodity prices or price increases with positive stock and bond returns.

---

**72** See Bodie (1983), Greer (1978), Halpern and Warsager (1998), and Becker and Finnerty (2000).
**73** For example, see Halpern and Warsager (1998).

Halpern and Warsager (1998) observed that commodity indices add their most value as inflation hedges in traditional stock and bond portfolios during periods of unexpected changes in inflation.

More ambiguous is a role of passive long-only commodity futures investments in increasing the expected return vis-à-vis a portfolio of traditional and other alternative investments. Erb and Harvey (2005) claimed that the average historical excess returns of individual commodity futures is approximately zero. They suggest that the measured positive excess return of portfolios of these futures for some time periods is a result not of a risk premium but of the portfolio weighting selected and of rebalancing to it.

Long-term investors with liabilities indexed to inflation, such as defined-benefit plans, may be able to improve their risk-return trade-off by including commodities in the portfolio.[74] For university endowments, which support the inflation-sensitive costs of operating a university, commodities can have a role as a good risk diversifier in a portfolio that needs inflation protection. The role of commodities in a private wealth client's portfolio awaits further study, but passive investment programs have generally been infrequently marketed to that group.

Below, using the methodology familiar from the section on real estate, we provide some quantitative information on the *ex post* role of commodities as a risk diversifier.

In Exhibit 20, the benefits of commodity investment are examined by using the GSCI (a long-only futures-based investable commodity index) in combination with equities, bonds, and hedge funds in various weights for the period January 1990 through December 2004.[75]

| Exhibit 20 | Commodities Performance in Portfolios 1990–2004 | | | | | |
|---|---|---|---|---|---|---|
| **Measure** | **Portfolio I** | **Portfolio II** | **Portfolio III** | **Portfolio IV** | **Portfolio V** | **Portfolio VI** |
| Annualized return | 9.64% | 9.51% | 9.99% | 7.86% | 8.07% | 8.56% |
| Annualized std. dev. | 7.94% | 7.19% | 6.87% | 8.29% | 7.55% | 7.16% |
| Sharpe ratio | 0.67 | 0.73 | 0.83 | 0.43 | 0.50 | 0.60 |
| Minimum monthly return | −6.25% | −6.18% | −6.28% | −5.61% | −5.67% | −5.77% |
| Correlation with GSCI | −0.07 | 0.47 | 0.22 | −0.03 | 0.48 | 0.24 |

*Notes*:
Portfolio I: 50% S&P 500, 50% Lehman Gov./Corp. Bond.
Portfolio II: 40% S&P 500, 40% Lehman Gov./Corp., and 20% GSCI.
Portfolio III: 40% S&P 500, 40% Lehman Gov./Corp., 10% GSCI, 10% HFCI.
Portfolio IV: 50% MSCI World, 50% Lehman Global Bond.
Portfolio V: 40% MSCI World, 40% Lehman Global, 20% GSCI.
Portfolio VI: 40% MSCI World, 40% Lehman Global, 10% GSCI, 10% HFCI.
*Source*: CISDM (2005b).

As presented in Exhibit 13 from a stand-alone perspective, whether risk-adjusted or not, commodities underperformed U.S. and world bond and equity markets during the sample period. However, the low or negative correlations of GSCI returns with returns to the S&P 500 (−0.08), Lehman Government/Corporate Bond Index (0.03),

---

**74** See Nijman and Swinkels (2003), pp. 1–36.
**75** The GSCI futures contract has been the most active commodity index futures listed in the United States for 2004 in terms of outstanding open interest and total volume.

HFCI (0.09), MSCI World Index (−0.06), and Lehman Global Bond Index (0.06) suggested diversification benefits and the potential for improvement in the Sharpe ratio by including commodities. Exhibit 20 supports those conclusions.

Exhibit 21 examines the evidence for a more recent time period. When added to a U.S. portfolio of stocks and bonds, the GSCI helps reduce the standard deviation of the portfolio from 7.93 percent (Portfolio I) to 7.60 percent (Portfolio II). Additionally, risk-adjusted performance (Sharpe ratio) improves significantly from 0.06 (Portfolio I) to 0.39 (Portfolio II). Similarly, when added to a global stock/bond portfolio, the GSCI reduces volatility from 8.56 percent (Portfolio IV) to 8.26 percent (Portfolio V) and increases the Sharpe ratio from 0.09 to 0.38. Adding more assets, such as hedge funds, to the portfolio results in worse performance (Portfolio VI versus Portfolio V).

| **Exhibit 21** | Recent Commodities Performance in Portfolios 2000–2004 | | | | | |
| --- | --- | --- | --- | --- | --- | --- |
| **Measure** | **Portfolio I** | **Portfolio II** | **Portfolio III** | **Portfolio IV** | **Portfolio V** | **Portfolio VI** |
| Annualized return | 3.15% | 5.66% | 4.81% | 3.43% | 5.88% | 5.03% |
| Annualized std. dev. | 7.93% | 7.60% | 6.94% | 8.56% | 8.26% | 7.57% |
| Sharpe ratio | 0.06 | 0.39 | 0.30 | 0.09 | 0.38 | 0.31 |
| Minimum monthly return | −4.36% | −5.05% | −4.12% | −4.94% | −5.40% | −4.46% |
| Correlation with GSCI | −0.04 | 0.55 | 0.30 | 0.03 | 0.56 | 0.33 |

*Notes:*
Portfolio I: 50% S&P 500, 50% Lehman Gov./Corp. Bond.
Portfolio II: 40% S&P 500, 40% Lehman Gov./Corp., 20% GSCI.
Portfolio III: 40% S&P 500, 40% Lehman Gov./Corp., 10% GSCI, 10% HFCI.
Portfolio IV: 50% MSCI World, 50% Lehman Global Bond.
Portfolio V: 40% MSCI World, 40% Lehman Global, 20% GSCI.
Portfolio VI: 40% MSCI World, 40% Lehman Global, 10% GSCI, 10% HFCI.
*Source*: CISDM (2005b).

This discussion has focused on passive long-only exposures. Commodities also offer potential for active management that may involve short as well as long positions. For example, research for the United States has indicated that the benefits to adding commodity futures, particularly metals and agricultural futures (both managed and unmanaged), to a portfolio accrue almost exclusively when the U.S. Federal Reserve (the central bank) is following a restrictive monetary policy.[76] Such results suggest an active strategy based on central bank actions and monetary conditions. As another example, an investor who believes that a commodity's price reverts to the underlying production costs might implement an active long–short commodity program based on divergences from production cost value. Frequently, active programs involve momentum strategies that typically go long after recent prior returns have been positive and short after recent prior returns have been negative.

Active programs may be executed within a separately managed account or a private commodity pool. Private commodity pools will be the focus of the section on managed futures programs later in the reading.

In the next section we discuss one of the most important types of alternative investments, the hedge fund.

---

**76** See Jensen, Mercer, and Johnson (2002).

## 6    HEDGE FUNDS

Hedge funds as a group have become a booming segment of the alternative investment market, with appeal to many segments of the private wealth and institutional investor markets. The impact of hedge funds has been broad in scope. The trading activity of hedge funds constitutes a substantial portion of trading volume in a number of traditional investment markets. Services to hedge funds, known as "prime brokerage," have become an important and actively contested revenue source among major sell-side investment firms.[77] The competition from hedge funds has caused an increasing number of equity and bond mutual funds to seek approval from shareholders to make increased use of derivative strategies and short selling.[78]

The first hedge fund was established in the late 1940s as a long–short hedged equity vehicle. More recently, institutional investors—corporate and public pension funds, endowments and trusts, and bank trust departments—have included hedge funds as one segment of a well-diversified portfolio.

There is no precise legal or universally accepted definition of a hedge fund, and hedge funds can take many forms. Originally, hedge funds were private partnerships that took long and short equity positions to reduce net market exposure in exchange for accepting a lower rate of investment return. In other words, they were "hedged" funds. Today, the term "hedge fund" is much broader. Rather than indicating use of hedging in the portfolio, the organizational and structural characteristics of the portfolio define it as a hedge fund.

Generally, hedge funds intentionally adopt structures that permit them to be loosely regulated pooled investment vehicles, although a trend toward greater regulatory oversight is in motion.[79] The nature of hedge funds as private pools has permitted this investment vehicle to avoid certain reporting and other requirements, as well as some restrictions on incentive fees, that apply to many other investment vehicles. For example, unlike traditional mutual funds, most hedge fund vehicles can take aggressive long or short positions and use leverage aggressively.

Managed futures are now frequently classified as hedge funds. However, this reading will discuss them in a separate section to give them adequate coverage.

Each hedge fund strategy is constructed to take advantage of certain market opportunities. Hedge funds use different investment strategies and thus are often classified according to investment style. There is substantial diversity in risk attributes and investment opportunities among styles, which reflects the flexibility of the hedge fund format. In general, this diversity benefits investors by increasing the range of choices among investment attributes. We will explain the diversity in more detail.

### 6.1  The Hedge Fund Market

The hedge fund market has experienced tremendous growth in the past 15 years and keeps evolving. The market has witnessed a proliferation of hedge funds and products offered by hedge funds. As more hedge funds with similar strategies enter the market, returns on their once-unique strategies start to shrink. Liquidity and capacity

---

**77  Prime brokerage** (or prime brokering) is a suite of services that is often specified to include support in accounting and reporting, leveraged trade execution, financing, securities lending (related to short-selling activities), and start-up advice (for new entities).

**78**  See Laise (2006), pp. D1, D2.

**79**  As of 2006 in the United States, the SEC requires hedge fund advisors to register with it, which subjects them to random audits, record-keeping and compliance requirements, and information filing requirements. As of early 2006, it was estimated that 15–20 percent of U.S. hedge fund advisors were exempt from SEC registration requirements (Kara Scannell, "Making Hedge Funds Less Secret," *Wall Street Journal*, 3 February 2006, pp. C1, C5).

constraints have affected some hedge funds and driven some of them to become—voluntarily or involuntarily—defunct. Some have been able to return the money to their investors, but others, unfortunately, could not and did not. Nevertheless, new hedge funds continue to be established and to try their new strategies, with the successful ones being mimicked by imitators. Although many hedge funds maintain that their strategies seek "absolute returns" that require no benchmark, some institutional investors who invest in hedge funds are asking for relative performance evaluation, which requires some benchmarking.

### 6.1.1 *Types of Hedge Fund Investments*

Many style classifications of hedge funds exist; the following classification of hedge fund style will be the basis for most of our discussion. Keep in mind that industry usage applies the term "arbitrage" somewhat loosely to mean, roughly, a "low-risk" rather than a "no-risk" investment operation.

- *Equity market neutral*: Equity market-neutral managers attempt to identify overvalued and undervalued equity securities while neutralizing the portfolio's exposure to market risk by combining long and short positions. Portfolios are typically structured to be market, industry, sector, and dollar neutral. This is accomplished by holding long and short equity positions with roughly equal exposure to the related market or sector factors. The market opportunity for equity market-neutral programs comes from 1) their flexibility to take short as well as long positions in securities without regard to the securities' weights in a benchmark and 2) the existence of pockets of inefficiencies (i.e., mispricing relative to intrinsic value) in equity markets, particularly as related to overvalued securities. Because many investors face constraints relative to shorting stocks, situations of overvaluation may be slower to correct than those of undervaluation.

- *Convertible arbitrage*: Convertible arbitrage strategies attempt to exploit anomalies in the prices of corporate convertible securities, such as convertible bonds, warrants, and convertible preferred stock. Managers in this category buy or sell these securities and then hedge part or all of the associated risks. The simplest example is buying convertible bonds and hedging the equity component of the bonds' risk by shorting the associated stock. The cash proceeds from the short sale remain with the hedge fund's prime broker but earn interest, and the hedge fund may earn an extra margin through leverage when the bonds' current yield exceeds the borrowing rate of money from the prime broker. The risks include changes in the price of the underlying stock, changes in expected volatility of the stock, changes in the level of interest rates, and changes in the credit standing of the issuer. In addition to collecting the coupon on the underlying convertible bond, convertible arbitrage strategies typically make money if the expected volatility of the underlying asset increases or if the price of the underlying asset increases rapidly. Depending on the hedge strategy, the strategy will also make money if the credit quality of the issuer improves.

- *Fixed-income arbitrage*: Managers dealing in fixed-income arbitrage attempt to identify overvalued and undervalued fixed-income securities primarily on the basis of expectations of changes in the term structure of interest rates or the credit quality of various related issues or market sectors. Fixed-income portfolios are generally neutralized against directional market movements because the portfolios combine long and short positions.

- *Distressed securities*: Portfolios of distressed securities are invested in both the debt and equity of companies that are in or near bankruptcy. Distressed debt and equity securities are fundamentally different from nondistressed securities.

Most investors are unprepared for the legal difficulties and negotiations with creditors and other claimants that are common with distressed companies. Traditional investors prefer to transfer those risks to others when a company is in danger of default. Furthermore, many investors are prevented by charter from holding securities that are in default or at risk of default. Because of the relative illiquidity of distressed debt and equity, short sales are difficult, so most funds are long.

▪ *Merger arbitrage*: Merger arbitrage, also called "deal arbitrage," seeks to capture the price spread between current market prices of corporate securities and their value upon successful completion of a takeover, merger, spin-off, or similar transaction involving more than one company. In merger arbitrage, the opportunity typically involves buying the stock of a target company after a merger announcement and shorting an appropriate amount of the acquiring company's stock.

▪ *Hedged equity*: Hedged equity strategies attempt to identify overvalued and undervalued equity securities. Portfolios are typically not structured to be market, industry, sector, and dollar neutral, and they may be highly concentrated. For example, the value of short positions may be only a fraction of the value of long positions and the portfolio may have a net long exposure to the equity market. Hedged equity is the largest of the various hedge fund strategies in terms of assets under management.[80]

▪ *Global macro*: Global macro strategies primarily attempt to take advantage of systematic moves in major financial and nonfinancial markets through trading in currencies, futures, and option contracts, although they may also take major positions in traditional equity and bond markets. For the most part, they differ from traditional hedge fund strategies in that they concentrate on major market trends rather than on individual security opportunities. Many global macro managers use derivatives, such as futures and options, in their strategies. Managed futures are sometimes classified under global macro as a result.

▪ *Emerging markets*: These funds focus on the emerging and less mature markets. Because short selling is not permitted in most emerging markets and because futures and options are not available, these funds tend to be long.

▪ *Fund of funds*: A **fund of funds** (FOF) is a fund that invests in a number of underlying hedge funds. A typical FOF invests in 10–30 hedge funds, and some FOFs are even more diversified. Although FOF investors can achieve diversification among hedge fund managers and strategies, they have to pay two layers of fees—one to the hedge fund manager, and the other to the manager of the FOF.[81]

There is no single standard classification system or set of labels for hedge fund strategies. One provider of hedge fund benchmarks classifies strategies into the following five broad groups:[82]

▪ *Relative value*, in which the manager seeks to exploit valuation discrepancies through long and short positions. This label may be used as a supercategory for, for example, equity market neutral, convertible arbitrage, and hedged equity.

---

**80** The equivalent classification termed "equity long-short" represented 28.2 percent of the Credit Suisse/ Tremont Hedge Fund Index as of early 2006 (www.hedgeindex.com accessed 12 March 2006).
**81** Returns on FOFs have been found to be more positively correlated with equity markets than returns on hedge funds individually; see Kat (2005), pp. 51–57.
**82** This list follows the categories established for the EACM100® Index of hedge funds by EACM Advisors I LC.

- *Event driven*, in which the manager focuses on opportunities created by corporate transactions (e.g., mergers). Merger arbitrage and distressed securities would be included in this group.

- *Equity hedge*, in which the manager invests in long and short equity positions with varying degrees of equity market exposure and leverage.

- *Global asset allocators*, which are opportunistically long and short a variety of financial and/or nonfinancial assets.

- *Short selling*, in which the manager shorts equities in the expectation of a market decline.

The five most widely used hedge fund strategies, accounting for 85–90 percent of assets under management in the hedge fund industry as of the early 2000s, are three equity-based strategies (equity market neutral, hedged equity, and merger arbitrage), one fixed-income strategy (convertible arbitrage), and global macro, which uses all types of assets, including currencies and commodities.

The compensation structure of hedge funds comprises a percentage of net asset value (NAV) as a management fee plus an incentive fee. The management fee is also known as an "asset under management" or **AUM fee**. The management fee generally ranges from 1 percent to 2 percent. The incentive fee is a percentage of profits as specified by the terms of the investment. It has traditionally been 20 percent but has recently averaged approximately 17.5 percent.[83] Recently, roughly 50 percent of hedge funds were using a management fee of 1 percent, 1.5 percent, or 2 percent combined with an incentive fee of 20 percent.

The great majority of funds have a high-water mark provision that applies to the payment of the incentive fee. Intuitively, a **high-water mark** (HWM) is a specified net asset value level that a fund must exceed before performance fees are paid to the hedge fund manager. Once the first incentive fee has been paid, the highest month-end NAV establishes a high-water mark. If the NAV then falls below the HWM, no incentive fee is paid until the fund's NAV exceeds the HWM; then the incentive fee for a "1 plus 20" structure (a 1 percent management fee plus a 20 percent incentive fee) is 20 percent of the positive difference between the ending NAV and the HWM NAV. The new, higher NAV establishes a new HWM. A minority of funds also specify that no incentive fee is earned until a specified minimum rate of return (hurdle rate) is earned.

The purpose of a HWM provision is to ensure that the hedge fund manager earns an incentive fee only once for the same gain. For the hedge fund manager, the HWM is like a call option on a fraction of the increase in the value of the fund's NAV. Many hedge fund managers depend on earning the incentive fee. Given a 15 percent gain, a 1 and 20 fund would earn about 4 percent of the asset versus 1 percent if no incentive fee were earned.

Hedge fund investors also often take the opportunities offered them to withdraw capital from a fund on a losing streak. A hedge fund far under its HWM is frequently dissolved. According to Credit Suisse/Tremont, more than 20 percent of hedge funds were liquidated in 2003 after a year in which more than 70 percent of hedge funds in their database failed to earn an incentive fee.[84]

FOFs impose management fees and incentive fees. A "1.5 plus 10" structure would not be uncommon.

Much debate has surrounded the fee structures of hedge funds. One perspective is that to the extent a hedge fund investor is not paying for "beta" (exposure to systematic risk), as the investor might do with a traditional long-only mutual fund,

---

**83** As reported by Black (2005, p. 186) based on the CISDM database as of January 2004.
**84** Ibid.

a higher fee structure is warranted. Another rationale is that to the extent a hedge fund contributes to controlling a portfolio's downside risk, somewhat like a protective put, the fund manager should earn a premium, somewhat like an insurance premium.

All else being equal, between two similarly sized hedge funds following the same strategy, the expectation is that the fund charging the lower management fee will deliver superior performance, unless the higher fee manager in a particular case can make a convincing case that he or she can deliver future superior investment performance. Not uncommonly, hedge fund managers with superior past track records ask for and obtain higher-than-average incentive fees. The investor needs to ask whether the hedge fund manager will repeat as a winner.

Hedge funds also prescribe a minimum initial holding or **lock-up period** for investments during which no part of the investment can be withdrawn. Lock-up periods of one to three years are common. Thereafter, the fund will redeem the investments of investors only within specified exit windows—for example, quarterly after the lock-up period has ended. The rationale for these provisions is that the hedge fund manager needs to be insulated to avoid unwinding positions unfavorably. FOFs usually do not impose lock-up periods and may permit more frequent investor exits. However to offer that additional liquidity, the FOF manager must hold a cash buffer that may reduce expected returns.

### 6.1.2  *Size of the Hedge Fund Market*

According to *Forbes* magazine, almost one-quarter of the U.S. largest 1,800 pension funds, endowments, and foundations held hedge fund investments in 2003, up from 12 percent in 2000.[85] It is estimated that money under management for hedge funds grew from less than US$50 billion in 1990 to approximately US$600 billion in 2002; the number of hedge funds increased to more than 6,000.[86] Hedge Fund Research estimated, as reported in *Forbes*, that in 2004, US$800 billion was invested in 6,300 hedge funds—900 of them less than a year old. However, 10 percent of hedge funds tracked by HedgeFund.net became defunct in that year. It is estimated that more than 8,000 hedge funds were managing more than US$1 trillion in 2005.

## 6.2  Benchmarks and Historical Performance

Many investors are concerned that hedge funds do not provide a means for monitoring and tracking these investments that are available for other, more traditional investments.[87] In the traditional stock and bond markets, Morningstar and Lipper provide active manager-based benchmarks of mutual fund performance. Similarly, in the alternative investment industry, CISDM (the Center for International Securities and Derivatives Markets), Hedge Fund Research (HFR), Dow Jones, Standard & Poor's, and Morgan Stanley provide monthly or daily indices that track the performance of active manager-based benchmarks of hedge fund performance.

Recently, research has also focused on developing indices for strategies (e.g., tracking portfolios) that try to separate the contribution to performance of the strategy from the contribution to performance of the manager's specific talent.[88] In most cases, evidence exists for abnormal returns based on such indices. However, investors should be cautioned that abnormal returns simply reflect that the reference benchmark is not a complete tracking portfolio for the hedge fund so the abnormal returns are simply the result of additional, nonmeasured risks.

---

**85** *Forbes*, 24 May 2004.
**86** See SEC (2003).
**87** Siegel (2003) found it surprising, given that the inherent nature of hedge fund investing is hostile to benchmarking, that hedge funds or their clients need benchmarks.
**88** See Schneeweis and Kazemi (2001).

### 6.2.1 *Benchmarks*

Hedge fund benchmarks include both monthly and daily series. In alphabetical order, a sample of monthly hedge fund indices includes the following:

- *CISDM of the University of Massachusetts.* The CISDM hedge fund and managed futures indices are based on managers reporting to the CISDM hedge fund and managed futures databases. The indices cover a broad set of hedge fund and managed futures trading strategies. Publication of returns in each style classification began in 1994 with data beginning in 1990. The broadest CISDM hedge fund index is equally weighted—the CISDM Equal Weighted Hedge Fund Index.

- *Credit Suisse/Tremont.* These indices cover more than 10 strategies and are based on a set of more than 400 funds selected from the TASS database. The Credit Suisse/Tremont Index discloses its construction methods and identifies all the funds within it. Credit Suisse/Tremont accepts only funds (not separate accounts) with a minimum of US$10 million under management and an audited statement. The Credit Suisse/Tremont Hedge Fund Index was launched in 1999 with data beginning in 1994 and is asset weighted (i.e., weights depend on assets under management).

- *EACM Advisors.* This group provides the EACM100˚ Index, which is an equally weighted composite of 100 hedge funds selected to be representative of five broad strategies representing 13 substrategy styles. Funds are assigned categories on the basis of how closely they match the strategy definitions. Names in the funds are not disclosed. The index is equally weighted and rebalanced annually. It was launched in 1996 with data beginning in 1990.

- *Hedge Fund Intelligence Ltd.* Hedge Fund Intelligence supplies the EuroHedge and HSBC AsiaHedge series of equally weighted indices. The EuroHedge series consists of hedge funds that are at least 50 percent managed in developed European countries or that are solely invested in developed European countries. The series began in 2002. The HSBC AsiaHedge series contains hedge funds that are at least 50 percent managed in the Asia-Pacific area or that are solely invested in the Asia-Pacific area. The series began in 1998.

- *HedgeFund.net.* Also called the "Tuna" indices, this covers more than 30 strategies. They are equally weighted indices based on the HedgeFund.net database.

- *HFR.* This company provides equally weighted hedge fund indices based on managers reporting to the HFR database of hedge fund returns segregated into a number of categories and subcategories. FOFs are not included in the composite index but are in a separate index. The indices were launched in 1994 with data beginning in 1990. Funds are assigned to categories based on the descriptions in their offering memoranda.

- *MSCI.* These indices are classified according to five basic categories and include a composite index. Within each category, indices are segregated on the basis of asset class and geographical region. Funds included need to have a minimum of US$15 million in AUM, although there is no restriction on whether a fund is open or closed. The indices are supported by a platform that allows subscribers to access the data at a more detailed level (industry focus, fund size, open versus closed, etc.). Indices are equally weighted except at higher levels of aggregation, where both equally weighted and asset-weighted versions are available.

A sample of available daily indices includes the following:

- *Dow Jones Hedge Fund Strategy benchmarks.* These benchmarks currently cover six hedge fund strategies. Funds within each category must meet asset size, years in existence, and statistically based style purity constraints. Funds that meet these restrictions are asked to participate in the index. However, only those managers who also agree to meet reporting constraints are included. The benchmarks were launched in 2001 as the Zurich Institutional Benchmark Series. The Dow Jones indices are available in an investable form through a separate asset company not directly affiliated with Dow Jones and are approximately equally weighted.

- *HFR hedge fund indices.* These indices are based on managers reporting to HFR. The indices cover a number of categories and subcategories and were launched in 2003.

- *MSCI Hedge Invest Index.* This index is based on over 100 hedge funds that represent 24 hedge fund strategies and have weekly liquidity.[89] The MSCI Hedge Invest Index is available in an investable form through a separate asset company not directly affiliated with MSCI. The index was launched in July 2003.

- *Standard & Poor's Hedge Fund Indices.* These indices cover three styles with three strategies each. The indices are equally weighted and are rebalanced annually. Standard & Poor's discloses the construction method and the number of funds that are in each strategy. It performs due diligence on all funds in the indices and publishes daily returns. The S&P Hedge Fund Indices are available in an investable form through a separate asset company not directly affiliated with Standard & Poor's.

**Comparison of Major Manager-Based Hedge Fund Indices**    The general distinguishing feature of various hedge fund series is whether they report monthly or daily series, are investable or noninvestable, and list the actual funds used in benchmark construction. Of the current indices, only Dow Jones, Standard & Poor's, MSCI, and HFR provide a daily return series. Of these daily indices, only Dow Jones and Standard & Poor's publicly list the funds in the indices. Another important feature of the daily indices is that they are generally constructed from managed accounts of an asset manager rather than from the funds themselves.

For the monthly return series, the EACM Advisors, CISDM, HFR, and MSCI indices have many different classifications and subclassifications, whereas the Credit Suisse/Tremont and Standard & Poor's have relatively few classifications. The CISDM indices do not report a "hedge fund composite" return each month.

It is natural to want to express the performance of hedge funds with a single number. However, defining the hedge fund universe is both a difficult and unproductive exercise. There is no general agreement among institutional investors regarding which investment strategies are considered hedge fund strategies and what weights should be given to each strategy.

There are many differences in the construction of the major manager-based hedge fund indices. Principal differences are as follows:

- *Selection criteria.* Decision rules determine which hedge funds are included in the index. Examples of selection criteria include length of track record, AUM, and restrictions on new investment. For example, MSCI, Dow Jones, and Standard & Poor's have specific rule-based processes for manager selection.

- *Style classification.* Indices have various approaches to how each hedge fund is assigned to a style-specific index and whether or not a fund that fails to satisfy the style classification methodology is excluded from the index.

---

**89** As of 6 April 2004.

- *Weighting scheme.* Indices have different schemes to determine how much weight a particular fund's return is given in the index. Common weighting schemes are equally weighting and dollar weighting on the basis of AUM. Many indices report both equal-weighted and asset-weighted versions.

- *Rebalancing scheme.* Rebalancing rules determine when assets are reallocated among the funds in an equally weighted index. For example, some funds are rebalanced monthly; others use annual rebalancing.

- *Investability.* An index may be directly or only indirectly investable. The majority of monthly manager-based hedge fund indices are not investable, whereas most of the daily hedge fund indices are investable but often in association with other financial firms.

**Alpha Determination and Absolute-Return Investing**   Performance appraisal has emerged as a major issue in the hedge fund industry. Hedge funds have often been promoted as absolute-return vehicles. **Absolute-return vehicles** have been defined as investments that have no direct benchmark portfolios. Estimates of alpha, however, must be made relative to a benchmark portfolio.[90] Problems in alpha determination have been discussed widely; for example, differences in the selected benchmark can result in large differences in reported alpha.[91] One perspective is that all active management is about performance relative to some investable benchmark.[92] Another important issue in evaluating claims of alpha is whether account is being taken of all sources of systematic risk the fund may be exposed to. Alpha is the residual after returns to systematic risks have been removed. Simple models for systematic risk that have been applied to long-only equity portfolios may not be relevant for a hedge fund strategy.

The lack of a clear hedge fund benchmark, however, is not indicative of an inability to determine comparable returns for a hedge fund strategy. Hedge fund strategies within a particular style often trade similar assets with similar methodologies and are sensitive to similar market factors. Two principal means of establishing comparable portfolios are 1) using a single-factor or multifactor methodology and 2) using optimization to create tracking portfolios with similar risk and return characteristics. Kazemi and Schneeweis (2001) created passive indices, from both factors that underlie the strategy and financial instruments that are used in the strategy, to track the return of a hedge fund strategy. Their results indicate that active hedge fund management shows evidence of positive alpha relative to cited tracking portfolios.

### 6.2.2 *Historical Performance*

In this section, we provide summary information on the performance of various hedge fund strategies. Exhibit 22 shows the performance of a number of assets and combinations of assets (traditional assets and hedge funds) over the period 1990–2004.[93] These assets include CSDIM's Hedge Fund Composite Index and several measures of U.S. and global stock and bond performance.

---

90 Alpha is defined as the return relative to an investment's expected return given a benchmark portfolio and the investment's beta with respect to the benchmark.

91 Refer to the reading on evaluating portfolio performance for the alpha determination in traditional investments; see Schneeweis (1998) for alpha determination in hedge funds.

92 See Waring and Siegel (2005).

93 The annual and monthly returns are presented in their nominal form. Annualized standard deviations are derived by multiplying the monthly data by the square root of 12.

| Exhibit 22 | Hedge Fund Performance 1990–2004 |
| --- | --- |

| Measure | HFCI | S&P 500 | Lehman Gov./ Corp. | MSCI World | Lehman Global |
| --- | --- | --- | --- | --- | --- |
| Annualized return | 13.46% | 10.94% | 7.77% | 7.08% | 8.09% |
| Annualized std. dev. | 5.71% | 14.65% | 4.46% | 14.62% | 5.23% |
| Sharpe ratio | 1.61 | 0.45 | 0.78 | 0.19 | 0.73 |
| Minimum monthly return | −6.92% | −14.46% | −4.19% | −13.32% | −3.66% |
| Correlation with HFCI | 1.00 | 0.59 | 0.16 | 0.56 | 0.04 |

*Source*: CISDM (2005c).

For the entire period, the HFCI had the superior return performance relative to other traditional asset classes. During the sharp decline of the S&P 500 between mid 2000 and late 2002, the HFCI had a small but positive trend. The minimum monthly return for the HFCI for the entire period, at −6.92 percent, represents a smaller loss than that of the worst monthly return for either U.S. or world equities. The HFCI has a higher Sharpe ratio than any of the other reported assets. Note that the HFCI's correlation of 0.59 with the S&P 500 is consistent with substantial long equity market exposure as well as the potential for risk-diversification benefits (because the correlation is considerably below 1).

As Exhibit 23 shows, for the five-year period ending in 2004, the HFCI outperformed U.S. and world equities but not bonds. The minimum monthly return for the HFCI during the period is smaller than for all other reported asset classes.

| Exhibit 23 | Recent Hedge Fund Performance 2000–2004 |
| --- | --- |

| Measure | HFCI | S&P 500 | Lehman Gov./ Corp. | MSCI World | Lehman Global |
| --- | --- | --- | --- | --- | --- |
| Annualized return | 6.84% | −2.30% | 8.00% | −2.05% | 8.51% |
| Annualized std. dev. | 4.83% | 16.35% | 4.76% | 15.62% | 6.00% |
| Sharpe ratio | 0.86 | −0.31 | 1.11 | −0.30 | 0.97 |
| Minimum monthly return | −2.94% | −10.87% | −4.19% | −10.98% | −3.66% |
| Correlation with HFCI | 1.00 | 0.52 | 0.11 | 0.60 | 0.21 |

*Source*: CISDM (2005c).

The risk and return benefit of a wide range of hedge fund indices and their correlations with stock and bond indices are given in Exhibit 24. As the dispersion of Sharpe ratios and of correlations of hedge fund styles with stocks and bonds in Exhibit 24 shows, in 1990–2004, there was considerable variation in the risk and return characteristics among styles. As expected, those hedge fund groups whose strategies call for eliminating stock or bond market risk (e.g., equity market neutral or fixed-income arbitrage) have low correlations with, respectively, stock or bond indices. Those hedge fund strategies with equity exposure (e.g., event driven and hedged equity) have moderate correlations with the S&P 500.

| Exhibit 24 | Performance of Hedge Fund Strategies and Traditional Assets 1990–2004 |
| --- | --- |

| Strategy or Index | Annual Return (%) | Annual Standard Deviation (%) | Sharpe Ratio | Minimum Monthly Return (%) | Correlation w/S&P 500 | Correlation w/ Lehman Gov./ Corp. |
| --- | --- | --- | --- | --- | --- | --- |
| HFCI | 13.46 | 5.71 | 1.61 | −6.92 | 0.59 | 0.17 |
| Event driven | 13.46 | 5.59 | 1.64 | −9.37 | 0.59 | 0.07 |
| Equity hedge | 15.90 | 9.34 | 1.24 | −9.70 | 0.64 | 0.10 |
| Equity market neutral | 9.24 | 2.50 | 1.98 | −1.07 | 0.09 | 0.24 |
| Merger/risk arbitrage | 9.07 | 4.86 | 0.99 | −8.78 | 0.48 | 0.10 |
| Distressed securities | 15.28 | 6.07 | 1.81 | −9.71 | 0.42 | 0.04 |
| Fixed-income arbitrage | 7.62 | 3.61 | 0.92 | −6.61 | 0.06 | −0.06 |
| Convertible arbitrage | 10.23 | 3.96 | 1.50 | −3.42 | 0.19 | 0.13 |
| Global macro | 16.98 | 8.38 | 1.51 | −5.41 | 0.26 | 0.34 |
| Short selling | −0.61 | 19.39 | −0.25 | −14.62 | −0.76 | −0.01 |
| S&P 500 | 10.94 | 14.65 | 0.45 | −14.46 | 1.00 | 0.13 |
| Lehman Gov./Corp. | 7.77 | 4.46 | 0.78 | −4.19 | 0.13 | 1.00 |
| MSCI World | 7.08 | 14.62 | 0.19 | −13.32 | 0.86 | 0.09 |
| Lehman Global | 8.09 | 5.23 | 0.73 | −3.66 | 0.11 | 0.74 |

*Source*: CISDM (2005c).

Research has shown that the actual performance of hedge fund strategies depends on the market conditions affecting that strategy. As shown in Exhibit 25, equity-based hedge fund strategies are correlated with several equity and bond market factors. Credit-sensitive strategies (e.g., distressed securities) are correlated with similar factors (e.g., high-yield debt returns) as credit-sensitive bond instruments. Because relative-value strategies (e.g., equity market neutral) and systematic managed futures strategies (which are discussed in detail later) are sensitive to different return factors from those to which hedged equity strategies and the S&P 500 are sensitive, one expects them to have low correlations with the S&P 500 and they may be considered risk diversifiers.[94] Because equity hedge funds load on similar return factors as the S&P 500, they offer less diversification than many relative-value strategies and can be more rightly considered return enhancers.

| Exhibit 25 | Factor Correlations 1990–2004 |
| --- | --- |

| Hedge Fund | S&P 500 | Lehman Gov./ Corp. | Lehman Corp. High Yield | Stock Volatility | Bond Volatility |
| --- | --- | --- | --- | --- | --- |
| HFCI | 0.59 | 0.17 | 0.51 | −0.42 | −0.13 |
| Event driven | 0.59 | 0.07 | 0.69 | −0.42 | −0.02 |
| Equity hedge | 0.64 | 0.10 | 0.43 | −0.33 | −0.04 |

*(continued)*

[94] Although some research (Schneeweis and Pescatore, 1999) has focused on CTAs as offering exposure to long volatility, unless specifically designed to capture volatility, systematic CTA strategies often make returns in periods of low-volatility in high-trend markets. Systematic commodity trading programs (e.g., CTAs) are positively correlated with various passive trend-following indices. See CISDM (2005d) and www.cisdm.som.umass.edu for information.

| Hedge Fund | S&P 500 | Lehman Gov./ Corp. | Lehman Corp. High Yield | Stock Volatility | Bond Volatility |
|---|---|---|---|---|---|
| Equity market neutral | 0.09 | 0.24 | −0.03 | −0.13 | −0.23 |
| Merger/risk arbitrage | 0.48 | 0.10 | 0.50 | −0.31 | −0.01 |
| Distressed securities | 0.42 | 0.04 | 0.70 | −0.41 | −0.01 |
| Fixed-income arbitrage | 0.06 | −0.06 | 0.34 | −0.36 | −0.18 |
| Convertible arbitrage | 0.19 | 0.13 | 0.47 | −0.12 | −0.15 |
| Global macro | 0.26 | 0.34 | 0.23 | −0.27 | −0.26 |
| Short selling | −0.78 | −0.01 | −0.50 | 0.20 | −0.15 |

*Notes*: Stock and bond volatility was measured as, respectively, monthly volatility of daily returns of the S&P 500 and Lehman Brothers bond index.
*Source*: CISDM (2005c).

The different sensitivities of various hedge fund strategies to various market factors result in different correlations among hedge fund strategies themselves. The correlations between various hedge fund strategies are given in Exhibit 26. Diversification among hedge fund strategies should therefore also reduce the volatility of hedge fund–based investment portfolios.

### 6.2.3 *Interpretation Issues*[95]

Hedge fund indices often have meaningfully different performance within a given time period. This raises the challenging question of which index is most appropriate for the investor's purposes.

Despite the differences in returns, comparable hedge fund indices appear to be sensitive to the same set of risk factors. The return differences among indices often reflect differences in the weights of different strategy groups.

The hedge fund investor should be aware of the following issues in selecting and using hedge fund indices.

**Biases in Index Creation**   The use of manager-based hedge fund indices in performance appraisal and asset allocation is based on the premise that the indices neutrally reflect the underlying performance of the strategy. A primary concern is that most databases are self-reported; that is, the hedge fund manager chooses which databases to report to and provides the return data. Although the correlations among hedge fund indices based on similar strategies are generally moderately high in the period covered by Exhibit 26 (e.g., above 0.80), in certain cases, the correlations fall below 0.20. There are several possible explanations for low correlations between "similar strategy" indices. One is the size and age restrictions some indices impose. Another may be the weighting schemes.

Value weighting may result in a particular index taking on the return characteristics of the best-performing hedge funds in a particular time period: As top-performing funds grow from new inflows and high returns and poorly performing funds are closed, the top-performing funds represent an increasing share of the index. Fung and Hsieh (2001) pointed out that the indices that are value weighted may reflect current popularity with investors because the asset values of the various funds change as a result of asset purchases and price. Popularity may reflect the most recent results, creating a momentum effect in returns. The ability of an investor to track an index subject to momentum is problematic.

---

[95] Discussion in this section draws on Schneeweis, Kazemi, and Martin (2002).

**Exhibit 26** Correlations between Hedge Fund Strategies 1990–2004

| | HFCI | Event Driven | Equity Hedge | Equity Market Neutral | Merger/ Risk Arbitrage | Distressed Securities | Fixed- Income Arbitrage | Convert. Arbitrage | Global Macro | Short Selling | S&P 500 | Lehman Gov./ Corp. | MSCI World | Lehman Global |
|---|---|---|---|---|---|---|---|---|---|---|---|---|---|---|
| HFCI | 1.00 | | | | | | | | | | | | | |
| Event driven | 0.76 | 1.00 | | | | | | | | | | | | |
| Equity hedge | 0.90 | 0.70 | 1.00 | | | | | | | | | | | |
| Equity market neutral | 0.32 | 0.13 | 0.27 | 1.00 | | | | | | | | | | |
| Merger/risk arbitrage | 0.52 | 0.82 | 0.50 | 0.06 | 1.00 | | | | | | | | | |
| Distressed securities | 0.66 | 0.87 | 0.56 | 0.14 | 0.57 | 1.00 | | | | | | | | |
| Fixed-income arbitrage | 0.38 | 0.34 | 0.19 | 0.13 | 0.12 | 0.42 | 1.00 | | | | | | | |
| Convert. arbitrage | 0.47 | 0.55 | 0.34 | 0.15 | 0.35 | 0.56 | 0.37 | 1.00 | | | | | | |
| Global macro | 0.72 | 0.33 | 0.46 | 0.34 | 0.16 | 0.29 | 0.27 | 0.21 | 1.00 | | | | | |
| Short selling | −0.64 | −0.66 | −0.77 | 0.00 | −0.50 | −0.54 | −0.09 | −0.28 | −0.18 | 1.00 | | | | |
| S&P 500 | 0.59 | 0.59 | 0.64 | 0.09 | 0.48 | 0.42 | 0.06 | 0.19 | 0.26 | −0.78 | 1.00 | | | |
| Lehman Gov./ Corp. | 0.17 | 0.07 | 0.10 | 0.24 | 0.10 | 0.04 | −0.06 | 0.13 | 0.34 | −0.01 | 0.13 | 1.00 | | |
| MSCI World | 0.56 | 0.54 | 0.62 | 0.07 | 0.42 | 0.39 | 0.09 | 0.17 | 0.24 | −0.71 | 0.86 | 0.09 | 1.00 | |
| Lehman Global | 0.05 | −0.03 | 0.06 | 0.21 | 0.04 | −0.06 | −0.16 | 0.00 | 0.19 | −0.03 | 0.11 | 0.74 | 0.22 | 1.00 |

*Source:* CISDM (2005c).

Equal-weighted indices may reflect potential diversification of hedge funds better than value-weighted indices. For funds designed to track equal-weighted indices, however, the costs of rebalancing to index weights make it difficult to create an investable form. Only recently have hedge fund indices been created that are investable. Some such indices have the express goal of tracking a comparable but noninvestable index.[96] The creation of a single, all-encompassing hedge fund index that reflects some natural, market-based equilibrium assumption as to the proper holdings of hedge funds and is appropriate for all purposes does not appear to be feasible. Many hedge fund investors use custom or negotiated benchmarks.

An appropriate benchmark reflects the particular style of an investment manager and can serve as a surrogate for the manager in studies of risk and return performance and asset allocation. Of great concern for investors is whether an index reflects the actual relative sensitivity of hedge funds to various market conditions, such that each index provides information on the true diversification benefits of the underlying hedge fund strategies. Many studies have used both single-factor and multifactor models in identifying market factors and option-like payoffs that describe the sources of hedge fund returns.[97] However, the sensitivity of various hedge fund indices to these economic factors may change over time, so the changing styles and changing assets under management (if asset-weighted) in an index may make historical results relative to that index conditional at best.

**Relevance of Past Data on Performance**   The usefulness of historical hedge fund data is a topic of controversy. As is true for stock and bond analyses, hedge funds with similar investment styles generate similar returns, and there is little evidence of superior individual manager skill within a particular style group.[98] Research has also shown that the volatility of returns is more persistent through time than the level of returns.[99] This research shows that the best forecast of future returns is one that is consistent with prior volatility, not one that is consistent with prior returns.[100] There are a host of methodological concerns, however, with interpreting the results of such studies.

The composition of hedge fund indices also changes greatly, so the past returns of an index reflect the performance of a different set of managers from today's or tomorrow's managers. This may be a more severe problem for value-weighted indices than for equal-weighted indices because value-weighted indices are more heavily weighted in the recent best-performing fund(s).

**Survivorship Bias**   Survivorship bias is often raised as a major concern for investors in hedge funds. **Survivorship bias** results when managers with poor track records exit the business and are dropped from the database whereas managers with good records remain. If survivorship bias is large, then the historical return record of the average surviving manager is higher than the average return of all managers over the test period. Because a diversified portfolio would have likely consisted of funds that were destined to fail as well as funds destined to succeed, studying only survivors results in overestimation of historical returns. It is estimated that this bias is in the range of at least 1.5–3 percent per year.[101]

---

**96**  See the Dow Jones Hedge Fund Strategy Benchmarks at www.djhedgefundindexes.com.

**97**  See Fung and Hsieh (1997a) and Schneeweis and Pescatore (1999).

**98**  See Bodie, Kane, and Marcus (2005) for a summary. To the degree that superior return persistence is shown, the result arises primarily from consistency among poor performers rather than superior performers; see Brown et al. (1999).

**99**  See Schneeweis (1998) and Park and Staum (1998).

**100**  The ability of historical data to classify managers into similar trading strategies is still an open question. Fung and Hsieh (1997a) and others have used various factor analytic programs to group managers. In contrast, various fund management companies place managers into relevant groups on the basis of direct evaluation. Future research is required to see which of the relevant methods provides the least bias.

**101**  See Brown et al. (1999) and Fung and Hsieh (2000).

Survivorship bias varies among hedge fund strategies. For instance, survivorship bias is minor for event-driven strategies, is higher for hedged equity, and is considerable for currency funds. More importantly, for the largest hedge fund group, equity hedge funds, overestimation of historical performance because of survivorship bias has been previously reported to range from 1.5 percent to 2 percent. However, the bias may be concentrated in certain periods (e.g., following the August 1998 Long-Term Capital Management crisis). Thus, the levels of survivorship bias exhibited in past data may, depending on economic conditions and strategy, over- or underestimate future bias. Finally, data for U.S. equity hedge funds indicate that for particular hedge fund strategies, although the relative return performance of the "dead" funds was less than that of the "alive" funds, the survivorship bias may differ greatly among funds, with some nonsurvivor funds showing no return bias.

Moreover, the problem of survivorship bias may be reduced by conducting superior due diligence. For instance, one explanation for the proliferation of FOFs is that managers of these funds may be able to avoid managers destined to fail, thereby mitigating the survivorship bias problem. Investors may be willing to bear an additional layer of management fees to reduce exposure to the ill-fated managers. As a result, once the FOFs have screened funds, survivorship bias may be reduced significantly.

**Stale Price Bias**    In asset markets, lack of security trading may lead to what is called **stale price bias**. For securities with stale prices, measured correlations may be lower than expected, and depending on the time period chosen, measured standard deviation may be higher or lower than would exist if actual prices existed.

Even in traditional asset markets, prices are often computed from factor models, appraisal values, and so on, so that reported prices do not reflect current market prices. In fact, for CTAs and many hedge fund strategies, prices reflect market-traded prices to a greater extent than in many traditional asset portfolios. There is little evidence that stale prices present a significant bias in hedge fund returns.

**Backfill Bias (Inclusion Bias)**    Backfill bias can result when missing past return data for a component of an index are filled at the discretion of the component (e.g., a hedge fund for a hedge fund index) when it joins the index. As with survivorship bias, backfill bias makes results look too good because only components with good past results will be motivated to supply them.[102] The issue of this bias has been raised particularly with respect to certain hedge fund indices.[103]

---

**Example 10**

## Hedge Fund Benchmarks

CBA, a large charitable organization, is planning to make an investment in one or more hedge funds. Alex Carr, CIO of CBA, is evaluating information prepared by the organization's senior analyst, Kim Park, CFA.

Carr asks Park why a U.S.-focused market-neutral long–short hedge fund CBA is considering has resisted accepting a U.S equity index as a benchmark.

1.  Prepare a response to Carr's question to Park.

2.  Recommend an alternative to using a stock index benchmark for a market-neutral long–short fund.

---

**102** See Malkiel and Saha (2005) and references therein. Another bias the authors identified is end-of-life bias, which arises from the option a hedge fund has to stop reporting results. One might anticipate that predominantly poorly performing hedge funds would choose to do that.
**103** See Malkiel and Saha (2005).

3. Discuss the impact the following factors have on index creation with respect to hedge funds:

   A. survivorship bias

   B. value-weighted indices

   C. stale price bias

**Solution to 1:**

Market-neutral long–short hedge funds consider themselves to be absolute return vehicles, in that their performance should not be linked to that of the stock market. Such a fund should have effectively zero systematic risk.

**Solution to 2:**

For those hedge funds using absolute-return strategies that are indifferent to the direction of the market, a hurdle rate may be used as a standard for performance.

**Solution to 3:**

A. Survivorship bias occurs when returns of managers who have failed or exited the market are not included in the data analyzed over a specific timeframe. This results in overestimation of historical returns in the range of 1.5–3.0 percent per year. The timing of survivorship bias may be concentrated during certain economic periods, which further complicates analysis of persistence of returns over shorter timeframes. A manager's investment performance reflects not only skill but the starting point of market opportunities and valuations levels—such factors constitute age effects (or vintage effects) in hedge fund performance. Over a long horizon, the starting point should generally decrease in importance. However, hedge funds have average track records of only two to five years. Age effects make it difficult to compare the performance of hedge funds that have track records of different lengths.

B. Indices that are value weighted, as opposed to equally weighted, may take on the return characteristics of the best-performing hedge fund over a given period. These indices thus reflect the weights of popular bets by hedge fund managers, because the asset values of the various funds change as a result of asset purchases as well as price appreciation.

C. Lack of security trading leads to stale prices for those securities and can cause measured standard deviation to be over- or understated, depending on the time period being studied. This could result in measured correlations being lower than expected. This issue is not a significant concern in the creation of hedge fund indices because monthly data are used and for many hedge fund strategies, the underlying holdings are relatively liquid, so positions reflect market-traded prices.

## 6.3 Hedge Funds: Investment Characteristics and Roles

Hedge funds have been described as skill-based investment strategies. Skill-based investment strategies obtain returns primarily from the firm's competitive advantages in information or its interpretation. To the extent that a hedge fund's returns derive primarily from an individual manager's skill or superior depth of information, its returns may be uncorrelated or weakly correlated with the long-term return of the traditional stock and bond markets.

The investor needs to keep in mind, however, that the flip side of skill in producing investment success is market opportunity. The supply of market opportunities can and does vary for particular investment strategies as investment industry, economic, and financial market conditions evolve. To take an obvious example, the opportunities for merger arbitrage hedge funds are heavily influenced by corporate merger activities.

### 6.3.1 *Investment Characteristics*

A number of empirical studies have directly assessed the return drivers of traditional and alternative investments. For instance, for traditional stocks and bonds, a common set of factors has been used to explain stock and bond returns.[104] Similarly, academic research indicates that for hedge funds, a common set of return drivers based on trading strategy factors (e.g., option-like payoffs) and location factors (e.g., payoffs from a buy-and-hold policy) help to explain returns of each strategy.[105]

Results show that, as for traditional "long-bias" stock and bond investments, the returns of some long-bias equity-based and fixed income–based hedge fund strategies are affected primarily by changes in the risk and return of the underlying stock and bond markets and should, therefore, be regarded less as portfolio return diversifiers than as portfolio return enhancers. Hedge fund strategies that attempt to be less affected by the direction of the underlying stock and bond markets (e.g., equity market neutral or bond arbitrage) may be regarded more as diversifiers for traditional stock and bond portfolios.

Studies that used direct replication of underlying strategies also support market factors and option-like payoff variables (e.g., put options) as describing certain hedge fund strategies.[106] The bottom line is that analysis of the underlying factors used in trading strategies is important, given the investor's economic forecast and market expectations, when deciding which hedge funds to include in a portfolio. Investors may consider allocation to various strategies warranted by economic factors directly driving hedge fund returns and may even consider allocations to new strategies based on new economic conditions driving hedge fund returns.

### 6.3.2 *Roles in the Portfolio*[107]

Hedge funds constitute a diverse set of strategies. Because the strategies are skill based, most investors will accord manager selection great scrutiny. Investors put varying emphases on style selection. For a given portfolio, the diversification benefits of adding hedge funds in different style groups can be quite distinct.

FOF investments have been popular as entry-level investments because they essentially delegate individual manager selection to the FOF manager and provide professional management. They also shorten the due diligence process to a single manager. FOFs may be diversified funds composed of various hedge fund strategies or style pure. A significant consideration is that FOF investing involves two layers of management and incentive fees.

Research indicates that an equally weighted diversified portfolio of five to seven randomly selected equity securities will result in a portfolio standard deviation similar to that of the investment population from which it is drawn. Similarly, for hedge funds, a randomly selected equal-weighted portfolio of five to seven hedge funds has a standard deviation similar to that of the population from which it is drawn.[108] Thus, as is true for equity portfolios, multimanager hedge fund portfolios may have

---

**104** See Fama and French (1996).
**105** See Fung and Hsieh (1997a), Schneeweis and Spurgin (1998), Schneeweis and Pescatore (1999), and Agarwal and Naik (2000).
**106** See Mitchell and Pulvino (2000).
**107** Discussion in this section draws on CISDM (2005c).
**108** See Henker (1998).

risk levels similar to that of a larger population of hedge funds. Also important is that a portfolio of randomly selected hedge funds has a correlation in excess of 0.90 with that of a typical hedge fund benchmark. Therefore, the use of a smaller subset of hedge funds can represent the performance of the EACM 100, just as a smaller portfolio of stocks or mutual funds can represent, respectively, the performance of the S&P 500 or mutual fund indices.

**The Role of Hedge Funds as Diversifiers**    A first caution is that, as discussed in detail in the reading on asset allocation, the allocations produced by mean–variance optimization (MVO) are sensitive to errors in return estimates. The different historical index returns among various index providers raise a warning that basing allocations on historical hedge fund index returns in MVO may be unreliable.[109] Hedge fund strategies often have option characteristics that present a further challenge when relying on MVO.

The use of hedge fund indices in overall asset allocation is based, in part, on the assumption that FOFs created to track certain hedge fund strategies perform similarly to the benchmarks used in asset allocation analysis. In short, there are a number of issues involved in portfolio creation at the strategy level as well as among strategies. These issues include 1) persistence in historical performance, 2) portfolio rebalancing, and 3) impact of return distribution features beyond mean and standard deviation—that is, "higher moments."

If one assumes that a portfolio tracks the performance of a particular index, then an investor may use hedge fund indices together with other traditional indices to improve risk–return trade-offs.

**Historical Performance**    The benefit of including hedge funds in diversified portfolios is illustrated in Exhibit 27. For the 1990–2004 period, when the HFCI is added to U.S. stocks, bonds, or a portfolio of U.S. stocks and bonds, the risk-adjusted return improves. For instance, the Sharpe ratio of a balanced portfolio with U.S. stocks and bonds (0.67, Portfolio I) increases to 0.87 when hedge funds are added (Portfolio II). Similarly, when hedge funds are added to a balanced portfolio of world equities and bonds (Portfolio III), the Sharpe ratio increases significantly from 0.43 to 0.65 (Portfolio IV). The correlation between the HFCI and the U.S. stock/bond portfolio (Portfolio I) is 0.59 and between the HFCI and the world stock/bond portfolio (Portfolio III) is 0.51.

| Exhibit 27 | Hedge Fund Performance in Portfolios 1990–2004 | | | |
|---|---|---|---|---|
| **Measure** | **Portfolio I** | **Portfolio II** | **Portfolio III** | **Portfolio IV** |
| Annualized return | 9.64% | 10.43% | 7.86% | 9.01% |
| Annualized std. dev. | 7.94% | 7.09% | 8.29% | 7.28% |
| Sharpe ratio | 0.67 | 0.87 | 0.43 | 0.65 |
| Minimum monthly return | −6.25% | −6.39% | −5.61% | −5.87% |
| Correlation w/HFCI | 0.59 | 0.69 | 0.51 | 0.62 |

*Notes:*
Portfolio I: 50% S&P 500, 50% Lehman Gov./Corp. Bond.
Portfolio II: 40% S&P 500, 40% Lehman Gov./Corp., 20% HFCI.
Portfolio III: 50% MSCI World, 50% Lehman Global Bond.
Portfolio IV: 40% MSCI World, 40% Lehman Global, 20% HFCI.
*Source*: CISDM (2005c).

---

**109** It is important to note that use of historical returns in optimization modeling may not reflect expected risk and return relationships. If factor-based regression models are used to forecast expected rates of return, then the consistency of the sensitivities of various index models to factors is an issue of concern.

Hedge funds achieved historically high returns in the first half of the 1990s, which suggests that the more recent record should be examined closely. Exhibit 28 considers the period 2000–2004. The annualized return of hedge funds for this period (6.84 percent, Exhibit 23) is lower than for the 1990–2004 period (13.46 percent, Exhibit 22), but the benefits that hedge funds add to the portfolios are similar to those for the period that includes the early 1990s.

| Exhibit 28 | Recent Hedge Fund Performance in Portfolios 2000–2004 | | | |
|---|---|---|---|---|
| **Measure** | **Portfolio I** | **Portfolio II** | **Portfolio III** | **Portfolio IV** |
| Annualized return | 3.15% | 3.92% | 3.45% | 4.16% |
| Annualized std. dev. | 7.93% | 6.94% | 8.55% | 7.48% |
| Sharpe ratio | 0.06 | 0.18 | 0.09 | 0.19 |
| Minimum monthly return | −4.36% | −3.62% | −4.94% | −4.08% |
| Correlation w/HFCI | 0.57 | 0.66 | 0.62 | 0.70 |

*Notes*:
Portfolio I: 50% S&P 500, 50% Lehman Gov./Corp. Bond.
Portfolio II: 40% S&P 500, 40% Lehman Gov./Corp Bond, 20% HFCI.
Portfolio III: 50% MSCI World, 50% Lehman Global Bond.
Portfolio IV: 40% MSCI World, 40% Lehman Global, 20% HFCI.
*Source*: CISDM (2005c).

In interpreting data such as those in Exhibit 28 showing that the inclusion of hedge funds effected a mean–variance improvement, researchers such as Kat and Amin (2003) have shown that including hedge funds can also frequently lead to lower skewness and higher kurtosis, which are exactly opposite to the attributes (positive skewness and moderate kurtosis) that investors are presumed to want.

**Example 11**

## Skewness and Hedge Funds[110]

In 2002, the S&P 500 dropped by more than 20 percent and distressed debt hedge funds as a group achieved poor returns. Equity market-neutral funds also achieved poor returns, which was explained as relating to lower market liquidity.

1. Explain why distressed debt hedge funds might have performed poorly in 2002.

2. Explain how lower market liquidity might have negatively affected long–short market-neutral hedge funds.

### Solution to 1:

Major declines in equity markets lead to widening credit spreads and, all else being equal, to capital losses on high-yield bonds. Distressed debt hedge funds are exposed to the risk of increased credit spreads and, as a result, fared poorly in 2002.

---

**110** This discussion draws on Kat (2005), who also discussed a program of buying and rolling over out-of-the-money stock index put options, which tend to deliver positively skewed returns.

> **Solution to 2:**
>
> Maintaining market neutrality involves dynamic portfolio adjustments. Declines in market liquidity increase the cost of shorting equity markets.

The following are techniques for neutralizing negative skewness in a portfolio resulting from hedge fund positions that a portfolio manager may consider:[111]

- Adopt a mean–variance, skewness and kurtosis–aware approach to hedge fund selection. An example is given in Kat (2005), who discussed combining global macro and equity market-neutral hedge strategies with traditional assets. Global macro funds have tended to have positive skewness with only moderate correlation with equities but relatively high kurtosis and volatility; equity market-neutral strategies tend to act as volatility and kurtosis reducers in the portfolio. In other words, smart hedge fund selection may be able to reduce the problem of negative skewness.

- Invest in managed futures. Managed futures programs are generally trend following in nature, which tends to produce skewness characteristics that are opposite to those of many hedge funds.

### 6.3.3 *Other Issues*[112]

In addition to market factors affecting a broad range of investment vehicles, individual fund factors may affect expected performance. Academic and practitioner research has tested various fund-specific factors—such as onshore/offshore, age, and size—on manager performance. Results from this research support the following: 1) Young funds outperform old funds on a total-return basis, or at least old funds do not outperform young ones; 2) on average, large funds underperform small funds; 3) FOFs may provide closer approximation to return estimation than indices do.[113]

Unfortunately, as in any tests of fund effects, one has the problem of disaggregating effects for a large number of funds, each with different strategies, starting periods, and so on. In fact, although it is not the purpose of this reading to conduct a detailed analysis of each of these effects, the following discussion indicates that simple relationships between hedge fund returns and each of the aforementioned fund factors must be analyzed closely before final conclusions can be made.

- *Performance fees and lock-up impacts.* Periods of severe drawdown (e.g., 1998) may influence funds to dissolve rather than face the prospect of not earning the incentive fees because of HWM provisions. There is some evidence of an impact of lock-up periods on hedge fund performance. In the case of U.S. hedge funds, funds with quarterly lock-ups have higher returns than similar-strategy funds with monthly lock-ups.

- *Funds of funds.* FOF returns may differ from overall hedge fund performance because of various issues, including a less direct impact of survivorship bias on FOFs because hedge funds that dissolve are included in the returns of the FOFs (there still is some survivorship bias, in that FOFs may remove themselves from datasets because of, for example, poor performance). FOFs may thus provide a more accurate prediction of future fund returns than that provided by the more generic indices.

---

**111** This discussion is based on Kat (2005).
**112** Discussion in this section draws on Schneeweis, Kazemi, and Martin (2002).
**113** See Howell (2001), Liang (2000), and Fung and Hsieh (2002).

However, classification and style drift are issues with FOFs. A number of FOFs reported as diversified by category differ greatly not only in their correlation with standard indices but also in their sensitivity to general economic factors. Investors must use factors to test "style drift" of generic FOFs.

As a result, the use of FOFs that change over time in response to rebalancing may not fit well into strict asset allocation modeling. For instance, new FOFs (U.S. diversified FOFs) starting in the years 1992 onward were found to have lower correlations with FOFs starting in 1991 or earlier, but as years progressed, the correlations increased. This indicates that new FOFs are constructed differently from old funds. This is expected. New FOFs can be more flexible in fund selection. As time passes, however, older FOFs can redistribute cash or funds in such a way that they resemble the new fund construction. Thus, simple averaging across FOFs without taking the year of origination into account may not be appropriate.

Over time, hedge fund correlations with hedged equity have risen and hedge fund correlations with global macro strategies have fallen, indicating an increase in FOFs' use of hedged equity and a decrease in the use of global macro. These results emphasize that FOFs may be timing one market and have become less useful in asset allocation strategies than previously because of their factor sensitivity and composition change—in contrast to more style-pure hedge fund indices or strategies.

- *Effect of fund size.* On the one hand, there are potential advantages to a hedge fund having a large asset base. The fund may be able to attract and retain more talented people than a small fund and receive more attention from, for example, its prime broker. On the other hand, a smaller fund may be more nimble. With smaller positions, the market impact cost of its trades may be less. Depending on the particular strategies pursued, there may be an optimal market size for the fund in relation to market opportunities available for its strategy at a given time. The investor should, following the paradigm for due diligence illustrated in Example 2, examine the current market opportunities in relation to the fund's size.

  Research has generally supported the conclusion that, overall, larger funds have earned lower mean returns and lower risk-adjusted returns than small funds. However, the relationships of performance to fund size have been found to have exceptions according to hedge fund strategy. Because market opportunities and assets under management in a strategy change, the best advice may be to evaluate the effect of fund size on a case-by-case basis. The investor should also investigate differences in mortality rates among hedge funds by size within the strategy.

- *Age (vintage) effects.* The usual performance statistics hide the time dimension behind hedge fund performance. Investors should be sensitive to the fact that because of vintage effects, it may be difficult to compare the performance of funds with different lengths of track record. Comparisons of a fund with the performance of the median manager of the same vintage in a hedge fund's style group can be revealing.

**Hedge Fund Due Diligence**   Hedge funds have historically been loosely regulated entities without the mandated and often standardized disclosure requirements of other investment vehicles, such as unit trusts in the United Kingdom and mutual funds in the United States. Although hedge funds typically provide an annual audited financial statement and performance review, they rarely disclose their existing portfolio positions. Possible concerns that arise from this lack of disclosure (see Anson, 2002a) include the following:

- Authenticity of the hedge fund manager's performance is doubtful if investors cannot verify the performance with a position report.

- Risk monitoring and management are difficult for investors without disclosure of trading and portfolio positions by the hedge fund manager. Without full disclosure of the holdings, investors cannot aggregate risk across their entire investment program to understand the implications at the portfolio level.

Because hedge fund operations and/or strategies may also be somewhat opaque, reducing investment risk in hedge fund investing starts with due diligence.

Again, the framework for due diligence presented in Example 2—covering market opportunity, investment process, organization, people, terms and structure, service providers, documents, and write-ups—applies here. The investor may interview the hedge fund and/or submit a questionnaire. The Alternative Investments Management Association provides the following due diligence checklist as a guide for investors evaluating hedge fund managers.[114] Investors should try to learn the following information:

I. Structure of the Hedge Fund

   a. Legal entity: type and ownership structure

   b. Name and address of hedge fund manager

   c. Domicile: onshore or offshore

      i. Branch offices or other locations (and their functions)

   d. Regulatory registrations (e.g., investment advisor or commodity trading advisor)

   e. Personnel: responsible officers and employees (including their biographies)

   f. Auditors, legal counsel, and prime broker information

II. Strategy of the Hedge Fund

   a. Style (e.g., event driven, global macro)

   b. Instruments used under each strategy (e.g., which derivatives)

   c. Benchmark, hurdle rate, high-water mark, etc.

   d. Competitive niche or any uniqueness about the fund

      i. The source of investment ideas or strategy

      ii. How the strategy works under different market conditions

      iii. Market conditions in which the strategy works best

      iv. Any capacity constraint for the strategy

   e. Current investments: types and positions

III. Performance Data

   a. List of all funds and performance since inception

   b. Information on the performance of the funds and explanations

IV. Risk

   a. What and how risks are measured and managed

      i. Personnel involved

   b. Specific risk-control measures, if any (e.g., position limits, derivatives, counterparty credit limits)

   c. Past, current, and future use of leverage

---

114 See www.aima.org.

   **V.** Research

      **a.** Any change in strategy in the past resulting from research findings

      **b.** Efforts put into research for investment/trading ideas

      **c.** Budget and personnel (internal and external) for research

  **VI.** Administration

      **a.** Law suits, litigations, regulatory actions against the fund or its managers

      **b.** Significant employees and employee turnover

      **c.** Personnel arrangement for the account: responsible account executive

      **d.** Disaster recovery plan

 **VII.** Legal

      **a.** Fee structure: management and incentive fees (Is high-water mark applicable?)

      **b.** Lock-up

      **c.** Subscription amount: maximum and minimum

      **d.** Drawback provision

**VIII.** References

      **a.** Professional: auditor, prime broker, legal counsel

      **b.** Existing investors

---

**Example 12**

## An Investor Does Due Diligence on a Hedge Fund

Alois Winkelmann is conducting due diligence on a U.S.-based hedge fund, Tricontinent Investors, for the Malvey Charitable Trust (MCT). Among the facts Winkelmann gathers are the following:

### Structure

The fund employs three people—the two principals, Bryce Smith and Henrietta Duff, and an administrative assistant. Smith's prior work experience is 10 years as an equity analyst at North Country Trust Company and, prior to that, three years as an associate in a Syracuse, New York, law firm. He holds a BBA and an LLB. Duff worked for three years as an equity growth fund manager at a medium-size mutual fund complex. Prior to that, she was a corporate finance associate at a leading investment bank. Duff holds an AB in English and an MBA with a concentration in finance. The principals have at-will employment contracts. The fund's relationship with its prime broker extends back two years. The fund has used only one prime broker since it was formed. The prime broker is a prestigious firm ranked number two by prime brokerage business.

### Hedge Fund Strategy

- The fund invests in both fixed-income and equity markets.
- The fund buys U.S. 10-year Treasury notes and borrows short term abroad in markets that have particularly low interest rates to earn, currently, a positive spread.
- The fund conducts merger arbitrage involving the securities of the target and acquirer.

**Legal**

The fund has a 1 and 20 fee structure and a two-year lock-up period.

Based only on the information supplied, identify and discuss the risk factors in this hedge fund investment.

**Solution:**

- The firm is a small shop with limited management and research resources.
- Either principal could leave the firm on short notice because of the at-will nature of their employment contracts.
- The hedge fund has only a two-year track record available for evaluation.
- Neither principal has prior experience in either fixed-income investing or merger arbitrage, although Duff's investment banking experience may be somewhat relevant.
- The fixed-income strategy could become unprofitable if the U.S. dollar weakens against the currencies of the markets in which Tricontinent is borrowing short term.
- The fixed-income strategy could become less profitable or unprofitable if the spread between long-term and short-term interest rates decreases.

## 6.4 Performance Evaluation Concerns

The reading on evaluating portfolio performance covers the basic concepts of performance evaluation, with components of performance measurement, performance attribution, and performance appraisal. This section provides further comments and illustrations in the context of hedge funds. In reviewing the performance of a hedge fund, some factors an investor needs to consider are:

- the returns achieved;
- volatility, not only standard deviation but also downside volatility;
- what performance appraisal measures to use;
- correlations (to gain information on diversification benefits in a portfolio context);
- skewness and kurtosis because these affect risk and may qualify the conclusions drawn from a performance appraisal measure; and
- consistency, including the period specificity of performance.

**Returns**  Hedge funds typically report data to hedge fund data providers monthly, and the default compounding frequency for hedge fund performance evaluation and reporting is monthly. The rate of return reported by hedge funds is the nominal monthly-holding-period return computed as follows:

$$\text{Rate of return} = \big[\big(\text{Ending value of portfolio}\big) - \big(\text{Beginning value of portfolio}\big)\big] / \big(\text{Beginning value of portfolio}\big)$$

These returns are typically compounded over 12 monthly periods (or 4 periods if the data are reported quarterly) to obtain the annualized rate of return. The reporting and compounding frequency can materially affect hedge funds' apparent performance for a number of reasons, including the following:

- Many hedge funds allow entry or exit to their funds quarterly or even less frequently.
- In calculating drawdowns, no compounding is typically applied to the loss.

The issues of leverage and the use of derivatives in return calculation also arise in hedge fund performance evaluation. The calculation convention followed in the hedge fund industry is to "look through" the leverage as if the asset were fully paid. Thus, as the beginning value in the above equation for rate of return, the return on a levered position is based on the amount actually paid plus any borrowing used to fund the purchase. The ending value is, of course, calculated on a consistent basis. Thus, leverage affects the weighting of an asset in the portfolio but not the return on the individual asset. The same principle of deleveraging applies to the computation of the rate of return when derivatives are included in the hedge fund portfolio.[115]

Investors sometimes examine the rolling returns to a hedge fund. The **rolling return**, *RR*, is simply the moving average of the holding-period returns for a specified period (e.g., a calendar year) that matches the investor's time horizon. For example, if the investor's time horizon is 12 months, the rolling return would be calculated using

$$RR_{n,t} = \left( R_t + R_{t-1} + R_{t-2} + \ldots + R_{t-(n-1)} \right) \Big/ n$$

so

$$RR_{12,t} = \left( R_t + R_{t-1} + R_{t-2} + \ldots + R_{t-11} \right) \Big/ 12$$

Rolling returns provide some insight into the characteristics and qualities of returns. In particular, they show how consistent the returns are over the investment period and identify any cyclicality in the returns.

**Volatility and Downside Volatility**   As in traditional investments, the standard deviation of returns is a common measure of risk in hedge fund performance. The standard deviation of hedge fund returns is computed in the usual fashion and typically based on monthly returns. The annualized standard deviation is usually computed as the standard deviation of the monthly return times the square root of 12, making the assumption of serially uncorrelated returns. The use of the standard deviation of monthly returns as a measure of risk also makes the implicit assumption that the return distribution follows the normal distribution, at least to a close approximation. As already mentioned, however, hedge funds appear to have more instances of extremely high and extremely low returns than would be expected with a normal distribution (i.e., positive excess kurtosis) and some funds also display meaningful skewness. When those conditions hold, standard deviation incorrectly represents the actual risk of a hedge fund's strategies.

Downside deviation, or semideviation, is an alternative risk measure that mitigates one critique of standard deviation, namely, that it penalizes high positive returns. Downside deviation computes deviation from a specified threshold (i.e., below a specified return, $r^*$); only the negative deviations are included in the calculation. The threshold can be zero (separating gains from losses) or the prevailing short-term rate

---

[115] Because derivatives require only a good faith deposit, which is interest yielding, there is no real capital investment involved. The computed rate of return under the assumption that the full value of the derivatives constitutes the investment base is, at best, a pseudo rate of return. Yau, Savanayana, and Schneeweis (1990) examined the impact of different rates of return of derivative investments based on differing computations of the rates of return and found significantly different results in portfolio optimization and hedging programs.

or any rate chosen by the user. Semideviation uses the average monthly return as the threshold. Once the threshold is determined, the computation resembles that of the standard deviation. Using downside deviation instead of standard deviation recognizes a distinction between good and bad volatility:

$$\text{Downside deviation} = \sqrt{\frac{\sum_{i=1}^{n}\left[\min\left(r_t - r^*, 0\right)\right]^2}{n-1}}$$

where min(A,B) means "A or B, whichever is smaller."

Another popular risk measure is drawdown. As discussed in the reading on risk management, drawdown in the field of hedge fund management is the difference between a portfolio's point of maximum net asset value (its high-water mark) and any subsequent low point (until new "high water" is reached). *Maximum* drawdown is the largest difference between a high-water point and a subsequent low.[116] A portfolio may also be said to be in a position of drawdown from a decline from a high-water mark until a new high-water mark is reached. How long this period lasts is relevant to evaluating hedge fund performance—in particular, its record of recovering from losses.

**Performance Appraisal Measures**    The most extensively used industry measure to date has been the Sharpe ratio, which measures the average amount of return in excess of the risk-free rate per unit of standard deviation of return. The reading on evaluating portfolio performance gives a definition and a discussion, but we may present it as follows, with reference to the *ex post* performance in a given year:

$$\text{Sharpe ratio} = \left(\text{Annualized rate of return} - \text{Annualized risk-free}\right.$$
$$\left.\text{rate}\right)/\text{Annualized standard deviation}$$

In this application, a one-year T-bill yield is usually used to determine the annualized risk-free rate.

The Sharpe ratio has a number of limitations that the hedge fund investor needs to understand:

- The Sharpe ratio is time dependent; that is, the overall Sharpe ratio increases proportionally with the square root of time. An annual Sharpe ratio will therefore be $\sqrt{12}$ bigger than a monthly Sharpe ratio if returns are serially uncorrelated.[117]

- It is not an appropriate measure of risk-adjusted performance when the investment has an asymmetrical return distribution, with either negative or positive skewness.[118]

- Illiquid holdings bias the Sharpe ratio upward.

- Sharpe ratios are overestimated when investment returns are serially correlated (i.e., returns trend), which causes a lower estimate of the standard deviation. This occurs with certain hedge fund strategies that may have a problem with stale pricing or illiquidity. Distressed securities may be an example.

---

116 See Lhabitant (2002), p. 254.
117 See Lhabitant (2004).
118 A number of researchers insist that the Sharpe ratio should be interpreted together with the higher moments of the return distribution. For example, Brooks and Kat (2002) found that high Sharpe ratios tend to go together with negative skewness and high kurtosis.

- The Sharpe ratio is primarily a risk-adjusted performance measure for stand-alone investments and does not take into consideration the correlations with other assets in a portfolio.

- The Sharpe ratio has not been found to have predictive ability for hedge funds in general. Being a "winner" according to the Sharpe ratio over a past period cannot be relied on to predict future success.

- The Sharpe ratio can be gamed; that is, the reported Sharpe ratio can be increased without the investment really delivering higher risk-adjusted returns. Specifically, Spurgin (2001) showed the following means to gaming the Sharpe ratio:

  1. Lengthening the measurement interval. This will result in a lower estimate of volatility; for example, the annualized standard deviation of daily returns is generally higher than the weekly, which is, in turn, higher than the monthly.

  2. Compounding the monthly returns but calculating the standard deviation from the (not compounded) monthly returns.

  3. Writing out-of-the-money puts and calls on a portfolio. This strategy can potentially increase the return by collecting the option premium without paying off for several years. Strategies that involve taking on default risk, liquidity risk, or other forms of catastrophe risk have the same ability to report an upwardly biased Sharpe ratio. (Examples are the Sharpe ratios of market-neutral hedge funds before and after the 1998 liquidity crisis.) This is similar to trading negative skewness for a greater Sharpe ratio by improving the mean or standard deviation of the investment.[119]

  4. Smoothing of returns. Using certain derivative structures, infrequent marking to market of illiquid assets, and pricing models that understate monthly gains or losses can reduce reported volatility.

  5. Getting rid of extreme returns (best and worst monthly returns each year) that increase the standard deviation. Operationally, this entails a total-return swap: One pays the best and worst returns for one's benchmark index each year, and the counterparty pays a fixed cash flow and hedges the risk in the open market. If swaps are not available, one can do it directly with options.

The **Sortino ratio** replaces standard deviation in the Sharpe ratio with downside deviation. Instead of using the mean rate of return to calculate the downside deviation, the investor's minimum acceptable return or the risk-free rate is typically used. The reading on risk management has further comments on this measure. The Sortino ratio is

$$\text{Sortino ratio} = (\text{Annualized rate of return} -$$
$$\text{Annualized risk-free rate}) / \text{Downside deviation}$$

The **gain-to-loss ratio** measures the ratio of positive returns to negative returns over a specified period of time. The higher the gain-to-loss ratio (in absolute value), the better:

$$\text{Gain-to-loss ratio} = (\text{Number months with positive returns} /$$
$$\text{Number months with negative returns}) \times$$
$$(\text{Average up-month return} /$$
$$\text{Average down-month return})$$

---

**119** See Spurgin (2001) and Anson (2002a) for theoretical proofs and examples.

In addition, two major appraisal measures based on drawdowns as indicators of risk, the Calmar ratio and the Sterling ratio, have been applied to hedge fund analysis.[120]

**Correlations**    Correlations provide information on portfolio diversification. However, correlations are most meaningful when assets' or strategies' returns are normally distributed. This fact is an additional reason to consider skewness and kurtosis.

**Skewness and Kurtosis**    To review, skewness is a measure of asymmetry in the distribution of returns. A symmetrical distribution has a skewness of zero; all else being equal, a positive value of skewness is desirable. Kurtosis evaluates the relative incidence of returns clustered near the mean return versus returns extremely far away from the mean. If one investment has higher kurtosis than another, it tends to have more instances of extreme returns.

**Consistency**    Another element in evaluating hedge funds is consistency of results. Consistency analysis is most relevant when comparing funds of the same style or strategy. It is important to look at the number of months that the strategy has had positive (or negative) returns, the number of months that the strategy has had positive (negative) returns when the market is up (down), and the average monthly returns in up and down markets. For consistency, a fund should have a greater percentage of positive returns and less negative returns than the benchmark in all market conditions. We illustrate with the data given in Exhibit 29. In computing the rolling returns, the relevant holding period for the investor is assumed to be six months. This is simply for illustration purposes. In practice, the rolling returns should match the investor's investment horizon.

| **Exhibit 29** | Hypothetical Hedge Fund Consistency Data | | | | | | | |
|---|---|---|---|---|---|---|---|---|
| Month | Hedge Fund Return (%) | Index Return (%) | (HF Return − Hurdle Rate)$^2$ | (Index Return − Hurdle Rate)$^2$ | 1+ HF Return | 1+ Index Return | Rolling Six-Month Return of HF | Rolling Six-Month Return of Index |
| January | 2.5 | 1.0 | 0.0000 | 0.0000 | 1.0250 | 1.0100 | | |
| February | 1.5 | 1.3 | 0.0000 | 0.0000 | 1.0150 | 1.0130 | | |
| March | −1.0 | −1.6 | 2.0070 | 4.0671 | 0.9900 | 0.9840 | | |
| April | −1.2 | −2.4 | 2.6137 | 7.9338 | 0.9880 | 0.9760 | | |
| May | −1.0 | −4.2 | 2.0070 | 21.3139 | 0.9900 | 0.9580 | | |
| June | 0.9 | 2.0 | 0.0000 | 0.0000 | 1.0090 | 1.0200 | 0.0028 | −0.0065 |
| July | −1.0 | 2.5 | 2.0070 | 0.0000 | 0.9900 | 1.0250 | −0.0030 | −0.0040 |
| August | 0.7 | −2.1 | 0.0000 | 6.3338 | 1.0070 | 0.9790 | −0.0043 | −0.0097 |
| September | 1.1 | 2.0 | 0.0000 | 0.0000 | 1.0110 | 1.0200 | −0.0008 | −0.0037 |
| October | 2.1 | 0.5 | 0.0000 | 0.0000 | 1.0210 | 1.0050 | 0.0047 | 0.0012 |
| November | 1.5 | 3.1 | 0.0000 | 0.0000 | 1.0150 | 1.0310 | 0.0088 | 0.0133 |

---

120 The **Calmar ratio** is the compound annualized rate of return over a specified time period divided by the absolute value of maximum drawdown over the same time period. Frequently, the time horizon is set at three years (36 months), but if three years of data are not available, the available data are used. The **Sterling ratio** is the compound annualized rate of return over a specified time period divided by the average yearly maximum drawdown over the same time period less an arbitrary 10 percent. To calculate this average yearly drawdown, the data period is divided into separate 12-month periods and the maximum drawdown is calculated for each and averaged. The convention for the time horizon follows that of the Calmar ratio.

| Exhibit 29 | Continued |
|---|---|

| Month | Hedge Fund Return (%) | Index Return (%) | (HF Return – Hurdle Rate)² | (Index Return – Hurdle Rate)² | 1+ HF Return | 1+ Index Return | Rolling Six-Month Return of HF | Rolling Six-Month Return of Index |
|---|---|---|---|---|---|---|---|---|
| December | 1.5 | 0.2 | 0.0000 | 0.0470 | 1.0150 | 1.0020 | 0.0098 | 0.0103 |
| Sum | 7.6 | 2.3 | 8.6348 | 39.6955 | | | | |
| Mean | 0.63 | 0.19 | | | | | 0.0026 | 0.0001 |
| Product | | | | | 1.0777 | 1.0203 | | |

*Notes:* The hurdle rate is 5 percent per year or 0.4167 percent per month. Deviation from the hurdle rate squared is computed if the fund/index return is less than the hurdle rate; otherwise, it will be equal to zero. The rolling six-month return is computed as $RR_t = (R_t + R_{t-1} + \ldots + R_{t-5})/6$.

Exhibit 30 shows the computation of the performance statistics of a hypothetical hedge fund for 12 months from the data given in Exhibit 29.

| Exhibit 30 | Return and Risk Calculations |
|---|---|

| | Hedge Fund | Index |
|---|---|---|
| **1. Return** | | |
| Total fund return = $[(1 + r_1)(1 + r_2)\ldots(1 + r_{12})] - 1 = 1.0777 - 1 = 0.0777$ | | |
| Total index return = $1.0203 - 1 = 0.0203$ | 7.77% | 2.03% |
| Geometric mean per year: | | |
| Fund = $(1.0777^{1/12} - 1) \times 12 = 7.50\%$ | | |
| Index = $(1.0203^{1/12} - 1) \times 12 = 2.02\%$ | 7.50% | 2.02% |
| Rolling six-month returns mean = $(RR_{6,1} + RR_{6,2} + RR_{6,3} + RR_{6,4} + RR_{6,5} + RR_{6,6} + RR_{6,7})/7$ | | |
| where $RR_{6,t} = (R_t + R_{t-1} + R_{t-2} + R_{t-3} + R_{t-4} + R_{t-5})/6$ | | |
| Fund = $(0.0028 - 0.0030 - 0.0043 - 0.0008 + 0.0047 + 0.0088 + 0.0098)/7 = 0.0026$ | | |
| Index = $(-0.0065 - 0.0040 - 0.0097 - 0.0037 + 0.0012 + 0.0133 + 0.0103)/7 = 0.0001$ | 0.26% | 0.01% |
| Rolling six-month returns (max) | 0.98% | 1.33% |
| Rolling six-month returns (min) | −0.43% | −0.97% |
| **2. Risk** | | |
| Annualized standard deviation | 4.62% | 7.87% |
| Annualized downside deviation: | | |
| Hurdle rate = 5% per year | | |
| Fund = $\sqrt{8.6348/(12-1)} \times \sqrt{12} = 3.07$ | | |
| Index = $\sqrt{39.6955/(12-1)} \times \sqrt{12} = 6.58$ | 3.07% | 6.58% |
| **3. Appraisal** | | |
| Sharpe ratio (per year) = (Return – 5%)/Standard deviation: | | |
| Fund = $(7.5 - 5)/4.62 = 0.54$ | | |
| Index = $(2.02 - 5)/7.87 = -0.38$ | 0.54 | −0.38 |

*(continued)*

| Exhibit 30 | Continued | | |
|---|---|---|---|

| | | Hedge Fund | Index |
|---|---|---|---|
| Sortino ratio (per year) = (Return − 5%)/Downside deviation: | | | |
| Fund = (7.5 − 5)/3.07 = 0.81 | | | |
| Index = (2.02 − 5)/6.58 = −0.45 | | 0.81 | −0.45 |
| Gain/Loss: | | | |
| Fund = (1.475/−1.05) × (8/4) = −2.82 | | | |
| Index = (1.575/−2.575) × (8/4) = −1.22 | | −2.82 | −1.22 |
| *4. Consistency* | | | |
| Number of months | | 12 | 12 |
| Number of positive months | | 8 | 8 |
| Percentage of positive months | | 66.67% | 66.67% |
| Average return in up-months | | 1.48% | 1.58% |
| Number of negative months | | 4 | 4 |
| Percentage of negative months | | 33.33% | 33.33% |
| Average return in down-months | | −1.05% | −2.58% |
| Average monthly return in index up-months: | | | |
| Fund = (2.5 + 1.5 + 0.9 − 1.0 + 1.1 + 2.1 + 1.5 + 1.5)/8 = 1.263. | | | |
| Index = (1.0 + 1.3 + 2.0 + 2.5 + 2.0 + 0.5 + 3.1 + 0.2)/8 = 1.575. | | 1.26% | 1.58% |
| Average monthly return in index down-months = (−1.0 − 1.2 − 1.0 + 0.7)/4 = −0.625. | | −0.63% | −2.58% |
| *5. Correlation between Fund and Index Returns—12 Months* | | | 0.53 |

*Note*: The arithmetic means used in the computation of standard deviation were computed as 0.63 percent and 0.19 percent for, respectively, the fund and the index.

# 7   MANAGED FUTURES

Managed futures have been used as an investment alternative since the late 1960s.[121] More recently, such institutional investors as corporate and public pension funds, endowments, trusts, and bank trust departments have been including managed futures as one segment of a well-diversified portfolio.

**Managed futures** are private pooled investment vehicles that can invest in cash, spot, and derivative markets for the benefit of their investors and have the ability to use leverage in a wide variety of trading strategies. Like hedge funds, managed futures programs are actively managed. Similar to hedge funds, with which they are often grouped, managed futures programs are often structured as limited partnerships open only to accredited investors (institutions and high-net-worth individuals). Compensation arrangements for managed futures programs are also similar to those of hedge funds. The primary distinguishing differences between hedge funds and managed futures is that, for the most part, managed futures trade exclusively in derivative markets (future, forward, or option markets) whereas hedge funds tend to be more active in spot markets while using futures markets for hedging. Because hedge funds often trade in individual securities whereas managed futures primarily trade

---

**121** Books that provide information on the structural and performance history of managed futures include Fox-Andrews and Meaden (1995), Peters and Warwick (1997), and Chance (1996).

market-based futures and options contracts on broader or more generic baskets of assets, one can view hedge funds as concentrating on inefficiencies in micro (security) stock and bond markets whereas managed futures look for return opportunities in macro (index) stock and bond markets. In addition, in some jurisdictions, managed futures programs have been historically more highly regulated than hedge funds.

## 7.1 The Managed Futures Market

Managed futures programs are an industry comprising specialist professional money managers. In the United States, such programs are run by general partners known as commodity pool operators (CPOs), who are, or have hired, professional commodity trading advisors to manage money in the pool. In the United States, both CPOs and CTAs are registered with the U.S. Commodity Futures Trading Commission and National Futures Association (a self-regulatory body).

### 7.1.1 Types of Managed Futures Investments

Managed futures have been described as skill-based investment strategies. Skill-based strategies obtain returns from the unique skill or strategy of the trader. Like hedge funds, managed futures have also been described as absolute-return strategies.

In addition to private commodity pools, managed futures programs are also available in separately managed accounts (sometimes known as "CTA managed accounts"). Publicly traded commodity funds open to smaller investors are also available. Managed futures programs may use a single manager or multiple managers.

Managed futures funds share the compensation structure of hedge funds consisting of a management fee plus incentive fee, with a 2 plus 20 arrangement the most common structure.

Managed futures may be classified according to investment style. They are often classified into subgroups on the basis of investment style (e.g., systematic or discretionary), markets traded (e.g., currency or financial), or trading strategy (e.g., trend following or contrarian). Managed futures are at times viewed as a subset of global macro hedge funds, in that they also attempt to take advantage of systematic moves in major financial and nonfinancial markets, primarily through trading futures and option contracts.

The trading strategies of managed futures include the following:

- *Systematic trading strategies* trade primarily according to a rule-based trading model usually based on past prices. Most systematic CTAs invest by using a trend-following program, although some trade according to a contrarian, or countertrend, program. In addition, trend-following CTAs may concentrate on short-term trends, medium-term trends, long-term trends, or a combination thereof.

- *Discretionary trading strategies* trade financial, currency, and commodity futures and options. Unlike systematic strategies, they involve portfolio manager judgment. Discretionary trading models include those based on fundamental economic data and on trader beliefs. Traders often use multiple criteria in making trading decisions.

By the markets emphasized in trading, managed futures may be classified as:

- *Financial* (trading financial futures/options, currency futures/options, and forward contracts).

- *Currency* (trading currency futures/options and forward contracts).

- *Diversified* (trading financial futures/options, currency futures/options, and forward contracts, as well as physical commodity futures/options).

A market classification can also be used to distinguish subcategories of systematic and discretionary trading strategies.

### 7.1.2 *Size of the Managed Futures Market*

Worldwide, the managed futures industry has grown from less than US$1 billion under management in 1980 to approximately US$130 billion under management in 2004.[122] To put this last figure in perspective, consider that the managed futures industry is probably somewhat less than 10 percent the size of the hedge fund industry as judged by assets under management.

## 7.2 Benchmarks and Historical Performance

The benchmarks for managed futures are similar to those for hedge funds, in that indices represent performance of a group of managers who use a similar trading strategy or style.

### 7.2.1 *Benchmarks*

Investable benchmarks for actively managed derivative strategies exist. Such indices replicate the return to a mechanical, trend-following strategy in a number of financial and commodity futures markets. For example, the Mount Lucas Management Index takes both long and short positions in a number of futures markets based on a technical (moving-average) trading rule that is, in effect, an active momentum strategy.

The CISDM CTA trading strategy benchmarks are examples of benchmarks based on peer groups of CTAs. The dollar-weighted (CTA$) and equal-weighted (CTAEQ) CISDM indices reflect manager returns for all reporting managers in the CISDM database on, respectively, a dollar-weighted and equal-weighted basis. The CISDM CTA indices include indices for systematic versus discretionary strategies, for groups based on market emphasis (financial, currency, diversified), and for trend following versus contrarian. For example, the CTA trend-following index may include financial, currency, and diversified trend-following CTAs.

### 7.2.2 *Historical Performance*

The performance of managed futures on an individual basis and as a group is of interest. For the 1990–2004 period, the annualized standard deviations of individual CTAs in the CISDM alternative investment database were, on average, comparable to the averaged annualized standard deviations of U.S. blue chip stocks.[123] As Exhibit 31 shows, on a portfolio basis, for the 1990–2004 period, the volatility of the CTA$ Index (9.96 percent) was less than that of either the S&P 500 (14.65 percent) or MSCI World Index (14.62 percent) but greater than that of U.S. or global bonds (4.46 percent and 5.23 percent, respectively). The Sharpe ratio for the CTA$ was better than those of equities but not those of bonds. Exhibit 32 shows that results for a more recent period (2000–2004) are qualitatively similar. Noteworthy is that the correlations of the CISDM CTA$ with the equity indices are slightly negative; the correlations of the CISDM CTA$ with U.S. and global bonds are similar at 0.42 and 0.46, respectively.

---

**122** These numbers do not include the large amount of funds traded through hedge funds (e.g., global asset allocators) or proprietary trading desks of large investment houses, insurance companies, or banks that use strategies similar to those of independent CTAs. The estimate is from Barclays Trading Group.

**123** The average annualized standard deviation of the individual CTAs that have complete data for 1990–2004 in the CISDM database is 27.06 percent vs. 28.54 percent for the individual component stocks in the DJIA (CISDM 2005d). Annualized standard deviations are derived by multiplying the monthly data by the square root of 12.

| Exhibit 31 | CTA Performance 1990–2004 |
| --- | --- |

| Measure | CISDM CTA$ | HFCI | S&P 500 | Lehman Gov./Corp. | MSCI World | Lehman Global |
| --- | --- | --- | --- | --- | --- | --- |
| Annualized return | 10.85% | 13.46% | 10.94% | 7.77% | 7.08% | 8.09% |
| Annualized std. dev. | 9.96% | 5.71% | 14.65% | 4.46% | 14.62% | 5.23% |
| Sharpe ratio | 0.66 | 1.61 | 0.45 | 0.78 | 0.19 | 0.73 |
| Minimum monthly return | −6.00% | −6.92% | −14.46% | −4.19% | −13.32% | −3.66% |
| Correlation w/CTA$ | 1.00 | 0.19 | −0.10 | 0.29 | −0.11 | 0.27 |

*Note*: CTA$ is the dollar-weighted CTA universe.
*Source*: CISDM (2005d).

| Exhibit 32 | Recent CTA Performance 2000–2004 |
| --- | --- |

| Measure | CISDM CTA$ | HFCI | S&P 500 | Lehman Gov./Corp. | MSCI World | Lehman Global |
| --- | --- | --- | --- | --- | --- | --- |
| Annualized return | 7.89% | 6.84% | −2.30% | 8.00% | −2.05% | 8.51% |
| Annualized std. dev. | 8.66% | 4.83% | 16.35% | 4.76% | 15.62% | 6.00% |
| Sharpe ratio | 0.60 | 0.86 | −0.31 | 1.11 | −0.30 | 0.97 |
| Minimum monthly return | −5.12% | −2.94% | −10.87% | −4.19% | −10.98% | −3.66% |
| Correlation w/CTA$ | 1.00 | 0.18 | −0.25 | 0.42 | −0.18 | 0.46 |

*Source*: CISDM (2005d).

Exhibit 33 displays the correlations among CTA investment strategies, which range from moderate to highly positive. The correlation of trend-following with discretionary is among the lowest at 0.51. In general, the correlations among CTA strategies appear to be influenced by the degree to which the strategies are trend following or discretionary. The overall dollar-weighted and equal-weighted indices are highly correlated with diversified, financial, and trend-following strategies and distinctly less correlated with currency and discretionary strategies.

| Exhibit 33 | Correlations of CISDM CTA Universe Strategies 1990–2004 |
| --- | --- |

| | CTA$ | CTAEQ | Currency | Discretionary | Diversified | Financial | Trend Following |
| --- | --- | --- | --- | --- | --- | --- | --- |
| CTA$ | 1.00 | | | | | | |
| CTAEQ | 0.94 | 1.00 | | | | | |
| Currency | 0.66 | 0.62 | 1.00 | | | | |
| Discretionary | 0.63 | 0.54 | 0.44 | 1.00 | | | |
| Diversified | 0.94 | 0.93 | 0.54 | 0.60 | 1.00 | | |
| Financial | 0.93 | 0.88 | 0.59 | 0.47 | 0.84 | 1.00 | |
| Trend following | 0.96 | 0.95 | 0.64 | 0.51 | 0.92 | 0.93 | 1.00 |

*Source*: CISDM (2005d).

Exhibit 34 complements the information that was provided in Exhibit 31 by adding performance information on the CTA strategies, including correlations with U.S. equity and bond indices. Across CTA strategies, correlations with U.S. equities are low and correlations with U.S. bonds are low or moderate.

| **Exhibit 34** | Performance of CISDM CTA Universe Strategies and Traditional Assets 1990–2004 | | | | | |
|---|---|---|---|---|---|---|
| **Strategy or Class** | **Return (%)** | **Standard Deviation (%)** | **Sharpe Ratio** | **Minimum Monthly Return (%)** | **Correlation w/S&P 500** | **Correlation w/Lehman Gov./Corp.** |
| CISDM CTA$ | 10.85 | 9.96 | 0.66 | −6.00 | −0.10 | 0.29 |
| CISDM CTAEQ | 9.33 | 9.58 | 0.53 | −5.43 | −0.16 | 0.26 |
| CISDM Currency | 9.24 | 11.80 | 0.42 | −8.17 | 0.05 | 0.15 |
| CISDM Discretionary | 11.78 | 6.51 | 1.15 | −4.57 | −0.05 | 0.21 |
| CISDM Diversified | 9.56 | 11.42 | 0.46 | −7.53 | −0.14 | 0.27 |
| CISDM Financial | 11.76 | 12.83 | 0.58 | −8.56 | −0.09 | 0.35 |
| CISDM Trend following | 11.30 | 16.24 | 0.43 | −10.38 | −0.16 | 0.29 |
| S&P 500 | 10.94 | 14.65 | 0.50 | −14.46 | 1.00 | 0.10 |
| Lehman Gov./Corp. | 7.77 | 4.46 | 0.80 | −4.19 | 0.10 | 1.00 |

*Source*: CISDM (2005d).

### 7.2.3  *Interpretation Issues*

In evaluating historical managed futures return data, the investor should be aware of the upward bias that survivorship can impart. Research has found return differences on the order of 3.5 percent between the surviving CTAs and the full sample that includes defunct CTAs.[124] The differential performance between survivor and nonsurvivor samples (on an absolute basis and a risk-adjusted basis) comes chiefly from differences in return performance in the months just prior to CTA dissolution. The ability of investment professionals to forecast which managers may not survive could result in dramatic differences in investment results.[125]

## 7.3  Managed Futures: Investment Characteristics and Roles

Similar to hedge funds, managed futures are active skill-based strategies that investors can examine for the potential to improve a portfolio's risk and return characteristics. In the following sections, we present more details on these investments.

### 7.3.1  *Investment Characteristics*

This discussion of investment characteristics will focus on the market opportunities that may be exploited by CTAs. Derivative markets are zero-sum games.[126] As a result, the long-term return to a passively managed, unlevered futures position should be the risk-free return on invested capital less management fees and transaction costs. For derivative-based investment strategies like managed futures to produce excess returns,

---

**124** See Fung and Hsieh (1997b) and McCarthy et al. (1996).
**125** For research in the area of manager default, see Diz (1999).
**126** The term "zero sum" refers to the fact that derivatives markets reallocate uncertain cash flows among market participants without enhancing aggregate cash flows in any way. See Gastineau and Kritzman (1999).

on average, there must be a sufficient number of hedgers or other users of the markets who systematically earn less than the risk-free rate. Hedgers, for example, may pay a risk premium to liquidity providers for the insurance they obtain. If that condition is met, managed futures may be able to earn positive excess returns (i.e., be the winning side in the zero-sum transactions).

The zero-sum nature of derivatives markets also does not restrict CTAs from attempting to conduct arbitrage when relationships are out of equilibrium. Institutional characteristics and differential carrying costs among investors may permit managed fund traders to take advantage of short-term pricing differences between theoretically identical stock, bond, futures, options, and cash market positions. CTAs may also attempt to take advantage of the opportunity of trading in trending markets.

Most actively managed derivative strategies follow momentum strategies. In equity markets, research has begun to support the notion that short-term momentum-based strategies may be able to produce excess returns; the evidence related to the market opportunity in futures markets is less well developed.[127] Government policy intervention in interest rate and currency markets may cause trending in currency and fixed-income markets. Some corporate risk management approaches may result in trading that creates short-term trending. Trading techniques based on capturing these price trends, whatever the source, may be profitable. There is also evidence that momentum trading imparts the desirable characteristic of positive skewness to managed fund returns.

Because of the ease with which futures traders take short positions, futures traders can attempt to earn positive excess returns in falling as well as rising markets. Some of the most impressive periods of return for CTAs have been during periods of poor performance in the equity markets (e.g., October 1987). Access to options markets permits managed futures and hedge fund traders to create positions that attempt to exploit changes in market volatility of the underlying asset (volatility being one of the determinants of option value). Such strategies are not available to investors who are restricted to using cash markets.

Because managed futures can replicate many strategies available to a cash market investor at a lower cost—and allow strategies that are unavailable to cash investors—factor models for this group must include the factors that may be unique to managed futures and hedge fund trading opportunities.[128] To the degree that different factors explain managed futures returns and stock/bond returns, managed futures may provide investors exposure to unique sources of return. The presence of such risk factors also provides an economic rationale for managed futures' diversification capabilities when added to a portfolio of equities and bonds.

### 7.3.2 *Roles in the Portfolio*

As for the other alternative investments, we now offer historical evidence on the potential of managed futures as part of a portfolio. Managed futures appear to be useful in diversifying risk even in a diversified portfolio of stocks, bonds, and hedge funds.

Exhibit 35 shows that, for the period 1990–2004, managed futures would have been a valuable addition to a stock/bond/hedge fund portfolio in relation both to U.S. and global stocks and bonds. The Sharpe ratio of Portfolios III and VI, which include at least a 10 percent investment in managed futures, dominate those invested only in stocks, bonds, and hedge funds, whether the stocks and bonds are U.S. or global (see Portfolio III versus Portfolio II for the U.S. comparison and Portfolio VI versus Portfolio V for the global comparison). The portfolios with managed futures also improve on the portfolios invested only in stocks and bonds (Portfolio I for the U.S., Portfolio IV for global).

---

**127** See Lee and Swaminathan (2000) and references therein for the evidence on momentum strategies in U.S. equity markets.
**128** For a discussion of whether managed futures returns are the natural result of market forces or are based primarily on trader skills, see Schneeweis and Spurgin (1996).

| Exhibit 35 | Managed Futures Performance in Portfolios 1990–2004 | | | | | |
|---|---|---|---|---|---|---|
| Measure | Portfolio I | Portfolio II | Portfolio III | Portfolio IV | Portfolio V | Portfolio VI |
| Annualized return | 9.64% | 10.43% | 10.54% | 7.86% | 9.01% | 9.26% |
| Annualized std. deviation | 7.94% | 7.09% | 6.48% | 8.29% | 7.28% | 6.65% |
| Sharpe ratio | 0.67 | 0.87 | 0.97 | 0.43 | 0.65 | 0.75 |
| Minimum monthly return | −6.25% | −6.39% | −5.21% | −5.61% | −5.87% | −4.75% |
| Correlation w/CISDM CTA$ | −0.01 | 0.02 | n/c | −0.01 | 0.02 | n/c |

*Notes*:
Portfolio I = 50% S&P 500, 50% Lehman Gov./Corp. Bond.
Portfolio II = 40% S&P 500, 40% Lehman Gov./Corp., 20% HFCI.
Portfolio III = 90% Portfolio II, 10% CTA$.
Portfolio IV = 50% MSCI World, 50% Lehman Global Bond.
Portfolio V = 40% MSCI World, 40% Lehman Global, 20% HFCI.
Portfolio VI = 90% Portfolio V, 10% CTA$.
n/c = not computed.
*Source*: CISDM (2005d).

Exhibit 36 breaks out the results for the five most recent years covered in Exhibit 35. For 2000–2004 also, managed futures would have provided better risk-adjusted performance than the comparison portfolios. The Sharpe ratio of an equally weighted stock and bond portfolio is 0.06, and the Sharpe ratio of an equally weighted stock and bond portfolio with a 20 percent hedge fund component is 0.18, whereas adding a 10 percent CTA allocation to the stock/bond/hedge fund portfolio resulted in a Sharpe ratio of 0.27.[129]

| Exhibit 36 | Recent Managed Futures Performance in Portfolios 2000–2004 | | | | | |
|---|---|---|---|---|---|---|
| Measure | Portfolio I | Portfolio II | Portfolio III | Portfolio IV | Portfolio V | Portfolio VI |
| Annualized return | 3.15% | 3.92% | 4.37% | 3.45% | 4.16% | 4.58% |
| Annualized std. deviation | 7.93% | 6.94% | 6.22% | 8.55% | 7.48% | 6.81% |
| Sharpe ratio | 0.06 | 0.18 | 0.27 | 0.09 | 0.19 | 0.28 |
| Minimum monthly return | −4.36% | −3.62% | −3.07% | −4.94% | −4.08% | −3.48% |
| Correlation w/CTA$ | −0.13 | −0.10 | n/c | 0.00 | 0.02 | n/c |

*Notes*:
Portfolio I = 50% S&P 500, 50% Lehman Gov./Corp. Bond.
Portfolio II = 40% S&P 500, 40% Lehman Gov./Corp., 20% HFCI.
Portfolio III = 90% Portfolio II, 10% CTA$.
Portfolio IV = 50% MSCI World, 50% Lehman Global Bond.
Portfolio V = 40% MSCI World, 40% Lehman Global, 20% HFCI.
Portfolio VI = 90% Portfolio V, 10% CTA$.
n/c = not computed.
*Source*: CISDM (2005d).

---

**129** Considerable research exists on the risk reduction benefits of managed futures. In short, the academic (Schneeweis et al., 1996) and practitioner (Schneeweis, 1996) literature has shown that the returns of managed futures have a low correlation with the returns of traditional investment vehicles, such as stocks and bonds. Recent research has shown that when managed futures returns were segmented according to whether the stock/bond market rose or fell, managed futures had a negative correlation when these cash markets posted significant negative returns and a positive correlation when these cash markets reported significant positive returns. Thus, managed futures may also offer unique asset allocation properties in differing market environments.

The performance of managed futures has also been examined in the peer-reviewed literature. The conclusions appear to be investment-vehicle dependent and, to some extent, time-period and strategy dependent. On the one hand, a number of studies found that publicly traded commodity funds have been poor investments either on a stand-alone basis or as part of a diversified portfolio.[130] On the other hand, some research has concluded that private commodity pools and CTA-based managed accounts do have value either as stand-alone investments, as part of a portfolio, or in both roles.[131] Note that many CTAs prefer not to offer their services through public or private pools, so distinctions as to investment vehicle matter in interpreting results.[132]

It appears that an investor can fairly closely track the performance of a CTA-based managed futures index by using a small random selection of CTAs. Henker and Martin (1998) provided empirical evidence that a naively (e.g., randomly) chosen CTA portfolio replicates comparison CTA benchmark indices. They showed that a portfolio of randomly selected CTAs has a correlation in excess of 0.90 with that of a commonly cited benchmark (the Managed Account Reports dollar-weighted CTA index). Henker and Martin also showed that for CTAs, as for equity securities, a randomly selected equally weighted portfolio of 8–10 CTAs has a standard deviation similar to that of the population from which it is drawn.

These results, taken as a whole, suggest that the forecasted returns to a CTA-based managed futures index can be useful for determining the optimal asset allocation to managed futures when the investor will invest with a relatively limited number of CTAs.[133] Henker and Martin also concluded, as did Billingsley and Chance (1996), that fewer than 10 CTAs are needed to achieve most of the benefits of including CTAs in an existing stock and bond portfolio.

### 7.3.3 *Other Issues*

Performance persistence in CTA managers has been actively debated in the academic community.[134] Although there is little evidence that a strategy of investing in winners and avoiding losers will be successful over time, there is some evidence of performance persistence. McCarthy et al. (1996), showed that the relative riskiness of a CTA—the CTA's beta with respect to an index of CTAs—is a good predictor of future relative returns.[135] Thus, past CTA performance may be valuable in forecasting CTA and multi-advisor CTA portfolios' return and risk parameters, especially at the portfolio level. In terms of public policy, public disclosure of individual CTAs as well as benchmark information may be of benefit to potential investors who want to forecast expected risk-adjusted performance of public commodity funds.

Because managed futures frequently use derivatives and leverage in their strategies, investors should conduct the same due diligence as described in the hedge fund section. Particular attention should be paid to the risk management practices of the CTA.

---

**130** For example, Elton et al. (1987, 1990) and Edwards and Park (1996).

**131** See Edwards and Park (1996), Edwards and Liew (1999), and McCarthy, Schneeweis, and Spurgin (1996).

**132** The value of commodity funds, in contrast to investing directly with CTAs, has been questioned by Schneeweis (1996). Schneeweis, however, also concludes that the results are strategy and time-period dependent. Given that commodity funds are often multimanager in form, the benefits of commodity fund investment relative to multiple CTA investment is primarily a function of the fee structure.

**133** See also Park and Staum (1998).

**134** See Brown and Goetzmann (1995).

**135** Similar results were reported by Brorsen (1998).

**Example 13**

## Adding Managed Futures to the Strategic Asset Allocation

Andrew Cassano, CIO of a large charitable organization, is meeting with his senior analyst, Lori Wood, to discuss managed futures. Wood presents Cassano with information taken from Exhibits 31 and 35.

| Exhibit 31 | CTA Performance 1990–2004 (excerpt) | | | |
|---|---|---|---|---|
| Measure | CTA$ | HFCI | MSCI World Index | Lehman Global Bond Index |
| Annualized return | 10.85% | 13.46% | 7.08% | 8.09% |
| Annualized std. dev. | 9.96% | 5.71% | 14.62% | 5.23% |
| Correlation w/CTA$ | 1.00 | 0.19 | −0.11 | 0.27 |

*Note*: CTA$ is the dollar-weighted CISDM CTA universe.
*Source*: CISDM (2005d).

| Exhibit 35 | Managed Futures Performance in Portfolios 1990–2004 (excerpt) | | |
|---|---|---|---|
| Measure | Portfolio IV | Portfolio V | Portfolio VI |
| Annualized return | 7.86% | 9.01% | 9.26% |
| Annualized std. dev. | 8.29% | 7.28% | 6.65% |
| Sharpe ratio | 0.43 | 0.65 | 0.75 |
| Minimum monthly return | −5.61% | −5.87% | −4.75% |
| Correlation w/CTA$ | −0.01 | 0.02 | n/a |

*Notes*:
Portfolio IV = 50% MSCI World, 50% Lehman Global Bond.
Portfolio V = 40% MSCI World, 40% Lehman Global, 20% HFCI.
Portfolio VI = 90% Portfolio V, 10% CTA$.
*Source*: CISDM (2005d).

1. Using data from these two exhibits, determine whether the addition of managed futures to a portfolio comprising world equities, global bonds, and hedge fund strategies would improve the risk/return profile of that portfolio. Justify your response with reference to two statistics provided in the exhibits.

   Cassano addresses Wood as follows: "You've explained why the Sharpe ratio may not be the most representative indicator of risk with respect to hedge fund strategies. Are there other statistics that could be useful as potential predictors of performance persistence for CTA managers?"

2. With respect to Cassano's question, recommend another statistic that research has shown to be a useful predictor of performance persistence among CTAs.

   Cassano states: "If managed futures are a subset of hedge funds, including them in the portfolio may be redundant if we also invest in other hedge funds. We won't gain any diversification benefits."

3. Critique Cassano's statement and justify your response with reference to data in the two exhibits.

### Solution to 1:

The Sharpe ratio for Portfolio VI, which incorporates an allocation of 10 percent to managed futures, improves on the Sharpe ratio of Portfolio V. Therefore, managed futures appear to be valuable when added to a portfolio of world equities, global bonds, and hedge fund strategies. All measures of risk provided (Sharpe ratio, standard deviation, and minimum monthly return) are superior for Portfolio VI.

### Solution to 2:

Research has indicated that the relative riskiness of a CTA (i.e., the commodity trading advisor's beta with respect to an index of CTAs) is a good predictor of future relative returns. Thus, past CTA performance may be valuable in forecasting CTA and multi-advisor CTA portfolios' return and risk parameters, especially at the portfolio level.

### Solution to 3:

The correlation of the hedge fund composite with the CISDM CTA$ composite in Exhibit 31 is only 0.19, suggesting that combining investments in these vehicles would provide significant diversification benefits. This is also demonstrated in the low correlation of the first two portfolios with the CTA$ Index (shown in Exhibit 35), which indicates that the derivative trading strategies of managed futures may provide unique sources of return when compared with hedge fund strategies that have relatively high exposure to traditional equity and bond markets.

---

The next section discusses investment strategies based on the equity and, especially, the debt of distressed companies.

## DISTRESSED SECURITIES

**8**

**Distressed securities** are the securities of companies that are in financial distress or near bankruptcy. In the United States, investing in distressed securities involves purchasing the claims of companies that have already filed for Chapter 11 (protection for reorganization) or are in immediate danger of doing so.[136] Under Chapter 11 protection, companies try to avoid Chapter 7 (protection for liquidation) through an out-of-court debt restructuring with their creditors.

Investment strategies using distressed securities exploit the fact that many investors are unable to hold below-investment-grade securities because of regulatory or investment policy restrictions. Furthermore, relatively few analysts cover distressed securities markets and bankruptcies, resulting in unresearched investment opportunities for knowledgeable investors who are prepared to do their homework. Skill in influencing management and skill in negotiation are other qualities that can be rewarded in this field.

Debt and equity are traditional asset classes. Yet, because of the special characteristics and risks of the debt and equity of distressed companies and the strategies that use them, distressed securities investing is widely viewed as an alternative investment. Contributing to this perspective is the fact that among the most active investors in the field are hedge funds and private equity funds.

---

**136** "Chapter" in this context refers to a section of the U.S. Bankruptcy Code.

## 8.1 The Distressed Securities Market

Distressed securities investing has a long history—in the United States, dating back to at least the 1930s, when Max L. Heine formed an investment firm specializing in selectively acquiring the debt and real estate of bankrupt railroads. Through the 1980s and early 1990s, individual professional investors, private buyout funds, and others became increasingly active in the securities (and sometimes real assets) of troubled and bankrupt companies in many industries. With the explosive growth in hedge funds, with their flexibility to take short and long positions across all markets, and an abundant supply of troubled companies, by the 2000s, distressed securities investing had become well established as a set of skill-based strategies. The market opportunities for this strategy increase with higher default rates on speculative-grade bonds (which have historically averaged about 5 percent per year in the United States) and decrease with the number of distressed debt investors competing for mispriced securities.

### 8.1.1 Types of Distressed Securities Investments

Investors may access distressed securities investing through two chief structures:

- *Hedge fund structure.* This is the dominant type. For the hedge fund manager, it offers the advantage of being able to take in new capital on a continuing basis. The AUM fee and incentive structure, particularly when there is no hurdle rate associated with the incentive fee, may be more lucrative than with other structures. Investors generally enjoy more liquidity (that is, can withdraw capital more easily) than with other structures.

- *Private equity fund structure.* Private equity funds have a fixed term (i.e., a mandated dissolution date) and are closed end (they close after the offering period has closed). This structure has advantages where the assets are highly illiquid or difficult to value. An NAV fee structure may be problematic when it is difficult to value assets. When assets are illiquid, hedge fund–style redemption rights may be inappropriate to offer.

There are also structures that are hybrids of the hedge fund and private equity fund structures. In addition, distressed securities investing may be conducted in traditional investment structures, such as separately managed accounts, and even in open-end investment companies (mutual funds).[137] As a result of this variety, the investor can find information about distressed securities investing in hedge fund and private equity sources and elsewhere.

Distressed securities managers may themselves invest or trade in many types of assets, including the following:

- the publicly traded debt and equity securities of the distressed company;
- newly issued equity of a company emerging from reorganization that appears to be undervalued (**orphan equity**);
- bank debt and trade claims, because banks and suppliers owed money by the distressed company may want to realize the cash value of their claims. When the company is in reorganization, these instruments would be bankruptcy claims;
- "lender of last resort" notes; and
- a variety of derivative instruments for hedging purposes—in particular, for hedging the market risk of a position.

---

**137** In such traditional structures as mutual funds, long-only type investing would be expected.

### 8.1.2 *Size of the Distressed Securities Market*

The appropriate measure of the size of the distressed securities marketplace is elusive. One measure would aggregate all the assets under management related to distressed securities in whatever investment structure such assets are managed. Nevertheless, the size of the high-yield bond market can give an indication of the potential supply of opportunities, because distressed debt is one part of that market—in particular, the highest-risk part. Based on a maximum quality rating of Ba1 (as determined by Moody's Investors Services), the U.S. high-yield market consisted of US$548 billion at face value and US$552 billion at market value as of the end of May 2004. This size can be compared with the market size of only US$69 billion at face value as of the end of 1991.

## 8.2 Benchmarks and Historical Performance

Hedge fund industry data are the chief source for evaluating modern distressed securities investing.

### 8.2.1 *Benchmarks*

In the context of hedge funds, distressed securities investing is often classed as a substyle of event-driven strategies. All major hedge fund indices that we discussed in the hedge fund section have a subindex for distressed securities; For example, the EACM, CISDM, and HFR indices all have distressed securities subindices. In the United States, returns to the Altman–NYU Salomon Center Defaulted Public Bond and Bank Loan Index also provide a comparison point for evaluating a long-only value strategy in distressed debt.

### 8.2.2 *Historical Performance*

The returns on distressed securities investing can be quite rewarding. Exhibit 37 presents historical performance for distressed securities and high-yield fixed-income securities. Using the monthly HFR Distressed Securities Index for the period January 1990–December 2004, Exhibit 37 shows that the return distribution for distressed securities is distinctly non-normal. In particular, it reflects significant downside risk, with a negative skewness of −0.68. The negative skewness indicates that, for distressed securities, large negative returns are more likely than large positive returns. Hence, there is a bias to the downside. In addition, the monthly return distribution displays a large degree of kurtosis (5.55). This indicates that these securities are exposed to large outlier events. The two statistics together indicate significant downside risk. Consequently, the Sharpe ratio, which is based on the normal distribution assumption, may not capture the complete risk–return trade-off of distressed securities investing.

| **Exhibit 37** | **Monthly Returns of High-Yield and Distressed Securities 1990–2004** | |
|---|---|---|
| **Moment** | **HFR Fixed-Income High-Yield Index** | **HFR Distressed Securities Index** |
| Mean | 0.80% | 1.23% |
| Standard deviation | 1.84% | 1.77% |
| Skewness | −0.80 | −0.68 |
| Kurtosis | 6.63 | 5.55 |

*Source*: www.hedgefundresearch.com.

The monthly return distribution of high-yield debt displays similar risk characteristics, with a negative skewness of –0.80 and a kurtosis of 6.63. Overall, high-yield
debt investing, although producing favorable returns over the period, was subject to
considerable credit and, probably, event risk. These risks were greater, however, than
those observed for the distressed securities investing.

Exhibit 38 shows that for the same period, distressed securities outperformed all
stock and bond investments and with a standard deviation of 6.13 percent, compared
with the S&P 500's 14.65 percent. The Sharpe ratio for the HRF Distressed Securities
Index is 1.59, which is greater than the ratio for all the other assets. High mean returns
with low standard deviation seem to be an attractive characteristic of this strategy.
Moreover, the minimum one-month return is less negative for distressed securities
than for U.S. and world equities. Low correlation with world stock and bond investments suggest that adding distressed securities to a portfolio of world stocks and bonds
might increase return and reduce risk. Because returns of distressed securities display
negative skewness and high kurtosis (see Exhibit 37), however, risk represented by
standard deviation is probably understated.

| Exhibit 38 | Distressed Securities Performance 1990–2004 | | | | |
|---|---|---|---|---|---|
| Measure | HFR Distressed Securities | S&P 500 | Lehman Global Bond | MSCI World | Lehman Gov./Corp. Bond |
| Annualized return | 14.76% | 10.94% | 8.09% | 7.08% | 7.77% |
| Annualized std. dev. | 6.13% | 14.65% | 5.23% | 14.62% | 4.46% |
| Sharpe ratio | 1.59 | 0.45 | 0.72 | 0.19 | 0.78 |
| Minimum monthly return | –8.5% | –14.46% | –3.66% | –13.32% | –4.19% |

*Sources*: www.hedgefundresearch.com and CISDM.

In terms of performance, this strategy depends a great deal on the business cycle
and how well the economy is doing. When the economy is not doing well, bankruptcies increase and this strategy does well. An important risk factor that may not be
captured by the performance data is event risk. The ability to correctly predict whether
an event will occur will ensure the success of the strategy.

### 8.2.3 Interpretation Issues

In estimating the size of the distressed debt market, we gave figures for the high-yield
debt market. Non-investment-grade or high-yield bonds are not necessarily on the
brink of default; thus, they are not necessarily distressed. Distressed bonds constitute
the highest credit-risk segment of the high-yield bond market.[138] Furthermore, distressed securities include distressed equities and strategies based on these instruments.

## 8.3 Distressed Securities: Investment Characteristics and Roles

Although certain types of distressed securities investing may be considered for
risk-diversification potential, some of its typical risks are not well captured by such
measures as correlation and standard deviation, which are usually the guideposts in

---

**138** Distressed debt has sometimes been defined arbitrarily as bonds trading at spreads of 1,000 bps or
more above government bonds. See Yago and Trimbath (2003).

portfolio optimization. Investors look to distressed securities investing primarily for the possibility of high returns from security selection (exploiting mispricing), activism, and other factors.

### 8.3.1 *Investment Characteristics*

The market opportunity that distressed securities investing offers to some investors arises from the problems that corporate distress poses to other investors. Many investors are barred either by regulations or by their investment policy statements from any substantial holdings in below-investment-grade debt. These investors must sell debt that has crossed the threshold from investment grade to high yield (so-called **fallen angels**). Banks and trade creditors may prefer to convert their claims to cash rather than participate as creditors in a possibly long reorganization process. Failed leveraged buyouts have also been a source of distressed securities opportunities.[139] The impetus of some investors to off-load distressed debt creates opportunities for bargain hunters.

Old equity claims may be wiped out in a reorganization, replaced by new shares issued to creditors, and sold to the public as the company emerges from reorganization. These shares may be shunned by investors and analysts, and thus be mispriced. Distressed securities may offer a fertile ground for experts in credit analysis, turnarounds, business valuation, and bankruptcy proceedings to earn returns based on their skill and experience.[140]

A common theme in distressed securities investing is that it often demands access to specialist skills and deep experience in credit analysis and business valuation. Distressed companies are potentially near the end of their life as going concerns. The investor needs to assess not only potential outcomes for the company as a going concern but also the bare-bones liquidation value of the company. The investor needs to understand the sources of the company's problems, its core business, and its financing structure. A distressed securities fund's abilities in this regard are one element in due diligence.

For a private or institutional investor investing indirectly via a hedge fund or other vehicle, this type of investment inherits the liquidity characteristics specified in the structure of the vehicle. Discussion of the types of risk involved in distressed securities investing follows an overview of strategies in the next section.

### 8.3.2 *Roles in the Portfolio*

According to the 2005 Commonfund Benchmarks Study of U.S. educational endowments, overall allocation to distressed debt among the institutions surveyed was 5 percent for the year ended 30 June 2005.[141] Investors, private and institutional, are making substantial allocations to this alternative investment and need to understand the ranges of distressed securities strategies available and their risk characteristics.

From the perspective of the direct investor in distressed securities, there are a number of different strategies that may be adopted. As we discuss them, the reader should be aware that the hedge fund and private equity businesses and benchmark vendors use a variety of classifications and some differences in definition. The aim here is to convey the gist of what the various approaches involve.

---

**139** See Anson (2002b) for a detailed discussion of leveraged buyouts and this type of opportunity.
**140** In fact, according to a study published by New York University's Salomon Center and the Georgetown School of Business, newly distributed stocks emanating from Chapter 11 proceedings during the 1980–93 period outperformed the relevant market indices by more than 20 percent during their first 200 days of trading.
**141** See Jacobius (2006b), pp. 3, 40.

**Long-Only Value Investing**    The simplest approach involves investing in perceived undervalued distressed securities in the expectation that they will rise in value as other investors see the distressed company's prospects improve. When the distressed securities are public debt, this approach is **high-yield investing**. When the securities are orphan equities, this approach is **orphan equities investing**.

**Distressed Debt Arbitrage**    **Distressed debt arbitrage** (or distressed arbitrage) involves purchasing the traded bonds of bankrupt companies and selling the common equity short. The hedge fund manager attempts to buy the debt at steep discounts. If the company's prospects worsen, the value of the company's debt and equity should decline, but the hedge fund manager hopes that the equity, in which the fund has a short position, will decline to a greater degree. Indeed, as a residual claim, the value of equity may be wiped out. If the company's prospects improve, the portfolio manager hopes that debt will appreciate at a higher rate than the equity because the initial benefits to a credit improvement accrue to bonds as the senior claim. Typically, the company will have already suspended any dividends, but debtholders will receive accrued interest. This approach has been popular with hedge funds.

**Private Equity**    This has also been called an "active" approach because it involves corporate activism. It has, in fact, a number of variations. The investor usually first becomes a major creditor of the target company to obtain influence on the board of directors or, if the company is already in reorganization or liquidation, on the creditor committee. The investor buys the debt at deep discounts. The investor then influences and assists in the recovery or reorganization process. The objective of this focused active involvement is to increase the value of the troubled company by deploying the company's assets more efficiently than in the past. If the investor obtains new shares in the company as part of the reorganization, the investor hopes to sell them subsequently at a profit.

A variation of the active approach is converting distressed debt to private equity in a **prepackaged bankruptcy**.[142] This type of operation is typically conducted by private equity firms. The firm (or team of firms, because the capital commitment may be major) takes a dominant position in the distressed debt of a public company. Working with the company and other creditors, the firm seeks to have a prepackaged bankruptcy in which the firm becomes the majority owner of a private company on favorable terms (the previous public equityholders losing their complete stake in the company).[143] After restoring the company to better health, the firm has a company that can be sold to private or public investors. An example discussed by Anson is the conversion in 2001 of Loews Cineplex Entertainment Corporation from a public to a private company by two buyout firms (the buyout firms subsequently sold their interest, and as of 2005, Loews is still a private company).

Distressed securities investors following an active approach will be quite proactive or aggressive in protecting and increasing the value of their claims.[144] Practitioners of the private equity approach are often referred to as "vulture" investors, and their funds, as "vulture funds" or "vulture capital." Nevertheless, if the company is turned around, other parties may benefit, and the vultures are bearing risk that presumably other investors wish to transfer to them.

---

**142** The term "prepackaged bankruptcy" refers to the case in which the debtor seeks agreement from creditors on the terms of a reorganization before filing formally for a Chapter 11 reorganization. More details are given later.

**143** See Anson (2002b). Another operation Anson discusses is private equity firms making a cash bid for the assets of a company in reorganization at a discount to perceived value.

**144** See Branch and Ray (2002).

## Example 14

### Turnaround Partners

Often, distressed securities investors solicit the help of experienced executives to manage the troubled companies. In the case of the WorldCom/MCI bankruptcy, one such investor was quoted in the *Wall Street Journal*, when the investor urged Michael D. Capellas, the former chairman and CEO of Compaq Corporation, to join Worldcom Inc., as saying, "You run the business and we'll run the bankruptcy process."[145]

Investors need to assess the risks that a particular distressed securities strategy may entail. The risks may include one or more of the following:

- *Event risk.* Any number of unexpected company-specific or situation-specific risks may affect the prospects for a distressed securities investment. Because the event risk in this context is company specific, it has a low correlation with the general stock market.

- *Market liquidity risk.* Market liquidity in distressed securities is significantly less than for other securities, although the liquidity has improved in recent years. Also, market liquidity, dictated by supply and demand for such securities, can be highly cyclical in nature. This is a major risk in distressed securities investing.

- *Market risk.* The economy, interest rates, and the state of equity markets are not as important as the liquidity risks.

- *J factor risk.* Barnhill, Maxwell, and Shenkman (1999) referred to the judge's track record in adjudicating bankruptcies and restructuring as "**J factor risk**." The judge's involvement in the proceedings and the judgments will decide the investment outcome of investing in bankruptcy. Branch and Ray (2002) noted that the judge factor is also an important variable in determining which securities, debt or equity, of a Chapter 11-protected company to invest in.

Other risks may also be present. Some are associated with the legal proceedings of a reorganization: The actions of the trustees as well as the identity of creditors can affect the investment outcome. The distressed securities investor may lack information about the other investors and their motivations. Tax issues may arise in reorganizations.[146]

A normality assumption is not appropriate in evaluating this class of strategies. It has become quite well known that the return distribution from this strategy is not normally distributed (it has negative skewness and positive kurtosis); thus, if normal distribution is assumed, risk measurement tends to underestimate the likelihood of downside returns.

Distressed securities are illiquid and almost nonmarketable at the time of purchase. As the companies turn around, values of the distressed securities may go up gradually. Typically, it takes a relatively long time for this strategy to play out; thus, valuing the holdings may be a problem. It is difficult to estimate the true market values of the distressed securities, and stale pricing is inevitable. Stale valuation makes the distressed securities appear less risky. The risk of this strategy is probably understated, and its Sharpe ratio overstated.

---

145 *Wall Street Journal*, 16 April 2004.
146 See Branch and Ray (2002) and Feder and Lagrange (2002) for more information.

Whether a distressed securities investment will be successful or not depends on many factors. The outcome depends heavily on the legal process and may take years. Of course, the vulture investor's timeframe is often months, not years. The role played by vulture investors has a significant bearing on the outcome. If vulture investors do not participate in the restructuring (as in the case of MCI, where two of the vulture investors named to the board declined to take board seats) or if they decide to sell prior to the final settlement, the flood of shares into the market will create further downward pressure on the stock price. This may have a significant impact on the whole industry. Because any move by vulture investors may be heeded by other investors, they take great care not to divulge their intentions.

Thus, investing in distressed securities/bankruptcies requires legal, operational, and financial analysis. From an investment perspective, the relevant analysis involves an evaluation of the source of distress. The source could be the operations, finances, or both. This is a complex task, and each distressed situation requires a unique approach and solution. As a result, distressed investing involves company selection. In this reading, we focus on the legal aspects.

### 8.3.3  Other Issues

In this section, we describe the bankruptcy process to highlight how the process may affect the investment outcome and considerations that investors need to ponder.

**Bankruptcy in the United States versus Other Countries**[147]   For all practical purposes, the relevant legislation for distressed investment in the United States is the Bankruptcy Reform Act of 1978, which applies to all bankruptcies filed since 1 October 1979. This enactment is referred to as "The Bankruptcy *Code*," or "United States *Code*" (Branch and Ray, 2002). In the *Code*, there are several chapters of the substantive law of bankruptcy. Chapters 1, 3, and 5 generally apply to all cases, whereas Chapters 7, 9, 11, 12, and 13 provide specific treatment for particular types of cases. Of particular interest to distressed securities investors are Chapters 7 and 11, which provide specific treatments for, respectively, liquidations and reorganizations.

Branch and Ray pointed out that a U.S. Chapter 7 bankruptcy is *conceptually* (emphasis ours) similar to the bankruptcy procedures followed in most other countries. That is, when a person seeks protection under Chapter 7, that person's assets are collected and liquidated and the proceeds are distributed to creditors by an appointed bankruptcy trustee. The debtor is normally discharged from the debts that were incurred prior to bankruptcy. As in most other countries, under Chapter 7, rehabilitation of the debtor is not especially important. It is in this sense that the U.S. Chapter 7 is conceptually similar to other countries.

In contrast, Chapter 11 emphasizes rehabilitation of the debtor and provides an opportunity for the reorganization (restructuring) of the debtor. This is the distinctive feature of U.S. bankruptcy that separates it from most of the rest of the world (although a similar code exists in Canada called the Companies' Creditors Arrangement Act, or CCAA). This is where opportunity arises for distressed debt investors. In Chapter 11, the debtor (a business seeking relief and protection) retains control of its assets (which will immediately pass into a bankruptcy estate under the supervision of the court) and continues its operations. While under this protection, the debtor, now known as a "debtor-in-possession," seeks to pay off creditors (often at a discount) over a period of time according to a plan approved by the bankruptcy

---

[147] We do not intend to provide a complete treatment of the bankruptcy process but to provide an overview of the process so that investors can recognize the complexities involved and make intelligent investment decisions without being confused by the legal technicalities. For a detailed treatment, see Branch and Ray (2002).

court. Some of the liabilities may be discharged. By filing Chapter 11, a debtor can protect its productive assets from being seized by creditors and have time to plan the turnaround of the business.

A Chapter 11 case can be initiated voluntarily by a debtor or involuntarily by certain of the debtor's creditors or their indenture trustee. The indenture trustee—typically a bank, trust company, or other secure, respected institution—is named in the indenture agreement (contract between bondholders and the bond issuer) as the bondholders' agent charged with enforcing the terms of the indenture.

A plan of reorganization is submitted to the court for approval. The plan is typically proposed by the debtor with the blessings of creditors, especially the senior creditors. In most cases, the debtor works with its creditors to formulate a plan of reorganization. This plan details how much and over what period of time the creditors will be paid. Prospective distressed securities investors should pay attention to the exclusivity period. The exclusivity period occurs at the beginning of each case. During this time (set at 120 days but often extended by the court), only the debtor can file a plan of reorganization. After the exclusivity period expires, any party with an interest in the bankruptcy can file a plan proposing how the estate's creditors are to be paid under Chapter 11. Creditors and shareholders of the debtor eventually must approve the plan and have it confirmed by the bankruptcy judge. The judge can refuse to confirm a case if the plan is not proposed in good faith or if each creditor receives less than it would receive in a Chapter 7 liquidation. The judge can overrule the disapproval by some dissenting creditors, however, on economic grounds or for other considerations, such as social or legal grounds. This is commonly referred to as the "cram down." Thus, a cram down is basically a compromise between the debtor and certain classes of creditors when they cannot come to an agreement on the reorganization plan. Referred to as the "impaired class," those who object to the reorganization plan are those who believe their interest in the reorganization is impaired by the proposed plan.

Put another way, an approved reorganization plan by the court of law may not necessarily make economic sense, and such an erroneous presumption may be costly to distressed investing. The uncertain nature of the outcome of legal proceedings makes analysis of such investment challenging, and it must be accompanied by extensive due diligence.[148]

**Absolute Priority Rule**   In the United States, a reorganization plan must follow the rule of priority with respect to the order of claims by its security holders. In general, claims from senior secured debtholders (typically, bank loans) will be satisfied first. The debtor's bondholders come next. The distribution may be split between senior and subordinated bondholders. Last on the list are the debtor's shareholders.

In a cram down in which the court overrules the objection of a dissenting class of creditors, the priority rule becomes absolute. The rule is absolute in the sense that, to be "fair and equitable" to a class of dissenting unsecured creditors, the plan must provide either that the unsecured creditors receive property of a value equal to the allowed amount of the claim or that the holder of any claim or interest junior to the dissenting class does not receive or retain any property on account of the junior claim. In other words, the classes ranked below the dissenting unsecured class must receive nothing if the dissenting class is to be crammed down. It is in this sense that the law treats the holders of claims or interest with similar legal rights fairly and equitably, even if they do not accept the proposed plan.

There is an exception to the absolute priority rule, which is referred to as "the new value exception." In the new value exception, the debtor's shareholders seek to retain all or a portion of their equity interest by making what amounts to a capital

---

148 According to Branch and Ray (2002), only one out of eight cases that file for Chapter 11 is able to reorganize successfully in the United States.

contribution. In exchange for their contribution, they retain their interest even in the face of a dissenting vote by a senior class of creditors. The U.S. Supreme Court has held, however, that the new value exception does not permit contribution of such value without competitive bidding or some other mechanism to establish the adequacy of the contribution. Branch and Ray (2002) concluded that this ruling removes substantial uncertainty over whether or not a lower class of creditors can receive distribution under a plan of reorganization by contributing new value to the bankruptcy confirmation process. In other words, it helps reduce uncertainty in purchasing an interest in a Chapter 11 debtor.

Most of the time, holders of senior secured debts are "made whole" whereas the debtor's shareholders often receive nothing on their original equity capital. This is the residual risk that equity shareholders ultimately must bear.

**Relationship between Chapter 7 and Chapter 11**    Why must distressed investors pay attention to Chapter 7 filings? Chapter 11 reorganization can start from a Chapter 7 filing, whether voluntarily or involuntarily. A debtor against whom an involuntary Chapter 7 is filed has a right to convert the case to a Chapter 11 proceeding. Similarly, a Chapter 7 debtor that filed a voluntary petition can convert the case to a Chapter 11, unless the case started as a Chapter 11. In addition, the court can convert a Chapter 11 case to Chapter 7 or dismiss the case for cause (e.g., the inability of the debtor to carry out a plan) at any point in the case. The latter uncertainty adds much risk to bankruptcy investors.

**Prepackaged Bankruptcy Filing**    In a prepackaged bankruptcy filing, the debtor agrees in advance with its creditors on a plan or reorganization before it formally files for protection under Chapter 11. Creditors usually agree to make concessions in return for equity in the reorganized company. This is tantamount to obtaining advance approval of an exchange offer of public debt with less stringent requirements than those found in the public indenture. This way, a debtor expedites the bankruptcy process to emerge as a new organization.

Whether it is Chapter 7 or Chapter 11, a filing for protection under law will affect the value of the debtor. Especially under forced bankruptcy (i.e., involuntary Chapter 7 filing by creditors), its reputation is severely impaired by the stigma of being forced into bankruptcy.

---

**Example 15**

### Distressed Securities Investing

Gloria Richardson is CIO of a multi-billion-dollar home office for the Nelson family. She is discussing the revision of the governing investment policy statement to permit the investment in distressed securities. Susan Nelson represents the family in policy matters.

Nelson states: "Distressed securities sound like a very high-risk investment strategy because the strategy focuses on companies in bankruptcy. Is that why few investors choose to invest in distressed securities? What are the origins of distressed securities, and how are investors involved? Who researches these situations?"

1. Discuss the suitability of investing in distressed securities for buy-side (institutional) investors and evaluate the participation of sell-side analysts in researching distressed securities.

Nelson is still concerned about the downside risk of investing in distressed securities. Nelson states: "I'm a patient investor, and I want our family's philanthropic contributions to extend into perpetuity, but it seems that the strategy of investing in distressed securities has higher risk in every aspect than investing in traditional equities and bonds."

2. Judge the suitability of investing in distressed securities for the home office. Justify your response with reference to time horizon and Nelson's statement regarding risk.

## Solution to 1:

Some buy-side investors, such as pension plans, cannot or may choose not to hold below-investment-grade securities because of the securities' relatively high risk in comparison with other asset classes. However, results suggest that institutional investors with higher risk tolerances and long time horizons may receive stable returns from distressed securities with relatively low risk in the long run.

As a result of the inability of some institutional investors to allocate funds to distressed securities, few sell-side analysts cover this area of the market. Given this limited following of distressed securities, undercovered and undervalued market opportunities exist that knowledgeable investors can exploit to earn high returns.

## Solution to 2:

Given Nelson's statement, investing in distressed securities could provide a potentially attractive strategy for the family's home office. Because the investment time horizon is long term, there should be no inherent obstacle regarding the amount of time it may take for a distressed securities investment to work out. Additionally, Nelson is incorrect in stating that distressed securities are riskier than traditional asset classes in all respects. Although long-term returns for distressed securities show negative monthly returns for 20 percent of all months studied, the maximum 1-month and 12-month drawdowns are smaller for distressed securities than for U.S. and world equities and bonds. If Nelson understands and accepts these risks, such investments may be appropriate.

# SUMMARY

Alternative investments have become a large portion of the portfolios of both individual and institutional investors. This reading presented six groups of alternative investments: real estate, private equity, commodities, hedge funds, managed futures, and distressed securities.

■ Common features of alternative investments include relative illiquidity, which tends to be associated with a return premium as compensation; diversifying potential relative to a portfolio of stocks and bonds; high due diligence costs; and the difficulty of performance evaluation.

■ Checkpoints in due diligence for alternative investment selection should cover market opportunity, investment process, organization, people, terms and structure, service providers, documents, and write-up.

■ Special concerns for advisors to private wealth clients include tax issues, determining suitability, communication with the client, decision risk (the risk of changing strategies at the point of maximum loss), and concentrated equity positions of the client in a closely held company.

- The physical real estate market is characterized by a relative lack of liquidity, large lot size, and high transaction costs.

- Real estate investments can be viewed in terms of direct ownership and indirect ownership. Direct ownership includes investment in residences, business real estate, and agricultural land. Indirect ownership includes vehicles such as REITs.

- Advantages to real estate investment include tax benefits, the use of leverage, control over property, diversification, potential as an inflation hedge, and low volatility of returns.

- Disadvantages to real estate investment include the inability to subdivide real estate investments, high information costs, high commissions, maintenance and operating costs, location risk, and political risk related to tax deductions.

- Private equity investments are highly illiquid, and investors must be willing to hold these securities for long periods.

- Private equity investments include start-up companies, middle-market private companies, and private investment in public entities.

- Private equity investors include angel investors, venture capitalists, and larger companies in the same industry.

- There are two broad approaches to investing in commodities: direct and indirect. Direct commodity investment entails purchase of the physical commodities or use of derivatives with direct exposure to changes in spot prices. In contrast, indirect investment in commodities involves the acquisition of indirect claims on commodities.

- Futures contract–based commodity indices have three separate components of return: price, collateral, and roll return.

- Price return derives from changes in commodity futures prices, which comes from the changes in the underlying spot prices via the cost-of-carry model. In other words, when the spot price goes up (down), so does the futures price, giving rise to a positive (negative) return to a long futures position.

- Collateral return is related to the assumption that when an investor invests in the commodity futures index, the full value of the underlying futures contracts is invested at a risk-free interest rate.

- Roll return or roll yield arises from rolling long futures positions forward through time and may capture a positive return when the term structure of futures prices is downward sloping.

- The inflation-hedging ability of commodity investing appears to differ according to the commodity.

- Hedge funds are skill-based investment strategies in various forms, including limited partnerships. The funds use different investment strategies and thus are often classified according to investment style. Within each style category, hedge funds are classified according to the underlying markets traded or the unique trading style—for example, relative value, event driven, hedged equity, and global macro.

- Within each style classification, there are a number of subgroups. For instance, within the hedge fund relative-value style classification, subgroups include market-neutral long–short equity, convertible hedging, and fixed-income arbitrage (or bond hedging).

- Hedge funds can provide return and diversification benefits, but the risks are not usually well represented by standard deviation.

- Managed futures are actively managed investment vehicles which share many features of hedge funds (e.g., compensation arrangements and availability to only accredited investors). However, managed futures programs primarily trade futures and options contracts, whereas hedge funds typically are more active in spot markets.

- Managed futures programs include systematic trading strategies (based on trading rules applied to price data) and discretionary trading strategies (which incorporate manager judgment).

- Distressed securities are securities of companies that are in financial distress or near bankruptcy. The securities could be equity, debt, trade, or other claims.

- Distressed securities investment exploits the fact that many investors are unable to hold below-investment-grade securities. Furthermore, few analysts cover the distressed market.

- Risks of distressed securities investing include event risk, "judge" factor risk, liquidity risk, market risk, and other risks.

# PRACTICE PROBLEMS FOR READING 31

1. Compare the relative liquidity characteristics of direct versus indirect investment in real estate. Discuss three factors that affect the liquidity of both forms of investment.

## The following information relates to Questions 2–3

| | | | | | | |
|---|---|---|---|---|---|---|
| **Real Estate Performance 1990–2004** | | | | | | |
| Measure | NAREIT Index | NAREIT Index Hedged | NCREIF Index | NCREIF Index Unsmoothed | S&P 500 | Lehman Aggregate Bond Index |
| Annualized return | 12.71% | 8.96% | 6.14% | 7.27% | 10.94% | 7.70% |
| Annualized std. dev. | 12.74% | 11.93% | 3.37% | 8.95% | 14.65% | 3.91% |
| Sharpe ratio | 0.66 | 0.39 | 0.55 | 0.33 | 0.45 | 0.87 |
| Minimum quarterly return | −14.19% | −10.16% | −5.33% | −18.55% | −17.28% | −2.87% |
| Correlation w/NAREIT | 1.00 | 0.94 | −0.001 | 0.21 | 0.35 | 0.18 |
| Correlation w/NAREIT hedged | 0.94 | 1.00 | 0.00 | 0.24 | 0.00 | 0.14 |
| Correlation w/NCREIF | 0.00 | 0.00 | 1.00 | 0.71 | 0.01 | −0.18 |
| Correlation w/NCREIF unsmoothed | 0.21 | 0.24 | 0.71 | 1.00 | −0.01 | −0.27 |

*Source*: CISDM (2005a).

2. **A.** Summarize the major categories of direct and indirect investment in real estate.

   **B.** Using the data in the table, evaluate the historical relative diversification benefits of both forms of investment when added to a 50 percent stock/50 percent bond portfolio. Use the NCREIF Index unsmoothed to represent direct investment and the NAREIT Index to represent indirect investment.

3. The board trustees of Elite Corporation's US$50 million pension fund are meeting to discuss a presentation they recently received from their pension consultant, who is recommending that they diversify their current 50/50 stock/ bond asset allocation to include a 10 percent allocation to real estate. Although the trustees would like to reduce portfolio risk without sacrificing a significant amount of return, the trustees have previously been reluctant to change the asset allocation because they are concerned about "making a mistake we can't easily fix" if the economic environment changes.

   One trustee, Maya Semyonova, makes reference to the table above and some notes that provide an overview of how the various indices are constructed. Semyonova states: "To address our stated risk and return objectives and given the superior historical benefits of direct investing in real estate, represented by the unsmoothed NCREIF Index, I recommend that we reallocate 10 percent from our bond investments indexed to the Lehman Aggregate to a direct real estate asset."

Practice Problems and Solutions: 1–19 taken from *Managing Investment Portfolios: A Dynamic Process*, Third Edition, John L. Maginn, CFA, Donald L. Tuttle, CFA, Jerald E. Pinto, CFA, and Dennis W. McLeavey, CFA, editors. Copyright © 2007 by CFA Institute. All other problems and solutions copyright © CFA Institute.

A second trustee, John Pearson, responds with a different recommendation: "I believe we should reallocate 10 percent from the 50 percent S&P 500 allocation to REITs to achieve our goals."

**A.** Critique Semyonova's recommendation with reference to the return, risk, diversification, and liquidity characteristics of the two asset classes that Semyonova is referring to.

**B.** Critique Pearson's recommendation with reference to the return, risk, diversification, and liquidity characteristics of the two asset classes that Pearson is referring to.

**C.** Of the reallocation scenarios suggested by Semyonova and Pearson, choose the one most appropriate for Elite Corporation's pension fund based on the trustees' objectives. Justify your choice with reference to returns, risks, and issues concerning construction of real estate and REIT indices.

**4.** Roger Guidry, CIO of a university endowment fund, is reviewing investment data related to the endowment's investment in energy commodities.

| Year | GSCI Total Annual Return | GSCI Collateral Yield | GSCI Roll Yield | GSCI Spot Annual Return |
|------|--------------------------|-----------------------|-----------------|-------------------------|
| 1 | 29.1% | 9.6% | ? | 6.1% |
| 2 | −30.5% | ? | −14.2% | −24.3% |

**A.** Calculate the roll yield for Year 1.

**B.** Calculate the collateral yield for Year 2.

Guidry notes that the collateral yield is positive in both scenarios, although the GSCI total annual return for Year 2 is −30.5 percent. He asks for an explanation with regard to the positive collateral yield.

**C.** Justify the positive collateral yield by discussing the concepts of margin and implied yield.

A consultant tells Guidry: "Commodities exhibit positive event risk."

**D.** Justify the consultant's statement by discussing the relationship between commodity prices and event risk.

| Commodity Index Performance 1990–2004 | | | | | |
|---------------------------------------|------|---------|----------------------------|-------------------|---------------------|
| Measure | GSCI | S&P 500 | Lehman Gov./ Corp. Bond | MSCI World Equity | Lehman Global Bond |
| Annualized return | 7.08% | 10.94% | 7.77% | 7.08% | 8.08% |
| Annualized std. dev. | 19.26% | 14.65% | 4.46% | 14.62% | 5.23% |
| Sharpe ratio | 0.15 | 0.45 | 0.78 | 0.19 | 0.72 |
| Minimum monthly return | −14.41% | −14.46% | −4.19% | −13.32% | −3.66% |
| Correlation with GSCI | 1.00 | −0.08 | 0.03 | −0.06 | 0.06 |

*Source*: CISDM (2005b).

**5.** Capital market analysts John Lake and Julie McCoy are reviewing the information in the table above. Lake and McCoy note that the Sharpe ratio for the GSCI is significantly lower than that of the S&P 500 and the Lehman

Government/Corporate Bond indices. They also note that the minimum monthly returns for the GSCI and S&P 500 are similar.

Lake states to McCoy: "Based on the historical record, I don't understand why we would invest in the GSCI when the annualized return for the GSCI is lower than that of the S&P 500 and Lehman Government/Corporate indices, the minimum monthly return is similar to that of the S&P 500, and the Sharpe ratio is significantly lower than either of the domestic equity or bond asset classes. The risk measure in the Sharpe ratio should completely capture a commodity index's risk."

**A.** Critique Lake's statement.

McCoy shows Lake the table below and suggests that these more recent data, which show a significant outperformance of commodity returns versus domestic and international equities and bonds, make a much stronger case for investing in commodities. McCoy also states that the low correlations of commodities with the other asset classes indicate that inclusion of commodities will provide significant diversification benefits to the portfolio.

| | Recent Commodity Index Performance 2000–2004 | | | | |
| Measure | GSCI | S&P 500 | Lehman Gov./ Corp. Bond | MSCI World Equity | Lehman Global Bond |
| --- | --- | --- | --- | --- | --- |
| Annualized return | 13.77% | −2.30% | 8.00% | −2.05% | 8.47% |
| Annualized std. dev. | 22.10% | 16.35% | 4.76% | 15.62% | 6.02% |
| Sharpe ratio | 0.50 | −0.31 | 1.11 | −0.30 | 0.96 |
| Minimum monthly return | −14.41% | −10.87% | −4.19% | −10.98% | −3.66% |
| Correlation with GSCI | 1.00 | −0.05 | 0.05 | 0.00 | 0.10 |

*Source*: CISDM (2005b).

**B.** Judge the validity of McCoy's conclusions regarding returns and correlations of the various asset classes.

6. Explain the practical effects of the following possible characteristics of a hedge fund index:

**A.** survivorship bias.

**B.** value weighting.

**C.** stale price bias.

7. Ian Parkinson, as chief pension officer of a large defined-benefit plan, is considering presenting a recommendation that the pension plan make its first investments in three different types of hedge funds: 1) market neutral, 2) convertible arbitrage, and 3) global macro.

An analyst who works for Parkinson comes by with the table given below and makes the following comment: "The returns for global macro are very impressive. In fact, there are other strategies that have significantly outperformed the S&P 500, equity market-neutral, and convertible arbitrage over the past 15 years. I think that, based on their returns, we should focus specifically on the other strategies."

### Performance of Hedge Fund Strategies and Traditional Assets 1990–2004

| Fund or Asset | Annual Return (%) | Annual Standard Deviation (%) | Sharpe Ratio | Minimum Monthly Return (%) | Correlation with S&P 500 | Correlation with Lehman Gov./Corp. Bond |
|---|---|---|---|---|---|---|
| HFCI | 13.46 | 5.71 | 1.61 | 6.92 | 0.59 | 0.17 |
| Event driven | 13.46 | 5.59 | 1.64 | −9.37 | 0.59 | 0.07 |
| Equity hedge | 15.90 | 9.34 | 1.24 | −9.70 | 0.64 | 0.10 |
| Equity market neutral | 9.24 | 2.50 | 1.98 | −1.07 | 0.09 | 0.24 |
| Merger/risk arbitrage | 9.07 | 4.86 | 0.99 | −8.78 | 0.48 | 0.10 |
| Distressed | 15.28 | 6.07 | 1.81 | −9.71 | 0.42 | 0.04 |
| Fixed-income arbitrage | 7.62 | 3.61 | 0.92 | −6.61 | 0.06 | −0.06 |
| Convertible arbitrage | 10.23 | 3.96 | 1.50 | −3.42 | 0.19 | 0.13 |
| Global macro | 16.98 | 8.38 | 1.51 | −5.41 | 0.26 | 0.34 |
| Short selling | −0.61 | 19.39 | −0.25 | −14.62 | −0.76 | −0.01 |
| S&P 500 | 10.94 | 14.65 | 0.45 | −14.46 | 1.00 | 0.13 |
| Lehman Gov./Corp. Bond | 7.77 | 4.46 | 0.78 | −4.19 | 0.13 | 1.00 |
| MSCI World | 7.08 | 14.62 | 0.19 | −13.32 | 0.86 | 0.09 |
| Lehman Global Bond | 8.09 | 5.23 | 0.73 | −3.66 | 0.11 | 0.74 |

*Note*: HFCI is the Hedge Fund Composite Index and was constructed by equally weighting the EACM 100, the HFR Fund Weighted Composite Index, and Credit Suisse/Tremont Hedge Fund Index.
*Source*: CISDM (2005c).

 

    **A.** Describe the three alternative strategies that Parkinson is considering, and evaluate each with respect to their level of market risk and credit risk. Interpret their correlations with the S&P 500 and the Lehman Government/ Corporate Bond indices as presented in the table above.

    **B.** Critique the analyst's statement.

**8.** Interpret a "1 and 20" fee structure with reference to high-water marks and drawdowns.

**9.** Susan DiMarco is evaluating a hedge fund that has a high level of portfolio turnover and a short investment record. The hedge fund makes a contractual stipulation with limited partners regarding a lock-up period that is quite common in the hedge fund industry. A colleague, Jane Farkas, who has reviewed the fund, makes the following statement to DiMarco: "Well, if we're unhappy with performance, we can always fire the hedge fund manager. If they trade frequently, as indicated by their high portfolio turnover, our investment must have high liquidity." Judge the validity of Farkas's statement.

**10.** Jane Farkas tells Susan DiMarco that she has seen exciting data on the performance of market-neutral, convertible arbitrage, and global macro hedge funds. Farkas states: "The Sharpe ratios of all of these hedge fund strategies are much higher than for traditional equities or bonds, which means they have a great risk/return profile. We should definitely plan a major investment in hedge funds."

DiMarco responds: "There are several reasons that the Sharpe ratio may be misleading."

  A. Discuss the situations that could cause an upward bias in the calculation of the Sharpe ratio.

  B. Evaluate the reasons that statistically indicate that the Sharpe ratio is not the most appropriate measure of risk for hedge funds.

# The following information relates to Questions 11–12[1]

| Month | Hedge Fund Returns (%) | Index Returns (%) |
|---|---|---|
| January | 3.50 | −2.40 |
| February | 4.00 | −4.00 |
| March | −2.00 | −1.60 |
| April | −2.00 | 3.00 |
| May | −1.00 | −4.20 |
| June | 0.90 | 2.00 |
| July | −1.00 | 2.50 |
| August | 1.70 | −2.10 |
| September | 2.70 | −2.00 |
| October | 3.70 | 0.50 |
| November | 0.40 | 3.10 |
| December | −3.20 | 0.20 |

11. **A.** Calculate the average rolling returns for the hedge fund if the investor's investment horizon is nine months.

   **B.** Explain how rolling returns can provide additional information about the hedge fund's performance.

12. **A.** Compute the annualized downside deviations for the hedge fund and the index, and contrast them to the standard deviation. The annualized standard deviations for the hedge fund and the index are, respectively, 8.64 percent and 9.19 percent.

   **B.** Compute the Sortino ratio and, based on this statistic, evaluate the performance of the hedge fund against the performance of the index portfolio.

13. Andrew Cassano, CIO of a large charitable organization, is meeting with his senior analyst, Lori Wood, to discuss managed futures. Cassano believes that it would be beneficial to evaluate this alternative investment category before making a final decision with respect to hedge fund investment.

   Wood states: "Although managed futures are sometimes considered a subset of hedge funds, there are some differences that make them worthy of consideration."

   **A.** Determine which absolute-return hedge fund strategy to which managed futures are mostly closely related (i.e., managed futures are often considered a subgroup of this hedge fund strategy).

---

1 This table shows monthly returns for a hedge fund and an index portfolio. For the purpose of computation, the hurdle rate is the U.S. T-bill rate, assumed to be 5 percent per year.

   **B.** Briefly discuss a primary similarity and a primary difference between managed futures and many other hedge fund strategies.

   **C.** Contrast the characteristics of two managed futures styles: systematic and discretionary.

14. Cassano asks: "If managed futures strategies are often momentum based, how do they achieve excess returns differently from traditional stock or bond investment vehicles?" Formulate an answer to Cassano's question.

15. List and discuss the sources of return available to managed futures programs through the use of derivative trading strategies.

16. Contrast "fallen angels" to high-yield debt.

17. Evaluate the role of investors in both the private equity and relative-value strategies—specifically, with respect to investing in distressed securities.

18. Formulate a description of the results of a prepackaged bankruptcy with reference to a) "prebankruptcy" creditors of the company, b) "prebankruptcy" shareholders, and c) vulture investors.

19. Critique the following statement: "When the economy has been faltering and may be going into recession, it is typically a good time to invest in distressed securities."

# The following information relates to Questions 20–25

Franciszek Magerski is a portfolio manager who specializes in alternative investments. He recently joined Harman, Klyde, and Palson (HKP), private wealth managers. Although he has managed institutional portfolios, Magerski has no experience with private wealth clients. A partner at HKP tells Magerski: "Alternative investing and due diligence for private wealth clients is similar to that for institutional clients. Private clients have the same issues of time horizon, but different liquidity needs."

Magerski is assigned to modify a portfolio having a current allocation of 50 percent equity and 50 percent fixed income. The equity portion consists of common stocks from the S&P 500 and is benchmarked to that index. The fixed-income portion consists of high-grade U.S. corporate bonds and U.S. Treasury securities and closely tracks the Lehman Aggregate Bond Index.

Magerski intends to improve the risk-return profile of the portfolio by including alternative investments. Some recent characteristics of equities, fixed-income securities, U.S. treasury bills, and four potential alternative asset classes are shown in Exhibit 1. Magerski will use the Sharpe ratio to initially select three alternative investments for the portfolio.

| Exhibit 1 | Characteristics of Asset Classes | | | |
|---|---|---|---|---|
| Asset Class | Annual Return (%) | Standard Deviation of Returns (%) | Correlation with U.S. Stocks | Correlation with U.S. Bonds |
| U.S. Common Stocks | 11.0 | 15.0 | 1.00 | 0.12 |
| U.S. Bonds | 7.5 | 4.0 | 0.12 | 1.00 |
| Real Estate–NCREIF–unsmoothed | 8.0 | 9.0 | −0.01 | −0.27 |
| Hedge Funds–market neutral | 6.0 | 2.5 | 0.09 | 0.21 |
| Commodities–GSCI | 7.0 | 19.0 | −0.06 | 0.04 |
| Private Equity | 20.0 | 22.0 | 0.50 | 0.30 |
| U.S. Treasury Bills | 3.5 | — | — | — |

Although the new equity and fixed-income allocation will form the passive core of the portfolio, the alternative segment allows for active management, alpha generation, and additional diversification benefits. Magerski's associate, Julio Chavez, states that diversification is improved by adding real estate to an equity/fixed-income portfolio and points to the correlations between real estate and bonds and stocks as shown in Exhibit 1. Magerski expresses some concern with the real estate data because it refers to the NCREIF–unsmoothed index. Chavez states that the unsmoothed index provides a better indication of the benefits of real estate investment than the NCREIF (smoothed) Index.

Chavez also mentions that because the Sharpe ratios for hedge funds are generally higher than for traditional equities or bonds, a substantial allocation should be made to hedge funds. Magerski disagrees with Chavez and responds that the Sharpe ratio for a hedge fund may be biased and not always an appropriate performance measure for risk-adjusted return.

Magerski also tells Chavez there are several issues to consider when selecting hedge fund investments, including fee structure and liquidity. The hedge fund under consideration is an equity market-neutral fund with a fee structure consisting of a 2 percent management fee and a 15 percent incentive fee. The fund's initial amount of assets under management and the initial high-water mark are $100 million. When performance fees are paid, the incentive fee will, as is the standard industry practice, apply to the entire amount under management. Also, the lock-up period is five years and the long period is very beneficial to private wealth investors in the fund.

Magerski has received a research report recommending a large commodity allocation to manage portfolio risk and serve as an inflation hedge. The report notes, however, that some commodities are not effective as inflation hedges. Magerski is considering following this recommendation and continues reading the report so as to better understand which specific commodities would serve as the best inflation hedge.

**20.** Is the HKP partner's statement regarding differences between private clients and institutional clients correct?

**A.** Yes.

**B.** No, because their time horizon issues are different.

**C.** No, because their liquidity needs are not different.

**21.** Using the Sharpe ratio, which of the following alternative investments has the *most* beneficial risk profile?

**A.** Real Estate.

**B.** Hedge Funds.

**C.** Private Equity.

**22.** Chavez's preference for the unsmoothed version of the NCREIF Index instead of the smoothed version is most likely because the:

**A.** smoothed version includes the effect of leverage on returns.

**B.** smoothed version is based on actual unreliable market values.

**C.** bias arising from infrequent appraisals is corrected in the unsmoothed version.

**23.** Magerski's concern about a biased Sharpe ratio for hedge funds is most likely because:

**A.** eliminating extreme returns reduces the standard deviation of returns.

**B.** smoothing returns can overstate true gains and losses and calculated volatility.

**C.** lengthening the measurement interval from weekly data to monthly data increases the estimate of annualized standard deviation of returns.

**24.** Is Magerski's statement regarding the hedge fund incentive fee and the benefit of the lock-up period correct?

    **A.** No regarding both the incentive fee and the lock-up period.

    **B.** No regarding the incentive fee, and yes regarding the lock-up period.

    **C.** Yes regarding the incentive fee, and no regarding the lock-up period.

**25.** The report's comment about some commodities being ineffective as inflation hedges most likely relates to:

    **A.** livestock.

    **B.** changes, rather than levels, of inflation.

    **C.** storable commodities directly related to the level of economic activity.

# The following information relates to Questions 26–31

The board of trustees of Cochran Corporation's US$150 million pension fund is meeting with a consultant, Ferdinand Clyburn. They plan to discuss altering the fund's current asset allocation of 50 percent equity and 50 percent bonds to include investments such as real estate, private equity, and commodities. The portfolio is currently invested in funds indexed to the S&P 500 Index and the Lehman Brothers' U.S. Aggregate Index. The board gives Clyburn the following investment policy mandate:

> Select an asset allocation that will increase the expected return on the portfolio without reducing liquidity.

Before Clyburn's presentation begins, Esme Howard, a trustee, asks the following question:

> "What are the return-distribution characteristics associated with alternative investment strategies that reduce downside risk?"

Clyburn begins his presentation with a discussion of real estate investing. He states that if the board decides to invest *directly* in real estate, then the optimal asset allocation should be based on either the National Council of Real Estate Investment Fiduciaries (NCREIF) Index (without correction) or the NCREIF Index (unsmoothed). He recommends the NCREIF (unsmoothed) because the NCREIF (without correction) historically suffers from a bias.

He further states that if the board decides to invest *indirectly* in real estate, the optimal asset allocation should be based on the National Association of Real Estate Investment Trusts (NAREIT) Index.

Based on the expected return data in Exhibit 1, Clyburn provides the board with alternative asset allocation strategies that include real estate. The potential asset allocations under consideration are displayed in Exhibit 2.

| Exhibit 1 | Expected Returns for Selected Indexes |
|---|---|
| **Asset Class** | **Expected Annualized Return (%)** |
| NAREIT Index | 9.87 |
| NCREIF Index (unsmoothed) | 9.90 |
| S&P 500 Index | 11.16 |
| Lehman Brothers U.S. Aggregate Index | 7.70 |

| Exhibit 2 | Asset Allocation Strategies That Include Real Estate | | |
|---|---|---|---|
| **Allocation Strategy** | **Stock Allocation (%)** | **Bond Allocation (%)** | **Real Estate Allocation** |
| Strategy 1 | 40 | 50 | 10% invested in the NAREIT Index |
| Strategy 2 | 40 | 40 | 20% invested in the NAREIT Index |
| Strategy 3 | 40 | 40 | 20% invested directly based on the NCREIF Index (unsmoothed) |

Clyburn then provides an overview of private equity investing, with a primary focus on venture capital and buyout funds. In response to the presentation, trustee Rex Bolger asks the following question for clarification:

Bolger question #1:        "What are the common features of private equity investing?"

Finally, Clyburn reviews the implications of investing in commodities on the risk-return profile of the pension fund's portfolio. He states that a major reason for including commodities in a portfolio is to provide protection against unexpected inflation. Bolger then asks another question:

Bolger question #2:        "Historically, have all types of commodity investments been equally effective in protecting a portfolio against inflation?"

Clyburn explains that the appropriate benchmark to assess the performance of a commodity futures investment strategy is a commodity index. However, he stresses that the return on a commodity index futures contract is not the same as the return on the underlying commodity, and is composed of three components: the spot return, the collateral return, and the roll return. Clyburn presents the data in Exhibit 3 to illustrate the behavior of these components.

| Exhibit 3 | Market Data on Commodity Futures and Spot Prices (US$) | | |
|---|---|---|---|
| **Contract Maturity** | **Futures Price as of April** | **Futures Price as of March** | **Change in Spot Price March to April** |
| June | 41.85 | 40.01 | 0.90 |
| September | 40.76 | 39.07 | 0.90 |
| December | 39.54 | 38.56 | 0.90 |

26. Which of the following is the *most* appropriate response to Howard's question?
    A.  Positive skewness and low kurtosis.
    B.  Positive skewness and high kurtosis.
    C.  Negative skewness and high kurtosis.

27. The real estate index bias indicated by Clyburn is *most likely* an:
    A.  overestimation of the return volatility.
    B.  underestimation of the return volatility.
    C.  overweighting of residential real estate.

28. Given the board's investment policy mandate and Exhibits 1 and 2, the *most* appropriate asset allocation is:

    **A.** Strategy 1.

    **B.** Strategy 2.

    **C.** Strategy 3.

29. Which of the following is the *least* appropriate response to Bolger's first question?

    **A.** High due diligence costs.

    **B.** Limited diversification potential.

    **C.** Complexity of valuation and assessment.

30. Which of the following is the *most* appropriate response to Bolger's second question?

    **A.** Yes.

    **B.** No, indirect commodity investments have been the most effective.

    **C.** No, direct commodity investments that are related to the intensity of economic activity have been the most effective.

31. Assuming a fully collateralized futures position with a collateral return of US$0.15, the one-month return on a long position in the September contract shown in Exhibit 3 is *closest* to:

    **A.** $0.64.

    **B.** $0.94.

    **C.** $1.84.

# The following information relates to Questions 32–37

Guy Northrup is an investment advisor with Stoneford Partners, a private wealth management firm. The advisors at Stoneford Partners are considering adding several hedge funds to their investment list. Northrup and his colleague, Sasha Slate, meet with their supervisor to discuss hedge fund investing.

## Hedge Fund Characteristics

During the meeting Northrup comments: "Although fund of funds have lock-up periods similar to other hedge funds, investors in fund of funds typically pay lower fees overall."

Northrup reviews information about a hedge fund, Peeble Creek. Northrup notes they have $400 million under management and a 1.5 plus 20 fee structure without a high-water mark provision. Slate explains that a high-water mark caps the annual fee to the fund manager.

## Performance Evaluation

The group's discussion changes to focus on evaluating the performance of hedge funds. During the discussion Northrup makes two observations:

Observation 1: As top-performing funds grow from new inflows and poorly performing funds close, value weighting the components of a hedge fund index will cause an index to have return characteristics similar to those of its best-performing funds over a given time period.

Observation 2: Transaction costs do not affect the ability to rebalance an investable, equally weighted hedge fund index.

The supervisor comments that the presence of some attributes may indicate the manager is trying to "game" the hedge fund's Sharpe ratio. Northrup notes the following changes in investment and reporting attributes for three hedge funds shown in Exhibit 1.

| Exhibit 1 | Three Hedge Funds and Attributes That May Affect Sharpe Ratio | | |
|---|---|---|---|
| **Attributes** | **Fund A** | **Fund B** | **Fund C** |
| Change in the length of measurement interval | From monthly to quarterly | From monthly to quarterly | From quarterly to monthly |
| Percent of assets subject to stale pricing | Increase from 5% to 10% | Decrease from 10% to 5% | Increase from 5% to 10% |
| Option trading | Write out-of-money calls | Buy out-of-money calls | Write in-the-money calls |

## Managed Futures

After the meeting, Northrup tells his supervisor that the firm should consider managed futures as a diversification tool for client portfolios. His supervisor replies: "That may be a good idea because there are possibilities to earn positive excess returns using managed futures:

■ First, hedgers may pay a risk premium to liquidity providers, such as Commodity Trading Advisors (CTA), for the insurance that the hedgers obtain.

■ Second, CTAs are more likely to be able to conduct profitable arbitrage trades between stock, bond, futures, options, and cash markets because of differential carrying costs between investors."

32. Are Northrup's comments about fund of funds' lock-up periods and lower fees *most likely* correct?

    A. No.

    B. Yes, for lower fees only.

    C. Yes, for lock-up periods only.

33. Which of the following *best* describes Peeble Creek's fee structure? Peeble Creek receives:

    A. a one-time fee of 1.5 percent of the investor's commitment and receives 20 percent of annual profits.

    B. an annual compensation of 1.5 percent of the fund's assets and an additional 20 percent of the fund's annual profits.

    C. an annual compensation of 1.5 percent of the investor's commitment and an additional 20 percent of the fund's cumulative returns at portfolio liquidation.

34. Is Slate's explanation about high-water marks correct?

    A. Yes.

    B. No, because the high-water mark provides a minimum fee to the manager.

    C. No, because the high-water mark determines if this period's incentive fee is paid.

35. Are Northrup's observations about value weighting and transaction costs for hedge funds indices correct?

    A. No.

    **B.**  Yes, for value weighting only.

    **C.**  Yes, for transaction costs only.

**36.** Which of the hedge funds in Exhibit 1 has attributes that provide the greatest opportunity to game its Sharpe ratio?

    **A.**  Fund A.

    **B.**  Fund B.

    **C.**  Fund C.

**37.** Are both of the supervisors' explanations of excess returns in managed futures investing correct?

    **A.**  Yes.

    **B.**  No, only the first statement is correct because differential carrying costs do not exist between CTAs and other investors.

    **C.**  No, only the second statement is correct because CTAs, seeking liquidity, pay a premium to hedgers.

# The following information relates to Questions 38–43

The University Endowment Fund is considering making an investment in hedge funds. Its investment committee is meeting to decide which of the following four hedge funds should be selected:

- COE Fund, a "fund of funds;"

- Savior Capital, an "equity market neutral" fund;

- Alphameric Advisors, a "distressed debt arbitrage" fund;

- MarketView LLC, a "long-only value investing in distressed securities" fund.

During the meeting, committee members made the following statements:

| | |
|---|---|
| Statement 1: | "The Sharpe ratio is not the best performance measure for hedge funds because it is based on the assumption of normality of returns." |
| Statement 2: | "Alphameric Advisors' investment style involves selling the traded debt of the distressed company under consideration, and buying the debt of non-distressed companies." |
| Statement 3: | "It is better to use an equally weighted hedge fund index to reflect the potential diversification of hedge funds rather than a value-weighted index. This is because value weighting may result in the index taking on the return characteristics of the best-performing hedge funds, creating a momentum effect in returns." |
| Statement 4: | "The Sortino ratio is the best means to examine the consistency of hedge fund returns." |

One of the investment committee members noted that MarketView LLC has a "2 and 20 fee structure with a high-water mark provision," and wondered what that meant.

**38.** Given the hedge funds' investment styles, which of the following is *most likely* to display negative skewness and high kurtosis in its investment returns?

    **A.**  Savior Capital.

    **B.**  MarketView LLC.

    **C.**  Alphameric Advisors.

**39.** Given the hedge funds' investment styles, which of the following would be *most likely* to reduce the beta of the endowment fund's equity portfolio if the hedge fund investment replaces average-beta equity assets?

    **A.** COE Fund.

    **B.** Savior Capital.

    **C.** MarketView LLC.

**40.** Statement 1 is:

    **A.** correct.

    **B.** incorrect, because the Sharpe ratio accommodates a skewed distribution.

    **C.** incorrect, because the Sharpe ratio takes into account distributions with high kurtosis.

**41.** Statement 2 is:

    **A.** correct.

    **B.** incorrect, because this investment style involves a long position in the distressed company's traded debt and a short position in its equity.

    **C.** incorrect, because this investment style involves a long position in the distressed company's traded debt and a short position in non-distressed companies' debt.

**42.** Statement 3 is:

    **A.** correct.

    **B.** incorrect, because the higher survivorship bias of an equally weighted index will lead it to understate historical returns.

    **C.** incorrect, because changes in the index's composition tend to affect an equally weighted index less than a value-weighted index.

**43.** Statement 4 is:

    **A.** correct.

    **B.** incorrect, because it would be better to use rolling returns.

    **C.** incorrect, because it would be better to use the downside deviation.

# SOLUTIONS FOR READING 31

1.  Direct (physical) investments in real estate tend to be much less liquid than investments in REITs (which are indirect investments). Reasons for the illiquidity of direct investments include the following:

    ● The large transaction sizes when buying/selling commercial/industrial buildings and land or residential apartment buildings is in contrast to the flexibility of trading small amounts in REITs on public exchanges.

    ● The lack of availability and timeliness of information with respect to direct real estate investment results in extensive valuation and due diligence issues, whereas REITs are exchange traded in real time on a daily basis, and information about them is readily available and accessible.

    ● The high transaction costs of direct investments in terms of broker commissions and the financing costs of buying physical assets require long-term investment horizons. Exchange-traded REITs have low transaction costs, and reallocation of funds is easy.

2.  **A.** Direct investment in real estate includes individual residences, agricultural land, and commercial real estate. The category of commercial real estate can be subdivided into industrial, office, retail, and apartment complexes. Indirect investment is achieved via REITs, which can be subdivided into equity, mortgage, and hybrid (a combination of first two) investment trusts.

    **B.** Using the unsmoothed NCREIF Index as a benchmark for direct investment in commercial real estate indicates that the long-term (1990–2004) correlation of direct real estate investment with the S&P 500 is slightly negative; the correlation of direct real estate investment with bonds (the Lehman Aggregate Bond Index) is significantly negative, indicating that adding physical real estate to a 50 percent stock/50 percent bond portfolio would have provided very substantial diversification benefits.

    The correlations of the NAREIT Index with both the S&P 500 and bonds were both moderately positive for the period examined. This fact indicates that indirect investment in real estate had diversification benefits relative to a 50/50 stock bond portfolio, but that the diversification benefits were not as large as those resulting from direct real estate investment.

3.  **A.** Semyonova's recommendation can be critiqued along the following dimensions:

    ■ *Return*: The long-term returns for bonds and direct investment in real estate (unsmoothed NCREIF) are similar (7.70 percent and 7.27 percent); therefore, reallocating 10 percent of bond investments to direct real estate investment would not sacrifice much return.

    ■ *Risk*: a) The standard deviation for the unsmoothed NCREIF Index is more than twice that for the Lehman Aggregate; therefore, this reallocation does not reduce risk as measured by standard deviation. b) Downside volatility, as represented in this table by the minimum quarterly return, is much greater for real estate than for bonds. c) The NCREIF Index is a compilation of many types of real estate, whereas the trustees would have to choose a specific asset, possibly incurring higher risk than indicated by the NCREIF data.

    ■ *Diversification*: The correlation between the Lehman Aggregate and the unsmoothed NCREIF Index is significantly negative, which would indicate good potential for diversification.

- *Liquidity*: Investment in physical real estate is the least liquid of the asset classes shown in the table. A transaction could probably not be reversed quickly or easily.

**B.** Pearson's recommendations can be criticized along the following dimensions:

- *Return*: The unhedged return of REITs is almost 2 percentage points greater than the return of the S&P 500, whereas the hedged return is about 2 percentage points less than the S&P. Therefore, taking into account the equity return component of the NAREIT Index, this reallocation could represent a slight sacrifice in return.

- *Risk*: The standard deviation of the NAREIT Index and the hedged NAREIT Index was approximately 2 and 3 percentage points below that of the S&P 500, respectively. Thus no matter which index we use to represent indirect real estate investment, the reallocation would satisfy the objective of risk reduction, based on historical experience. Additionally, downside risk (as measured by the minimum quarterly return) was much less for REITs than for the S&P 500, so the reallocation could reduce downside risk as well.

- *Diversification*: The correlation between the S&P 500 and the hedged NAREIT Index is zero, indicating that REITs have sources of return that are different from those for large-cap equities, which would enhance diversification.

- *Liquidity*: REITs and S&P 500 equities are exchange traded and, therefore, are both liquid.

**C.** The second scenario—that is, reallocation of 10 percent of large-cap equities to REITs—is the best choice to fulfill the trustees' stated goals for the following reasons:

- *Return*: Using the long-term data provided in the table, the first scenario (based on unsmoothed NCREIF data) would have a mean return of $10.94\% \times 0.5 + 7.70\% \times 0.4 + 7.27\% \times 0.1 = 9.28\%$, whereas the second scenario (using hedged NAREIT) would yield 9.12 percent. If the unhedged NAREIT returns are used in the calculation, the expected return rises to 9.5 percent. Therefore, a 10 percent investment in REITs (even those least correlated with equities—e.g., mortgage REITs) and corresponding 10 percent reduction in S&P 500 stocks would represent a return similar to that of the first scenario.

- *Risk*: The second scenario is superior in terms of risk reduction because it maintains a higher allocation to bonds, which show a much lower correlation with unhedged REITs than does the S&P 500. Additionally, the minimum quarterly return is worst (most negative) for the unsmoothed NCREIF Index and the S&P 500. Therefore, the second scenario would reduce allocation to an asset class with high downside risk and reallocate money to REITs, which have a lower downside risk. Finally, REITs are highly liquid and can be easily divested, whereas physical real estate necessitates a long-term commitment and entails high transaction costs. *Note*: Although bonds have a negative correlation with the NCREIF Index (the first scenario), which suggests a superior reduction in risk through diversification, the three points provided here indicate that the reallocation from equities to REITS more closely fulfills the stated objectives of the trustees.

- *Index construction*: The choice of real estate index is pertinent to the assumptions used in calculating expected results for asset allocation decisions. The use of the unsmoothed NCREIF Index can be substantiated because more frequent, market-based (transaction) data are more timely and accurate than the smoothed, annually calculated, appraisal-based data. This method suggests higher expected returns—and significantly greater risk.

  The use of the hedged NAREIT Index could be justified by the concept of eliminating double counting (the equity return component in equity REITs). Additionally, the use of mortgage and hybrid REITs would reduce the redundancy of the more highly correlated equity REITs. Nevertheless, equity REITs compose about 95 percent of the NAREIT Index, so the unhedged data show a significant increase in return with less risk, as demonstrated by the high Sharpe ratio of the NAREIT Index relative to most other asset classes.

4. **A.** The roll yield for Year 1 is 29.1% − 9.6% − 6.1% = 13.4%.

   **B.** The collateral yield for Year 2 is −30.5% − (−14.2%) − (−24.3%) = 8.0%.

   **C.** Collateral yield is earned because of the assumption that when investing in a commodity futures index, the full value of the underlying futures contract is invested at a risk-free rate as the investor posts 100 percent margin with T-bills. Therefore, the position is fully collateralized, and for every dollar invested in the commodity futures index, the investor receives a dollar of commodity exposure plus interest on a dollar invested in T-bills. This is the "implied yield" or "collateral return."

   **D.** Changes in commodity futures prices are highly correlated with changes in spot prices. In periods of financial, economic, or political distress, and sometimes after natural disasters, short-term commodity prices tend to rise because most such events create shocks with respect to physical commodities that reduce current supply and cause prices to rise. This is called "positive event risk."

5. **A.** Two points can be made that relate to the value of the GSCI as a risk diversifier and the interpretation of the Sharpe ratio. First, the negative correlation of the GSCI with the S&P 500 and the low positive correlation of the GSCI with the Lehman Government/Corporate Bond Index suggest good risk reduction benefits when the GSCI is added to a portfolio of U.S. stocks and bonds. Second, in interpreting the low Sharpe ratio for the GSCI, account must be taken of the appropriateness of the Sharpe ratio for measuring commodity returns. The validity of standard deviation as a measure of risk in the denominator of the Sharpe ratio is compromised when returns are skewed and/or have high kurtosis. Because the data presented does not address skewness or kurtosis, Lake's statement on standard deviation is speculative.

   **B.** McCoy is evaluating a short time series. Because investment performance depends on the time period studied, the high returns generated by commodities in 2000–2004 may not be representative of long-term performance. In fact, we know this is the case when the data are compared with data for the longer period documented in Problem 4. This does not necessarily suggest that investment in commodities is not appropriate. However, it raises a caveat about comparing expectations of future returns for a period when the economic environment may be different from that of the short-term period that generated the results in the table given. This information also suggests that commodities may provide benefits as a tactical asset class.

The same concerns with respect to the short timeframe covered by the table can be expressed for the correlation data. However, the values are virtually the same for the longer-term data, which suggests that commodity returns are not correlated with the other asset classes; as a result, inclusion of commodities in the portfolio could provide both long-and short-term diversification benefits.

6. A. Survivorship bias occurs when returns of managers who have failed or exited the market are not included in the data analyzed over a specific timeframe. This results in overestimation of historical returns in the range of 1.5–3.0 percent per year. The timing of survivorship bias may be concentrated during certain economic periods, further complicating analysis of persistence of returns over short timeframes. Additionally, age (vintage) effects make it difficult to compare performance of hedge funds that have track records of different lengths. This is especially important when researching hedge funds, which have average track records of two to five years.

B. Indices that are value weighted as opposed to equally weighted may take on the return characteristics of the best-performing hedge fund in them over a given period. These indices thus reflect the weights of popular bets by hedge fund managers, because the asset values of the various funds change as a result of asset purchases as well as price appreciation.

C. Lack of security trading leads to stale price bias and can cause measured standard deviation to be over-or understated, depending on the time period being studied. This could result in measured correlations being lower than expected. This issue is not a significant concern in the creation of hedge fund indices because monthly data are used. Furthermore, the underlying holdings in many hedge fund strategies are relatively liquid; therefore, positions reflect market prices.

7. A. Equity market-neutral strategies identify over-and undervalued stocks while neutralizing the fund's exposure to market risk by combining long and short positions with similar exposure to related market or sector factors. Therefore, as their name suggests, they have little or no market risk. They also have low credit risk because their long–short positions result in net low leverage. As expected, there is virtually no correlation between funds using this strategy and the S&P 500.

Convertible arbitrage strategies exploit anomalies in the prices of corporate convertible bonds, warrants, and preferred stock. The convertible arbitrage funds buy or sell these securities and then hedge the risk of changes in price and volatility of the underlying securities, changes in interest rates, and changes in the issuers' credit ratings. The many small, individual positions taken, and hedging of these risks, result in low market exposure. However, this strategy also increases credit risk considerably because hedging via derivative instruments creates high leverage exposure. Convertible arbitrage strategies have a relatively low correlation with the S&P 500 or the Lehman Government/Corporate Bond Index because hedging the risks mitigates underlying market exposure.

Global macro strategies trade on systematic moves in major financial and nonfinancial markets by using futures and options contracts. They may also take positions in traditional equity and fixed-income markets. Because they tend to make large bets on the direction of currencies, commodities, or stock and bond markets globally, they have high market exposure. Given their extensive use of leverage via futures and options, they are also exposed to significant credit (leverage) risk. Because of their large positions with regard to anticipated changes in market levels, the correlation of global macro with the S&P 500 and Lehman Government/Corporate Bond Index tends to be greater than those of the first two strategies discussed here.

**B.** The usefulness of historical hedge fund data continues to be controversial. Research has shown that the volatility of returns is more persistent through time than the level of returns. Issues such as survivorship and backfill bias have a significant impact on historical tests of performance persistence. Additionally, lock-up periods, restrictions on redemptions/withdrawals, and the relatively short track record of many hedge funds complicate the extrapolation of past performance to expected (future) performance of hedge funds.

**8.** The fee structures charged by hedge fund managers often have two components: management fees and incentive fees. The "1 and 20" refers to a 1 percent per year management fee based on net asset value plus a 20 percent incentive, or profit-sharing, fee that is earned only if assets exceed a specified value. This value may be the high-water mark of the fund—that is, the highest previous NAV. Typically, drawdowns (declines/losses in net asset value) must be recouped before any incentive fees are charged.

**9.** Farkas's statement is not valid because the hedge fund has a lock-up period. During this time, the investor cannot redeem any part of the investment. Additionally, once the lock-up period has expired, redemption rights may be limited to a quarterly or semiannual schedule and the investor generally must give advance notice, ranging from 30 to 90 days, of an intention to redeem.

**10. A.** Any of the following reasons could cause an upward bias in the Sharpe ratio:

- Lengthening the measurement interval: This will result in a lower estimate of volatility. For example, the annualized standard deviation of daily returns is generally higher than of weekly returns, which is, in turn, higher than of monthly returns.

- Compounding the monthly returns but calculating the standard deviation from the (not compounded) monthly returns.

- Writing out-of-the-money puts and calls on a portfolio: This strategy can potentially increase the return by collecting the option premium without paying off for several years. Strategies that involve taking on default risk, liquidity risk, or other forms of catastrophe risk have the same ability to report an upwardly biased Sharpe ratio. (An example is the Sharpe ratios of market-neutral hedge funds before and after the 1998 liquidity crisis.) This is akin to trading negative skewness for a greater Sharpe ratio by improving the mean or standard deviation of the investment.

- Smoothing of returns: Using certain derivative structures, infrequent marking to market of illiquid assets, or using pricing models that understate monthly gains or losses can reduce reported volatility.

- Eliminating extreme returns: Because such returns increase the reported standard deviation of a hedge fund, a manager may chose to attempt to eliminate the best and the worst monthly returns each year to reduce the standard deviation. Operationally, this entails a total-return swap, in which one pays the best and worst returns for one's benchmark index each year and the counterparty pays a fixed cash flow and hedges the risk in the open market. If swaps are not available, one can do it directly with options.

**B.** Because of the option-like payoff characteristics of many hedge fund strategies, their returns are not normally distributed, but normality is an assumption inherent in the computation of standard deviation in the denominator of the Sharpe ratio. Hedge fund returns, on average, display some skewness (asymmetry of the return distribution), as well as high kurtosis (relatively frequent extreme returns). These effects are not captured by standard deviation, the risk measure used in the Sharpe ratio. Also, Sharpe ratios are overestimated when investment returns are serially correlated (i.e., returns trend), which causes a lower estimate of the standard deviation. This occurs with certain momentum (trend-following) hedge fund strategies and those that may have a problem with stale pricing or illiquidity (e.g., distressed securities).

**11. A.** The hedge fund's average nine-month rolling return:

$$RR_{9,1} = (2.7 + 1.7 - 1 + 0.9 - 1 - 2 - 2 + 4 + 3.5)/9 = 0.7556\%$$
$$RR_{9,2} = 0.7778\%$$
$$RR_{9,3} = 0.3778\%$$
$$RR_{9,4} = 0.2444\%$$
$$\text{Average} = (0.7556 + 0.7778 + 0.3778 + 0.2444)/4 = 0.54\%$$

**B.** Rolling returns can show how consistent the returns are over the investment period and whether there is any cyclicality in the returns.

**12. A.** A hurdle rate of 5% per year equates to a monthly hurdle rate of 5%/12 = 0.4167%.

The downside deviation for the hedge fund = $\sqrt{28.78/(12-1)} \times \sqrt{12} = 5.60\%$.

The downside deviation for the index = $\sqrt{65.04/(12-1)} \times \sqrt{12} = 8.42\%$.

The downside deviation is lower than the standard deviation because downside deviation takes into account only the deviations on the downside. The downside deviation of the hedge fund is lower than that of the index in this case.

**B.** Annualized return for the hedge fund = 0.6133% × 12 = 7.360%.

Annualized return for the index = −0.449% × 12 = −5.388%.

The Sortino ratio for the hedge fund = (7.36 − 5)/5.6 = 0.42.

The Sortino ratio for the index = (−5.39 − 5)/8.42 = −1.23.

The Sortino ratio of the hedge fund is much higher than that of the index, indicating that it provides greater return per unit of downside risk.

**13. A.** Managed futures are often considered a subgroup of global macro hedge funds because both strategies attempt to take advantage of systematic moves in major financial and nonfinancial markets.

**B.** The primary similarity between managed futures and absolute-return hedge fund strategies is that they seek positive returns regardless of market direction. Managed futures strategies invest exclusively in the forward and derivatives markets on a leveraged basis by trading futures and options contracts in the financial, commodity, and currency markets. In contrast, other hedge fund strategies invest in underlying markets; some, depending on their strategies, also use derivatives.

C. Systematic trading strategies are rule based and frequently trend following. Discretionary trading strategies rely on portfolio manager judgment rather than rules and include strategies based on fundamental economic data and trader beliefs.

14. The theory of market efficiency suggests that news is simultaneously available to all market participants and is quickly incorporated into market prices. However, research in behavioral finance indicates that investors may systematically underreact to information; consequently, security prices may trend, particularly in traditional investment vehicles (stocks and bonds). Actively managed derivative strategies that follow momentum, or trend-based, models have been shown to be profitable by capturing these trends.

15. Similarly to market-neutral funds, managed futures programs can replicate many strategies available to cash market investors at lower transaction costs and can also trade on strategies by using derivatives that are unavailable to cash market investors. Research has shown that when returns are segmented according to whether the stock/bond markets rose or fell, managed futures have a negative correlation with cash market portfolios when cash market portfolios post significant negative returns and are positively correlated when cash portfolios reported significant positive returns. Therefore, managed futures may offer unique asset allocation characteristics in different market environments.

Also, hedging demands of cash market participants may create investment situations where hedgers are required to offer derivative investors a risk premium, or positive return, for holding open long or short offsetting positions. Option traders may be able to create positions that offer this "risk premium" for holding various option contracts when cash market participants increase purchases of options to protect themselves in markets with trending prices or volatility. This return (i.e., the convenience yield) can be earned simply by buying and holding a derivatives portfolio.

16. The term "fallen angels" refers to debt securities that were originally deemed investment grade when issued by financially healthy companies but have subsequently been downgraded to below investment grade. In contrast, companies with high risk profiles and existing senior debt issues can seek additional (subordinated) financing via originally issued high-yield securities.

17. The private equity approach of investing is considered an active approach. New investors in the debt and/or equity of a troubled company (distressed securities) participate on creditor committees and assist in the recovery or reorganization process to maximize their return on investment. Under the relative-value approach, passive investors buy the distressed securities and either hold them until they appreciate to the desired level or trade them within a relatively short period of time.

18. The results of a prepackaged bankruptcy have different effects on the various parties involved:

A. In a prepackaged bankruptcy, the prebankruptcy creditors of the company have already agreed in advance with the debtor company on a plan or reorganization before the debtor company actually files for bankruptcy. This may involve the creditors making concessions in return for equity of the reorganized company.

**B.** Prebankruptcy shareholders do not have nearly as much leverage as the creditors. The prebankruptcy shareholders typically lose their entire stake in the company because in a prepackaged bankruptcy, a private equity firm (the vulture investor) seeks to become a majority owner of a new private company.

**C.** The vulture investor is bearing a lot of risk in a transaction like this but may come out with a substantial profit if things work out well. The vulture investor hopes to end up with a healthy company that can be sold to private or public investors.

**19.** The statement is correct. When the economy is in a downturn, there are more bankruptcies, thereby increasing the supply of distressed securities at relatively low (or falling) prices.

**20.** B is correct. Private clients have different time horizon issues compared to institutional investors such as pension funds. The partner is correct in stating that private clients have different liquidity needs than institutional investors.

**21.** B is correct. Using the data in Exhibit 1, the Sharpe ratio for hedge funds = (6 − 3.5)/2.5 = 1.0. For real estate the ratio is (8 − 3.5)/9 = 0.50, and for private equity it is (20 − 3.5)/22 = 0.75.

**22.** C is correct. Unsmoothing the data corrects bias in returns calculated from infrequent appraisals and property transactions.

**23.** A is correct. Magerski's concern relates to the potential for the Sharpe ratio to be gamed. Standard deviation of returns is reduced when extreme returns are eliminated. Smoothing returns understates gains and losses and reduces volatility. Lengthening the measurement interval generally decreases the estimate of annualized standard deviation of returns.

**24.** A is correct. The incentive fee applies to the difference between the ending period net asset value and the net assets at the high water mark, not to the entire amount under management. Five years is an exceedingly long lock-up period during which investors will not be able to withdraw any funds.

**25.** A is correct. Commodity classes such as livestock and agriculture exhibit negative correlation with unexpected inflation as measured by monthly changes in the inflation rate. Thus they are poor inflation hedges. Storable commodities directly linked to economic activity exhibit positive correlation with changes in inflation and have superior inflation-hedging properties.

**26.** A is correct. The two characteristics of the returns distribution associated with alternative investment strategies that reduce downside risk are positive skewness and low kurtosis.

**27.** B is correct. The returns on the NCREIF Index are based on appraisals that underestimate the volatility in underlying values.

**28.** B is correct. Strategy 2 (40% stock/40% bonds/20% NAREIT Index) satisfies the board's mandate because:

- the expected portfolio return of 9.52% (0.4 × 11.16% + 0.4 × 7.70% + 0.2 × 9.87%) is greater than the current allocation's expected return of 9.43% (0.5 × 11.16% + 0.5 × 7.70%), and

- indirect investments in real estate via REITs would not result in reduced liquidity because REITs are very liquid.

**29.** B is correct. One of the common features of private equity investing is the high level of diversification potential due to low correlations with traditional investment classes.

30. C is correct. Historically, direct commodity investments that are (directly) related to the intensity of economic activity have had significant, positive return correlations with inflation.

31. C is correct. Total return = Roll return + Spot return + Collateral return = (Change in futures price – Change in spot price) + Change in spot price + Collateral return = Change in futures price + Collateral return = (40.76 – 39.07 – 0.90) + 0.90 + 0.15 = (40.76 – 39.07) + 0.15 = 1.84.

32. A is correct. Contrary to Northrup's comment, fund of funds usually do not impose lock-up periods (or minimum initial holding period) and their fees are higher as investors pay two layers of fees: one to the FOF and the other to the underlying hedge fund managers.

33. B is correct. 1.5 plus 20 refers to a 1.5 percent management fee for assets under management (AUM) plus a 20% incentive fee for the managers; without a high-water mark provision, managers receive 20% of annual profits.

34. C is correct. The high-water mark is a specified net asset value level that a fund must exceed before performance/incentive fees are paid to the hedge fund manager. Once the first incentive fee has been paid, the highest month-end NAV establishes a high-water mark.

35. B is correct. Value weighting may result in a particular index taking on the return characteristics of the best-performing hedge funds in a particular time period. The second observation is incorrect as the transaction costs make it difficult to rebalance an equally weighted index.

36. A is correct. Use of a longer measurement interval will help to lower annualized volatility estimates; illiquid assets or stale prices bias the Sharpe ratio upward; use of out-of-the-money options can potentially increase returns by collecting premiums now while paying off at a later time.

37. A is correct. Both statements are correct. Hedgers may pay a risk premium to liquidity providers for the insurance they obtain so managed futures may be able to earn positive excess returns. Differential carrying costs among investors may permit managed fund traders to take advantage of short-term pricing differences between theoretically identical stock, bond, futures, options, and cash market positions.

38. B is correct. The historical returns of (a long-only position in) distressed securities have been shown to have negative skewness and high kurtosis.

39. B is correct. Equity market-neutral portfolios are supposed to have no systematic risk as a result of holding both long and short positions in stocks.

40. A is correct. The Sharpe ratio is based on a normality assumption, and hedge fund returns typically have negative skewness and high kurtosis.

41. B is correct. In distressed debt arbitrage the investor buys the distressed company's debt at steep discount and shorts its equity. Therefore, if the situation worsens and the debt is discounted further, the short position in equity will fall relatively more than the debt.

42. A is correct. As strategies become popular, more money flows into them causing those to become overweighted in a value-weighted index. On the other hand, in an equally weighted index, as a result of rebalancing, the overweighting is not a major issue.

43. B is correct. Rolling returns can provide an understanding into the consistency and cyclicality of hedge fund returns.

# Swaps

*by Robert L. McDonald*

| LEARNING OUTCOME | |
|---|---|
| **Mastery** | **The candidate should be able to** |
| ☐ | **a** evaluate commodity hedging strategies that rely on swaps and describe their inherent risk exposures. |

## INTRODUCTION

Thus far we have talked about derivatives contracts that settle on a single date. A forward contract, for example, fixes a price for a transaction that will occur on a specific date in the future. However, many transactions occur repeatedly. Firms that issue bonds make periodic coupon payments. Multinational firms frequently exchange currencies. Firms that buy commodities as production inputs or that sell them make payments or receive income linked to commodity prices on an ongoing basis.

These situations raise the question: If a manager seeking to reduce risk confronts a risky payment *stream*—as opposed to a single risky payment—what is the easiest way to hedge this risk? One obvious answer to this question is that we can enter into a separate forward contract for each payment we wish to hedge. However, it might be more convenient, and entail lower transaction costs, if there were a single transaction that we could use to hedge a stream of payments.

A **swap** is a contract calling for an exchange of payments over time. One party makes a payment to the other depending upon whether a price turns out to be greater or less than a reference price that is specified in the swap contract. A swap thus provides a means to hedge a stream of risky payments. By entering into an oil swap, for example, an oil buyer confronting a stream of uncertain oil payments can lock in a fixed price for oil over a period of time. The swap payments would be based on the difference between a fixed price for oil and a market price that varies over time.

From this description, you can see that there is a relationship between swaps and forward contracts. In fact, a forward contract is a single-payment swap. It is possible to price a multi-date swap—determine the fixed price for oil in the above example—by using information from the set of forward prices with different maturities (i.e., the strip). We will see that swaps are nothing more than forward contracts coupled with borrowing and lending money.

## 1  AN EXAMPLE OF A COMMODITY SWAP

We begin our study of swaps by presenting an example of a simple commodity swap. Our purpose here is to understand the economics of swaps. In particular we wish to understand how a swap is related to forwards, why someone might use a swap, and how market-makers hedge the risk of swaps. In later sections we present swap-price formulas and examine interest rate swaps, total return swaps, and more complicated commodity swap examples.

An industrial producer, IP Inc., is going to buy 100,000 barrels of oil 1 year from today and 2 years from today. Suppose that the forward price for delivery in 1 year is $20/barrel and in 2 years is $21/barrel. We need interest rates in this discussion, so suppose that the 1- and 2-year zero-coupon bond yields are 6% and 6.5%.

IP can use forward contracts to guarantee the cost of buying oil for the next 2 years. Specifically, IP could enter into long forward contracts for 100,000 barrels in each of the next 2 years, committing to pay $20/barrel in 1 year and $21/barrel in 2 years. The present value of this cost is

$$\frac{\$20}{1.06} + \frac{\$21}{1.065^2} = \$37.383$$

IP could invest this amount today and ensure that it had the funds to buy oil in 1 and 2 years. Alternatively, IP could pay an oil supplier $37.383, and the supplier would commit to delivering one barrel in each of the next two years. A single payment today for a single delivery of oil in the future is a prepaid forward. A single payment today to obtain *multiple* deliveries in the future is a **prepaid swap**.

Although it is possible to enter into a prepaid swap, buyers might worry about the resulting credit risk: They have fully paid for oil that will not be delivered for up to 2 years. (The prepaid forward has the same problem.) For the same reason, the swap counterparty would worry about a postpaid swap, where the oil is delivered and full payment is made after 2 years. A more attractive solution for both parties is to defer payment until the oil is delivered, while still fixing the total price.

Note that there are many feasible ways to have the buyer pay; any payment stream with a present value of $37.383 is acceptable. Typically, however, a swap will call for equal payments in each year. The payment per year per barrel, $x$, will then have to be such that

$$\frac{x}{1.06} + \frac{x}{1.065^2} = \$37.383$$

To satisfy this equation, the payments must be $20.483 in each year. We then say that the 2-year swap price is $20.483. *However, any payments that have a present value of $37.383 are acceptable.*

### Physical versus Financial Settlement

Thus far we have described the swap as if the swap counterparty supplied physical oil to the buyer. Figure 1 shows a swap that calls for physical settlement. In this case $20.483 is the per-barrel cost of oil.

**Figure 1**

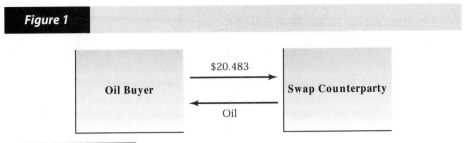

Illustration of a swap where the oil buyer pays $20.483/year and receives one barrel of oil each year.

However, we could also arrange for *financial settlement* of the swap. With financial settlement, the oil buyer, IP, pays the swap counterparty the difference between $20.483 and the spot price (if the difference is negative, the counterparty pays the buyer), and the oil buyer then buys oil at the spot price. For example, if the market price is $25, the swap counterparty pays the buyer

$$\text{Spot price} - \text{Swap price} = \$25 - \$20.483 = \$4.517$$

If the market price is $18, the spot price less the swap price is

$$\text{Spot price} - \text{Swap price} = \$18 - \$20.483 = -\$2.483$$

In this case, the oil buyer makes a payment to the swap counterparty. Whatever the market price of oil, the net cost to the buyer is the swap price, $20.483:

$$\underbrace{\text{Spot price} - \text{Swap price}}_{\text{Swap payment}} - \underbrace{\text{Spot price}}_{\text{Spot purchase of oil}} = -\text{Swap price}$$

Figure 2 depicts cash flows and transactions when the swap is settled financially. *The results for the buyer are the same whether the swap is settled physically or financially.* In both cases, the net cost to the oil buyer is $20.483.

**Figure 2**

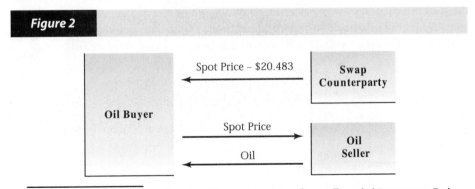

Cash flows from a transaction where the oil buyer enters into a financially settled 2-year swap. Each year the buyer pays the spot price for oil and receives spot price − $20.483. The buyer's net cost of oil is $20.483/barrel.

We have discussed the swap on a per-barrel basis. For a swap on 100,000 barrels, we simply multiply all cash flows by 100,000. In this example, 100,000 is the **notional amount** of the swap, meaning that 100,000 barrels is used to determine the magnitude of the payments when the swap is settled financially.

## Why Is the Swap Price Not $20.50?

The swap price, $20.483, is close to the average of the two oil forward prices, $20.50. However, it is not exactly the same. Why?

Suppose that the swap price were $20.50. The oil buyer would then be committing to pay $0.50 more than the forward price the first year and would pay $0.50 less than the forward price the second year. Thus, *relative to the forward curve, the buyer would have made an interest-free loan to the counterparty.* There is implicit lending in the swap.

Now consider the actual swap price of $20.483/barrel. Relative to the forward curve prices of $20 in 1 year and $21 in 2 years, we are overpaying by $0.483 in the first year and we are underpaying by $0.517 in the second year. Therefore, the swap is equivalent to being long the two forward contracts, coupled with an agreement to lend $0.483 to the swap counterparty in 1 year, and receive $0.517 in 2 years. This loan has the effect of equalizing the net cash flow on the two dates.

The interest rate on this loan is $0.517/0.483 - 1 = 7\%$. Where does 7% come from? We assumed that 6% is the 1-year zero yield and 6.5% is the 2-year yield. Given these interest rates, 7% is the 1-year implied forward yield from year 1 to year 2. By entering into the swap, we are lending the counterparty money for 1 year beginning in 1 year. If the deal is priced fairly, the interest rate on this loan should be the implied forward interest rate.

## The Swap Counterparty

The swap counterparty is a dealer, who hedges the oil price risk resulting from the swap. The dealer can hedge in several ways. First, imagine that an oil seller would like to lock in a fixed selling price of oil. In this case, the dealer locates the oil buyer and seller and serves as a go-between for the swap, receiving payments from one party and passing them on to the other. In practice the fixed price paid by the buyer exceeds the fixed price received by the seller. This price difference is a bid-ask spread and is the dealer's fee.

Figure 3 illustrates how this transaction would work with financial settlement. The oil seller receives the spot price for oil and receives the swap price less the spot price, on net receiving the swap price. The oil buyer pays the spot price and receives the spot price less the swap price. The situation where the dealer matches the buyer and seller is called a **back-to-back transaction** or "matched book" transaction. The dealer bears the credit risk of both parties but is not exposed to price risk.

---

**Figure 3**

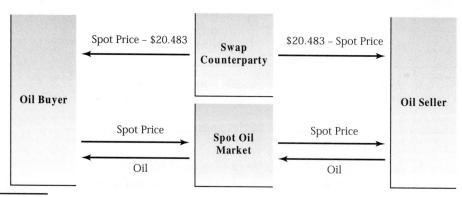

Cash flows from a transaction where an oil buyer and seller each enters into a financially settled 2-year swap. The buyer pays the spot price for oil and receives spot price – $20.483 each year as a swap payment. The oil seller receives the spot price for oil and receives $20.483 – spot price as a swap payment.

A more interesting situation occurs when the dealer serves as counterparty and hedges the transaction using forward markets. Let's see how this would work.

After entering the swap with the oil buyer, the dealer has the obligation to pay the spot price and receive the swap price. If the spot price rises, the dealer can lose money. The dealer has a short position in 1- and 2-year oil.

The natural hedge for the dealer is to enter into long forward or futures contracts to offset this short exposure. Table 1 illustrates how this strategy works. As we discussed earlier, there is an implicit loan in the swap and this is apparent in Table 1. The net cash flow for the hedged dealer is a loan, where the dealer receives cash in year 1 and repays it in year 2.

---

### Table 1

Positions and cash flows for a dealer who has an obligation to receive the fixed price in an oil swap and who hedges the exposure by going long year 1 and year 2 oil forwards.

| Year | Payment from Oil Buyer | Long Forward | Net |
|------|------------------------|--------------|-----|
| 1 | $20.483 − Year 1 spot price | Year 1 spot price − $20 | $0.483 |
| 2 | $20.483 − Year 2 spot price | Year 2 spot price − $21 | −$0.517 |

---

This example shows that *hedging the oil price risk in the swap does not fully hedge the position.* The dealer also has interest rate exposure. If interest rates fall, the dealer will not be able to earn a sufficient return from investing $0.483 in year 1 to repay $0.517 in year 2. Thus, in addition to entering oil forwards, it would make sense for the dealer to use Eurodollar contracts or forward rate agreements to hedge the resulting interest rate exposure.

The following box shows an extreme example of a hedged transaction—allegedly used to hide debt and manipulate earnings—involving Enron and JPMorgan Chase.

---

### ENRON'S HIDDEN DEBT

When energy giant Enron collapsed in the fall of 2001, there were charges that other companies had helped Enron mislead investors. In July 2003, the Securities and Exchange Commission announced that JPMorgan Chase and Citigroup had each agreed to pay more than $100 million to settle allegations that they had helped Enron commit fraud. Specifically, the SEC alleged that both banks had helped Enron characterize loan proceeds as operating income.

The basic outline of the transaction with JPMorgan Chase is as follows. Enron entered into "prepaid forward sales contracts" (essentially a prepaid swap) with an entity called Mahonia; Enron received a lump-sum payment and agreed to deliver natural gas in the future. Mahonia in turn received a lump-sum payment from Chase and agreed to deliver natural gas in the future. Chase, which controlled Mahonia, then hedged its Mahonia transaction with Enron. With all transactions netted out, Enron had no commodity exposure, and received its lump-sum initial payment from Mahonia in exchange for making future fixed installment payments to Chase. In other words, Enron in effect had a loan with Chase. Not only did Enron not record debt from these transactions, but the company reported operating income. The transaction is illustrated in the figure below.

The SEC complaint included a revealing excerpt from internal Chase e-mail:

WE ARE MAKING DISGUISED LOANS, USUALLY BURIED IN COMMODITIES OR EQUITIES DERIVATIVES (AND I'M SURE IN OTHER AREAS). WITH A FEW [sic] EXCEPTIONS, THEY ARE UNDERSTOOD TO BE DISGUISED LOANS AND APPROVED AS SUCH. (Capitalization in the original.)

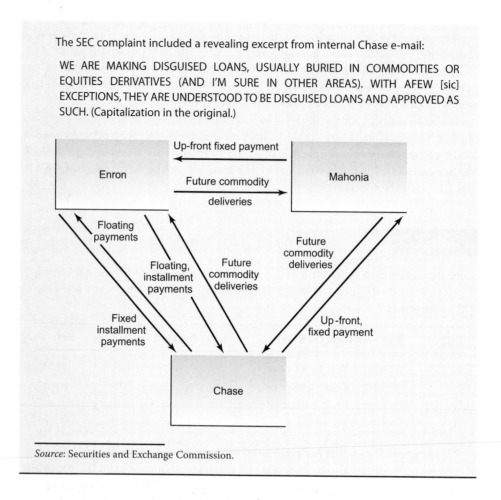

*Source:* Securities and Exchange Commission.

## The Market Value of a Swap

When the buyer first enters the swap, its market value is zero, meaning that either party could enter or exit the swap without having to pay anything to the other party (apart from commissions and bid-ask spreads). From the oil buyer's perspective, the swap consists of two forward contracts plus an agreement to lend money at the implied forward rate of 7%. The forward contracts and forward rate agreement have zero value, so the swap does as well.

Once the swap is struck, however, its market value will generally no longer be zero, for two reasons. First, the forward prices for oil and interest rates will change over time. New swaps would no longer have a fixed price of $20.483; hence, one party will owe money to the other should one party wish to exit or *unwind* the swap.

Second, even if oil and interest rate forward prices do not change, the value of the swap will remain zero only *until the first swap payment is made.* Once the first swap payment is made, the buyer has overpaid by $0.483 relative to the forward curve, and hence, in order to exit the swap, the counterparty would have to pay the oil buyer $0.483. Thus, even if prices do not change, the market value of swaps can change over time due to the implicit borrowing and lending.

A buyer wishing to exit the swap could negotiate terms with the original counterparty to eliminate the swap obligation. An alternative is to leave the original swap in place and enter into an offsetting swap with whoever offers the best price. The original swap called for the oil buyer to pay the fixed price and receive the floating price; the offsetting swap has the buyer receive the fixed price and pay floating. The original obligation would be cancelled except to the extent that the fixed prices are different.

However, the difference is known, so oil price risk is eliminated. (There is still credit risk when the original swap counterparty and the counterparty to the offsetting swap are different. This could be a reason for the buyer to prefer offsetting the swap with the original counterparty.)

To see how a swap can change in value, suppose that immediately after the buyer enters the swap, the forward curve for oil rises by $2 in years 1 and 2. Thus, the year-1 forward price becomes $22 and the year-2 forward price becomes $23. The original swap will no longer have a zero market value.

Assuming interest rates are unchanged, the new swap price is $22.483. (Problem 1 asks you to verify this.) The buyer could unwind the swap at this point by agreeing to sell oil at $22.483, while the original swap still calls for buying oil at $20.483. Thus, the net swap payments in each year are

$$\underbrace{\left(\text{Spot price} - \$20.483\right)}_{\text{Original swap}} + \underbrace{\left(\$22.483 - \text{Spot price}\right)}_{\text{New swap}} = \$2$$

The present value of this difference is

$$\frac{\$2}{1.06} + \frac{\$2}{\left(1.065\right)^2} = \$3.650$$

The buyer can receive a stream of payments worth $3.65 by offsetting the original swap with a new swap. Thus, $3.65 is the market value of the swap.

If interest rates had changed, we would have used the new interest rates in computing the new swap price.

The examples we have analyzed in this section illustrate the fundamental characteristics of swaps and their cash flows. In the rest of the reading, we will compute more realistic swap prices for interest rates, currencies, and commodities and see some of the ways in which we can modify the terms of a swap.

# INTEREST RATE SWAPS

**2**

OPTIONAL SEGMENT

Companies use interest rate swaps to modify their interest rate exposure. In this section we will begin with a simple example of an interest rate swap, similar to the preceding oil swap example. We will then present general pricing formulas and discuss ways in which the basic swap structure can be altered.

## A Simple Interest Rate Swap

Suppose that XYZ Corp. has $200m of floating-rate debt at LIBOR—meaning that every year XYZ pays that year's current LIBOR—but would prefer to have fixed-rate debt with 3 years to maturity. There are several ways XYZ could effect this change.

First, XYZ could change their interest rate exposure by retiring the floating-rate debt and issuing fixed-rate debt in its place. However, an actual purchase and sale of debt has transaction costs.

Second, they could enter into a strip of forward rate agreements (FRAs) in order to guarantee the borrowing rate for the remaining life of the debt. Since the FRA for each year will typically carry a different interest rate, the company will lock in a different rate each year and, hence, the company's borrowing cost will vary over time, even though it will be fixed in advance.

A third alternative is to obtain interest rate exposure equivalent to that of fixed rate debt by entering into a swap. XYZ is already paying a floating interest rate. They therefore want to enter a swap in which they receive a floating rate and pay the fixed rate, which we will suppose is 6.9548%. This swap is illustrated in Figure 4. Notice the similarity to the oil swap.

**Figure 4**

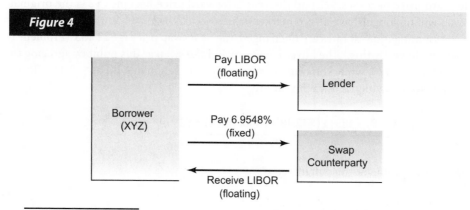

Illustration of cash flows for a company that borrows at LIBOR and swaps to fixed-rate exposure at 6.9548%.

In a year when the fixed 6.9548% swap rate exceeds 1-year LIBOR, XYZ pays 6.9548% – LIBOR to the swap counterparty. Conversely, when the 6.9548% swap rate is less than LIBOR, the swap counterparty pays LIBOR – 6.9548% to XYZ. On net, XYZ pays 6.9548%. Algebraically, the net interest payment made by XYZ is

$$\text{XYZ net payment} = \underbrace{\text{LIBOR}}_{\text{Floating payment}} + \underbrace{\text{LIBOR} - 6.9548\%}_{\text{Swap payment}} = -6.9548\%$$

The notional principal of the swap is $200m: It is the amount on which the interest payments—and, hence, the net swap payment—is based. The life of the swap is the **swap term** or **swap tenor**.

There are timing conventions with a swap similar to those for a forward rate agreement. At the beginning of a year, the borrowing rate for that year is known.

However, the interest payment on the loan is due at the end of the year. The interest rate determination date for the floating interest payment would therefore occur at the beginning of the period. As with an FRA we can think of the swap payment being made at the end of the period (when interest is due).

With the financially settled oil swap, only net swap payments—in this case the difference between LIBOR and 6.9548%—are actually made between XYZ and the counterparty. If one party defaults, they owe to the other party at most the present value of net swap payments they are obligated to make at current market prices. This means that a swap generally has less credit risk than a bond: Whereas principal is at risk with a bond, only net swap payments are at risk in a swap.

The swap in this example is a construct, making payments *as if* there were an exchange of payments between a fixed-rate and floating-rate bond. In practice, a fund manager might own fixed-rate bonds and wish to have floating-rate exposure while continuing to own the bonds. A swap in which a fund manager receives a floating rate in exchange for the payments on bonds the fund continues to hold is called an **asset swap**.

## Pricing and the Swap Counterparty

To understand the pricing of the swap, we will examine it from the perspective of both the counterparty and the firm. We first consider the perspective of the counterparty, who we assume is a market-maker.

The market-maker is a counterparty to the swap in order to earn fees, not to take on interest rate risk. Therefore, the market-maker will hedge the transaction. The market-maker receives the fixed rate from the company and pays the floating rate; the danger for the market-maker is that the floating rate will rise. The risk in this transaction can be hedged by entering into forward rate agreements. We express the time 0 implied forward rate between time $t_i$ and $t_j$ as $r_0(t_i, t_j)$ and the realized 1-year rate as $\tilde{r}_{t_i}$. The current 1-year rate, 6%, is known. With the swap rate denoted $R$, Table 2 depicts the risk-free (but time-varying) cash flows faced by the hedged market-maker.

---

**Table 2**

Cash flows faced by a market-maker who receives fixed and pays floating and hedges the resulting exposure using forward rate agreements.

| Year | Payment on Forward | Net Swap Payment | Net |
|------|--------------------|------------------|-----|
| 1 | — | $R - 6\%$ | $R - 6\%$ |
| 2 | $\tilde{r}_2 - 7.0024\%$ | $R - \tilde{r}_2$ | $R - 7.0024\%$ |
| 3 | $\tilde{r}_3 - 8.0071\%$ | $R - \tilde{r}_3$ | $R - 8.0071\%$ |

---

How is $R$ determined? Obviously a market-maker receiving the fixed rate would like to set a high swap rate, but the swap market is competitive. We expect $R$ to be bid down by competing market-makers until the present value of the hedged cash flows is zero. In computing this present value, we need to use the appropriate rate for each cash flow: The one-year rate for $R - 6\%$, the two-year rate for $R - 7.0024\%$, and so forth.

$$\frac{R - 6\%}{1.06} + \frac{R - 7.0024\%}{1.065^2} + \frac{R - 8.0071\%}{1.07^3} = 0$$

This formula gives us an $R$ of 6.9548%, which is the same as the par coupon rate on a 3-year bond! In fact, our swap-rate calculation is a roundabout way to compute a par bond yield. On reflection, this result should be no surprise. Once the borrower has entered into the swap, the net effect is exactly like borrowing at a fixed rate. Thus the fixed swap rate should be the rate on a coupon bond.

Notice that the unhedged net cash flows in Table 2 (the "net swap payment" column) can be replicated by borrowing at a floating rate and lending at a fixed rate. In other words, *an interest rate swap is equivalent to borrowing at a floating rate to buy a fixed-rate bond.*

The borrower's calculations are just the opposite of the market-maker's. The borrower continues to pay the floating rate on its floating-rate debt, and receives floating and pays fixed in the swap. Table 3 details the cash flows.

**Table 3**

Cash flows faced by a floating-rate borrower who enters into a 3-year swap with a fixed rate of 6.9548%.

| Year | Floating-Rate Debt Payment | Net Swap Payment | Net |
|------|---------------------------|------------------|------|
| 1 | $-6\%$ | $6\% - 6.9548\%$ | $-6.9548\%$ |
| 2 | $-\tilde{r}_2$ | $\tilde{r}_2 - 6.9548\%$ | $-6.9548\%$ |
| 3 | $-\tilde{r}_3$ | $\tilde{r}_3 - 6.9548\%$ | $-6.9548\%$ |

Since the swap rate is the same as the par 3-year coupon rate, the borrower is indifferent between the swap and a coupon bond, ignoring transaction costs. Keep in mind that the borrower could also have used forward rate agreements, locking in an escalating interest rate over time: 6% the first year, 7.0024% the second, and 8.0071% the third. By using interest rate forwards the borrower would have eliminated uncertainty about future borrowing rates and created an uneven but certain stream of interest payments over time. The swap provides a way to both guarantee the borrowing rate and lock in a constant rate in a single transaction.

## Computing the Swap Rate in General

We now examine more carefully the general calculations for determining the swap rate. Suppose there are $n$ swap settlements, occurring on dates $t_i$, $i = 1, ..., n$. The implied forward interest rate from date $t_{i-1}$ to date $t_i$, known at date 0, is $r_0(t_{i-1}, t_i)$. [We will treat $r_0(t_{i-1}, t_i)$ as *not* having been annualized; i.e., it is the return earned from $t_{i-1}$ to $t_i$.] The price of a zero-coupon bond maturing on date $t_i$ is $P(0, t_i)$.

The market-maker can hedge the floating-rate payments using forward rate agreements. The requirement that the hedged swap have zero net present value is

$$\sum_{i=1}^{n} P(0, t_i)\left[R - r_0\left(t_{i-1}, t_i\right)\right] = 0 \qquad (1)$$

where there are $n$ payments on dates $t_1, t_2, ..., t_n$. The cash flows $R - r_0(t_{i-1}, t_i)$ can also be obtained by buying a fixed-rate bond paying $R$ and borrowing at the floating rate.

Equation 1 can be rewritten as

$$R = \frac{\sum_{i=1}^{n} P(0, t_i) r\left(t_{i-1}, t_i\right)}{\sum_{i=1}^{n} P(0, t_i)} \qquad (2)$$

The expression $\sum_{i=1}^{n} P(0, t_i) r\left(t_{i-1}, t_i\right)$ is the present value of interest payments implied by the strip of forward rates. The expression $\sum_{i=1}^{n} P(0, t_i)$ is just the present value of a \$1 annuity when interest rates vary over time. Thus, the swap rate annuitizes the interest payments on the floating-rate bond.

We can rewrite Equation 2 to make it easier to interpret:

$$R = \sum_{i=1}^{n} \left[\frac{P(0, t_i)}{\sum_{j=1}^{n} P(0, t_j)}\right] r\left(t_{i-1}, t_i\right)$$

Since the terms in square brackets sum to one, this form of Equation 2 emphasizes that the fixed swap rate is a weighted average of the implied forward rates, where zero-coupon bond prices are used to determine the weights.

There is another, equivalent way to express the swap rate. The implied forward rate between times $t_1$ and $t_2$, $r_0(t_1, t_2)$, is given by the ratio of zero-coupon bond prices, i.e.,

$$r_0(t_1, t_2) = P(0, t_1)/P(0, t_2) - 1$$

Therefore Equation 1 can be rewritten

$$\sum_{i=1}^{n} P(0, t_i) \left[ R - r(t_{i-1}, t_i) \right] = \sum_{i=1}^{n} P(0, t_i) \left[ R - \frac{P(0, t_{i-1})}{P(0, t_i)} + 1 \right]$$

Setting this equation equal to zero and solving for $R$ gives us

$$R = \frac{1 - P_0(0, t_n)}{\sum_{i=1}^{n} P_0(0, t_i)} \tag{3}$$

You may recognize this as the formula for the coupon on a par coupon bond. This in turn can be rewritten as

$$R \sum_{i=1}^{n} P(0, t_i) + P(0, t_n) = 1$$

This is the valuation equation for a bond priced at par with a coupon rate of $R$.

The conclusion is *the swap rate is the coupon rate on a par coupon bond.* This result is intuitive since a firm that swaps from floating-rate to fixed-rate exposure ends up with the economic equivalent of a fixed-rate bond.

## The Swap Curve

The Eurodollar futures contract provides a set of 3-month forward LIBOR rates extending out 10 years. It is possible to use this set of forward interest rates to compute Equation 2 or 3. Zero-coupon bond prices can be constructed from implied forward rates.

The set of swap rates at different maturities implied by LIBOR is called the *swap curve.* There is an over-the-counter market in interest rate swaps, which is widely quoted. The swap curve should be consistent with the interest rate curve implied by the Eurodollar futures contract, which is used to hedge swaps.[1]

Here is how we construct the swap curve using the set of Eurodollar prices.[2] Column 2 of Table 4 lists 2 years of Eurodollar futures prices from June 2004. The next column shows the implied 91-day interest rate, beginning in the month in column 1.

---

**1** The Eurodollar contract is a futures contract, while a swap is a set of forward rate agreements. Because of convexity bias, the swap curve constructed from Eurodollar futures contracts following the procedure described in this section will be somewhat greater than the observed swap curve. This is discussed by Burghardt and Hoskins (1995) and Gupta and Subrahmanyam (2000).

**2** Collin-Dufresne and Solnik (2001) point out that the credit risk implicit in the LIBOR rate underlying the Eurodollar futures contract is different than the credit risk of an interest rate swap. LIBOR is computed as an average 3-month borrowing rate for international banks with good credit. Banks that experience credit problems are dropped from the sample. Thus, by construction, the pool of banks represented in the Eurodollar contract never experience a credit downgrade. A firm with a swap, by contrast, could be downgraded.

For example, the June price of 98.5558 implies a June to September quarterly interest rate of

$$(100 - 98.555)\frac{91}{90}\frac{1}{400} = 0.0037\%$$

---

**Table 4**

Three-month LIBOR forward rates implied by Eurodollar futures prices with maturity dates given in the first column. Prices are from June 2, 2004.

| Maturity Date, $t_i$ | Eurodollar Futures Price | Implied Quarterly Rate, $r(t, t_{i+1})$ | Implied June 2004 Price of $1 Paid on Maturity Date, $t$, $P(0, t_i)$ | Swap Rate |
|---|---|---|---|---|
| Jun-04 | 98.555 | 0.0037 | — | 1.4611% |
| Sep-04 | 98.010 | 0.0050 | 0.9964 | 1.7359% |
| Dec-04 | 97.495 | 0.0063 | 0.9914 | 2.0000% |
| Mar-05 | 97.025 | 0.0075 | 0.9851 | 2.2495% |
| Jun-05 | 96.600 | 0.0086 | 0.9778 | 2.4836% |
| Sep-05 | 96.235 | 0.0095 | 0.9695 | 2.6997% |
| Dec-05 | 95.910 | 0.0103 | 0.9603 | 2.8995% |
| Mar-06 | 95.650 | 0.0110 | 0.9505 | 3.0808% |

*Source*: Eurodollars futures prices from Datastream.

---

Column 4 reports the corresponding implied zero-coupon bond price. In the second row, the price is the cost in June of $1 paid in September. The third row is the June cost of $1 paid in December, and so forth. The fourth row is

$$\frac{1}{1.0037} \times \frac{1}{1.0050} \times \frac{1}{1.0063} = 0.9851$$

which is the June cost of $1 paid in March. The December swap rate, expressed as a quarterly rate, is the fixed quarterly interest rate from June through March, with swap payments in June, September, and December (the months in which the quarterly rate prevailing over the *next* 3 months is known). This is computed using Equation 3:

$$\frac{1 - 0.9851}{0.9964 + 0.9914 + 0.9851} = 0.50\%$$

Multiplying this by 4 to annualize the rate gives the 2.00% in the swap rate column of Table 4.

In Figure 5 we graph the entire swap curve against quarterly forward rates implied by the Eurodollar curve. The **swap spread** is the difference between swap rates and Treasury-bond yields for comparable maturities. Thus, Figure 5 also displays yields on government bonds.

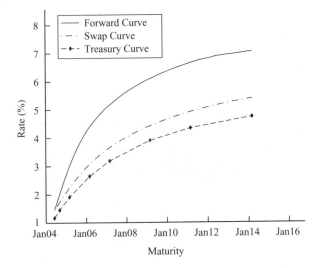

Forward 3-month interest rate curve implied by the Eurodollar strip, swap rates, and constant maturity Treasury yields for June 2, 2004.
*Source*: Datastream.

## The Swap's Implicit Loan Balance

An interest rate swap behaves much like the oil swap in Section 1. At inception, the swap has zero value to both parties. If interest rates change, the present value of the fixed payments and, hence, the swap rate will change. The market value of the swap is the difference in the present value of payments between the old swap rate and the new swap rate. For example, consider the 3-year swap in Table 3. If interest rates rise after the swap is entered into, the value of the existing 6.9548% swap will fall for the party receiving the fixed payment.

Even in the absence of interest rate changes, however, the swap in Table 3 changes value over time. Once the first swap payment is made, the swap acquires negative value for the market-maker (relative to the use of forwards) because in the second year the market-maker will make a net cash payment. Similarly, the swap will have positive value for the borrower (again relative to the use of forwards) after the first payment is made. In order to smooth payments, the borrower pays "too much" (relative to the forward curve) in the first year and receives a refund in the second year. *The swap is equivalent to entering into forward contracts and undertaking some additional borrowing and lending.*

The 10-year swap rate in Figure 5 is 5.3986%. We can use this value to illustrate the implicit borrowing and lending in the swap. Consider an investor who pays fixed and receives floating. This investor is paying a high rate in the early years of the swap, and, hence, is lending money. About halfway through the life of the swap, the Eurodollar forward rate exceeds the swap rate and the loan balance declines, falling to zero by the end of the swap. The fixed-rate recipient has a positive loan balance over the life of the swap because the Eurodollar futures rate is below the swap initially—so the fixed-rate recipient is receiving payments—and crosses the swap price once. The credit risk in this swap is therefore borne, at least initially, by the fixed-rate payer, who is lending to the fixed-rate recipient. The implicit loan balance in the swap is illustrated in Figure 6.

*Figure 6*

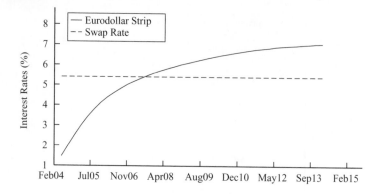

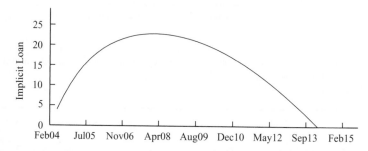

Eurodollar strip and the 10-year swap rate are plotted in the top panel, and implicit lending from being a fixed-rate recipient in the bottom panel. Swap payment dates are on the horizontal axis. *Source*: Datastream.

## Deferred Swaps

We can construct a swap that begins at some date in the future, but for which the swap rate is agreed upon today. This type of swap is called a **deferred swap**. To demonstrate this type of swap, we can compute the value of a 2-period swap that begins 1 year from today. The reasoning is exactly as before: The swap rate will be set by the market-maker so that the present value of the fixed and floating payments is the same. This gives us

$$\frac{R-0.070024}{1.065^2}+\frac{R-0.080071}{1.07^3}=0$$

Solving for $R$, the deferred swap rate is 7.4854%. In general, the fixed rate on a deferred swap beginning in $k$ periods is computed as

$$R=\frac{\sum_{i=k}^{T}P_0\left(0,t_i\right)r_0\left(t_{i-1},t_i\right)}{\sum_{i=k}^{T}P\left(0,t_i\right)}\tag{4}$$

This can also be written as

$$R=\frac{P\left(0,t_{k-1}\right)-P\left(0,t_n\right)}{\sum_{i=k}^{n}P\left(0,t_i\right)}\tag{5}$$

Equation 4 is equal to Equation 2 when $k = 1$.

## Why Swap Interest Rates?

Managers sometimes say that they would like to borrow short-term because short-term interest rates are on average lower than long-term interest rates. Leaving aside the question of whether this view makes sense theoretically, let's take for granted the desire to borrow at short-term interest rates. The problem facing the manager is that the firm may be unable to borrow significant amounts by issuing short-term debt.

When a firm borrows by issuing long-term debt, bondholders bear both interest rate risk and the credit risk of the firm. If the firm borrows short-term (for example, by issuing commercial paper), lenders primarily bear credit risk.

In practice, short-term lenders appear unwilling to absorb large issues from a single borrower because of credit risk. For example, money-market mutual funds that hold commercial paper will not hold large amounts of any one firm's commercial paper, preferring instead to diversify across firms. This diversification minimizes the chance that a single bankruptcy will significantly reduce the fund's rate of return.

Because short-term lenders are sensitive in this way to credit risk, a firm cannot borrow a large amount of money short-term without lenders demanding a higher interest rate. By contrast, long-term lenders to corporations—for example, pension funds and insurance companies—willingly assume both interest rate and credit risk. Thus there are borrowers who wish to issue short-term debt and lenders who are unwilling to buy it. Swaps provide a way around this problem, permitting the firm to separate credit risk and interest rate risk.

Suppose, for example, that a firm borrows long-term and then swaps into short-rate exposure. The firm receives the fixed rate, pays the fixed rate to bondholders, and pays the floating rate on the swap. The net payment is the short-term rate, which is the rate the firm wanted to pay.

Credit risk does not vanish; it is still mostly held by the long-term bondholders. The swap counterparty faces credit risk since the firm could go bankrupt when the value of the swap is positive to the counterparty (this would occur if interest rates had risen). The notional principal of the loan is not at risk for the swap counterparty, however, so the credit risk in the swap is less than for a short-term loan. Thus, by swapping its interest rate exposure, the firm pays the short-term interest rate, *but the long-term bondholders continue to bear most of the credit risk.*

If it seems odd to you that the firm can use a swap to convert a high fixed rate into a low floating rate, recognize that any time there is an upward-sloping yield curve, the short-term interest rate is below the long-term interest rate. If you reduce the period for which your borrowing rate is fixed (which happens when you swap fixed for floating), you borrow at the lower short-term interest rate instead of the higher long-term interest rate.

Swaps thus permit separation of two aspects of borrowing: credit risk and interest rate risk. To the extent these risks are acquired by those most willing to hold them, swaps increase efficiency.

## Amortizing and Accreting Swaps

We have assumed that the notional value of the swap remains fixed over the life of the swap. However, it is also possible to engage in a swap where the notional value is changing over time. For example, consider a floating-rate mortgage, for which every payment contains an interest and principal component. Since the outstanding principal is declining over time, a swap involving a mortgage would need to account for this. Such a swap is called an **amortizing swap** because the notional value is declining over time. It is also possible for the principal in a swap to grow over time. This is called an **accreting swap**.

Let $Q_t$ be the relative notional amount at time $t$. Then the basic idea in pricing a swap with a time-varying notional amount is the same as with a fixed notional amount: The present value of the fixed payments should equal the present value of the floating payments:

$$\sum_{i=1}^{n} Q_{t_i} P(0, t_i) \left[ R - r(t_{i-1}, t_i) \right] = 0 \tag{6}$$

where, as before, there are $n$ payments on dates $t_1, t_2, \ldots, t_n$. Equation 6 can be rewritten as

$$R = \frac{\sum_{i=1}^{n} Q_{t_i} P(0, t_i) r(t_{i-1}, t_i)}{\sum_{i=1}^{n} Q_{t_i} P(0, t_i)} \tag{7}$$

The fixed swap rate is still a weighted average of implied forward rates, only now the weights also involve changing notional principal.

Many other structures are possible for swaps based on interest rates or other prices. One infamous swap structure is described in the following box, which recounts the 1993 swap between Procter & Gamble and Bankers Trust.

### THE PROCTER & GAMBLE SWAP

In November 1993, consumer products company Procter & Gamble (P&G) entered into a 5-year $200m notional value swap with Bankers Trust. The contract called for P&G to receive a 5.3% fixed rate from Bankers Trust and pay the 30-day commercial paper rate less 75 basis points, plus a spread. Settlements were to be semiannual. The spread would be zero for the first settlement, and thereafter be fixed at the spread as of May 4, 1994.

The spread was determined by the difference between the 5-year constant maturity treasury (CMT) rate (the yield on a 5-year Treasury bond, but a constructed rate since there is not always a Treasury bond with exactly 5 years to expiration) and the price per $100 of maturity value of the 6.25% 30-year Treasury bond. The formula for the spread was

$$\text{Spread} = \max \left( \frac{\dfrac{5 - \text{Year CMT\%}}{0.0578} \times 98.5 - \text{Price of 30-year bond}}{100}, 0 \right)$$

At inception in November 1993, the 5-year CMT rate was 5.02% and the 30-year Treasury price was 102.57811. The expression in the max function evaluated to −.17 (−17 basis points), so the spread was zero.

If the spread were 0 on May 4, 1994, P&G would save 75 basis points per year on $200m for 4.5 years, an interest rate reduction worth approximately $7m. However, notice something important: If interest rates rise before the spread determination date, then the 5-year CMT goes up *and the price of the 30-year bond goes down*. Thus, the swap is really a bet on the *direction* of interest rates, not the difference in rates!

The swap is recounted in Smith (1997) and Srivastava (1998). Interest rates rose after P&G entered the swap. P&G and Bankers Trust renegotiated the swap in January 1994, and P&G liquidated the swap in March, with a loss of about $100m. P&G sued Bankers Trust, complaining in part that the risks of the swap had not been adequately disclosed by Bankers Trust.

In the end P&G and Bankers Trust settled, with P&G paying Bankers Trust about $35m. [Forster (1996) and Horwitz (1996) debate the implications of the trial and settlement.] The notion that Procter & Gamble might have been uninformed about the risk of the swap, and if so, whether this should have mattered, was controversial. U.S. securities laws are often said to protect "widows and orphans." Nobel-prize–winning economist Merton Miller wryly said of the case, "Procter is the widow and Gamble is the orphan."

# CURRENCY SWAPS

**3**

Firms sometimes issue debt denominated in a foreign currency. A firm may do this as a hedge against revenues received in that currency, or because perceived borrowing costs in that currency are lower. Whatever the reason, if the firm later wants to change the currency to which they have exposure, there are a variety of ways to do so. The firm can use forward contracts to hedge exchange rate risk, or it can use a **currency swap**, in which payments are based on the difference in debt payments denominated in different currencies.

To understand these alternatives, let's consider the example of a dollar-based firm that has euro-denominated 3-year fixed-rate debt. The annual coupon rate is $\rho$. The firm is obligated to make a series of payments that are fixed in euro terms but variable in dollar terms.

Since the payments are known, eliminating euro exposure is a straightforward hedging problem using currency forwards. We have cash flows of $-\rho$ each year, and $-(1 + \rho)$ in the maturity year. If currency forward prices are $F_{0,t}$, we can enter into long euro forward contracts to acquire at a known exchange rate the euros we need to pay to the lenders. Hedged cash flows in year $t$ are $-\rho F_{0,t}$.

As we have seen in other examples, the forward transactions eliminate risk but leave the firm with a variable (but riskless) stream of cash flows. The variability of hedged cash flows is illustrated in the following example.

## Example 1

Suppose the effective annual euro-denominated interest rate is 3.5% and the dollar-denominated rate is 6%. The spot exchange rate is $0.90/€. A dollar-based firm has a 3-year 3.5% euro-denominated bond with a €100 par value and price of €100. The firm wishes to guarantee the dollar value of the payments. Since the firm will make debt payments in euros, it buys the euro forward to eliminate currency exposure. Table 5 summarizes the transaction and reports the currency forward curve and the unhedged and hedged cash flows. The value of the hedged cash flows is

$$\frac{\$3.226}{1.06} + \frac{\$3.304}{1.06^2} + \frac{\$100.064}{1.06^3} = \$90$$

**Table 5**

Unhedged and hedged cash flows for a dollar-based firm with euro-denominated debt.

| Year | Unhedged Euro Cash Flow | Forward Exchange Rate | Hedged Dollar Cash Flow |
|------|------|------|------|
| 1 | −€3.5 | 0.922 | −$3.226 |
| 2 | −€3.5 | 0.944 | −$3.304 |
| 3 | −€103.5 | 0.967 | −$100.064 |

Example 1 verifies what we knew had to be true: Hedging does not change the value of the debt. The initial value of the debt in euros is €100. Since the exchange rate is $0.90/€, the debt should have a dollar value of $90, which it has.

As an alternative to hedging each euro-denominated payment with a forward contract, a firm wishing to change its currency exposure can enter into a currency swap, which entails making debt payments in one currency and receiving debt payments in a different currency. There is typically an exchange of principal at both the start and end of the swap. Compared with hedging the cash flows individually, the currency swap generates a different cash flow stream, but with equivalent value. We can examine a currency swap by supposing that the firm in Example 1 uses a swap rather than forward contracts to hedge its euro exposure.

**Example 2**

Make the same assumptions as in Example 1. The dollar-based firm enters into a swap where it pays dollars (6% on a $90 bond) and receives euros (3.5% on a €100 bond). The firm's euro exposure is eliminated. The market-maker receives dollars and pays euros. The position of the market-maker is summarized in Table 6. The present value of the market-maker's net cash flow is

$$\frac{\$2.174}{1.06} + \frac{\$2.096}{1.06^2} - \frac{\$4.664}{1.06^3} = 0$$

The market-maker's net exposure in this transaction is long a dollar-denominated bond and short a euro-denominated bond. Table 6 shows that after hedging there is a series of net cash flows with zero present value. As in all the previous examples, the effect of the swap is equivalent to entering into forward contracts, coupled with borrowing or lending. In this case, the firm is lending to the market-maker in the first 2 years, with the implicit loan repaid at maturity.

**Table 6**

Unhedged and hedged cash flows for a dollar-based firm with euro-denominated debt. The effective annual dollar-denominated interest rate is 6% and the effective annual euro-denominated interest rate is 3.5%.

| Year | Forward Exchange Rate ($/€) | Receive Dollar Interest | Pay Hedged Euro Interest | Net Cash Flow |
|------|------|------|------|------|
| 1 | 0.9217 | $5.40 | −€3.5 × 0.9217 | $2.174 |
| 2 | 0.9440 | $5.40 | −€3.5 × 0.9440 | $2.096 |
| 3 | 0.9668 | $95.40 | −€103.5 × 0.9668 | −$4.664 |

A currency swap is equivalent to borrowing in one currency and lending in the other, and the same is true of currency forwards.

## Currency Swap Formulas

Currency swap calculations are the same as those for the other swaps we have discussed. To see this, consider a swap in which a dollar annuity, $R$, is exchanged for an annuity in another currency, $R^*$. Given the foreign annuity, $R^*$, what is $R$?

We start with the observation that the present value of the two annuities must be the same. There are $n$ payments and the time-0 forward price for a unit of foreign currency delivered at time $t_i$ is $F_{0,t\,i}$. This gives

$$\sum_{i=1}^{n}\left[ RP_{0,t_i} - R^*\,F_{0,t_i}\,P_{0,t_i} \right] = 0$$

In calculating the present value of the payment $R^*$, we first convert to dollars by multiplying by $F_{0,ti}$. We can then compute the present value using the dollar-denominated zero-coupon bond price, $P_{0,ti}$. Solving for $R$ gives

$$R = \frac{\sum_{i=1}^{n} P_{0,t_i}\,R^*\,F_{0,t_i}}{\sum_{i=1}^{n} P_{0,t_i}} \qquad (8)$$

This expression is exactly like Equation 2, with the implied forward rate, $r_0(t_{i-1}, t_i)$, replaced by the foreign-currency-denominated annuity payment translated into dollars, $R^* F_{0,\,ti}$.

When coupon bonds are swapped, we have to account for the difference in maturity value as well as the coupon payment, which is an annuity. If the dollar bond has a par value of \$1, the foreign bond will have a par value of $1/x_0$, where $x_0$ is the current exchange rate expressed as dollars per unit of the foreign currency. If $R^*$ is the coupon rate on the foreign bond and $R$ is the coupon rate on the dollar bond, the present value of the difference in payments on the two bonds is

$$\sum_{i=1}^{n}\left[ RP_{0,t_i} - R^*\,F_{0,t_i}\,P_{0,t_i}/x_0 \right] + P_{0,t_n}\left(1 - F_{0,t_n}/x_0\right) = 0$$

The division by $x_0$ accounts for the fact that a \$1 bond is equivalent to $1/x_0$ bonds with a par value of 1 unit of the foreign currency. The dollar coupon in this case is

$$R = \frac{\sum_{i=1}^{n} P_{0,t_i} R^*\,F_{0,t_i}/x_0 + P_{0,t_n}\left(F_{0,t_n}/x_0 - 1\right)}{\sum_{i=1}^{n} P_{0,t_i}} \qquad (9)$$

The fixed payment, $R$, is the dollar equivalent of the foreign coupon plus the amortized value of the difference in the maturity payments of the two bonds.

## Other Currency Swaps

There are other kinds of currency swaps. The preceding examples assumed that all borrowing was fixed rate. Suppose the dollar-based borrower issues a euro-denominated loan with a *floating* interest rate. In this case there are two future unknowns: the exchange rate at which interest payments are converted, and—because the bond is floating rate—the amount of the interest payment. Swapping this loan to a dollar loan is still straightforward, however; we just require one extra hedging transaction.

We first convert the floating interest rate into a fixed interest rate with a *euro* interest rate swap. The resulting fixed-rate euro-denominated exposure can then be hedged with currency forwards and converted into dollar interest rate exposure. Given the assumptions in Table 6, the euro-denominated loan would swap to a 3.5% floating-rate loan. From that point on, we are in the same position as in the previous example.

In general, we can swap fixed-to-fixed, fixed-to-floating, floating-to-fixed, and floating-to-floating. The analysis is similar in all cases.

One kind of swap that might on its face seem similar is a **diff swap**, short for differential swap. In this kind of swap, payments are made based on the difference in floating interest rates in two different currencies, with the notional amount in a single currency. For example, we might have a swap with a $10m notional amount, but the swap would pay in dollars, based on the difference in a euro-denominated interest rate and a dollar-denominated interest rate. If the short-term euro interest rate rises from 3.5% to 3.8% with the dollar rate unchanged, the annual swap payment would be 30 basis points on $10m, or $30,000. This is like a standard interest rate swap, only for a diff swap, the reference interest rates are denominated in different currencies.

Standard currency forward contracts cannot be used to hedge a diff swap. The problem is that we can hedge the change in the foreign interest rate, but doing so requires a transaction denominated in the foreign currency. We can't easily hedge the exchange rate at which the value of the interest rate change is converted *because we don't know in advance how much currency will need to be converted.* In effect there is quantity uncertainty regarding the foreign currency to be converted. The diff swap is an example of a quanto swap.

**END OPTIONAL SEGMENT**

---

## 4    COMMODITY SWAPS

At the beginning of this reading we looked at a simple two-date commodity swap. Now we will look at commodity swaps more generally, present the general formula for a commodity swap—showing that the formula is exactly the same as for an interest rate swap—and look at some ways the swap structure can be modified.

### The Commodity Swap Price

The idea of a commodity swap, as discussed in Section 1, is that we use information in the commodity forward curve to fix a commodity price over a period of time. We can derive the swap price following the same logic as before.

Think about the position of the market-maker, who we suppose receives the fixed payment, $\bar{F}$, makes the floating payment, and hedges the risk of the floating payment. If there are $n$ swap payments, the resulting hedged cash flow is

$$\text{Hedged cash flow for payment } i = \bar{F} - F_{0,t_i}$$

With competitive market-makers, the present value of the net *hedged* swap payments will be zero (ignoring bid-ask spreads):

$$\sum_{i=1}^{n} P(0, t_i)\left(\bar{F} - F_{0,t_i}\right) \tag{10}$$

As before, $P(0, t_i)$ is the price of a zero-coupon bond paying \$1 at time $t_i$. Equation 10 implies that the present value of the swap payments equals the present value of the forward curve:

$$\bar{F} \sum_{i=1}^{n} P\left(0, t_i\right) = \sum_{i=1}^{n} P\left(0, t_i\right) F_{0,t_i}$$

Solving for the swap price, we obtain

$$\bar{F} = \frac{\sum_{i=1}^{n} P\left(0, t_i\right) F_{0,t_i}}{\sum_{i=1}^{n} P\left(0, t_i\right)} \qquad \text{(11)}$$

Compare Equation 11 with Equation 2 for an interest rate swap. *They are the same formula, except that the interest swap rate is a weighted average of implied forward interest rates and the commodity swap price is a weighted average of commodity forward prices.*

Because of seasonality in both price and quantity, natural gas provides an interesting context for examining commodity swaps. The swap curves for June 2002 and June 2004, computed using Equation 11, are plotted in Figure 7.

**Figure 7**

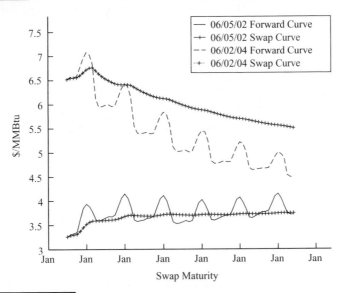

Six-year swap curves for June 5, 2002, and June 2, 2004, based on Henry Hub Natural Gas Futures and interest rates from Eurodollar futures. Each point on the swap curve represents the fixed price for a swap terminating in that month.
*Source*: Futures prices from Datastream.

## Swaps with Variable Quantity and Price

It might make sense for a gas buyer with seasonally varying demand (for example, someone buying gas for heating) to enter into a swap in which quantities vary over time. For example, a buyer might want three times the quantity in the winter months as in the summer months. A buyer also might be willing to fix different prices in different seasons—for example, if there is seasonal variation in the price of the output produced using gas as an input. How do we determine the swap price with seasonally varying quantities?

Let $Q_{ti}$ denote the quantity of gas purchased at time $t_i$. Once again, we can think about this from the perspective of the competitive market-maker. The market-maker who hedges the swap will enter into varying quantities of forward contracts in different months to match the variable quantity called for in the swap. The zero-profit condition is still that the fixed and floating payments have zero present value, only in this case they must be weighted by the appropriate quantities. Thus, we have

$$\sum_{i=1}^{n} P\left(0, t_i\right) Q_{t_i}\left(\overline{F} - F_{0, t_i}\right)$$

The swap price is thus

$$\overline{F} = \frac{\sum_{i=1}^{n} Q_{t_i} P\left(0, t_i\right) F_{0, t_i}}{\sum_{i=1}^{n} Q_{t_i} P\left(0, t_i\right)} \qquad (12)$$

This equation makes perfect sense: If we are going to buy more gas when the forward price is high, we have to weight more heavily the forward price in those months. When $Q_t = 1$, the formula is the same as Equation 11, when the quantity is not varying.

We can also permit prices to be time-varying. If we let the summer swap price be denoted by $\overline{F}_s$ and the winter price by $\overline{F}_w$, then the summer and winter swap prices can be any prices that satisfy the market-maker's zero present value condition:

$$\overline{F}_s \sum_{i\,\varepsilon\,\text{summer}} P\left(0, t_i\right) Q_{t_i} + \overline{F}_w \sum_{i\,\varepsilon\,\text{winter}} P\left(0, t_i\right) Q_{t_i}$$

$$= \sum_{i\,\varepsilon\,\text{summer}} P\left(0, t_i\right) Q_{t_i} F_{0, t_i} + \sum_{i\,\varepsilon\,\text{winter}} P\left(0, t_i\right) Q_{t_i} F_{0, t_i}$$

The notations $i\,\varepsilon$ summer and $i\,\varepsilon$ winter mean to sum over only the months in those seasons. This gives us one equation and two unknowns, $\overline{F}_w$ and $\overline{F}_s$. Once we fix one of the two prices, the equation will give us the other.

OPTIONAL
SEGMENT

**5**

# SWAPTIONS

An option to enter into a swap is called a **swaption**. We can see how a swaption works by returning to the two-date oil swap example in Section 1. The 2-year oil swap price was $20.483. Suppose we are willing to buy oil at $20.483/barrel, but we would like to speculate on the swap price being even lower over the next 3 months.

Consider the following contract: If in 3 months the fixed price for a swap commencing in 9 months (1 year from today) is $20.483 or above, we enter into the swap, agreeing to pay $20.483 and receive the floating price for 2 years. If, on the other hand, the market swap price is below $20.483, we have no obligation. If the swap price in 3 months is $19.50, for example, we could enter into a swap at that time at the $19.50 price, or we could elect not to enter any swap.

With this contract we are entering into the swap with $20.483 as the swap price only when the market swap price is greater; hence, this contract will have a premium. In this example, we would have purchased a **payer swaption**, since we have the right, but not the obligation, to pay a fixed price of $20.483 for 2 years of oil. The counterparty has sold this swaption.

When exercised, the swaption commits us to transact at multiple times in the future. It is possible to exercise the option and then offset the swap with another swap, converting the stream of swap payments into a certain stream with a fixed present value. Thus, the swaption is analogous to an ordinary option, with the present value of the swap obligations (the price of the prepaid swap) as the underlying asset.

The strike price in this example is $20.483, so we have an at-the-money swaption. We could make the strike price different from $20.483. For example, we could reduce the swaption premium by setting the strike above $20.483.

Swaptions can be American or European, and the terms of the underlying swap—fixed price, floating index, settlement frequency, and tenor—will be precisely specified.

---

**Example 3**

Suppose we enter into a European payer oil swaption with a strike price of $21. The underlying swap commences in 1 year and has two annual settlements. After 3 months, the fixed price on the underlying swap is $21.50. We exercise the option, obligating us to pay $21/barrel for 2 years. If we wish to offset the swap, we can enter into a swap to receive the $21.50 fixed price. In year 1 and year 2 we will then receive $21.50 and pay $21, for a certain net cash flow each year of $0.50. The floating payments cancel.

---

A **receiver swaption** gives you the right to pay the floating price and receive the fixed strike price. Thus, the holder of a receiver swaption would exercise when the fixed swap price is below the strike.

Although we have used a commodity swaption in this example, an interest rate or currency swaption would be analogous, with payer and receiver swaptions giving the right to pay or receive the fixed interest rate.

# TOTAL RETURN SWAPS

**6**

A **total return swap** is a swap in which one party pays the realized total return (dividends plus capital gains) on a reference asset, and the other party pays a floating return such as LIBOR. The two parties exchange only the difference between these rates. The party paying the return on the reference asset is the *total return payer.*

As with other swaps, there are multiple settlement dates over the life of the swap. The cumulative effect for the total return payer is of being short the reference asset and long an asset paying the floating rate. The cash flows on a total return swap are illustrated in Figure 8.

---

**Figure 8**

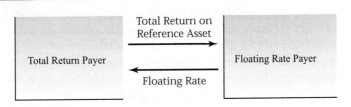

Cash flows for a total return swap. The total return payer pays the per-period total return on the reference asset, receiving the floating rate from the counterparty.

### Example 4

ABC Asset Management has a $2 billion investment in the S&P stock index. However, fund managers have become pessimistic about the market and would like to reduce their exposure to stocks from $2 billion to $1 billion. One way to do this is to sell $1 billion of stocks. However, the fund can retain the stock position but financially transfer the return of the stocks by engaging in a total return swap, obligating the fund to pay the total return (dividends plus capital gains) on the swapped stocks, while receiving a floating-rate return such as LIBOR on the swapped $1 billion notional amount. This avoids the transaction costs of a sale of physical stock.

Table 7 illustrates the payments on such a swap. In year 1, ABC earns 6.5% on the S&P index. However, on the portion it has swapped, it must pay the 6.5% in exchange for the 7.2% floating rate. The net payment of 0.7% leaves ABC as well off as if it had sold the index and invested in an asset paying the floating rate. In year 2, ABC receives 18%, compensating it for the difference between the 7.5% floating return and the 10.5% loss on the S&P index. Finally, in year 3 the S&P index does well, and ABC pays 16.5% to the counterparty.

### Table 7

Illustration of cash flows on a total return swap with annual settlement for 3 years.

| Year | S&P Capital Gain | S&P Dividend | Floating Rate | Net Payment to Total Return Payer |
|------|------------------|--------------|---------------|-----------------------------------|
| 1 | 5% | 1.5% | 7.2% | 0.7% |
| 2 | −12% | 1.5% | 7.5% | 18.0% |
| 3 | 22% | 1.5% | 7.0% | −16.5% |

You might wonder about the economics of a swap like this. The stock index on average earns a higher return than LIBOR. So if the fund swaps the stock index in exchange for LIBOR, it will on average make payments to the counterparty.

This observation is correct, but notice that the fund is paying the difference between the index return and a short-term interest rate—this difference is the risk premium on the index.

The average loss associated with swapping a stock index for LIBOR is the same as the average loss associated with selling the stock and buying a floating-rate note paying LIBOR. It is just that the swap makes the loss obvious since it requires a payment.

Some investors have used total return swaps to avoid taxes on foreign stocks. In many cases, countries impose withholding taxes on foreign investors, meaning that if a firm in country A pays a dividend, for example, country A withholds a fraction of that dividend from investors based in country B. A total return swap enables a country-B investor to own country-A stocks without physically holding them, and thus in many cases without having to pay withholding taxes. For example, a U.S. investor could first swap out of a U.S. stock index and then swap into a European stock index, effectively becoming the counterparty for a European investor wanting to swap out of European stock exposure. Because net swap payments are not always recognized by withholding rules, this transaction can be more tax-efficient than holding the foreign stocks directly.

Another use of total return swaps is the management of credit risk. A fund manager holding corporate debt can swap the return on a particular bond for a floating-rate return. If the company that issued the bond goes bankrupt, the debt holder receives a payment on the swap compensating for the fact that the bond is worth a fraction of its face value.

If you think about this use of total return swaps, it is a crude tool for managing credit risk specifically. The problem is that bond prices also change due to interest rate changes. A corporate bond holder might wish to retain interest rate risk but not bankruptcy risk. Thus, there are products called **default swaps**. These are essentially default options, in which the buyer pays a premium, usually amortized over a series of payments. If the reference asset experiences a "credit event" (for example, a failure to make a scheduled payment on a particular bond or class of bonds), then the seller makes a payment to the buyer. Frequently these contracts split the return on the bond into the portion due to interest rate changes (with Treasury securities used as a reference) and the portion due to credit quality changes, with the swap making payments based only on the latter.

END OPTIONAL SEGMENT

## SUMMARY

A swap is a contract calling for an exchange of payments, on one or more dates, determined by the difference in two prices. A single-payment swap is the same thing as a cash-settled forward contract. In the simplest swaps, a fixed payment is periodically exchanged for a floating payment. A firm can use a swap to lock in a long-term commodity price, a fixed interest rate, or a fixed exchange rate. Considering only the present value of cash flows, the same result is obtained using a strip of forward contracts and swaps. The difference is that hedging with a strip of forward contracts results in net payments that are time-varying. In contrast, hedging with a swap results in net payments that are constant over time. The value of a swap is zero at inception, though as swap payments are made over time, the value of the swap can change in a predictable way.

The fixed price in a swap is a weighted average of the corresponding forward prices. The swap formulas in different cases all take the same general form. Let $f_0(t_i)$ denote the forward price for the floating payment in the swap. Then the fixed swap payment is

$$R = \frac{\sum_{i=1}^{n} P(0, t_i) f_0(t_i)}{\sum_{i=1}^{n} P(0, t_i)} \tag{13}$$

Table 8 summarizes the substitutions to make in Equation 13 to get the various swap formulas shown in the reading. This formula can be generalized to permit time variation in the notional amount and the swap price, and the swap can start on a deferred basis.

---

**Table 8**

Equivalent forms of the swap-rate calculation. For the currency swap, $F_{0,t\,i}$ is the forward price for the foreign currency. For the commodity swap, $F_{0,t\,i}$ is the forward price for the commodity.

| To Obtain Formula for | Substitute in Equation 13 | Equation in Reading |
|---|---|---|
| Interest rate swap | $f_0(t_i) = r_0(t_{i-1}, t_i)$ | Equation 2 |
| Currency swap (annuity) | $f_0(t_i) = R^* F_{0,t_i}$ | Equation 8 |
| Commodity swap | $f_0(t_i) = F_{0,t_i}$ | Equation 11 |

An important characteristic of swaps is that they require only the exchange of net payments, and not the payment of principal. So if a firm enters an interest rate swap, for example, it is required only to make payments based on the difference in interest rates, not on the underlying principal. As a result, swaps have less credit risk than bonds.

Total return swaps involve exchanging the return on an asset for a floating rate such as LIBOR. The term *swap* is also used to describe agreements like the Procter & Gamble swap (page 157), which required payments based on the difference in interest rates and bond prices, as well as default swaps.

# PRACTICE PROBLEMS FOR READING 32

1. Consider the oil swap example in Section 1 with the 1- and 2-year forward prices of $22/barrel and $23/barrel. The 1- and 2-year interest rates are 6% and 6.5%. Verify that the new 2-year swap price is $22.483.

2. Suppose that oil forward prices for 1 year, 2 years, and 3 years are $20, $21, and $22. The 1-year effective annual interest rate is 6.0%, the 2-year interest rate is 6.5%, and the 3-year interest rate is 7.0%.

   A. What is the 3-year swap price?

   B. What is the price of a 2-year swap beginning in one year? (That is, the first swap settlement will be in 2 years and the second in 3 years.)

3. Consider the same 3-year oil swap. Suppose a dealer is paying the fixed price and receiving floating. What position in oil forward contracts will hedge oil price risk in this position? Verify that the present value of the locked-in net cash flows is zero.

4. Consider the 3-year swap in the previous example. Suppose you are the fixed-rate payer in the swap. How much have you overpaid relative to the forward price after the first swap settlement? What is the cumulative overpayment after the second swap settlement? Verify that the cumulative overpayment is zero after the third payment. (Be sure to account for interest.)

5. Consider the same 3-year swap. Suppose you are a dealer who is paying the fixed oil price and receiving the floating price. Suppose that you enter into the swap and immediately thereafter all interest rates rise 50 basis points (oil forward prices are unchanged). What happens to the value of your swap position? What if interest rates fall 50 basis points? What hedging instrument would have protected you against interest rate risk in this position?

# SOLUTIONS FOR READING 32

1. We first solve for the present value of the cost per two barrels:

$$\frac{\$22}{1.06} + \frac{\$23}{(1.065)^2} = 41.033$$

We then obtain the swap price per barrel by solving:

$$\frac{x}{1.06} + \frac{x}{(1.065)^2} = 41.033$$
$$\Leftrightarrow \quad x = 22.483$$

which was to be shown.

2. **A.** We first solve for the present value of the cost per three barrels, based on the forward prices:

$$\frac{\$20}{1.06} + \frac{\$21}{(1.065)^2} + \frac{\$22}{(1.07)^3} = 55.3413$$

We then obtain the swap price per barrel by solving:

$$\frac{x}{1.06} + \frac{x}{(1.065)^2} + \frac{x}{(1.07)^3} = 55.341$$
$$\Leftrightarrow \quad x = 20.9519$$

**B.** We first solve for the present value of the cost per two barrels (year 2 and year 3):

$$\frac{\$21}{(1.065)^2} + \frac{\$22}{(1.07)^3} = 36.473$$

We then obtain the swap price per barrel by solving:

$$\frac{x}{(1.065)^2} + \frac{x}{(1.07)^3} = 36.473$$
$$\Leftrightarrow \quad x = 21.481$$

3. Since the dealer is paying fixed and receiving floating, she generates the cash-flows depicted in column 2. Suppose that the dealer enters into three short forward positions, one contract for each year of the active swap. Her payoffs are depicted in column 3, and the aggregate net cash flow position is in column 4.

| Year | Net Swap Payment | Short Forwards | Net Position |
|------|------------------|----------------|--------------|
| 1 | $S_1 - \$20.9519$ | $\$20 - S_1$ | −0.9519 |
| 2 | $S_2 - \$20.9519$ | $\$21 - S_2$ | +0.0481 |
| 3 | $S_3 - \$20.9519$ | $\$22 - S_3$ | +1.0481 |

We need to discount the net positions to year zero. We have:

$$PV(netC\,F) = \frac{-0.9519}{1.06} + \frac{0.0481}{(1.065)^2} + \frac{1.0481}{(1.07)^3} = 0$$

Indeed, the present value of the net cash flow is zero.

4. The fair swap rate was determined to be $20.952. Therefore, compared to the forward curve price of $20 in one year, we are overpaying $0.952. In year two, this overpayment has increased to $0.952 × 1.070024 = 1.01866, where we used the appropriate forward rate to calculate the interest payment. In year two, we underpay by $0.048, so that our total accumulative overpayment is $0.97066. In year three, this overpayment has increased again to $0.97066 × 1.08007 = 1.048. However, in year three, we receive a fixed payment of $20.952, which underpays relative to the forward curve price of $22 by $22 − $20.952 = 1.048. Therefore, our cumulative balance is indeed zero, which was to be shown.

5. Since the dealer is paying fixed and receiving floating, she generates the cash-flows depicted in column 2. Suppose that the dealer enters into three short forward positions, one contract for each year of the active swap. Her payoffs are depicted in column 3, and the aggregate net position is summarized in column 4.

| Year | Net Swap Payment | Short Forwards | Net Position |
|------|------------------|----------------|--------------|
| 1 | $S_1$ − $20.952 | $20 − $S_1$ | −0.952 |
| 2 | $S_1$ − $20.952 | $21 − $S_1$ | +0.048 |
| 3 | $S_1$ − $20.952 | $22 − $S_1$ | +1.048 |

We need to discount the net positions to year zero, taking into account the uniform shift of the term structure. We have:

$$PV\left(netC\ F\right) = \frac{-0.9519}{1.065} + \frac{0.0481}{\left(1.07\right)^2} + \frac{1.0481}{\left(1.075\right)^3} = -0.0081$$

The present value of the net cash flow is negative: The dealer never recovers from the increased interest rate he faces on the overpayment of the first swap payment.

$$PV\left(netC\ F\right) = \frac{-0.9519}{1.055} + \frac{0.0481}{\left(1.06\right)^2} + \frac{1.0481}{\left(1.065\right)^3} = +0.0083$$

The present value of the net cash flow is positive. The dealer makes money, because he gets a favorable interest rate on the loan he needs to take to finance the first overpayment.

The dealer could have tried to hedge his exposure with a forward rate agreement or any other derivative protecting against interest rate risk.

| Index | | | |
|---|---|---|---|
| Seoul | | | |
| Johan. (Comp) | | | |
| Mumbai | | | |
| Singapore | | | |
| Sydney | | | |
| Shanghai B | 2971.0 | 1.1% | |
| Hong Kong | 4644.0 | 0.9% | −10.5% |
| Toronto | 316.8 | 0.7% | −6.9% |
| Stockholm | 22,700.9 | 0.5% | −4.2% |
| Mexico City | 13,524.8 | 0.1% | 4.1% |

# 33

# Commodity Forwards and Futures

*by Robert L. McDonald*

## LEARNING OUTCOMES

| Mastery | The candidate should be able to: |
|---|---|
| ☐ | **a** discuss pricing factors for commodity forwards and futures, including storability, storage costs, production and demand, and explain their influence on lease rates and the forward curve; |
| ☐ | **b** identify and explain how to exploit arbitrage situations that result from the convenience yield of a commodity and from commodity spreads across related commodities; |
| ☐ | **c** compare the basis risk of commodity futures with that of financial futures. |

Tolstoy observed that all happy families are all alike; each unhappy family is unhappy in its own way. An analogous idea in financial markets might be: Financial forwards are all alike; each commodity forward, however, has some unique economic characteristic that must be understood in order to appreciate forward pricing in that market. In this reading we will see how commodity forwards and futures differ from, and are similar to, financial forwards and futures.

In our discussion of forward pricing for financial assets we relied heavily on the fact that for financial assets, the price of the asset today is the present value of the asset at time $T$, less the value of dividends to be received between now and time $T$. We will explore the extent to which this relationship also is true for commodities.

## INTRODUCTION TO COMMODITY FORWARDS

**1**

Consider the formula for a forward price on a financial asset:

$$F_{0,T} = S_0 e^{(r-\delta)T} \tag{1}$$

where $S_0$ is the spot price of the asset, $r$ is the continuously compounded interest rate, and $\delta$ is the continuous dividend yield on the asset. The difference between the forward price and spot price reflects the cost and benefits of delaying payment for, and receipt of, the asset. In this reading we treat forward and futures prices as the same.

On any given day, for many commodities there are futures contracts available that expire in a number of different months. The set of prices for different expiration dates for a given commodity is called the **forward curve** or the **forward strip** for that date. Table 1 displays futures prices with up to 6 months to maturity for several commodities. Let's consider these prices and try to interpret them using Equation 1. To provide a reference interest rate, 3-month LIBOR on May 5, 2004, was 1.22%, or about 0.3% for 3 months. From May to July, the forward price of corn rose from 314.25 to 319.75. This is a 2-month increase of 319.75/314.25 − 1 = 1.75%, an annual rate of approximately 11%, far in excess of the 1.22% annual interest rate. In the context of the formula for pricing financial forwards, Equation 1, we would need to have a continuous dividend yield, $\delta$, of −9.19% in order to explain this rise in the forward price over time.

In that case, we would have

$$F_{\text{July}} = 314.25e^{[0.0122-(-0.0919)]\times(1/6)} = 319.75$$

How do we interpret a negative dividend yield?

**Table 1**

Futures prices for various commodities, May 5, 2004. Corn and soybeans are from the CBOT and unleaded gasoline, oil, and gold from NYMEX.

| Expiration Month | Corn (Cents/ Bushel) | Soybeans (Cents/ Bushel) | Gasoline (Cents/ Gallon) | Crude Oil (Dollars/ Barrel) | Gold (Dollars/ Ounce) |
|---|---|---|---|---|---|
| May | 314.25 | 1034.50 | — | — | 393.40 |
| June | — | — | 131.25 | 39.57 | 393.80 |
| July | 319.75 | 1020.00 | 127.15 | 39.36 | 394.30 |
| August | — | 959.00 | 122.32 | 38.79 | 394.80 |
| September | 316.75 | 845.50 | 116.57 | 38.13 | — |
| October | — | — | 109.64 | 37.56 | 395.90 |
| November | — | 786.50 | 105.49 | 37.04 | — |

*Source*: Futures data from Datastream.

Perhaps even more puzzling, given our discussion of financial futures, is the subsequent drop in the corn futures price from July to September, and the behavior of soybean, gasoline, and crude oil prices, which all decline with time to expiration. It is possible to tell plausible stories about this behavior. Corn and soybeans are harvested over the summer, so perhaps the expected increase in supply accounts for the reduction over time in the futures price. In May 2004, the war in Iraq had driven crude oil prices to high levels. We might guess that producers would respond by increasing supply and consumers by reducing demand, resulting in lower expected oil prices in subsequent months. Gasoline is distilled from oil, so gasoline prices might behave similarly. Finally, in contrast to the behavior of the other commodities, gold prices rise steadily over time at a rate close to the interest rate.

It seems that we can tell stories about the behavior of forward prices over time. But how do we reconcile these explanations with our understanding of financial forwards, in which forward prices depend on the interest rate and dividends, and explicit expectations of future prices do not enter the forward price formula?

The behavior of forward prices can vary over time. Two terms often used by commodity traders are **contango** and **backwardation**. If on a given date the forward curve is upward-sloping—i.e., forward prices more distant in time are higher—then we say the market is in contango. We observe this pattern with gold in Table 1. If the forward curve is downward sloping, as with gasoline, we say the market is in backwardation. Forward curves can have portions in backwardation and portions in contango, as does that for corn.

It would take an entire book to cover commodities in depth. Our goal here is to understand the *logic* of forward pricing for commodities and where it differs from the logic of financial forward pricing. What is the forward curve telling us about the market for the commodity?

## EQUILIBRIUM PRICING OF COMMODITY FORWARDS

**2**

As with forward prices on financial assets, commodity forward prices are the result of a present value calculation. To understand this, it is helpful to consider synthetic commodities.

Just as we could create a synthetic stock with a stock forward contract and a zero-coupon bond, we can also create a synthetic commodity by combining a forward contract with a zero-coupon bond. Consider the following investment strategy: Enter into a long commodity forward contract at the price $F_{0,T}$ and buy a zero-coupon bond that pays $F_{0,T}$ at time $T$. Since the forward contract is costless, the cost of this investment strategy at time 0 is just the cost of the bond, or

$$\text{Time 0 cash flow} = -e^{-rT} F_{0,T} \tag{2}$$

At time $T$, the strategy pays

$$\underbrace{S_T - F_{0,T}}_{\text{Forward contract payoff}} + \underbrace{F_{0,T}}_{\text{Bond payoff}} = S_T$$

where $S_T$ is the time $T$ price of the commodity. This investment strategy creates a *synthetic commodity*, in that it has the same value as a unit of the commodity at time $T$. Note that, from Equation 2, the cost of the synthetic commodity is the prepaid forward price, $e^{-rT} F_{0,T}$.

Valuing a synthetic commodity is easy if we can see the forward price. Suppose, however, that we do not know the forward price. Computing the time 0 value of a unit of the commodity received at time $T$ is a standard problem: You discount the expected commodity price to determine its value today. Let $E_0(S_T)$ denote the expected time-$T$ price as of time 0, and let $\alpha$ denote the appropriate discount rate for a time-$T$ cash flow of $S_T$. Then the present value is

$$E_0(S_T)e^{-\alpha T} \tag{3}$$

The important point is that *Equations 2 and 3 represent the same value*. Both reflect what you would pay today to receive one unit of the commodity at time $T$. Equating the two expressions, we have

$$e^{-rT} F_{0,T} = E_0(S_T)e^{-\alpha T} \tag{4}$$

Rearranging this equation, we can write the forward price as

$$F_{0,T} = e^{rT} E_0 \left( S_T \right) e^{-\alpha T}$$
$$= E_0 \left( S_T \right) e^{(r-\alpha)T} \tag{5}$$

Equation 5 demonstrates the link between the expected commodity price, $E_0(S_T)$, and the forward price. As with financial forwards, the forward price is a biased estimate of the expected spot price, $E_0(S_T)$, with the bias due to the risk premium on the commodity, $\alpha - r$.[1]

Equation 4 deserves emphasis: *The time-T forward price discounted at the risk-free rate back to time 0 is the present value of a unit of commodity received at time T.* This calculation is useful when performing NPV calculations involving commodities for which forward prices are available. Thus, for example, an industrial producer who buys oil can calculate the present value of future oil costs by discounting oil forward prices at the risk-free rate. The present value of future oil costs is not dependent upon whether or not the producer hedges. We will see an example of this calculation later in the reading.

If a commodity cannot be physically stored, the no-arbitrage pricing principles cannot be used to obtain a forward price. Without storage, Equation 5 determines the forward price. However, it is difficult to implement this formula, which requires forecasting the expected future spot price and estimating $\alpha$. Moreover, even when physically possible, storage may be costly. Given the difficulties of pricing commodity forwards, our goal will be to interpret forward prices and to understand the economics of different commodity markets.

In the rest of the reading, we will further explore similarities and differences between forward prices for commodities and financial assets. Some of the most important differences have to do with storage: whether the commodity can be stored and, if so, how costly it is to store. The next section provides an example of forward prices when a commodity cannot be stored.

## 3    NONSTORABILITY: ELECTRICITY

The forward market for electricity illustrates forward pricing when storage is not possible. Electricity is produced in different ways: from fuels such as coal and natural gas, or from nuclear power, hydroelectric power, wind power, or solar power. Once it is produced, electricity is transmitted over the power grid to end-users. Electricity has characteristics that distinguish it not only from financial assets, but from other commodities as well. What is special about electricity?

First, electricity is difficult to store, hence it must be consumed when it is produced or else it is wasted.[2] Second, at any point in time the maximum supply of electricity is fixed. You can produce less but not more. Third, demand for electricity varies substantially by season, by day of week, and by time of day.

---

**1** Historical commodity and futures data, necessary to estimate expected commodity returns, are relatively hard to obtain. Bodie and Rosansky (1980) examine quarterly futures returns from 1950 to 1976, while Gorton and Rouwenhorst (2004) examine monthly futures returns from 1959 to 2004. Both studies construct portfolios of synthetic commodities—T-bills plus commodity futures—and find that these portfolios earn the same average return as stocks, are on average negatively correlated with stocks, and are positively correlated with inflation. These findings imply that a portfolio of stock and synthetic commodities would have the same expected return and less risk than a diversified stock portfolio alone.
**2** There are ways to store electricity. For example, it is possible to use excess electricity to pump water uphill and then, at a later time, release it to generate electricity. Storage is uncommon, expensive, and entails losses, however.

To illustrate the effects of nonstorability, Table 2 displays 1-day ahead hourly prices for 1 megawatt-hour of electricity in New York City. The 1-day ahead forward price is $28.37 at 3 A.M., and $62.71 at 3 P.M. Since you have learned about arbitrage, you are possibly thinking that you would like to buy electricity at the 3 A.M. price and sell it at the 3 P.M. price. However, there is no way to do so. Because electricity cannot be stored, its price is set by demand and supply at a point in time. There is also no way to buy winter electricity and sell it in the summer, so there are seasonal variations as well as intraday variations. Because of peak-load plants that operate only when prices are high, power suppliers are able to temporarily increase the supply of electricity. However, expectations about supply are already reflected in the forward price.

Given these characteristics of electricity, what does the electricity forward price represent? The prices in Table 2 are best interpreted using Equation 5. The large price swings over the day primarily reflect changes in the expected spot price, which in turn reflects changes in demand over the day.

| Table 2 | | | | | | | |

Day-ahead price, by hour, for 1 megawatt-hour of electricity in New York City, September 7, 2004.

| Time | Price | Time | Price | Time | Price | Time | Price |
|------|-------|------|-------|------|-------|------|-------|
| 0000 | $35.68 | 0600 | $40.03 | 1200 | $61.46 | 1800 | $57.81 |
| 0100 | $31.59 | 0700 | $49.64 | 1300 | $61.47 | 1900 | $62.18 |
| 0200 | $29.85 | 0800 | $53.48 | 1400 | $61.74 | 2000 | $60.12 |
| 0300 | $28.37 | 0900 | $57.15 | 1500 | $62.71 | 2100 | $54.25 |
| 0400 | $28.75 | 1000 | $59.04 | 1600 | $62.68 | 2200 | $52.89 |
| 0500 | $33.57 | 1100 | $61.45 | 1700 | $60.28 | 2300 | $45.56 |

*Source*: Bloomberg.

Notice two things. First, the swings in Table 2 could not occur with financial assets, which are stored. (It is so obvious that financial assets are stored that we usually don't mention it.) As a consequence, the 3 A.M. and 3 P.M. forward prices for a stock will be almost identical. If they were not, it would be possible to engage in arbitrage, buying low at 3 A.M. and selling high at 3 P.M. Second, whereas the forward price for a stock is largely redundant in the sense that it reflects information about the current stock price, interest, and the dividend yield, the forward prices in Table 2 provide information we could not otherwise obtain, revealing information about the future price of the commodity. This illustrates the forward market providing **price discovery**, with forward prices revealing information, not otherwise obtainable, about the future price of the commodity.

## PRICING COMMODITY FORWARDS BY ARBITRAGE: AN EXAMPLE                    **4**

Electricity represents the extreme of nonstorability. However, many commodities are storable. To see the effects of storage, we now consider the very simple, hypothetical example of a forward contract for pencils. We use pencils as an example because they are familiar and you will have no preconceptions about how such a forward should work, because it does not exist.

Suppose that pencils cost $0.20 today and for certain will cost $0.20 in 1 year. The economics of this assumption are simple. Pencil manufacturers produce pencils from wood and other inputs. If the price of a pencil is greater than the cost of production, more pencils are produced, driving down the market price. If the price falls, fewer pencils are produced and the price rises. The market price of pencils thus reflects the cost of production. An economist would say that the supply of pencils is *perfectly elastic*.

There is nothing inherently inconsistent about assuming that the pencil price is expected to stay the same. However, before we proceed, note that a constant price would *not* be a reasonable assumption about the price of a nondividend-paying stock. A nondividend-paying stock must be expected to appreciate, or else no one would own it. At the outset, there is an obvious difference between this commodity and a financial asset.

One way to describe this difference between the pencil and the stock is to say that, in equilibrium, stocks and other financial assets must be held by investors, or *stored*. This is why the stock price appreciates on average; appreciation is necessary for investors to willingly store the stock.

The pencil, by contrast, need not be stored. The equilibrium condition for pencils requires that price equals marginal production cost. This distinction between a storage and production equilibrium is a central concept in our discussion of commodities.[3]

Now suppose that the continuously compounded interest rate is 10%. What is the forward price for a pencil to be delivered in 1 year? Before reading any further, you should stop and decide what you think the answer is. (Really. Please stop and think about it!)

One obvious possible answer to this question, drawing on our discussion of financial forwards, is that the forward price should be the future value of the pencil price: $e^{0.1} \times \$0.20 = \$0.2210$. However, *common sense suggests that this cannot be the correct answer*. You *know* that the pencil price in one year will be $0.20. If you entered into a forward agreement to buy a pencil for $0.221, you would feel foolish in a year when the price was only $0.20.

Common sense also rules out the forward price being less than $0.20. Consider the forward seller. No one would agree to sell a pencil for a forward price of less than $0.20, knowing that the price will be $0.20.

Thus, it seems as if both the buyer and seller perspective lead us to the conclusion that the forward price must be $0.20.

## An Apparent Arbitrage and Resolution

If the forward price is $0.20, is there an arbitrage opportunity? Suppose you believe that the $0.20 forward price is too low. You would want to buy the pencil forward and short-sell a pencil. Table 3 depicts the cash flows in this reverse cash-and-carry arbitrage. The result seems to show that there is an arbitrage opportunity.

We seem to have reached an impasse. Common sense suggests a forward price of $0.20, but the application in Table 3 of our formulas suggests that any forward price less than $0.221 leads to an arbitrage opportunity, where we would make $\$0.221 - F_{0,1}$ per pencil.

Once again it is time to stop and think before proceeding. Examine Table 3 closely; there is a problem.

---

**3** You may be thinking that you have pencils in your desk and therefore you do, in fact, store pencils. However, you are storing them to save yourself the inconvenience of going to the store each time you need a new one, not because you expect pencils to be a good financial investment akin to stock. When storing pencils for convenience, you will store only a few at a time. Thus, for the moment, suppose that no one stores pencils. We return to the concept of storing for convenience in Section 6.

The arbitrage assumes that you can short-sell a pencil by borrowing it today and returning it in a year. However, recall that pencils cost $0.20 today and will cost $0.20 in a year. Borrowing one pencil and returning one pencil in a year is an interest-free loan of $0.20. *No one will lend you the pencil without charging you an additional fee.*

If you are to short-sell, there must be someone who is both holding the asset and willing to give up physical possession for the period of the short-sale. Unlike stock, nobody holds pencils in a brokerage account. It is straightforward to borrow a financial asset and return it later, in the interim paying dividends to the owner. However, if you borrow an unused pencil and return an unused pencil at some later date, the owner of the pencil loses interest for the duration of the pencil loan since the pencil price does not change.

### Table 3

Apparent reverse cash-and-carry arbitrage for a pencil. These calculations *appear* to demonstrate that there is an arbitrage opportunity if the pencil forward price is below $0.221. However, there is a logical error in the table.

| | Cash Flows | |
| --- | --- | --- |
| **Transaction** | **Time 0** | **Time 1** |
| Long forward @ $0.20 | 0 | $0.20 - F_{0,1}$ |
| Short-sell pencil | +$0.20 | -$0.20 |
| Lend short-sale proceeds @ 10% | -$0.20 | $0.221 |
| **Total** | 0 | $0.221 - F_{0,1}$ |

Thus, *the apparent arbitrage in the above table has nothing at all to do with forward contracts on pencils.* If you find someone willing to lend you pencils for a year, you should borrow as many as you can and invest the proceeds in T-bills. You will earn the interest rate and pay nothing to borrow the money.

You might object that pencils do provide a flow of services—namely, making marks on paper. However, this service flow requires having physical possession of the pencil and it also uses up the pencil. A stock loaned to a short-seller continues to earn its return; the pencil loaned to the short-seller earns no return for the lender. Consequently, the pencil borrower must make a payment to the lender to compensate the lender for lost time value of money.

## Pencils Have a Positive Lease Rate

How do we correct the arbitrage analysis in Table 3? We have to recognize that the lender of the pencil has invested $0.20 in the pencil. In order to be kept financially whole, *the lender of a pencil will require us to pay interest.* The pencil therefore has a *lease rate* of 10%, since that is the interest rate. With this change, the corrected reverse cash-and-carry arbitrage is in Table 4.

When we correctly account for the lease payment, this transaction no longer earns profits when the forward price is $0.20 or greater. If we turn the arbitrage around, buying the pencil and shorting the forward, the cash-and-carry arbitrage is depicted in Table 5. These calculations show that any forward price greater than $0.221 generates arbitrage profits.

Using no-arbitrage arguments, we have ruled out arbitrage for forward prices less than $0.20 (go long the forward and short-sell the pencil) and greater than $0.221 (go short the forward and long the pencil). However, what if the forward price is between $0.20 and $0.221?

If there is an active lending market for pencils, we can narrow the no-arbitrage price even further: We can demonstrate that the forward price *must* be $0.20. The lease rate of a pencil is 10%. Therefore a pencil *lender* can earn 10% by buying the pencil and lending it. The lease payment for a short seller is a dividend for the lender. Imagine that the forward price is $0.21. We would buy a pencil and sell it forward, *and simultaneously lend the pencil*. To see that this strategy is profitable, examine Table 6.

### Table 4

Reverse cash-and-carry arbitrage for a pencil. This table demonstrates that there is an arbitrage opportunity if the pencil forward price is below $0.20. It differs from Table 3 in properly accounting for lease payments.

| | Cash Flows | |
|---|---|---|
| **Transaction** | **Time 0** | **Time 1** |
| Long forward @ $.20 | 0 | $0.20 − $F_{0,1}$ |
| Short-sell pencil @ lease rate of 10% | +$0.20 | −$0.221 |
| Lend short-sale proceeds @ 10% | −$0.20 | $0.221 |
| **Total** | 0 | $0.20 − $F_{0,1}$ |

### Table 5

Cash-and-carry arbitrage for a pencil, showing that there is an arbitrage opportunity if the forward pencil price exceeds $0.221.

| | Cash Flows | |
|---|---|---|
| **Transaction** | **Time 0** | **Time 1** |
| Short forward @ $.20 | 0 | $F_{0,1}$ − $0.20 |
| Buy pencil @ $.20 | −$0.20 | +$0.20 |
| Borrow @ 10% | +$0.20 | −$0.221 |
| **Total** | 0 | $F_{0,1}$ − $0.221 |

Income from lending the pencil provides the missing piece: Any forward price greater than $0.20 now results in arbitrage profits. Since we also have seen that any forward price less than $0.20 results in arbitrage profits, we have pinned down the forward price as $0.20.

Finally, what about Equation 5, which we claimed holds for all commodities and assets? To apply this equation to the pencil, recognize that the appropriate discount rate, $\alpha$, for a risk-free pencil is $r$, the risk-free rate. Hence, we have

$$F_{0,T} = E_0\left(S_T\right)e^{(r-\alpha)T} = 0.20 \times e^{(0.10-0.10)} = 0.20$$

Thus, Equation 5 gives us the correct answer.

The pencil is obviously a special example, but this discussion establishes the important point that in order to understand arbitrage relationships for commodity forwards, we have to think about the cost of borrowing and income from lending an asset. Borrowing and leasing costs also determine the pricing of financial forwards, but the cash flow associated with borrowing and lending financial assets is the dividend yield, which is readily observable. The commodity analogue to dividend income is *lease income*, which may not be directly observable. We now discuss leasing more generally.

Cash-and-carry arbitrage with pencil lending. When the pencil is loaned, interest is earned and the no-arbitrage price is $0.20.

| Transaction | Cash Flows | |
| --- | --- | --- |
| | Time 0 | Time 1 |
| Short forward @ $0.20 | 0 | $F_{0,1}$ – $0.20 |
| Buy pencil @ $0.20 | –$0.20 | +$0.20 |
| Lend pencil @ 10% | 0 | 0.021 |
| Borrow @ 10% | +$0.20 | –$0.221 |
| **Total** | 0 | $F_{0,1}$ – $0.20 |

# THE COMMODITY LEASE RATE

## 5

The discussion of pencil forwards raises the issue of a lease market. How would such a lease market work in general?

## The Lease Market for a Commodity

Consider again the perspective of a commodity lender, who in the previous discussion required that we pay interest to borrow the pencil. More generally, here is how a lender will think about a commodity loan: "If I lend the commodity, I am giving up possession of a unit worth $S_0$. At time $T$, I will receive a unit worth $S_T$. *I am effectively making an investment of $S_0$ in order to receive the random amount $S_T$.*"

How would you analyze this investment? Suppose that $\alpha$ is the expected return on a stock that has the same risk as the commodity; $\alpha$ is therefore the appropriate discount rate for the cash flow $S_T$. The NPV of the investment is

$$\text{NPV} = E_0\left(S_T\right)e^{-\alpha T} - S_0 \tag{6}$$

Suppose that we expect the commodity price to increase at the rate $g$, so that

$$E_0\left(S_T\right) = S_0 e^{gT}$$

Then from Equation 6, the NPV of the commodity loan, without payments, is

$$\text{NPV} = S_0 e^{(g-\alpha)T} - S_0 \tag{7}$$

If $g < \alpha$, the commodity loan has a negative NPV. However, suppose the lender demands that the borrower return $e^{(\alpha-g)T}$ units of the commodity for each unit borrowed. If one unit is loaned, $e^{(\alpha-g)T}$ units will be returned. This is like a continuous proportional lease payment of $\alpha - g$ to the lender. Thus, the lease rate is the difference between the commodity discount rate and the expected growth rate of the commodity price, or

$$\delta_l = \alpha - g \tag{8}$$

With this payment, the NPV of a commodity loan is

$$\text{NPV} = S_0 e^{(\alpha-g)T} e^{(g-\alpha)T} - S_0 = 0 \tag{9}$$

Now the commodity loan is a fair deal for the lender. The commodity lender must be compensated by the borrower for the opportunity cost associated with lending. When the future pencil price was certain to be \$0.20, the opportunity cost was the risk-free interest rate, 10%.

Note that if $S_T$ were the price of a nondividend-paying stock, its expected rate of appreciation would equal its expected return, so $g = \alpha$ and no payment would be required for the stock loan to be a fair deal.[4] Commodities, however, are produced; as with the pencil, their expected price appreciation need not equal $\alpha$.

## Forward Prices and the Lease Rate

Suppose we have a commodity where there is an active lease market, with the lease rate given by Equation 8. What is the forward price?

The key insight, as in the pencil example, is that *the lease payment is a dividend.* If we borrow the asset, we have to pay the lease rate to the lender, just as with a dividend-paying stock. If we buy the asset and lend it out, we receive the lease payment. Thus, the formula for the forward price with a lease market is

$$F_{0,T} = S_0 e^{(r-\delta_l)T} \tag{10}$$

Tables 7 and 8 verify that this formula is the no-arbitrage price by performing the cash-and-carry and reverse cash-and-carry arbitrages. In both tables we tail the position in order to offset the lease income.

The striking thing about Tables 7 and 8 is that on the surface they are *exactly* like those that depict arbitrage transactions for a dividend-paying stock. In an important sense, however, the two sets of tables are quite different. With the stock, the dividend yield, $\delta$, is an observable characteristic of the stock, reflecting payment received by the owner of the stock *whether or not the stock is loaned.*

With pencils, by contrast, the lease rate, $\delta_l = \alpha - g$, is income earned only if the pencil is loaned. In fact, notice in Tables 7 and 8 that the arbitrageur never stores the commodity! Thus, Equation 10 holds whether or not the commodity can be, or is, stored.

One of the implications of Tables 7 and 8 is that the lease rate has to be consistent with the forward price. Thus, when we observe the forward price, we can infer what the lease rate would have to be if a lease market existed. Specifically, if the forward price is $F_{0,T}$, the annualized lease rate is

$$\delta_l = r - \frac{1}{T} \ln\left(F_{0,T}/S\right) \tag{11}$$

If instead we use an effective annual interest rate, $r$, the effective annual lease rate is

$$\delta_l = \frac{(1+r)}{\left(F_{0,T}/S\right)^{1/T}} - 1 \tag{12}$$

The denominator in this expression annualizes the forward premium.

---

**4** For a nondividend-paying stock, the present value of the future stock price is the current stock price.

| Table 7 |
| --- |

Cash-and-carry arbitrage with a commodity for which the lease rate is $\delta_l$. The implied no-arbitrage restriction is $F_{0,T} \leq S_0 e^{(r-\delta_l)T}$.

| | Cash Flows | |
| --- | --- | --- |
| **Transaction** | **Time 0** | **Time $T$** |
| Short forward @ $F_{0,T}$ | 0 | $F_{0,T} - S_T$ |
| Buy $e^{-\delta_l T}$ commodity units and lend @ $\delta_l$ | $-S_0 e^{-\delta_l T}$ | $+S_T$ |
| Borrow @ $r$ | $+S_0 e^{-\delta_l T}$ | $-S_0 e^{(r-\delta_l)T}$ |
| **Total** | 0 | $F_{0,T} - S_0 e^{(r-\delta_l)T}$ |

| Table 8 |
| --- |

Reverse cash-and-carry arbitrage with a commodity for which the lease rate is $\delta_l$. The implied no-arbitrage restriction is $F_{0,T} \geq S_0 e^{(r-\delta_l)T}$.

| | Cash Flows | |
| --- | --- | --- |
| **Transaction** | **Time 0** | **Time $T$** |
| Long forward @ $F_{0,T}$ | 0 | $S_T - F_{0,T}$ |
| Short $e^{-\delta_l T}$ commodity units with lease rate $\delta_l$ | $+S_0 e^{-\delta_l T}$ | $-S_T$ |
| Lend @ $r$ | $-S_0 e^{-\delta_l T}$ | $+S_0 e^{(r-\delta_l)T}$ |
| **Total** | 0 | $S_0 e^{(r-\delta_l)T} - F_{0,T}$ |

In some markets, consistent and reliable quotes for the spot price are not available, or are not comparable to forward prices. In such cases, the near-term forward price can be used as a proxy for the spot price, $S$.

By definition, contango—an upward-sloping forward curve—occurs when the lease rate is less than the risk-free rate. Backwardation—a downward-sloping forward curve—occurs when the lease rate exceeds the risk-free rate.

# 6

# CARRY MARKETS

Sometimes it makes sense for a commodity to be stored, at least temporarily. Storage is also called **carry**, and a commodity that is stored is said to be in a **carry market**.

One reason for storage is seasonal variation in either supply or demand, which causes a mismatch between the time at which a commodity is produced and the time at which it is consumed. With some agricultural products, for example, supply is seasonal (there is a harvest season) but demand is constant over the year. In this case, storage permits consumption to occur throughout the year.

With natural gas, by contrast, there is high demand in the winter and low demand in the summer, but relatively constant production over the year. This pattern of use and production suggests that there will be times when natural gas is stored.

## Storage Costs and Forward Prices

Storage is not always feasible (for example, fresh strawberries are perishable) and when technically feasible, storage is almost always costly. When storage is feasible, how do storage costs affect forward pricing? Put yourself in the position of a commodity merchant who owns one unit of the commodity and ask whether you would be willing to store this unit until time $T$. You face the choice of selling it today, receiving $S_0$, or selling it at time $T$. If you elect to sell at time $T$, you can sell forward (to guarantee the price you will receive), and you will receive $F_{0,T}$. This is a cash-and-carry.

The cash-and-carry logic with storage costs suggests that *you will store only if the present value of selling at time $T$ is at least as great as that of selling today.* Denote the future value of storage costs for one unit of the commodity from time 0 to $T$ as $\lambda(0,T)$. Indifference between selling today and at time $T$ requires

$$\underbrace{S_0}_{\text{Revenue from selling today}} = e^{-rT}\underbrace{\left[F_{0,T} - \lambda(0,T)\right]}_{\text{Net revenue from selling at time }T}$$

This relationship in turn implies that if storage is to occur, the forward price is at least

$$F_{0,T} \geq S_0 e^{rT} + \lambda(0,T) \tag{13}$$

In the special case where storage costs are paid continuously and are proportional to the value of the commodity, storage cost is like a continuous negative dividend of $\lambda$, and we can write the forward price as

$$F_{0,T} = S_0 e^{(r+\lambda)T} \tag{14}$$

When there are no storage costs ($\lambda = 0$), Equations 13 and 14 reduce to the familiar forward pricing formula.

When there are storage costs, the forward price is higher. Why? The selling price must compensate the commodity merchant for both the financial cost of storage (interest) and the physical cost of storage. With storage costs, the forward curve can rise faster than the interest rate. We can view storage costs as a negative dividend in that, instead of receiving cash flow for holding the asset, you have to pay to hold the asset.

> **Example 1**
>
> Suppose that the November price of corn is $2.50/bushel, the effective monthly interest rate is 1%, and storage costs per bushel are $0.05/month. Assuming that corn is stored from November to February, the February forward price must compensate owners for interest and storage. The future value of storage costs is
>
> $$\$0.05 + (\$0.05 \times 1.01) + (\$0.05 \times 1.01^2) = (\$0.05/.01) \times \left[(1 + 0.01)^3 - 1\right]$$
> $$= \$0.1515$$
>
> Thus, the February forward price will be
>
> $$2.50 \times (1.01)^3 + 0.1515 = 2.7273$$
>
> Practice Problem 3 asks you to verify that this is a no-arbitrage price.

Keep in mind that just because a commodity *can* be stored does not mean that it *should* (or will) be stored. Pencils were not stored because storage was not economically necessary: A constant new supply of pencils was available to meet pencil demand. Thus, Equation 13 describes the forward price *when storage occurs*. Whether and when a commodity is stored are peculiar to each commodity.

## Storage Costs and the Lease Rate

Suppose that there is a carry market for a commodity, so that its forward price is given by Equation 13. What is the lease rate in this case?

Again put yourself in the shoes of the commodity lender. If you lend the commodity, you are saved from having to pay storage cost. Thus, the lease rate should equal the *negative* of the storage cost. In other words, the lender will pay the borrower! In effect, the commodity borrower is providing "virtual storage" for the commodity lender, who receives back the commodity at a point in the future. The lender making a payment to the borrower generates a negative dividend.

## The Convenience Yield

The discussion of commodities to this point has ignored business reasons for holding commodities. For example, suppose you are a food manufacturer for whom corn is an essential input. You will hold an inventory of corn. If you end up holding too much corn, you can sell the excess. However, if you hold too little and run out of corn, you must stop producing, idling workers and machines. Your physical inventory of corn in this case has value—it provides insurance that you can keep producing in case there is a disruption in the supply of corn.

In this situation, corn holdings provide an extra nonmonetary return that is sometimes referred to as the **convenience yield**.[5] You will be willing to store corn with a lower rate of return than if you did not earn the convenience yield. What are the implications of the convenience yield for the forward price?

Suppose that someone approached you to borrow a commodity from which you derived a convenience yield. You would think as follows: "If I lend the commodity, I am bearing interest cost, saving storage cost, and losing the value I derive from having

---

**5** The term *convenience yield* is defined differently by different authors. Convenience yield generally means a return to physical ownership of the commodity. In practice it is sometimes used to mean the lease rate. In this book, the lease rate of a commodity can be inferred from the forward price using Equation 11.

a physical inventory. I was willing to bear the interest cost already; thus, I will pay a commodity borrower storage cost *less the convenience yield.*"

Suppose the continuously compounded convenience yield is $c$, proportional to the value of the commodity. The commodity lender saves $\lambda - c$ by not physically storing the commodity; hence, the commodity borrower pays $\delta = c - \lambda$, compensating the lender for convenience yield less storage cost. Using an argument identical to that in Table 8 we conclude that the forward price must be no less than

$$F_{0,T} \geq S_0 e^{(r-\delta)T} = S_0 e^{(r+\lambda-c)T}$$

This is the restriction imposed by a reverse cash-and-carry, in which the arbitrageur borrows the commodity and goes long the forward.

Now consider what happens if you perform a cash-and-carry, buying the commodity and selling it forward. If you are an average investor, you will not earn the convenience yield (it is earned only by those with a business reason to hold the commodity). You could try to lend the commodity, reasoning that the borrower could be a commercial user to whom you would pay storage cost less the convenience yield. But those who earn the convenience yield likely already hold the optimal amount of the commodity. *There may be no way for you to earn the convenience yield when performing a cash-and-carry.* Those who do not earn the convenience yield will not own the commodity.

Thus, *for an average investor,* the cash-and-carry has the cash flows[6]

$$F_{0,T} - S_T + S_T - S_0 e^{(r+\lambda)T} = F_{0,T} - S_0 e^{(r+\lambda)T}$$

This expression implies that the forward price must be below $S_0 e^{(r+\lambda)T}$ if there is to be no cash-and-carry arbitrage.

In summary, from the perspective of an arbitrageur, the price range within which there is no arbitrage is

$$S_0 e^{(r+\lambda-c)T} \leq F_{0,T} \leq S_0 e^{(r+\lambda)T} \tag{15}$$

The convenience yield produces a no-arbitrage *region* rather than a no-arbitrage *price*. The observed lease rate will depend upon both storage costs and convenience. Also, bid-ask spreads and trading costs will further expand the no-arbitrage region in Equation 15.

As another illustration of convenience yield, consider again the pencil example of Section 4. In reality, everyone stores a few pencils in order to be sure to have one available. You can think of this benefit from storage as the convenience yield of a pencil. However, because the supply of pencils is perfectly elastic, the price of pencils is fixed at $0.20. Convenience yield in this case does not affect the forward price, but it does explain the decision to store pencils.

The difficulty with the convenience yield in practice is that convenience is hard to observe. The concept of the convenience yield serves two purposes. First, it explains patterns in storage—for example, why a commercial user might store a commodity when the average investor will not. Second, it provides an additional parameter to better explain the forward curve. You might object that we can invoke the convenience yield to explain *any* forward curve, and therefore the concept of the convenience yield is vacuous. While convenience yield can be tautological, it is a meaningful economic concept and it would be just as arbitrary to assume that there is never convenience. Moreover, the upper bound in Equation 15 depends on storage costs but not the convenience yield. Thus, the convenience yield only explains anomalously low forward prices, and only when there is storage.

---

**6** In this expression, we assume we tail the holding of the commodity by buying $e^{\lambda T}$ units at time 0, and selling off units of the commodity over time to pay storage costs.

We will now examine particular commodities to illustrate the concepts from the previous sections.

# GOLD FUTURES

**7**

Gold is durable, relatively inexpensive to store (compared to its value), widely held, and actively produced through gold mining. Because of transportation costs and purity concerns, gold often trades in certificate form, as a claim to physical gold at a specific location. There are exchange-traded gold futures, specifications for which are in Figure 1.[7]

---

**Figure 1**

| | |
|---|---|
| Underlying | Refined gold bearing approved refiner stamp |
| Where traded | New York Mercantile Exchange |
| Size | 100 troy ounces |
| Months | Feb, Apr, Aug, Oct, out two years. Jun, Dec, out five years |
| Trading ends | Third-to-last business day of maturity month |
| Delivery | Any business day of the delivery month |

Specifications for the NYMEX gold futures contract.

---

Figure 2 is a newspaper listing for the NYMEX gold futures contract. Figure 3 graphs the futures prices for all available gold futures contracts—the forward curve—for the first Wednesday in June, from 2001 to 2004. (Newspaper listings for most futures contracts do not show the full set of available expiration dates, so Figure 3 is constructed using more expiration dates than are in Figure 2.) What is interesting about the gold forward curve is how relatively uninteresting it is, with the forward price steadily increasing with time to maturity.

---

**Figure 2**

| | Open | High | Low | Settle | Chg | Lifetime High | Lifetime Low | Open Int |
|---|---|---|---|---|---|---|---|---|
| **Gold** (CMX)-100 troy oz.; $ per troy oz. | | | | | | | | |
| July | — | — | — | 401.90 | -3.70 | 400.20 | 380.50 | 4 |
| Aug | 406.00 | 407.10 | 399.70 | 402.10 | -3.70 | 433.00 | 324.70 | 139,287 |
| Oct | 407.50 | 408.00 | 401.20 | 403.40 | -3.70 | 432.00 | 332.00 | 11,310 |
| Dec | 408.50 | 409.90 | 402.00 | 404.80 | -3.70 | 436.50 | 290.00 | 62,036 |
| Fb05 | 408.50 | 408.50 | 405.00 | 406.40 | -3.70 | 435.00 | 331.50 | 6,614 |
| Aug | 411.00 | 411.00 | 411.00 | 411.80 | -3.70 | 416.50 | 379.00 | 2,290 |
| Dec | 420.00 | 420.00 | 420.00 | 415.90 | -3.70 | 441.50 | 298.40 | 6,387 |

Est vol 52,000; vol Mon 31,225; open int 262,052, -1,522

*Source*: Listing for the NYMEX gold futures contract from the *Wall Street Journal*, July 21, 2004.

---

**7** Gold is usually denominated in troy ounces (480 grains), which are approximately 9.7% heavier than the more familiar avoirdupois ounce (437.5 grains). Twelve troy ounces make 1 troy pound, which weighs approximately 0.37 kg.

From our previous discussion, the forward price implies a lease rate. Short sales and loans of gold are common in the gold market, and gold borrowers in fact have to pay the lease rate. On the lending side, large gold holders (including some central banks) put gold on deposit with brokers, in order that it may be loaned to short-sellers. The gold lenders earn the lease rate.

The lease rate for gold, silver, and other commodities is computed in practice using Equation 12 and is reported routinely by financial reporting services. Table 9 shows the 6-month and 1-year lease rates for the four gold forward curves depicted in Figure 3, computed using Equation 12.

**Figure 3**

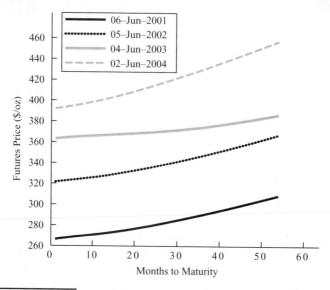

The forward curve for gold on four dates, from NYMEX gold futures prices.
*Source*: Futures data from Datastream.

**Example 2**

Here are the details of computing the 6-month lease rate for June 6, 2001. Gold futures prices are in Table 9. The June and September Eurodollar futures prices on this date were 96.09 and 96.13. Thus, 3-month LIBOR from June to September was $(100 - 96.09)/400 \times 91/90 = 0.988\%$, and from September to December was $(100 - 96.13)/400 \times 91/90 = 0.978\%$. The June to December interest rate was therefore $(1.00988) \times (1.00978) - 1 = 1.9763\%$, or $1.019763^2$ annualized. Using Equation 12, the annualized 6-month lease rate is therefore

$$6\text{-month lease rate} = \left( \frac{1.019763^2}{\left( 269/265.7 \right)^{(1/0.5)}} \right) - 1 = 1.456\%$$

## Gold Investments

If you wish to hold gold as part of an investment portfolio, you can do so by holding physical gold or synthetic gold—i.e., holding T-bills and going long gold futures. Which should you do? If you hold physical gold without lending it, and if the lease rate is positive, you forgo the lease rate. You also bear storage costs. With synthetic gold, on the other hand, you have a counterparty who may fail to pay so there is credit risk. Ignoring credit risk, however, synthetic gold is generally the preferable way to obtain gold price exposure.

Table 9 shows that the 6-month annualized gold lease rate is 1.46% in June 2001. Thus, by holding physical gold instead of synthetic gold, an investor would lose this 1.46% return.[8] In June 2003 and 2004, however, the lease rate was about −0.10%. If storage costs are about 0.10%, an investor would be indifferent between holding physical and synthetic gold. The futures market on those dates was compensating investors for storing physical gold.

**Table 9**

Six-month and 12-month gold lease rates for four dates, computed using Equation 12. Interest rates are computed from Eurodollar futures prices.

| Date | Gold Futures Prices ($) | | | Lease Rates | |
|---|---|---|---|---|---|
| | June | Dec | June | 6 Month | 1 Year |
| June 6, 2001 | 265.7 | 269.0 | 271.7 | 1.46% | 1.90% |
| June 5, 2002 | 321.2 | 323.9 | 326.9 | 0.44% | 0.88% |
| June 4, 2003 | 362.6 | 364.9 | 366.4 | −0.14% | 0.09% |
| June 2, 2004 | 391.6 | 395.2 | 400.2 | −0.10% | 0.07% |

*Source*: Futures data from Datastream.

Some nonfinancial holders of gold will obtain a convenience yield from gold. Consider an electronics manufacturer who uses gold in producing components. Suppose that running out of gold would halt production. It would be natural in this case to hold a buffer stock of gold in order to avoid a stock-out of gold, i.e., running out of gold. For this manufacturer, there *is* a return to holding gold—namely, a lower probability of stocking out and halting production. Stocking out would have a real financial cost, and the manufacturer is willing to pay a price—the lease rate—to avoid that cost.

## Evaluation of Gold Production

Suppose we have an operating gold mine and we wish to compute the present value of future production. As discussed in Section 2, the present value of the commodity received in the future is simply the present value—computed at the risk-free rate—of the forward price. We can use the forward curve for gold to compute the value of an operating gold mine.

Suppose that at times $t_i$, $i = 1, \ldots, n$, we expect to extract $n_{ti}$ ounces of gold by paying an extraction cost $x(t_i)$. We have a set of $n$ forward prices, $F_{0, ti}$. If the continuously compounded annual risk-free rate from time 0 to $t_i$ is $r(0, t_i)$, the value of the gold mine is

---

**8** The cost of 1 ounce of physical gold is $S_0$. However, from Equation 10, the cost of 1 ounce of gold bought as a prepaid forward is $S_0 e^{-\delta_l T}$. Synthetic gold is proportionally cheaper by the lease rate, $\delta_l$.

$$\text{PV gold production} = \sum_{i=1}^{n} n_{t_i} \left[ F_{0,t_i} - x(t_i) \right] e^{-r(0,t_i)t_i} \tag{16}$$

This equation assumes that the gold mine is certain to operate the entire time and that the quantity of production is known. Only price is uncertain. Note that in Equation 16, by computing the present value of the forward price, we compute the prepaid forward price.

**Example 3**

Suppose we have a mining project that will produce 1 ounce of gold every year for 6 years. The cost of this project is $1,100 today, the marginal cost per ounce at the time of extraction is $100, and the continuously compounded interest rate is 6%.

We observe the gold forward prices in the second column of Table 10, with implied prepaid forward prices in the third column. Using Equation 16, we can use these prices to perform the necessary present value calculations.

$$\text{Net present value} = \sum_{i=1}^{6} \left[ F_{0,i} - 100 \right] e^{-0.06 \times i} - \$1100$$

$$= \$119.56 \tag{17}$$

**Table 10**

Gold forward and prepaid forward prices on 1 day for gold delivered at 1-year intervals, out to 6 years. The continuously compounded interest rate is 6% and the lease rate is assumed to be a constant 1.5%.

| Expiration Year | Forward Price ($) | Prepaid Forward Price ($) |
|---|---|---|
| 1 | 313.81 | 295.53 |
| 2 | 328.25 | 291.13 |
| 3 | 343.36 | 286.80 |
| 4 | 359.17 | 282.53 |
| 5 | 375.70 | 278.32 |
| 6 | 392.99 | 274.18 |

# 8    SEASONALITY: THE CORN FORWARD MARKET

Corn in the United States is harvested primarily in the fall, from September through November. The United States is a leading corn producer, generally exporting rather than importing corn. Figure 4 shows a newspaper listing for corn futures.

Given seasonality in production, what should the forward curve for corn look like? Corn is produced at one time of the year, but consumed throughout the year. In order to be consumed when it is not being produced, corn must be stored. Thus, to understand the forward curve for corn we need to recall our discussion of storage and carry markets.

As discussed in Section 6 storage is an economic decision in which there is a trade-off between selling today and selling tomorrow. If we can sell corn today for $2/bu and in 2 months for $2.25/bu, the storage decision entails comparing the price we can get today with the present value of the price we can get in 2 months. In addition to interest, we need to include storage costs in our analysis.

---

**Figure 4**

|  | Open | High | Low | Settle | Chg | Lifetime High | Lifetime Low | Open Int |
|---|---|---|---|---|---|---|---|---|
| **Corn** (CBT)-5,000 bu.; cents per bu. | | | | | | | | |
| Sept | 236.50 | 237.50 | 232.75 | 234.00 | −3.00 | 341.00 | 229.75 | 162,000 |
| Dec | 244.75 | 246.00 | 240.75 | 242.00 | −3.00 | 341.50 | 232.50 | 307,442 |
| Mr05 | 252.25 | 254.00 | 248.75 | 250.25 | −2.50 | 342.00 | 239.00 | 52,447 |
| May | 258.00 | 259.75 | 255.00 | 256.00 | −3.00 | 344.00 | 243.50 | 16,608 |
| July | 262.00 | 263.25 | 259.00 | 260.00 | −2.50 | 342.00 | 246.50 | 13,717 |
| Sept | 262.75 | 263.00 | 260.00 | 260.25 | −2.75 | 299.00 | 260.00 | 3,058 |
| Dec | 262.50 | 262.75 | 260.00 | 260.50 | −2.75 | 288.50 | 235.00 | 10,707 |

Est vol 74,710; vol Mon 71,892; open int 566,664, +1,488.

*Source*: Listing for the CBOT corn futures contract from the *Wall Street Journal*, July 21, 2004.

---

An equilibrium with some current selling and some storage requires that corn prices be expected to rise at the interest rate plus storage costs, which implies that there will be an upward trend in the price between harvests. While corn is being stored, the forward price should behave as in Equation 14, rising at interest plus storage costs.

Once the harvest begins, storage is no longer necessary; if supply and demand remain constant from year to year, the harvest price will be the same every year. The corn price will fall to that level at harvest, only to begin rising again after the harvest.

The market conditions we have described are graphed in Figure 5, which depicts a hypothetical forward curve as seen from time 0. Between harvests, the forward price of corn rises to reward storage, and it falls at each harvest. Let's see how this graph was constructed.

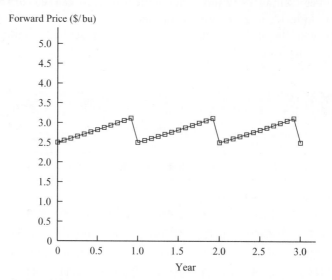

**Figure 5**

A hypothetical forward curve for corn, assuming the harvest occurs at years 0, 1, 2, etc.

---

The corn price is $2.50 initially, the continuously compounded interest rate is 6%, and storage cost is 1.5%/month. The forward price after $n$ months (where $n < 12$) is

$$F_{0,n} = \$2.50 \times e^{(0.005 + 0.015) \times n}$$

Thus, the 12-month forward price is $\$2.50e^{0.06+0.18} = \$3.18$. After 1 year, the process starts over.

Farmers will plant in anticipation of receiving the harvest price, which means that it is the harvest price that reflects the cost of producing corn. The price during the rest of the year equals the harvest price plus storage. In general we would expect those storing corn to plan to deplete inventory as harvest approaches and to replenish inventory from the new harvest.

This is a simplified version of reality. Perhaps most important, the supply of corn varies from year to year. When there is a large crop, producers will expect corn to be stored not just over the current year, but into the next year as well. If there is a large harvest, therefore, we might see the forward curve rise continuously until year 2. To better understand the possible behavior of corn, let's look at real corn prices.

Table 11 shows the June forward curves for corn over a 10-year period. Some clear patterns are evident. First, notice that from December to March to May (columns 3–5), the futures price rises every year. We would expect there to be storage of corn during this period, with the futures price compensating for storage. A low current price suggests a large supply. Thus, when the near-July price is low, we might also expect storage across the coming harvest. Particularly in the years with the lowest July prices (1999–2002), there is a pronounced rise in price from July to December. When the price is unusually high (1996 and 2004), there is a drop in price from July to December. Behavior is mixed in the other years.[9] We can also examine the July-December price relationship in the following year. In 6 of the 10 years, the distant-December price

---

**9** It is possible to have low current storage and a large expected harvest, which would cause the December price to be lower than the July price, or high current storage and a poor expected harvest, which would cause the July price to be below the December price.

(column 8) is below the distant July price (column 6). The exceptions occur in years with relatively low current prices (1998–2001). These patterns are generally consistent with storage of corn between harvests, and storage across harvests only occasionally.

Futures prices for corn (from the Chicago Board of Trade) for the first Wednesday in June, 1995–2004. The last column is the 18-month forward price. Prices are in cents per bushel.

| | Contract Expiration Month | | | | | | | |
| | Current Year | | | Following Year | | | | |
| Date | July | Sept | Dec | Mar | May | July | Sept | Dec |
|------|------|------|------|------|------|------|------|------|
| 07-Jun-1995 | 265.50 | 272.25 | 277.75 | 282.75 | 285.25 | 286.00 | 269.50 | 253.50 |
| 05-Jun-1996 | 435.00 | 373.25 | 340.75 | 346.75 | 350.50 | 348.00 | 298.00 | 286.50 |
| 04-Jun-1997 | 271.25 | 256.50 | 254.75 | 261.00 | 265.50 | 269.00 | 257.00 | 255.00 |
| 03-Jun-1998 | 238.00 | 242.25 | 245.75 | 253.75 | 259.00 | 264.00 | 261.00 | 268.00 |
| 02-Jun-1999 | 216.75 | 222.00 | 230.75 | 239.75 | 244.50 | 248.25 | 248.00 | 251.50 |
| 07-Jun-2000 | 219.75 | 228.50 | 234.50 | 239.25 | 242.50 | 248.50 | 254.50 | 259.00 |
| 06-Jun-2001 | 198.50 | 206.00 | 217.25 | 228.25 | 234.50 | 241.75 | 245.00 | 251.25 |
| 05-Jun-2002 | 210.25 | 217.25 | 226.75 | 234.50 | 237.25 | 240.75 | 235.00 | 239.00 |
| 04-Jun-2003 | 237.50 | 236.25 | 237.75 | 244.00 | 248.00 | 250.00 | 242.25 | 242.50 |
| 02-Jun-2004 | 321.75 | 319.75 | 319.25 | 322.50 | 325.50 | 324.50 | 296.50 | 279.00 |

*Source*: Futures data from Datastream.

Finally, compare prices for the near-July contract (the first column) with those for the distant-December contract (the last column). Near-term prices are quite variable, ranging from 216.75 to 435.00 cents per bushel. In December of the following year, however, prices range only from 239 to 286.50. In fact, in 7 of the 10 years, the price is between 251 and 268. The lower variability of distant prices is not surprising: It is difficult to forecast a harvest more than a year into the future. Thus, the forward price is reflecting the market's expectation of a normal harvest 1 year hence.

If we assume that storage costs are approximately \$0.03/month/bushel, the forward price in Table 11 never violates the no-arbitrage condition

$$F_{0,T+s} < F_{0,T} e^{rs} + \lambda(T, T+s) \qquad (18)$$

which says that the forward price from $T$ to $T + s$ cannot rise faster than interest plus storage costs.

# NATURAL GAS                                                                9

Natural gas is another market in which seasonality and storage costs are important. The natural gas futures contract, introduced in 1990, has become one of the most heavily traded futures contracts in the United States. The asset underlying one contract is 1 month's worth of gas, delivered at a specific location (different gas contracts call for delivery at different locations). Figure 6 shows a newspaper listing for natural gas futures, and Figure 7 details the specifications for the Henry Hub contract.

---

**Figure 6**

| | Open | High | Low | Settle | Chg | Lifetime High | Lifetime Low | Open Int |
|---|---|---|---|---|---|---|---|---|
| **Natural Gas** (NYM) -10,000 MMBtu.; $ per MMBtu | | | | | | | | |
| Aug | 5.815 | 5.960 | 5.797 | 5.837 | .019 | 6.825 | 3.120 | 40,430 |
| Sept | 5.865 | 5.990 | 5.835 | 5.877 | .013 | 6.780 | 3.100 | 60,098 |
| Oct | 5.910 | 6.040 | 5.898 | 5.934 | .015 | 6.800 | 3.100 | 40,028 |
| Nov | 6.250 | 6.360 | 6.240 | 6.274 | .016 | 6.940 | 3.270 | 19,225 |
| Dec | 6.560 | 6.660 | 6.530 | 6.584 | .016 | 7.110 | 3.460 | 25,005 |
| Ja05 | 6.740 | 6.835 | 6.730 | 6.757 | .016 | 7.230 | 3.520 | 21,758 |
| Feb | 6.705 | 6.800 | 6.705 | 6.722 | .017 | 7.145 | 3.400 | 15,510 |
| Mar | 6.575 | 6.650 | 6.560 | 6.592 | .018 | 6.970 | 3.640 | 17,636 |
| Apr | 5.980 | 6.010 | 5.974 | 5.987 | .013 | 6.200 | 3.400 | 13,388 |
| May | 5.890 | 5.900 | 5.870 | 5.874 | .017 | 6.020 | 3.500 | 11,510 |
| June | 5.900 | 5.910 | 5.890 | 5.890 | .017 | 6.030 | 3.530 | 8,340 |
| July | 5.960 | 5.960 | 5.935 | 5.927 | .017 | 6.070 | 3.560 | 11,657 |
| Aug | 5.960 | 5.960 | 5.950 | 5.937 | .008 | 6.080 | 3.230 | 8,036 |
| Oct | 5.990 | 5.990 | 5.990 | 5.952 | .008 | 6.080 | 3.540 | 6,627 |
| Nov | 6.150 | 6.160 | 6.150 | 6.124 | — | 6.240 | 3.790 | 6,770 |
| Dec | 6.350 | 6.350 | 6.350 | 6.302 | –.007 | 6.400 | 3.960 | 6,249 |
| Jl06 | 5.520 | 5.520 | 5.520 | 5.488 | –.012 | 5.520 | 3.580 | 3,074 |
| Ap07 | 5.264 | 5.264 | 5.264 | 5.189 | –.005 | 5.264 | 4.747 | 3,187 |
| May | 5.109 | 5.109 | 5.109 | 5.034 | –.005 | 5.130 | 4.712 | 767 |
| June | 5.111 | 5.111 | 5.111 | 5.039 | –.002 | 5.111 | 4.000 | 376 |
| Oct | 5.090 | 5.090 | 5.090 | 5.057 | .013 | 5.090 | 4.891 | 312 |

Est vol 76,493; vol Mon 61,746; open int 380,824, +3,187.

*Source*: Listing for the NYMEX natural gas futures contract from the *Wall Street Journal*, July 21, 2004.

---

**Figure 7**

| | |
|---|---|
| Underlying | Natural gas delivered at Sabine Pipe Lines Co.'s Henry Hub, Louisiana |
| Where traded | New York Mercantile Exchange |
| Size | 10,000 million British thermal units (MMBtu) |
| Months | 72 consecutive months |
| Trading ends | Third-to-last business day of month prior to maturity month |
| Delivery | As uniformly as possible over the delivery month |

*Specifications for the NYMEX Henry Hub natural gas contract.*

---

Natural gas has several interesting characteristics. First, gas is costly to transport internationally, so prices and forward curves vary regionally. Second, once a given well has begun production, gas is costly to store. Third, demand for gas in the United States is highly seasonal, with peak demand arising from heating in winter months.

Thus, there is a relatively steady stream of production with variable demand, which leads to large and predictable price swings. Whereas corn has seasonal production and relatively constant demand, gas has relatively constant supply and seasonal demand.

Figure 8 displays 3-year (2001) and 6-year (2002–2004) strips of gas futures prices for the first Wednesday in June from 1997 to 2000. Seasonality is evident, with high winter prices and low summer prices. The 2003 and 2004 strip shows seasonal cycles combined with a downward trend in prices, suggesting that the market considered prices in that year as anomalously high. For the other years, the average price for each coming year is about the same.

**Figure 8**

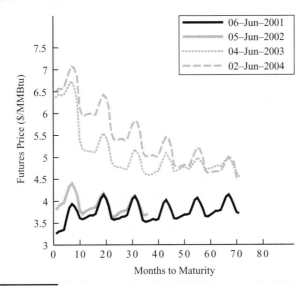

Forward curves for natural gas for the first Wednesday in June from 2001 to 2004. Prices are dollars per MMBtu, from NYMEX.
*Source*: Futures data from Datastream.

Gas storage is costly and demand for gas is highest in the winter. The steady rise of the forward curve during the fall months suggests that storage occurs just before the heaviest demand. Table 12 shows prices for October through December. The monthly increase in gas prices over these months ranges from $0.13 to $0.23. Assuming that the interest rate is about 0.15% per month and that you use Equation 13, storage cost in November 2004, λ, would satisfy

$$6.947 = 6.759e^{0.0015} + \lambda$$

implying an estimated storage cost of λ = $0.178 in November 2004. You will find different imputed marginal storage costs in each year, but this is to be expected if marginal storage costs vary with the quantity stored.

**Table 12**

June natural gas futures prices for October, November, and December in the same year, for 2001 to 2004.

| Date | Oct | Nov | Dec |
|------|-----|-----|-----|
| 06-Jun-2001 | 2.173 | 2.305 | 2.435 |
| 05-Jun-2002 | 3.352 | 3.617 | 3.850 |
| 04-Jun-2003 | 6.428 | 6.528 | 6.658 |
| 02-Jun-2004 | 6.581 | 6.759 | 6.947 |

*Source*: Futures data from Datastream.

Because of the expense in transporting gas internationally, the seasonal behavior of the forward curve can vary in different parts of the world. In tropical areas where gas is used for cooking and electricity generation, the forward curve is relatively flat because demand is relatively flat. In the Southern Hemisphere, where seasons are reversed from the Northern Hemisphere, the forward curve will peak in June and July rather than December and January.

Recent developments in energy markets could alter the behavior of the natural gas forward curve in the United States. Power producers have made greater use of gas-fired peak-load electricity plants. These plants have increased summer demand for natural gas and may permanently alter seasonality.

# 10  OIL

Both oil and natural gas produce energy and are extracted from wells, but the different physical characteristics and uses of oil lead to a very different forward curve than that for gas. Oil is easier to transport than gas. Transportation of oil takes time, but oil has a global market. Oil is also easier to store than gas. Thus, seasonals in the price of crude oil are relatively unimportant. Specifications for the NYMEX light oil contract are shown in Figure 9. Figure 10 shows a newspaper listing for oil futures. The NYMEX forward curve on four dates is plotted in Figure 11.

**Figure 9**

| | |
|---|---|
| Underlying | Specific domestic crudes delivered at Cushing, Oklahoma |
| Where traded | New York Mercantile Exchange |
| Size | 1000 U.S. barrels (42,000 gallons) |
| Months | 30 consecutive months plus long-dated futures out 7 years |
| Trading ends | Third-to-last business day preceding the 25th calendar day of month prior to maturity month |
| Delivery | As uniformly as possible over the delivery month |

*Specifications for the NYMEX light, sweet crude oil contract.*

**Figure 10**

| | | | | | | Lifetime | | |
|---|---|---|---|---|---|---|---|---|
| | Open | High | Low | Settle | Chg | High | Low | Open Int |
| **Crude Oil, Light Sweet** (NYM)-1,000 bbls.; $ per bbl. | | | | | | | | |
| Aug | 41.63 | 42.30 | 40.51 | 40.86 | −0.78 | 42.30 | 20.84 | 29,478 |
| Sept | 41.41 | 41.75 | 40.31 | 40.44 | −1.00 | 41.90 | 20.82 | 236,034 |
| Oct | 40.85 | 41.05 | 39.80 | 39.88 | −1.00 | 41.30 | 23.75 | 68,764 |
| Nov | 40.38 | 40.45 | 39.52 | 39.45 | −0.93 | 40.70 | 24.75 | 35,763 |
| Dec | 39.85 | 40.10 | 39.00 | 39.04 | −0.89 | 40.30 | 16.35 | 60,672 |
| Ja05 | 39.34 | 39.50 | 39.20 | 38.55 | −0.86 | 39.50 | 23.25 | 23,149 |
| Feb | 38.89 | 39.05 | 38.65 | 38.13 | −0.83 | 39.15 | 23.85 | 13,656 |
| Mar | 38.49 | 38.53 | 38.20 | 37.74 | −0.80 | 38.65 | 23.05 | 14,312 |
| Apr | 38.05 | 38.20 | 37.85 | 37.37 | −0.78 | 38.50 | 23.25 | 10,589 |
| June | 37.30 | 37.45 | 36.60 | 36.68 | −0.73 | 37.55 | 22.40 | 22,138 |
| Sept | 36.65 | 36.65 | 36.65 | 35.96 | −0.67 | 36.85 | 24.00 | 8,357 |
| Dec | 36.00 | 36.05 | 35.90 | 35.44 | −0.61 | 36.30 | 17.00 | 47,774 |
| Dc06 | 34.15 | 34.15 | 34.15 | 33.58 | −0.58 | 34.15 | 19.10 | 34,365 |
| Dc07 | 32.75 | 32.75 | 32.75 | 32.19 | −0.55 | 32.75 | 19.50 | 12,536 |
| Dc08 | 31.75 | 31.80 | 31.70 | 31.22 | −0.55 | 32.00 | 19.75 | 11,967 |
| Dc09 | 31.20 | 31.20 | 31.20 | 30.48 | −0.55 | 31.20 | 22.50 | 10,916 |
| Dc10 | 30.85 | 30.95 | 30.63 | 30.18 | −0.55 | 31.00 | 27.15 | 15,928 |

Est vol 204,514, vol Mon 248,398; open int 708,255, −1,567.

*Source*: Listing for the NYMEX crude oil futures contract from the *Wall Street Journal*, July 21, 2004.

**Figure 11**

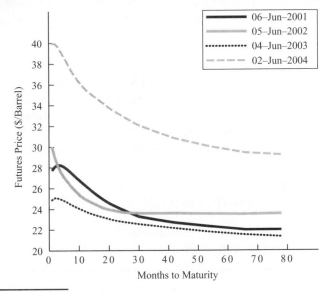

*Seven-year strip of NYMEX crude oil futures prices, $/barrel, for four different dates.*
*Source*: Futures data from Datastream.

On the four dates in the figure, near-term oil prices range from $25 to $40, while the 7-year forward price in each case is between $22 and $30. The long-run forward price is less volatile than the short-run forward price, which makes economic sense. In the short run, an increase in demand will cause a price increase since supply is fixed. A supply shock (such as production restrictions by the Organization of Petroleum Exporting Countries [OPEC]) will cause the price to increase. In the long run, however, both supply and demand have time to adjust to price changes with the result that price movements are attenuated. The forward curve suggests that market participants in June 2004 did not expect the price to remain at $40/barrel.

## 11    COMMODITY SPREADS

Some commodities are inputs in the creation of other commodities, which gives rise to **commodity spreads**. Soybeans, for example, can be crushed to produce soybean meal and soybean oil (and a small amount of waste). A trader with a position in soybeans and an opposite position in equivalent quantities of soybean meal and soybean oil has a **crush spread** and is said to be "trading the crush."

Similarly, crude oil is refined to make petroleum products, in particular heating oil and gasoline. The refining process entails distillation, which separates crude oil into different components, including gasoline, kerosene, and heating oil. The split of oil into these different components can be complemented by a process known as "cracking"; hence, the difference in price between crude oil and equivalent amounts of heating oil and gasoline is called the **crack spread**.

Oil can be processed in different ways, producing different mixes of outputs. The spread terminology identifies the number of gallons of oil as input, and the number of gallons of gasoline and heating oil as outputs. Traders will speak of "5-3-2," "3-2-1," and "2-1-1" crack spreads. The 5-3-2 spread, for example, reflects the profit from taking 5 gallons of oil as input, and producing 3 gallons of gasoline and 2 gallons of heating oil. A petroleum refiner producing gasoline and heating oil could use a futures crack spread to lock in both the cost of oil and output prices. This strategy would entail going long oil futures and short the appropriate quantities of gasoline and heating oil futures. Of course there are other inputs to production and it is possible to produce other outputs, such as jet fuel, so the crack spread is not a perfect hedge.

### Example 4

Suppose we consider buying oil in July and selling gasoline and heating oil in August. On June 2, 2004, the July futures price for oil was $39.96/barrel, or $0.9514/gallon (there are 42 gallons per barrel). The August futures prices for unleaded gasoline and heating oil were $1.2427/gallon and $1.0171/gallon. The 3-2-1 crack spread tells us the gross margin we can lock in by buying 3 gallons of oil and producing 2 gallons of gasoline and 1 of heating oil. Using these prices, the spread is

$$(2 \times \$1.2427) + \$1.0171 - (3 \times \$0.9514) = \$0.6482$$

or $0.6482/3 = $0.2161/gallon. In this calculation we made no interest adjustment for the different expiration months of the futures contract.

There are crack spread options trading on NYMEX. Two of these options pay based on the difference between the price of heating oil and crude oil, and the price of gasoline and heating oil, both in a 1:1 ratio.

# HEDGING STRATEGIES

**12**

In this section we discuss some of the complications that can arise when using commodity futures and forwards to hedge commodity price exposure. One such complication is the problem of quantity uncertainty, where, for example, a farmer growing corn does not know the ultimate yield at the time of planting. Other issues can arise. Since commodities are heterogeneous and often costly to transport and store, it is common to hedge a risk with a commodity contract that is imperfectly correlated with the risk being hedged. This gives rise to *basis risk*: The price of the commodity underlying the futures contract may move differently than the price of the commodity you are hedging. For example, because of transportation cost and time, the price of natural gas in California may differ from that in Louisiana, which is the location underlying the principal natural gas futures contract (see again Figure 7). In some cases, one commodity may be used to hedge another. As an example of this we discuss the use of crude oil to hedge jet fuel. Finally, weather derivatives provide another example of an instrument that can be used to cross-hedge. We discuss degree-day index contracts as an example of such derivatives.

## Basis Risk

Exchange-traded commodity futures contracts call for delivery of the underlying commodity at specific locations and specific dates. The actual commodity to be bought or sold may reside at a different location and the desired delivery date may not match that of the futures contract. Additionally, the *grade* of the deliverable under the futures contract may not match the grade that is being delivered.

This general problem of the futures or forward contract not representing exactly what is being hedged is called *basis risk*. Basis risk is a generic problem with commodities because of storage and transportation costs and quality differences. Basis risk can also arise with financial futures, as for example when a company hedges its own borrowing cost with the Eurodollar contract.

An individual stock can be hedged with an index futures contract. If we regress the individual stock return on the index return, the resulting regression coefficient provides a hedge ratio that minimizes the variance of the hedged position.

In the same way, suppose we wish to hedge oil delivered on the East Coast with the NYMEX oil contract, which calls for delivery of oil in Cushing, Oklahoma. The variance-minimizing hedge ratio would be the regression coefficient obtained by regressing the East Coast price on the Cushing price. Problems with this regression are that the relationship may not be stable over time or may be estimated imprecisely.

Another example of basis risk occurs when hedgers decide to hedge distant obligations with near-term futures. For example, an oil producer might have an obligation to deliver 100,000 barrels per month at a fixed price for a year. The natural way to hedge this obligation would be to buy 100,000 barrels per month, locking in the price and supply on a month-by-month basis. This is called a **strip hedge**. We engage in a strip hedge when we hedge a stream of obligations by offsetting each individual obligation with a futures contract matching the maturity and quantity of the obligation. For the oil producer obligated to deliver every month at a fixed price, the hedge would entail buying the appropriate quantity each month, in effect taking a long position in the strip.

An alternative to a strip hedge is a **stack hedge**. With a stack hedge, we enter into futures contracts with a *single* maturity, with the number of contracts selected so that changes in the *present value* of the future obligations are offset by changes in the value of this "stack" of futures contracts. In the context of the oil producer with a monthly delivery obligation, a stack hedge would entail going long 1.2 million barrels using the near-term contract. (Actually, we would want to tail the position and go long less than 1.2 million barrels, but we will ignore this.) When the near-term contract matures, we reestablish the stack hedge by going long contracts in the new near month. This process of stacking futures contracts in the near-term contract and rolling over into the new near-term contract is called a **stack and roll**. If the new near-term futures price is below the expiring near-term price (i.e., there is backwardation), rolling is profitable.

Why would anyone use a stack hedge? There are at least two reasons. First, there is often more trading volume and liquidity in near-term contracts. With many commodities, bid-ask spreads widen with maturity. Thus, a stack hedge may have lower transaction costs than a strip hedge. Second, the manager may wish to speculate on the shape of the forward curve. You might decide that the forward curve looks unusually steep in the early months. If you undertake a stack hedge and the forward curve then flattens, you will have locked in all your oil at the relatively cheap near-term price, and implicitly made gains from not having locked in the relatively high strip prices. However, if the curve becomes steeper, it is possible to lose.

The box below recounts the story of Metallgesellschaft A. G. (MG), in which MG's large losses on a hedged position might have been caused, at least in part, by the use of a stack hedge.

---

### METALLGESELLSCHAFT A. G.

In 1992, a U.S. subsidiary of the German industrial firm Metallgesellschaft A. G. (MG) had offered customers fixed prices on over 150 million barrels of petroleum products, including gasoline, heating oil, and diesel fuel, over periods as long as 10 years. To hedge the resulting short exposure, MG entered into futures and swaps.

Much of MG's hedging was done using short-dated NYMEX crude oil and heating oil futures. Thus, MG was using stack hedging, rolling over the hedge each month.

During much of 1993, the near-term oil market was in contango (the forward curve was upward sloping). As a result of the market remaining in contango, MG systematically lost money when rolling its hedges and had to meet substantial margin calls. In December 1993, the supervisory board of MG decided to liquidate both its supply contracts and the futures positions used to hedge those contracts. In the end, MG sustained losses estimated at between $200 million and $1.3 billion.

The MG case was extremely complicated and has been the subject of pointed exchanges among academics—see in particular Culp and Miller (1995), Edwards and Canter (1995), and Mello and Parsons (1995). While the case is complicated, several issues stand out. First, was the stack-and-roll a reasonable strategy for MG to have undertaken? Second, should the position have been liquidated when it was and in the manner it was liquidated (as it turned out, oil prices increased—which would have worked in MG's favor—following the liquidation). Third, did MG encounter liquidity problems from having to finance losses on its hedging strategy? While the MG case has receded into history, hedgers still confront the issues raised by this case.

---

## Hedging Jet Fuel with Crude Oil

Jet fuel futures do not exist in the United States, but firms sometimes hedge jet fuel with crude oil futures along with futures for related petroleum products.[10] In order to perform this hedge, it is necessary to understand the relationship between crude

---

[10] For example, Southwest Airlines reportedly used a combination of crude oil and heating oil futures to hedge jet fuel. See Melanie Trottman, "Southwest Airline's Big Fuel-Hedging Call Is Paying Off," *Wall Street Journal*, January 16, 2004, p. B4.

oil and jet fuel prices. If we own a quantity of jet fuel and hedge by holding $H$ crude oil futures contracts, our mark-to-market profit depends on the change in the jet fuel price and the change in the futures price:

$$\left(P_t - P_{t-1}\right) + H\left(F_t - F_{t-1}\right) \tag{19}$$

where $P_t$ is the price of jet fuel and $F_t$ the crude oil futures price. We can estimate $H$ by regressing the change in the jet fuel price (denominated in cents per gallon) on the change in the crude futures price (denominated in dollar per barrel). Doing so using daily data for January 2000–June 2004 gives (standard errors are in parentheses)

$$P_t - P_{t-1} = \underset{(0.069)}{0.009} + \underset{(0.094)}{2.037}\left(F_t - F_{t-1}\right) R^2 = 0.287 \tag{20}$$

The futures price used in this regression is the price of the current near-term contract. The coefficient on the futures price change tells us that, on average, when the crude futures price increases by \$1, a gallon of jet fuel increases by \$0.02. Suppose that as part of a particular crack spread, 1 gallon of crude oil is used to produce 1 gallon of jet fuel. Then, other things equal, since there are 42 gallons in a barrel, a \$1 increase in the price of a barrel of oil will generate a \$1/42 = \$0.0238 increase in the price of jet fuel. This is approximately the regression coefficient.

The $R^2$ in Equation 19 is 0.287, which implies a correlation coefficient of about 0.50. The hedge would therefore have considerable residual risk.

## Weather Derivatives

Weather derivatives provide another illustration of cross-hedging. Weather as a business risk can be difficult to hedge. For example, weather can affect both the prices of energy products and the amount of energy consumed. If a winter is colder than average, home-owners and businesses will consume extra electricity, heating oil, and natural gas, and the prices of these products will tend to be high as well. Conversely, during a warm winter, energy prices and quantities will be low. While it is possible to use futures markets to hedge prices of commodities such as natural gas, hedging the quantity is more difficult.

There are many other examples of weather risk: ski resorts are harmed by warm winters, soft drink manufacturers are harmed by a cold spring, summer, or fall, and makers of lawn sprinklers are harmed by wet summers. In all of these cases, firms could hedge their risk using **weather derivatives**—contracts that make payments based upon realized characteristics of weather—to cross-hedge their specific risk.

The payoffs for weather derivatives are based on weather-related measurements. An example of a weather contract is the degree-day index futures contract traded at the Chicago Mercantile Exchange. A **heating degree-day** is the maximum of zero and the difference between the average daily temperature and 65 degrees Fahrenheit. A **cooling degree-day** is the maximum of the difference between the average daily temperature and 65 degrees Fahrenheit, and zero. Sixty-five degrees is a moderate temperature. At higher temperatures, air conditioners may be used, while at lower temperatures, heating may be used. A monthly degree-day index is constructed by adding the daily degree-days over the month. The futures contract then settles based on the cumulative heating or cooling degree-days (the two are separate contracts) over the course of a month. The size of the contract is \$100 times the degree-day index. As of September 2004, degree-day index contracts were available for over 20 cities in the United States, Europe, and Japan. There are also puts and calls on these futures.

With city-specific degree-day index contracts, it is possible to create and hedge payoffs based on average temperatures, or using options, based on ranges of average temperatures. If Minneapolis is unusually cold but the rest of the country is normal, the heating degree-day contract for Minneapolis will make a large payment that will compensate the holder for the increased consumption of energy. Notice that in this scenario a natural gas price contract (for example) would not provide a sufficient hedge, since unusual cold in Minneapolis alone would not have much effect on national energy prices.

## SUMMARY

At a general level, commodity forward prices can be described by the same formula as financial forward prices:

$$F_{0,T} = S_0 e^{(r-\delta)T} \tag{21}$$

For financial assets, $\delta$ is the dividend yield. For commodities, $\delta$ is the commodity *lease rate*—the return that makes an investor willing to buy and then lend a commodity. Thus, for the commodity owner who lends the commodity, it is like a dividend. From the commodity borrower's perspective, it is the cost of borrowing the commodity. As with financial forwards, commodity forward prices are biased predictors of the future spot price when the commodity return contains a risk premium.

While the dividend yield for a financial asset can typically be observed directly, the lease rate for a commodity can typically be estimated *only by observing the forward price*. The forward curve provides important information about the commodity.

Commodities are complex because every commodity market differs in the details. Forward curves for different commodities reflect different properties of storability, storage costs, production, and demand. Electricity, gold, corn, natural gas, and oil all have distinct forward curves, reflecting the different characteristics of their physical markets. These idiosyncrasies will be reflected in the commodity lease rate. When there are seasonalities in either the demand or supply of a commodity, the commodity will be stored (assuming this is physically feasible), and the forward curve for the commodity will reflect storage costs. Some holders of a commodity receive benefits from physical ownership. This benefit is called the commodity's *convenience yield*. The convenience yield creates different returns to ownership for different investors, and may or may not be reflected in the forward price. The convenience yield can lead to no-arbitrage regions rather than a no-arbitrage price. It can also be costly to short-sell commodities with a significant convenience yield.

## PRACTICE PROBLEMS FOR READING 33

1.  Suppose the gold spot price is $300/oz., the 1-year forward price is 310.686, and the continuously compounded risk-free rate is 5%.

    **A.**  What is the lease rate?

    **B.**  What is the return on a cash-and-carry in which gold is not loaned?

    **C.**  What is the return on a cash-and-carry in which gold is loaned, earning the lease rate?

2.  Assume that the continuously compounded interest rate is 6% and the storage cost of widgets is $0.03 quarterly (payable at the end of the quarter). Here is the forward price curve for widgets:

| 2004 | 2005 | | | | 2006 | |
|------|------|------|------|------|------|------|
| Dec | Mar | Jun | Sep | Dec | Mar | Jun |
| 3.000 | 3.075 | 3.152 | 2.750 | 2.822 | 2.894 | 2.968 |

    **A.**  What are some possible explanations for the shape of this forward curve?

    **B.**  What annualized rate of return do you earn on a cash-and-carry entered into in December 2004 and closed in March 2005? Is your answer sensible?

    **C.**  What annualized rate of return do you earn on a cash-and-carry entered into in December 2004 and closed in September 2005? Is your answer sensible?

3.  Consider Example 1 on p. 183. Suppose the February forward price had been $2.80. What would the arbitrage be? Suppose it had been $2.65. What would the arbitrage be? In each case, specify the transactions and resulting cash flows in both November and February. What are you assuming about the convenience yield?

# SOLUTIONS FOR READING 33

1. **A.** The spot price of gold is \$300.00 per ounce. With a continuously compounded annual risk-free rate of 5%, and at a one-year forward price of 310.686, we can calculate the lease rate according to the formula:

$$\delta_l = r - \frac{1}{T}\ln\left(\frac{F_{0,T}}{S_0}\right) = 0.05 - \ln\left(\frac{310.686}{300}\right) = 0.015$$

**B.** Suppose gold cannot be loaned. Then our cash and carry "arbitrage" is:

| Transaction | Time 0 | Time T = 1 |
|---|---|---|
| Short forward | 0 | $310.686 - S_T$ |
| Buy gold | −\$300 | $S_T$ |
| Borrow @ 0.05 | \$300 | −\$315.38 |
| Total | 0 | −4.6953 |

The forward price bears an implicit lease rate. Therefore, if we try to engage in a cash and carry arbitrage, but if we do not have access to the gold loan market, and thus to the additional revenue on our long gold position, it is not possible for us to replicate the forward price. We incur a loss.

**C.** If gold can be loaned, we engage in the following cash and carry arbitrage:

| Transaction | Time 0 | Time T = 1 |
|---|---|---|
| Short forward | 0 | $310.686 - S_T$ |
| Buy tailed gold position, lend @ 0.015 | −\$295.5336 | $S_T$ |
| Borrow @ 0.05 | \$295.5336 | −\$310.686 |
| Total | 0 | 0 |

Therefore, we now just break even: Since the forward was fairly priced, taking the implicit lease rate into account, this result should not surprise us.

2. **A.** The forward prices reflect a market for widgets in which seasonality is important. Let us look at two examples, one with constant demand and seasonal supply, and another one with constant supply and seasonal demand.

One possible explanation might be that widgets are extremely difficult to produce and that they need one key ingredient that is only available during July/August. However, the demand for the widgets is constant throughout the year. In order to be able to sell the widgets throughout the year, widgets must be stored after production in August. The forward curve reflects the ever increasing storage costs of widgets until the next production cycle arrives. Once produced, widget prices fall again to the spot price.

Another story that is consistent with the observed prices of widgets is that widgets are in particularly high demand during the summer months. The storage of widgets may be costly, which means that widget producers are reluctant to build up inventory long before the summer. Storage occurs slowly over the winter months and inventories build up sharply just before the highest demand during the summer months. The forward prices reflect those storage cycle costs.

**B.** Let us take the December 2004 forward price as a proxy for the spot price in December 2004. We can then calculate with our cash and carry arbitrage tableau:

| Transaction | Time 0 | Time $T = 3/12$ |
|---|---|---|
| Short March forward | 0 | $3.075 - S_T$ |
| Buy December forward (= buy spot) | −3.00 | $S_T$ |
| Pay storage cost | | −0.03 |
| Total | −3.00 | 3.045 |

We can calculate the annualized rate of return as:

$$\frac{3.045}{3.00} = e^{(r) \times T}$$

$$\Leftrightarrow \ln\left(\frac{3.045}{3.00}\right) = r \times 3/12$$

$$r = 0.05955$$

which is the prevailing risk-free interest rate of 0.06. This result seems to make sense.

**C.** Let us again take the December 2004 forward price as a proxy for the spot price in December 2004. We can then calculate with our cash and carry arbitrage tableau:

| Transaction | Time 0 | Time $T = 9/12$ |
|---|---|---|
| Short Sep forward | 0 | $2.75 - S_T$ |
| Buy spot | −3.00 | $S_T$ |
| Pay storage cost Sep | | −0.03 |
| FV (Storage Jun) | | −0.0305 |
| FV (Storage Mar) | | −0.0309 |
| Total | −3.00 | 2.6586 |

We can calculate the annualized rate of return as:

$$\frac{2.6586}{3.00} = e^{(r) \times T} \Leftrightarrow \ln\left(\frac{2.6586}{3.00}\right) = r \times 9/12$$

$$r = -0.16108$$

This result does not seem to make sense. We would earn a negative annualized return of 16% on such a cash and carry arbitrage. Therefore, it is likely that our naive calculations do not capture an important fact about the widget market. In particular, we will buy and hold the widgets through a time where the forward curve indicates that there is a significant convenience yield attached to widgets.

It is tempting, although premature, to conclude that a reverse cash and carry arbitrage may make a positive 16% annualized return.

**3.** If the February corn forward price is $2.80, the observed forward price is too expensive relative to our theoretical price of $2.7273. We will therefore sell the February contract short, and create a synthetic long position, engaging in cash and carry arbitrage:

| Transaction | Nov | Dec | Jan | Feb |
|---|---|---|---|---|
| Short Feb forward | 0 | | | $2.80 - S_T$ |
| Buy spot | −2.50 | | | $S_T$ |
| Borrow purchasing cost | +2.50 | | | −2.57575 |
| Pay storage cost Dec, | | −0.05 | | −0.051005 |
|    borrow storage cost | | +0.05 | | |
| Pay storage cost Jan, | | | −0.05 | −0.0505 |
|    borrow storage cost | | | +0.05 | |
| Pay storage cost Feb | | | | −0.05 |
| Total | 0 | 0 | 0 | 0.072745 |

We made an arbitrage profit of 0.07 dollar.

If the February corn forward price is $2.65, the observed forward price is too low relative to our theoretical price of $2.7273. We will therefore buy the February contract, and create a synthetic short position, engaging in reverse cash and carry arbitrage:

| Transaction | Nov | Dec | Jan | Feb |
|---|---|---|---|---|
| Long Feb forward | 0 | | | $S_T - 2.65$ |
| Sell spot | 2.50 | | | $-S_T$ |
| Lend short sale proceeds | −2.50 | | | +2.57575 |
| Receive storage cost | | +0.05 | | +0.051005 |
| Dec, lend them | | −0.05 | | |
| Receive storage cost | | | +0.05 | +0.0505 |
| Jan, lend them | | | −0.05 | |
| Receive cost Feb | | | | +0.05 |
| Total | 0 | 0 | 0 | 0.077255 |

We made an arbitrage profit of 0.08 dollar. It is important to keep in mind that we ignored any convenience yield that there may exist to holding the corn. We assumed the convenience yield is zero.

# 14

# Risk Management

Effective risk management identifies, assesses, and controls numerous sources of risk, both financial and nonmarket related, in an effort to achieve the highest possible level of reward for the risks incurred. With the increasingly complex nature of investment management firms and investment portfolios, sophisticated risk management techniques have been developed to provide analysts with the necessary tools to properly measure the varying facets of risk.

The first reading in this study session describes a framework for risk management, focusing on the concepts and tools for measuring and managing market risk and credit risk. The study session continues with an overview of currency management, as global investing involves not only exposure to local market returns but also to exchange rate movements.

## READING ASSIGNMENTS

**Reading 34** *Risk Management*

*Managing Investment Portfolios: A Dynamic Process*, Third Edition, John L. Maginn, CFA, Donald L. Tuttle, CFA, Jerald E. Pinto, CFA, and Dennis W. McLeavey, CFA, editors

**Reading 35** *Currency Risk Management*

*Global Investments*, Sixth Edition, by Bruno Solnik and Dennis McLeavey, CFA

# 34

# Risk Management

*by Don M. Chance, CFA, Kenneth Grant, and John Marsland, CFA*

## LEARNING OUTCOMES

| Mastery | The candidate should be able to: |
|---------|----------------------------------|
| ☐ | **a** discuss the main features of the risk management process, risk governance, risk reduction, and an enterprise risk management system; |
| ☐ | **b** evaluate the strengths and weaknesses of a company's risk management process; |
| ☐ | **c** describe the characteristics of an effective risk management system; |
| ☐ | **d** evaluate a company's or a portfolio's exposures to financial and nonfinancial risk factors; |
| ☐ | **e** calculate and interpret value at risk (VAR) and explain its role in measuring overall and individual position market risk; |
| ☐ | **f** compare the analytical (variance–covariance), historical, and Monte Carlo methods for estimating VAR and discuss the advantages and disadvantages of each; |
| ☐ | **g** discuss the advantages and limitations of VAR and its extensions, including cash flow at risk, earnings at risk, and tail value at risk; |
| ☐ | **h** compare alternative types of stress testing and discuss the advantages and disadvantages of each; |
| ☐ | **i** evaluate the credit risk of an investment position, including forward contract, swap, and option positions; |
| ☐ | **j** demonstrate the use of risk budgeting, position limits, and other methods for managing market risk; |
| ☐ | **k** demonstrate the use of exposure limits, marking to market, collateral, netting arrangements, credit standards, and credit derivatives to manage credit risk; |
| ☐ | **l** discuss the Sharpe ratio, risk-adjusted return on capital, return over maximum drawdown, and the Sortino ratio as measures of risk-adjusted performance; |
| ☐ | **m** demonstrate the use of VAR and stress testing in setting capital requirements. |

*Managing Investment Portfolios: A Dynamic Process*, Third Edition, John L. Maginn, CFA, Donald L. Tuttle, CFA, Jerald E. Pinto, CFA, and Dennis W. McLeavey, CFA, editors. Copyright © 2007 by CFA Institute.

# 1 INTRODUCTION

Investment is an intrinsically risky activity. Indeed, risk taking is an innate characteristic of human activity and as old as humankind itself. Without risk, we have little possibility of reward. We thus need to treat risk management as a critical component of the investment process. Specifically, with regard to both individual investments and entire portfolios, we should examine and compare the full spectrum of risks and expected returns to ensure that to the greatest extent possible the exposures we assume are at all times justified by the rewards we can reasonably expect to reap. Proper identification, measurement, and control of risk are key to the process of investing, and we put our investment objectives at risk unless we commit appropriate resources to these tasks.

A portfolio manager must be familiar with risk management not only as it relates to portfolio management but also as it relates to managing an enterprise, because a portfolio manager is a responsible executive in an enterprise (his investment firm). He must also understand the risks and risk management processes of companies in which he invests. The risk management framework presented in this reading is an inclusive one, applicable to the management of both enterprise and portfolio risk.

Although portfolio managers and enterprises may occasionally hedge their risks or engage in other risk-reducing transactions, they should not, and indeed cannot, restrict their activities to those that are risk free, as discussed in more detail later. The fact that these entities engage in risky activities raises a number of important questions:

■ What is an effective process for identifying, measuring, and managing risk?

■ Which risks are worth taking on a regular basis, which are worth taking on occasion, and which should be avoided altogether?

■ How can our success or lack of success in risk taking be evaluated?

■ What information should be reported to investors and other stakeholders concerning the risk of an enterprise or a portfolio?

The answers to these questions and many others collectively define the process of *risk management.* Over the course of this reading, we endeavor to explain this process and some of its most important concepts. Consistent with the book's focus on portfolio management, this reading concentrates on managing risks arising from transactions that are affected by interest rates, stock prices, commodity prices, and exchange rates. We also survey the other risks that most enterprises face and illustrate the discussion from a variety of perspectives. The reading is organized as follows. Section 2 defines and explains a risk management framework. Section 3 discusses what constitutes good risk management. Sections 4, 5, and 6 discuss the individual steps in the risk management process, and we conclude with a summary.

# 2 RISK MANAGEMENT AS A PROCESS

We can formally define risk management as follows:

> Risk management is a process involving the identification of exposures to risk, the establishment of appropriate ranges for exposures (given a clear understanding of an entity's objectives and constraints), the continuous measurement of these exposures (either present or contemplated), and the execution of appropriate adjustments whenever exposure levels fall outside of target ranges. The process is continuous and may require alterations in any of these activities to reflect new policies, preferences, and information.

This definition highlights that risk management should be a *process*, not just an activity. A process is continuous and subject to evaluation and revision. Effective risk management requires the constant and consistent monitoring of exposures, with an eye toward making adjustments, whenever and wherever the situation calls for them.[1] Risk management in its totality is all at once a proactive, anticipative, and reactive process that continuously monitors and controls risk.

Exhibit 1 illustrates the *practical application of the process* of risk management as it applies to a hypothetical business enterprise. We see at the top that the company faces a range of financial and nonfinancial risks; moving down the exhibit, we find that the company has responded to this challenge by establishing a series of risk management policies and procedures. First, it defines its risk tolerance, which is the level of risk it is willing and able to bear.[2] It then identifies the risks, drawing on all sources of information, and attempts to measure these risks using information or data related to all of its identified exposures. The process of risk measurement can be as simple as Exhibit 1 illustrates, but more often than not it involves expertise in the practice of modeling and sometimes requires complex analysis. Once the enterprise has built effective risk identification and measurement mechanisms, it is in a position to adjust its risk exposures, wherever and whenever exposures diverge from previously identified target ranges. These adjustments take the form of risk-modifying transactions (broadly understood to include the possible complete transfer of risk). The execution of risk management transactions is itself a distinct process; for portfolios, this step consists of trade identification, pricing, and execution. The process then loops around to the measurement of risk and continues in that manner, and to the constant monitoring and adjustment of the risk, to bring it into or maintain it within the desired range.

| **Exhibit 1** | **Risk Management Process: The Practice of Risk Management** |
| --- | --- |

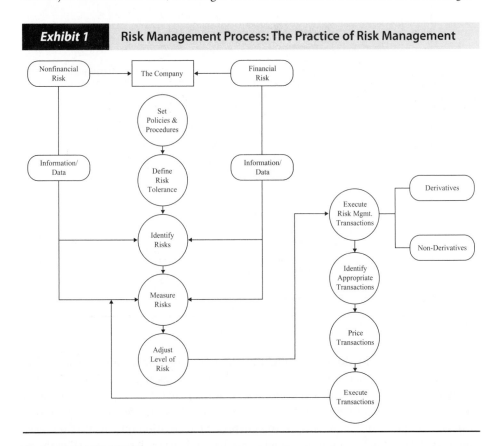

---

1 For brevity, we often refer to an exposure to risk or **risk exposure** (the state of being exposed to or vulnerable to a risk) as simply an *exposure*.

2 An enterprise may have different risk tolerances for different types of risk in a manner that does not readily permit averaging, so we should view risk tolerance in this context as potentially multidimensional.

In applying the risk management process to portfolio management, managers must devote a considerable amount of attention to measuring and pricing the risks of financial transactions or positions, particularly those involving derivatives. Exhibit 2 illustrates this process of pricing and measuring risk, expanding on the detail given in Exhibit 1. In Exhibit 2, we see at the top that in pricing the transaction, we first identify the source(s) of uncertainty. Then we select the appropriate pricing model and enter our desired inputs to derive our most accurate estimate of the instrument's model value (which we hope reflects its true economic value). Next, we look to the marketplace for an indication of where we can actually execute the transaction. If the execution price is "attractive" (i.e., the market will buy the instrument from us at a price at or above, or sell it to us at a price at or below, the value indicated by our model), it fits our criteria for acceptance; if not, we should seek an alternative transaction. After executing the transaction, we would then return to the process of measuring risk.

| Exhibit 2 | Risk Management Process: Pricing and Measuring Risk |
| --- | --- |

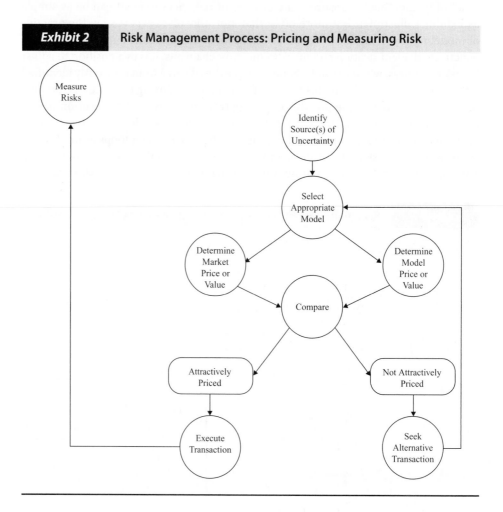

Our discussion of Exhibit 1 highlighted that risk management involves adjusting levels of risk to appropriate levels, not necessarily eliminating risk altogether. It is nearly impossible to operate a successful business or investment program without taking risks. Indeed, a company that accepted no risk would not be an operating business. Corporations take risks for the purpose of generating returns that increase their owners' wealth. Corporation owners, the shareholders, risk their capital with the same objective in mind. *Companies that succeed in doing the activities they should be able to do well, however, cannot afford to fail overall because of activities in which they have no expertise.* Accordingly, many companies hedge risks that arise from areas in which they have no expertise or comparative advantage. In areas in which they do have an edge (i.e., their primary line of business), they tend to hedge only tactically. They hedge when they think they have sufficient information to suggest that a lower risk position is appropriate. They manage risk, increasing it when they perceive a competitive advantage and decreasing it when they perceive a competitive disadvantage. In essence, they attempt to efficiently allocate risk. Similarly, portfolio managers attempt to efficiently use risk to achieve their return objectives.

We have illustrated that risk management involves far more than risk reduction or hedging (one particular risk-reduction method). Risk management is a general practice that involves risk modification (e.g., risk reduction or risk expansion) as deemed necessary and appropriate by the custodians of capital and its beneficial owners.

For the risk management process to work, managers need to specify thoughtfully the business processes they use to put risk management into practice. We refer to these processes collectively as risk governance, the subject of the next section.

## RISK GOVERNANCE

3

Senior management is ultimately responsible for *every* activity within an organization. Their involvement is thus essential for risk management to succeed. The process of setting overall policies and standards in risk management is called risk governance. Risk governance involves choices of governance structure, infrastructure, reporting, and methodology. The quality of risk governance can be judged by its transparency, accountability, effectiveness (achieving objectives), and efficiency (economy in the use of resources to achieve objectives).

Risk governance begins with choices concerning governance structure. Organizations must determine whether they wish their risk management efforts to be centralized or decentralized. Under a centralized risk management system, a company has a single risk management group that monitors and ultimately controls all of the organization's risk-taking activities. By contrast, a decentralized system places risk management responsibility on individual business unit managers. In a decentralized approach, each unit calculates and reports its exposures independently. Decentralization has the advantage of allowing the people closer to the actual risk taking to more directly manage it. Centralization permits economies of scale and allows a company to recognize the offsetting nature of distinct exposures that an enterprise might assume in its day-to-day operations. For example, suppose one subsidiary of a company buys from Japan and another subsidiary sells to Japan, with both engaged in yen-denominated transactions. Each subsidiary would perceive some foreign exchange exposure. From a centralized viewpoint, however, these risks have offsetting effects, thereby reducing the overall need to hedge.

Moreover, even when exposures to a single risk factor do not directly offset one another, enterprise-level risk estimates may be lower than those derived from individual units because of the risk-mitigating benefits of diversification. For example, one corporate division may borrow U.S. dollars at five-year maturities, and another division may fund its operation by issuing 90-day commercial paper. In theory, the corporation's overall sensitivity to rising interest rates may be less than the sum of that reported by each division, because the five-year and 90-day rate patterns are less than perfectly correlated.

In addition, centralized risk management puts the responsibility on a level closer to senior management, where we have argued it belongs. It gives an overall picture of the company's risk position, and ultimately, the overall picture is what counts. This centralized type of risk management is now called **enterprise risk management** (ERM) or sometimes firmwide risk management because its distinguishing feature is a firmwide or across-enterprise perspective.[3] In ERM, an organization must consider each risk factor to which it is exposed—both in isolation and in terms of any interplay among them.

Risk governance is an element of **corporate governance** (the system of internal controls and procedures used to manage individual companies). As risk management's role in corporate governance has become better appreciated, the importance of ERM has risen proportionately. Indeed, for risk-taking entities (this means nearly the entire economic universe), it is contradictory to suggest that an organization has sound corporate governance without maintaining a clear and continuously updated understanding of its exposures at the enterprise level. Senior managers who have an adequate understanding of these factors are in a superior governance position to those who do not, and over time this advantage is almost certain to accrue to the bottom line. Therefore, the risk management system of a company that chooses a decentralized risk management approach requires a mechanism by which senior managers can inform themselves about the enterprise's overall risk exposures.

At the enterprise level, companies should control not only the sensitivity of their earnings to fluctuations in the stock market, interest rates, foreign exchange rates, and commodity prices, but also their exposures to credit spreads and default risk, to gaps in the timing match of their assets and liabilities, and to operational/systems failures, financial fraud, and other factors that can affect corporate profitability and even survival.

### Example 1

## Some Risk Governance Concerns of Investment Firms

Regardless of the risk governance approach chosen, effective risk governance for investment firms demands that the trading function be separated from the risk management function. An individual or group that is independent of the trading function must monitor the positions taken by the traders or risk takers and price them independently. The risk manager has the responsibility for monitoring risk levels for all portfolio positions (as well as for portfolios as a whole) and executing any strategies necessary to control the level of risk. To do this, the risk manager must have timely and accurate information, authority, and independence from the trading function. That is not to say that the trading function will not need its own risk management expertise in order to allocate capital in an optimal fashion and maximize risk-adjusted profit. Ideally, the risk manager will work with the trading desks in the development of risk management specifications, such that everyone in the organization is working from a common point of reference in terms of measuring and controlling exposures.

Effective risk governance for an investment firm also requires that the back office be fully independent from the front office, so as to provide a check on the accuracy of information and to forestall collusion. (The **back office** is concerned with transaction processing, record keeping, regulatory compliance, and other administrative functions; the **front office** is concerned with trading and sales.) Besides being independent, the back office of an investment firm must have a high level of competence, training, and knowledge because failed trades, errors, and over-sights can lead to significant losses that may be amplified by leverage. The back office must effectively coordinate with external service suppliers, such

---

**3** The Committee of Sponsoring Organizations of the Treadway Commission defines ERM as follows: "Enterprise risk management is a process, effected by an entity's board of directors, management, and other personnel, applied in strategy setting and across the enterprise, designed to identify potential events that may affect the entity, and manage risk to be within its risk appetite, to provide reasonable assurance regarding the achievement of entity objectives" (2004, p. 2).

as the firm's **global custodian**. The global custodian effects **trade settlement** (completion of a trade wherein purchased financial instruments are transferred to the buyer and the buyer transfers money to the seller), safekeeping of assets, and the allocation of trades to individual custody accounts. Increasingly, financial institutions are seeking risk reduction with cost efficiencies through **straight-through processing** (STP) systems that obviate manual and/or duplicative intervention in the process from trade placement to settlement.

An effective ERM system typically incorporates the following steps:

1. Identify each *risk factor* to which the company is exposed.

2. Quantify each exposure's size in money terms.

3. Map these inputs into a risk estimation calculation.[4]

4. Identify overall risk exposures as well as the contribution to overall risk deriving from each risk factor.

5. Set up a process to report on these risks periodically to senior management, who will set up a committee of division heads and executives to determine capital allocations, risk limits, and risk management policies.

6. Monitor compliance with policies and risk limits.

Steps 5 and 6 help enormously in allowing an organization to quantify the magnitude and distribution of its exposures and in enabling it to use the ERM system's output to more actively align its risk profile with its opportunities and constraints on a routine, periodic basis.

As a final note, effective ERM systems always feature centralized data warehouses, where a company stores all pertinent risk information, including position and market data, in a technologically efficient manner. Depending on the organization's size and complexity, developing and maintaining a high-quality data warehouse can require a significant and continuing investment. In particular, the process of identifying and correcting errors in a technologically efficient manner can be enormously resource intensive—especially when the effort requires storing historical information on complex financial instruments. It is equally clear, however, that the return on such an investment can be significant.

# IDENTIFYING RISKS

**4**

As indicated above, economic agents of all types assume different types of exposures on a near-continuous basis. Moreover, these risk exposures take very different forms, each of which, to varying extents, may call for customized treatment. Effective risk management demands the separation of risk exposures into specific categories that reflect their distinguishing characteristics. Once a classification framework is in place, we can move on to the next steps in the risk management process: identification, classification, and measurement.

Although the list is far from exhaustive, many company (or portfolio) exposures fall into one of the following categories: market risk (including interest rate risk, exchange rate risk, equity price risk, commodity price risk); credit risk; liquidity risk; operational risk; model risk; settlement risk; regulatory risk; legal/contract risk; tax risk; accounting risk; and sovereign/political risk. These risks may be grouped into

---

**4** For example, using Value at Risk or another of the concepts that we will discuss later.

financial risks and nonfinancial risks as shown in Exhibit 3.[5] **Financial risk** refers to all risks derived from events in the external financial markets; **nonfinancial risk** refers to all other forms of risk.

| Exhibit 3 | The Sources of Risk |
| --- | --- |

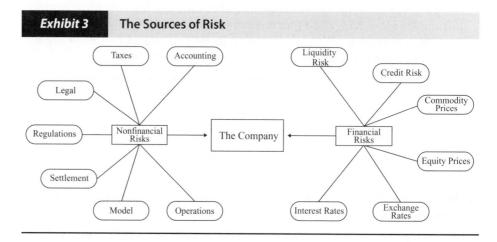

Example 2 illustrates a simple analysis of risk exposures. In the example, we have detailed the subtypes of market risk; each one may pose unique issues of measurement and management.

## Example 2

## An Analysis of Risk Exposures

Liam McNulty is the risk manager for a large multinational agricultural concern, Agripure. The company grows its own corn, wheat, and soybeans but pays large sums to third parties for pesticides, fertilizer, and other supplies. For this, it must borrow heavily to finance its purchases. Customers typically purchase Agripure's goods on credit. Moreover, Agripure buys and sells its products and raw materials worldwide, often transacting in the domestic currency of its customers and suppliers. Finally, to finance its own expansion, Agripure intends to issue stock.

Recommend and justify the risk exposures that McNulty should report as part of an enterprise risk management system for Agripure.

## Solution:

McNulty should report on the following risk exposures:

- Market risk, including these subtypes:
    - Commodity price risk, because Agripure has exposures in raw materials and finished products.
    - Foreign exchange risk, because it buys and sells products world-wide, often transacting in the home currency of the entity on the other side of the transaction.
    - Equity market risk, because Agripure's expansion financing is affected by the price it receives for its share issuance.

---

**5** A notable risk that could be included in a comprehensive listing (particularly as pertains to commercial enterprises) is **business risk**, defined by Ross, Westerfield, and Jordan (1993, p. 527) as "the equity risk that comes from the nature of the firm's operating activities." For example, the risk for a hotel business that arises from variability in room occupancy rates would be classified as business risk. In a later section on other risks, we also discuss two types of risks related to netting.

> - Interest rate risk, because Agripure has exposures in financing its raw material purchases and because its customers typically purchase their goods on credit.
> - Credit risk, because Agripure's customers typically purchase their goods on credit.
> - Operational risk, because as an agricultural producer Agripure is subject to weather-related risk (an external event).

In the following sections, we discuss each of these risks in detail.

## 4.1 Market Risk

**Market risk** is the risk associated with interest rates, exchange rates, stock prices, and commodity prices. It is linked to supply and demand in various marketplaces. Although we may distinguish among interest rate risk, currency risk, equity market risk, and commodity risk when discussing measurement and management issues, for example, these subtypes all have exposure to supply and demand. Much of the evolution that has taken place in the field of risk management has emanated from a desire to understand and control market risks, and we will have a good deal to say about this topic throughout the balance of this reading.

One set of market risk takers with special requirements for market risk are defined-benefit (DB) pension funds, which manage retirement assets generally under strict regulatory regimes. Pension fund risk management necessarily concerns itself with funding the stream of promised payments to pension plan participants. Therefore, a DB plan must measure its market exposures not purely on the basis of its assets but also in terms of the risks of pension assets in relation to liabilities. Other investors as well can have strong asset/liability management concerns.[6] This has important implications for exposure measurement, risk control, capital allocation and risk budgeting, which we will address later.

## 4.2 Credit Risk

Apart from market risk, credit risk is the primary type of financial risk that economic agents face. **Credit risk** is the risk of loss caused by a counterparty or debtor's failure to make a promised payment. This definition reflects a traditional binary concept of credit risk, by and large embodied by default risk (i.e., the risk of loss associated with the nonperformance of a debtor or counterparty). For the last several years, however, credit markets have taken on more and more of the characteristics typically associated with full-scale trading markets. As this pattern has developed, the lines between credit risk and market risk have blurred as markets for credit derivatives have developed.[7] For example, the holder of a traded credit instrument could suffer a loss as a result of a short-term supply–demand imbalance without the underlying probability of default changing. Some subset of market participants often suffers losses whether credit is improving or deteriorating because it is now quite easy to take long and short positions in credit markets. Finally, note that pricing conventions for credit typically take the form of spreads against market benchmarks, for example, government bond yields or swap rates.[8] Thus when a given credit instrument is said

---

**6** See the readings on managing institutional investor portfolios and asset allocation in particular.

**7** A **credit derivative** is a contract in which one party has the right to claim a payment from another party in the event that a specific credit event occurs over the life of the contract.

**8** A **swap rate** is the interest rate applicable to the pay-fixed-rate side of an interest rate swap. See Chance (2003) to review the basics of swaps.

to be priced at 150 over, it typically means that the instrument can be purchased to yield 150 basis points over the rate on the market benchmark (e.g., the government bond with the same maturity).

Until the era of over-the-counter derivatives, credit risk was more or less exclusively a concern in the bond and loan markets. Exchange-traded derivatives are guaranteed against credit loss. OTC derivatives, however, contain no explicit credit guaranty and, therefore, subject participants to the threat of loss if their counterparty fails to pay.

Before OTC derivatives became widely used, bond portfolio managers and bank loan officers were the primary credit risk managers. They assessed credit risk in a number of ways,[9] including the qualitative evaluation of corporate fundamentals through the review of financial statements, the calculation of credit scores, and by relying on consensus information that was and still is widely available for virtually every borrower. The synthesis of this "credit consensus" resides with rating agencies and credit bureaus, which were historically, and to some extent still are, the primary sources of information on credit quality. The proliferation and complexity of financial instruments with credit elements in the OTC derivatives market, however, has placed new demands on the understanding of credit risk. Indeed, the need to better understand credit risk has led to significant progress in developing tools to measure and manage this risk.

## 4.3 Liquidity Risk

**Liquidity risk** is the risk that a financial instrument cannot be purchased or sold without a significant concession in price because of the market's potential inability to efficiently accommodate the desired trading size.[10] In some cases, the market for a financial instrument can dry up completely, resulting in a total inability to trade an asset. This risk is present in both initiating and liquidating transactions, for both long and short positions, but can be particularly acute for liquidating transactions—especially when such liquidation is motivated by the need to reduce exposures in the wake of large losses. Those wishing to sell securities under these circumstances can find the market bereft of buyers at prices acceptable to the seller, particularly in periods of unusually high market stress. Perhaps less frequently, short sellers in need of covering losing positions are at risk to short squeezes. This situation is often exacerbated by the fact that for most cash instruments, short sellers establish positions by borrowing the securities in question from brokerage firms and other entities that typically can require the securities to be returned with little or no advance warning. Although derivatives can be used to effectively sell an asset or liquidate a short position, they often will not help in managing liquidity risk. If the underlying is illiquid, there is a good possibility that the universe of associated derivative instruments may also be illiquid.

For traded securities, the size of the **bid–ask spread** (the spread between the bid and ask prices), stated as a proportion of security price, is frequently used as an indicator of liquidity.[11] When markets are illiquid, dealers expect to sell at relatively high prices and buy at relatively low prices to justify their assumption of exposure to liquidity risk. However, bid–ask quotations apply only to specified, usually small size, trades, and are thus an imprecise measure of liquidity risk. Other, more complex measures of liquidity have been developed to address the issue of trading volume. For

---

**9** Credit risk in the more general context of fixed-income securities is discussed in more detail in Fabozzi (2004a), Chapter 15. Many of the principles of credit risk analysis for fixed-income securities also apply to derivatives.

**10** Liquidity has been used in various senses. For example, **funding risk** (the risk that liabilities funding long asset positions cannot be rolled over at reasonable cost) has sometimes been referred to as a type of liquidity risk; liquidity in this sense relates to the availability of cash. One would still distinguish between market liquidity risk (discussed in the reading) and funding liquidity risk.

**11** For example, see Amihud and Mendelson (1986). We must state the bid–ask spread as a proportion of stock price to control for differences in securities' prices.

example, Amihud's (2002) illiquidity ratio measures the price impact per $1 million traded in a day, expressed in percentage terms. Note, however, that no explicit transaction volume is available for many OTC instruments. Less formally, one of the best ways to measure liquidity is through the monitoring of transaction volumes, with the obvious rule of thumb being that the greater the average transaction volume, the more liquid the instrument in question is likely to be. Historical volume patterns, however, may not repeat themselves at times when the liquidity they imply is most needed.

Liquidity risk is a serious problem and often is difficult to observe and quantify. It is not always apparent that certain securities are illiquid: Some that are liquid when purchased (or sold short) can be illiquid by the time they are sold (or repurchased to cover short positions). Valuation models rarely encompass this liquidity risk in estimating fair value. Those models that do attempt to incorporate transaction costs do so in a nonformulaic manner. Of course, these problems typically reach their apex when the markets themselves are under stress and the need for liquidity is most acute. Liquidity assessments that fail to consider the problems that might arise during periods of market stress are incomplete from a risk management perspective. For all of these reasons, liquidity risk is one of the more complex aspects of risk management.

We now turn our attention to nonfinancial risks, starting with operational risk.

## 4.4 Operational Risk

**Operational risk**, sometimes called operations risk, is the risk of loss from failures in a company's systems and procedures or from external events. These risks can arise from computer breakdowns (including bugs, viruses, and hardware problems), human error, and events completely outside of companies' control, including "acts of God" and terrorist actions.

Computer failures are quite common, but the development of backup systems and recovery procedures has reduced their impact in recent years. Technology bugs and viruses are potentially quite risky but have become more manageable with the proper personnel, software, and systems. Even the smallest business has learned to back up files and take them off the premises. Larger businesses have much more extensive computer risk management practices.

Human failures include the typically manageable unintentional errors that occur in every business, along with more critical and potentially disastrous incidences of willful misconduct.

---

**Example 3**

### An Operational Risk for Financial Services Companies: The Rogue Trader

Among the more prominent examples of operational risk for financial service companies is that of the so-called rogue trader: an individual who has either assumed an irresponsibly high level of risk, engaged in unauthorized transactions, or some combination of the two. The risks associated with this type of activity increase the longer it goes undetected, and often the very lack of controls that creates the opportunity for a rogue trader in the first place renders it difficult to quickly determine that a problem exists. In some extreme cases, such as an incident that occurred in the Singapore office of Barings Bank, a rogue trader can cause an entire organization to fold. The incidence of high-profile rogue trading episodes has multiplied since the early 1990s, but in nearly all of these episodes, the problem's major source was a lack of rudimentary corporate controls and oversight.[12]

---

12 For more on the subject of operational risk in financial services companies, see Marshall (2001).

Our definition of operational risk includes losses from external events. Insurance typically covers damage from fires, floods and other types of natural disasters, but insurance provides only cash compensation for losses. If a flood destroys the trading room of a bank, the monies recovered likely will not come close to paying for the loss of customers who may take their trading business elsewhere. Hence, most companies have backup facilities they can activate in such cases. The 1993 World Trade Center bombing in New York City led many companies to establish backup systems in the event of another terrorist attack, which sadly took place on a greater scale eight years later. The speed with which trading enterprises, including the New York Stock Exchange, domiciled inside or near the World Trade Center reestablished full-scale operations after such a devastating attack is but one indication of the increased importance placed on operational risk management by these enterprises.

In some cases, companies manage operational risk by using insurance contracts, which involves a transfer of risk. A few types of derivative contracts even pay off for operational losses, but the market for these has not fully developed. These instruments are essentially insurance contracts. Most companies manage operational risk, however, by monitoring their systems, taking preventive actions, and having a plan in place to respond if such events occur.

## 4.5 Model Risk

**Model risk** is the risk that a model is incorrect or misapplied; in investments, it often refers to valuation models. Model risk exists to some extent in any model that attempts to identify the fair value of financial instruments, but it is most prevalent in models used in derivatives markets.

Since the development of the seminal Black–Scholes–Merton option pricing model, both derivatives and derivative pricing models have proliferated.[13] The development of so many models has brought model risk to prominence. If an investor chooses an inappropriate model, misinterprets the results, or uses incorrect inputs, the chance of loss increases at the same time that control over risk is impaired. Therefore, investors must scrutinize and objectively validate all models they use.

## 4.6 Settlement (Herstatt) Risk

The payments associated with the purchase and sale of cash securities such as equities and bonds, along with cash transfers executed for swaps, forwards, options, and other types of derivatives, are referred to collectively as settlements. The process of settling a contract involves one or both parties making payments and/or transferring assets to the other. We define **settlement risk** as the risk that one party could be in the process of paying the counterparty while the counterparty is declaring bankruptcy.[14]

Most regulated futures and options exchanges are organized in such a way that they themselves (or a closely affiliated entity) act as the central counterparty to all transactions. This facility usually takes the form of a clearing house, which is backed by large and credible financial guarantees. All transactions on the exchange take place between an exchange member and the central counterparty, which removes settlement risk from the transaction. The possibility always exists, however, that the exchange member is acting in an agency capacity and/or that its end client fails to settle. Clearly in these circumstances, the responsibility falls to the exchange member to make good and bear any loss on the trade.

---

**13** See Chance (2003).
**14** Note that settlement can also fail because of operational problems even when the counterparty is creditworthy; the risk in that case would be an operational risk.

OTC markets, including those for bonds and derivatives, do not rely on a clearing house. Instead, they effect settlement through the execution of agreements between the actual counterparties to the transaction. With swaps and forward contracts, settlements take the form of two-way payments. Two-way payments create the problem that one party could be in the process of paying its counterparty while that counterparty is declaring bankruptcy and failing to make its payment. Netting arrangements, used in interest rate swaps and certain other derivatives, can reduce settlement risk. In such arrangements, the financial instrument is periodically marked to market (under an agreed-upon methodology) and the "loser" pays the "winner" the difference for the period. This mechanism reduces the magnitude of any settlement failures to the net payment owed plus the cost of replacing the defaulted contract. Transactions with a foreign exchange component, however (e.g., currency forwards and currency swaps, but also spot trades), do not lend themselves to netting. Furthermore, such contracts often involve two parties in different countries, increasing the risk that one party will be unaware that the other party is declaring bankruptcy. The risk has been called Herstatt risk because of a famous incident in 1974 when Bank Herstatt failed at a time when counterparties were sending money to it.

Fortunately, bankruptcy does not occur often. Furthermore, through continuously linked settlement (CLS) in which payments on foreign exchange contracts are executed simultaneously, this risk has been even further mitigated.[15]

## 4.7 Regulatory Risk

**Regulatory risk** is the risk associated with the uncertainty of how a transaction will be regulated or with the potential for regulations to change. Equities (common and preferred stock), bonds, futures, and exchange-traded derivatives markets usually are regulated at the federal level, whereas OTC derivative markets and transactions in alternative investments (e.g., hedge funds and private equity partnerships) are much more loosely regulated. Federal authorities in most countries take the position that these latter transactions are private agreements between sophisticated parties, and as such should not be regulated in the same manner as publicly traded markets. Indeed, in some circumstances, unsophisticated investors are excluded altogether from participating in such investments.

With regard to derivatives, companies that are regulated in other ways may have their derivatives business indirectly regulated. For example, in the United States, banks are heavily regulated by federal and state banking authorities, which results in indirect regulation of their derivatives business. Beyond these de facto restrictions, however, in most countries, the government does not regulate the OTC derivatives business.[16]

Regulation is a source of uncertainty. Regulated markets are always subject to the risk that the existing regulatory regime will become more onerous, more restrictive, or more costly. Unregulated markets face the risk of becoming regulated, thereby imposing costs and restrictions where none existed previously. Regulatory risk is difficult to estimate because laws are written by politicians and regulations are written by civil servants; laws, regulations, and enforcement activities may change with changes in political parties and regulatory personnel. Both the regulations and their enforcement often reflect attitudes and philosophies that may change over time. Regulatory risk and the degree of regulation also vary widely from country to country.

Regulatory risk often arises from the arbitrage nature of derivatives and structured transactions. For example, a long position in stock accompanied by borrowing can replicate a forward contract or a futures contract. Stocks are regulated by securities regulators, and loans are typically regulated by banking oversight entities. Forward

---

**15** The execution takes place in a five-hour window (three hours in Asia Pacific), representing the overlapping business hours of different settlement systems. For more information, see www.cls-group.com.

**16** Of course, contract law always applies to any such transaction.

contracts are essentially unregulated. Futures contracts are regulated at the federal level in most countries, but not always by the same agency that regulates the stock market. Equivalent combinations of cash securities and derivatives thus are not always regulated in the same way or by the same regulator. Another example of inconsistent or ambiguous regulatory treatment might arise from a position spanning different geographic regions, such as the ownership of a NASDAQ-listed European-domiciled technology company in a European stock portfolio.

## 4.8 Legal/Contract Risk

Nearly every financial transaction is subject to some form of contract law. Any contract has two parties, each obligated to do something for the other. If one party fails to perform or believes that the other has engaged in a fraudulent practice, the contract can be abrogated. A dispute would then likely arise, which could involve litigation, especially if large losses occur. In some cases, the losing party will claim that the counterparty acted fraudulently or that the contract was illegal in the first place and, therefore, should be declared null and void. The possibility of such a claim being upheld in court creates a form of **legal/contract risk**: the possibility of loss arising from the legal system's failure to enforce a contract in which an enterprise has a financial stake.

Derivative transactions often are arranged by a dealer acting as a principal. The legal system has upheld many claims against dealers, which is not to say that the dealer has always been in the wrong but simply that dealers have sometimes put themselves into precarious situations. Dealers are indeed often advisors to their counterparties, giving the impression that if the dealer and counterparty enter into a contract, the counterparty expects the contract to result in a positive outcome. To avoid that misunderstanding, dealers may go to great lengths to make clear that they are the opposite party, not an advisor. Dealers also write contracts more carefully to cover the various contingencies that have been used against them in litigation. But a government or regulator might still take the legal view that a dealer has a higher duty of care for a less experienced counterparty. Contract law is in most circumstances federally or nationally governed. As such, the added possibility exists in arbitrage transactions that different laws might apply to each side of the transaction, thus adding more risk.

## 4.9 Tax Risk

**Tax risk** arises because of the uncertainty associated with tax laws. Tax law covering the ownership and transaction of financial instruments can be extremely complex, and the taxation of derivatives transactions is an area of even more confusion and uncertainty. Tax rulings clarify these matters on occasion, but on other occasions, they confuse them further. In addition, tax policy often fails to keep pace with innovations in financial instruments. When this happens, investors are left to guess what type and level of taxation will ultimately apply, creating the risk that they have guessed wrongly and could later be subject to back taxes. In some cases, transactions that appear upfront to be exempt from taxation could later be found to be taxable, thereby creating a future expense that was unanticipated (and perhaps impossible to anticipate) at the time that the transaction was executed. We noted, in discussing regulatory risk, that equivalent combinations of financial instruments are not always regulated the same way. Likewise, equivalent combinations of financial instruments are not always subject to identical tax treatment. This fact creates a tremendous burden of inconsistency and confusion, but on occasion the opportunity arises for arbitrage gains, although the tax authorities often quickly close such opportunities.

Like regulatory risk, tax risk is affected by the priorities of politicians and regulators. Many companies invest considerable resources in lobbying as well as hiring tax experts and consultants to control tax risk.

## 4.10  Accounting Risk

**Accounting risk** arises from uncertainty about how a transaction should be recorded and the potential for accounting rules and regulations to change. Accounting statements are a key, if not primary, source of information on publicly traded companies. In the United States, accounting standards are established primarily by the Financial Accounting Standards Board (FASB). Legal requirements in the area of accounting are enforced for publicly traded companies by federal securities regulators and by the primary stock exchange associated with the security. Non-U.S. domiciled companies that raise capital in the United States are also subject to these standards and laws. The law demands accurate accounting statements, and inaccurate financial reporting can subject corporations and their principals to civil and criminal litigation for fraud. In addition, the market punishes companies that do not provide accurate accounting statements, as happened for Enron and its auditor Arthur Andersen.

The International Accounting Standards Board (IASB) sets global standards for accounting. The FASB and the IASB have been working together toward convergence of accounting standards worldwide with 2005 targeted for harmonization. Historically, accounting standards have varied from country to country, with some countries requiring a higher level of disclosure than others.

**Example 4**

## Accounting Risk: The Case of Derivative Contracts

Accounting for derivative contracts has raised considerable confusion. When confusion occurs, companies run the risk that the accounting treatment for transactions could require adjustment, which could possibly lead to a need to restate earnings. Earnings restatements are almost always embarrassing for a company, because they suggest either a desire to hide information, the company's failure to fully understand material elements of its business, or some combination of the two. Restatements are very detrimental to corporate valuations because they cause investors to lose confidence in the accuracy of corporate financial disclosures. Beyond that, if negligence or intent to mislead was involved, the company could face civil and criminal liabilities as well.

Confusion over the proper accounting for derivatives gives rise to accounting as a source of risk. As with regulatory and tax risk, sometimes equivalent combinations of derivatives are not accounted for uniformly. The accounting profession typically moves to close such loopholes, but it does not move quickly and certainly does not keep pace with the pace of innovation in financial engineering, so problems nearly always remain.

The IASB in IAS 39 (International Accounting Standard No. 39) requires the inclusion of derivatives and their associated gains and losses on financial statements, as does the FASB in SFAS 133 (Statement of Financial Accounting Standard No. 133). These rulings contain some areas of confusion and inconsistency, however, affording considerable room for interpretation.[17]

---

17 Gastineau, Smith, and Todd (2001) provides excellent information on accounting for derivatives in the United States.

Most companies deal with accounting risk by hiring personnel with the latest accounting knowledge. In addition, companies lobby and communicate actively with accounting regulatory bodies and federal regulators in efforts to modify accounting rules in a desired direction and to make them clearer. Companies have tended to fight rules requiring more disclosure, arguing that disclosure per se is not always beneficial and can involve additional costs. A trade-off exists between the rights of corporations to protect proprietary information from competitors and the need to adequately inform investors and the public. This controversy is unlikely to go away, suggesting that accounting risk will always remain.

## 4.11 Sovereign and Political Risks

Although they are covered indirectly above in areas such as regulatory, accounting, and tax risk, we can also isolate, and to a certain extent evaluate, the risks associated with changing political conditions in countries where portfolio managers may choose to assume exposure. Although this topic merits more discussion than can reasonably be devoted in this space, we can broadly define two types of exposures.

**Sovereign risk** is a form of credit risk in which the borrower is the government of a sovereign nation. Like other forms of credit risk, it has a current and a potential component, and like other forms, its magnitude has two components: the likelihood of default and the estimated recovery rate. Of course, the task of evaluating sovereign risk is in some ways more complex than that of evaluating other types of credit exposure because of the additional political component involved. Like other types of borrowers, debtor nations have an asset/liability/cash flow profile that competent analysts can evaluate. In addition to this profile, however, lenders to sovereigns (including bondholders) must consider everything from the country's willingness to meet its credit obligations (particularly in unstable political environments) to its alternative means of financing (seeking help from outside entities such as the International Monetary Fund, imposing capital controls, etc.) and other measures it might take, such as currency devaluation, to stabilize its situation.

The presence of sovereign risk is real and meaningful, and perhaps the most salient example of its deleterious effects can be found in Russia's 1998 default. This episode represented the first time in many decades that a nation of such size and stature failed to meet its obligations to its lenders. Moreover, although the country was experiencing considerable trauma at that time—in part as the result of a contagion in emerging markets—it is abundantly clear that Russia was *unwilling* rather than *unable* to meet these obligations. The end result was a global financial crisis, in which investors lost billions of dollars and the country's robust development arc was slowed down for the better part of a decade.

**Political risk** is associated with changes in the political environment. Political risk can take many forms, both overt (e.g., the replacement of a pro-capitalist regime with one less so) and subtle (e.g., the potential impact of a change in party control in a developed nation), and it exists in every jurisdiction where financial instruments trade.

## 4.12 Other Risks

Companies face nonfinancial and financial risks other than those already mentioned. **ESG risk** is the risk to a company's market valuation resulting from environmental, social, and governance factors. Environmental risk is created by the operational decisions made by the company managers, including decisions concerning the products and services to offer and the processes to use in producing those products and services. Environmental damage may lead to a variety of negative financial and other consequences. Social risk derives from the company's various policies and practices regarding human resources, contractual arrangements, and the workplace. Liability from discriminatory workplace policies and the disruption of business resulting from labor strikes are examples of this type of risk. Flaws in corporate governance policies and procedures increase governance risk, with direct and material effects on a company's value in the marketplace.

One little-discussed but very large type of risk that some investment companies face is that of performance netting risk, often referred to simply as netting risk. **Performance netting risk**, which applies to entities that fund more than one strategy, is the potential for loss resulting from the failure of fees based on net performance to fully cover contractual payout obligations to individual portfolio managers that have positive performance when other portfolio managers have losses and when there are asymmetric incentive fee arrangements with the portfolio managers. The problem is best explained through an example.

Consider a hedge fund that charges a 20 percent incentive fee of any positive returns and funds two strategies equally, each managed by independent portfolio managers (call them Portfolio Managers A and B). The hedge fund pays Portfolio Managers A and B 10 percent of any gains they achieve. Now assume that in a given year, Portfolio Manager A makes $10 million and Portfolio Manager B loses the same amount. The net incentive fee to the hedge fund is zero because it has generated zero returns. Unless otherwise negotiated, however (and such clauses are rare), the hedge fund remains obligated to pay Portfolio Manager A $1 million. As a result, the hedge fund company has incurred a loss, despite breaking even overall in terms of returns.[18] Note that the asymmetric nature of incentive fee contracts (i.e., losses are not penalized as gains are rewarded) plays a critical role in creating the problem the hedge fund faces. Because such arrangements are effectively a call option on a percentage of profits, in some circumstances they may provide an incentive to take excessive risk (the value of a call option is positively related to the underlying's volatility). Nevertheless, such arrangements are widespread.

Performance netting risk occurs only in multistrategy, multimanager environments and only manifests itself when individual portfolio managers within a jointly managed product generate actual losses over the course of a fee-generating cycle—typically one year. Moreover, an investment entity need not be flat or down on the year to experience netting-associated losses. For any given level of net returns, its portion of fees will by definition be higher if all portfolio managers generate no worse than zero performance over the period than they would if some portfolio managers generate losses. As mentioned earlier, an asymmetric incentive fee contract must exist for this problem to arise.

Performance netting risk applies not just to hedge funds but also to banks' and broker/dealers' trading desks, commodity trading advisors, and indeed, to any environment in which individuals have asymmetric incentive fee arrangements but the entity or unit responsible for paying the fees is compensated on the basis of net results. Typically this risk is managed through a process that establishes absolute negative performance thresholds for individual accounts and aggressively cuts risk for individual portfolio managers at performance levels at, near, or below zero for the period in question.[19]

Distinct from performance netting risk, **settlement netting risk** (or again, simply netting risk) refers to the risk that a liquidator of a counterparty in default could challenge a netting arrangement so that profitable transactions are realized for the benefit of creditors.[20] Such risk is mitigated by netting agreements that can survive legal challenge.

# MEASURING RISK

**5**

Having spent some time identifying some of the major sources of risk, both financial and nonfinancial, we now turn our attention toward the measurement of those risks. In particular, we look at some techniques for measuring market risk and credit risk.

---

**18** The asymmetric nature of the incentive fee contract (currently typical for hedge funds) plays a critical role in this example; were the arrangement symmetric, with negative returns penalized as positive returns are rewarded, the issue discussed would disappear.

**19** For more information on this topic, see Grant (2004).

**20** See www.foa.co.uk/documentation/netting/index.jsp.

Subsequently, we briefly survey some of the issues for measuring nonfinancial risk, a very difficult area but also a very topical one—particularly after the advent of the Basel II standards on risk management for international banks, which we will discuss.

## 5.1  Measuring Market Risk

Market risk refers to the exposure associated with actively traded financial instruments, typically those whose prices are exposed to the changes in interest rates, exchange rates, equity prices, commodity prices, or some combination thereof.[21]

Over the years, financial theorists have created a simple and finite set of statistical tools to describe market risk. The most widely used and arguably the most important of these is the standard deviation of price outcomes associated with an underlying asset. We usually refer to this measure as the asset's **volatility**, typically represented by the Greek letter sigma ($\sigma$). Volatility is often an adequate description of portfolio risk, particularly for those portfolios composed of instruments with linear payoffs.[22] In some applications, such as indexing, volatility relative to a benchmark is paramount. In those cases, our focus should be on the volatility of the deviation of a portfolio's returns in excess of a stated benchmark portfolio's returns, known as **active risk**, **tracking risk**, tracking error volatility, or by some simply as tracking error.

As we will see shortly, the volatility associated with individual positions, in addition to being a very useful risk management metric in its own right, can be combined with other simple statistics, such as correlations, to form the building blocks for the portfolio-based risk management systems that have become the industry standard in recent years. We cover these systems in the next section of this reading.

A portfolio's exposure to losses because of market risk typically takes one of two forms: sensitivity to adverse movements in the value of a key variable in valuation (primary or first-order measures of risk) and risk measures associated with *changes in* sensitivities (secondary or second-order measures of risk). Primary measures of risk often reflect linear elements in valuation relationships; secondary measures often take account of curvature in valuation relationships. Each asset class (e.g., bonds, foreign exchange, equities) has specific first- and second-order measures.

Let us consider measures of primary sources of risk first. For a stock or stock portfolio, **beta** measures sensitivity to market movements and is a linear risk measure. For bonds, **duration** measures the sensitivity of a bond or bond portfolio to a small parallel shift in the yield curve and is a linear measure, as is **delta** for options, which measures an option's sensitivity to a small change in the value of its underlying. These measures all reflect the expected change in price of a financial instrument for a unit change in the value of another instrument.

Second-order measures of risk deal with the change in the price sensitivity of a financial instrument and include convexity for fixed-income portfolios and gamma for options. **Convexity** measures how interest rate sensitivity changes with changes in interest rates.[23] **Gamma** measures the delta's sensitivity to a change in the underlying's value. Delta and gamma together capture first- and second-order effects of a change in the underlying.

For options, two other major factors determine price: volatility and time to expiration, both first-order or primary effects. Sensitivity to volatility is reflected in **vega**, the change in the price of an option for a change in the underlying's volatility. Most early option-pricing models (e.g., the Black–Scholes–Merton model) assume that

---

21 The definition of market risk given here is the one used in the practice of risk management. The term market risk, however, is often used elsewhere to refer to the risk of the market as a whole, which is usually known as systematic risk. In this reading, we define market risk as risk management professionals do.

22 The contrast is with instruments such as options that have nonlinear or piecewise linear payoffs. See Chance (2003) for more on the payoff functions of options.

23 Convexity is covered in some detail in Fabozzi (2004a), Chapter 7.

volatility does not change over the life of an option, but in fact, volatility does generally change. Volatility changes are sometimes easy to observe in markets: Some days are far more volatile than others. Moreover, new information affecting the value of an underlying instrument, such as pending product announcements, will discernibly affect volatility. Because of their nonlinear payoff structure, options are typically very responsive to a change in volatility. Swaps, futures, and forwards with linear payoff functions are much less sensitive to changes in volatility. Option prices are also sensitive to changes in time to expiration, as measured by **theta**, the change in price of an option associated with a one-day reduction in its time to expiration.[24] Theta, like vega, is a risk that is associated exclusively with options. Correlation is a source of risk for certain types of options—for example, options on more than one underlying (when the correlations between the underlyings' returns constitute a risk variable).[25]

Having briefly reviewed traditional notions of market risk measurement, we introduce a new topic, one that took the industry by storm: value at risk.

## 5.2 Value at Risk

During the 1990s, value at risk—or VAR, as it is commonly known—emerged as the financial service industry's premier risk management technique.[26] JPMorgan (now JPMorgan Chase) developed the original concept for internal use but later published the tools it had developed for managing risk (as well as related information).[27] Probably no other risk management topic has generated as much attention and controversy as has value at risk. In this section, we take an introductory look at VAR, examine an application, and look at VAR's strengths and limitations.

VAR is a probability-based measure of loss potential for a company, a fund, a portfolio, a transaction, or a strategy. It is usually expressed either as a percentage or in units of currency. Any position that exposes one to loss is potentially a candidate for VAR measurement. VAR is most widely and easily used to measure the loss from market risk, but it can also be used—subject to much greater complexity—to measure the loss from credit risk and other types of exposures.

We have noted that VAR is a probability-based measure of loss potential. This definition is very general, however, and we need something more specific. More formally: **Value at risk (VAR)** is an estimate of the loss (in money terms) that we expect to be exceeded with a given level of probability over a specified time period.[28]

Readers are encouraged to think very carefully about the implications of this definition, which has a couple of important elements. First, we see that VAR is an estimate of the loss that we expect to be exceeded. Hence, it measures a minimum loss. The actual loss may be much worse without necessarily impugning the VAR model's accuracy. Second, we see that VAR is associated with a given probability. Say the VAR is €10,000,000 at a probability of 5 percent for a given time period. All else equal, if we lower the probability from 5 percent to 1 percent, the VAR will be larger in magnitude because we now are referring to a loss that we expect to be exceeded with only a 1 percent probability. Third, we see that VAR has a time element and that as such, VARs cannot be compared directly unless they share the same time interval. There is a big difference

---

24 For more information on theta, see Chance (2003).

25 For more information, see Chance (2003).

26 The terminology "Value-at-Risk" is expressed in different ways. For example, sometimes hyphens are used and sometimes it is just written as "Value at Risk." Sometimes it is abbreviated as VAR and sometimes as VaR. Those who have studied econometrics should be alert to the fact that the letters VAR also refer to an estimation technique called Vector Autoregression, which has nothing to do with Value at Risk. We shall use the abbreviation "VAR."

27 RiskMetrics Group has now spun off from JPMorgan and is an independent company. See www.riskmetrics.com.

28 In the terminology of statistics, VAR with an $x$ percent probability for a given time interval represents the $x$th percentile of the distribution of outcomes (ranked from worst to best) over that time period.

among potential losses that are incurred daily, weekly, monthly, quarterly, or annually. Potential losses over longer periods should be larger than those over shorter periods, but in most instances, longer time periods will not increase exposure in a linear fashion.

Consider the following example of VAR for an investment portfolio: *The VAR for a portfolio is $1.5 million for one day with a probability of 0.05.* Recall what this statement says: *There is a 5 percent chance that the portfolio will lose at least $1.5 million in a single day.* The emphasis here should be on the fact that *the $1.5 million loss is a minimum.* With due care, it is also possible to describe VAR as a maximum: The probability is 95 percent that the portfolio will lose no more than $1.5 million in a single day. We see this equivalent perspective in the common practice of stating VAR using a confidence level: For the example just given, we would say that *with 95 percent confidence* (or *for a 95 percent confidence level*), *the VAR for a portfolio is $1.5 million for one day.*[29] We prefer to express VAR in the form of a minimum loss with a given probability. This approach is a bit more conservative, because it reminds us that the loss could be worse.[30]

### 5.2.1 *Elements of Measuring Value at Risk*

Although VAR has become an industry standard, it may be implemented in several forms, and establishing an appropriate VAR measure requires the user to make a number of decisions about the calculation's structure. Three important ones are picking a probability level, selecting the time period over which to measure VAR, and choosing the specific approach to modeling the loss distribution.[31]

The probability chosen is typically either 0.05 or 0.01 (corresponding to a 95 percent or 99 percent confidence level, respectively). The use of 0.01 leads to a more conservative VAR estimate, because it sets the figure at the level where there should be only a 1 percent chance that a given loss will be worse than the calculated VAR. The trade-off, however, is that the VAR risk estimate will be much larger with a 0.01 probability than it will be for a 0.05 probability. In the above example, we might have to state that the VAR is $2.1 million for one day at a probability of 0.01. The risk manager selects 0.01 or 0.05; no definitive rule exists for preferring one probability to the other. For portfolios with largely linear risk characteristics, the two probability levels will provide essentially identical information. However, the tails of the loss distribution may contain a wealth of information for portfolios that have a good deal of optionality or nonlinear risks, and in these cases risk managers may need to select the more conservative probability threshold.

The second important decision for VAR users is choosing the time period. VAR is often measured over a day, but other, longer time periods are common. Banking regulators prefer two-week period intervals. Many companies report quarterly and annual VARs to match their performance reporting cycles. Investment banks, hedge funds, and dealers seem to prefer daily VAR, perhaps because of the high turnover in their positions. Regardless of the time interval selected, the longer the period, the greater the VAR number will be because the magnitude of potential losses varies directly with the time span over which they are measured. The individual or individuals responsible for risk management will choose the time period.

Once these primary parameters are set, one can proceed to actually obtain the VAR estimate. This procedure involves another decision: the choice of technique. The basic idea behind estimating VAR is to identify the probability distribution characteristics of

---

**29** This would be referred to as 95% one-day VAR.

**30** For a long position, the maximum possible loss is the entire value of the portfolio. For a short position, or a portfolio with both long and short positions, it is impossible to state the maximum possible loss because at least in theory, a short faces the possibility of unlimited losses.

**31** As we will learn in this section, users can select from three basic VAR methodologies, each of which uses a slightly different algorithm to estimate exposure.

portfolio returns. Consider the information in Exhibit 4, which is a simple probability distribution for the return on a portfolio over a specified time period. Suppose we were interested in the VAR at a probability of 0.05. We would add up the probabilities for the class intervals until we reached a cumulative probability of 0.05. Observe that the probability is 0.01 that the portfolio will lose at least 40 percent, 0.01 that the portfolio will lose between 30 percent and 40 percent, and 0.03 that the portfolio will lose between 20 percent and 30 percent. Thus, the probability is 0.05 that the portfolio will lose at least 20 percent. Because we want to express our risk measure in units of money, we would then multiply 20 percent by the portfolio's initial market value to obtain VAR. The VAR for a probability of 0.01 would be 40 percent multiplied by the market value. From a confidence-level perspective, we estimate with 99 percent confidence that our portfolio will lose no more than 40 percent of its value over the specified time period.

| Exhibit 4 | Sample Probability Distribution of Returns on a Portfolio |
|---|---|
| **Return on Portfolio** | **Probability** |
| Less than −40% | 0.010 |
| −40% to −30% | 0.010 |
| −30% to −20% | 0.030 |
| −20% to −10% | 0.050 |
| −10% to −5% | 0.100 |
| −5% to −2.5% | 0.125 |
| −2.5% to 0% | 0.175 |
| 0% to 2.5% | 0.175 |
| 2.5% to 5% | 0.125 |
| 5% to 10% | 0.100 |
| 10% to 20% | 0.050 |
| 20% to 30% | 0.030 |
| 30% to 40% | 0.010 |
| Greater than 40% | 0.010 |
|  | 1.000 |

Exhibit 4 offers a simplified representation of the information necessary to estimate VAR. This method for calculating VAR is rather cumbersome, and the information is not always easy to obtain. As such, the industry has developed a set of three standardized methods for estimating VAR: the analytical or variance–covariance method, the historical method, and the Monte Carlo simulation method. We will describe and illustrate each of these in turn.

### 5.2.2  The Analytical or Variance–Covariance Method

The analytical or variance–covariance method begins with the assumption that portfolio returns are normally distributed. Recall from your study of portfolio management that a normal distribution can be completely described by its expected value and standard deviation.

Consider the standard normal distribution, a special case of the normal distribution centered on an expected value of zero and having a standard deviation of 1.0. We can convert any outcome drawn from a nonstandard normal distribution to a standard normal value by taking the outcome of interest, subtracting its mean, and dividing the result by its standard deviation. The resulting value then conforms to the standard normal distribution.[32] With the standard normal distribution, 5 percent of possible outcomes are likely to be smaller than −1.65.[33] Therefore, to calculate a 5 percent VAR for a portfolio (i.e., VAR at a probability of 0.05), we would estimate its expected return and subtract 1.65 times its estimated standard deviation of returns. So, the key to using the analytical or variance–covariance method is to estimate the portfolio's expected return and standard deviation of returns. An example follows.[34]

Suppose the portfolio contains two asset classes, with 75 percent of the money invested in an asset class represented by the S&P 500 Index and 25 percent invested in an asset class represented by the NASDAQ Composite Index.[35] Recall that a portfolio's expected return is a weighted average of the expected returns of its component stocks or asset classes. A portfolio's variance can be derived using a simple quadratic formula that combines the variances and covariances of the component stocks or asset classes. For example, assume that $\mu_S$ and $\mu_N$ are the expected returns of the S&P 500 and NASDAQ, respectively; $\sigma_S$ and $\sigma_N$ are their standard deviations; and $\rho$ is the correlation between the two asset classes. The expected return, $\mu_P$, and variance, $\sigma_P^2$, of the combined positions are given as

$$\mu_P = w_S \mu_S + w_N \mu_N$$
$$\sigma_P^2 = w_S^2 \sigma_S^2 + w_N^2 \sigma_N^2 + 2\rho w_S w_N \sigma_S \sigma_N$$

where $w$ indicates the percentage allocated to the respective classes. The portfolio's standard deviation is just the square root of its variance. Exhibit 5 provides estimates of the portfolio's expected value and standard deviation using actual numbers, where we obtain $\mu_P$ of 0.135 and $\sigma_P$ of 0.244.

| Exhibit 5 | Estimating the Expected Return and Standard Deviation of a Portfolio Combining Two Asset Classes | | |
|---|---|---|---|
| | **S&P 500** | **NASDAQ** | **Combined Portfolio** |
| Percentage invested ($w$) | 0.75 | 0.25 | 1.00 |
| Expected annual return ($\mu$) | 0.12 | 0.18 | 0.135[a] |
| Standard deviation ($\sigma$) | 0.20 | 0.40 | 0.244[b] |
| Correlation ($\rho$) | 0.90 | | |

[a]Expected return of portfolio: $\mu_P = w_S \mu_S + w_N \mu_N = 0.75(0.12) + 0.25(0.18) = 0.135$
[b]Standard deviation of portfolio:

$$\sigma_P^2 = w_S^2 \sigma_P^2 + w_S^2 \sigma_P^2 + 2\rho w_S w_N \sigma_S \sigma_N$$
$$= (0.75)^2 (0.20)^2 + (0.25)^2 (0.40)^2 + 2(0.90)(0.75)(0.25)(0.20)(0.40) = 0.0595$$
$$\sigma_P = \left(\sigma_P^2\right)^{1/2} = (0.0595)^{1/2} = 0.244$$

Note that the example provided above is quite simplistic, involving only two assets, and thus only two variances and one covariance. As such, the calculation of portfolio variance is relatively manageable. As the number of instruments in the portfolio

---

**32** For example, suppose you were interested in knowing the probability of obtaining a return of −15 percent or less when the expected return is 12 percent and the standard deviation is 20 percent. You would calculate the standard normal value, called a "$z$", as $(−0.15 − 0.12)/0.20 = −1.35$. Then you would look up this value in a table or use a spreadsheet function, such as Microsoft Excel's "=normsdist()" function. In this case, the probability is 0.0885.
**33** See DeFusco, McLeavey, Pinto, and Runkle (2004), pp. 255–56.
**34** For more detailed information, see DeFusco et al. (2004), Chapter 11.
**35** The extension to three or more classes is relatively straightforward once one knows how to calculate the variance of a portfolio of more than two assets. We shall focus here on the two-asset-class case.

increases, however, the calculation components expand dramatically and the equation quickly becomes unwieldy. The important thing to remember is that in order to derive the variance for a portfolio of multiple financial instruments, all we require are the associated variances and covariances, along with the ability to calculate their quadratic relationship.

If we are comfortable with the assumption of a normal distribution and the accuracy of our estimates of the expected returns, variances, and correlations, we can confidently use the analytical-method estimate of VAR. Exhibit 6 illustrates the calculation of this estimate. VAR is first expressed in terms of the return on the portfolio. With an expected return of 0.135, we move 1.65 standard deviations along the $x$-axis in the direction of lower returns. Each standard deviation is 0.244. Thus we would obtain $0.135 - 1.65(0.244) = -0.268$.[36] At this point, VAR could be expressed as a loss of 26.8 percent. We could say that there is a 5 percent chance that the portfolio will lose at least 26.8 percent in a year. It is also customary to express VAR in terms of the portfolio's currency unit. Therefore, if the portfolio is worth $50 million, we can express VAR as $50,000,000(0.268) = $13.4 million.

This figure is an annual VAR. If we prefer a daily VAR, we can adjust the expected return to its daily average of approximately $0.135/250 = 0.00054$ and the standard deviation to its daily value of $0.244/\sqrt{250} = 0.01543$, which are based on the assumption of 250 trading days in a year and statistical independence between days. Then the daily VAR is $0.00054 - 1.65(0.01543) = -0.0249$. On a dollar basis, the daily VAR is $50,000,000(0.0249) = $1.245 million.

| Exhibit 6 | Annual VAR for a Portfolio with Expected Return of 0.135 and Standard Deviation of 0.244 |
| --- | --- |

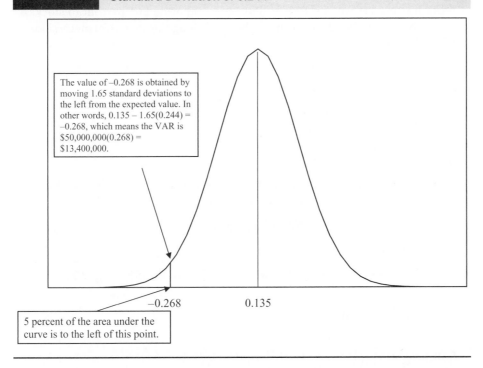

For a 1 percent VAR, we would move 2.33 standard deviations in the direction of lower returns. Thus the annual VAR would be $0.135 - 2.33(0.244) = -0.434$ or $50,000,000(0.434) = $21.7 million. The daily VAR would be $0.00054 - 2.33(0.01543) = -0.035$ or $50,000,000(0.035) = $1.75 million.

---

**36** The reader can confirm that 1.65 and 2.33 standard deviations give the correct VAR at the 5 percent and 1 percent probability levels, respectively, using the Microsoft Excel function "=normsdist()".

Some approaches to estimating VAR using the analytical method assume an expected return of zero. This assumption is generally thought to be acceptable for daily VAR calculations because expected daily return will indeed tend to be close to zero. Because expected returns are typically positive for longer time horizons, shifting the distribution by assuming a zero expected return will result in a larger projected loss, so the VAR estimate will be greater. Therefore, this small adjustment offers a slightly more conservative result and avoids the problem of having to estimate the expected return, a task typically much harder than that of estimating associated volatility. Another advantage of this adjustment is that it makes it easier to adjust the VAR for a different time period. For example, if the daily VAR is estimated at $100,000, the annual VAR will be $100,000\sqrt{250} = \$1,581,139$. This simple conversion of a shorter-term VAR to a longer-term VAR (or vice versa) does not work, however, if the average return is not zero. In these cases, one would have to convert the average return and standard deviation to the different time period and compute the VAR from the adjusted average and standard deviation.

### Example 5

## VAR with Different Probability Levels and Time Horizons

Consider a portfolio consisting of stocks as one asset class and bonds as another. The expected return on the portfolio's stock portion is 12 percent, and the standard deviation is 22 percent. The expected return on the bond portion is 5 percent, and the standard deviation is 7 percent. All of these figures are annual. The correlation between the two asset classes is 0.15. The portfolio's market value is $150 million and is allocated 65 percent to stocks and 35 percent to bonds. Determine the VAR using the analytical method for the following cases:

1. a 5 percent yearly VAR.

2. a 1 percent yearly VAR.

3. a 5 percent weekly VAR.

4. a 1 percent weekly VAR.

### Solutions:

First, we must calculate the annual portfolio expected return and standard deviation. Using $S$ to indicate stocks and $B$ to indicate bonds, we have

$$\mu_p = w_S\mu_S + w_B\mu_B = 0.65(0.12) + 0.35(0.05) = 0.0955$$

$$\sigma_P^2 = w_S^2\sigma_S^2 + w_B^2\sigma_B^2 + 2\rho w_S w_B\sigma_S\sigma_B$$

$$= (0.65)^2(0.22)^2 + (0.35)^2(0.07)^2 + 2(0.15)(0.65)(0.35)(0.22)(0.07)$$

$$= 0.0221$$

$$\sigma_p = \sqrt{0.0221} = 0.1487$$

### Solution to 1:

For a 5 percent yearly VAR, we have $\mu_p - 1.65\sigma_p = 0.0955 - 1.65(0.1487) = -0.1499$. Then the VAR is $150,000,000(0.1499) = \$22.485$ million.

### Solution to 2:

For a 1 percent yearly VAR, we have $\mu_p - 2.33\sigma_p = 0.0955 - 2.33(0.1487) = -0.251$. Then the VAR is $150,000,000(0.251) = \$37.65$ million.

---

**Solution to 3:**

For weekly VAR, we adjust the expected return to $0.0955/52 = 0.00184$ and the standard deviation to $0.1487/\sqrt{52} = 0.02062$.

The 5 percent weekly VAR is then $\mu_p - 1.65\sigma = 0.00184 - 1.65(0.02062) = -0.03218$. Then the VAR is $\$150{,}000{,}000(0.03218) = \$4.827$ million.

**Solution to 4:**

The 1 percent weekly VAR is $\mu_p - 2.33\sigma_p = 0.00184 - 2.33(0.02062) = -0.0462$. Then the VAR is $\$150{,}000{,}000(0.0462) = \$6.93$ million.

---

The analytical or variance–covariance method's primary advantage is its simplicity. Its primary disadvantage is its reliance on several simplifying assumptions, including the normality of return distributions. In principle, there is no reason why the calculation demands a normal distribution, but if we move away from the normality assumption, we cannot rely on variance as a complete measure of risk. Distributions can deviate from normality because of skewness and kurtosis. Skewness is a measure of a distribution's deviation from the perfect symmetry (the normal distribution has a skewness of zero). A positively skewed distribution is characterized by relatively many small losses and a few extreme gains and has a long tail on its right side. A negatively skewed distribution is characterized by relatively many small gains and a few extreme losses and has a long tail on its left side. When a distribution is positively or negatively skewed, the variance–covariance method of estimating VAR will be inaccurate.

In addition, many observed distributions of returns have an abnormally large number of extreme events. This quality is referred to in statistical parlance as leptokurtosis but is more commonly called the property of fat tails.[37] Equity markets, for example, tend to have more frequent large market declines than a normal distribution would predict. Therefore, using a normality assumption to estimate VAR for a portfolio that features fat tails could understate the actual magnitude and frequency of large losses. VAR would then fail at precisely what it is supposed to do: measure the risk associated with large losses.

A related problem that surfaces with the analytical or variance–covariance method is that the normal distribution assumption is inappropriate for portfolios that contain options. The return distributions of options portfolios are often far from normal. Remember that a normal distribution has an unlimited upside and an unlimited downside. Call options have unlimited upside potential, as in a normal distribution, but their downside is a fixed value (the call's premium) and the distribution of call returns is highly skewed. Put options have a large but limited upside and a fixed downside (the put's premium), and the distribution of put returns is also highly skewed. In the same vein, covered calls and protective puts have return distributions that are sharply skewed in one direction or the other.

Therefore, when portfolios contain options, the assumption of a normal distribution to estimate VAR presents a significant problem. One common solution is to estimate the option's price sensitivity using its delta. Recall that delta expresses a linear relationship between an option's price and the underlying's price (i.e., Delta = Change in option price/Change in underlying). A linear relationship lends itself more easily to treatment with a normal distribution. That is, a normally distributed random variable remains normally distributed when multiplied by a constant. In this case, the constant is the delta. The change in the option price is assumed to equal the change in the underlying price multiplied by the delta. This trick converts the normal distribution for the return on the underlying into a normal distribution for the option return. As such, the use of delta to estimate the option's price sensitivity for VAR purposes has led some to call the analytical method (or variance–covariance method) the **delta-normal method**. The use of delta is appropriate only for small changes in the underlying, however. As

---

**37** See DeFusco, McLeavey, Pinto, and Runkle (2004), Chapter 5.

an alternative, some users of the delta-normal method add the second-order effect, captured by gamma. Unfortunately, as these higher-order effects are added, the relationship between the option price and the underlying's price begins to approximate the true nonlinear relationship. At that point, using a normal distribution becomes completely inappropriate. Therefore, using the analytical method could cause problems if a portfolio has options or other financial instruments that do not follow the normal distribution. Moreover, it is often difficult, if not impossible, to come up with a single second-order estimate that both is accurate and fits seamlessly into a variance/covariance VAR model.

### 5.2.3 *The Historical Method*

Another widely used VAR methodology is the historical method. Using historical VAR, we calculate returns for a given portfolio using actual daily prices from a user-specified period in the recent past, graphing these returns into a histogram. From there, it becomes easy to identify the loss that is exceeded with a probability of 0.05 (or 0.01 percent, if preferred).

Consider the portfolio we have been examining, consisting of 75 percent invested in the S&P 500 and 25 percent invested in the NASDAQ Composite Index. Exhibit 7, a histogram, shows the daily returns on this portfolio for a recent calendar year. First, we note that the distribution is similar, but by no means identical, to that of a normal distribution. This portfolio has a few more returns slightly lower than the midpoint of the return sample than it would if its distribution were perfectly normal. With the historical method, however, we are not constrained to using the normal distribution. We simply collect the historical data and identify the return below which 5 (or 1) percent of returns fall. Although we could attempt to read this number from the histogram, it is much easier to simply rank-order the returns and determine the VAR figure from the sorted returns and the portfolio's dollar value.

| **Exhibit 7** | **Historical Daily Returns on a Portfolio Invested 75 Percent in S&P 500 and 25 Percent in NASDAQ** |
| --- | --- |

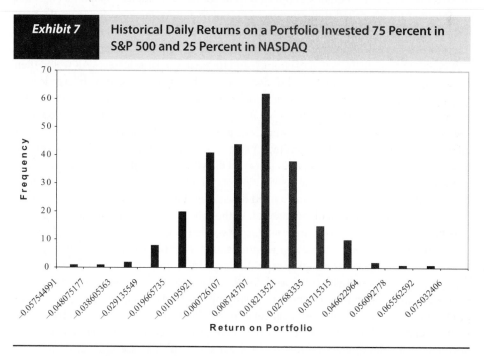

The year examined here contains 248 returns. Having 5 percent of the returns in the distribution's lower tail would mean that about 12 return observations should be less than the VAR estimate. Thus the approximate VAR figure would be indicated by the 12th-worst return. A rank ordering of the data reveals that the 12th-worst return is −0.0294. For a $50,000,000 portfolio, the one-day VAR would thus be 0.0294($50,000,000) = $1.47 million.[38]

---

**38** Technically, the VAR would fall between the 12th- and 13th-worst returns. Using the 13th-worst return gives a more conservative VAR. Alternatively, we might average the 12th- and 13th-worst returns.

The historical method is also sometimes called the **historical simulation method**. This term is somewhat misleading because the approach involves not a *simulation* of the past returns but rather what *actually happened* in the past. In this context, note that a portfolio that an investor might have held in the past might not be the same as the one that investor will have in the future. When using the historical method, one must always keep in mind that the purpose of the exercise is to apply *historical* price changes to the *current* portfolio.[39] In addition, instruments such as bonds and most derivatives behave differently at different times in their lives, and any accurate historical VAR calculation must take this into account by adjusting current bond/derivative pricing parameters to simulate their current characteristics across the period of analysis. For example, a historical VAR calculation that goes back one year for a portfolio that contains bonds that mature in the year 2027 should actually use otherwise identical bonds maturing in 2026 as proxies; these bonds are the most accurate representations of the current risk profile because they would have presented themselves one year ago in time. When a company uses a different portfolio composition to calculate its historical VAR than the one it actually had in the past, it may be more appropriate to call the method a historical simulation.

The historical method has the advantage of being **nonparametric** (i.e., involving minimal probability-distribution assumptions), enabling the user to avoid any assumptions about the type of probability distribution that generates returns. The disadvantage, however, is that this method relies completely on events of the past, and whatever distribution prevailed in the past might not hold in the future. In particular, periods of unusually large negative returns, such as the 23 percent one-day decline in the Dow Jones Industrial Average on 19 October 1987, might be questionable as an assumption for the future. This problem applies to the other types of VAR methodologies as well, however, including the analytical method and Monte Carlo simulation, both of which derive their inputs, more often than not, entirely from the historical prices associated with the securities contained in the portfolio.

### Example 6

## Calculating VAR Using the Historical Method

For simplicity, we use a one-stock portfolio. Exhibit 8 shows the 40 worst monthly returns on IBM stock during the last 20 years, in descending order, as of 2011 (minus signs omitted):

| Exhibit 8 | IBM Stock: Worst Monthly Returns | | |
|---|---|---|---|
| 0.26190 | 0.11692 | 0.09077 | 0.07537 |
| 0.22645 | 0.11553 | 0.08926 | 0.07298 |
| 0.20511 | 0.10838 | 0.08585 | 0.07260 |
| 0.19462 | 0.10805 | 0.08481 | 0.07247 |
| 0.18802 | 0.10687 | 0.08422 | 0.07075 |
| 0.17183 | 0.10503 | 0.08356 | 0.06894 |
| 0.16415 | 0.09873 | 0.08234 | 0.06782 |
| 0.14834 | 0.09550 | 0.08197 | 0.06746 |
| 0.14773 | 0.09276 | 0.08143 | 0.06501 |
| 0.12444 | 0.09091 | 0.07547 | 0.06437 |

---

**39** For example, in the two-asset portfolio we illustrated here, the weights were 75 percent S&P 500 and 25 percent NASDAQ. If the company were going forward with a different set of weights, it would obviously need to use the weights it planned to use in the future when calculating the VAR by the historical method.

For both calculations below, assume the portfolio value is $100,000.

1.  Calculate a 5 percent monthly VAR using the historical method.

2.  Calculate a 1 percent monthly VAR using the historical method.

### Solutions:

First, we note that during the last 20 years, there were 240 monthly returns. We see here only the worst 40 returns. Therefore, although we lack the entire distribution of returns, we do have enough to calculate the VAR.

### Solution to 1:

Out of 240 returns, the 5 percent worst are the 12 worst returns. Therefore, the historical VAR would be about the 12th-worst return. From the exhibit, we see that this return is –0.11553. So, the one-month VAR is 0.11553($100,000) = $11,553.

### Solution to 2:

The 1 percent worst returns include 2.4 returns. We would probably use the second-worst return, which is –0.22645. The VAR is 0.22645($100,000) = $22,645. Alternatively, we might average the second- and third-worst returns to obtain (–0.22645 + –0.20511)/2 = –0.21578. Then the one-month VAR would be 0.21578($100,000) = $21,578.

---

The excerpt from The Goldman Sachs Group, Inc. Form 10-K that follows in Example 7 shows how this investment firm reports its VAR. We see that Goldman Sachs reports average values for 5 percent daily VAR for its last three fiscal years. In addition, the firm reports the high and low daily VAR values for the last fiscal year along with the year end values for the last two fiscal years. Goldman Sachs reports VARs for these four risk categories (interest rate, equity prices, currency rates, and commodity prices) as well as its firm-wide risk exposure (total VAR). Total VAR is less than the sum of the individual VARs because Goldman Sachs' exposures to the various risk categories are less than perfectly correlated. The **diversification effect** reported in the Average Daily VAR table in Example 7 equals the difference between the total VAR and the sum of the individual VARs. For example, for 2010, the diversification effect is $134 – ($93 + $68 + $32 + $33) = –$92.

### Example 7

## Value at Risk and the Management of Market Risk at Goldman Sachs

The following excerpt is from the 2010 Form 10-K of Goldman Sachs:

### Value-at-Risk

VaR is the potential loss in value of inventory positions due to adverse market movements over a defined time horizon with a specified confidence level. We typically employ a one-day time horizon with a 95% confidence level. Thus, we would expect to see reductions in the fair value of inventory positions at least as large as the reported VaR once per month. The VaR model captures risks including interest rates, equity prices, currency rates and commodity prices. As such, VaR facilitates comparison across portfolios of different risk characteristics. VaR also captures the diversification of aggregated risk at the firmwide level.

Inherent limitations to VaR include:

- VaR does not estimate potential losses over longer time horizons where moves may be extreme.
- VaR does not take account of the relative liquidity of different risk positions.
- Previous moves in market risk factors may not produce accurate predictions of all future market moves.

The historical data used in our VaR calculation is weighted to give greater importance to more recent observations and reflect current asset volatilities. This improves the accuracy of our estimates of potential loss. As a result, even if our inventory positions were unchanged, our VaR would increase with increasing market volatility and vice versa.

Given its reliance on historical data, VaR is most effective in estimating risk exposures in markets in which there are no sudden fundamental changes or shifts in market conditions.

We evaluate the accuracy of our VaR model through daily backtesting (i.e., comparing daily trading net revenues to the VaR measure calculated as of the prior business day) at the firmwide level and for each of our businesses and major regulated subsidiaries.

VaR does not include:

- positions that are best measured and monitored using sensitivity measures; and
- the impact of changes in counterparty and our own credit spreads on derivatives as well as changes in our own credit spreads on unsecured borrowings for which the fair value option was elected.

## Stress Testing

We use stress testing to examine risks of specific portfolios as well as the potential impact of significant risk exposures across the firm. We use a variety of scenarios to calculate the potential loss from a wide range of market moves on the firm's portfolios. These scenarios include the default of single corporate or sovereign entities, the impact of a move in a single risk factor across all positions (e.g., equity prices or credit spreads) or a combination of two or more risk factors.

Unlike VaR measures, which have an implied probability because they are calculated at a specified confidence level, there is generally no implied probability that our stress test scenarios will occur. Instead, stress tests are used to model both moderate and more extreme moves in underlying market factors. When estimating potential loss, we generally assume that our positions cannot be reduced or hedged (although experience demonstrates that we are generally able to do so).

Stress test scenarios are conducted on a regular basis as part of the firm's routine risk management process and on an ad hoc basis in response to market events or concerns. Stress testing is an important part of the firm's risk management process because it allows us to highlight potential loss concentrations, undertake risk/reward analysis, and assess and mitigate our risk positions.

## Limits

We use risk limits at various levels in the firm (including firmwide, product and business) to govern risk appetite by controlling the size of our exposures to market risk. Limits are reviewed frequently and amended on a permanent or temporary basis to reflect changing market conditions, business conditions or tolerance for risk.

The Firmwide Risk Committee sets market risk limits at firmwide and product levels and our Securities Division Risk Committee sets sub-limits for market-making and investing activities at a business level. The purpose of the firmwide limits is to assist senior management in controlling the firm's overall risk profile. Sub-limits set the desired maximum amount of exposure that may be managed by any particular business on a day-to-day basis without additional levels of senior management approval, effectively leaving day-to-day trading decisions to individual desk managers and traders. Accordingly, sub-limits are a management tool designed to ensure appropriate escalation rather than to establish maximum risk tolerance. Sub-limits also distribute risk among various businesses in a manner that is consistent with their level of activity and client demand, taking into account the relative performance of each area.

Our market risk limits are monitored daily by Market Risk Management, which is responsible for identifying and escalating, on a timely basis, instances where limits have been exceeded. The business-level limits that are set by the Securities Division Risk Committee are subject to the same scrutiny and limit escalation policy as the firmwide limits.

When a risk limit has been exceeded (e.g., due to changes in market conditions, such as increased volatilities or changes in correlations), it is reported to the appropriate risk committee and a discussion takes place with the relevant desk managers, after which either the risk position is reduced or the risk limit is temporarily or permanently increased.

## Metrics

We analyze VaR at the firmwide level and a variety of more detailed levels, including by risk category, business, and region. The tables below present average daily VaR and year-end VaR by risk category.

### Average Daily VaR (in millions)

| Risk Categories | Year Ended | | |
| --- | --- | --- | --- |
|  | December 2010 | December 2009 | November 2008 |
| Interest rates | $ 93 | $176 | $ 142 |
| Equity prices | 68 | 66 | 72 |
| Currency rates | 32 | 36 | 30 |
| Commodity prices | 33 | 36 | 44 |
| Diversification effect[1] | (92) | (96) | (108) |
| **Total** | **$134** | **$218** | **$ 180** |

1. Equals the difference between total VaR and the sum of the VaRs for the four risk categories. This effect arises because the four market risk categories are not perfectly correlated.

Our average daily VaR decreased to $134 million in 2010 from $218 million in 2009, principally due to a decrease in the interest rates category which was primarily due to reduced exposures, lower levels of volatility and tighter spreads.

Our average daily VaR increased to $218 million in 2009 from $180 million in 2008, principally due to an increase in the interest rates category and a reduction in the diversification benefit across risk categories, partially offset by a decrease in the commodity prices category. The increase in the interest rates category was primarily due to wider spreads. The decrease in the commodity prices category was primarily due to lower energy prices.

### Year-End VaR and High and Low VaR (in millions)

| Risk Categories | As of December | | Year Ended December 2010 | |
|---|---|---|---|---|
| | 2010 | 2009 | High | Low |
| Interest rates | $ 78 | $ 122 | $123 | $ 76 |
| Equity prices | 51 | 99 | 186 | 39 |
| Currency rates | 27 | 21 | 62 | 14 |
| Commodity prices | 25 | 33 | 62 | 18 |
| Diversification effect[1] | (70) | (122) | | |
| **Total** | **$111** | **$ 153** | **$223** | **$105** |

1. Equals the difference between total VaR and the sum of the VaRs for the four risk categories. This effect arises because the four market risk categories are not perfectly correlated.

Our daily VaR decreased to $111 million as of December 2010 from $153 million as of December 2009, principally due to a decrease in the equity prices and interest rates categories, partially offset by a decrease in the diversification benefit across risk categories. The decreases in the equity prices and interest rates categories were primarily due to reduced exposures and lower levels of volatility.

During the year ended December 2010, the firmwide VaR risk limit was exceeded on one occasion in order to facilitate a client transaction and was resolved by a reduction in the risk position on the following day. Separately, during the year ended December 2010, the firmwide VaR risk limit was reduced on one occasion reflecting lower risk utilization.

During the year ended December 2009, the firmwide VaR risk limit was exceeded on two successive days. It was resolved by a reduction in the risk position without a permanent or temporary VaR limit increase. Separately, during the year ended December 2009, the firmwide VaR risk limit was raised on one occasion and reduced on two occasions as a result of changes in the risk utilization and the market environment.

The chart below reflects the VaR over the last four quarters.

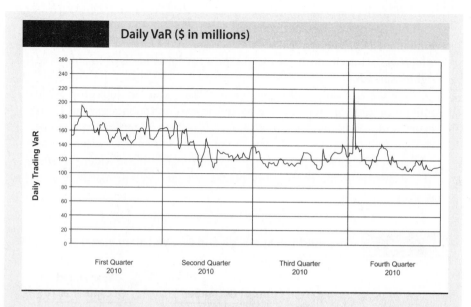

**Daily VaR ($ in millions)**

The chart below presents the frequency distribution of our daily trading net revenues for substantially all inventory positions included in VaR for the year ended December 2010.

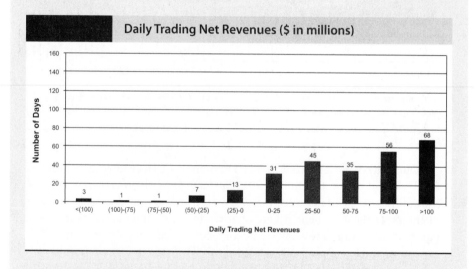

**Daily Trading Net Revenues ($ in millions)**

As noted above, daily trading net revenues are compared with VaR calculated as of the end of the prior business day. Trading losses incurred on a single day exceeded our 95% one-day VaR on two occasions during 2010. Trading losses incurred on a single day did not exceed our 95% one-day VaR during 2009.

*Source*: Goldman Sachs 2010 Form 10-K, pp. 85-87.

The next section addresses the third method of estimating VAR, Monte Carlo simulation.

### 5.2.4 *The Monte Carlo Simulation Method*

The third approach to estimating VAR is Monte Carlo simulation. In general, Monte Carlo simulation produces random outcomes so we can examine what might happen given a particular set of risks. It is used widely in the sciences as well as in business to study a variety of problems. In the financial world in recent years, it has become an extremely important technique for measuring risk. Monte Carlo simulation generates random outcomes according to an assumed probability distribution and a set of input parameters. We can then analyze these outcomes to gauge the risk associated with the events in question. When estimating VAR, we use Monte Carlo simulation to produce random portfolio returns. We then assemble these returns into a summary distribution from which we can determine at which level the lower 5 percent (or 1 percent, if preferred) of return outcomes occur. We then apply this figure to the portfolio value to obtain VAR.

Monte Carlo simulation uses a probability distribution for each variable of interest and a mechanism to randomly generate outcomes according to each distribution. Our goal here is to gain a basic understanding of the technique and how to use it. Therefore, we illustrate it without explaining the full details of how to generate the random values.

Suppose we return to the example of our $50 million portfolio invested 75 percent in the S&P 500 and 25 percent in the NASDAQ Composite Index. We assume, as previously, that this portfolio should have an annual expected return of 13.5 percent and a standard deviation of 24.4 percent. We shall now conduct a Monte Carlo simulation using the normal distribution with these parameters. Keep in mind that in practice, one advantage of Monte Carlo simulation is that it does not require a normal distribution, but the normal distribution is often used and we shall stay with it for illustrative purposes.

We use a random number generator to produce a series of random values, which we then convert into a normally distributed stream of outcomes representing a rate of return for this portfolio over a period of one year. Suppose the first value it produces is a return of −21.87 percent. This rate corresponds to an end-of-year portfolio value of $39.07 million. The second random return it produces is −4.79 percent, which takes the portfolio value to $47.61 million.[40] The third random return it produces is 31.38 percent, which makes the portfolio value $65.69 million. We continue this process a large number of times, perhaps several thousand or even several million. To keep the simulation to a manageable size for illustrative purposes, we generate only 300 outcomes.

Exhibit 9 shows the histogram of portfolio outcomes. Notice that even though we used a normal distribution to generate the outcomes, the resulting distribution does not look entirely normal. Of course, we should be surprised if it did because we used only 300 random outcomes, a relatively small sample.

To obtain the point in the lower tail that 5 percent of the outcomes exceed, we rank order the data and find the 15th-lowest outcome, which is a portfolio value of $34.25 million, corresponding to a loss of $15.75 million. This value is higher than the annual VAR estimated using the analytical method ($13.4 million). These two values would be identical (or nearly so) if we had employed a sufficiently large sample size in the Monte Carlo simulation so that the sample VAR would converge to the true population VAR.

---

**40** The random outcomes are independent, not sequential. Each outcome thus represents a return relative to the full initial portfolio value of $50 million.

| Exhibit 9 | Simulated Values after One Year for a Portfolio Invested 75 Percent in S&P 500 and 25 Percent in NASDAQ |

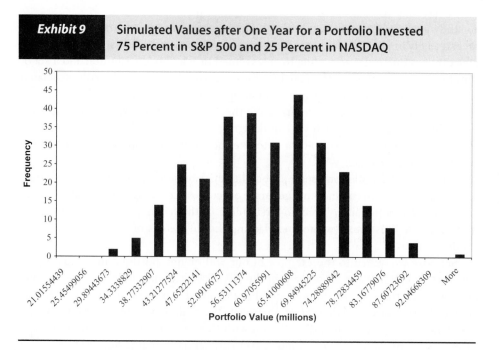

In Monte Carlo simulation, we can make any distributional assumption that we believe is appropriate. In many practical applications, it is inappropriate to assume a normal return distribution. In particular, for many derivatives dealers, the problems in managing the risk of these instruments are compounded by the fact that an extremely large number of random variables may affect the value of their overall position. These variables are often not normally distributed, and furthermore, they often interact with each other in complex ways. Monte Carlo simulation is often the only practical means of generating the information necessary to manage the risk. With tens of thousands of transactions on the books of most dealers, however, Monte Carlo simulation can require extensive commitments of computer resources.

### 5.2.5 "Surplus at Risk": VAR as It Applies to Pension Fund Portfolios

You will recall from earlier points in our discussion that pension funds face a slightly different set of challenges in the measurement of market exposures, primarily because of the fact that the assets must fund pension obligations whose present value is itself subject to interest rate risk and other risks.[41] The difference between the value of the pension fund's assets and liabilities is referred to as the **surplus**, and it is this value that pension fund managers seek to enhance and protect. If this surplus falls into negative territory, the plan sponsor must contribute funds to make up the deficit over a period of time that is specified as part of the fund's plan.

In order to reflect this set of realities in their risk estimations, pension fund managers typically apply VAR methodologies not to their portfolio of assets but to the surplus. To do so, they simply express their liability portfolio as a set of short securities and calculate VAR on the net position. VAR handles this process quite elegantly, and once this adjustment is made, all three VAR methodologies can be applied to the task.

---

**41** An example of a defined-benefit pension plan's obligation is the promise to pay, for each year of service, a certain percentage of a vested participant's average salary in their final five years of service; this promise may include cost-of-living adjustments.

## 5.3 The Advantages and Limitations of VAR

Although value at risk has become the industry standard for risk assessment, it also has widely documented imperfections. VAR can be difficult to estimate, and different estimation methods can give quite different values. VAR can also lull one into a false sense of security by giving the impression that the risk is properly measured and under control. VAR often underestimates the magnitude and frequency of the worst returns, although this problem often derives from erroneous assumptions and models. As we discuss later, VAR for individual positions does not generally aggregate in a simple way to portfolio VAR. Also, VAR fails to incorporate positive results into its risk profile, and as such, it arguably provides an incomplete picture of overall exposures.

Users of VAR should routinely test their system to determine whether their VAR estimates prove accurate in predicting the results experienced over time. For example, if daily VAR at 0.05 is estimated at $1 million, then over a reasonable period of time, such as a year, a loss of at least $1 million should be exceeded approximately 250(0.05) = 12.5 days. If the frequency of losses equal to or greater than this amount is markedly different, then the model is not accomplishing its objectives. This process of comparing the number of violations of VAR thresholds with the figure implied by the user-selected probability level is part of a process known as **backtesting**. It is extremely important to go through this exercise, ideally across multiple time intervals, to ensure that the VAR estimation method adopted is reasonably accurate. For example, if the VAR estimate is based on daily observations and targets a 0.05 probability, then in addition to ensuring that approximately a dozen threshold violations occur during a given year, it is also useful to check other, shorter time intervals, including the most recent quarter (for which, given 60-odd trading days, we would expect approximately three VAR exceptions—i.e., losses greater than the calculated VAR), and the most recent month (20 observations, implying a single VAR exception). Note that the results should not be expected to precisely match the probability level predictions but should at a minimum be of similar magnitude. If the results vary much from those that the model predicts, then users must examine the reasons and make appropriate adjustments.

An accurate VAR estimate can also be extremely difficult to obtain for complex organizations. In the simple example we used previously, VAR was driven solely by the large- and small-cap U.S. stocks. For a large international bank, however, the exposures might be to a variety of domestic and international interest rate markets, numerous exchange rates, perhaps some equity markets, and even some commodity markets. A bank could have exposure to literally thousands of risks. Consolidating the effects of these exposures into a single risk measure can be extremely difficult. Nonetheless, most large banks manage to do so.

VAR has the attraction of quantifying the potential loss in simple terms and can be easily understood by senior management. Regulatory bodies have taken note of VAR as a risk measure, and some require that institutions provide it in their reports. In the United States, the Securities and Exchange Commission now requires publicly traded companies to report how they are managing financial risk. VAR is one acceptable method of reporting that information.

Another advantage of VAR is its versatility. Many companies use VAR as a measure of their capital at risk. They will estimate the VAR associated with a particular activity, such as a line of business, an individual asset manager, a subsidiary, or a division. Then, they evaluate performance, taking into account the VAR associated with this risky activity. In some cases, companies allocate capital based on VAR. For example, a pension fund might determine its overall acceptable VAR and then inform each asset class manager that it can operate subject to its VAR not exceeding a certain amount. The manager's goal is to earn the highest return possible given its VAR allocation. This activity is known as risk budgeting; we cover it in more detail in a later section.

In summary, VAR has notable advantages and disadvantages. Controversy and criticism have surrounded it.[42] Nevertheless, if a risk manager uses VAR with full awareness of its limitations, he should definitely gain useful information about risk. Even if VAR gives an incorrect measure of the loss potential, the risk manager can take this risk measurement error into account when making the key overall decisions—provided, of course, that the magnitude of the error can be measured and adjusted for with some level of precision, e.g., through backtesting a VAR method against historical data. The controversy remains, but VAR as a risk measure is unlikely to ever be completely rejected. It should not, however, be used in isolation. VAR is often paired with stress testing, discussed in a subsequent section. Remember too that no risk measure can precisely predict future losses. It is important to ensure that the inputs to the VAR calculation are as reliable as possible and relevant to the current investment mix.

## 5.4 Extensions and Supplements to VAR

Risk managers have developed several useful extensions and supplements to VAR. In this section, we review several of the more noteworthy.

A key concern to risk managers is the evaluation of the portfolio effect of a given risk. The ability to isolate the effect of a risk, particularly in complex portfolios with high correlation effects, is very important. We can use incremental VAR (IVAR) to investigate the effect. **Incremental VAR** measures the incremental effect of an asset on the VAR of a portfolio by measuring the difference between the portfolio's VAR while including a specified asset and the portfolio's VAR with that asset eliminated.[43] We can also use IVAR to assess the incremental effect of a subdivision on an enterprise's overall VAR. Although IVAR gives an extremely limited picture of the asset's or portfolio's contribution to risk, it nonetheless provides useful information about how adding the asset will affect the portfolio's overall risk as reflected in its VAR.

Some variations of VAR are **cash flow at risk** (CFAR) and **earnings at risk (EAR)**. CFAR and EAR measure the risk to a company's cash flow or earning, respectively, instead of its market value as in the case of VAR. CFAR is the minimum cash flow loss that we expect to be exceeded with a given probability over a specified time period. EAR is defined analogously to CFAR but measures risk to accounting earnings. CFAR and EAR can be used when a company (or portfolio of assets) generates cash flows or profits but cannot be readily valued in a publicly traded market, or when the analyst's focus is on the risk to cash flow and earnings, for example, in a valuation. CFAR and EAR can complement VAR's perspective on risk.

Another useful tool to supplement VAR is the **tail value at risk** (TVAR), also known as the conditional tail expectation. TVAR is defined as the VAR plus the expected loss in excess of VAR, when such excess loss occurs. For example, given a 5 percent daily VAR, TVAR might be calculated as the average of the worst 5 percent of outcomes in a simulation.

---

**42** A well-known critic of VAR has likened its use to flying an aircraft with a potentially flawed altimeter. With an altimeter, a pilot may think he knows the correct altitude. Without an altimeter, the pilot will look out the window. Of course, this argument presumes that there are no clouds below. The probability of hitting trees or a mountain is the joint probability that the aircraft is too low and that the altimeter gives a false signal, which is less than the simple probability that the aircraft is too low. Aware of the potential for the altimeter to be flawed, the pilot will also seek information from other sources, which themselves are less than 100 percent accurate. So will the risk manager when using VAR. Both will gauge the risk against their tolerance for risk and take appropriate action. We look at some of these other sources of risk information in the next section.

**43** For more details, see Crouhy, Galai, and Mark (2001), Chapter 6.

VAR developed initially as a measure for market risk, which is the risk associated with the primary market forces of interest rates, exchange rates, stock prices, and commodity prices. With some difficulty, VAR can be extended to handle credit risk, the risk that a counterparty will not pay what it owes. More recent extensions of VAR have tended to focus on modeling assets with nonnormal underlying distributions. The use of conditional normal distribution based on different regimes is a very intriguing concept, but the mathematics used in this area can be daunting.[44]

## 5.5 Stress Testing

Managers often use stress testing (a term borrowed from engineering) to supplement VAR as a risk measure. The main purpose of VAR analysis is to quantify potential losses under normal market conditions. Stress testing, by comparison, seeks to identify unusual circumstances that could lead to losses in excess of those typically expected. Clearly, different scenarios will have attached probabilities of occurring that vary from the highly likely to the almost totally improbable. It is, therefore, the natural complement to VAR analysis. Two broad approaches exist in stress testing: scenario analysis and stressing models.

### 5.5.1 *Scenario Analysis*

Scenario analysis is the process of evaluating a portfolio under different states of the world. Quite often it involves designing scenarios with deliberately large movements in the key variables that affect the values of a portfolio's assets and derivatives.

One type of scenario analysis, that of **stylized scenarios**, involves simulating a movement in at least one interest rate, exchange rate, stock price, or commodity price relevant to the portfolio. These movements might range from fairly modest changes to quite extreme shifts. Many practitioners use standard sets of stylized scenarios to highlight potentially risky outcomes for the portfolio. Some organizations have formalized this process; for example, the Derivatives Policy Group recommends its members look at the following seven scenarios:

- parallel yield curve shifting by ±100 basis points (1 percentage point);
- yield curve twisting by ±25 basis points;[45]
- each of the four combinations of the above shifts and twists;
- implied volatilities changing by ±20 percent from current levels;
- equity index levels changing by ±10 percent;
- major currencies moving by ±6 percent and other currencies by ±20 percent;
- swap spread changing by ±20 basis points.

In 1988, the Chicago Mercantile Exchange introduced a system call SPAN to calculate collateral requirements based on their members' total portfolios of futures and options. The objective of this system was to stress portfolios under a variety of scenarios. SPAN has become a very popular system among futures and options exchanges worldwide to set margin requirements. It offers a very useful, generalized form of scenario analysis that combines elements of VAR with some specified overlay based on real-world observation of the relationship among financial instruments.

---

44 For an extremely entertaining tour of some of the pitfalls of traditional risk analysis and some solutions, see Osband (2002).

45 A **twist** is a nonparallel movement in the yield curve. An example of a twist is a 25-bps increase in short rates and no change in long rates, which would result in a flattening of the yield curve.

Scenario analysis is a very useful enhancement to VAR, enabling those interested in risk analysis to identify and analyze specific exposures that might affect a portfolio. The results, of course, are only as good as implied by the accuracy of the scenarios devised. One problem with the stylized scenario approach is that the shocks tend to be applied to variables in a sequential fashion. In reality, these shocks often happen at the same time, have much different correlations than normal, or have some causal relationship connecting them.

Another approach to scenario analysis involves using **actual extreme events** that have occurred in the past. Here, we might want to put our portfolio through price movements that simulate the stock market crash of October 1987; the collapse of Long-Term Capital Management in 1998; the technology stock bubble of the late 1990s; the abrupt bursting of said bubble, beginning in the spring of 2000; or the market reaction to the terrorist attacks of 11 September 2001. This type of scenario analysis might be particularly useful if we think that the occurrence of extreme market breaks has a higher probability than that given by the probability model or historical time period being used in developing the VAR estimate. Stress testing of actual extreme events forces one to direct attention to these outcomes.

We might also create scenarios based on **hypothetical events**—events that have never happened in the markets or market outcomes to which we attach a small probability. These types of scenarios are very difficult to analyze and may generate confusing outcomes, so it is important to carefully craft hypothetical analyses if they are to generate information that adds value to the risk management processes.

Having devised a series of appropriate scenarios, the next step in the process is to apply them to the portfolio. The key task here is to understand the instruments' sensitivities to the underlying risk factors being stressed. This process is often a complex one that demands an understanding of the portfolio's risk parameters such that we can make appropriate approximations from standardized risk characteristics such as betas, deltas, gammas, duration, and convexity. Market liquidity is often a consideration also, especially when the underlying valuation models for assets assume arbitrage-free pricing, which assumes the ability to transact in any quantity. In addition, liquidity often dries up completely in a market crisis.

### 5.5.2  Stressing Models

Given the difficulty in estimating the sensitivities of a portfolio's instruments to the scenarios we might design, another approach might be to use an existing model and apply shocks and perturbations to the model inputs in some mechanical way. This approach might be considered more scientific because it emphasizes a range of possibilities rather than a single set of scenarios, but it will be more computationally demanding. It is also possible to glean some idea of the likelihood of different scenarios occurring.

The simplest form of stressing model is referred to as **factor push**, the basic idea of which to is to push the prices and risk factors of an underlying model in the most disadvantageous way and to work out the combined effect on the portfolio's value. This exercise might be appropriate for a wide range of models, including option-pricing models such as Black–Scholes–Merton, multifactor equity risk models, and term structure factor models. But factor push also has its limitations and difficulties—principally the enormous model risk that occurs in assuming the underlying model will function in an extreme risk climate.

Other approaches include **maximum loss optimization**—in which we would try to optimize mathematically the risk variable that will produce the maximum loss—and **worst-case scenario analysis**—in which we can examine the worst case that we actually expect to occur.

Overall stress testing is a valuable complement to VAR analysis and can highlight weaknesses in risk management procedures.

## 5.6 Measuring Credit Risk

Credit risk is present when there is a positive probability that one party owing money to another will renege on the obligation (i.e., the counterparty could default). If the defaulting party has insufficient resources to cover the loss or the creditor cannot impose a claim on any assets the debtor has that are unrelated to the line of business in which the credit was extended, the creditor can suffer a loss.[46] A creditor might be able to recover some of the loss, perhaps by having the debtor sell assets and pay the creditors a portion of their claim.

Credit losses have two dimensions: the likelihood of loss and the associated amount of loss (reflecting, of course, the amount of credit outstanding and the associated recovery rate). The likelihood of loss is a probabilistic concept: In every credit-based transaction, a given probability exists that the debtor will default. When a default does occur, however, creditors are often able to recover at least a portion of their investment, and as such, it is necessary and appropriate to assess the magnitude of this recovery (i.e., the recovery rate) in order to fully understand the risk profile of the credit dynamic. In relation to data on market risk, the amount of information available on credit losses is much smaller. Credit losses occur infrequently, and as such, the empirical data set from which to draw exposure inferences is quite limited. Although some statistical data are available, historical recovery rates can be unreliable. It can be hard to predict what an asset could be sold for in bankruptcy proceedings, and claims are not always paid in the order specified by bankruptcy law.

In the risk management business, exposure must often be viewed from two different time perspectives. We must assess first the risk associated with immediate credit events and second the risk associated with events that may happen later. With respect to credit, the risk of events happening in the immediate future is called **current credit risk** (or, alternatively, jump-to-default risk); it relates to the risk that amounts due at the present time will not be paid. For example, some risk exists that the counterparty could default on an interest or swap payment due immediately. Assuming, however, that the counterparty is solvent and that it will make the current payment with certainty, the risk remains that the entity will default at a later date. This risk is called potential credit risk, and it can differ quite significantly from current credit risk; the relationship between the two is a complex one. A company experiencing financial difficulties at present could, with sufficient time, work out its problems and be in better financial condition at a later date. Regardless of which risk is greater, however, a creditor must assess credit risk at different points in time. In doing so, the creditor must understand how different financial instruments have different patterns of credit risk, both across instruments and across time within a given instrument. This point will be discussed later in this section.

Another element of credit risk, which blends current and potential credit risk, is the possibility that a counterparty will default on a current payment to a different creditor. Most direct lending or derivative-based credit contracts stipulate that if a borrower defaults on any outstanding credit obligations, the borrower is in default on them all (this is known as a **cross-default provision**). Creditors stipulate this condition as one means of controlling credit exposure; in particular, it allows them to act quickly to mitigate losses to counterparties unable to meet any of their obligations. For example, suppose Party A owes Party B, but no payments are due for some time. Party A, however, currently owes a payment to Party C and is unable to pay. A is, therefore, in default to Party C. Depending on what actions C takes, A may be forced into bankruptcy. If so, then B's claim simply goes into the pool of other claims on A. In that case, A has technically defaulted to B without actually having a payment due.

---

46 The personal assets of a corporation's owners are shielded from creditors by the principle of limited liability, which can also apply to certain partnerships. The law supporting limited liability is a fundamental one in most societies and supports the notion that default is a right. Indeed, option-pricing theory has been used to value this right as the option that it actually is.

In a previous section, we discussed how VAR is used to measure market risk. VAR is also used, albeit with greater difficulty, to measure credit risk. This measure is sometimes called **credit VAR**, default VAR, or credit at risk. Like ordinary VAR, it reflects the minimum loss with a given probability during a period of time. A company might, for example, quote a credit VAR of €10 million for one year at a probability of 0.05 (or a confidence level of 95 percent). In other words, the company has a 5 percent chance of incurring default-related losses of at least €10 million in one year. Note that credit VAR cannot be separated from market VAR because credit risk arises from gains on market positions held. Therefore, to accurately measure credit VAR, a risk manager must focus on the upper tail of the distribution of market returns, where the return to the position is positive, in contrast to market risk VAR, which focuses on the lower tail. Suppose the 5 percent upper tail of the market risk distribution is €5 million. The credit VAR can be roughly thought of as €5 million, but this thinking assumes that the probability of loss is 100 percent and the net amount recovered in the event of a loss is zero. Further refinements incorporating more-accurate measures of the default probability and recovery rate should lead to a lower and more accurate credit VAR. In addition, the explosion of volume and liquidity in the credit derivatives market has vastly increased the amount of information available to risk managers with respect to the problem of understanding how the marketplace values credit risk on a real-time basis. Nevertheless, estimating credit VAR is more complicated than estimating market VAR because credit events are rare and recovery rates are hard to estimate. Credit risk is less easily aggregated than market risk; the correlations between the credit risks of counterparties must be considered.

In the next sections, we present the perspective of option pricing theory on credit risk and the measurement of credit risk exposures for certain derivative contracts.

### 5.6.1 Option-Pricing Theory and Credit Risk

Option theory enables us to better understand the nature of credit risk. In this section, we will see that the stock of a company with leverage can be viewed as a call option on its assets. This approach will lead to the result that a bond with credit risk can be viewed as a default-free bond plus an implicit short put option written by the bondholders for the stockholders.

Consider a company with assets with a market value of $A_0$ and debt with a face value of $F$. The debt is in the form of a single zero-coupon bond due at time $T$. The bond's market value is $B_0$. Thus the stock's market value is

$$S_0 = A_0 - B_0$$

At time $T$, the assets will be worth $A_T$ and the company will owe $F$. If $A_T \geq F$, the company will pay off its debt, leaving the amount $A_T - F$ for the stockholders. Thus $S_T$ will be worth $A_T - F$. If the assets' value is insufficient to pay off the debt ($A_T < F$), the stockholders will discharge their obligation by turning over the assets to the bondholders. Thus the bondholders will receive $A_T$, which is less than their claim of $F$, and the stockholders will receive nothing. The company is, therefore, bankrupt. Exhibit 10 illustrates these results by showing the payoffs to the two suppliers of capital.

| **Exhibit 10** | Payoffs to the Suppliers of Capital to the Company | | |
|---|---|---|---|
| | | **Payoffs at Time $T$** | |
| **Source of Capital** | **Market Value at Time 0** | $A_T < F$ | $A_T \geq F$ |
| Bondholders | $B_0$ | $A_T$ | $F$ |
| Stockholders | $S_0$ | $0$ | $A_T - F$ |
| Total | $B_0 + S_0 = A_0$ | $A_T$ | $A_T$ |

Notice that the payoffs to the stockholders resemble those of a call option in which the underlying is the assets, the exercise price is $F$, and the option expires at time $T$, the bond maturity date. Indeed, the stock of a company with a single zero-coupon bond issue is a call option on the assets.

To better understand the nature of stock as a call option, let us recall the concept of put–call parity,[47] where $p_0 + S_0 = c_0 + X/(1 + r)^T$. The put price plus the underlying price equals the call price plus the present value of the exercise price. So, working this through for our own problem, we find the correspondences shown in Exhibit 11.

| Exhibit 11 | Equity as a Call Option on the Value of a Company | |
|---|---|---|
| **Variable** | **Traditional Framework** | **Current Framework** |
| Underlying | $S_0$ (stock) | $A_0$ (value of assets) |
| Exercise price | $X$ | $F$ (face value of bond) |
| Time to expiration | $T$ | $T$ (maturity of bond) |
| Risk-free rate | $r$ | $r$ |
| Call price | $c_0$ | $S_0$ (value of stock) |
| Put price | $p_0$ | $p_0$ |

Note the last line. We see that in the traditional framework, there is a put option, which we know is an option to sell the underlying at a fixed price. In fact, we know from put–call parity that $p_0 = c_0 - S_0 + X/(1 + r)^T$. The put is equivalent to a long call, a short position in the underlying stock, and a long position in a risk-free bond with face value equal to the exercise price. In the current framework, the standard expression of put–call parity is $p_0 + A_0$ (put plus underlying) = $S_0 + F/(1 + r)^T$ (stock plus present value of bond principal). Turning this expression around and reversing the order of the put and bond, we obtain

$$A_0 = S_0 + F/(1+r)^T - p_0$$

Noting, however, that by definition the asset value, $A_0$, equals the stock's market value, $S_0$, plus the bond's market value, $B_0$,

$$A_0 = S_0 + B_0$$

we see that the bond's market value must be equivalent to

$$B_0 = F/(1+r)^T - p_0$$

The first term on the right-hand side is equivalent to a default-free zero-coupon bond paying $F$ at maturity. The second term is a short put. The bondholders' claim, which is subject to default, can thus be viewed as a default-free bond and a short put on the assets. In other words, the bondholders have implicitly written the stockholders a put on the assets. From the stockholders' perspective, this put is their right to fully discharge their liability by turning over the assets to the bondholders, even though those assets could be worth less than the bondholders' claim. In legal terminology, this put option is called the stockholders' right of limited liability.

The existence of this implicit put option is the difference between a default-free bond and a bond subject to default. This approach to understanding credit risk forms the basis for models that use option-pricing theory to explain credit risk premiums,

---

**47** See Chance (2003), Chapter 4.

probabilities of default, and the valuation of companies that use leverage. In practice, the capital structures of most companies are more complex than the one used here, but practical applications of model variants appear in the financial industry.

### 5.6.2 The Credit Risk of Forward Contracts

Recall that forward contracts involve commitments on the part of each party. No cash is due at the start, and no cash is paid until expiration, at which time one party owes the greater amount to the other. The party that owes the larger amount could default, leaving the other with a claim of the defaulted amount. Each party assumes the other's credit risk. Prior to expiration, no current credit risk exists, because no current payments are owed, but there is potential credit risk in connection with the payments to be made at expiration. Current credit risk arises when the contract is at its expiration. Below we will examine how potential credit risk changes during the life of the contract as the value of the underlying changes.

From the perspective of a given party, a forward contract's market value can be easily calculated as the present value of the amount owed to the party minus the present value of the amount it owes. So, the market value at a given time reflects the potential credit risk. This is another reason why the calculation of market value is important: It indicates the amount of a claim that would be subject to loss in the event of a default.

For example, look at a forward contract that expires in one year. The underlying asset price is $100 and the risk-free interest rate is 5 percent. We can determine that the forward price is $100(1.05) = $105. We could then assume that three months later, the asset price is $102. We can determine that the long forward contract's value at that time is $102 − $105/(1.05)^{0.75} = $0.7728. This is the value to the long because the contract is a claim on the asset, which is currently worth $102, and an obligation to pay $105 for it in nine months. To the holder of the long position, this contract is worth $0.7728, and to the holder of the short position, it is worth −$0.7728.

Which party bears the potential credit risk? The long's claim is positive; the short's claim is negative. Therefore, the long currently bears the credit risk. As it stands right now, the value of the long's claim is $0.7728. No payment is currently due, and hence no current credit risk exists, but the payments that are due later have a present value of $0.7728. Actual default may or may not occur at expiration. Moreover, at expiration, the amount owed is unlikely to be this same amount. In fact, if the spot price falls enough, the situation will have turned around and the long could owe the short the greater amount. Nonetheless, in assessing the credit risk three months into the contract, the long's claim is $0.7728. This claim has a probability of not being paid and also has the potential for recovery of a portion of the loss in the event of default. If the counterparty declares bankruptcy before the contract expires, the claim of the non-defaulting counterparty is the forward contract's market value at the time of the bankruptcy, assuming this value is positive. So, if the short declares bankruptcy at this time, the long has a claim worth $0.7728. If the long declares bankruptcy, the long holds an asset worth $0.7728.

### 5.6.3 The Credit Risk of Swaps

A swap is similar to a series of forward contracts. The periodic payments associated with a swap imply, however, that credit risk will be present at a series of points during the contract's life. As with forward contracts, the swap's market value can be calculated at any time and reflects the present value of the amount at risk for a credit loss (i.e., the potential credit risk).

Consider, for example, the case of a plain vanilla interest rate swap with a one-year life and quarterly payments at LIBOR. Using the term structure, we can determine that the swap has a fixed rate of 3.68 percent, leading to quarterly fixed payments of $0.0092 per $1 notional principal. We then can move forward 60 days into the life of the swap and, with a new term structure, we can determine that the swap's market value is $0.0047 per $1 notional principal. To the party that is long (i.e., paying fixed and receiving floating), the swap has a positive market value. To the counterparty, which pays floating and receives fixed, the claim has a market value of −$0.0047.

As with a forward contract, the market value indicates the present value of the payments owed to the party minus the present value of the payments the party owes. Only 60 days into the life of a swap with quarterly payments, no payment is due for 30 more days. Thus there is no current credit risk. There is, however, potential credit risk. The market value of $0.0047 represents the amount that is at risk of loss for default. Of course, if default occurs, it will be at a later date when the amount will probably be different. Moreover, the market value could reverse its sign. At this time, the amount owed by the short to the long is greater, but at a later date, the amount owed by the long to the short could be greater. As with forward contracts, if the party to which the value is negative defaults, the counterparty has a claim of that value. If the party to which the value is positive defaults, the defaulting party holds an asset with the positive market value. Also, the counterparty could default to someone else, thereby being forced to declare bankruptcy before a payment on this swap is due. In that case, the swap's market value at that time is either the claim of the creditor or the asset held by the bankrupt party in bankruptcy proceedings.

The credit risk of swaps can vary greatly across product types within this asset class and over a given swap's lifetime. For interest rate and equity swaps, the potential credit risk is largest during the middle period of the swap's life. During the beginning of a swap's life, typically we would assume that the credit risk is small because, presumably, the involved counterparties have performed sufficient current credit analysis on one another to be comfortable with the arrangement or otherwise they would not engage in the transaction. At the end of the life of the swap, the credit risk is diminished because most of the underlying risk has been amortized through the periodic payment process. There are fewer payments at the end of a swap than at any other time during its life; hence, the amount a party can lose because of a default is smaller. This leaves the greatest exposure during the middle period, a point at which 1) the credit profile of the counterparties may have changed for the worse and 2) the magnitude and frequency of expected payments between counterparties remain material. One exception to this pattern involves currency swaps, which often provide for the payment of the notional principal at the beginning and at the end of the life of the transaction. Because the notional principal tends to be a large amount relative to the payments, the potential for loss caused by the counterparty defaulting on the final notional principal payment is great. Thus, whereas interest rate swaps have their greatest credit risk midway during the life of the swap, currency swaps have their greatest credit risk between the midpoint and the end of the life of the swap.

### 5.6.4 *The Credit Risk of Options*

Forward contracts and swaps have bilateral default risk. Although only one party will end up making a given payment, each party could potentially be the party owing the net amount. Options, on the other hand, have unilateral credit risk. The buyer of an option pays a cash premium at the start and owes nothing more unless, under the buyer's sole discretion, he decides to exercise the option. Once the premium is paid, the seller assumes no credit risk from the buyer. Instead, credit risk accrues entirely to the buyer and can be quite significant. If the buyer exercises the option, the seller must meet certain terms embedded in the contract. If the option is a call, the seller must deliver the underlying or pay an equivalent cash settlement. If the option is a put, the seller must accept delivery of the underlying and pay for it or meet these obligations in the form of cash payments. If the seller fails to fulfill her end of the obligation, she is in default. Like forward contracts, European options have no payments due until expiration. Hence, they have no current credit risk until expiration, although significant potential credit risk exists.

Consider a European call option for which the underlying security has a price of 52.75 and a standard deviation of 0.35. The exercise price is 50, the risk-free rate is 4.88 percent continuously compounded, and the option expires in nine months. Using the Black–Scholes–Merton model, we find that the value of the option is 8.5580. The holder thus has potential credit risk represented by a present claim of 8.5580. This amount can be thought of as the amount that is at risk, even though at expiration the option will probably be worth a different amount. In fact, the option might even expire out of the money, in which case it would not matter if the short were bankrupt. If the short declares bankruptcy before expiration, the long has a claim on the value of the option under bankruptcy law.

If the option were American, the value could be greater. Moreover, with American options, current credit risk could arise if the option holder decides to exercise the option early. This alternative creates the possibility of the short defaulting before expiration.

---

### Example 8

## Calculating Credit Risk Exposures

Calculate the amount at risk of a credit loss in the following situations:

1. A U.S. party goes long a forward contract on €1 denominated in dollars in which the underlying is the euro. The original term of the contract was two years, and the forward rate was $0.90. The contract now has 18 months or 1.5 years to maturity. The spot or current exchange rate is $0.862. The U.S. interest rate is 6 percent, and the euro interest rate is 5 percent. The interest rates are based on discrete compounding/discounting. At the point when the contract has 1.5 years remaining, the value of the contract to the long per $1 notional principal equals the spot exchange rate, $0.862, discounted at the international interest rate for 1.5 years, minus the forward rate, $0.90, discounted at the domestic interest rate for 1.5 years:[48]

$$\frac{\$0.862}{(1.05)^{1.5}} - \frac{\$0.90}{(1.06)^{1.5}} = -\$0.0235$$

Evaluate the credit risk characteristics of this situation.

2. Consider a plain vanilla interest rate swap with two months to go before the next payment. Six months after that, the swap will have its final payment. The swap fixed rate is 7 percent, and the upcoming floating payment is 6.9 percent. All payments are based on 30 days in a month and 360 days in a year. Two-month LIBOR is 7.250 percent, and eight-month LIBOR is 7.375 percent. The present value factors for two and eight months can be calculated as follows:

$$\frac{1}{1+0.0725(60/360)} = 0.9881$$

$$\frac{1}{1+0.07375(240/360)} = 0.9531$$

---

[48] See Chance (2003), pp. 58–59.

The next floating payment will be 0.069(180/360) = 0.0345. The present value of the floating payments (plus hypothetical notional principal) is 1.0345(0.9881) = 1.0222. Given an annual rate of 7 percent, the fixed payments will be 0.07(180/360) = 0.035.

The present value of the fixed payments (plus hypothetical notional principal) is, therefore, 0.035(0.9881) + 1.035(0.9531) = 1.0210. Determine the amount at risk of a credit loss and state which party currently bears the risk. Assume a $1 notional principal.

3. A dealer has sold a call option on a stock for $35 to an investor. The option is currently worth $46, as quoted in the market. Determine the amount at risk of a credit loss and state which party currently bears the risk.

### Solution to 1:

The position has a negative value to the long, so the credit risk is currently borne by the short. From the short's point of view, the contract has a value of $0.0235 per $1 notional principal. No payments are due for 18 months, but the short's claim on the long is worth $0.0235 more than the long's claim on the short. Therefore, this amount is the current value of the amount at risk for a credit loss. Of course, the amount could, and probably will, change over the life of the contract. The credit risk exposure might even shift to the other party.

### Solution to 2:

The market value of the swap to the party paying fixed and receiving floating is 1.0222 − 1.0210 = 0.0012. This value is positive to the party paying fixed and receiving floating; thus this party currently assumes the credit risk. Of course, the value will change over the life of the swap and may turn negative, meaning that the credit risk is then assumed by the party paying floating and receiving fixed.

### Solution to 3:

All of the credit risk is borne by the investor (the owner of the call), because he will look to the dealer (the seller) for the payoff if the owner exercises the option. The current value of the amount at risk is the market price of $46.

---

Derivatives' credit risk can be quite substantial, but this risk is considerably less than that faced by most lenders. When a lender makes a loan, the interest and principal are at risk. The loan principal corresponds closely to the notional principal of most derivative contracts. With the exception of currency swaps, the notional principal is never exchanged in a swap. Even with currency swaps, however, the risk is much smaller than on a loan. If a counterparty defaults on a currency swap, the amount owed to the defaulting counterparty serves as a type of collateral because the creditor is not required to pay it to the defaulting party. Therefore, the credit risk on derivative transactions tends to be quite small relative to that on loans. On forward and swap transactions, the netting of payments makes the risk extremely small relative to the notional principal and to the credit risk on a bond or loan of equivalent principal.

## 5.7 Liquidity Risk

One of the implicit assumptions in risk management with VAR is that positions can be liquidated when they approach or move outside pre-agreed risk limits. In practice, some assets are far more liquid than others and practitioners will often liquidity-adjust VAR estimates accordingly. Wide bid–ask spreads in proportion to price are an obvious measure of the cost of trading an illiquid instrument or underlying security. But some instruments simply trade very infrequently at any price—a far more complex problem, because infrequently quoted prices often give the statistical illusion of low or lower volatility. This dynamic is counterintuitive, because we would expect instruments that are illiquid to have a higher bid–ask spread and higher volatilities.

A famous case of underestimating liquidity risk is the failure of the hedge fund Long-Term Capital Management (LTCM) in 1998. LTCM was set up by a group of bond traders and academics and was engaged in arbitrage or relative value trading on world fixed-income markets through the use of the swap market. The total equity in the fund peaked at around $5 billion, but this amount was leveraged around 25 times (perhaps substantially more when the full impact of derivatives is considered). The BIS estimated that the notional value of the swaps entered into by LTCM was around 2.4 percent of the entire world swap market. LTCM failed to appreciate the market moves that would occur when it attempted to liquidate positions, particularly those in illiquid, emerging, fixed-income markets. The New York Federal Reserve was forced to act for fear of a global financial crisis and organized a consortium of 14 international banks to manage the assets of the fund. In the end, and after substantial financial help, LTCM's investors lost more than 90 percent of their equity.

## 5.8 Measuring Nonfinancial Risks

Nonfinancial risks are intrinsically very difficult to measure. Indeed, some of the nonfinancial exposures we have discussed, such as regulatory risk, tax risk, legal risk, and accounting risk, could easily be thought of as not measurable in any precise mathematical way. They are unlike market risk and the VAR concept because we usually lack an observable distribution of losses related to these factors.

Some of these risks could be thought of as more suitable for insurance than measurement and hedging. Like a flood that occurs every 50 years, they might well affect a large number of instruments or contracts. Here, it is possible to learn from best practice in the insurance industry. Insurance companies usually have sufficient assets and are capitalized to withstand these uncertain events. Where it is possible to model a source of risk, actuaries often use techniques like extreme value theory, but even these techniques are only as good as the historical data on which they are based.

### 5.8.1 Operational Risk

Until a few years ago, the subject of operational risk received little attention, and ideas about actually measuring operational risk were practically unheard of. But a number of well-publicized losses at financial institutions, ranging from a breakdown of internal systems to rogue employees and in some cases employee theft, have put operational risk justifiably into the forefront.

Furthermore, the explicit mention of operational risk requirements in the Basel II banking regulations has created real advantages for banks that can credibly measure their operational risks. This, in turn, has led to an explosion in the academic literature relating to the measurement of operational risk and its role in enterprise risk systems.

### Example 9

### Basel II—A Brief Overview

The Basel banking regulations apply only to large international banks, but national governments use them as a guideline in formulating their own financial laws and regulations, so the regulations have much more widespread importance. In January 2001, the Basel Committee on Banking Supervision issued a proposal for a New Basel Capital Accord that would replace the 1988 Capital Accord. This first accord, "Basel I," was widely criticized for being too inflexible in applying an across-the-board 8 percent capital adequacy ratio that made no discrimination between a well risk-managed bank and one that was not.[49]

The Basel II proposal incorporates three mutually reinforcing pillars that allow banks and supervisors to evaluate properly the various risks that banks face:

- Pillar 1: Capital Requirements;
- Pillar 2: Supervisory Review;
- Pillar 3: Market Discipline.

The first pillar of Basel II moves away from a blanket, one-size-fits-all approach and allows banks to develop their own mathematically based financial models. Once these internally developed techniques have been successfully demonstrated to the regulators, banks are able to progress to higher levels of risk management that within the accord are offset by reduced regulatory capital charges. Key to these higher levels of risk management are advanced systems for managing credit risk and operational risk.

The second pillar, supervisory review, requires banks to meet Basel-recommended operational risk requirements that have been tailored by their host country. "Risky" banks, whose risk management systems score lowly in the areas of market risk and operational risk, face penalties. Better-risk-managed banks will have major competitive advantages over rivals, in that, all else equal, they are likely to be subject to reduced capital requirements per unit of risk.

The third pillar says that banks must fulfill the Basel requirements for transparency and disclosing company data. A key point here is that banks must reveal more detail about their profits and losses, which may lead to a supervisory authority reviewing risk systems and changing the capital allocation under the first pillar.

# MANAGING RISK

6

Having established methods for the identification and measurement of risk, we turn our attention to a critical stage of any solid risk management program: that of *managing* risk. The key components, which by now should be somewhat intuitive to you, are as follows:

- An effective risk governance model, which places overall responsibility at the senior management level, allocates resources effectively and features the appropriate separation of tasks between revenue generators and those on the control side of the business.

- Appropriate systems and technology to combine information analysis in such a way as to provide timely and accurate risk information to decision makers.

- Sufficient and suitably trained personnel to evaluate risk information and articulate it to those who need this information for the purposes of decision making.

---

49 A **capital adequacy ratio** is a measure of the adequacy of capital in relation to assets. The purpose of capital is to absorb unanticipated losses with sufficient margin to permit the entity to continue as a going concern. Basel I specified a capital adequacy ratio as a percent of the credit-risk-weighted assets on the bank's balance sheet, where bank assets were divided into four broad categories. For more details, see Saunders and Cornett (2003).

A recent advertisement for the RiskMetrics Group (www.riskmetrics.com) identified the following nine principles of effective risk management:

- There is no return without risk. Rewards go to those who take risks.
- Be transparent. Risk should be fully understood.
- Seek experience. Risk is measured and managed by people, not mathematical models.
- Know what you don't know. Question the assumptions you make.
- Communicate. Risk should be discussed openly.
- Diversify. Multiple risks will produce more consistent rewards.
- Show discipline. A consistent and rigorous approach will beat a constantly changing strategy.
- Use common sense. It is better to be approximately right than to be precisely wrong.
- Return is only half the equation. Decisions should be made only by considering the risk and return of the possibilities.

Risk management is in so many ways just good common business sense. It is quite remarkable, however, that commonsense rules are violated so easily and so often. But that problem is not unique to risk management.

Currently, two professional organizations are devoted to risk management. The Global Association of Risk Professionals (GARP) and the Professional Risk Managers' International Association (PRMIA) are actively involved in promoting knowledge in the field of risk management. You may wish to visit their websites at www.garp.com and www.prmia.org.

With these principles in mind, in the following section, we will discuss the various components of a well-adapted risk-control program.

## 6.1 Managing Market Risk

Let us assume we have correctly identified the sources of market risk that affect our business. Further assume that we have decided on an appropriate way to measure market risk and successfully deployed the systems we need to monitor our positions and measure our risk in a timely way. The result is an appropriate firmwide VAR estimate and associated breakdown by business area. Now we must ask ourselves the following questions: How do we know how much risk is acceptable for us to take? What is the overall exposure assumption capacity for the enterprise, and how close to full capacity should we run? We already know that VAR is not a measure of the maximum possible loss but only a probabilistic guide to the minimum loss we might expect with a certain frequency over a certain time frame.

Our **enterprise risk management** system will be incomplete without a well-thought-out approach to setting appropriate **risk tolerance** levels and identifying the proper corrective behavior to take if our actual risks turn out to be significantly higher or lower than is consistent with our risk tolerance. Note here that in many circumstances, it could cause as many problems to take too little risk as to take too much risk. As we noted at the beginning of this reading, companies are in business to take risk and taking too little risk will more than likely reduce the possible rewards; it could even make the company vulnerable to takeover. In a more extreme scenario, insufficient risk-taking may lead to situations in which the expected return stands little chance of covering variable (let alone fixed) costs.

Corrective behavior in the case of excessive market risk will almost always result in the need for additional hedging or the scaling back of tradable positions. Quite often, however, liquidity and other factors will prevent perfect hedging, perhaps exacerbating risk concerns rather than mitigating them.

### 6.1.1 *Risk Budgeting*

In recent years, companies and portfolio managers have begun to implement a new approach to risk management called **risk budgeting**. It focuses on questions such as, "Where do we want to take risk?" and "What is the efficient allocation of risk across various units of an organization or investment opportunities?" Risk budgeting is relevant in both an organizational and a portfolio management context.

To take an organizational perspective first, risk budgeting involves establishing objectives for individuals, groups, or divisions of an organization that take into account the allocation of an acceptable level of risk. As an example, the foreign exchange (FX) trading desk of a bank could be allocated capital of €100 million and permitted a daily VAR of €5 million. In other words, the desk is granted a budget, expressed in terms of allocated capital and an acceptable level of risk, expressed in euro amounts of VAR. In variations on this theme, instead of using VAR units an organization might allocate risk based on individual transaction size, the amount of working capital needed to support the portfolio, or the amount of losses acceptable for any given time period (e.g., one month). In any case, the innovation here is that the enterprise allocates risk capital before the fact in order to provide guidance on the acceptable amount of risky activities that a given unit can undertake.

A well-run risk-taking enterprise manages these limits carefully and constantly monitors their implementation. Any excesses are reported to management immediately for corrective action. Under this type of regime, management can compare the profits generated by each unit with the amount of capital and risk employed. So, to continue our example from above, say the FX trading desk made a quarterly profit of €20 million from its allocation. The bank's fixed-income trading desk was allocated capital of €200 million and permitted a daily VAR of €5 million; the fixed-income trading desk made €25 million in quarterly trading profits. We note that the allocated daily VARs for the two business areas are the same, so each area has the same risk budget, and that the fixed-income desk generated better returns on the VAR allocation, but worse on the allocation of actual capital, than did the FX desk. (The FX desk shows a €20/€100 = 20% return on capital versus €25/€200 = 12.5% for the fixed-income desk.) This type of scenario is quite common and highlights the complexities of the interaction between risk management and capital allocation. Risk and capital are finite resources that must be allocated carefully.

The sum of risk budgets for individual units will typically exceed the risk budget for the organization as a whole because of the impacts of diversification. Returning to our example, let us assume that for the enterprise in question, its FX and bond trading desks engage in activities that are only weakly correlated. In this case, our present allocation of capital and risk might make perfect sense. For example, the daily VAR of the two business areas combined might be €7 million (i.e., 70 percent of the combined risk allocation for the two desks), for which we again generate a total quarterly profit of €20,000,000 + €25,000,000 = €45 million.

Alternatively, say the two business areas are very highly correlated (their correlation coefficient equals 1) and their combined daily VAR is €5,000,000 + €5,000,000 = €10 million (i.e., 100 percent of the aggregate VAR allocation across desks). The combined profit is still €20,000,000 + €25,000,000 = €45 million. Under these circumstances— and particularly if the bank's management believes that the correlations will remain strong—management might consider closing down the fixed-income desk to generate 0.20(€100,000,000 + €200,000,000) = €60 million of returns on the 3(€5,000,000) = €15 million of VAR. Contrast this strategy with that of closing down the foreign exchange trading desk and allocating all of the capital and risk to the bond trading desk, which would produce 0.125(€200,000,000 + €100,000,000) = €37.5 million in profit for the €7.5 million in VAR, representing a lower return on capital and a higher return on VAR.

A risk-budgeting perspective has also been applied to allocating funds to portfolio managers. Consider an active investor who wants to allocate funds optimally to several domestic and nondomestic equity and fixed-income investment managers. Such an investor might focus on tracking risk as the primary risk measure and decide on an overall maximum acceptable level for it, such as 200 basis points. The expected information ratio (IR) for each manager is one possible measure of each manager's ability to add value, considering the managers in isolation.[50] In this application, however, it is appropriate for the investor to adjust each manager's IR to eliminate the effect of asset class correlations; such correlation-adjusted IRs will capture each manager's incremental ability to add value in a portfolio context. Using such correlation-adjusted IRs, we can determine the optimal tracking risk allocation for each investment manager (which, intuitively, is positively related to his correlation-adjusted IR).[51]

Through these two examples, we edge toward some understanding of risk-adjusted performance measures, which we will discuss in greater detail later in the reading. The point about risk budgeting is that it is a comprehensive methodology that empowers management to allocate capital and risk in an optimal way to the most profitable areas of a business, taking account of the correlation of returns in those business areas.

It once again bears mention that for many portfolio managers, risk budget allocations should be measured in relation to risk to the surplus—that is, the difference between the values of assets and liabilities.

### Example 10

## A Fund Management Company and Risk Budgeting

We can readily illustrate the methodology and underlying economics of risk budgeting with the example of a fund management company. We choose, for this example, a multistrategy hedge fund, because although mutual funds and other types of institutional money managers certainly face similar risk management issues, they are often bound by strict guidelines that tie their risk budgeting to factors such as the performance of a benchmark index and other mandated fund management protocols. For example, the Vanguard family of mutual funds offers a wide range of indexed mutual funds. These funds' associated risk budgets are very narrowly defined, as the managers are called on at all times to track the underlying index very closely in terms of securities held, associated portfolio weightings, and so forth. As investor funds flow in and out of these securities, portfolio managers execute trades that do little more than reestablish this replication balance. Of course, many institutional fund products allow for much broader deviations from market benchmarks; in most cases, however, risk budgeting will be constrained by certain principles associated with benchmarking.

Hedge funds with multiple portfolio managers (as well as, in some cases, the proprietary trading divisions of banks and broker/dealers) have many fewer risk constraints than indexed mutual funds; they have more freedom, therefore, in establishing risk budgets. Because of the absolute return (as opposed to benchmark-driven) nature of their performance, and because of issues such as performance netting risk covered earlier in this reading, it is very much in their interest to ensure that each portfolio in the enterprise operates within a well-conceived risk budget framework. Included among the critical components of such a program might be the following:

---

**50** The information ratio is active return divided by active risk; it measures active return per unit of active risk.

**51** See Waring, Whitney, Pirone, and Castile (2000) and references therein for further reading.

- **Performance Stopouts** A performance stopout is the maximum amount that a given portfolio is allowed to lose in a period (e.g., a month or a year).

- **Working Capital Allocations** Most funds will allocate a specific amount of working capital to each portfolio manager, both as a means of enforcing risk disciplines and also to ensure the ability to fund all operations.

- **VAR Limits** Discussed above.

- **Scenario Analysis Limits** The risk manager of the fund company may establish risk limits based on the scenario analysis discussed in the preceding section. Under such an approach, the portfolio manager would be compelled to construct a portfolio such that under specified scenarios, it did not produce losses greater than certain predetermined amounts.

- **Risk Factor Limits** Portfolio managers may be subject to limits on individual risk factors, as generated by a VAR analysis (e.g., VAR exposure to a certain risk cannot exceed, say, $X or X%) or driven by linear (e.g., duration, beta) or nonlinear (e.g., convexity, gamma) risk estimation methodologies.

- **Position Concentration Limits** Many risk managers seek to enforce diversification by mandating a specific maximum amount for individual positions.

- **Leverage Limits** A maximum amount of leverage in the portfolio may be specified.

- **Liquidity Limits** To help manage liquidity exposure, large funds will often also set position limits as a specified maximum percentage of daily volume, float, or open interest.

Of course, other types of limits are imposed on portfolio managers in a multistrategy environment, and by the same token, the risk-budgeting strategy of a given enterprise may include only a subset of the examples provided immediately above. Nevertheless, some subset of these limit structures is present in nearly every multistrategy fund vehicle, and it is difficult to imagine an effective risk control system that does not set limits.

## 6.2 Managing Credit Risk

It is important that creditors do a good job of measuring and controlling credit risk. Estimating default probabilities is difficult because of the infrequency of losses for many situations where credit risk exists. Moreover, credit losses differ considerably from losses resulting from market moves. Credit is a one-sided risk. If Party B owes Party A the amount of £1,000, B will end up paying A either £1,000 or some amount ranging from zero to £1,000. A's rate of return is certainly not normally distributed and not even symmetric. All of the risk is downside. Thus credit risk is not easily analyzed or controlled using such measures as standard deviation and VAR. Creditors need to regularly monitor the financial condition of borrowers and counterparties. In addition, they can use the risk management techniques for credit discussed below.

### 6.2.1 *Reducing Credit Risk by Limiting Exposure*

Limiting the amount of exposure to a given party is the primary means of managing credit risk. Just as a bank will not lend too much money to one entity, neither will a party engage in too many derivatives transactions with one counterparty. Exactly how much exposure to a given counterparty is "too much" is still not easy to quantify. Experienced risk managers often have a good sense of when and where to limit their exposure, and they make extensive use of quantitative credit exposure measures to guide them in this process. Banks have regulatory constraints on the amount of credit risk they can assume, which are specified in terms of formulas.

### 6.2.2  Reducing Credit Risk by Marking to Market

One device that the futures market uses to control credit risk is marking tradable positions to market. The OTC derivatives market also uses **marking to market** to deal with credit risk: Some OTC contracts are marked to market periodically during their lives. Recall that a forward contract or swap has a market value that is positive to one party and negative to another. When a contract calls for marking to market, the party for which the value is negative pays the market value to the party for which the value is positive. Then the fixed rate on the contract is recalculated, taking into account the new spot price, interest rate, and time to expiration.

Recall that we examined a one-year forward contract with an initial forward price of $105. Three months later, when the asset price was $102, its value was $0.7728 to the long. If the contract were marked to market at that time, the short would pay the long $0.7728. Then, the two parties would enter into a new contract expiring in nine months with a new forward price, which would be $102(1.05)^{0.75} = $105.80.

---

**Example 11**

### Repricing a Forward Contract

Consider a one-year forward contract established at a rate of $105. The contract is four months into its life. The spot price is $108, the risk-free rate is 4.25 percent, and the underlying makes no cash payments. The two parties decided at the start that they will mark the contract to market every four months. The market value of the contract is $108 - $105/(1.0425)^{8/12} = $5.873. Determine how the cash flows and resets would work under these circumstances.

### Solution:

The contract is positive to the long, so the short pays the long $5.873. The parties then reprice the contract. The new price is $108(1.0425)^{8/12} = $111.04. At this point, the forward price is reset to $111.04. The parties will then mark to market again at the eight-month point and reset the forward price. This price will then stay in force until expiration.

---

OTC options usually are not marked to market because their value is always positive to one side of the transaction. Of course, one party of the option certainly bears credit risk, but marking to market is usually done only with contracts with two-way credit risk. Option credit risk is normally handled by collateral.

### 6.2.3  Reducing Credit Risk with Collateral

The posting of collateral is a widely accepted credit exposure mitigant in both lending and derivatives transactions. One very prominent example of its use comes from futures markets, which require that all market participants post margin collateral. Beyond this, many OTC derivative markets have collateral posting provisions, with the collateral usually taking the form of cash or highly liquid, low-risk securities. A typical arrangement involves the routine, periodic posting of values sufficient to cover mark-to-market deficiencies. To illustrate, if a given derivatives contract has a positive value to Party A and a negative value to Party B, then Party B owes more than Party A, and Party B must put collateral into an account designated for this purpose. As the contract's market value changes, the amount of collateral that must be maintained will vary, increasing as the market value increases and vice versa. At some point, if the market value of the transaction changes sign (i.e., goes from positive to negative for one of the participants), the collateral position will typically reverse itself, with the entity previously posting collateral seeing a release of these assets and the other participant in the transaction experiencing a collateral obligation. In addition to market values, collateral requirements are sometimes also based on factors such as participants' credit ratings.

### 6.2.4  *Reducing Credit Risk with Netting*

One of the most common features used in two-way contracts with a credit risk component, such as forwards and swaps, is netting. This process, which we have already briefly discussed, involves the reduction of all obligations owed between counterparties into a single cash transaction that eliminates these liabilities. For example, if a payment is due and Party A owes more to Party B than B owes to A, the difference between the amounts owed is calculated and Party A pays the net amount owed. This procedure, called **payment netting**, reduces the credit risk by reducing the amount of money that must be paid. If Party A owes €100,000 to Party B, which owes €40,000 to A, then the net amount owed is €60,000, which A owes to B. Without netting, B would need to send €40,000 to A, which would send €100,000 to B. Suppose B was in the process of sending its €40,000 to A but was unaware that A was in default and unable to send the €100,000 to B. If the €40,000 is received by A, B might be unable to get it back until the bankruptcy court decides what to do, which could take years. Using netting, only the €60,000 owed by A to B is at risk.

In the examples we have seen so far, netting is applied on the payment date. The concept of netting can be extended to the events and conditions surrounding a bankruptcy. Suppose A and B are counterparties to a number of derivative contracts. On some of the contracts, the market value to A is positive, while on others, the market value to B is positive. If A declares bankruptcy, the parties can use netting to solve a number of problems. If A and B agree to do so before the bankruptcy, they can net the market values of *all* of their derivative contracts to determine one overall value owed by one party to another. It could well be the case that even though A is bankrupt, B might owe more to A than A owes to B. Then, rather than B being a creditor to A, A's claim on B becomes one of A's remaining assets. This process is referred to as **closeout netting**.

During this bankruptcy process, netting plays an important role in reducing a practice known in the financial services industry as cherry picking, which in this case would involve a bankrupt company attempting to enforce contracts that are favorable to it while walking away from those that are unprofitable. In our example, without netting, A could default on the contracts in which it owes more to B than B owes to A, but B could be forced to pay up on those contracts in which it owes more to A than A owes to B.

To be supported through the bankruptcy process, however, netting must be recognized by the legal system and works best when each party's rights and obligations are specified at the time before or contemporaneous to the executions of transactions. Most, but not all, legal jurisdictions recognize netting.

### 6.2.5  *Reducing Credit Risk with Minimum Credit Standards and Enhanced Derivative Product Companies*

As noted above, the first line of defense against credit risk is limiting the amount of business one party engages in with another. An important and related concept is to ensure that all credit-based business is undertaken with entities that have adequate levels of credit quality. The historical standard measures for such credit quality come from rating agencies such as Moody's Investors Service and Standard & Poor's. Some companies will not do business with an enterprise unless its rating from these agencies meets a prescribed level of credit quality. This practice can pose a problem for some derivatives dealers, most of which engage in other lines of business that expose them to a variety of other risks; for example, banks are the most common derivatives dealers. To an end user considering engaging in a derivative contract with a dealer, the potential for the dealer's other business to cause the dealer to default is a serious concern. Banks, in particular, are involved in consumer and commercial lending, which can be quite risky. In the United States, for example, we have seen banking crises involving bad loans to the real estate industry and underdeveloped countries.

The possibility that bad loans will cause a bank to default on its derivatives transactions is quite real, and credit ratings often reflect this possibility. In turn, ratings are a major determinant in business flows for banks that act as dealers. Hence, many derivatives dealers have taken action to control their exposure to rating downgrades. One such action is the formation of a type of subsidiary that is separate from the dealer's other activities. These subsidiaries are referred to as **enhanced derivatives products companies** (EDPCs), sometimes known as special purpose vehicles (SPVs). These companies are usually completely separate from the parent organization and are not liable for the parent's debts. They tend to be very heavily capitalized and are committed to hedging all of their derivatives positions. As a result of these features, these subsidiaries almost always receive the highest credit quality rating by the rating agencies. In the event that the parent goes bankrupt, the EDPC is not liable for the parent company's debts; if the EDPC goes under, however, the parent is liable for an amount up to its equity investment and may find it necessary to provide even more protection. Hence, an EDPC would typically have a higher credit rating than its parent. In fact, it is precisely for the purpose of obtaining the highest credit rating, and thus the most favorable financing terms with counterparties, that banks and broker dealers go through the expense of putting together EDPCs.

### 6.2.6 *Transferring Credit Risk with Credit Derivatives*

Another mechanism for managing credit risk is to transfer it to another party. Credit derivatives provide mechanisms for such transfers. Credit derivatives include such contracts as credit default swaps, total return swaps, credit spread options, and credit spread forwards. These transactions are typically customized, although the wording of contract provisions is often standardized. In a **credit default swap**, the protection buyer pays the protection seller in return for the right to receive a payment from the seller in the event of a specified credit event. In a **total return swap**, the protection buyer pays the total return on a reference obligation (or basket of reference obligations) in return for floating-rate payments. If the reference obligation has a credit event, the total return on the reference obligation should fall; the total return should also fall in the event of an increase in interest rates, so the protection seller (total return receiver) in this contract is actually exposed to both credit risk and interest rate risk. A **credit spread option** is an option on the yield spread of a reference obligation and over a referenced benchmark (such as the yield on a specific default-free security of the same maturity); by contrast, a **credit spread forward** is a forward contract on a yield spread. Credit derivatives may be used not only to eliminate credit risk but also to assume credit risk. For example, an investor may be well positioned to assume a credit risk because it is uncorrelated with other credit risks in her portfolio.[52]

## 6.3 Performance Evaluation

In order to maximize risk-adjusted return through the capital allocation process, we must measure performance against risks assumed and budgeted at both the business unit or substrategy level and enterprise or overall portfolio level. All business

---

[52] For more information on credit derivatives, see Fabozzi (2004b), Chapter 9, and Chance (2003), Chapter 9.

activities should be evaluated against the risk taken, and a considerable body of knowledge has developed concerning the evaluation of investment performance from a risk-adjusted perspective. Traditional approaches, which take into account return against a risk penalty, are now used in other areas of business activity besides portfolio management. Some banks and service providers have developed sophisticated performance evaluation systems that account for risk, and they have marketed these systems successfully to clients. Risk-adjusted performance, as measured against sensible benchmarks, is a critically important capital allocation tool because it allows for the comparison of results in terms of homogeneous units of exposure assumption. Absent these measurement tools, market participants with high risk profiles are likely to be given higher marks for positive performance than they arguably deserve because they derive more from increased exposure assumption than they do from superior portfolio management methodologies. Furthermore, most investment professionals are compensated on the basis of the performance of their portfolios, trading positions, or investment ideas, and it is appropriate to judge performance in risk-adjusted terms.

Following is a list of standard methodologies for expressing return in units of exposure assumption:

- **Sharpe Ratio** The seminal measure for risk-adjusted return, the Sharpe ratio has become the industry standard. The traditional definition of this measure is as follows:[53]

$$\text{Sharpe ratio} = \frac{\text{Mean portfolio return} - \text{Risk-free rate}}{\text{Standard deviation of portfolio return}}$$

  The basic idea, therefore, is entirely intuitive: The Sharpe ratio is the mean return earned in excess of the risk-free rate per unit of volatility or total risk. By subtracting a risk-free rate from the mean return, we can isolate the performance associated with risk-taking activities. One elegant outcome of the calculation is that a portfolio engaging in "zero risk" investment, such as the purchase of Treasury bills for which the expected return is precisely the risk-free rate, earns a Sharpe ratio of exactly zero.

  The Sharpe ratio calculation is the most widely used method for calculating risk-adjusted return. Nevertheless, it can be inaccurate when applied to portfolios with significant nonlinear risks, such as options positions. In part for these reasons, alternative risk-adjusted return methodologies have emerged over the years, including the following.

- **Risk-Adjusted Return on Capital (RAROC)** This concept divides the expected return on an investment by a measure of capital at risk, a measure of the investment's risk that can take a number of different forms and can be calculated in a variety of ways that may have proprietary features. The company may require that an investment's expected RAROC exceed a RAROC benchmark level for capital to be allocated to it.[54]

---

53 This traditional definition of the Sharpe ratio can be directly linked to the capital market line and related capital market theory concepts (see Elton, Gruber, Brown, and Goetzmann, 2003). Sharpe (1994), however, defines the Sharpe ratio as a general construct using the mean excess return in relation to a benchmark in the numerator and the standard deviation of returns in excess of the benchmark in the denominator (see the discussion of the information ratio in the reading on evaluating portfolio performance for an illustration of this usage). Using the risk-free rate as the benchmark, the numerator would be as given in the text but the denominator would be the standard deviation of returns in excess of the risk-free rate (which, in practice, would infrequently result in significant discrepancies).

54 For more information on RAROC, see Saunders and Cornett (2003).

■ **Return over Maximum Drawdown (RoMAD)** Drawdown, in the field of hedge fund management, is defined as the difference between a portfolio's maximum point of return (known in industry parlance as its "high-water" mark), and any subsequent low point of performance. *Maximum* drawdown is the largest difference between a high-water and a subsequent low. Maximum drawdown is a preferred way of expressing the risk of a given portfolio—particularly as associated track records become longer—for investors who believe that observed loss patterns over longer periods of time are the best available proxy for actual exposure.

  Return over maximum drawdown is simply the average return in a given year that a portfolio generates, expressed as a percentage of this drawdown figure. It enables investors to ask the following question: Am I willing to accept an occasional drawdown of $X$ percent in order to generate an average return of $Y$ percent? An investment with $X = 10$ percent and $Y = 15$ percent (RoMAD = 1.5) would be more attractive than an investment with $X = 40$ percent and $Y = 10$ percent (RoMAD = 0.25).

■ **Sortino Ratio** One school of thought concerning the measurement of risk-adjusted returns argues, with some justification, that portfolio managers should not be penalized for volatility deriving from outsized positive performance. The Sortino ratio adopts this perspective. The numerator of the Sortino ratio is the return in excess of the investor's minimum acceptable return (MAR). The denominator is the downside deviation using the MAR as the target return.[55] **Downside deviation** computes volatility using only rate of return data points below the MAR. Thus the expression for the Sortino ratio is

$$\text{Sortino ratio} = (\text{Mean portfolio return} - \text{MAR}) / \text{Downside deviation}$$

If the MAR is set at the risk-free rate, the Sortino ratio is identical to the Sharpe ratio, save for the fact that it uses downside deviation instead of the standard deviation in the denominator. A side-by-side comparison of rankings of portfolios according to the Sharpe and Sortino ratios can provide a sense of whether outperformance may be affecting assessments of risk-adjusted performance. Taken together, the two ratios can tell a more detailed story of risk-adjusted return than either will in isolation, but the Sharpe ratio is better grounded in financial theory and analytically more tractable. Furthermore, departures from normality of returns can raise issues for the Sortino ratio as much as for the Sharpe ratio.

These approaches are only a subset of the methodologies available to investors wishing to calculate risk-adjusted returns. Each approach has both its merits and its drawbacks. Perhaps the most important lesson to bear in mind with respect to this mosaic is the critical need to understand the inputs to any method, so as to be able to interpret the results knowledgeably, with an understanding of their possible limitations.

## 6.4 Capital Allocation

In addition to its unquestionable value in the task of capital preservation, risk management has become a vital, if not central, component in the process of allocating capital across units of a risk-taking enterprise. The use of inputs, such as volatility/correlation analysis, risk-adjusted return calculations, scenario analysis, etc., provides the

---

**55** Downside deviation, the term usually used in presenting the Sortino ratio, could also be called a target semideviation (using MAR as the target).

allocators of risk capital with a much more informed means of arriving at the appropriate conclusions on how best to distribute this scarce resource. The risk management inputs to the process can be used in formal, mathematical, "optimization" routines, under which enterprises input performance data into statistical programs that will then offer appropriate capital allocation combinations to make efficient use of risk. Quantitative output may simply serve as background data for qualitative decision-making processes. One way or another, however, risk management has become a vital input into the capital allocation process, and it is fair to describe this development as positive from a systemic perspective.

As part of the task of allocating capital across business units, organizations must determine how to measure such capital. Here there are multiple methodologies, and we will discuss five of them in further detail:

1. **Nominal, Notional, or Monetary Position Limits** Under this approach, the enterprise simply defines the amount of capital that the individual portfolio or business unit can use in a specified activity, based on the actual amount of money exposed in the markets. It has the advantage of being easy to understand, and, in addition, it lends itself very nicely to the critical task of calculating a percentage-based return on capital allocated. Such limits, however, may not capture effectively the effects of correlation and offsetting risks. Furthermore, an individual may be able to work around a nominal position using other assets that can replicate a given position. For these reasons, although it is often useful to establish notional position limits, it is seldom a *sufficient* capital allocation method from a risk control perspective.

2. **VAR-Based Position Limits** As an alternative or supplement to notional limits, enterprises often assign a VAR limit as a proxy for allocated capital. This approach has a number of distinct advantages, most notably the fact that it allocates capital in units of estimated exposure and thus acts in greater harmony with the risk control process. This approach has potential problems as well, however. Most notably, the limit regime will be only as effective as the VAR calculation itself; when VAR is cumbersome, less than completely accurate, not well understood by traders, or some combination of the above, it is difficult to imagine it providing rational results from a capital allocation perspective. In addition, the relation between overall VAR and the VARs of individual positions is complex and can be counterintuitive.[56] Nevertheless, VAR limits probably have an important place in any effective capital allocation scheme.

3. **Maximum Loss Limits** Irrespective of other types of limit regimes that it might have in place, it is crucial for any risk-taking enterprise to establish a maximum loss limit for each of its risk-taking units. In order to be effective, this figure must be large enough to enable the unit to achieve performance objectives but small enough to be consistent with the preservation of capital. This limit must represent a firm constraint on risk-taking activity. Nevertheless, even when risk-taking activity is generally in line with policy, management should recognize that extreme market discontinuities can cause such limits to be breached.

4. **Internal Capital Requirements** Internal capital requirements specify the level of capital that management believes to be appropriate for the firm. Some regulated financial institutions, such as banks and securities firms, typically also have regulatory capital requirements that, if they are higher, overrule internal requirements. Traditionally, internal capital requirements have been specified

---

56 For example, one cannot add the VAR of individual positions to obtain a conservative measure (i.e., maximum) of overall VAR because it is possible for the sum of the VARs to be greater than the VAR of the combined positions.

heuristically in terms of the capital ratio (the ratio of capital to assets). Modern tools permit a more rigorous approach. If the value of assets declines by an amount that exceeds the value of capital, the firm will be insolvent. Say a 0.01 probability of insolvency over a one-year horizon is acceptable. By requiring capital to equal at least one-year aggregate VAR at the 1 percent probability level, the capital should be adequate in terms of the firm's risk tolerance. If the company can assume a normal return distribution, the required amount of capital can be stated in standard deviation units (e.g., 1.96 standard deviations would reflect a 0.025 probability of insolvency). A capital requirement based on aggregate VAR has an advantage over regulatory capital requirements in that it takes account of correlations. Furthermore, to account for extraordinary shocks, we can stress test the VAR-based recommendation.

5. **Regulatory Capital Requirements** In addition, many institutions (e.g., securities firms and banks) must calculate and meet regulatory capital requirements. Wherever and whenever this is the case, it of course makes sense to allocate this responsibility to business units. Meeting regulatory capital requirements can be a difficult process, among other reasons because such requirements are sometimes inconsistent with rational capital allocation schemes that have capital preservation as a primary objective. Nevertheless, when regulations demand it, firms must include regulatory capital as part of their overall allocation process.

Depending on such factors as the type of enterprise, its corporate culture, fiduciary obligations, etc., the most effective approach to capital allocation probably involves a combination of most, if not all, of the above methodologies. The trick, of course, is to combine the appropriate ones in a rational and consistent manner that creates the proper incentives for balance between the dual objectives of profit maximization and capital preservation.

## 6.5  Psychological and Behavioral Considerations

Over the past several years, a body of research has emerged that seeks to model the behavioral aspects of portfolio management. This concept has important implications for risk management for two reasons. First, risk takers may behave differently at different points in the portfolio management cycle, depending on such factors as their recent performance, the risk characteristics of their portfolios, and market conditions. Second, and on a related note, risk management would improve if these dynamics could be modeled.

Although the topic merits more discussion than we can possibly include in this context, the main factor to consider from a risk management perspective is the importance of establishing a risk governance framework that anticipates the points in a cycle when the incentives of risk takers diverge from those of risk capital allocators. One prominent example (although by no means the only one) occurs when portfolio managers who are paid a percentage of their profits in a given year fall into a negative performance situation. The trader's situation does not deteriorate from a compensation perspective with incremental losses at this point (i.e., the trader is paid zero, no matter how much he loses), but of course the organization as a whole suffers from the trader's loss. Moreover, the risks at the enterprise level can be nonlinear under these circumstances because of concepts of netting risk covered earlier in this reading. These and other behavioral issues can be handled best by risk control and governance processes that contemplate them. One such example is limit setting, which can, with some thought, easily incorporate many of these issues.[57]

---

**57** Those interested in studying these topics further may wish to refer to Grant (2004) and Kiev (2002).

# SUMMARY

Financial markets reward competence and knowledge in risk management and punish mistakes. Portfolio managers must therefore study and understand the discipline of successful risk management. In this reading, we have introduced basic concepts and techniques of risk management and made the following points:

■ Risk management is a process involving the identification of the exposures to risk, the establishment of appropriate ranges for exposures, the continuous measurement of these exposures, and the execution of appropriate adjustments to bring the actual level and desired level of risk into alignment. The process involves continuous monitoring of exposures and new policies, preferences, and information.

■ Typically, risks should be minimized wherever and whenever companies lack comparative advantages in the associated markets, activities, or lines of business.

■ Risk governance refers to the process of setting risk management policies and standards for an organization. Senior management, which is ultimately responsible for all organizational activities, must oversee the process.

■ Enterprise risk management is a centralized risk management system whose distinguishing feature is a firm-wide or across-enterprise perspective on risk.

■ Financial risk refers to all risks derived from events in the external financial markets. Nonfinancial risk refers to all other forms of risk. Financial risk includes market risk (risk related to interest rates, exchange rates, stock prices, and commodity prices), credit risk, and liquidity risk. The primary sources of nonfinancial risk are operations risk, model risk, settlement risk, regulatory risk, legal risk, tax risk, and accounting risk.

■ Traditional measures of market risk include linear approximations such as beta for stocks, duration for fixed income, and delta for options, as well as second-order estimation techniques such as convexity and gamma. For products with option-like characteristics, techniques exist to measure the impact of changes in volatility (vega) and the passage of time (theta). Sensitivity to movements in the correlation among assets is also relevant for certain types of instruments.

■ Value at risk (VAR) estimates the minimum loss that a party would expect to experience with a given probability over a specified period of time. Using the complementary probability (i.e., 100 percent minus the given probability stated as a percent), VAR can be expressed as a maximum loss at a given confidence level. VAR users must make decisions regarding appropriate time periods, confidence intervals, and specific VAR methodologies.

■ The analytical or variance–covariance method can be used to determine VAR under the assumption that returns are normally distributed by subtracting a multiple of the standard deviation from the expected return, where the multiple is determined by the desired probability level. The advantage of the method is its simplicity. Its disadvantages are that returns are not normally distributed in any reliable sense and that the method does not work well when portfolios contain options and other derivatives.

■ The historical method estimates VAR from data on a portfolio's performance during a historical period. The returns are ranked, and VAR is obtained by determining the return that is exceeded in a negative sense 5 percent or 1 percent (depending on the user's choice) of the time. The historical method has the advantage of being simple and not requiring the assumption of a normal distribution. Its disadvantage is that accurate historical time-series information is not always easily available, particularly for instruments such as bonds and options, which behave differently at different points in their life spans.

■ Monte Carlo simulation estimates VAR by generating random returns and determining the 5 percent or 1 percent (depending on the user's choice) worst outcomes. It has the advantages that it does not require a normal distribution and can handle complex relationships among risks. Its disadvantage is that it can be very time consuming and costly to conduct the large number of simulations required for accuracy. It also requires the estimation of input values, which can be difficult.

■ VAR can be difficult to estimate, can give a wide range of values, and can lead to a false sense of security that risk is accurately measured and under control. VAR for individual positions do not generally aggregate in a simple way to portfolio VAR. VAR also puts all emphasis on the negative outcomes, ignoring the positive outcomes. It can be difficult to calculate VAR for a large complex organization with many exposures. On the other hand, VAR is a simple and easy-to-understand risk measure that is widely accepted. It is also adaptable to a variety of uses, such as allocating capital.

■ Incremental VAR measures the incremental effect of an asset on the VAR of a portfolio. Cash flow at risk and earnings at risk measure the risk to a company's cash flow or earnings instead of market value, as in the case of VAR. Tail value at risk is VAR plus the expected loss in excess of VAR, when such excess loss occurs. Stress testing is another important supplement to VAR.

■ Credit risk has two dimensions, the probability of default and the associated recovery rate.

■ Credit risk in a forward contract is assumed by the party to which the market value is positive. The market value represents the current value of the claim that one party has on the other. The actual payoff at expiration could differ, but the market value reflects the current value of that future claim.

■ Credit risk in swaps is similar to credit risk in forward contracts. The market value represents the current value of the claim on the future payments. The party holding the positive market value assumes the credit risk at that time. For interest rate and equity swaps, credit risk is greatest near the middle of the life of the swap. For currency swaps with payment of notional principal, credit risk is greatest near the end of the life of the swap.

■ Credit risk in options is one-sided. Because the seller is paid immediately and in full, she faces no credit risk. By contrast, the buyer faces the risk that the seller will not meet her obligations in the event of exercise. The market value of the option is the current value of the future claim the buyer has on the seller.

■ VAR can be used to measure credit risk. The interpretation is the same as with standard VAR, but a credit-based VAR is more complex because it must interact with VAR based on market risk. Credit risk arises only when market risk results in gains to trading. Credit VAR must take into account the complex interaction of market movements, the possibility of default, and recovery rates. Credit VAR is also difficult to aggregate across markets and counterparties.

■ Risk budgeting is the process of establishing policies to allocate the finite resource of risk capacity to business units that must assume exposure in order to generate return. Risk budgeting has also been applied to allocation of funds to investment managers.

- The various methods of controlling credit risk include setting exposure limits for individual counterparties, exchanging cash values that reflect mark-to-market levels, posting collateral, netting, setting minimum credit, using special-purpose vehicles that have higher credit ratings than the companies that own them, and using credit derivatives.

- Among the measures of risk-adjusted performance that have been used in a portfolio context are the Sharpe ratio, risk-adjusted return on capital, return over maximum drawdown, and the Sortino ratio. The Sharpe ratio uses standard deviation, measuring total risk as the risk measure. Risk-adjusted return on capital accounts for risk using capital at risk. The Sortino ratio measures risk using downside deviation, which computes volatility using only rate-of-return data points below a minimum acceptable return. Return over maximum drawdown uses maximum drawdown as a risk measure.

- Methods for allocating capital include nominal position limits, VAR-based position limits, maximum loss limits, internal capital requirements, and regulatory capital requirements.

## PRACTICE PROBLEMS FOR READING 34

1. Discuss the difference between centralized and decentralized risk management systems, including the advantages and disadvantages of each.

2. Stewart Gilchrist follows the automotive industry, including Ford Motor Company. Based on Ford's 2003 annual report, Gilchrist writes the following summary:

   Ford Motor Company has businesses in several countries around the world. Ford frequently has expenditures and receipts denominated in non-U.S. currencies, including purchases and sales of finished vehicles and production parts, subsidiary dividends, investments in non-U.S. operations, etc. Ford uses a variety of commodities in the production of motor vehicles, such as non-ferrous metals, precious metals, ferrous alloys, energy, and plastics/resins. Ford typically purchases these commodities from outside suppliers. To finance its operations, Ford uses a variety of funding sources, such as commercial paper, term debt, and lines of credit from major commercial banks. The company invests any surplus cash in securities of various types and maturities, the value of which are subject to fluctuations in interest rates. Ford has a credit division, which provides financing to customers wanting to purchase Ford's vehicles on credit. Overall, Ford faces several risks. To manage some of its risks, Ford invests in fixed-income instruments and derivative contracts. Some of these investments do not rely on a clearing house and instead effect settlement through the execution of bilateral agreements.

   Based on the above discussion, recommend and justify the risk exposures that should be reported as part of an Enterprise Risk Management System for Ford Motor Company.

3. NatWest Markets (NWM) was the investment banking arm of National Westminster Bank, one of the largest banks in the United Kingdom. On 28 February 1997, NWM revealed that a substantial loss had been uncovered in its trading books. During the 1990s, NatWest was engaged in trading interest rate options and swaptions on several underlying currencies. This trading required setting appropriate prices of the options by the traders at NatWest. A key parameter in setting the price of an interest rate option is the implied volatility of the underlying asset—that is, the interest rate on a currency. In contrast to other option parameters that affect the option prices, such as duration to maturity and exercise price, implied volatility is not directly observable and must be estimated. Many option pricing models imply that the implied volatility should be the same for all options on the same underlying, irrespective of their exercise price or maturity. In practice, however, implied volatility is often observed to have a curvilinear relationship with the option's moneyness (i.e., whether the option is out of the money, at the money, or in the money), a relationship sometimes called the *volatility smile.* Implied volatility tended to be higher for out-of-the-money options than for at-the-money options on the same underlying.

   NWM prices on certain contracts tended to consistently undercut market prices, as if the out-of-the money options were being quoted at implied volatilities that were too low. When trading losses mounted in an interest rate option contract, a trader undertook a series of off-market-price transactions between the options portfolio and a swaptions portfolio to transfer the losses to a type of contract where losses were easier to conceal. A subsequent investigation revealed that the back office did not independently value the trading positions in question and that lapses in trade reconciliation had occurred.

What type or types of risk were inadequately managed in the above case?

4. Sue Ellicott supervises the trading function at an asset management firm. In conducting an in-house risk management training session for traders, Ellicott elicits the following statements from traders:

> Trader 1: "Liquidity risk is not a major concern for buyers of a security as opposed to sellers."

> Trader 2: "In general, derivatives can be used to substantially reduce the liquidity risk of a security."

Ellicott and the traders then discuss two recent cases of a similar risk exposure in an identical situation that one trader (Trader A) hedged and another trader (Trader B) assumed as a speculation. A participant in the discussion makes the following statement concerning the contrasting treatment:

> Trader 3: "Our traders have considerable experience and expertise in analyzing the risk, and this risk is related to our business. Trader B was justified in speculating on the risk within the limits of his risk allocation."

State and justify whether each trader's statement is correct or incorrect.

5. A large trader on the government bond desk of a major bank loses €20 million in a year, in the process reducing the desk's overall profit to €10 million. Senior management, on looking into the problem, determines that the trader repeatedly violated his position limits during the year. They also determine that the bulk of the loss took place in the last two weeks of the year, when the trader increased his position dramatically and experienced 80 percent of his negative performance. The bank dismisses both the trader and his desk manager. The bank has an asymmetric incentive compensation contract arrangement with its traders.

A. Discuss the performance netting risk implications of this scenario.

B. Are there any reasons why the timing of the loss is particularly significant?

C. What mistakes did senior management make? Explain how these errors can be corrected.

6. Ford Credit is the branch of Ford Motor Company that provides financing to Ford's customers. For this purpose, it obtains funding from various sources. As a result of its interest rate risk management process, including derivatives, Ford Credit's debt reprices faster than its assets. This situation means that when interest rates are rising, the interest rates paid on Ford Credit's debt will increase more rapidly than the interest rates earned on assets, thereby initially reducing Ford Credit's pretax net interest income. The reverse will be true when interest rates decline.

Ford's annual report provides a quantitative measure of the sensitivity of Ford Credit's pretax net interest income to changes in interest rates. For this purpose, it uses interest rate scenarios that assume a hypothetical, instantaneous increase or decrease in interest rates of 1 percentage point across all maturities. These scenarios are compared with a base case that assumes that interest rates remain constant at existing levels. The differences between the scenarios and the base case over a 12-month period represent an estimate of the sensitivity of Ford Credit's pretax net interest income. This sensitivity as of year-end 2003 and 2002 is as follows:

| | Pretax Net Interest Income Impact Given a One Percentage Point Instantaneous *Increase* in Interest Rates (in Millions) | Pretax Net Interest Income Impact Given a One Percentage Point Instantaneous *Decrease* in Interest Rates (in Millions) |
|---|---|---|
| December 31, 2003 | ($179) | $179 |
| December 31, 2002 | ($153) | $156 |

*Source*: Annual Report of Ford Motor Company, 2003.

Describe the strengths and weaknesses of the interest rate risk analysis presented in the foregoing table.

**7. A.** An organization's risk management function has computed that a portfolio held in one business unit has a 1 percent weekly value at risk (VAR) of £4.25 million. Describe what is meant in terms of a minimum loss.

**B.** The portfolio of another business unit has a 99 percent weekly VAR of £4.25 million (stated using a confidence limit approach). Describe what is meant in terms of a maximum loss.

**8.** Each of the following statements about VAR is true *except*:

**A.** VAR is the loss that would be exceeded with a given probability over a specific time period.

**B.** Establishing a VAR involves several decisions, such as the probability and time period over which the VAR will be measured and the technique to be used.

**C.** VAR will be larger when it is measured at 5 percent probability than when it is measured at 1 percent probability.

**D.** VAR will be larger when it is measured over a month than when it is measured over a day.

**9.** Suppose you are given the following sample probability distribution of annual returns on a portfolio with a market value of $10 million.

| Return on Portfolio | Probability |
|---|---|
| Less than −50% | 0.005 |
| −50% to −40% | 0.005 |
| −40% to −30% | 0.010 |
| −30% to −20% | 0.015 |
| −20% to −10% | 0.015 |
| −10% to −5% | 0.165 |
| −5% to 0% | 0.250 |
| 0% to 5% | 0.250 |
| 5% to 10% | 0.145 |
| 10% to 20% | 0.075 |
| 20% to 30% | 0.025 |
| 30% to 40% | 0.020 |
| 40% to 50% | 0.015 |
| Greater than 50% | 0.005 |
| | 1.000 |

Based on this probability distribution, determine the following:

**A.** 1 percent yearly VAR.

**B.** 5 percent yearly VAR.

**10.** An analyst would like to know the VAR for a portfolio consisting of two asset classes: long-term government bonds issued in the United States and long-term government bonds issued in the United Kingdom. The expected monthly return on U.S. bonds is 0.85 percent, and the standard deviation is 3.20 percent. The expected monthly return on U.K. bonds, in U.S. dollars, is 0.95 percent, and the standard deviation is 5.26 percent. The correlation between the U.S. dollar returns of U.K. and U.S. bonds is 0.35. The portfolio market value is $100 million and is equally weighted between the two asset classes. Using the analytical or variance–covariance method, compute the following:

**A.** 5 percent monthly VAR.

**B.** 1 percent monthly VAR.

**C.** 5 percent weekly VAR.

**D.** 1 percent weekly VAR.

**11.** You invested $25,000 in the stock of Dell Computer Corporation in early 2011. You have compiled the monthly returns on Dell's stock during the period 2006–2010, as given below.

| 2006 | 2007 | 2008 | 2009 | 2010 |
|---|---|---|---|---|
| −0.0214 | −0.0347 | −0.1824 | −0.0723 | −0.1017 |
| −0.0106 | −0.0566 | −0.0070 | −0.1021 | 0.0264 |
| 0.0262 | 0.0158 | 0.0010 | 0.1114 | 0.1344 |
| −0.1196 | 0.0862 | −0.0648 | 0.2257 | 0.0786 |
| −0.0313 | 0.0675 | 0.2378 | −0.0043 | −0.1772 |
| −0.0362 | 0.0609 | −0.0512 | 0.1867 | −0.0953 |
| −0.1137 | −0.0203 | 0.1229 | −0.0255 | 0.0978 |
| 0.0401 | 0.0100 | −0.1156 | 0.1831 | −0.1110 |
| 0.0129 | −0.0230 | −0.2416 | −0.0360 | 0.1020 |
| 0.0652 | 0.1087 | −0.2597 | −0.0531 | 0.1099 |
| 0.1196 | −0.1980 | −0.0844 | −0.0228 | −0.0816 |
| −0.0789 | −0.0012 | −0.0833 | 0.0170 | 0.0250 |

Using the historical method, compute the following:

**A.** 5 percent monthly VAR.

**B.** 1 percent monthly VAR.

**12.** Consider a $10 million portfolio of stocks. You perform a Monte Carlo simulation to estimate the VAR for this portfolio. You choose to perform this simulation using a normal distribution of returns for the portfolio, with an expected annual return of 14.8 percent and a standard deviation of 20.5 percent. You generate 700 random outcomes of annual return for this portfolio, of which the worst 40 outcomes are given below.

| −0.400 | −0.320 | −0.295 | −0.247 |
|--------|--------|--------|--------|
| −0.398 | −0.316 | −0.282 | −0.233 |
| −0.397 | −0.314 | −0.277 | −0.229 |
| −0.390 | −0.310 | −0.273 | −0.226 |
| −0.355 | −0.303 | −0.273 | −0.223 |
| −0.350 | −0.301 | −0.261 | −0.222 |
| −0.347 | −0.301 | −0.259 | −0.218 |
| −0.344 | −0.300 | −0.253 | −0.216 |
| −0.343 | −0.298 | −0.251 | −0.215 |
| −0.333 | −0.296 | −0.248 | −0.211 |

Using the above information, compute the following:

A. 5 percent annual VAR.

B. 1 percent annual VAR.

13. A. A firm runs an investment portfolio consisting of stocks as well as options on stocks. Management would like to determine the VAR for this portfolio and is thinking about which technique to use. Discuss a problem with using the analytical or variance–covariance method for determining the VAR of this portfolio.

B. Describe a situation in which an organization might logically select each of the three VAR methodologies.

14. An organization's 5 percent daily VAR shows a number fairly consistently around €3 million. A backtest of the calculation reveals that, as expected under the calculation, daily portfolio losses in excess of €3 million tend to occur about once a month. When such losses do occur, however, they typically are more than double the VAR estimate. The portfolio contains a very large short options position.

A. Is the VAR calculation accurate?

B. How can the VAR figure best be interpreted?

C. What additional measures might the organization take to increase the accuracy of its overall exposure assessments?

15. Indicate which of the following statements about credit risk is (are) false, and explain why.

A. Because credit losses occur often, it is easy to assess the probability of a credit loss.

B. One element of credit risk is the possibility that the counterparty to a contract will default on an obligation to another (i.e., third) party.

C. Like the buyer of a European-style option, the buyer of an American-style option faces no current credit risk until the expiration of the option.

16. Ricardo Colón, an analyst in the investment management division of a financial services firm, is developing an earnings forecast for a local oil services company. The company's income is closely linked to the price of oil. Furthermore, the company derives the majority of its income from sales to the United States. The economy of the company's home country depends significantly on export oil sales to the United States. As a result, movements

in world oil prices in U.S. dollar terms and the U.S. dollar value of the home country's currency are strongly positively correlated. A decline in oil prices would reduce the company's sales in U.S. dollar terms, all else being equal. On the other hand, the appreciation of the home country's currency relative to the U.S. dollar would reduce the company's sales in terms of the home currency.

According to Colón's research, Raúl Rodriguez, the company's chief risk officer, has made the following statement:

"The company has rejected hedging the market risk of a decline in oil prices by selling oil futures and hedging the currency risk of a depreciation of the U.S. dollar relative to our home currency by buying home currency futures in U.S. markets. We have decided that a more effective risk management strategy for our company is to not hedge either market risk or currency risk."

    **A.** State whether the company's decision to not hedge market risk was correct. Justify your answer with one reason.

    **B.** State whether the company's decision to not hedge currency risk was correct. Justify your answer with one reason.

    **C.** Critique the risk management strategy adopted.

**17.** Tony Smith believes that the price of a particular underlying, currently selling at $96, will increase substantially in the next six months, so he purchases a European call option expiring in six months on this underlying. The call option has an exercise price of $101 and sells for $6.

    **A.** How much is the current credit risk, if any?

    **B.** How much is the current value of the potential credit risk, if any?

    **C.** Which party bears the credit risk(s), Tony Smith or the seller?

**18.** Following are four methods for calculating risk-adjusted performance: the Sharpe ratio, risk-adjusted return on capital (RAROC), return over maximum drawdown (RoMAD), and the Sortino ratio. Compare and contrast the measure of risk that each method uses.

## The following information relates to Questions 19–24

Monika Kreuzer chairs the risk management committee for DGI Investors, a European money management firm. The agenda for the 1 June committee meeting includes three issues concerning client portfolios:

**1.** Estimating a new value at risk (VAR) for the Stimson Industries portfolio.

**2.** Answering questions from Kalton Corporation managers.

**3.** Revising the VAR for Muth Company given new capital market expectations.

**1. VAR for Stimson Industries.** DGI currently provides a 5 percent yearly VAR on the equity portfolio that it manages for Stimson. The €50 million portfolio has an expected annual return of 9.6 percent and an annual standard deviation of 18.0 percent. With a standard normal distribution, 5 percent of the possible outcomes are 1.65 standard deviations or more below the mean. Using the analytical (variance–covariance) method for calculating VAR, DGI estimates the 5 percent yearly VAR to be €10.05 million. Assuming that monthly returns are independent, committee member Eric Stulz wants to estimate a 5 percent *monthly* VAR for Stimson's portfolio.

Stulz asks his fellow committee members for feedback on the following statements about VAR in a report he is preparing for Stimson Industries:

| Statement #1: | "Establishing a VAR involves several decisions, such as the probability and time period over which the VAR will be measured and the technique to be used." |
| Statement #2: | "A portfolio's VAR will be larger when it is measured at a 5 percent probability than when it is measured at a 1 percent probability." |
| Statement #3: | "A portfolio's VAR will be larger when it is measured over a month than when it is measured over a day." |

**2. Questions from Kalton Corporation Managers.** Kalton Corporation has two large derivatives positions with a London securities house. The first position is a long forward currency contract to buy pounds at €1.4500. The current exchange rate is €1.4000 per pound. The second position is a long put position on the DJ Euro STOXX Index with a strike price of 305.00. The current closing price of the index is 295.00. A Kalton manager has written, "I am concerned about the risks of these two large positions. Who is bearing the credit risks, Kalton Corporation or the counterparty (the London securities house)?" Kreuzer suggests that DGI reply: "Kalton Corporation is bearing the credit risk of the currency forward contract, but the London securities house is bearing the credit risk of the put option on the DJ Euro STOXX Index."

Because they believe that the credit risk in corporate bonds is going to decline, Kalton Corporation managers have decided to increase Kalton's credit risk exposure in corporate bonds. They have asked Kreuzer and the risk management committee to recommend derivatives positions to accomplish this change.

**3. Revising the VAR for Muth Company.** Kreuzer provides a variety of statistics to Muth, for whom DGI manages a portfolio composed of 50 percent in Asia-Pacific equities and 50 percent in European equities. One of the statistics that Kreuzer supplies Muth is a 5 percent monthly VAR estimate based on the analytical (variance–covariance) method. Kreuzer is concerned that changes in the market outlook will affect Muth's risk. DGI is updating its capital market expectations, which will include 1) an increase in the expected return on Asia-Pacific equities and 2) an increase in the correlation between Asia-Pacific equities and European equities. Kreuzer comments: "Considered independently, and assuming that other variables are held constant, each of these changes in capital market expectations will increase the monthly VAR estimate for the Muth portfolio."

Kreuzer also discusses the limitations and strengths of applying VAR to the Muth portfolio. She states that: "One of the advantages of VAR is that the VAR of individual positions can be simply aggregated to find the portfolio VAR." Kreuzer also describes how VAR can be supplemented with performance evaluation measures, such as the Sharpe ratio. She states: "The Sharpe ratio is widely used for calculating a risk-adjusted return, although it can be an inaccurate measure when applied to portfolios with significant options positions."

19. The monthly VAR that Stulz wants to estimate for the Stimson portfolio is *closest* to:

    A. €0.8 million.

    B. €2.9 million.

    C. €3.9 million.

20. Regarding the three statements in the report that Stulz is preparing for Stimson Industries, the statement that is *incorrect* is:

    A. Statement #1.

    B. Statement #2.

    C. Statement #3.

21. Regarding Kalton's two derivatives positions, is Kreuzer correct about which party is bearing the credit risk of the currency forward contract and the put option on the DJ Euro STOXX Index, respectively?

|  | Currency Forward Contract | Put Option on the DJ Euro STOXX Index |
|---|---|---|
| **A.** | No | No |
| **B.** | No | Yes |
| **C.** | Yes | Yes |

22. To make the desired change in Kalton's credit risk exposure in corporate bonds, Kreuzer could recommend that Kalton take a position as a:

   **A.** seller in a credit default swap.

   **B.** buyer in a credit default swap.

   **C.** buyer of a put option on a corporate bond.

23. Is Kreuzer correct in predicting the independent effects of the increase in the expected return and the increase in the correlation, respectively, on the calculated VAR of the Muth portfolio?

|  | Effect of Increase in the Expected Return | Effect of Increase in the Correlation |
|---|---|---|
| **A.** | No | No |
| **B.** | No | Yes |
| **C.** | Yes | No |

24. Are Kreuzer's statements about an advantage of VAR and about the Sharpe ratio, respectively, correct?

|  | Statement about an Advantage of VAR | Statement about the Sharpe Ratio |
|---|---|---|
| **A.** | No | No |
| **B.** | No | Yes |
| **C.** | Yes | Yes |

# SOLUTIONS FOR READING 34

1. Centralized risk control systems bring all risk management activities under the responsibility of a single risk control unit. Under decentralized systems, each business unit is responsible for its own risk control. The advantages of a centralized system are that it brings risk control closer to the key decision makers in the organization and enables the organization to better manage its risk budget by recognizing the diversification embedded across business units. The decentralized approach has the advantage of placing risk control in nearer proximity to the source of risk taking. However, it has the disadvantage of not accounting for portfolio effects across units.

2. The following risk exposures should be reported as part of an Enterprise Risk Management System for Ford Motor Company:

   ● *Market risks*

      ▪ Currency risk, because expenditures and receipts denominated in nondomestic currencies create exposure to changes in exchange rates.

      ▪ Interest rate risk, because the values of securities that Ford has invested in are subject to changes in interest rates. Also, Ford has borrowings and loans, which could be affected by interest rate changes.

      ▪ Commodity risk, because Ford has exposure in various commodities and finished products.

   ● *Credit risk*, because of financing provided to customers who have purchased Ford's vehicles on credit.

   ● *Liquidity risk*, because of the possibility that Ford's funding sources may be reduced or become unavailable and Ford may then have to sell its securities at a short notice with a significant concession in price.

   ● *Settlement risk*, because of Ford's investments in fixed-income instruments and derivative contracts, some of which effect settlement through the execution of bilateral agreements and involve the possibility of default by the counterparty.

   ● *Political risk*, because Ford has operations in several countries. This exposes it to political risk. For example, the adoption of a restrictive policy by a non-U.S. government regarding payment of dividends by a subsidiary in that country to the parent company could adversely affect Ford.

3. Two types of risk that were inadequately managed were model risk and operational risk. Systematic errors in a major input of the options pricing model, implied volatility, resulted in mispricing options and trading losses. Thus model risk was inadequately managed. Furthermore, the systems and procedures at NatWest failed to prevent or detect and bring to the attention of senior management the trading losses. Thus operational risk also was not well managed.

4. Trader 1's statement is incorrect. Buyers are concerned about the transaction costs of trades as much as sellers, so a security's liquidity is highly relevant to buyers. In certain cases, such as a short position in a stock with limited float, the liquidity risk for the purchase side of a trade can be considerable.

   Trader 2's statement is incorrect. Derivatives usually do not help in managing liquidity risk because the lack of liquidity in the spot market typically passes right through to the derivatives market.

   Trader 3's statement is correct. Businesses need to take risks in areas in which they have expertise and possibly a comparative advantage in order to earn profits. Risk management can entail taking risk as well as reducing risk.

5.  **A.**   Assuming that the desk pays its traders a percentage of the profits on their
        own trading books, the −€20 million loss generated by an individual trader
        implies that the rest of the desk made €30 million and that the bank will
        have to pay the other traders an incentive fee on this larger amount, even
        though it generated only €10 million in net revenues. By contrast, if every
        trader had made money and the revenues to the desk were €10 million,
        the incentive payouts to traders would have been much lower and the net
        profits to the bank much higher.

    **B.**   In the scenario described above, the trader in question appears to have
        increased his risk exposure at year-end. The asymmetric nature of the
        incentive fee arrangement may induce risk taking because it is a call option
        on a percentage of profits and the value of a call option increases in the
        volatility of the underlying. In this sense, the interests of the bank and the
        trader diverged to the detriment of the bank.

    **C.**   First and foremost, it is clear that senior management was out of touch with
        the risk dynamics of the desk because it should have known that the trader
        in question was over his limits at some points much earlier in the scenario.
        The fact that management discovered this violation only after the loss
        occurred reflects poor risk governance.

6.  *Strengths*: The sensitivity analysis reported by Ford is useful in highlighting the
    possible adverse effect of a 1 percent increase in interest rates on Ford Credit's
    net income. It also is based on an objective measure of interest rate risk,
    duration.

    *Weaknesses*: The sensitivity analysis reported in the table assumes that interest
    rate changes are instantaneous, small, parallel shifts in the yield curve. From a
    risk management perspective, one would have a special interest in the effects
    of larger interest rate changes, including major discontinuities in interest
    rates. The inclusion of value at risk would help fill this gap in the analysis.
    Furthermore, changes in the yield curve other than parallel shifts should
    be examined, such as nonparallel shifts (twists) in the yield curve. The text
    mentions the recommendation of the Derivatives Policy Group to examine both
    parallel shifts and twists of the yield curve.

7.  **A.**   There is a 1 percent chance that the portfolio will lose at least £4.25 million
        in any given week.

    **B.**   There is a 99 percent chance that the portfolio will lose no more than £4.25
        million in one week.

8.  Statement A, which is the definition of VAR, is clearly correct. Statement B
    is also correct, because it lists the important decisions involved in measuring
    VAR. Statement D is correct: The longer the time period, the larger the possible
    losses. Statement C, however, is incorrect. The VAR number would be larger for
    a 1 percent probability than for a 5 percent probability. Accordingly, the correct
    answer is C.

9.  **A.**   The probability is 0.005 that the portfolio will lose at least 50 percent in a
        year. The probability is 0.005 that the portfolio will lose between 40 percent
        and 50 percent in a year. Cumulating these two probabilities implies that the
        probability is 0.01 that the portfolio will lose at least 40 percent in a year. So,
        the 1 percent yearly VAR is 40 percent of the market value of $10 million,
        which is $4 million.

    **B.**   The probability is 0.005 that the portfolio will lose at least 50 percent in
        a year, 0.005 that it will lose between 40 and 50 percent, 0.010 that it will
        lose between 30 and 40 percent, 0.015 that it will lose between 20 and 30
        percent, and 0.015 that it will lose between 10 and 20 percent. Cumulating

these probabilities indicates that the probability is 0.05 that the portfolio will lose at least 10 percent in a year. So, the 5 percent yearly VAR is 10 percent of the market value of $10 million, which is $1 million.

10. First, we must calculate the monthly portfolio expected return and standard deviation. Using "1" to indicate the U.S. government bonds and "2" to indicate the U.K. government bonds, we have

$$\mu_p = w_1\mu_1 + w_2\mu_2 = 0.50(0.0085) + 0.50(0.0095) = 0.0090$$
$$\sigma_p^2 = w_1^2\sigma_1^2 + w_2^2\sigma_2^2 + 2w_1w_2\sigma_1\sigma_2\rho$$
$$= (0.50)^2(0.0320)^2 + (0.50)^2(0.0526)^2$$
$$+ 2(0.50)(0.50)(0.0320)(0.0526)(0.35)$$
$$= 0.001242$$
$$\sigma_p = \sqrt{0.001242} = 0.0352$$

A. For a 5 percent monthly VAR, we have $\mu_p - 1.65\sigma_p = 0.0090 - 1.65(0.0352) = -0.0491$. Then the VAR would be $100,000,000(0.0491) = $4.91 million.

B. For a 1 percent monthly VAR, we have $\mu_p - 2.33\sigma_p = 0.0090 - 2.33(0.0352) = -0.0730$. Then the VAR would be $100,000,000(0.0730) = $7.30 million.

C. There are 12 months or 52 weeks in a year. So, to convert the monthly return of 0.0090 to weekly return, we first multiply the monthly return by 12 to convert it to an annual return, and then we divide the annual return by 52 to convert it to a weekly return. So, the expected weekly return is 0.0090(12/52) = 0.0021. Similarly, we adjust the standard deviation to $0.0352\left(\sqrt{12}/\sqrt{52}\right) = 0.01691$. The 5 percent weekly VAR would then be $\mu_p - 1.65\sigma_p = 0.0021 - 1.65(0.01691) = -0.0258$. Then the VAR in dollars would be $100,000,000(0.0258) = $2.58 million.

D. The 1 percent weekly VAR would be $\mu_p - 2.33\sigma_p = 0.0021 - 2.33(0.01691) = -0.0373$. Then the VAR would be $100,000,000(0.0373) = $3.73 million.

11. A. For the five-year period, there are 60 monthly returns. Of the 60 returns, the 5 percent worst are the 3 worst returns. Therefore, based on the historical method, the 5 percent VAR would be the third worst return. From the returns given, the third worst return is −0.1980. So, the VAR in dollars is 0.1980($25,000) = $4,950.

B. Of the 60 returns, the 1 percent worst are the 0.6 worst returns. Therefore, we would use the single worst return. From the returns given, the worst return is −0.2597. So, the VAR in dollars is 0.2597($25,000) = $6,492.50.

12. A. Of the 700 outcomes, the worst 5 percent are the 35 worst returns. Therefore, the 5 percent VAR would be the 35th worst return. From the data given, the 35th worst return is −0.223. So, the 5 percent annual VAR in dollars is 0.223($10,000,000) = $2,230,000.

B. Of the 700 outcomes, the worst 1 percent are the 7 worst returns. Therefore, the 1 percent VAR would be the seventh worst return. From the data given, the seventh worst return is −0.347. So, the 1 percent annual VAR in dollars is 0.347($10,000,000) = $3,470,000.

13. A. The analytical or variance–covariance method begins with the assumption that portfolio returns are normally distributed. A normal distribution has an unlimited upside and an unlimited downside. The assumption of a normal distribution is inappropriate when the portfolio contains options because the return distributions of options are far from normal. Call options have unlimited upside potential, as in a normal distribution, but the downside

return is truncated at a loss of 100 percent. Similarly, put options have a limited upside and a large but limited downside. Likewise, covered calls and protective puts have limits in one direction or the other. Therefore, for the portfolio that has options, the assumption of a normal distribution to estimate VAR has a number of problems. In addition, it is very difficult to calculate a covariance between either two options or an option and a security with more linear characteristics—among other reasons because options have different dynamics at different points in their life cycle.

**B.** Portfolios with simple, linear characteristics, particularly those with a limited budget for computing resources and analytical personnel, might select the variance/covariance method. For more complex portfolios containing options and time-sensitive bonds, the historical method might be more appropriate. The Monte Carlo simulation method typically would not be a wise choice unless it were managed by an organization with a portfolio of complex derivatives that is willing to make and sustain a considerable investment in technology and human capital.

**14. A.** The observed outcomes are consistent with the VAR calculation's prediction on the frequency of losses exceeding the VAR. Therefore, the VAR calculation is accurate.

**B.** The VAR results indicate that under "normal" market conditions that would characterize 19 out of 20 days, the portfolio ought to lose less than €3 million. It provides no other information beyond this.

**C.** The portfolio certainly lends itself to scenario analysis. In this particular case, given the substantial short options position, it might be instructive to create a customized scenario under which the portfolio was analyzed in the wake of a large increase in option-implied volatility.

**15.** The fact that credit losses occur infrequently makes Statement A incorrect. Unlike a European-style option, which cannot be exercised prior to expiration and thus has no current credit risk, an American-style option does have the potential for current credit risk. Therefore, Statement C is incorrect. Statement B, however, is correct.

**16. A.** The decision not to hedge this risk was correct. Suppose the company had hedged this risk. If the price of oil were to increase, the favorable effect of the increase on income would be offset by the loss on the oil futures, but the home currency should appreciate against the U.S. dollar, leaving the company worse off. If the price of oil were to decrease, the unfavorable effect on income would be offset by the futures position and the home currency should depreciate, leaving the company better off. In short, the company would remain exposed to exchange rate risk associated with oil price movements.

**B.** The decision not to hedge this risk was correct. The company should remain exposed to market risk associated with exchange rate movements (i.e., currency risk). Hedging would remove currency risk but leave the company with market risk associated with oil price movements. If the home currency declined, the price of oil would likely decline because it is positively correlated with the U.S. dollar value of the home currency. That would be a negative for income. On the other hand, appreciation of the home currency is likely to be accompanied by an oil price increase, which would be positive for income.

**C.** The risk management strategy adopted is logical because it exploits a natural hedge. A decline in the price of oil (a negative) is likely to be accompanied by a depreciation of the home currency relative to the U.S.

dollar (a positive), and an increase in the price of oil (a positive) is likely to be accompanied by appreciation of the home currency (a negative). Hedging both currency and market risk would be an alternative risk management strategy to consider, but in comparison to the strategy adopted, it would incur transaction costs.

17. **A.** Because the option is a European-style option, it cannot be exercised prior to expiration. Therefore, there is no current credit risk.

   **B.** The current value of the potential credit risk is the current market value of the option, which is $6. Of course, at expiration, the option is likely to be worth a different amount and could even expire out of the money.

   **C.** Options have unilateral credit risk. The risk is borne by the buyer of the option, Tony Smith, because he will look to the seller for the payoff at expiration if the option expires in the money.

18. The Sharpe ratio uses standard deviation of portfolio return as the measure of risk. Standard deviation is a measure of total risk. RAROC uses capital at risk (defined in various ways) as the measure of risk. RoMAD uses maximum drawdown as a risk measure. Maximum drawdown is the difference between a portfolio's maximum point of return and the lowest point of return over a given time interval. The Sortino ratio measures risk using downside deviation, which computes volatility using only rate of return data points below a minimum acceptable return. In contrast to the Sharpe ratio, its focus is on downside risk.

19. C is correct. The monthly return is 9.6%/12 = 0.8%.

   The monthly standard deviation is $18.0\%/\sqrt{12} = 5.196\%$.

   The percent VAR is 0.8% − 1.65 (5.196%) = −7.7734%.

   The dollar VAR is 7.7734% (€50 million) = €3.8867 million, or €3.9 million.

20. B is correct. Stolz' Statement #2 is the only incorrect statement. The VAR will be larger for a 1 percent probability than for a 5 percent probability. A 1 percent probability is equivalent to a 99 percent confidence level. This requires movement 2.33 standard deviations in the direction of lower returns.

21. A is correct. Kreuzer is wrong on both. For the currency forward contract, the London securities house is bearing credit risk because the London house is the party that would be owed (or paid) at current prices. For option contracts, including puts, the option buyer is the only party with credit risk. So Kalton Corporation is bearing credit risk on its long put position.

22. A is correct. In a credit default swap, the protection seller would make payments to the protection buyer in the event of a specified credit event. Thus, the protection seller is assuming credit risk. The other positions would not give a desired increase in credit risk exposure in corporate bonds.

23. B is correct. Kreuzer's statement is incorrect with respect to the increase in expected return but correct with respect to the increased correlation. A 5% VAR would be equal to the expected monthly portfolio return minus 1.65 × (monthly portfolio standard deviation), or −VAR = $\mu_p$ − 1.65$\sigma_p$. The increase in expected return would result in a lower calculated VAR (smaller losses). An increase in the correlation would increase the portfolio standard deviation, which would result in a higher calculated VAR (larger losses).

24. B is correct. Kreuzer's statement about an advantage of VAR is wrong because the VAR for individual positions does not generally aggregate in a simple way into portfolio VAR. The correlation of the individual positions has to be taken into account. Kreuzer's statement about the Sharpe ratio is correct.

# Currency Risk Management

*by Bruno Solnik and Dennis McLeavey, CFA*

## LEARNING OUTCOMES

| Mastery | The candidate should be able to: |
|---|---|
| ☐ | **a** explain and demonstrate the use of foreign exchange futures to hedge the currency exposure associated with the principal value of a foreign investment; |
| ☐ | **b** justify the use of a minimum-variance hedge when local currency returns and exchange rate movements are correlated and interpret the components of the minimum-variance hedge ratio in terms of translation risk and economic risk; |
| ☐ | **c** evaluate the effect of basis risk on the quality of a currency hedge; |
| ☐ | **d** discuss the choice of contract maturity in constructing a currency hedge, including the advantages and disadvantages of different maturities; |
| ☐ | **e** explain the issues that arise when hedging multiple currencies; |
| ☐ | **f** discuss the use of options rather than futures/forwards to manage currency risk; |
| ☐ | **g** evaluate the effectiveness of a standard dynamic delta hedge strategy when hedging a foreign currency position; |
| ☐ | **h** discuss and justify methods for managing currency exposure, including the indirect currency hedge created when futures or options are used as a substitute for the underlying investment; |
| ☐ | **i** discuss the major types of currency management strategies specified in investment policy statements. |

The traditional international investment strategy is first to decide on an international asset allocation. An allocation breaks down a portfolio by both asset class (short-term deposit, bond, equity, sectors) and country or currency of investment (U.S. dollar, British pound, euro). The resulting allocation can be used to form a matrix of currencies and asset classes. Ten percent of a typical portfolio's value may be allocated to Japanese stocks, five percent to international bonds, and so forth. Specific bonds and stocks are selected using the various techniques discussed in previous readings. Once a portfolio is structured, it must be managed according to changes in expectations and risks.

Derivative instruments, such as options and futures, are used domestically to hedge risks. They protect a manager from being forced to arbitrage or liquidate a large part of her portfolio. For example, interest rate futures or options may be used to hedge a long-term bond portfolio if fears about a rise in interest rates suddenly materialize. The use of financial futures and options in controlling portfolio risk is described in textbooks that deal with domestic investment. The most important area of risk management in international investment is currency risk. This reading is therefore devoted to currency risk management. Most portfolio managers are often confronted with practical problems such as these:

- Currency risks can strongly affect the performance of an international portfolio. What proportion of the currency exposure should be hedged?

- A U.S. investor is bullish about her portfolio of Australian stocks but is concerned that the Australian dollar may drop sharply in the wake of local elections. On the other hand, the Australian dollar may appreciate strongly as a result of these elections.

- A Japanese investor holds British gilts. He expects the long-term U.K. interest rate to drop, which in turn would cause a depreciation of the pound that will offset the capital gain on the bond in pound terms.

This reading is intended to assist the reader in better handling situations of this kind. The first three sections of this reading deal with techniques of currency management using currency futures or forward contracts, currency options, and other methods. The last section deals with currency management in a portfolio context. We review strategic currency management, namely, the "neutral" or "long-term" policy for currency hedging. We also review tactical currency management, often referred to as *currency overlay*. In this final section, we discuss currencies as a separate asset class.

## 1  HEDGING WITH FUTURES OR FORWARD CURRENCY CONTRACTS

Either futures or forward currency contracts may be used to hedge a portfolio. They differ in several ways. Futures are exchange traded contracts while forwards are over-the-counter (OTC) contracts. Currency forwards are sometimes referred to as *currency swaps*. Portfolio managers tend to primarily use forward contracts in currency hedging. But forward and futures contracts allow a manager to take the same economic position. Therefore, in this reading, the generic term *futures* will denote both futures and forward (or swap) contracts.

### The Basic Approach: Hedging the Principal

Hedging with futures is very simple. An investor takes a position with a foreign exchange contract that offsets the currency exposure associated with the principal being hedged. In other words, a citizen of Country A who wants to hedge a portfolio of assets denominated in currency B would sell a futures contract to exchange currency B for currency A. The size of the contract would equal the market value ("principal") of the assets to be hedged. For example, a U.S. investor with £1 million invested in British gilts (treasury bonds) would sell futures for £1 million worth of dollars. The direction of a foreign exchange rate contract is often confusing because it involves the exchange rates of two currencies.

On the Chicago Mercantile Exchange (CME), investors can buy and sell contracts of £62,500 wherein the futures price is expressed in dollars per pound. The same size contract is also found on the London International Financial Futures Exchange (LIFFE). Let us assume that on September 12, a U.S. investor can buy or sell futures with delivery in December for 1.95 dollars per pound; the spot exchange rate is 2.00

dollars per pound. Throughout this chapter, we will use the shortcut notation "/" to mean "per"; hence, $2.00/£ means 2.00 dollars per pound. In order to hedge her £1 million principal, the investor must sell a total of 16 contracts. Now let us assume that a few weeks later, the futures and spot exchange rates drop to $1.85 and $1.90, respectively, whereas the pound value of the British assets rises to 1,010,000. The hedge is undertaken at time 0, and we study the rate of return on the portfolio from time 0 to a future time $t$. We introduce the following notation:

$V_t$ — is the value of the portfolio of foreign assets to hedge, measured in foreign currency at time $t$ (e.g., £1 million)

$V_t^*$ — is the value of the portfolio of foreign assets measured in domestic currency (e.g., $2 million)

$S_t$ — is the spot exchange rate: domestic currency value of one unit of foreign currency quoted at time $t$ (e.g., $2.00/£)

$F_t$ — is the futures exchange rate: domestic currency value of one unit of foreign currency quoted at time $t$ (e.g., $1.95/£)

$R$ — is the rate of return of the portfolio measured in foreign currency terms, $(V_t - V_0)/V_0$

$R^*$ — is the rate of return of the portfolio measured in domestic currency terms, $\left(V_t^* - V_0^*\right)/V_0^*$

$s$ — is the percentage movement in the exchange, $(S_t - S_0)/S_0$

In this example, the pound value of the British assets appreciates by 1 percent and the pound exchange rate drops by 5 percent, causing a loss in the dollar value on the portfolio of 4.05 percent (see Exhibit 1). In absolute dollar terms, this loss in portfolio value is $81,000:

$$V_t^* - V_0^* = V_t S_t - V_0 S_0 \tag{1}$$

Hence, $1,919,000 − $2,000,000 = (£1,010,000 × $1.90/£) − (£1,000,000 × $2.00/£) = −$81,000. On the other hand, the realized gain on the futures contract sale is $100,000, as follows:

$$\text{Realized gain} = V_0\left(- F_t + F_0\right) \tag{2}$$

---

**Exhibit 1**     **Relationships between Portfolio Value and Rate of Return**

|  | Period 0 | Period t | Rate of Return (%) |
|---|---|---|---|
| Portfolio value (in pounds) $V$ | 1,000,000 | 1,010,000 | 1.00 |
| Portfolio value (in dollars) $V^*$ | 2,000,000 | 1,919,000 | −4.05 |
| Exchange rate ($/pound) $S$ | 2.00 | 1.90 | −5.00 |
| Futures rate ($/pound) $F$ | 1.95 | 1.85 | −5.00 |

---

Hence, £1,000,000 × ($1.95/£ − $1.85/£) = $100,000. Therefore, the net profit on the hedged position is $19,000:

$$\text{Profit} = V_t S_t - V_0 S_0 - V_0\left(F_t - F_0\right) \tag{3}$$

Hence, Profit = −$81,000 + $100,000 = $19,000. The rate of return in dollars on the hedged position, $R_H$, can be found by dividing the profit in Equation 3 by the original portfolio value $V_0 S_0$. We find

$$R_H = \frac{V_t S_t - V_0 S_0}{V_0 S_0} - \frac{F_t - F_0}{S_0} = R^* - R_F \qquad (4)$$

where $R_F$ is the futures price movement as a percentage of the spot rate $(F_t - F_0)/S_0$.
In the example, we find

$$\text{Hedged return} = R_H = \frac{19{,}000}{2{,}000{,}000} = 0.95\%$$

This position is almost perfectly hedged, because the 1 percent return on the British asset is transformed into a 0.95 percent return in U.S. dollars, despite the drop in value of the British pound. The slight difference between the two numbers is explained by the fact that the investor hedged only the principal (£1 million), not the unexpected return on the British investment (equal here to 1 percent). The 5 percent drop in sterling value applied to this 1 percent return exactly equals 1% × 5% = 0.05 percent.

The exact relationship between dollar and pound returns on the foreign portfolio is as follows:

$$R^* = R + s(1 + R) \qquad (5)$$

Hence, $R^*$ = 1% − 5(1.01)% = −4.05 percent.

The currency contribution $R^* - R$ is equal to exchange rate variation plus the cross-product $sR$ (equal here to 0.05%). When the value of the portfolio in foreign currency fluctuates widely, the difference can become significant over long periods. This implies that the amount of currency hedging should be adjusted periodically to reflect movements in the value of the position to be hedged. A portfolio manager could decide to hedge the expected future value of the portfolio rather than its current (principal) value. This practice could be risky if expectations do not materialize, and therefore this approach is applied only for fixed-income securities to hedge both the principal value and the yield to be accrued. Still, periodic adjustment of the currency hedge would be required to cover unexpected capital gains or losses on the price of the fixed-income securities.

The hedge result could also be affected by the basis, that is, the difference between the futures and the spot prices. Basis risk is discussed later in this reading.

Another illustration of a hedged portfolio is provided in Example 1.

## Example 1

### Hedged Portfolio

You are French and own a portfolio of U.S. stocks worth $1 million. The current spot and one-month forward exchange rates are €1 per $. Interest rates are equal in both countries. You are worried that the results of U.S. elections could lead to a strong depreciation of the dollar and you decide to sell forward $1 million to hedge currency risk. A week later, your U.S. stock portfolio has gone up to $1.02 million, and the spot and forward exchange rates are now €0.95 per $. Analyze the return on your hedged portfolio.

### Solution:

The U.S. stock portfolio went up by 2 percent, but the dollar lost 5 percent relative to the euro. If the portfolio had not been hedged, its return in euros would have been

$$\frac{1{,}020{,}000 \times 0.95 - 1{,}000{,}000 \times 1}{1{,}000{,}000 \times 1} = -3.1\%$$

As per Equation 3, your profit on the hedge portfolio in euros is

$$\text{Profit} = 1,020,000 \times 0.95 - 1,000,000 \times 1 - 1,000,000$$
$$\times (0.95 - 1) = 19,000$$

The rate of return on the hedged portfolio in euros is equal to 19,000 per 1,000,000 = 1.9 percent, which is very close to the 2 percent portfolio rate of return in dollars. The difference comes from the fact that the dollar capital gain on the U.S. portfolio (2%) was not hedged and suffered the 5 percent currency loss.

We could also directly apply Equation 4:

$$R^* - R_F = -3.1\% + 5\% = 1.9\%$$

## Minimum-Variance Hedge Ratio

The objective of a currency hedge is to minimize the exposure to exchange rate movement. If the foreign investment were simply a foreign currency deposit—a fixed amount of local currency—it would be sufficient to sell forward an equivalent amount of foreign currency to eliminate currency risk. However, a problem appears when the foreign currency value of a foreign investment reacts *systematically* to an exchange rate movement. For example, a drop in the value of the British pound could lead to an increase in the value of a British company (measured in pounds). This is because this pound depreciation will increase the pound value of cash flows received from abroad, as well as make the company's products more attractive abroad. Another example is provided by bonds issued in a country that has an exchange rate target. A depreciation in its domestic currency will lead the country to raise its interest rates, pushing local bond prices down. In both cases, there is a covariance[1] between the asset return measured in local currency and the exchange rate movements. The covariance between asset returns and movements in the local currency value is negative in the first case and positive in the second case.

One objective is to search for minimum variability in the value of the hedged portfolio. Investors usually care about the rate of return on their investment and the variance thereof. So, if they decide to hedge, investors would like to set the hedge ratio $h$ to minimize the variance of the return on the hedged portfolio. Recall that the hedge ratio is the ratio of the size of the short futures position in foreign currency to the size of the currency exposure (value of the portfolio in foreign currency). For example, the hedge ratio is 1 if an investor has a portfolio of British gilts worth 1 million pounds and decides to sell forward 1 million pounds in futures currency contracts. It is easy to show that the rate of return on a hedged portfolio, $R_H$, is equal to the rate of return on the original portfolio (unhedged), $R^*$, minus $h$ times the percentage change on the futures price $R_F$:

$$R_H = R^* - h \times R_F \tag{6}$$

The return on a hedged portfolio with a 50 percent hedge ratio is illustrated in Example 2.

---

[1] Remember that the covariance between two variables is equal to the correlation times the product of the standard deviations of the two variables.

**Example 2**

## Portfolio with a 50 Percent Hedge Ratio

You are French and own a portfolio of U.S. stocks worth $1 million. The current spot and one-month forward exchange rates are €1 per $. Interest rates are equal in both countries. You are worried that the results of U.S. elections could lead to a strong depreciation of the dollar and decide to hedge 50 percent of the portfolio value against currency risk ($h = 0.5$). A week later, your U.S. stock portfolio has gone up to $1.01 million, and the spot and forward exchange rates are now €0.95 per $. Analyze the return on your hedged portfolio.

**Solution:**

The U.S. stock portfolio went up by 1 percent, but the dollar lost 5 percent relative to the euro. If the portfolio had not been hedged, its return in euros would have been

$$R^* = \frac{1,010,000 \times 0.95 - 1,000,000 \times 1}{1,000,000 \times 1} = -4.05\%$$

According to Equation 6, the return on your 50 percent–hedged portfolio is

$$R_H = R^* - h \times R_F = -4.05\% - 0.5 \times (-5\%) = -1.55\%$$

The optimal hedge ratio $h^*$, which minimizes the variance of $R_H$, is equal to the covariance of the portfolio return[2] to be hedged with the return on the futures, divided by the variance of the return on the futures:

$$h^* = \frac{\mathrm{cov}\left(R^*, R_F\right)}{\sigma_F^2} \qquad\qquad (7)$$

This optimal hedge ratio is sometimes called the *regression hedge ratio* because it can be estimated as the slope coefficient of the regression of the asset, or portfolio, return on the futures return:

$$R^* = a + h^* R_F + \text{Error term} \qquad\qquad (8)$$

where $R^*$ is the return on the asset or portfolio measured in the investor's domestic currency, $R_F$ is the return on the futures, and $a$ is a constant term.

To get a better understanding of this minimum-variance hedge ratio, it is useful to substitute the value of $R^*$ given in Equation 5 into Equation 6. From now on, we will further assume that the cross-product term of Equation 5 is small and will drop it.[3] We find

$$R_H = R + s - h R_F \qquad\qquad (9)$$

The futures exchange rate differs from the spot exchange rate by a "basis" equal to the interest rate differential. Let's first assume that the basis is zero (interest rates equal in the two currencies) and remains so over time. Hence, the futures exchange rate is

---

2 Previously, we used $R$ as the generic notation for any asset return. In this reading, we introduce the notations $h^*$ to denote the optimal hedge ratio and $R^*$ and $R$ to differentiate between returns measured in the investor's domestic currency ($R^*$) and in the foreign currency ($R$). Equation 8 should be applied to $R^*$, the asset return in domestic currency, which is the currency relevant to the domestic investor.

3 This assumes very frequent adjustment of the currency hedge to follow movements in the value of the portfolio.

equal to the spot exchange rate. Then the rate of return on a futures contract, $R_F = (F_t - F_0)/S_0$, is equal to the spot exchange rate movement, $s = (S_t - S_0)/S_0$. Equation 9 can now be written as follows:

$$R_H = R + s(1-h) \tag{10}$$

and the minimum-variance hedge ratio is equal to

$$h^* = \frac{\text{cov}(R^*, R_F)}{\sigma_F^2} = \frac{\text{cov}(R+s, s)}{\sigma_s^2} = 1 + \frac{\text{cov}(R, s)}{\sigma_s^2} \tag{11}$$

where $\sigma_s^2$ is the variance of the exchange rate movement. Equation 11 shows the minimum-variance hedge ratio as the sum of two components, $h_1$ and $h_2$, linked to different aspects of currency risk:

- Translation risk ($h_1 = 1$)

- Economic risk ($h_2 = \frac{\text{cov}(R, s)}{\sigma_s^2}$)

### Translation Risk

*Translation risk* comes from the translation of the value of the asset from the foreign currency to the domestic currency. It would be present even if the foreign currency value of the asset were constant (e.g., a deposit in foreign currency). The hedge ratio of translation risk is 1.

This is usually taken to mean that a currency hedge should achieve on a foreign asset the same rate of return in domestic currency as can be achieved on the foreign market in foreign currency terms. For example, a U.S. investor would try to achieve a dollar rate of return on a British gilts portfolio equal to what he could have achieved in terms of pounds. Creating a perfect currency hedge is equivalent to nullifying a currency movement and translating a foreign rate of return directly into a similar domestic rate of return. Considering only translation risk, the optimal amount to hedge is determined by finding the value of $h$ such that the hedged return in domestic currency terms $R_H$ closely tracks the return in foreign currency terms $R$.

Equation 10 can be written as

$$R_H - R = s(1-h) \tag{12}$$

To minimize the variance of $R_H - R$, we must obviously set a hedge ratio of 1. This is basically the strategy of "hedging the principal" outlined previously.

### Economic Risk

*Economic risk* comes when the foreign currency value of a foreign investment reacts systematically to an exchange rate movement. This is in addition to translation risk. Let's take again the example of a country that has an exchange rate target. A depreciation in its local currency will lead the country to raise its interest rates, pushing local bond prices down. So, there is a positive covariance between bond returns, measured in local currency, and the exchange rate movement. An investor from abroad will lose twice from the foreign currency depreciation. First, the percentage translation loss will be equal to the percentage depreciation of the foreign currency. Second, the value of the investment measured in foreign currency itself will drop.

The hedge ratio required to minimize this economic risk can be estimated by $\text{cov}(R, s)/\sigma_s^2$. This is the slope that we would get on a regression of the foreign currency return of the asset on the exchange rate movement.

### Hedging Total Currency Risk

If an investor worries about the total influence of a foreign exchange rate depreciation on her portfolio value, measured in domestic currency, she should hedge both translation and economic currency risk. In this approach, the objective is to minimize the overall influence of an exchange rate movement, whether direct or indirect, on the asset return in domestic currency. The objective is not to try to minimize the tracking error between $R_H$ and $R$ (translation risk).

Most portfolio managers care only about translation risk, so they adopt a unitary hedge ratio if they try to minimize the impact of currency risk. From a portfolio accounting standpoint, currency loss is simply stated as the difference in return when measured in domestic and foreign currencies, $R^* - R$. So, minimizing accounting currency losses is an objective choice. Also, the sensitivity of an asset value to an exchange rate movement has to be estimated from some economic model and/or from historical data. Even though estimates might be imprecise and unstable, hedging only translation risk might not be optimal from an economic viewpoint.

In practice, stock returns and currency movements are quite independent. If a foreign asset's returns are uncorrelated with short-term currency movements, a hedge ratio of unity is a reasonable strategy. Bonds returns and currency movements tend to exhibit a more significant correlation because currencies react to interest rate movements and vice versa. But the short-term correlation between bond returns and currency movements is still low.

### Implementation

As mentioned above, a regression between asset returns and currency returns is the simplest way to estimate the minimum-variance hedge ratio (Equations 8 and 11). This can be performed using time series such as 100 data points for past weekly returns. Taking the example of a U.S. investor calculating the optimal hedge ratio for his diversified British equity portfolio, the procedure would be as follows:

- Collect a weekly time series of the dollar price of the British pound (£:$).
- Calculate the weekly percentage price movement (rate of return) for this exchange rate.
- Collect a weekly time series of dollar returns on the British equity portfolio. As this is a diversified British equity portfolio, an easy alternative is to collect returns on a British stock index calculated in dollar terms (the investor's domestic currency).
- Run a simple regression (ordinary least square) between the equity return and the currency return. This can be done on a spreadsheet.
- The slope of this regression is the optimal hedge ratio $h^*$, as used in Example 3.

---

**Example 3**

## Portfolio with Minimum-Variance Hedge Ratio

You are French and own a portfolio of U.S. stocks worth $1 million. The current spot and one-month forward exchange rates are €1 per $. Interest rates are equal in both countries. You are worried that the results of U.S. elections could lead to a strong depreciation of the dollar. You have observed that U.S. stocks tend to react favorably to a depreciation of the dollar. A broker tells you that a regression of U.S. stock returns on the euro per dollar ($:€) percentage exchange rate movements has a slope of −0.20. In other words, U.S. stocks tend to go up by 1 percent when the dollar depreciates by 5 percent.

1. Discuss what your currency hedge ratio should be.
2. A week later, your U.S. stock portfolio has gone up to $1.01 million and the spot and forward exchange rates are now €0.95 per $. Analyze the return on your hedged portfolio.

**Solution to 1:**

These are the factors to consider:

■ To hedge only translation risk would require a hedge ratio of 1 (100%).

■ To hedge economic risk would require an additional hedge ratio of –20%.

The minimum-variance hedge ratio reflecting both translation and economic risk should therefore be 80 percent.

**Solution to 2:**

Let's now study the return on the optimally hedged portfolio under the proposed scenario. Using Equation 10, we find that the return on the hedged portfolio is equal to 0 percent (remember that we neglected the cross-product term). So, we have removed the overall impact of the currency movement. But we do not track the rate of return in foreign currency.

Alternatively, one could get a direct estimate of the economic risk by running a regression between the pound return on the British equity index, namely, the British equity return measured in local currency (the British pound) and the exchange rate movement. The slope of that regression added to 100 percent would also yield the optimal hedge ratio $h^*$.

One should be aware that this is only a statistical estimate based on past data. Qualitative considerations based on an economic assessment of future relationships between asset values and currencies could help refine this estimate.

## The Influence of the Basis

Note that the minimum-variance hedge, as described, is not necessarily optimal in a risk–return framework:

■ Futures and spot exchange rates differ by a basis. Changes in the basis can affect hedging strategies, creating *basis risk*.

■ Futures and spot exchange rates differ by a basis. Over time, the percentage movement in the futures and in the spot exchange rate will differ by this basis. In the long run, the return on the hedged portfolio will differ from the portfolio return achieved in foreign currency by the basis, even with a hedge ratio of 1.

These two aspects are now addressed.

### Basis Risk

Forward (or swap) and futures exchange rates are directly determined by two factors: the spot exchange rate and the interest rate differential between two currencies. The forward discount, or the premium—which is the percentage difference between the forward and the spot exchange rates—equals the interest rate differential for the same maturity as the forward contract. In futures jargon, we say that the basis equals the interest rate differential. If we express the exchange rate as the dollar value of one pound (e.g., $/£ = 2.00) and call $r_{\$}$ and $r_{£}$ the interest rates in dollars and pounds, respectively, with the same maturity as the futures contract, the relation known as interest rate parity is

$$\frac{F}{S} = \frac{1+r_{\$}}{1+r_{£}} \quad \text{and} \quad \frac{F-S}{S} = \frac{r_{\$} - r_{£}}{1+r_{£}} \tag{13}$$

Note that the interest rates in Equation 13 are period rates, not annualized. They equal the annualized rates multiplied by the number of days until maturity and divided by 360 days. Because interest rate parity is the result of arbitrage on very liquid markets, it technically holds at every instant. Changes in the basis have an impact on the quality of the currency hedge. Although currency risk is removed by hedging, some additional risk is taken in the form of *basis risk*. But this basis risk is quite small.

The correlation between futures and spot exchange rates is a function of the futures contract term. Futures prices for contracts near maturity closely follow spot exchange rates because at that point the interest rate differential is a small component of the futures price. To illustrate, consider the futures price of British pound contracts with 1, 3, and 12 months left until delivery. The spot exchange rate is currently $2.00 per pound, and the interest rates and the calculated values for the futures are as given in Exhibit 2. The 1-month futures price should equal $2.00 plus the 1-month interest rate differential applied to the spot rate. The interest rate differential for 1 month equals the annualized rate differential of −4 percent multiplied by 30 days and divided by 360 days, or divided by 12:

$$F = S + S\frac{r_{\$} - r_{£}}{1+r_{£}} = 2.00 - 2.00\frac{\dfrac{4}{12}\%}{1+\dfrac{14}{12}\%}$$

Hence, F = 1.993.

| Exhibit 2 | Importance of Interest Rate Differentials to Futures Prices | | |
|---|---|---|---|
| | **Maturity** | | |
| | **One Month** | **Three Months** | **Twelve Months** |
| Pound interest rate (%) | 14 | 13.5 | 13 |
| Dollar interest rate (%) | 10 | 10 | 10 |
| Futures price (dollars per pound) | 1.993 | 1.983 | 1.947 |
| Interest rate component (dollars) | −0.007 | −0.017 | −0.053 |
| Spot rate: £1 = $2.00. | | | |

We see, then, that even though the interest rate differential is very large, its effect on the one-month futures price is minimal, because the spot exchange rate is the driving force behind short-term forward exchange rate movements. This is less true for long-term contracts. More specifically, a reduction of 1 percentage point (100 basis points) in the interest rate differential causes a futures price movement of approximately 0.25 percentage point (3/12) for the three-month contract and 1 percentage point (12/12) for the one-year contract, as compared with 0.08 percentage point (1/12) for the one-month contract. So, basis risk is very small compared with the currency risk that is being hedged.

Another factor that can affect the quality of the hedge is that movement in the interest rate differential (basis) could be correlated with movement in the spot exchange rate itself.

### Expected Hedged Return and the Basis

We have so far focused on minimizing risk. A hedge ratio of 1 will minimize transaction risk. But in the long run, the return on the hedged portfolio will differ from the portfolio return achieved in foreign currency by the interest rate differential, even with a hedge ratio of 1. Although we can minimize, or even eliminate, the variance of $R_H - R$, it is impossible to set them equal. This is because we can hedge only with futures contracts with a price $F$ different from $S$. Over time, the percentage movement in the futures price used in the hedge, $R_F$, will differ from the percentage movement in the spot exchange rate, $s$, which affects the portfolio by the interest rate differential.

## Implementing Hedging Strategies

A major decision in selecting a currency hedge, whether it be with a forward (or swap) contract or with a futures contract, is the choice of contract terms. Short-term contracts track the behavior of the spot exchange rates better, have greater trading volume, and offer more liquidity than long-term contracts. On the other hand, short-term contracts must be rolled over if a hedge is to be maintained for a period longer than the initial contract. For long-term hedges, a manager can choose from three basic contract terms:

1. Short-term contracts, which must be rolled over at maturity
2. Contracts with a matching maturity, that is, contracts that match the expected period for which the hedge is to be maintained
3. Long-term contracts with a maturity extending beyond the hedging period

Contracts for any of the three terms may be closed by taking an offsetting position on the delivery date. This avoids actual physical delivery of a currency. Exhibit 3 depicts three such hedging strategies for an expected hedge period of six months. The results of the strategy depend on the evolution of interest rates and, hence, of the basis. Any contract maturity different from six months implies basis risk.

| Exhibit 3 | Three Hedging Strategies for an Expected Hedge Period of Six Months |

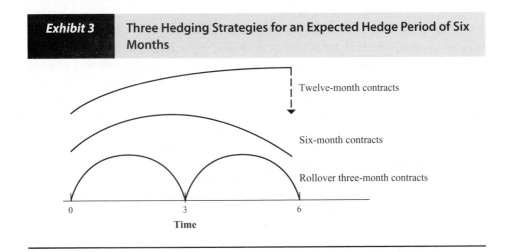

Another consideration in choosing a hedging strategy is transaction costs. Rolling over short-term contracts generates more commissions because of the larger number of transactions involved.

It must also be stressed that the market value of the investment to be hedged varies over time. To maintain a desired hedge ratio, the hedge amount should be adjusted frequently to reflect changes in asset market prices. Practically, this cannot be done on a continuous basis because of transaction costs. Forward contracts of small size can be expensive to arrange and will entail a staggering of maturity dates difficult to manage because they are arranged for a fixed duration (e.g., one month or six months). Futures are easier to use for frequent adjustments because they are of small size and traded with a few fixed maturity dates rather than a fixed duration.

Longer hedges can be built using currency swaps, which can be arranged with horizons of up to a dozen years. However, currency swaps are used primarily by corporations in the currency management of their assets and liabilities. Portfolio managers usually take a shorter horizon.

## Hedging Multiple Currencies

Cross-hedges are sometimes used for closely linked currencies. For example, a U.S. investor could use euro futures to hedge the currency risk in Swiss stocks, because the Swiss franc and the euro are highly correlated. Futures and forward currency contracts are actively traded only for the major currencies. International portfolios are often invested in assets in Hong Kong, Norway, Sweden, Singapore, and other countries where futures contracts in the local currency are sometimes not actively traded. In these cases, investors must try to find contracts on other currencies that are closely correlated with the investment currencies.

Some investment managers fear the depreciation of only one or two currencies in their portfolios and therefore hedge currency risk selectively. Other managers fear that their domestic currency will appreciate relative to all foreign currencies. For example, the strong U.S. dollar appreciation after 2000 was realized against all currencies. This domestic currency appreciation induced a negative currency contribution to the U.S. dollar return on all foreign portfolios. An overall currency hedge on their foreign investments would have drastically improved their performance by nullifying the negative currency contribution to the total dollar performance of non-U.S. portfolios.

Systematic currency hedging also reduces the total volatility of the portfolio, as noted in the reading on international diversification. A complete foreign currency hedge can be achieved by hedging the investments in each foreign currency. This is not feasible for many currencies, however, and is very cumbersome administratively. Also, it is not necessary to hedge each currency component in a multicurrency portfolio. In a portfolio with assets in many currencies, the residual risk of each currency is partly diversified away. Optimization techniques can be used to construct a hedge with futures contracts in only a few currencies (e.g., yen, euro, and sterling). Although the residual risk of individual currencies is not fully hedged, the portfolio is well protected against a general appreciation of the home currency.[4] Another alternative is to use contracts on a basket of currencies as offered by some banks.

The stability of the estimated hedge ratios is crucial in establishing effective hedging strategies, especially when cross-hedging is involved. Empirical studies indicate that hedges using futures contracts in the same currency as the asset to be hedged are very effective but that the optimal hedge ratios in cross-hedges that involve different currencies are somewhat unstable over time.[5]

---

**4** For an empirical examination of the multicurrency betas of international portfolios, see Adler and Simon (1986).

**5** See Eaker and Grant (1987), Dale (1981), and Grammatikos and Saunders (1983). The importance of basis risk (movements in interest rate differential) for determining the risk-minimizing hedge ratio has been illustrated by Briys and Solnik (1992). Kroner and Sultan (1993) derive risk-minimizing dynamic hedging strategies if the distribution of returns changes over time and follows some GARCH process.

In practice, a diversified international portfolio can be hedged using only the futures contracts available in a few currencies by following this procedure:

- Select the most independent major currencies with futures contracts available. For a U.S. investor, these may be the yen, the euro, and the pound. For a Swiss investor, these may be the yen, the euro, the pound, and the U.S. dollar.

- Calculate the hedge ratios jointly by running a multiple regression of the domestic currency returns of the portfolio (U.S. dollar return for a U.S. investor) on the futures returns in the selected currencies. With the example of three currencies, we have

$$R^* = a + h_1 R_{F1} + h_2 R_{F2} + h_3 R_{F3} + \text{Error term} \qquad \textbf{(14)}$$

- Use the estimates of the regression coefficients $h_1$, $h_2$, and $h_3$ as the hedge ratios in each currency. Because the spot currency movement is the major component of futures volatility, the hedge ratios obtained would be fairly close if we used currency movements in the regression instead of futures return.

Of course, this procedure requires historical data on the portfolio and will work well only if the estimated regression coefficients are stable over time.

# INSURING AND HEDGING WITH OPTIONS

# 2

Two approaches are used for reducing currency risk exposure with options. The traditional method exploits the asymmetric risk–return characteristic of an option, so that it is used as an *insurance* vehicle. The second approach takes into account the dynamics of the relationship between the option premium and the underlying exchange rate. This second approach is closer to a *hedging* technique.

## Insuring with Options

Many investors focus on the characteristics of options at expiration. Currency options are purchased in amounts equal to the principal to be hedged. It is not trivial to determine which options to use (calls or puts), because they involve the rate of exchange between two currencies. Consider a U.S. investor with £1 million of British assets. Let us assume that on the Philadelphia Stock Exchange he buys British pound puts for December with a strike price of 200 U.S. cents per pound. The contract size is £12,500. A British pound put gives him the right, but not the obligation, to sell British pounds at a fixed exercise (or strike) price with payment in dollars. Similarly, a British pound call gives him the right to buy British pounds with U.S. dollars. Note that a call to buy British pounds with U.S. dollars is equivalent to a put to sell U.S. dollars for British pounds. Options markets in some countries sometimes offer reverse contracts, so that investors must be sure they understand the position they are taking. In all cases, however, a good hedge implies buying options (puts or calls), not selling or writing them.

Suppose the spot exchange rate is $2.00 per pound. The strike price for the December put is 200 cents per pound (or $2.00 per pound), and the premium is 6 cents per pound. The investor must buy puts for £1 million, or 80 contracts. In this traditional approach, puts are treated as insurance devices. If the pound drops below $2.00 at expiration, a profit will be made on the put that exactly offsets the currency loss on the portfolio. If the pound drops to $1.90, the gain on the puts at expiration is

$$80 \times 12,500 \times (2.00 - 1.90) = \$100,000$$

The advantage of buying options rather than futures is that options simply expire if the pound appreciates rather than depreciates. For example, if the British pound moves up to $2.20, the futures contract will generate a loss of $200,000, nullifying the currency gain on the portfolio of assets. This does not happen with options that simply expire. Of course, investors must pay a price for this asymmetric risk structure, namely, the premium, which is the cost of having this insurance.

Note that the cost of the premium prevents a perfect hedge. In the previous example, the net profit on the put purchase equals the gain at expiration minus the premium. If we call $V_0$ the number of pounds, $P_0$ the premium per £, and $K$ the strike (or exercise) price, the net dollar profit on the put at the time of exercise $t$ is

$$\text{Net dollar profit} = V_0\left(K - S_t\right) - V_0 P_0 \text{ when } K > S_t$$
$$= -V_0 P_0 \text{ otherwise} \tag{15}$$

That is, when $K > S_t$, we have Net dollar profit = £ quantity × (Exercise price − Spot price) − £ quantity × Premium per pound, but the investor loses the premium otherwise.

Hence, if the pound drops to $1.90, the net dollar profit is

$$£1,000,000 \times \left(\$2.00/£ - \$1.90/£\right) - £1,000,000 \times \$0.06/£ = \$40,000$$

This profit does not cover the currency loss on the portfolio (equal to roughly $100,000), because the option premium cost $60,000. An alternative solution is to buy out-of-the-money puts with a lower exercise price and a lower premium. But with those, exchange rates would have to move that much more before a profit could be made on the options. In general, what is gained in terms of a lower premium is lost in terms of a lower strike price for the put option.

In fact, this approach does not allow for a good currency hedge except when variations in the spot exchange rate swamp the cost of the premium. Instead, this approach uses options as insurance contracts, and the premium is regarded as a sunk cost. Note, however, that options are usually resold on the market rather than left to expire; when the option is resold, part of the initial insurance premium is recovered. On the other hand, the approach still exploits the greatest advantage of options, namely, that an option can be allowed to expire if the currency moves in a favorable direction. Options protect a portfolio in case of adverse currency movements, as do currency futures, and maintain its performance potential in case of favorable currency movements, whereas futures hedge in both directions. The price of this asymmetric advantage is the insurance cost implicit in the time value of the option. To summarize, using options allows us to insure a portfolio against currency losses, rather than hedge it, and the option premium is the insurance cost. The use of currency options is illustrated in Example 4.

## Example 4

### Insuring with Options

You are a U.S. investor holding a portfolio of European assets worth €1 million. The current spot exchange rate is $1 = 1 euro but you fear a depreciation of the euro in the short term. The three-month forward exchange rate is $0.9960 = 1 euro. You are quoted the option premiums for calls euro and puts euro with a three-month maturity. These are options to buy (call) or sell (put) one euro at the dollar exercise price mentioned for each option. The contract size on the CME is €125,000. The quotations are as follows:

| Euro Options (All Prices in U.S. Cents per Euro) | | |
|---|---|---|
| Strike | Call Euro | Put Euro |
| 105 | 0.50 | 6.50 |
| 100 | 2.10 | 3.00 |
| 95 | 6.40 | 0.50 |

You decide to use options to insure your portfolio.

1. Should you buy (or sell) calls (or puts)? What quantity?

2. You decide to buy at-the-money puts, puts 100 (strike price of 100 U.S. cents) for €1 million. Suppose that you can borrow the necessary amount of dollars to buy these puts at a zero interest rate. Calculate the result at maturity of your strategy, assuming that the euro value of your portfolio remains at €1 million.

3. You have the choice of three different strike prices. What is the relative advantage of each option? What is the advantage relative to hedging, using forward currency contracts?

## Solution to 1:

To insure, you need to buy options. Here, you want to be able to translate euros at a fixed exchange rate, so you should buy euro puts for €1 million, or eight contracts.

## Solution to 2:

You buy at-the-money puts on €1 million. The cost (premium) is equal to

€1,000,000 × \$0.03/€ = \$30,000

If the euro rises in value, the put will expire worthless. If the euro depreciates, the gain on the option (per euro) will be equal to the difference between \$1 and the spot exchange rate at maturity (in dollars per euro). For example, if the spot exchange rate is \$0.90 = 1 euro, the gain on the puts will be

€1,000,000 × (\$1/€ − \$0.90/€) = \$100,000

But the original portfolio is now worth only \$900,000 (€1,000,000 × 0.90). The net result is a dollar portfolio value equal to

\$900,000 − \$30,000 + \$100,000 = \$970,000

The simulation of the dollar value of the position for a different value of the exchange rate at maturity is given in the first column of the following table. The portfolio is insured for down movements in the euro and benefits from up movements. But the cost of the insurance premium has to be deducted in all cases.

| Exchange Rate at Maturity (U.S. Cents per Euro) | Using Puts 100 | Using Puts 105 | Using Puts 95 | Hedging with Forward |
|---|---|---|---|---|
| 110 | 1,070,000 | 1,035,000 | 1,095,000 | 996,000 |
| 105 | 1,020,000 | 985,000 | 1,045,000 | 996,000 |
| 100 | 970,000 | 985,000 | 995,000 | 996,000 |
| 95 | 970,000 | 985,000 | 945,000 | 996,000 |
| 90 | 970,000 | 985,000 | 945,000 | 996,000 |

**Solution to 3:**

The preceding table simulates the results of using the various options as well as the forward. An "expensive" option (in-the-money, put 105) gives better downside protection at the expense of a lesser profit potential in case of an appreciation of the euro. A "cheap" option (out-of-the-money, put 95) provides less downside protection but a larger profit potential. Using forward contracts freezes the value of the portfolio at $996,000. You are well protected on the downside, but you cannot benefit from an appreciation of the euro. You will decide on the strategy, depending on your scenario for the euro exchange rate. If a depreciation of the euro seems very likely, you will hedge; if a depreciation seems very unlikely, you will buy out-of-the-money options, which are the cheapest. The other two strategies lie in between.

## Dynamic Hedging with Options

Listed options are traded continually, and positions are usually closed by reselling the option in the market instead of exercising it. The profit is therefore completely dependent on market valuation. The dynamic approach to currency option hedging recognizes this fact and is based on the relationship between changes in option premiums and changes in exchange rates.

The definition of a full currency-option hedge is simple and similar to the one given previously. A full hedge is a position in which every dollar loss from currency movement on a portfolio of foreign assets is covered by a dollar gain in the value of the options position.

We know that an option premium is related to the underlying exchange rate, but in a complex manner. Exhibit 4 shows the relationship we usually observe for a put. Beginning with a specific exchange rate, say, £:$ = 2.00, a put premium can go up or down in response to changes in the exchange rate. The slope of the curve at point A denotes the elasticity of the premium in response to any movements in the dollar exchange rate. In Exhibit 4, the premium is equal to 6 cents when the exchange rate is 200 U.S. cents per pound, and the slope of the tangent at point A equals −0.5. This slope is usually called delta ($\delta$).

| Exhibit 4 | Value of Pound Puts in Relation to the Exchange Rate |
|---|---|

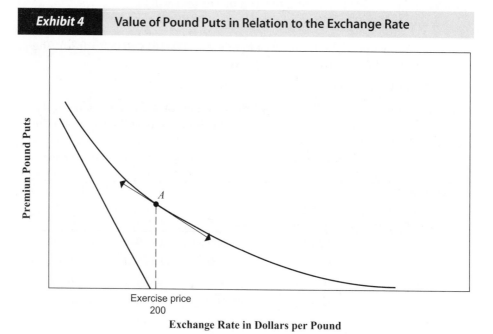

Exercise price
200

**Exchange Rate in Dollars per Pound**

In this example, a good hedge would be achieved by buying two pound puts for every pound of British assets. One pound put is defined here as a put option on one unit of British currency. One contract includes several pound puts, depending on the contract size. If the pound depreciated by 1 U.S. cent, each put would go up by approximately 0.5 cents, offsetting the currency loss on the portfolio. In general, if $n$ pound put options are purchased, the gain on the options position is

$$\text{Options gain} = n\left(P_t - P_0\right) \tag{16}$$

where $P_t$ is the put value at time $t$, and $P_0$ is the put value at time zero. For small movements in the exchange rate,

$$P_t - P_0 = \delta\left(S_t - S_0\right) \tag{17}$$

Hence, the gain on the options position is

$$\text{Options gain} = n\left(P_t - P_0\right) = n \times \delta \times \left(S_t - S_0\right) \tag{18}$$

Assuming that the value of the portfolio in foreign currency remains constant at $V_0$, the gain (loss if negative) on the portfolio in domestic currency is equal to

$$\text{Portfolio gain} = V_0 \times \left(S_t - S_0\right) \tag{19}$$

A good currency hedge is obtained by holding $n = -V_0/\delta$ options. The hedge ratio is equal to $-1/\delta$. The profit on the options position offsets the currency loss on the portfolio. In the example, the hedge ratio is equal to two as $\delta = -0.5$. One should buy two pound puts for every pound of portfolio value.

We must emphasize that $\delta$ and the hedge ratio vary with the exchange rate, so that the number of options held must be adjusted continually. This strategy is called the *delta hedge*.

Let's illustrate a delta hedge on the previous example. If the pound depreciates, options protect the portfolio, but its $\delta$ changes. For example, the slope $\delta$ could move to $-0.8$ if the pound drops to $1.95. Then the hedge ratio should be equal to $1/0.8 = 1.25$. To avoid overhedging, the investor must either sell some puts or switch to options with a lower exercise price (and lower $\delta$); in both cases, a profit will be realized. If the pound later reverses its downward trend, the puts will become worthless; however, most of the profit will have been realized previously and saved.

Transaction costs make continuous rebalancing impractical and expensive. In reality, a good hedge can be achieved only with periodic revisions in the options position, that is, when there is a significant movement in the exchange rate. Between revisions, options offer their usual asymmetric insurance within the general hedging strategy. This strategy may be regarded as a mixed hedging insurance strategy.

Implementing such a strategy requires a good understanding of option valuation and the precise estimation of the hedge ratio. As with futures, the strategy should take into account the expected return on the foreign portfolio, as well as its correlation with exchange rate movements.

## Implementation

Hedging strategies with options can be more sophisticated than those with forwards or futures for two reasons: The hedge ratio of options fluctuates but is constant for futures; and an investor can play with several maturities and exercise prices with options only.

A hedging strategy can combine futures and options.[6] Futures markets are very liquid and have low transaction costs. Options offer the advantage of an asymmetric risk structure but have higher costs, in terms of both the fair price for this insurance risk structure and their transaction costs.

If a hedging decision is necessary because an investor faces an increasing volatility in exchange rates and doesn't have a clear view of the direction of change, currency options are a natural strategy. In the scenario described at the beginning of this reading, Australian elections created uncertainties about the future of the Australian dollar. In that case, options would have allowed the investor to hedge a drop in the Australian dollar while maintaining the opportunity to profit in case it rose.

Where the direction of a currency movement is clearly forecasted, currency futures provide a cheaper hedge. In setting the hedge, however, investors should take into account the expected return on the portfolio and its correlation with currency movements.

# 3    OTHER METHODS FOR MANAGING CURRENCY EXPOSURE

Many methods are used to reduce currency exposure and to take positions in foreign markets without incurring excessive exchange risk. First, an investor can rearrange a portfolio so as to increase its risk level in a foreign market without increasing its currency exposure. For stocks, this means buying equities with higher betas (relative to the market index) and selling those with lower betas. This makes the portfolio more sensitive to local market movements without increasing its sensitivity to currency fluctuations. For bonds, this means adjusting the duration of the foreign portfolio to increase the portfolio's sensitivity to foreign interest rates without increasing its currency exposure.

An international portfolio manager who wants to invest in countries where the currency is expected to weaken has a few choices. She can buy common stock outright and hedge the exchange risk with currency futures or options, or buy options on the stock. For example, a U.S. investor may want to buy call options on the British firm ABC rather than ABC shares. The reason is simple: If ABC stock goes up by the same percentage as the British pound drops, the dollar value of a direct investment in ABC stock will remain unchanged. On the other hand, options on ABC will yield both a pound profit and a dollar profit. With options, currency fluctuations affect mostly the translation of the profit into dollars, not the principal. The price quotations given in Exhibit 5 illustrate how this strategy works.

The dollar profit of buying one share of ABC is zero because the currency loss on the principal offsets the capital gain in pounds. If the investor had instead purchased an option, the profit per share would have been $36 (= $52.50 − $16.50) despite the currency loss. Also, note that the initial investment in options is only $16.50 compared with $300 for shares. The difference could have been invested in U.S. cash instruments. Because the initial foreign currency investment in an option is very small, the currency impact is always limited compared with a direct investment in the asset.

---

**6** For a detailed description of currency options strategies, see the *Currency Options Strategy Manual* by the Chicago Mercantile Exchange, as well as various brochures prepared by options exchanges.

| Exhibit 5 | Price Quotations on ABC Shares | | |
|---|---|---|---|
| | Prices December 1 | Prices January 15 | Price Variation (%) |
| Dollars per pound | 1.50 | 1.25 | |
| Pounds per dollar | 0.667 | 0.800 | +20 |
| ABC stock (in pounds) | 200 | 240 | +20 |
| ABC stock (in dollars) | 300 | 300 | 0 |
| ABC February 200 options (in pounds) | 11.0 | 42 | |
| ABC February 200 options (in dollars) | 16.5 | 52.5 | |

A similar approach can be used to invest in an entire foreign market rather than only specific securities. This is done by buying stock index futures or options. Like any futures, stock index futures limit an investor's foreign currency exposure to the margin. Any realized profit can be repatriated immediately in the domestic currency. For example, a Swiss investor who is bullish on the U.S. stock market, but not on the U.S. dollar, can buy Standard & Poor's 500 Index futures. In addition, hedging the margin deposited in dollars against currency risk would provide the Swiss investor with complete currency protection. Stock index options can likewise be used. The use of stock index options is illustrated in Example 5. A similar strategy applies to bond investments. For example, a U.S. investor who is bullish on interest rates in the United Kingdom can buy gilt futures on the LIFFE rather than bonds, and thereby simultaneously hedge against exchange risk. Other alternatives include buying bond warrants.

### Example 5

## Buying Stock Index Futures

A European portfolio manager wishes to increase her exposure to Japanese stocks by €10 million, without taking much foreign exchange risk. Futures contracts are available on the TOPIX index. Each contract is for ¥1,000 times the index. The current futures price of the TOPIX index is 1,000, and the spot exchange rate is ¥100 per euro. What strategy could she adopt using those contracts?

### Solution:

She would buy TOPIX futures contracts to gain an overall exposure in the Japanese stock market corresponding to €10 million, or ¥1 billion at the current exchange rate. The number of contracts $N$ to be bought is determined as follows:

$$N = \frac{¥1,000,000,000}{\text{Multiplier} \times \text{Index value}} = \frac{¥1,000,000,000}{¥1,000 \times 1,000} = 1,000 \text{ contracts}$$

The futures contracts are not exposed to currency risk. However, she also has to deposit a margin in yen that can be hedged against currency risk.

Futures and options on foreign assets reduce currency exposure as long as an investor does not already own the assets in question. In addition, costs involved in taking such positions are less than those for actually buying foreign assets and hedging them with currency futures or options. On the other hand, if the assets are already part of a portfolio, more conventional methods of currency hedging are probably better, especially for assets that will remain in the portfolio for a long time.

Investors also should be aware of the currency impact on an investment strategy involving different types of instruments whose currency exposures are not identical. As an illustration, let's consider the following strategy. A U.S. investor buys Australian natural resource companies stock for A$1 million and sells stock index futures for the same amount to hedge the Australian stock market risk. The beta of this portfolio relative to the Australian market is assumed to be 1. The motivation for this strategy is the belief that natural resource stocks are undervalued relative to the Australian market. The U.S. investor believes that the portfolio will generate a positive alpha ("alpha strategy"). Such a position, which is long in stocks and short in futures, is not exposed to Australian stock market risk; however, it does require an Australian dollar net investment, and is therefore exposed to the risk of the Australian dollar. A depreciation of the Australian dollar would induce a currency loss in the stock position that would not be offset by a currency gain on the stock index futures.[7] This is illustrated in Example 6.

### Example 6

## Currency Risk for Alpha Strategies

On September 1, an American investor buys Australian natural resource companies stock for A$1 million and sells ASX stock index futures (December maturity) for the same amount to hedge the Australian stock market risk. The ASX contract has a multiplier of A$25. The current ASX futures price is 2,000. The investor sells 20 contracts.

The Australian dollar drops from 1.0 U.S. dollar on September 1 to 0.90 U.S. dollar on October 1. In the same period, the ASX index and the ASX futures price drop by 10 percent (in A$), while the portfolio only loses 7 percent (in A$). What is the profit or loss on this alpha strategy in Australian dollars and in U.S. dollars if the investor does not engage in currency hedging?

### Solution:

Calculations are detailed in the following table (the margin deposit is neglected here). The investor would have realized a gain of A$30,000 corresponding to the 3 percent return difference between the portfolio and the market (alpha). If the US$/A$ exchange rate had remained stable at 1, this would have translated into a US$30,000 profit. Instead, the 10 percent depreciation of the Australian dollar induced a loss of 73,000 U.S. dollars. To reduce the impact of currency movements, the investor should have hedged the stock portfolio against currency risk.

|  | **Futures Market** | **Stock Market** |
|---|---|---|
| **September 1** (A$:US$ = 1) | Sell 20 December ASX futures at 2,000 | Buy natural resource stocks; cost = A$1,000,000, US$1,000,000 |
| **October 1** (A$:US$ = 0.9) | *Market declines 10%, but natural resource stocks decline 7%* | Sell natural resource stocks; proceeds = A$930,000, US$837,000 |
|  | Buy 20 December ASX futures at 1,800 |  |
|  | Profit on futures = A$100,000, US$90,000 | Loss on stocks = A$70,000, US$163,000 |
|  | **Net loss on trade = US$73,000** |  |

---

**7**  As a matter of fact, there will even be an additional small currency loss in the initial margin deposited for the futures contracts.

Several investment vehicles and strategies may be used either to take advantage of or to hedge against monetary factors. Many of these strategies have been discussed before, so we already know that they usually involve a combination of investments in money, capital, and speculative markets. For example, a British investor expecting a weak U.S. dollar and falling U.S. interest rates could buy long-term U.S. bonds, or zero coupons, to maximize the sensitivity of her portfolio to U.S. interest rate movements and, at the same time, to hedge against exchange risk with currency futures or options. A matrix of alternative investments in the U.S. dollar fixed-income markets is given in Exhibit 6. Each quadrant represents a specific scenario concerning U.S. interest rates and the U.S. dollar. Group I, for example, represents a set of strategies designed to capitalize on a strong U.S. dollar and falling dollar interest rates.

---

**Exhibit 6    A Strategy Matrix of Alternative Investments in the U.S. Dollar Fixed-Income Markets**

**Dollar strength**

**Group I**

A. Long-maturity bonds
B. Long-maturity mortgage-related securities
C. CATS
D. Zero-coupon bonds
E. Money market plus bond options/futures/ warrants
F. Bond warrants
G. Financial options—bull strategies
H. Financial futures—bull strategies
I. Currency options—$ bull strategies
J. Currency futures—$ bull strategies
Government yield curve arbitrage— bull strategies

**Group II**

A. Money market
B. Eurodollar FRNs
C. Repurchase agreements
D. "Cash and carry"
E. Hedged nondollar money market
F. Short-maturity bonds
G. Financial options—bear strategies
H. Financial futures—bear strategies
Government yield curve arbitrage— bear strategies
Currency options—$ bull strategies
Currency futures—$ bull strategies

**Falling dollar interest rates**

**Rising dollar interest rates**

**Group IV**

A. Hedged long-maturity bonds
B. GNMA for ward plus base-currency money market
C. Reverse repos (overnight) plus base-currency money market
D. Government yield curve arbitrage— bull strategies
CATS
Zero-coupon bonds
Bond warrants
Financial options—bull strategies
Financial futures—bull strategies
Currency options—$ bear strategies
Currency futures—$ bear strategies

**Group III**

A. Hedged money market
B. Hedged Eurodollar FRNs
C. Reverse repos to maturity plus base-currency money market (for loss-constrained portfolios)
D. Currency options—$ bear strategies
E. Currency futures—$ bear strategies
F. Government yield curve arbitrage— bear strategies
Financial options—bear strategies
Financial futures—bear strategies

**Dollar weakness**

---

Securities/strategies are generally listed with the more traditional, or less risky, at the top of each group; the more highly leveraged, or risky, are toward the bottom of the list. In some instances, the same instruments/strategies appear in more than one quadrant. In such cases, they appear only with a code letter in that quadrant where they are especially appropriate. They appear without a code letter in the other quadrants.
*Source*: J. Hanna and P. Niculescu. "The Currency and Interest Rate Strategy Matrix: An Investment Tool for Multicurrency Investors," Bond Market Research, Salomon Brothers Inc., September 1982. Reprinted with permission.

The purpose in outlining strategies is to help an investor to take advantage of his specific forecasts with respect to interest rates and currencies. Of course, the actual performance of these strategies depends on the accuracy of the investor's forecasts. A similar strategy matrix can be designed for nondollar investments, although the absence of speculative markets in some currencies sometimes limits the range of strategies an investor can choose.

# 4    STRATEGIC AND TACTICAL CURRENCY MANAGEMENT

Currency management must be addressed at the strategic and tactical level. Investors must decide on the foreign currency exposure they wish to retain in the long run. This is a strategic policy decision, where a "neutral" allocation is decided in the absence of specific priors on currencies. Such a policy results in a neutral or benchmark hedge ratio for the long run. In the short run, the amount of currency hedging can deviate from this benchmark based on tactical considerations. Tactical management of the currency exposure is often delegated to currency overlay managers. Some investors even regard currency as a special asset class with attractive risk–return characteristics.

## Strategic Hedge Ratio

Investors must decide on the amount of currency exposure that should be hedged in their strategic allocation. For private investors, the approach to currency management is specified in the investment policy statement. For institutional investors, the strategic currency decision takes the form of a benchmark hedge ratio assigned to managers. Unfortunately, theory does not provide a clear-cut answer for the optimal hedge ratio to be used (see the reading on international diversification). In the absence of simple, widely accepted recommendations for a passive benchmark, simple hedging rules with a fixed hedge ratio are commonly adopted.

A traditional approach is simply to choose the hedging policy that minimizes the variance (risk) of the international portfolio. With the additional assumption that the correlation between asset returns and currency returns is small and unstable, this choice leads to a benchmark hedge ratio of 100 percent. All currency risk should be hedged. Basically, currency risk is treated as additional uncertainty with unpredictable return; it should be eliminated to the extent possible. Several large institutional investors use such a benchmark hedge ratio (e.g., CalPERS in 2007). However, several factors could be taken into account to determine the benchmark hedge ratio.

### Total Portfolio Risk

The traditional approach is to focus solely on the risk of the international segment of the total portfolio. But currencies provide an element of diversification to domestic assets. The contribution of currency risk should be measured at the level of the total portfolio (domestic and international investments), not at the level of international investments taken in isolation. It is often claimed that currency risk does not add a significant amount of uncertainty to the total portfolio when the international allocation is small (typically 10%). So the optimal passive hedge ratio is likely to depend on the proportion of international assets in the total portfolio: The lower the proportion of international assets, the lower the benchmark hedge ratio.

### Asset Types

Different asset prices react differently to currency movements. Correlation between asset returns and currency returns can be different across asset types. Stock prices from emerging countries are more sensitive to the value of the local currency than stock prices from developed countries. International bond portfolios could justify a different benchmark hedge ratio than international equity portfolios. The lower the correlation between portfolio return and currency movements, the lower the benchmark hedge ratio should be.

### Investment Horizon

It is often stated that exchange rates revert to fundamentals over the long run, so currency risk tends to diminish over long horizons. Hence, long-term investors should worry less about currency risk and possibly adopt a no-hedging policy. But empirical work indicates that it might take a very long time for exchange rates to revert to fundamentals. The longer the investor's time horizon, the lower the benchmark hedge ratio should be.

### Prior Beliefs on Currencies

Some investors believe that their own base currency is structurally weak (strong). This would lead them to adopt a lesser (higher) hedge ratio. In the old days (e.g., 1960s and 1970s), currencies like the French franc or British pound were regarded as depreciating currencies, and few investors from those countries considered any amount of currency hedging.

### Costs

There are two components in hedging cost. The first one is related to trading, namely, transaction costs in the form of fees, commissions, and bid–ask spreads. Currency hedging entails rather small transaction costs but poses a cumbersome administrative burden. The administrative and monitoring tasks should not be underestimated. The hedging policy is dynamic; contracts in many currencies have to be rolled over periodically and adjusted to changes in the asset portfolio. There is also the need for active multicurrency cash management as margins change and profits/losses are realized at contract expirations. Some money managers believe that removing currency risk is not worth the cost and effort. The second cost component is the interest differential, as described in earlier chapters. To hedge, one has to sell foreign currencies forward at their forward price, which differs from the spot exchange rate used to value assets. For example, when a Japanese investor hedges her U.S. assets against currency risk, she sells dollars forward against yen and must pay the U.S. dollar interest rate while receiving the yen interest rate. The difference (or basis) is the spread between the two interest rates. In 2007, the interest rate spread between the United States and Japan was on the order of 4 percent. This is not a transaction cost, but it is still a sure cost to be borne by a hedger. Hedging will become attractive only if the actual dollar depreciation is larger than this basis. Up to 2007, Japan has structurally been a low-interest-rate country, making foreign currency hedging less attractive for Japanese investors.[8] In general, the higher the perceived costs of hedging, the lower the benchmark hedge ratio should be.

### Is Regret the Proper Measure for Currency Risk?

Currencies are an emotional investment. A wrong hedging decision can lead to a vast amount of regret. For example, a U.S. investor who decided not to hedge currency risk would have incurred a currency loss of some 40 percent on Eurozone

---

[8] This is a different argument from the forecast that the yen might be "temporarily" overvalued (undervalued), leading to a tactical decision to decrease (increase) the hedge ratio used by Japanese investors.

assets from late 1998 to late 2000, with huge regret at not having been fully hedged. Conversely, a fully hedged investor would have missed the 50 percent appreciation of the euro from late 2001 to late 2004; again, there is a huge regret at not having made the "right" hedging decision.[9] Basically, *regret risk* stems from a comparison of the ex post return of the adopted hedging policy relative to the best hedging policy that could have been chosen. Ex post, *if the foreign currency depreciates* by any amount, the best hedging alternative would have been to be fully hedged. *If the foreign currency appreciates* by any amount, the best hedging alternative would have been to be unhedged. To minimize regret risk, a simple hedging rule would be to hedge 50 percent. Such a decision will turn out to be almost always wrong ex post, but the amount of regret would be minimized.[10] Several practitioners have justified a 50 percent naïve hedge ratio on such intuitive grounds. For example:

> The 50% hedge benchmark is gaining in popularity around the world as it offers specific benefits. It avoids the potential for large underperformance that is associated with "polar" benchmark, i.e. being fully unhedged when the Canadian dollar is strong or being fully hedged when it is weak. This minimizes the "regret" that comes with holding the wrong benchmark in the wrong conditions.[11]

Regret aversion pushes the benchmark toward 50 percent; the higher the investor's regret aversion, the closer to 50 percent the benchmark should be.

In summary, there is no obvious hedging benchmark, and the choice depends on many factors, such as the characteristics of the portfolio, the investor's horizon, and his risk and regret aversions. The diversity of benchmark hedge ratios is reflected in Exhibit 7, which gives the distribution of benchmark hedge ratios for 563 institutional investors delegating the currency hedging decision to overlay managers. Each column gives the distribution of the benchmark hedge ratio for investors from a given base currency, that is, a region (e.g., the first column is the distribution for U.S. investors) as well as the number of accounts in that base currency. The last column gives the distribution of all accounts. The 0 percent, 50 percent, and 100 percent hedging policies are the most common benchmarks, but their acceptance varies across investors' country of residence.

## Currency Overlay

The currency management of the international portfolio is often delegated to a specialized manager called the *currency overlay manager*. This decision is based on the assumption that the primary manager of the international assets does not have the currency expertise of the currency overlay specialist. The composition of the portfolio is periodically transferred to the currency overlay manager, who decides on the positions taken in currencies and manages currency risk. In the currency overlay approach, currencies are regarded as financial prices that require the expertise of a specialist. Note that the currency overlay manager could be an external manager or simply a specialized team among the organization managing the portfolio. A client who uses several managers for an international portfolio can delegate the management of the aggregate currency position to a single currency overlay manager.

---

**9** Furthermore, selling short an appreciating foreign currency leads to cash losses on the forward position that have to be covered by the sale of assets—a forced decision that is highly visible, painful, and easily criticized.

**10** Michenaud and Solnik (2006) propose a modelization of optimal currency hedging under risk and regret aversion. See also Gardner and Willoud (1995) and Statman (2005).

**11** Chrispin (2004) p.2.

| Exhibit 7 | Distribution of Benchmark Hedge Ratio for Investors from Different Base Currencies |
|---|---|

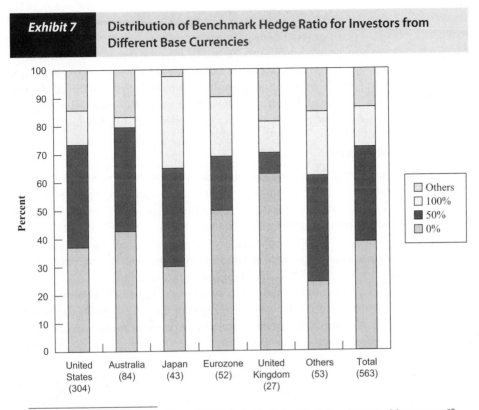

*Source*: Based on Harris, L., "Is There Still Alpha to Be Gained in Active Currency Management?" Russell/Mellon, 2005.

The role of the currency overlay manager is to manage currency risks within the existing portfolio, hedging part or all of the currency exposure of the international portfolio. It is not to take naked speculative positions in currencies. Typically, the client assigns to the currency overlay manager a benchmark hedge ratio that reflects the investor's desired neutral currency exposure. The tactical currency management on the portfolio is delegated to the currency overlay manager. The client also sets some parameters indicating how much an active currency overlay manager can deviate from the assigned benchmark. This is done in the forms of bounds on the actual hedge ratio used by the currency overlay manager or a maximum level of tracking error relative to the benchmark. Other parameters include the set of currencies and instruments that can be used by the manager.

Several types of tactical approaches are used in currency overlay.

### Management of the Currency Risk Profile

Exchange rate movements are assumed to be unpredictable and no attempt is made to forecast future returns. But currency risk is managed through dynamic hedging or option-based approaches. The strategy attempts to create an asymmetric risk profile protecting from downside losses while allowing capture of some upside potential. This is pure active risk management.

### Technical Approach

The currency markets are the most liquid markets in the world. But many of the major market participants are very different from those found on equity and bond markets. These market participants do not follow the usual paradigm of return and risk optimization. For example, central banks intervene to manage their cash positions in various currencies and to satisfy some inflation or balance of payments objectives. Corporate treasurers participate when business transactions create cash inflows or outflows in foreign currency. In many cases, the supply and demand for currencies that affect the exchange rate are non-profit-driven and may result in some temporary market inefficiencies in the price quoted for currencies. Some currency overlay managers claim that they can exploit these inefficiencies. They develop models that attempt to identify predictable price patterns in exchange rates and in their volatility. These technical models are used to generate superior returns within controlled currency risk management.

### Fundamental Approach

Economic analysis could help detect undervalued or overvalued currencies. The basic idea is that economic data can help predict future exchange rate movements. A fair value is determined for each currency, and the hedge ratio is adjusted upward (downward) when a foreign currency trades above (below) its fair value. Of course, sophisticated models have been developed that incorporate both the technical and fundamental approach in a risk-controlled framework. Ultimately, the success of these strategies depends on the predictability of exchange rates.

Currency overlay is a complex process in which costs must be minimized. While diversified equity portfolios are invested in a large number of countries and currencies, liquid currency forward and option contracts exist only for major currencies. It is feasible to hedge the currency risk on investments in many emerging markets, but the cost can be significant and the instruments are often illiquid. Hence, active currency managers typically use only a few major currencies and often resort to cross-hedging. For example, hedging in euros could be used to cover investments in Swedish kronor.

It should be stressed that an investment management approach that separates the asset allocation decision from currency exposure decisions is not ideal. Jorion (1994) proposed a mean-variance analysis of currency overlay. He found that currency overlays are suboptimal. It is better to optimize simultaneously the asset allocation and the currency hedging decision rather than to adopt a two-step currency overlay approach. In the two-step, suboptimal approach, asset allocation is optimized first (without taking currencies into consideration) and currency hedging is optimized second, assuming the asset allocation as given (currency overlay). But if the correlation between currency movements and asset returns is small, the difference between the optimal and the two-step approach will be small in terms of risk optimization.

## Currencies as an Asset Class

Currency overlay is restricted to the management of the currency exposure of an existing portfolio. The next step is to offer funds that specialize in currency management. The definition of what constitutes an asset class is beyond the scope of this reading. But there is no doubt that the currency market is huge and liquid, and that the drivers of exchange rates are somewhat different from those of other asset classes. The correlation between currency movements and equity returns is low. Even the correlation between currency movements and bond returns is relatively low. Hence, managers are now offering hedge funds and products that solely invest in currency instruments. They apply strategies outlined above to generate superior returns (alpha) with low correlation with other asset classes. But the objectives are somewhat different from those of a traditional currency overlay manager:

■ Traditional currency overlay managers focus primarily on hedging an existing portfolio against currency risks. They manage the currency exposure of a portfolio to generate an attractive risk profile compared to a passive hedging benchmark.

■ Currency funds typically use a LIBOR or other cash benchmark, on an absolute return basis. They will use currencies to generate a positive alpha. These funds are sometimes called *currency for alpha* funds.

# SUMMARY

- Currency futures, forwards, and option contracts are used primarily to protect a portfolio against currency risks. Managers adapt their hedging strategies to their expectations of an asset's performance in foreign currency and of exchange rate movements.

- The basic approach to the use of currency futures contracts is to hedge the foreign currency value of the foreign asset. Managers would sell short currencies in the amount of an asset's value. Ideally, investors should hedge the future value of an investment, taking into account the expected price change and income.

- The hedge ratio is the ratio of the size of the short futures position in foreign currency to the value of the portfolio in foreign currency.

- The covariance between the asset return and the exchange rate movement should be considered. A minimum-variance hedge sets a hedge ratio that minimizes both translation risk and economic risk. Translation risk comes from the fact that the principal value of a foreign asset is translated at the exchange rate, so that a movement in the exchange rate affects the domestic currency value of the asset. Economic risk comes from the fact that the foreign currency value of a foreign asset can be influenced by a movement in the exchange rate.

- The interest rate differential is the forward basis, the percentage difference between the futures and the spot exchange rates. Basis risk affects the quality of currency hedging.

- Because a currency hedge must use futures (or forward) exchange rates, not spot exchange rates, the return on the hedged asset will differ over time from the return on the asset measured in foreign currency by the interest rate differential.

- Hedging strategies for multicurrency portfolios usually involve the use of futures in the major currencies. The instability of the estimated hedge ratios reduces the effectiveness of hedging strategies.

- Currency options are used for their asymmetric risk–return characteristics. They provide insurance against adverse currency movements while retaining the profit potential in case of a favorable currency movement. There is a cost associated with this attractive insurance characteristic. More dynamic hedging strategies can also be implemented using currency options. They require option valuation models to estimate the hedge ratio.

- Other methods can be used to manage the currency exposure of international portfolios. Leveraged instruments on foreign assets, such as futures and options, have little currency exposure, because the capital invested in foreign currency is very small compared with the value of the underlying asset. The impact of a currency movement on a combined position of several assets and contracts should be studied carefully.

- Currency management must be addressed at the strategic and tactical level. Investors must decide on the foreign currency exposure they wish to retain in the long run. This is a strategic policy decision, where a "neutral" allocation is decided in the absence of specific priors on currencies. Many factors can affect the choice of a strategic hedge ratio.

■ A currency overlay approach is sometimes used in international investment management. Some clients delegate the currency management of the international portfolio to a specialized currency overlay manager. This strategy is based on the assumption that the primary manager of the international assets does not have the currency expertise of the currency overlay specialist. The composition of the portfolio is periodically transferred to the currency overlay manager, who decides on the positions taken in currencies and manages currency risk.

# PRACTICE PROBLEMS FOR READING 35

*Note*: In these problems, the notation / is used to mean "per." For example, ¥158/$ means "¥158 per $."

1. A U.S. investor holds a portfolio of Japanese stocks worth ¥160 million. The spot exchange rate is ¥158/$, and the three-month forward exchange rate is ¥160/$. The investor fears that the Japanese yen will depreciate in the next month but wants to keep the Japanese stocks. What position can the investor take based on three-month forward exchange rate contracts? List all the factors that will make the hedge imperfect.

2. Consider a German portfolio manager who holds a portfolio of U.S. stocks currently worth $5 million. In order to hedge against a potential depreciation of the dollar, the portfolio manager proposes to sell December futures contracts on the dollar that currently trade at €1.02/$ and expire in two months. The spot exchange rate is currently €0.974/$. A month later, the value of the U.S. portfolio is $5,150,000, and the spot exchange rate is €1.1/$, while the futures exchange rate is €1.15/$.

   A. Evaluate the effectiveness of the hedge by comparing the fully hedged portfolio return with the unhedged portfolio return.

   B. Calculate the return on the portfolio, assuming a 50 percent hedge ratio.

3. Consider a U.S. portfolio manager who holds a portfolio of French stocks currently worth €10 million. In order to hedge against a potential depreciation of the euro, the portfolio manager proposes to sell December futures contracts on the euro that currently trade at $1/€ and expire in two months. The spot exchange rate is currently $1.1/€. A month later, the value of the French portfolio is €10,050,000 and the spot exchange rate is $1.05/€, while the futures exchange rate is $0.95/€.

   A. Evaluate the effectiveness of the hedge by comparing the fully hedged portfolio return with the unhedged portfolio return.

   B. Calculate the return on the portfolio, assuming a 35 percent hedge ratio.

4. A Dutch investor holds a portfolio of Japanese stocks worth ¥160 million. The current three-month dollar/euro forward exchange rate is $1.2/€, and the current three-month $:¥ forward exchange rate is ¥160/$. Explain how the Dutch investor could hedge the €:¥ exchange risk, using $:¥ and €:$ forward contracts.

5. The current yield curve is much lower in the United States than in Great Britain. You read in the newspaper that it is unattractive for a U.S. investor to hedge currency risk on British assets. The same journal states that British investors should hedge the currency risk on their U.S. investments. What do you think?

6. Salomon Brothers proposes to investors a contract called a *range forward contract*. Here is an example of such a U.S. dollar/British pound contract:

   The contract has a size of £100,000 and a maturity of three months. At maturity, the investor will purchase the pounds at a price that is a function of the spot exchange rate.

   • If the spot exchange rate at maturity is less than $1.352/£, the investor will pay $1.352 to get one pound.

- If the spot exchange rate at maturity is between $1.352/£ and $1.470/£, the investor will pay the current spot exchange rate to get one pound.

- If the spot exchange rate at maturity is more than $1.470/£, the investor will pay $1.470 to get one pound.

Assume that you are a British exporter who will receive $10 million in three months that will have to be transferred into British pounds at the time. Currently, the spot and forward exchange rates are $1.4200/£ and $1.4085/£, respectively.

**A.** Explain why such a range forward contract could be attractive if you fear a depreciation of the dollar during the three months.

**B.** Explain why Salomon Brothers can sell such a contract at a very low price.

7. You are a British exporter who knows in December that you will receive $15 million in three months (March). The current spot exchange rate is $1.5/£, and the March forward exchange rate is also $1.5/£. Calls on the British pound are quoted by your bank for the exact amount that you desire, as follows:

| March Sterling Options (All Prices in $ per £) | |
| --- | --- |
| **Strike** | **Call £** |
| 1.50 | 0.03 |
| 1.55 | 0.015 |
| 1.60 | 0.005 |

Calculate the £ value of the $15 million received in three months, assuming that the £:$ spot exchange rate in March is equal to 1.3, 1.4, 1.5, 1.6, 1.7, and 1.8 dollar per pound. Perform this calculation under five different scenarios about your hedging decision in December:

- You do nothing.

- You hedge with forward contracts.

- You insure with calls 150.

- You insure with calls 155.

- You insure with calls 160.

Put all of these figures in a table, and discuss the relative advantages of the various strategies.

8. The HFS Trustees have decided to invest in international equity markets and have hired Jacob Hind, a specialist manager, to implement this decision. He has recommended that an unhedged equities position be taken in Japan, providing the following comment and data to support his views:

Appreciation of a foreign currency increases the returns to a U.S. dollar investor. Because appreciation of the yen from 100¥/$ to 98¥/$ is expected, the Japanese stock position should not be hedged.

| Market Rates and Hind's Expectations | United States | Japan |
| --- | --- | --- |
| Spot rate (direct quote) | n/a | 100 |
| Hind's 12-month currency forecast | n/a | 98 |
| One-year Eurocurrency rate (% per annum) | 6.00 | 0.80 |
| Hind's 1-year inflation forecast (% per annum) | 3.00 | 0.50 |

Assume that the investment horizon is one year and that there are no costs associated with currency hedging. State and justify whether Hind's recommendation should be followed. Show any calculations.

## SOLUTIONS FOR READING 35

*Note*: In these problems, the notation / is used to mean "per." For example, ¥158/$ means "¥158 per $."

1. To lock in the rate at which yen can be converted into U.S. dollars, the investor should enter into a contract to sell ¥160 million forward at a forward exchange rate of $:¥ = 160. The hedge will be imperfect for the following reasons:

   - If the price of the Japanese stocks changes. For example, if the value of the portfolio suddenly goes up to ¥180 million, the investor will have underhedged ¥20 million. To remain fully hedged, the investor should continually adjust the amount hedged.

   - Another reason for an imperfect hedge is the possibility of a change in the forward basis caused by a change in interest rate differential.

2. **A.** The return on the unhedged portfolio in dollar terms is

   $$\frac{5,150,000 - 5,000,000}{5,000,000} = 0.03 = 3.0\%$$

   The return on the unhedged portfolio in euro terms is

   $$\frac{(5,150,000)(1.1) - (5,000,000)(0.974)}{(5,000,000)(0.974)} = 0.1632 = 16.32\%$$

   The return on the hedged portfolio in euro terms is determined as follows:

   $$\text{The portfolio profit in euros} = (5,150,000)(1.1) - (5,000,000)(0.974)$$
   $$= €5,665,000 - €4,870,000 = €795,000$$

   $$\text{The loss on the futures contract in euros} = (5,000,000)(1.02 - 1.15)$$
   $$= -€650,000$$

   $$\text{The net profit on the hedged position} = €795,000 - €650,000$$
   $$= €145,000$$

   $$\text{The return on the hedged portfolio in euros} = €145,000/€4,870,000$$
   $$= 0.0298$$
   $$= 2.98\%$$

   This indicates that the position is almost perfectly hedged because a return of 3 percent in dollars has been transformed into a return of 2.98 percent in euros.

   **B.** The return on a portfolio with a hedge ratio of 0.5 is calculated as follows:

   Profit in euros = (0.5)(−€650,000) + €795,000 = €470,000

   Return on partially hedged portfolio = €470,000/€4,870,000 = 0.0965 = 9.65%

3. **A.** The return on the unhedged portfolio in euros is

   $$\frac{10,050,000 - 10,000,000}{10,000,000} = 0.005 = 0.5\%$$

The return on the unhedged portfolio in dollar terms is

$$\frac{(10{,}050{,}000)(1.05)-(10{,}000{,}000)(1.1)}{(10{,}000{,}000)(1.1)}=-0.0407=-4.07\%$$

The return on the hedged portfolio in dollar terms is determined as follows:

$$\text{The portfolio loss in dollars}=(10{,}050{,}000)(1.05)-(10{,}000{,}000)(1.1)$$
$$=\$10{,}552{,}500-\$11{,}000{,}000$$
$$=-\$447{,}500$$

$$\text{The gain on the futures contract in dollars}=(10{,}000{,}000)(1-0.95)$$
$$=\$500{,}000$$

$$\text{The net profit on the hedged position}=\$500{,}000-\$447{,}500$$
$$=\$52{,}500$$

$$\text{The return on the hedged portfolio in dollars}=\$52{,}500/\$11{,}000{,}000$$
$$=0.0048$$
$$=0.48\%$$

This indicates that the position is almost perfectly hedged because a return of 0.5% in euros has been transformed into a return of 0.48% in dollars.

**B.** The return on a portfolio with a hedge ratio of 0.35 is calculated as follows:

$$\text{Profit in dollars}=(0.35)(\$500{,}000)-\$447{,}500=-\$272{,}500$$

$$\text{Return on partially hedged portfolio}=-\$272{,}500/\$11{,}000{,}000$$
$$=-0.0248$$
$$=-2.48\%$$

4.  The investor should sell ¥160 million forward against euros, a transaction that combines two forward operations:

- Sell ¥160 million for $1 million ($1,000,000 = ¥160,000,000/¥160/$)
- Sell $1 million for €833,333 = $1,000,000/$1.20/€

5.  An American investor hedging the British pound risk has to "pay" the interest rate differential (British minus U.S. interest rate), while a British investor hedging the U.S. dollar risk "receives" it. It seems to be the reason why the journal suggests that Americans should *not* hedge their British investments, but that British investors should hedge their U.S. investments.

   If the interest rate differential simply reflects the expected depreciation of the pound relative to the dollar, there is no *expected* "cost" of hedging in the sense intended by the journal. Furthermore, short-term currency swings can be very large relative to the interest rate differential, so risk should also be considered. To hedge currency *risk* could turn out to be a good decision, even if you have to pay an interest rate differential.

   The journal could also be suggesting that a currency with a higher interest rate tends to appreciate. Even if this statement is true on the average, exchange rates are very volatile. A currency hedge still allows the reduction of the risk of a loss.

6.  **A.**  Traditional ways for the exporter to hedge against a decline in the value of the dollar would be to i) buy puts on the dollar or, equivalently, ii) buy calls on the pound. The Range Forward Contract ensures that the exporter will

not pay more than $1.470/£, even if the dollar depreciates strongly relative to the pound. Typically the range forward insurance costs nothing. On the other hand, a traditional call on the pound is costly in that it involves payment of a call premium. The same applies to put options on the pound. The disadvantage of the range forward is that the exporter will not fully benefit from an appreciation of the dollar. In the case of options, the exporter can allow the option to expire worthless if the dollar appreciates. With a range forward contract, the exporter will benefit up to an exchange rate of $1.352/£, but not beyond that rate. So, the exporter sacrifices some profit potential to get "free" insurance.

**B.** This contract is the sum of

- a call pound, giving the exporter the right to buy pounds at $1.470/£; and

- a put pound, giving Salomon Brothers the right to sell pounds at $1.352/£.

In other words, the exporter buys a call with a strike of $1.470/£ and sells a put with a strike of $1.352/£. The fair value of the Range Forward Contract should be the difference between the call premium and the put premium. The fair value should be much smaller than that of the call alone. Typically, the strike prices are chosen so that the option costs nothing.

**7.** Again, assume that we buy the calls by borrowing pounds at a zero interest rate. For example, to "insure" with $1.50 strike calls on the £, we need to buy calls on £10 million. The cost is $300,000, which we finance with £200,000, given the spot exchange rate.

The following table provides portfolio values at various exchange rates. To explain, portfolio values are calculated at an exchange rate of $1.7/£.

**A.** Unhedged portfolio value:

$$\$15,000,000/\$1.7 \text{ per pound} = £8,823,529$$

**B.** Hedged portfolio value, using forward contract $1.5 per pound:

$$\$15,000,000/\$1.5 \text{ per pound} = £10,000,000$$

**C.** Insured portfolio, using March 1.50 calls: Once again, remember that you can insure using a put to sell $ for £, or buying a call to buy £ using $. The call option will be exercised if Current price > Strike price. Otherwise, it will expire worthless, and you lose only the option premium:

$$\text{Option premium} = \frac{15,000,000}{1.5}(0.03) = \$300,000$$

or

$$£200,000 = \$300,000/1.5 \text{ .}$$

Current price = $1.7/£ and the Strike price = $1.5/£. The option is exercised because it allows the exporter to buy pounds at a cheaper rate:

$$\text{Profit on call} = \frac{15,000,000}{1.5} - \frac{15,000,000}{1.7} = £1,176,471$$

The dollar depreciation leads to a currency loss:

$$= \frac{15,000,000}{1.7} - \frac{15,000,000}{1.5} = -£1,176,471$$

The net profit on the position = £1,176,471 − £1,176,471 − £200,000 = −£200,000

The portfolio value = £10,000,000 − £200,000 = £9,800,000

| Rounded Portfolio Value (in £ Thousand): | | | | | |
|---|---|---|---|---|---|
| Exchange Rate (\$/£) | Unhedged | Hedged | Insured with Call (150) | Insured with Call (155) | Insured with Call (160) |
| 1.3 | 11,538 | 10,000 | 11,338 | 11,438 | 11,505 |
| 1.4 | 10,714 | 10,000 | 10,514 | 10,614 | 10,681 |
| 1.5 | 10,000 | 10,000 | 9,800 | 9,900 | 9,967 |
| 1.6 | 9,375 | 10,000 | 9,800 | 9,577 | 9,342 |
| 1.7 | 8,824 | 10,000 | 9,800 | 9,577 | 9,342 |
| 1.8 | 8,333 | 10,000 | 9,800 | 9,577 | 9,342 |

- Hedging with forward contracts allows the exporter to eliminate the risk of a decline in the dollar. However, it also means that the British exporter will not benefit if the dollar appreciates.

- Options allow the exporter to "insure" rather than "hedge." In other words, a floor is set on the total amount of pounds that the exporter will receive. If the dollar is "strong," the exporter will benefit. However, an insurance has a cost that has to be borne in all cases (i.e., the premium paid to purchase the option).

- An *expensive* option (in-the-money; in this case, the \$1.50 call) provides better protection in the case of a "weak" dollar, but reduces the profit potential in case of a "strong" dollar.

- A *cheap* option (the out-of-the-money \$1.60 call) provides less protection in case of a "weak" dollar, but only slightly reduces the profit potential in case of a "strong" dollar.

The choice between the following five alternatives depends on the expectations and risk aversion of the exporter. We can rank them in decreasing order of protection against a drop in the dollar (e.g., from \$1.50 to \$1.70 per pound), as follows:

   i. Hedge—Portfolio value £10,000,000

   ii. Call 150—Portfolio value £9,800,000

   iii. Call 155—Portfolio value £9,577,000

   iv. Call 160—Portfolio value £9,342,000

   v. No Hedge—Portfolio value £8,824,000

8. Appreciation of a foreign currency will, indeed, increase the dollar returns that accrue to a U.S. investor. However, the amount of the expected appreciation must be compared with the forward premium or discount on that currency in order to determine whether or not hedging should be undertaken.

In the present example, the yen is forecast to appreciate from 100 to 98 (2%). However, the forward premium on the yen, as given by the differential in one-year Eurocurrency rates, suggests an appreciation of over 5%:

Forward premium $= \left[ (1.06)/(1.008) \right] - 1 = 5.16\%$

Or, using interest rate parity, the implied forward rate for the yen is

$$(100)\left[\frac{1.008}{1.06}\right] = ¥95.09/\$$$

Thus, the manager's strategy to leave the yen unhedged is not appropriate. The manager should hedge, because, by doing so, a higher rate of yen appreciation can be locked in. Given the one-year Eurocurrency rate differentials, the yen position should be left unhedged only if the yen is forecast to appreciate to an exchange rate of less than 95.09 yen per U.S. dollar.

| Index | | |
|---|---|---|
| [Open Indices] | | 2011 |
| Seoul | | |
| Taiwan (Comp) | 19,249 | -11.1% |
| Mumbai | 30,124 | |
| Singapore | 18,193.7 | -4.5% |
| Sydney | 2971.0 | -4.7% |
| Shanghai B | 4644.0 | -10.5% |
| Hong Kong | 316.8 | -6.9% |
| Toronto | 22,700.9 | -4.2% |
| Stockholm | 13,524.8 | 4.1% |
| Mexico City | | |

# 15

# Risk Management Applications of Derivatives

This study session addresses risk management strategies using forwards and futures, option strategies, floors and caps, and swaps. Collectively referred to as derivatives, these investment vehicles can be used for a variety of risk management purposes, including modification of portfolio duration and beta, implementation of changes in asset allocation, and creation of cash market instruments. Derivative strategies have proven useful to both investors and borrowers, which accounts for their broad appeal. A growing number of security types now have embedded derivatives, and portfolio managers must be able to account for their effect on the return/risk profile of the security. After completing this study session, the candidate will better understand the advantages and disadvantages of derivative strategies, including the difficulties in creating and maintaining a dynamic hedge.

## READING ASSIGNMENTS

**Reading 36**  ***Risk Management Applications of Forward and Futures Strategies***

*Analysis of Derivatives for the Chartered Financial Analyst®*
*Program*, by Don M. Chance, CFA

**Reading 37**  ***Risk Management Applications of Option Strategies***

*Analysis of Derivatives for the Chartered Financial Analyst®*
*Program*, by Don M. Chance, CFA

**Reading 38**  ***Risk Management Applications of Swap Strategies***

*Analysis of Derivatives for the Chartered Financial Analyst®*
*Program*, by Don M. Chance, CFA

# 36

# Risk Management Applications of Forward and Futures Strategies

*by Don M. Chance, CFA*

## LEARNING OUTCOMES

| Mastery | The candidate should be able to: |
|---------|----------------------------------|
| ☐ | **a** demonstrate the use of equity futures contracts to achieve a target beta for a stock portfolio and calculate and interpret the number of futures contracts required; |
| ☐ | **b** construct a synthetic stock index fund using cash and stock index futures (equitizing cash); |
| ☐ | **c** explain the use of stock index futures to convert a long stock position into synthetic cash; |
| ☐ | **d** demonstrate the use of equity and bond futures to adjust the allocation of a portfolio between equity and debt; |
| ☐ | **e** demonstrate the use of futures to adjust the allocation of a portfolio across equity sectors and to gain exposure to an asset class in advance of actually committing funds to the asset class; |
| ☐ | **f** explain exchange rate risk and demonstrate the use of forward contracts to reduce the risk associated with a future receipt or payment in a foreign currency; |
| ☐ | **g** explain the limitations to hedging the exchange rate risk of a foreign market portfolio and discuss two feasible strategies for managing such risk. |

# INTRODUCTION

**1**

In preceding readings, we examined the characteristics and pricing of forwards, futures, options, and swaps. On occasion, we made reference to possible ways in which these instruments could be used. In the readings that follow, we examine more specifically the strategies and applications that are commonly used with these instruments. Here we focus on forward and futures contracts. These instruments are quite similar. Both involve commitments for one party to buy and the other to sell an underlying instrument at a future date at a price agreed on at the start of the contract. The underlying instrument might be an interest payment, a bond, a stock, or a currency. Forward contracts are customized agreements between two parties: The terms are agreed on

*Analysis of Derivatives for the Chartered Financial Analyst® Program,* by Don M. Chance, CFA. Copyright © 2003 by CFA Institute.

by both parties in a formal legal contract that exists in an environment outside of regulatory constraints. Each party is subject to potential default on the part of the other. Futures contracts, on the other hand, are standardized instruments created on a futures exchange, protected against credit losses by the clearinghouse, and subject to federal regulatory oversight.

In this reading, we examine a number of scenarios in which parties facing risk management problems use forward and futures contracts to alter the risk of their positions. In some situations we use forwards and in others we use futures. For cases in which either would suffice, we pick the instrument that is most commonly used in that type of situation. Although we shall not devote a great deal of space up front to justifying why we picked the instrument we did, we shall provide some discussion of this point in Section 6.

After completing this reading, you may be surprised to observe that we do not cover an important class of derivative strategies, those that are called *arbitrage*. This omission is not because they are not important enough to cover or that they are not risk management strategies; in fact, we have *already* covered them. When we covered the pricing of forwards, futures, options, and swaps, we explained how these instruments are priced by combining the underlying and risk-free bonds to replicate the derivative or by combining a long position in the underlying and a short position in the derivative to replicate a risk-free position. From there we obtained a formula that gives us the correct price of the derivative. An arbitrage profit is possible if the derivative is not priced according to the formula. We have already looked at how those strategies are executed. We should not expect to encounter arbitrage opportunities very often in practice. They are quickly captured by derivatives trading firms, which themselves cannot expect to be able to *consistently* claim such opportunities before they disappear.[1]

Businesses make products and provide services as they attempt to increase shareholder wealth. In doing so, they face a variety of risks. Managing risk lies at the heart of what companies do. All companies specialize in managing the risk of whatever market their primary business is in: Airlines deal with the risk associated with the demand for air travel, software companies deal with the risk associated with the demand for new computer programs, movie companies deal with the risk associated with the demand for their films. But these companies also deal with other risks, such as the risk of interest rates and exchange rates. Usually these companies take calculated risks in their primary lines of business and avoid risks they do not feel qualified to take, such as interest rate risk and exchange rate risk. Naturally this approach involves a practice called **hedging**.

Hedging involves taking a market position to protect against an undesirable outcome. Suppose a company has a strong belief that interest rates will increase. It engages in a forward rate agreement (FRA) transaction to lock in the rate on a loan it will take out at a later date. This position protects the company from the undesirable outcome of an increase in interest rates, but it also prevents the company from enjoying any decline in rates. In that sense, the position is as much a speculative position as if a speculator had made the following prediction: *We believe that interest rates will rise to an unacceptable level, and we intend to trade on that basis to make money.* By engaging in the FRA to hedge this outcome, the company trades to make a profit from its FRA that will help offset any increase in the interest rate on its future loan. But by locking in a rate, it forgoes the possibility of benefiting from a decline in interest

---

**1** Suppose market participants assume that arbitrage opportunities are so infrequent and difficult to capture before they are gone that no one monitors market prices looking for arbitrage opportunities. Then these arbitrage opportunities will begin to occur more frequently. A market in which arbitrage opportunities are rare, and therefore prices are fair and accurate, is ironically a market in which participants believe they can indeed uncover and exploit arbitrage opportunities. Thus, an arbitrage-free market requires disbelievers.

rates. The company has made a bet that rates will rise. If they fall, the company has lost the bet and lost money on its FRA that offsets the benefit of the lower interest rate on this loan planned for a later date.

In this reading we shall not overindulge in the use of the term hedging. We shall say that companies do more than hedge: *They manage risk.* They carefully consider scenarios and elect to adjust the risk they face to a level they feel is acceptable. In many cases, this adjustment will involve the reduction of risk; in some cases, however, the scenario will justify increasing the company's risk. In all cases, the company is just altering the risk from its current level to the level the company desires. And that is what managing risk is all about.

This reading is divided into five main parts. Sections 2 and 3 focus on the management of interest rate and equity market risk, respectively. Section 4 combines interest rate and equity risk management applications by looking at how investors can manage an asset portfolio using futures. Section 5 looks at the management of foreign currency risk. In Section 6 we examine the general question of whether to use forwards or futures to manage risk, and in Section 7 we look at a few final issues.

# STRATEGIES AND APPLICATIONS FOR MANAGING INTEREST RATE RISK

**2**

OPTIONAL SEGMENT

Almost every business borrows money from time to time. A company borrowing at a fixed rate may think it is immune to interest rate risk, but that is not the case. Risk arises from the possibility that interest rates can increase from the time the company decides to take the loan to the time it actually takes the loan. Most companies make plans to borrow based on their cash needs at specific future dates. The rates they pay on these loans are important determinants of their future cash needs, as reflected in their planned interest payments. Exposure to interest rate risk is, therefore, a major concern. Failing to manage interest rate risk can hinder the planning process, as well as result in unexpected demands on cash necessitated by unexpectedly higher interest payments.

## 2.1 Managing the Interest Rate Risk of a Loan Using an FRA

There are several situations in which a company might want to manage the interest rate risk of a loan. The two we look at here involve a company planning to take out a loan at a later date. In one situation, the loan has a single interest rate and a single interest payment. In another situation, a company takes out a floating-rate loan in which the interest rate is reset periodically.

### 2.1.1 *Single-Payment Loan*

Exhibit 1 presents the case of Global BioTechnology (GBT), which determines that it will need to borrow money at a later date at a rate of LIBOR plus 200 basis points. Fearing an increase in interest rates between now and the day it takes out the loan, it enters into a long position in an FRA. The FRA has a fixed rate, called the FRA rate. If the underlying rate at expiration is above the FRA rate, GBT as the holder of the long position will receive a lump sum of cash based on the difference between the FRA rate and the market rate at that time. This payment will help offset the higher rate GBT would be paying on its loan. If the rate in the market falls below the FRA rate, however, GBT will end up paying the counterparty, which will offset the lower rate GBT will be paying on its loan. The end result is that GBT will pay approximately a fixed rate, the FRA rate.

| Exhibit 1 | Using an FRA to Lock in the Rate on a Loan |
|-----------|---------------------------------------------|

## Scenario (15 April)

Global BioTechnology (GBT) is a U.S. corporation that occasionally undertakes short-term borrowings in U.S. dollars with the rate tied to LIBOR. To facilitate its cash flow planning, it uses an FRA to lock in the rate on such loans as soon as it determines that it will need the money.

On 15 April, GBT determines that it will borrow $40 million on 20 August. The loan will be repaid 180 days later on 16 February, and the rate will be at LIBOR plus 200 basis points. Because GBT believes that interest rates will increase, it decides to manage this risk by going long an FRA. An FRA will enable it to receive the difference between LIBOR on 20 August and the FRA rate quoted by the dealer on 15 April. The quoted rate from the dealer is 5.25 percent. GBT wants to lock in a 7.25 percent rate: 5.25 percent plus 200 basis points.

## Action

GBT confirms that it will borrow $40 million at LIBOR plus 200 basis points on 20 August. GBT goes long an FRA at a rate of 5.25 percent to expire on 20 August with the underlying being 180-day LIBOR.

## Scenario (20 August)

At contract expiration, 180-day LIBOR is 6 percent.

## Outcome and Analysis

The FRA payoff is given by the general formula:

$$\text{Notional principal} \times$$

$$\left[ \frac{\left( \begin{array}{c} \text{Underlying rate} \\ \text{at expiration} \end{array} - \text{Forward contract rate} \right) \left( \dfrac{\text{Days in underlying rate}}{360} \right)}{1 + \text{Underlying rate} \left( \dfrac{\text{Days in underlying rate}}{360} \right)} \right]$$

$$\text{or } \$40{,}000{,}000 \times \left[ \frac{(0.06 - 0.0525)(180/360)}{1 + 0.06(180/360)} \right] = \$145{,}631$$

GBT receives this amount in cash. Therefore, to obtain $40 million in cash, it has to borrow $40,000,000 − $145,631 = $39,854,369 at LIBOR plus 200 basis points, 0.06 + 0.02 = 0.08, or 8 percent.

On 16 February GBT pays back $39,854,369[1 + 0.08(180/360)] = $41,448,544. So, it effectively pays a rate of

$$\left( \frac{\$41{,}448{,}544}{\$40{,}000{,}000} - 1 \right) \left( \frac{360}{180} \right) = 0.0724$$

The net effect is that GBT receives $40 million on 20 August and pays back $41,448,544 on 16 February, a rate of 7.24 percent. This rate was effectively locked in on 15 April at the FRA rate of 5.25 percent plus the 200 basis points GBT pays over LIBOR.

Shown below are the results for possible LIBORs on 20 August of 2 percent, 4 percent, ..., 10 percent.

| | | | LIBOR + | Amount | |
|---|---|---|---|---|---|
| LIBOR on 20 August | FRA Payoff | Amount Borrowed | 200 bps Loan Rate | Repaid on 16 February | Effective Loan Rate |
| 0.02 | −$643,564 | $40,643,564 | 0.04 | $41,456,435 | 0.0728 |
| 0.04 | −245,098 | 40,245,098 | 0.06 | 41,452,451 | 0.0726 |
| 0.06 | 145,631 | 39,854,369 | 0.08 | 41,448,544 | 0.0724 |
| 0.08 | 528,846 | 39,471,154 | 0.10 | 41,444,712 | 0.0722 |
| 0.10 | 904,762 | 39,095,238 | 0.12 | 41,440,952 | 0.0720 |

**Exhibit 1 Continued**

In this problem, the FRA rate is 5.25 percent. In the exhibit, we described an outcome in which the underlying rate, 180-day LIBOR, is 6 percent. GBT ends up paying 6% + 2% = 8% on the loan, but the FRA pays off an amount sufficient to reduce the effective rate to 7.24 percent. Note the table at the end of the exhibit showing other possible outcomes. In all cases, the rate GBT pays is approximately the FRA rate of 5.25 percent plus 200 basis points. This rate is not precisely 7.25 percent, however, because of the way in which the FRA is constructed to pay off at expiration. When LIBOR on 20 August is above 5.25 percent, the FRA payoff on that day reduces the amount that has to be borrowed at LIBOR plus 200 basis points. This reduction works to the advantage of GBT. Conversely, when rates are below 5.25 percent, the amount that must be borrowed increases but that amount is borrowed at a lower rate. Thus, there is a slight asymmetric effect of a few basis points that prevents the effective loan rate from precisely equaling 7.25 percent.

In a similar manner, a lender could lock in a rate on a loan it plans to make by going short an FRA. Lenders are less inclined to do such transactions, however, because they cannot anticipate the exact future borrowing needs of their customers. In some cases, banks that offer credit lines at floating rates might wish to lock in lending rates using FRAs. But because the choice of whether to borrow is the borrower's and not the lender's, a lender that uses an FRA is taking considerable risk that the loan will not even be made. In that case, the lender would do better to use an option so that, in the worst case, it loses only the option premium.

## Example 1

ABTech plans to borrow $10 million in 30 days at 90-day LIBOR plus 100 basis points. To lock in a borrowing rate of 7 percent, it purchases an FRA at a rate of 6 percent. This contract would be referred to as a 1 × 4 FRA because it expires in one month (30 days) and the underlying Eurodollar matures four months (120 days) from now. Thirty days later, LIBOR is 7.5 percent. Demonstrate that ABTech's effective borrowing rate is 7 percent if LIBOR in 30 days is 7.5 percent.

### Solution:

If LIBOR is 7.5 percent at the expiration of the FRA in 30 days, the payoff of the FRA is

$$\text{Notional principal} \times$$

$$\left[ \frac{\left( \begin{array}{c} \text{Underlying rate} \\ \text{at expiration} \end{array} - \text{Forward contract rate} \right)\left( \dfrac{\text{Days in underlying rate}}{360} \right)}{1 + \text{Underlying rate}\left( \dfrac{\text{Days in underlying rate}}{360} \right)} \right]$$

which is

$$\$10,000,000 \times \left[ \frac{(0.075 - 0.06)(90/360)}{1 + 0.075(90/360)} \right] = \$36,810$$

Because this amount is a cash inflow, ABTech will not need to borrow a full $10,000,000. Instead, it will borrow $10,000,000 − $36,810 = $9,963,190.

The amount it will pay back in 90 days is

$$\$9,963,190\left[ 1 + (0.075 + 0.01)(90/360) \right] = \$10,174,908$$

The effective rate is, therefore,

$$\left( \frac{\$10,174,908}{\$10,000,000} - 1 \right)\left( \frac{360}{90} \right) \approx 0.07$$

ABTech borrows at LIBOR plus 100 basis points. Therefore, using an FRA, it should be able to lock in the FRA rate (6 percent) plus 100 basis points, which it does.

### 2.1.2 Floating-Rate Loan

In the example above, the loan involved only a single payment and, therefore, we had only one setting of an interest rate to worry about. Many loans are floating-rate loans, meaning that their rates are reset several times during the life of the loan. This resetting of the rate poses a series of risks for the borrower.

Suppose a corporation is taking out a two-year loan. The rate for the initial six months is set today. The rate will be reset in 6, 12, and 18 months. Because the current rate is already in place, there is nothing the corporation can do to mitigate that risk.[2] It faces, however, the risk of rising interest rates over the remaining life of the loan, which would result in higher interest payments.

One way to control this risk is to enter into a series of FRA transactions with each component FRA tailored to expire on a date on which the rate will be reset. This strategy will not lock in the *same* fixed rate for each semiannual period, but different rates for each period will be locked in. Another alternative would be to use futures. For example, for a LIBOR-based loan, the Eurodollar futures contract would be appropriate. Nonetheless, the use of futures to manage this risk poses significant problems. One problem is that the Eurodollar futures contract has expirations only on specific days during the year. The Chicago Mercantile Exchange offers contract expirations on the current month, the next month, and a sequence of months following the pattern of March, June, September, and December. Thus, it is quite likely that no contracts would exist with expirations that align with the later payment reset dates. The Eurodollar futures contract expires on the second London business day before

---

2  If a corporation were planning to take out a floating-rate loan at a later date, it would also be concerned about the first interest rate and might attempt to lock in that rate. In the example used here, we placed the company in a situation in which it already knows its initial rate and, therefore, is worried only about the remaining rate resets.

the third Wednesday of the month. This date might not be the exact day of the month on which the rate is reset. In addition, the Eurodollar futures contract is based only on the 90-day Eurodollar rate, whereas the loan rate is pegged to the 180-day rate. Although many dealer firms use the Eurodollar futures contract to manage the risk associated with their over-the-counter derivatives, they do so using sophisticated techniques that measure and balance the volatility of the futures contract to the volatility of their market positions. Moreover, they adjust their positions rapidly in response to market movements. Without that capability, borrowers who simply need to align their interest rate reset dates with the dates on which their derivatives expire can do so more easily with swaps. We cover how this is done in the reading on risk management. Nevertheless, an understanding of how FRAs are used will help with an understanding of this application of swaps.

## 2.2 Strategies and Applications for Managing Bond Portfolio Risk

In Section 2.1, we dealt with the risk associated with short-term borrowing interest rates, which obviously affects short-term borrowers and lenders. The risk associated with longer-term loans primarily takes the form of bond market risk. Here we shall take a look at a firm managing a government bond portfolio, that is, a lending position. The firm can manage the risk associated with interest rates by using futures on government bonds. In the next three sections, we explore how to measure the risk of a bond portfolio, measure the risk of bond futures, and balance those risks.

### 2.2.1 *Measuring the Risk of a Bond Portfolio*

The sensitivity of a bond to a general change in interest rates is usually captured by assuming that the bond price changes in response to a change in its yield, which is driven by the general level of rates. The responsiveness of a bond price to a yield change is captured in two ways: duration and basis point value.[3]

**Duration** is a measure of the size and timing of the cash flows paid by a bond. It quantifies these factors by summarizing them in the form of a single number, which is interpreted as an average maturity of the bond. To speak in terms of an average maturity of a bond of a given specific maturity sounds somewhat strange, but remember that a coupon bond is really just a combination of zero-coupon bonds.[4] The average maturity of these component zero-coupon bonds is the duration. The average is not an ordinary average but a weighted average, with the weights based on the present values of the respective cash payments on the bonds. Hence, the weights are not equal, and the large principal repayment places the greatest emphasis on the final payment.

Suppose the bond price is B, the yield is $y_B$, and Macaulay duration is $DUR_B$. Then the relationship between the change in the bond price and its yield is given as

$$\Delta B \approx -DUR_B B \frac{\Delta y_B}{1 + y_B}$$

---

**3** Readers may first wish to review some fixed-income securities material. See especially Chapter 7 of *Fixed Income Analysis for the Chartered Financial Analyst Program*, Frank J. Fabozzi (Frank J. Fabozzi Associates, 2000).

**4** This analogy comes about because the coupons and final principal on a bond can be viewed as zero-coupon bonds, each maturing on the date on which a coupon or the final principal is paid. The value of a coupon or the final principal is analogous to the face value of a zero-coupon bond. In the U.S. Treasury bond market, companies buy coupon bonds and sell claims on the individual coupons and principal, which are referred to as Treasury strips.

where the Greek symbol $\Delta$ indicates "change in" and where the overall relationship is shown as an approximation ($\approx$). For this relationship to be exact requires that the yield change be very small.[5] The left-hand side, $\Delta B$, is the change in the bond price. The negative sign on the right-hand side is consistent with the inverse relationship between the bond price and its yield.[6]

A somewhat simplified version of the above equation is

$$\Delta B \approx -MDUR_B B \Delta y_B$$

where $MDUR_B = DUR_B/(1 + y_B)$. $MDUR_B$ is called the **modified duration** and is just an adjustment of the duration for the level of the yield. We shall use the relationship as captured by the modified duration.[7]

As an example, suppose the bond price is \$922.50, modified duration is 5.47 years, and the yield increases by 15 basis points. Then the price change should be approximately

$$\Delta B \approx -5.47(\$922.50)(0.0015) = -\$7.57$$

In response to a 15 basis point increase in yield, the bond price should decrease by approximately \$7.57. So the new bond price would be predicted to be \$922.50 − \$7.57 = \$914.93.

The relationship between the bond price and its yield is sometimes stated another way. We often speak in terms of the change in the bond price for a 1 basis point change in yield. This value is sometimes referred to as **basis point value (BPV)**, **present value of a basis point (PVBP)**, or **price value of a basis point** (again PVBP). We refer to this concept as PVBP, defined as

$$PVBP_B \approx MDUR_B B(0.0001)$$

The multiplication by 0.0001 enables PVBP to capture how much the bond price changes for a 1 basis point change. In the example above, the PVBP for our bond is

$$PVBP_B \approx (5.47)(\$922.50)(0.0001) = \$0.5046$$

So for a 1 basis point change, the bond price would change by approximately \$0.5046. Accordingly, a 15 basis point change produces a price change of 15(\$0.5046) = \$7.57. Both duration and PVBP measure the same thing, however, and we shall use only duration.

Duration and PVBP are usually thought of with respect to individual bonds, but in practice, they are typically used at the portfolio level. Hence, we should care more about the duration of a bond portfolio than about the duration of an individual bond. With respect to yield, we do not usually speak in terms of the yield of a bond portfolio, but in this case we must. A given bond portfolio can be thought of as a series of cash flows that can be captured in terms of a representative bond. Thus, we might describe this bond as a bond portfolio with a market value of \$922.5 million, a modified duration of 5.47 years, and a portfolio yield that is a complex weighted average of the yields on the component bonds of the portfolio. The portfolio yield can change by a certain number of basis points. That yield change is a weighted average of the yield changes on the component bonds. Given such a yield change, the bond

---

**5** If the yield change is not sufficiently small, it may be necessary to incorporate second-order effects, which are captured by a bond's convexity.

**6** The above relationship is based on annual coupons. If the coupons are paid semiannually, then $1 + y_B$ should be $1 + y_B/2$. In this case, the duration will be stated as the number of semiannual, rather than annual, periods.

**7** The duration before dividing by $1 + y_B$ is sometimes called the **Macaulay duration**, to distinguish it from the modified duration. It is named for Frederick Macaulay, one of the economists who first derived it.

portfolio value will change in an approximate manner according to the duration formula shown above.

The way a bond price changes according to a yield change indicates its responsiveness to interest rates. Given a bond futures contract, we can also measure its sensitivity to interest rate changes.

### 2.2.2 *Measuring the Risk of Bond Futures*

Having measured the responsiveness of a bond portfolio to an interest rate change, we now need to measure the responsiveness of a futures contract to an interest rate change. Most bond futures contracts are based on a hypothetical benchmark bond. The Chicago Board of Trade's U.S. Treasury bond futures contract is based on a 6 percent bond with at least 15 years from the futures expiration to maturity or the first call date. Even though the benchmark bond has a 6 percent coupon, any bond meeting the maturity requirement can be delivered. At any time, a single bond exists that the holder of the short position would find optimal to deliver if current conditions continued. That bond is called the **cheapest to deliver** and can be thought of as the bond on which the futures contract is based. In other words, the cheapest to deliver bond is the underlying. The responsiveness of the futures contract to an interest rate change is equivalent to the responsiveness of that bond on the futures expiration day to an interest rate change.

We can think of this concept as the responsiveness of the underlying bond in a forward context. This responsiveness can be measured as that bond's modified duration on the futures expiration and, as such, we can use the price sensitivity formula to capture the sensitivity of the futures contract to a yield change. Accordingly, we shall, somewhat loosely, refer to this as the implied duration of the futures contract, keeping in mind that what we mean is the duration of the underlying bond calculated as of the futures expiration. Moreover, we also mean that the underlying bond has been identified as the cheapest bond to deliver and that if another bond takes its place, the duration of that bond must be used. We use the term *implied* to emphasize that a futures contract does not itself have a duration but that its duration is implied by the underlying bond. In addition to the duration, we also require an **implied yield** on the futures, which reflects the yield on the underlying bond implied by pricing it as though it were delivered at the futures contract expiration.

Hence, we can express the sensitivity of the futures price to a yield change as

$$\Delta f \approx -MDUR_f f \, \Delta y_f \tag{1}$$

where $MDUR_f$ is the implied modified duration of the futures, f is the futures price, and $\Delta y_f$ is the basis point change in the implied yield on the futures.

Now that we have a measure of the responsiveness of a bond portfolio and the responsiveness of a bond futures contract to interest rate changes, we should be able to find a way to balance the two to offset the risk.

### 2.2.3 *Balancing the Risk of a Bond Portfolio against the Risk of Bond Futures*

We now make the simple assumption that a single interest rate exists that drives all interest rates in the market. We assume that a 1 basis point change in this interest rate will cause a 1 basis point change in the yield on the bond portfolio and a 1 basis point change in the implied yield on the futures. We will relax that assumption later. For now, consider a money manager who holds a bond portfolio of a particular market value and will not be adding to it or removing some of it to balance the risk. In other words, the manager will not make any transactions in the actual bonds themselves. The manager can, however, trade any number of futures contracts to adjust the risk. Let $N_f$ be the number of futures contracts traded. To balance the risk, suppose we combine the change in the value of the bond portfolio and the change in the value of $N_f$ futures and set these equal to zero: $\Delta B + N_f \Delta f = 0$. Solving for $N_f$ produces $N_f = -\Delta B / \Delta f$. Substituting our formulas for $\Delta B$ and $\Delta f$, we obtain

$$N_f = -\left(\frac{MDUR_B}{MDUR_f}\right)\left(\frac{B}{f}\right)\left(\frac{\Delta y_B}{\Delta y_f}\right) = -\left(\frac{MDUR_B}{MDUR_f}\right)\left(\frac{B}{f}\right)$$

where we assume that $\Delta y_B / \Delta y_f = 1$; or in other words, the bond portfolio yield changes one-for-one with the implied yield on the futures.[8]

Now let us go back to the major simplifying assumption we made. We assumed that an interest rate change occurs in the market and drives the yield on the bond and the implied yield on the futures one-for-one. In reality, this assumption is unlikely to hold true. Suppose, for example, the rate driving all rates in the United States is the overnight Fed funds rate.[9] If this rate changes by 1 basis point, not all rates along the term structure are likely to change by 1 basis point. What actually matters, however, is not that all rates change by the same amount but that the yield on the bond portfolio and the implied yield on the futures change by the same amount for a 1 basis point change in this rate. If that is not the case, we need to make an adjustment.

Suppose the yield on the bond portfolio changes by a multiple of the implied yield on the futures in the following manner:

$$\Delta y_B = \beta_y \Delta y_f \tag{2}$$

We refer to the symbol $\beta_y$ as the **yield beta**. It can be more or less than 1, depending on whether the bond yield is more sensitive or less sensitive than the implied futures yield. If we take the formula we previously obtained for $\Delta B$, substitute $\beta_y \Delta y_f$ where we previously had $\Delta y_B$, and use this new variation of the formula in the formula $N_f = -\Delta B / \Delta f$, we obtain

$$N_f = -\left(MDUR_B / MDUR_f\right)\left(B/f\right)\beta_y \tag{3}$$

This is the more general formula, because $\beta_y = 1.0$ is just the special case we assumed at the start.

We can modify Equation 3 so that it gives us the number of futures contracts needed to change our portfolio's modified duration to meet a target. What we have done so far *completely* balances the risk of the futures position against the risk of the bond portfolio, eliminating the risk. In the practice of risk management, however, we might not always want to eliminate the risk; we might want to adjust it only a little. At some times we might even want to increase it.

The risk of the overall bond portfolio reflects the duration of the bonds and the duration of the futures. Suppose we consider a target overall modified duration of the portfolio, $MDUR_T$. This amount is our desired overall modified duration. Because the portfolio consists of bonds worth B and futures, which have zero value, the overall portfolio value is B.[10] Now we introduce the notion of a dollar duration, which is the duration times the market value. The target dollar duration of our portfolio is set equal to the dollar duration of the bonds we hold and the dollar duration of the futures contracts:

---

**8** Technically, this equation is the ratio of two approximate formulas, but we remove the approximation symbol from this point onward.

**9** The overnight Fed funds rate is the rate that banks charge each other to borrow and lend excess reserves for one night.

**10** Recall that futures contracts have value through the accumulation of price changes during a trading day. At the end of the day, all gains and losses are paid out through the marking-to-market process and the value then goes back to zero. We assume we are at one of those points at which the value is zero.

$$B(MDUR_T) = B(MDUR_B) + f(MDUR_f)N_f$$

Solving for $N_f$, we obtain

$$N_f = \left(\frac{MDUR_T - MDUR_B}{MDUR_f}\right)\left(\frac{B}{f}\right)$$

Observe that if we wish to increase the modified duration from $MDUR_B$ to something higher, then $MDUR_T$ is greater than $MDUR_B$ and the overall sign of $N_f$ will be positive, so we buy futures. This relationship should make sense: Buying futures would add volatility and increase duration. If we wish to reduce the modified duration from $MDUR_B$ to something lower, then $MDUR_T$ will be less than $MDUR_B$ and the sign of $N_f$ will be negative, meaning that we need to sell futures. Selling futures would reduce duration and volatility. In the extreme case in which we want to eliminate risk completely, we want $MDUR_T$ to equal zero. In that case, the above formula reduces to the original one we obtained earlier in this section for the case of completely eliminating risk. In a similar manner, if the bond and futures yields do not change one-for-one, we simply alter the above formula to

$$N_f = \left(\frac{MDUR_T - MDUR_B}{MDUR_f}\right)\left(\frac{B}{f}\right)\beta_y \qquad \textbf{(4)}$$

to incorporate the yield beta.

Now we explore how to use what we have learned in this section.

### 2.2.4  *Managing the Risk of a Government Bond Portfolio*

A money manager can use Equation 4 to determine the number of futures contracts to buy or sell to adjust the duration of a portfolio. Such a transaction might be done in anticipation of a strong or weak market in bonds over a temporary period of time. In Exhibit 2, we illustrate the case of a pension fund that wants to increase the portfolio duration. We see that the futures transaction was successful in increasing the duration but not as precisely as planned. In fact, even without doing the futures transaction, the portfolio duration was not exactly as the company had believed. Duration is not an exact measure, nor does the bond price change occur precisely according to the duration formula.[11]

| **Exhibit 2** | **Using Bond Futures to Manage the Risk of a Bond Portfolio** |

## Scenario (7 July)

A portion of the pension fund of United Energy Services (UES) is a portfolio of U.S. government bonds. On 7 July, UES obtained a forecast from its economist that over the next month, interest rates are likely to make a significant unexpected decline. Its portfolio manager would like to take a portion of the bond portfolio and increase the duration to take advantage of this forecasted market movement.

Specifically, UES would like to raise the duration on $75 million of bonds from its current level of 6.22 to 7.50. Both of these durations and all durations used in this problem are modified durations. UES has identified an appropriate Treasury bond futures contract that is currently priced at $82,500 and has an

*(continued)*

---

**11** For this reason, we stated that the bond price change, given the duration and yield change, is *approximately* given by the formula in the text.

| Exhibit 2 | Continued |
| --- | --- |

implied modified duration of 8.12. UES has estimated that the yield on the bond portfolio is about 5 percent more volatile than the implied yield on the futures. Thus, the yield beta is 1.05.

## Action

To increase the duration, UES will need to buy futures contracts. Specifically, the number of futures contracts UES should use is

$$N_f = \left( \frac{MDUR_T - MDUR_B}{MDUR_f} \right) \left( \frac{B}{f} \right) \beta_y$$

$$= \left( \frac{7.50 - 6.22}{8.12} \right) \left( \frac{\$75,000,000}{\$82,500} \right) 1.05 = 150.47$$

Because fractional contracts cannot be traded, UES will buy 150 contracts.

## Scenario (6 August)

The implied yield on the futures has decreased by 35 basis points, and the futures price has now moved to $85,000.[12] The yield on the bond portfolio has decreased by 40 basis points, and the portfolio has increased in value by $1,933,500.

## Outcome and Analysis

The profit on the futures transaction is found by multiplying the number of futures contracts by the difference between the new price and the old price:

$$\text{Profit on futures contract} = N_f \left( \text{New futures price} - \text{Old futures price} \right)$$

In this case, the profit on the futures contract is 150($85,000 − $82,500) = $375,000. Thus, the overall gain is $1,933,500 + $375,000 = $2,308,500.

How effective was the transaction? To answer this question, we compare the *ex post* duration to the planned duration. The purpose was to increase the duration from 6.22 to a planned 7.50. The return on the portfolio was

$$\frac{\$1,933,500}{\$75,000,000} = 0.0258$$

or 2.58 percent without the futures transaction, and

$$\frac{\$2,308,500}{\$75,000,000} = 0.0308$$

or 3.08 percent with the futures transaction. What does this set of calculations imply about the portfolio's *ex post* duration? Recall that duration is a measure of the percentage change in portfolio value with respect to a basis point change in yield. The *ex post* duration[13] of the portfolio can be measured by dividing the percentage change in portfolio value by the 40 basis point change in the portfolio yield:

$$\frac{0.0258}{0.0040} = 6.45$$

---

**12** In the examples in this reading, bond futures prices move to a new level in the course of the scenario. These new futures prices come from the cost-of-carry model (assuming there is no mispricing in the market).
**13** Of course, the *ex post* duration without the futures transaction is not exactly 6.22 because duration is an inexact measure, and the actual bond price change may not be precisely what is given by the modified duration formula.

| Exhibit 2 | *Continued* |

without the futures transaction and

$$\frac{0.0308}{0.0040} = 7.70$$

with the futures transaction. UES came fairly close to achieving its desired increase in duration using futures.

In the example here, the fund increased its modified duration during a time when interest rates fell and the bond portfolio value increased. It leveraged itself to take advantage of a favorable outlook. Not all such decisions work out so well. Suppose in this example the economist had a different forecast, and as a result, UES wanted to eliminate all interest rate risk. So let us rework the problem under the assumption that the fund put on a full hedge, thereby reducing the modified duration to zero.

With $MDUR_T = 0$, the number of futures contracts would be

$$N_f = \left(\frac{0 - 6.22}{8.12}\right)\left(\frac{\$75,000,000}{\$82,500}\right)1.05 = -731.19$$

Thus, the fund would sell 731 contracts. The profit from the futures transaction[14] would be $-731(\$85,000 - \$82,500) = -\$1,827,500$. The overall transaction earned a profit of $\$1,933,500 - \$1,827,500 = \$106,000$, a gain of

$$\frac{\$106,000}{\$75,000,000} = 0.0014$$

or 0.14 percent. Thus, shorting the futures contracts virtually wiped out all of the gain from the decrease in interest rates. Our *ex ante* objective was to reduce the modified duration to zero. The *ex post* modified duration, however, turned out to be

$$\frac{0.0014}{0.0040} = 0.35$$

Thus, the modified duration was reduced almost to zero.

### Example 2

Debt Management Associates (DMA) offers fixed-income portfolio management services to institutional investors. It would like to execute a duration-changing strategy for a €100 million bond portfolio of a particular client. This portfolio has a modified duration of 7.2. DMA plans to change the modified duration to 5.00 by using a futures contract priced at €120,000, which has an implied modified duration of 6.25. The yield beta is 1.15.

**A.** Determine how many futures contracts DMA should use and whether it should buy or sell futures.

**B.** Suppose that the yield on the bond has decreased by 20 basis points at the horizon date. The bond portfolio increases in value by 1.5 percent. The futures price increases to €121,200. Determine the overall gain on the portfolio and the *ex post* modified duration as a result of the futures transaction.

---

**14** Notice that in calculating the profit from a futures transaction, we multiply the number of futures contracts by the futures price at the close of the strategy minus the original futures price. It is important to maintain the correct sign for the number of futures contracts. This formulation always results in a positive number for $N_f$ times the futures selling price and a negative number for $N_f$ times the futures buying price, which should make sense. Of course, as previously noted, we also ignore the marking-to-market feature of futures contracts.

### Solution to A:

The appropriate number of futures contracts is

$$N_f = \left(\frac{5-7.2}{6.25}\right)\left(\frac{100,000,000}{120.000}\right)1.15 = -337.33$$

So DMA should sell 337 contracts.

### Solution to B:

The value of the bond portfolio will be €100,000,000(1.015) = €101,500,000. The profit on the futures transaction is −337(€121,200 − 120,000) = −€404,400; a loss of €404,400. Thus, the overall value of the position is €101,500,000 − €404,400 = €101,095,600, a return of approximately 1.1 percent. The bond yield decreases by 20 basis points and the portfolio gains 1.1 percent. The *ex post* modified duration would be 0.0110/0.0020 = 5.50.

Changing the duration—whether increasing it, reducing it partially, or reducing it all the way to zero—is an inexact process. More importantly, however, risk management by adjusting duration is only a means of implementing a strategy in response to an outlook. No one can guarantee that the outlook will not be wrong.

### 2.2.5  *Some Variations and Problems in Managing Bond Portfolio Risk*

In the examples used here, the bond portfolio consisted of government bonds. Of course, corporate and municipal bonds are widely held in bond portfolios. Unfortunately, there is no corporate bond futures contract.[15] A municipal bond futures contract exists in the United States, based on an index of municipal bonds, but its volume is relatively light and the contract may not be sufficiently liquid for a large-size transaction.[16] Government bond futures contracts tend to be relatively liquid. In fact, in the United States, different contracts exist for government securities of different maturity ranges, and most of these contracts are relatively liquid.

If one uses a government bond futures to manage the risk of a corporate or municipal bond portfolio, there are some additional risks to deal with. For instance, the relationship between the yield change that drives the futures contract and the yield change that drives the bond portfolio is not as reliable. The yield on a corporate or municipal bond is driven not only by interest rates but also by the perceived default risk of the bond. We might believe that the yield beta is 1.20, meaning that the yield on a corporate bond portfolio is about 20 percent more volatile than the implied yield that drives the futures contract. But this relationship is usually estimated from a regression of corporate bond yield changes on government bond yield changes. This relationship is less stable than if we were running a regression of government bond yield changes on yield changes of a different government bond, the one underlying the futures.

In addition, corporate and municipal bonds often have call features that can greatly distort the relationship between duration and yield change and also make the measurement of duration more complicated. For example, when a bond's yield decreases, its price should increase. The duration is meant to show approximately how much the bond's price should increase. But when the bond is callable and the yield enters into

---

**15** There have been attempts to create futures contracts on corporate bonds, but these contracts have not been successful in generating enough trading volume to survive.
**16** In the Commodity Futures Trading Commission's fiscal year 2001, the Chicago Board of Trade's municipçal bond futures contract traded about 1,400 contracts a day. Each contract is worth about $100,000 of municipal bonds. Thus, the average daily volume amounts to about $140 million of municipal bonds—not a very large amount relative to the size of the municipal bond market.

the region in which a call becomes more likely, its price will increase by far less than predicted by the duration. Moreover, the call feature complicates the measurement of duration itself. Duration is no longer a weighted-average maturity of the bond.

Finally, we should note that corporate and municipal bonds are subject to default risk that is not present in government bonds. As the risk of default changes, the yield spread on the defaultable bond relative to the default-free government bond increases. This effect further destabilizes the relationship between the bond portfolio value and the futures price so that duration-based formulas for the number of futures contracts tend to be unreliable.

It is tempting to think that if one wants to increase (decrease) duration and buys (sells) futures contracts, that at least the transaction was the right type even if the number of futures contracts is not exactly correct. The problem, however, is that changes in the bond portfolio value that are driven by changes in default risk or the effects of call provisions will not be matched by movements in the futures contract. The outcome will not always be what is expected.

Another problem associated with the modified duration approach to measuring and managing bond portfolio risk is that the relationship between duration and yield change used here is an instantaneous one. It captures *approximately* how a bond price changes in response to an immediate and very small yield change. As soon as the yield changes or an instant of time passes, the duration changes. Then the number of futures contracts required would change. Thus, the positions described here would need to be revised. Most bond portfolio managers do not perform these kinds of frequent adjustments, however, and simply accept that the transaction will not work precisely as planned.

We should also consider the alternative that the fund could adjust the duration by making transactions in the bonds themselves. It could sell relatively low-duration bonds and buy relatively high-duration bonds to raise the duration to the desired level. There is still no guarantee, however, that the actual duration will be exactly as desired. Likewise, to reduce the duration to zero, the fund could sell out the entire bond portfolio and place the proceeds in cash securities that have low duration. Reducing the duration to essentially zero would be easier to do than increasing it, because it would not be hard to buy bonds with essentially zero duration. Liquidating the entire portfolio, however, would be quite a drastic thing to do, especially given that the fund would likely remain in that position for only a temporary period.

Raising the duration by purchasing higher-duration bonds would be a great deal of effort to expend if the position is being altered only temporarily. Moreover, the transaction costs of buying and selling actual securities are much greater than those of buying and selling futures.

In this reading, we shall consider these adjustments as advanced refinements that one should understand before putting these types of transactions into practice. Although we need to be aware of these technical complications, we shall ignore them in the examples here.

END OPTIONAL SEGMENT

Now let us take a look at managing risk in the equity market.

# STRATEGIES AND APPLICATIONS FOR MANAGING EQUITY MARKET RISK    3

Even though interest rates are volatile, the stock market is even more volatile. Hence, the risk associated with stock market volatility is greater than that of bond market volatility. Fortunately, the stock market is generally more liquid than the bond market, at least compared with long-term and corporate and municipal bonds. The risk associated with stock market volatility can be managed relatively well with futures contracts. As we have previously noted, these contracts are based on stock market indices and not individual stocks. Although futures on individual stocks are available, most diversified investors manage risk at the portfolio level, thereby preferring futures on broad-based indices. Accordingly, this will be our focus in this reading. We look more specifically at the risk of managing individual stocks in the reading on risk management applications of option strategies.

## 3.1 Measuring and Managing the Risk of Equities

Futures provide the best way to manage the risk of diversified equity portfolios. Although the standard deviation, or volatility, is a common measure of stock market risk, we prefer a measure that more accurately reflects the risk of a diversified stock portfolio. One reason for this preference is that we shall use futures that are based on broadly diversified portfolios. The most common risk measure of this type is the **beta**,[17] often denoted with the Greek symbol β. Beta is an important factor in capital market and asset pricing theory and, as we see here, it plays a major role in risk management. Although you may have encountered beta elsewhere, we shall take a quick review of it here.

Beta measures the relationship between a stock portfolio and the market portfolio, which is an abstract hypothetical measure of the portfolio containing *all* risky assets, not just stocks. The market portfolio is the most broadly diversified portfolio of all. We know, however, that it is impossible to identify the composition of the true market portfolio. We tend to use proxies, such as the S&P 500 Index, which do not really capture the true market portfolio. Fortunately, for the purposes of risk management, precision in the market portfolio does not matter all that much. Obviously there are no futures contracts on the true market portfolio; there can be futures contracts only on proxies such as the S&P 500. That being the case, it is appropriate to measure the beta of a portfolio relative to the index on which the futures is based.

Beta is a relative risk measure. The beta of the index we use as a benchmark is 1.0. Ignoring any asset-specific risk, an asset with a beta of 1.10 is 10 percent more volatile than the index. A beta of 0.80 is 20 percent less volatile than the index. Beta is formally measured as

$$\beta = \frac{cov_{SI}}{\sigma_I^2}$$

where $cov_{SI}$ is the covariance between the stock portfolio and the index and $\sigma_I^2$ is the variance of the index. Covariance is a measure of the extent to which two assets, here the portfolio and the index, move together.[18] If the covariance is positive (negative), the portfolio and the index tend to move in the same (opposite) direction. By itself, the magnitude of the covariance is difficult to interpret, but the covariance divided by the product of the standard deviations of the stock and the index produces the familiar measure called the correlation coefficient. For beta, however, we divide the covariance by the variance of the index and obtain a measure of the volatility of the portfolio relative to the market.

---

**17** At this point, we must distinguish this beta from the yield beta. When we use the term "yield beta," we mean the relationship of the yield on the instrument being hedged to the implied yield on the futures. When we use the term "beta" without a modifier, we mean the relationship of a stock or portfolio to the market.

**18** More specifically, the covariance measures the extent to which the *returns* on the stock and the index move together.

It is important to emphasize that beta measures only the portfolio volatility relative to the index. Thus, it is a measure only of the risk that cannot be eliminated by diversifying a portfolio. This risk is called the systematic, nondiversifiable, or market risk. A portfolio that is not well diversified could contain additional risk, which is called the nonsystematic, diversifiable, or asset-specific risk.[19] Systematic risk is the risk associated with broad market movements; nonsystematic risk is the risk unique to a company. An example of the former might be a change in interest rates by the Federal Reserve; an example of the latter might be a labor strike on a particular company. Because it captures only systematic risk, beta may seem to be a limited measure of risk, but the best way to manage nonsystematic risk, other than diversification, is to use options, as we do in the reading on risk management applications of option strategies. At this point, we focus on managing systematic or market risk.

As a risk measure, beta is similar to duration. Recall that we captured the dollar risk by multiplying the modified duration by the dollar value of the portfolio. For the bond futures contract, we multiplied its implied modified duration by the futures price. We called this the dollar-implied modified duration. In a similar manner, we shall specify a dollar beta by multiplying the beta by the dollar value of the portfolio. For the futures, we shall multiply its beta by the futures price, f. For the futures contract, beta is often assumed to be 1.0, but that is not exactly the case, so we will specify it as $\beta_f$. The dollar beta of the futures contract is $\beta_f f$. The dollar beta of the stock portfolio is written as $\beta_S S$, where $\beta_S$ is the beta of the stock portfolio and S is the market value of the stock portfolio.

If we wish to change the beta, we specify the desired beta as a target beta of $\beta_T$. Because the value of the futures starts off each day as zero, the dollar beta of the combination of stock and futures if the target beta is achieved is $\beta_T S$.[20] The number of futures we shall use is $N_f$, which is the unknown that we are attempting to determine. We set the target dollar beta to the dollar beta of the stock portfolio and the dollar beta of $N_f$ futures:

$$\beta_T S = \beta_S S + N_f \beta_f f$$

We then solve for $N_f$ and obtain

$$N_f = \left(\frac{\beta_T - \beta_S}{\beta_f}\right)\left(\frac{S}{f}\right) \tag{5}$$

Observe that if we want to increase the beta, $\beta_T$ will exceed $\beta_S$ and the sign of $N_f$ will be positive, which means that we must buy futures. If we want to decrease the beta, $\beta_T$ will be less than $\beta_S$, the sign of $N_f$ will be negative, and we must sell futures. This relationship should make sense: Selling futures will offset some of the risk of holding the stock. Alternatively, buying futures will add risk as $\beta_T > \beta_S$ and $N_f > 0$.

In the special case in which we want to completely eliminate the risk, $\beta_T$ would be zero and the formula would reduce to

$$N_f = -\left(\frac{\beta_S}{\beta_f}\right)\left(\frac{S}{f}\right)$$

In this case, the sign of $N_f$ will always be negative, which makes sense. To hedge away all of the risk, we definitely need to sell futures.

---

[19] We also sometimes use the term "idiosyncratic risk."

[20] Recall that the market value of the portfolio will still be the same as the market value of the stock, because the value of the futures is zero. The futures value becomes zero whenever it is marked to market, which takes place at the end of each day. In other words, the target beta does not appear to be applied to the value of the futures in the above analysis because the value of the futures is zero.

In the practical implementation of a stock index futures trade, we need to remember that stock index futures prices are quoted on an order of magnitude the same as that of the stock index. The actual futures price is the quoted futures price times a designated multiplier. For example, if the S&P 500 futures price is quoted at 1225, the multiplier of $250 makes the actual futures price 1225($250) = $306,250. This amount would be the value of f in the above formulas. In some situations, the futures price will simply be stated, as for example $306,250. In that case, we can assume the price is quoted as f = $306,250 and the multiplier is 1.

We also need to remember that the futures contract will hedge only the risk associated with the relationship between the portfolio and the index on which the futures contract is based. Thus, for example, a portfolio consisting mostly of small-cap stocks should not be paired with a futures contract on a large-cap index such as the S&P 500. Such a transaction would manage only the risk that large-cap stocks move with small-cap stocks. If any divergence occurs in the relationship between these two sectors, such as large-cap stocks going up and smallcap stocks going down, a transaction designed to increase (decrease) risk could end up decreasing (increasing) risk.

Recall also that dividends can interfere with how this transaction performs. Index futures typically are based only on price indices; they do not reflect the payment and reinvestment of dividends. Therefore, dividends will accrue on the stocks but are not reflected in the index. This is not a major problem, however, because dividends in the short-term period covered by most contracts are not particularly risky.

## 3.2 Managing the Risk of an Equity Portfolio

To adjust the beta of an equity portfolio, an investment manager could use Equation 5 to calculate the number of futures contracts needed. She can use the formula to either increase or decrease the portfolio's systematic risk. The manager might increase the beta if she expects the market to move up, or decrease the beta if she expects the market to move down. Also, the betas of equity portfolios change constantly by virtue of the market value of the portfolio changing.[21] Therefore, futures can be used to adjust the beta from its actual level to the desired level.

Exhibit 3 illustrates the case of a pension fund that wants to increase its equity portfolio beta during a period in which it expects the market to be strong. It increases its beta from 0.90 to 1.10 by purchasing 29 futures contracts. Betas, however, are notoriously difficult to measure. We see after the fact that the beta actually was increased to 1.15. As long as we buy (sell) futures contracts, however, we will increase (decrease) the beta.

| **Exhibit 3** | **Using Stock Index Futures to Manage the Risk of a Stock Portfolio** |
|---|---|

### Scenario (2 September)

BB Holdings (BBH) is a U.S. conglomerate. Its pension fund generates market forecasts internally and receives forecasts from an independent consultant. As a result of these forecasts, BBH expects the market for large-cap stocks to be stronger than it believes everyone else is expecting over the next two months.

---

21 Consider, for example, a portfolio in which $3 million is invested in stock with a beta of 1.0 and $1 million is invested in cash with a beta of 0.0 and a rate of 5 percent. The equity market weight is, therefore, 0.75, and the overall beta is 1.0(0.75) + 0.0(0.25) = 0.75. Now suppose the following year, the stock increases by 20 percent. Then the stock value will be $3.6 million and the cash balance will be $1.05 million. The overall portfolio value will be $4.65 million, so the equity market weight will be 3.6/4.65 = 0.77. Thus, 77 percent of the portfolio will now have a beta of 1.0(0.77), and the overall beta will have drifted upward to 0.77.

| **Exhibit 3** | **Continued** |
|---|---|

## Action

BBH decides to adjust the beta on $38,500,000 of large-cap stocks from its current level of 0.90 to 1.10 for the period of the next two months. It has selected a futures contract deemed to have sufficient liquidity; the futures price is currently $275,000 and the contract has a beta of 0.95. The appropriate number of futures contracts to adjust the beta would be

$$N_f = \left(\frac{\beta_T - \beta_S}{\beta_f}\right)\left(\frac{S}{f}\right) = \left(\frac{1.10 - 0.90}{0.95}\right)\left(\frac{\$38,500,000}{\$275,000}\right) = 29.47$$

So it buys 29 contracts.

## Scenario (3 December)

The market as a whole increases by 4.4 percent. The stock portfolio increases to $40,103,000. The stock index futures contract rises to $286,687.50,[22] an increase of 4.25 percent.

## Outcome and Analysis

The profit on the futures contract is 29($286,687.50 − $275,000.00) = $338,937.50. The rate of return for the stock portfolio is

$$\frac{\$40,103,000}{\$38,500,000} - 1 = 0.0416$$

or 4.16 percent. Adding the profit from the futures gives a total market value of $40,103,000.00 + $338,937.50 = $40,441,937.50. The rate of return for the stock portfolio is

$$\frac{\$40,441,937.50}{\$38,500,000.00} - 1 = 0.0504$$

or 5.04 percent. Because the market went up by 4.4 percent and the overall gain was 5.04 percent, the effective beta of the portfolio was

$$\frac{0.0504}{0.044} = 1.15$$

Thus, the effective beta is quite close to the target beta of 1.10.

---

Of course, be aware that increasing the beta increases the risk. Therefore, if the beta is increased and the market falls, the loss on the portfolio will be greater than if beta had not been increased. Decreasing the beta decreases the risk, so if the market rises, the portfolio value will rise less. As an example, consider the outcome described in Exhibit 3. Suppose that instead of being optimistic, the fund manager was very pessimistic and wanted to decrease the beta to zero. Therefore, the target beta, $\beta_T$, is 0.0. Then the number of futures contracts would be

$$N_f = \left(\frac{0.0 - 0.90}{0.95}\right)\frac{\$38,500,000}{\$275,000.00} = -132.63$$

So the fund sells 133 futures. Given the same outcome as in Exhibit 3, the profit on the futures contracts would be

---

22 In the examples in this reading, stock futures prices move to a new level in the course of the scenario. These new futures prices come from the cost-of-carry model (assuming there is no mispricing in the market).

$$-133(\$286{,}687.50 - \$275{,}000.00) = -\$1{,}554{,}437.50$$

There would be a loss of more than \$1.5 million on the futures contracts. The market value of the stock after it moved up was \$40,103,000, but with the futures loss, the market value is effectively reduced to \$40,103,000.00 − \$1,554,437.50 = \$38,548,562.50. This is a return of

$$\frac{\$38{,}548{,}562.50}{\$38{,}500{,}000.00} - 1 = 0.0013$$

Thus, the effective beta is

$$\frac{0.0013}{0.044} = 0.030$$

The beta has been reduced almost to zero. This reduction costs the company virtually all of the upward movement, but such a cost is to be expected if the beta were changed to zero.

---

**Example 3**

Equity Analysts Inc. (EQA) is an equity portfolio management firm. One of its clients has decided to be more aggressive for a short period of time. It would like EQA to move the beta on its \$65 million portfolio from 0.85 to 1.05. EQA can use a futures contract priced at \$188,500, which has a beta of 0.92, to implement this change in risk.

**A.** Determine the number of futures contracts EQA should use and whether it should buy or sell futures.

**B.** At the horizon date, the equity market is down 2 percent. The stock portfolio falls 1.65 percent, and the futures price falls to \$185,000. Determine the overall value of the position and the effective beta.

**Solution to A:**

The number of futures contracts EQA should use is

$$N_f = \left(\frac{1.05 - 0.85}{0.92}\right)\left(\frac{\$65{,}000{,}000}{\$188{,}500}\right) = 74.96$$

So EQA should buy 75 contracts.

**Solution to B:**

The value of the stock portfolio will be \$65,000,000(1 − 0.0165) = \$63,927,500. The profit on the futures transaction is 75(\$185,000 − \$188,500) = −\$262,500. The overall value of the position is \$63,927,500 − \$262,500 = \$63,665,000.

Thus, the overall return is $\dfrac{\$63{,}665{,}000}{\$65{,}000{,}000} - 1 = -0.0205$

Because the market went down by 2 percent, the effective beta is 0.0205/0.02 = 1.025.

---

## 3.3 Creating Equity out of Cash

Stock index futures are an excellent tool for creating synthetic positions in equity, which can result in significant transaction cost savings and preserve liquidity. In this section, we explore how to create a synthetic index fund and how to turn cash into synthetic equity.

The relationship between a futures or forward contract and the underlying asset is determined by a formula that relates the risk-free interest rate to the dividends on the underlying asset. Entering into a hypothetical arbitrage transaction in which we buy stock and sell futures turns an equity position into a risk-free portfolio. In simple terms, we say that

Long stock + Short futures = Long risk-free bond

We can turn this equation around to obtain[23]

Long stock = Long risk-free bond + Long futures

If we buy the risk-free bonds and buy the futures, we replicate a position in which we would be buying the stock. This synthetic replication of the underlying asset can be a very useful transaction when we wish to construct a synthetic stock index fund, or when we wish to convert into equity a cash position that we are required to maintain for liquidity purposes. Both of these situations involve holding cash and obtaining equity market exposure through the use of futures.

### 3.3.1 *Creating a Synthetic Index Fund*

A synthetic index fund is an index fund position created by combining risk-free bonds and futures on the desired index. Suppose a U.S. money manager would like to offer a new product, a fund on an index of U.K. stock as represented by the Financial Times Stock Exchange (FTSE) 100 Index. The manager will initiate the fund with an investment of £100 million. In other words, the U.S. money manager would offer clients an opportunity to invest in a position in British stock with the investment made in British pounds.[24] The manager believes the fund is easier to create synthetically using futures contracts.

To create this synthetic index fund, we need to know several more pieces of information. The dividend yield on the U.K. stocks is 2.5 percent, and the FTSE 100 Index futures contract that we shall use expires in three months, has a quoted price of £4,000, and has a multiplier of £10.[25] The U.K. risk-free interest rate is 5 percent.[26] When the futures contract expires, it will be rolled over into a new contract.

To create this synthetic index fund, we must buy a certain number of futures. Let the following be the appropriate values of the inputs:

$V$ = amount of money to be invested, £100 million
$f$ = futures price, £4,000
$T$ = time to expiration of futures, 0.25
$\delta$ = dividend yield on the index, 0.025

---

**23** We turn the equation around by noting that to remove a short futures position from the left-hand side, we should buy futures. If we add a long futures position to the left-hand side, we have to add it to the right-hand side.

**24** If you are wondering why U.S. investors would like to invest in a position denominated in British pounds rather than dollars, remember that the currency risk can be a source of diversification. Adding a position in the U.K. equity market provides one tier of diversification, while adding the risk of the dollar/pound exchange rate adds another tier of diversification, especially because the exchange rate is likely to have a low correlation with the U.S. stock market.

**25** Recall that the multiplier is a number multiplied by the quoted futures price to obtain the actual futures price. In this section, accurately pricing the futures contract is important to the success of these strategies. For example, assume the S&P 500 is at 1,000 and the multiplier is $250, so the full price is (1,000)($250) = $250,000. We wish to trade a futures contract priced at f, where f is based on the index value of 1,000 grossed up by the risk-free rate and reduced by the dividends. It is far easier to think of f in terms of its relationship to S without the multiplier. In one case, however, we shall let the multiplier be 1, so you should be able to handle either situation.

**26** It might be confusing as to why we care about the U.K. interest rate and not the U.S. interest rate. This transaction is completely denominated in pounds, and the futures contract is priced in pounds based on the U.K. dividend yield and interest rate. Hence, the U.K. interest rate plays a role here, and the U.S. interest rate does not.

r = risk-free rate, 0.05

q = multiplier, £10

We would like to replicate owning the stock and reinvesting the dividends. How many futures contracts would we need to buy and add to a long bond position? We designate $N_f$ as the required number of futures contracts and $N_f^*$ as its rounded-off value.

Now observe that the payoff of $N_f^*$ futures contracts will be $N_f^*q(S_T - f)$. This equation is based on the fact that we have $N_f^*$ futures contracts, each of which has a multiplier of q. The futures contracts are established at a price of f. When it expires, the futures price will be the spot price, $S_T$, reflecting the convergence of the futures price at expiration to the spot price.

The futures payoff can be rewritten as $N_f^*qS_T - N_f^*qf$. The minus sign on the second term means that we shall have to pay $N_f^*qf$. The (implied) plus sign on the first term means that we shall receive $N_f^*qS_T$. Knowing that we buy $N_f^*$ futures contracts, we also want to know how much to invest in bonds. We shall call this V* and calculate it based on $N_f^*$. Below we shall show how to calculate $N_f^*$ and V*. If we invest enough money in bonds to accumulate a value of $N_f^*qf$, this investment will cover the amount we agree to pay for the FTSE: $N_f^* \times q \times f$. The present value of this amount is $N_f^*qf/(1 + r)^T$.

Because the amount of money we start with is V, we should have V equal to $N_f^*qf/(1 + r)^T$. From here we can solve for $N_f^*$ to obtain

$$N_f^* = \frac{V(1+r)^T}{qf} \quad \text{(rounded to an integer)} \tag{6}$$

But once we round off the number of futures, we do not truly have V dollars invested. The amount we actually have invested is

$$V^* = \frac{N_f^*qf}{(1+r)^T} \tag{7}$$

We can show that investing V* in bonds and buying $N_f^*$ futures contracts at a price of f is equivalent to buying $N_f^*q/(1 + \delta)^T$ units of stock.

As noted above, if we have bonds maturing to the value $N_f^*qf$, we have enough cash on hand to pay the obligation of $N_f^*qf$ on our futures contract. The futures contract will pay us the amount $N_f^*qS_T$. If we had actually purchased units of stock, the reinvestment of dividends into new units means that we would end up with the equivalent of $N_f^*q$ units, and means that we implicitly started off with $N_f^*q/(1 + \delta)^T$ units.

In short, this transaction implies that we synthetically start off with $N_f^*q/(1 + \delta)^T$ units of stock, collect and reinvest dividends, and end up with $N_f^*q$ units. We emphasize that all of these transactions are synthetic. We do not actually own the stock or collect and reinvest the dividends. We are attempting only to replicate what would happen if we actually owned the stock and collected and reinvested the dividends.

Exhibit 4 illustrates this transaction. The interest plus principal on the bonds is a sufficient amount to buy the stock in settlement of the futures contract, so the fund ends up holding the stock, as it originally wanted.

| Exhibit 4 | Constructing a Synthetic Index Fund |

## Scenario (15 December)

On 15 December, a U.S. money manager for a firm called Strategic Money Management (SMM) wants to construct a synthetic index fund consisting of a position of £100 million invested in U.K. stock. The index will be the FTSE 100,

| Exhibit 4 | Continued |
|---|---|

which has a dividend yield of 2.5 percent. A futures contract on the FTSE 100 is priced at £4,000 and has a multiplier of £10. The position will be held until the futures expires in three months, at which time it will be renewed with a new three-month futures. The U.K. risk-free rate is 5 percent. Both the risk-free rate and the dividend yield are stated as annually compounded figures.

## Action

The number of futures contracts will be

$$N_f = \frac{V(1+r)^T}{qf} = \frac{£100,000,000(1.05)^{0.25}}{£10(4,000)} = 2,530.68$$

Because we cannot buy fractions of futures contracts, we round $N_f$ to $N_f^* = 2,531$. With this rounding, we are actually synthetically investing

$$\frac{2,531(£10)£4,000}{(1.05)^{0.25}} = £100,012,622$$

in stock. So we put this much money in risk-free bonds, which will grow to £100,012,622$(1.05)^{0.25}$ = £101,240,000. The number of units of stock that we have effectively purchased at the start is

$$\frac{N_f^*q}{(1+\delta)^T} = \frac{2,531(10)}{(1.025)^{0.25}} = 25,154.24$$

If the stock had actually been purchased, dividends would be received and reinvested into additional shares. Thus, the number of shares would grow to 25,154.24$(1.025)^{0.25}$ = 25,310.

## Scenario (15 March)

The index is at $S_T$ when the futures expires.

## Outcome and Analysis

The futures contracts will pay off the amount

$$\text{Futures payoff} = 2,531(£10)(S_T - £4,000) = £25,310S_T - £101,240,000$$

This means that the fund will pay £101,240,000 to settle the futures contract and obtain the market value of 25,310 units of the FTSE 100, each worth $S_T$. Therefore, the fund will need to come up with £101,240,000, but as noted above, the money invested in risk-free bonds grows to a value of £101,240,000.

SMM, therefore, pays this amount to settle the futures contracts and effectively ends up with 25,310 units of the index, the position it wanted in the market.

---

There are a few other considerations to note. One is that we rounded according to the usual rules of rounding, going up if the fraction is 0.5 or greater. By rounding up, we shall have to invest more than V in bonds. If we rounded down, we shall invest less than V. It does not really matter whether we always round up on 0.5 or greater, but that is the rule we shall use here. It should also be noted that this transaction does not capture the dividends that would be earned if one held the underlying stocks directly. The yield of 2.5 percent is important in the computations here, but the fund does not earn these dividends. All this transaction does is capture the performance of the index.

Because the index is a price index only and does not include dividends, this synthetic replication strategy can capture only the index performance without the dividends.[27] Another concern that could be encountered in practice is that the futures contract could expire later than the desired date. If so, the strategy will still be successful if the futures contract is correctly priced when the strategy is completed. Consistent with that point, we should note that any strategy using futures will be effective only to the extent that the futures contract is correctly priced when the position is opened and also when it is closed. This point underscores the importance of understanding the pricing of futures contracts.

### 3.3.2  *Equitizing Cash*

The strategy of combining risk-free bonds and futures is used not only to replicate an index; it is also used to take a given amount of cash and turn it into an equity position while maintaining the liquidity provided by the cash. This type of transaction is sometimes called equitizing cash. Consider an investment fund that has a large cash balance. It would like to invest in equity but either is not allowed to do so or cannot afford to take the risk that it might need to liquidate a large amount of stock in a short period of time, which could be difficult to do or might result in significant losses. Nonetheless, the fund is willing to take the risk of equity market exposure provided it can maintain the liquidity. The above transaction can be altered just slightly to show how this is done.

Suppose the fund in Exhibit 4 is actually a U.K. insurance company that has about £100 million of cash invested at the risk-free rate. It would like to gain equity market exposure by investing in the FTSE 100 index. By policy, it is allowed to do so, provided that it maintains sufficient liquidity. If it engages in the synthetic index strategy described above, it maintains about £100 million invested in cash in the form of risk-free bonds and yet gains the exposure to about £100 million of U.K. stock. In the event that it must liquidate its position, perhaps to pay out insurance claims, it need only liquidate the U.K. risk-free bonds and close out the futures contracts. Given the liquidity of the futures market and the obvious liquidity of the risk-free bond market, doing so would be relatively easy.

There is one important aspect of this problem, however, over which the fund has no control: the pricing of the futures. Because the fund will take a long position in futures, the futures contract must be correctly priced. If the futures contract is overpriced, the fund will pay too much for the futures. In that case, the risk-free bonds will not be enough to offset the excessively high price effectively paid for the stock. If, however, the futures contract is underpriced, the fund will get a bargain and will come out much better.

Finally, we should note that these strategies can be illustrated with bond futures to gain bond market exposure, but they are more commonly implemented using stock index futures to gain equity market exposure.

**Example 4**

Index Advantage (INDEXA) is a money management firm that specializes in turning the idle cash of clients into equity index positions at very low cost. INDEXA has a new client with about $500 million of cash that it would like to invest in the small-cap equity sector. INDEXA will construct the position using a futures contract on a small-cap index. The futures price is 1,500, the

**27** The values of some stock indices, called total return indices, include reinvested dividends. If a futures contract on the total return index is used, then the strategy would capture the dividends. Doing so would, however, require a few changes to the formulas given here.

multiplier is $100, and the contract expires in six months. The underlying small-cap index has a dividend yield of 1 percent. The risk-free rate is 3 percent per year.

**A.** Determine exactly how the cash can be equitized using futures contracts.

**B.** When the futures contract expires, the index is at $S_T$. Demonstrate how the position produces the same outcome as an actual investment in the index.

### Solution to A:

INDEXA should purchase

$$N_f = \frac{\$500,000,000(1.03)^{0.5}}{\$100(1,500)} = 3,382.96$$

futures contracts. Round this amount to $N_f^* = 3,383$. Then invest

$$\frac{3,383(\$100)(1,500)}{(1.03)^{0.5}} = \$500,005,342$$

in risk-free bonds paying 3 percent interest. Note that this is not exactly an initial investment of $500 million, because one cannot purchase fractions of futures contracts. The bonds will grow to a value of $500,005,342(1.03)^{0.5} = $507,450,000. The number of units of stock effectively purchased through the use of futures is

$$\frac{N_f^* q}{(1+\delta)^T} = \frac{3,383(100)}{(1.01)^{0.5}} = 336,621.08$$

If 336,621.08 shares were actually purchased, the accumulation and reinvestment of dividends would result in there being 336,621.08 $(1.01)^{0.5} = 338,300$ shares at the futures expiration.

### Solution to B:

At expiration, the payoff on the futures is

$$3,383(100)(S_T - 1500) = 338,300 S_T - \$507,450,000$$

In other words, to settle the futures, INDEXA will owe $507,450,000 and receive the equivalent of 338,300 units of stock worth $S_T$.

## 3.4 Creating Cash out of Equity

Because we have the relation Long stock + Short futures = Long risk-free bonds, we should be able to construct a synthetic position in cash by selling futures against a long stock position. Indeed we have already done a similar transaction when we sold futures to reduce the stock portfolio beta to zero. Therefore, if we wish to sell stock, we can do so by converting it to synthetic cash. This move can save transaction costs and avoid the sale of large amounts of stock at a single point in time.

Suppose the market value of our investment in stock is V, and we would like to create synthetic cash roughly equivalent to that amount. We shall sell futures, with the objective that at the horizon date, we shall have $V(1 + r)^T$. Money in the amount of V will have grown in value at the risk-free rate. Each unit of the index is priced at S. The number of units of the index we shall effectively convert to cash would appear to be (V/S), but because of reinvested dividends, we actually end up with $(1 + \delta)^T$ units of stock for every unit we start with. Hence, the number of units we are effectively converting to cash is $(V/S)(1 + \delta)^T$.

As in the example of the synthetic index fund, we shall again have a problem in that the number of futures contracts must be rounded off to an integer. Keeping that in mind, the payoff of the futures contracts will be $qN_f^*(S_T - f) = qN_f^*S_T - qN_f^*f$. If the number of units of stock is $(V/S)(1 + \delta)^T$, then the value of the overall position (long stock plus short futures) will be $(V/S)(1 + \delta)^T S_T + qN_f^*S_T - qN_f^*f$. Because we are trying to convert to risk-free bonds (cash), we need to find a way to eliminate the $S_T$ term. We just solve for the value of $N_f^*$ that will cause the first two terms to offset.[28]

We obtain a previous equation, Equation 6

$$N_f^* = -\frac{V(1+r)^T}{qf} \qquad \text{(rounded to an integer)}$$

As usual, the minus sign means that $N_f^*$ is less than zero, which means we are selling futures. Because of rounding, the amount of stock we are actually converting is

$$V^* = \frac{-N_f^*qf}{(1+r)^T} \tag{8}$$

Therefore, if we use $N_f^*$ futures contracts, we have effectively converted stock worth $V^*$ to cash. This will not be the exact amount of stock we own, but it will be close. As in the case of the synthetic index fund, reinvestment of dividends means that the number of units of stock will be $-N_f^*q/(1 + \delta)^T$ at the start and $-N_f^*q$ when the futures expires. In Exhibit 5, we illustrate the application of this strategy for a pension fund that would like to convert $50 million of stock to synthetic cash.

| **Exhibit 5** | **Creating Synthetic Cash** |
|---|---|

## Scenario (2 June)

The pension fund of Interactive Industrial Systems (IIS) holds a $50 million portion of its portfolio in an indexed position of the NASDAQ 100, which has a dividend yield of 0.75 percent. It would like to convert that position to cash for a two-month period. It can do this using a futures contract on the NASDAQ 100, which is priced at 1484.72, has a multiplier of $100, and expires in two months. The risk-free rate is 4.65 percent.

## Action

The fund needs to use

$$N_f = \frac{-V(1+r)^T}{qf} = -\frac{\$50,000,000(1.0465)^{2/12}}{\$100(1484.72)} = -339.32$$

futures contracts. This amount should be rounded to $N_f^* = -339$. Because of rounding, the amount of stock synthetically converted to cash is really

$$\frac{-N_f^*qf}{(1+r)^T} = \frac{339(\$100)(1484.72)}{(1.0465)^{2/12}} = \$49,952,173$$

This amount should grow to $\$49,952,173(1.0465)^{2/12} = \$50,332,008$. The number of units of stock is

$$\frac{-N_f^*q}{(1+\delta)^T} = \frac{339(\$100)}{(1.0075)^{2/12}} = 33,857.81$$

---

[28] In order to get this solution, we must take the result that $f = S(1 + r)^T/(1 + \delta)^T$ and turn it around so that $S = f(1 + \delta)^T/(1 + r)^T$ to find the value of S.

| Exhibit 5 | Continued |
|---|---|

at the start, which grows to $33,857.81(1.0075)^{2/12} = 33,900$ units when the futures expires.

## Scenario (4 August)

The stock index is at $S_T$ when the futures expires.

## Outcome and Analysis

The payoff of the futures contract is

$$-339(\$100)(S_T - 1484.72) = -\$33,900S_T + \$50,332,008$$

As noted, dividends are reinvested and the number of units of the index grows to 33,900 shares. The overall position of the fund is

Stock worth 33,900S

Futures payoff of $-33,900S_T + \$50,332,008$

or an overall total of $50,332,008. This is exactly the amount we said the fund would have if it invested $49,952,173 at the risk-free rate of 4.65 percent for two months. Thus, the fund has effectively converted a stock position to cash.

---

**Example 5**

Synthetics Inc. (SYNINC) executes a variety of synthetic strategies for pension funds. One such strategy is to enable the client to maintain a liquid balance in cash while retaining exposure to equity market movements. A similar strategy is to enable the client to maintain its position in the market but temporarily convert it to cash. A client with a $100 million equity position wants to convert it to cash for three months. An equity market futures contract is priced at $325,000, expires in three months, and is based on an underlying index with a dividend yield of 2 percent. The risk-free rate is 3.5 percent.

**A.** Determine the number of futures contracts SYNINC should trade and the effective amount of money it has invested in risk-free bonds to achieve this objective.

**B.** When the futures contracts expire, the equity index is at $S_T$. Show how this transaction results in the appropriate outcome.

**Solution to A:**

First note that no multiplier is quoted here. The futures price of $325,000 is equivalent to a quoted price of $325,000 and a multiplier of 1.0. The number of futures contracts is

$$N_f = -\frac{\$100,000,000(1.035)^{0.25}}{\$325,000} = -310.35$$

Rounding off, SYNINC should sell 310 contracts. This is equivalent to selling futures contracts on stock worth

$$\frac{310(\$325,000)}{(1.035)^{0.25}} = \$99,887,229$$

and is the equivalent of investing \$99,887,229 in risk-free bonds, which will grow to a value of \$99,887,229$(1.035)^{0.25}$ = \$100,750,000. The number of units of stock being effectively converted to cash is (ignoring the minus sign)

$$\frac{N_f{}^*q}{(1+\delta)^T} = \frac{310(1)}{(1.02)^{0.25}} = 308.47$$

The accumulation and reinvestment of dividends would make this figure grow to 308.47$(1.02)^{0.25}$ = 310 units when the futures expires.

### Solution to B:

At expiration, the profit on the futures is $-310(S_T - \$325,000) = -310S_T + \$100,750,000$. That means SYNINC will have to pay $310S_T$ and will receive \$100,750,000 to settle the futures contract. Due to reinvestment of dividends, it will end up with the equivalent of 310 units of stock, which can be sold to cover the amount $-310S_T$. This will leave \$100,750,000, the equivalent of having invested in risk-free bonds.

---

You might be wondering about the relationship between the number of futures contracts given here and the number of futures contracts required to adjust the portfolio beta to zero. Here we are selling a given number of futures contracts against stock to effectively convert the stock to a risk-free asset. Does that not mean that the portfolio would then have a beta of zero? In Section 3.2, we gave a different formula to reduce the portfolio beta to zero. These formulas do not appear to be the same. Would they give the same value of $N_f$? In the example here, we sell the precise number of futures to completely hedge the stock portfolio. The stock portfolio, however, has to be identical to the index. It cannot have a different beta. The other formula, which reduces the beta to zero, is more general and can be used to eliminate the systematic risk on any portfolio. Note, however, that only systematic risk is eliminated. If the portfolio is not fully diversified, some risk will remain, but that risk is diversifiable, and the expected return on that portfolio would still be the risk-free rate. If we apply that formula to a portfolio that is identical to the index on which the futures is based, the two formulas are the same and the number of futures contracts to sell is the same in both cases.[29]

Finally, we should note that we could have changed the beta of the portfolio by making transactions in individual securities. To raise (lower) the beta we could sell (buy) low-beta stocks and buy (sell) high-beta stocks. Alternatively, we could do transactions in the portfolio itself and the risk-free asset. To reduce the beta to zero, for example, we could sell the entire portfolio and invest the money in the risk-free asset. To increase the beta, we could reduce any position we hold in the risk-free asset, even to the point of borrowing by issuing the risk-free asset.[30] In this reading, we illustrate how these transactions can be better executed using derivatives, which have lower transaction costs and generally greater liquidity. There is no guarantee that either approach will result in the portfolio having the exact beta the investor desired. Betas are notoriously difficult to measure. But executing the transactions in derivatives provides an attractive alternative to having to make a large number of transactions in individual securities. In light of the fact that many of these adjustments are intended

---

**29** A key element in this statement is that the futures beta is the beta of the underlying index, multiplied by the present value interest factor using the risk-free rate. This is a complex and subtle point, however, that we simply state without going into the mathematical proof.

**30** Students of capital market theory will recognize that the transactions we describe in this paragraph are those involving movements up and down the capital market line, which leads to investors finding their optimal portfolios. This kind of trading activity in turn leads to the well-known capital asset pricing model.

to be only temporary, it makes far more sense to do the transactions in derivatives than to make the transactions in the underlying securities, provided that one is willing to keep re-entering positions upon contract expirations.

# ASSET ALLOCATION WITH FUTURES

**4**

It has been widely noted that the most important factor in the performance of an asset portfolio is the allocation of the portfolio among asset classes. In this reading, we do not develop techniques for determining the best allocation among asset classes any more than we attempt to determine what beta to set as a target for our stock portfolio or what duration to set as a target for our bond portfolio. We focus instead on how derivative strategies can be used to implement a plan based on a market outlook. As we saw previously in this reading, we can adjust the beta or duration effectively with lower cost and greater liquidity by using stock index or bond futures. In this section, we look at how to allocate a portfolio among asset classes using futures.

## 4.1 Adjusting the Allocation among Asset Classes

Consider the case of a $300 million portfolio that is allocated 80 percent ($240 million) to stock and 20 percent ($60 million) to bonds. The manager wants to change the allocation to 50 percent ($150 million) stock and 50 percent ($150 million) bonds. Therefore, the manager wants to reduce the allocation to stock by $90 million and increase the allocation to bonds by $90 million. The trick, however, is to use the correct number of futures contracts to set the beta and duration to the desired level. To do this, the manager should sell stock index futures contracts to reduce the beta on the $90 million of stock from its current level to zero. This transaction will effectively convert the stock to cash. She should then buy bond futures contracts to increase the duration on the cash from its current level to the desired level.

Exhibit 6 presents this example. The manager sells 516 stock index futures contracts and buys 772 bond futures contracts. Two months later, the position is worth $297,964,852. As we show, had the transactions been done by selling stocks and buying bonds, the portfolio would be worth $297,375,000, a difference of only about 0.2 percent relative to the original market value. Of course, the futures transactions can be executed in a more liquid market and with lower transaction costs.

| **Exhibit 6** | **Adjusting the Allocation between Stocks and Bonds** |
|---|---|

### Scenario (15 November)

Global Asset Advisory Group (GAAG) is a pension fund management firm. One of its funds consists of $300 million allocated 80 percent to stock and 20 percent to bonds. The stock portion has a beta of 1.10 and the bond portion has a duration of 6.5. GAAG would like to temporarily adjust the asset allocation to 50 percent stock and 50 percent bonds. It will use stock index futures and bond futures to achieve this objective. The stock index futures contract has a price of $200,000 (after accounting for the multiplier) and a beta of 0.96. The bond futures contract has an implied modified duration of 7.2 and a price of $105,250. The yield beta is 1. The transaction will be put in place on 15 November, and the horizon date for termination is 10 January.

*(continued)*

**Exhibit 6**     **Continued**

## Action

The market value of the stock is 0.80($300,000,000) = $240,000,000. The market value of the bonds is 0.20($300,000,000) = $60,000,000. Because it wants the portfolio to be temporarily reallocated to half stock and half bonds, GAAG needs to change the allocation to $150 million of each.

Thus, GAAG effectively needs to sell $90 million of stock by converting it to cash using stock index futures and buy $90 million of bonds by using bond futures. This would effectively convert the stock into cash and then convert that cash into bonds. Of course, this entire series of transactions will be synthetic; the actual stock and bonds in the portfolio will stay in place.

Using Equation 5, the number of stock index futures, denoted as $N_{sf}$, will be

$$N_{sf} = \left(\frac{\beta_T - \beta_S}{\beta_f}\right)\frac{S}{f_s}$$

where $\beta_T$ is the target beta of zero, $\beta_S$ is the stock beta of 1.10, $\beta_f$ is the futures beta of 0.96, S is the market value of the stock involved in the transaction of $90 million, and $f_s$ is the price of the stock index futures, $200,000. We obtain

$$N_{sf} = \left(\frac{0.00 - 1.10}{0.96}\right)\frac{\$90,000,000}{\$200,000} = -515.63$$

Rounding off, GAAG sells 516 contracts.

Using Equation 4, the number of bond futures, denoted as $N_{bf}$, will be

$$N_{bf} = \left(\frac{MDUR_T - MDUR_B}{MDUR_f}\right)\frac{B}{f_b}$$

where $MDUR_T$ is the target modified duration of 6.5, $MDUR_B$ is the modified duration of the existing bonds, $MDUR_f$ is the implied modified duration of the futures (here 7.2), B is the market value of the bonds of $90 million, and $f_b$ is the bond futures price of $105,250. The modified duration of the existing bonds is the modified duration of a cash position. The sale of stock index futures provides $90 million of synthetic cash that is now converted into bonds using bond futures. Because no movement of actual cash is involved in these futures market transactions, the modified duration of cash is effectively equal to zero. We obtain

$$N_{bf} = \left(\frac{6.5 - 0.0}{7.2}\right)\left(\frac{\$90,000,000}{\$105,250}\right) = 771.97$$

So GAAG buys 772 contracts.

## Scenario (10 January)

During this period, the stock portion of the portfolio returns −3 percent and the bond portion returns 1.25 percent. The stock index futures price goes from $200,000 to $193,600, and the bond futures price increases from $105,250 to $106,691.

## Outcome and Analysis

The profit on the stock index futures transaction is −516($193,600 − $200,000) = $3,302,400. The profit on the bond futures transaction is 772($106,691 − $105,250) = $1,112,452. The total profit from the futures transaction is, therefore, $3,302,400 + $1,112,452 = $4,414,852. The market value of the stocks and bonds will now be

| Exhibit 6 | Continued |
|---|---|

Stocks: $240,000,000(1-0.03)$ = $232,800,000

Bonds: $60,000,000(1.0125)$ = $ 60,750,000

Total: $293,550,000

Thus, the total portfolio value, including the futures gains, is $293,550,000 + $4,414,852 = $297,964,852. Had GAAG sold stocks and then converted the proceeds to bonds, the value would have been

Stocks: $150,000,000(1-0.03)$ = $145,500,000

Bonds: $150,000,000(1.0125)$ = $151,875,000

Total: $297,375,000

This total is a slight difference of about 0.2 percent relative to the market value of the portfolio using derivatives.

---

Exhibit 7 shows a variation of this problem in which a portfolio management firm wants to convert a portion of a bond portfolio to cash to meet a liquidity requirement and another portion to a higher duration. On the portion it wants to convert to cash, it sells 104 futures contracts. This is the correct amount to change the duration to 0.25, the approximate duration of a short-term money market instrument. It then buys 33 futures contracts to raise the duration on the other part of the portfolio. The net is that it executes only one transaction of 71 contracts, and the end result is a portfolio worth $3,030,250 at the end of the period. Had the transactions been done by selling and buying securities, the portfolio would have been worth $3,048,000, or about the same amount. Another question we shall examine is whether this strategy actually meets the liquidity requirement.

We note in Exhibit 7 that the manager wants to convert a portion of the portfolio to cash to increase liquidity. By selling the futures contracts, the manager maintains the securities in long-term bonds but reduces the volatility of those bonds to the equivalent of that of a short-term instrument. We might, however, question whether liquidity has actually been improved. If cash is needed, the fund would have to sell the long-term bonds and buy back the futures. The latter would not present a liquidity problem, but the sale of the long-term bonds could be a problem. Reducing the duration to replicate a short-term instrument does not remove the problem that long-term instruments, which are still held, may have to be liquidated. What it does is convert the volatility of the instrument to that of a short-term instrument. This conversion in no way handles the liquidity problem. It simply means that given an interest rate change, the position will have the sensitivity of a short-term instrument.

| Exhibit 7 | Adjusting the Allocation between One Bond Class and Another |
|---|---|

## Scenario (15 October)

Fixed Income Money Advisors (FIMA) manages bond portfolios for wealthy individual investors. It uses various tactical strategies to alter its mix between long- and short-term bonds to adjust its portfolio to a composition appropriate for its outlook for interest rates. Currently, it would like to alter a $30 million segment of its portfolio that has a modified duration of 6.5. To increase liquidity,

*(continued)*

| Exhibit 7 | Continued |
| --- | --- |

it would like to move $10 million into cash but adjust the duration on the remaining $20 million to 7.5. These changes will take place on 15 October and will likely be reversed on 12 December.

## Action

The bond futures contract that FIMA will use is priced at $87,500 and has an implied modified duration of 6.85. To convert $10 million of bonds at a duration of 6.5 into cash requires adjusting the duration to that of a cash equivalent. A cash equivalent is a short-term instrument with a duration of less than 1.0. The equivalent instruments that FIMA would use if it did the transactions in cash would be six-month instruments. The average duration of a six-month instrument is three months or 0.25. The interest rate that drives the long-term bond market is assumed to have a yield beta of 1.0 with respect to the interest rate that drives the futures market.

FIMA could solve this problem in either of two ways. It could lower the duration on $10 million of bonds from 6.5 to 0.25. Then it could raise the duration on $20 million from 6.5 to 7.5. If FIMA converts $10 million to a duration of 0.25 and $20 million to a duration of 7.5, the overall duration would be $(10/30)0.25 + (20/30)7.50 = 5.08$. As an alternative, FIMA could just aim for lowering the overall duration to 5.08, but we shall illustrate the approach of adjusting the duration in two steps.

Thus, FIMA needs to lower the duration on $10 million from 6.5 to 0.25. Accordingly, the appropriate number of futures contracts is

$$N_f = \left(\frac{MDUR_T - MDUR_B}{MDUR_f}\right)\left(\frac{B}{f}\right) = \left(\frac{0.25 - 6.50}{6.85}\right)\left(\frac{\$10,000,000}{\$87,500}\right) = -104.28$$

So, FIMA should sell 104 contracts.

To increase the duration on $20 million from 6.5 to 7.5, the appropriate number of futures contracts is

$$N_f = \left(\frac{MDUR_T - MDUR_B}{MDUR_f}\right)\left(\frac{B}{f}\right) = \left(\frac{7.5 - 6.5}{6.85}\right)\left(\frac{\$20,000,000}{\$87,500}\right) = 33.37$$

Thus, FIMA should buy 33 futures contracts.

Because these transactions involve the same futures contract, the net effect is that FIMA should sell 71 contracts. Therefore, FIMA does just one transaction to sell 71 contracts.

## Scenario (12 December)

During this period, interest rates rose by 2 percent and the bonds decreased in value by 13 percent (6.5 duration times 2 percent). The futures price fell to $75,250. Thus, the $30 million bond portfolio fell by $30,000,000(0.13) = $3,900,000.

## Outcome and Analysis

The profit on the futures contracts is −71($75,250 − $87,500) = $869,750. So the overall loss is $3,900,000 − $869,750 = $3,030,250. The change in the portfolio value of 13 percent was based on an assumed yield change of 2 percent (6.5 duration times 0.02 = 0.13). A portfolio with a modified duration of 5.08 would, therefore, change by approximately 5.08(0.02) = 0.1016, or 10.16 percent. The portfolio thus would decrease by $30,000,000(0.1016) = $3,048,000.

---

**Exhibit 7**   *Continued*

The difference in this result and what was actually obtained is $17,750, or about 0.06 percent of the initial $30 million value of the portfolio. Some of this difference is due to rounding and some is due to the fact that bonds do not respond in the precise manner predicted by duration.

---

In Exhibit 8, we illustrate a similar situation involving a pension fund that would like to shift the allocation of its portfolio from large-cap stock to mid-cap stock. With futures contracts available on indices of both the large-cap and mid-cap sectors, the fund can do this by selling futures on the large-cap index and buying futures on the mid-cap index. The results come very close to replicating what would happen if it undertook transactions in the actual stocks. The futures transactions, however, take place in a market with much greater liquidity and lower transaction costs.

---

**Exhibit 8**   **Adjusting the Allocation between One Equity Class and Another**

## Scenario (30 April)

The pension fund of US Integrated Technology (USIT) holds $50 million of large-cap domestic equity. It would like to move $20 million from large-cap stocks to mid-cap stocks. The large-cap stocks have an average beta of 1.03. The desired beta of mid-cap stocks is 1.20. A futures contract on large-cap stocks has a price of $263,750 and a beta of 0.98. A futures contract on mid-cap stocks has a price of $216,500 and a beta of 1.14. The transaction will be initiated on 30 April and terminated on 29 May.

To distinguish the futures contracts, we use $N_{Lf}$ and $N_{Mf}$ as the number of large-cap and mid-cap futures contracts, $f_L$ and $f_M$ as the prices of large-cap and mid-cap futures contracts ($263,750 and $216,500, respectively), $\beta_L$ and $\beta_M$ as the betas of large-cap and mid-cap stocks (1.03 and 1.20, respectively), and $\beta_{Lf}$ and $\beta_{Mf}$ as the betas of the large-cap and mid-cap futures (0.98 and 1.14, respectively).

## Action

USIT first wants to convert $20 million of stock to cash and then convert $20 million of cash into mid-cap stock. It can use large-cap futures to convert the beta from 1.03 to zero and then use mid-cap futures to convert the beta from 0 to 1.20.

To convert the large-cap stock to cash will require

$$N_{Lf} = \left( \frac{\beta_T - \beta_L}{\beta_{Lf}} \right) \left( \frac{S}{f_L} \right) = \left( \frac{0.0 - 1.03}{0.98} \right) \left( \frac{\$20,000,000}{\$263,750} \right) = -79.70$$

So USIT sells 80 large-cap futures contracts. At this point, it has changed the beta to zero. Now it uses mid-cap futures to convert the beta from 0.0 to 1.20:

$$N_{Mf} = \left( \frac{\beta_M - \beta_T}{\beta_{Mf}} \right) \left( \frac{B}{f_M} \right) = \left( \frac{1.20 - 0.0}{1.14} \right) \left( \frac{\$20,000,000}{\$216,500} \right) = 97.24$$

So USIT buys 97 mid-cap futures contracts.

*(continued)*

| Exhibit 8 | Continued |
|-----------|-----------|

### Scenario (29 May)

Large-cap stocks increase by 2.47 percent, and the large-cap futures price increases to $269,948. Mid-cap stocks increase by 2.88 percent, and the mid-cap futures price increases to $222,432. The $50 million large-cap portfolio is now worth $50,000,000(1.0247) = $51,235,000.

### Outcome and Analysis

The profit on the large-cap futures contracts is −80($269,948 − $263,750) = −$495,840. The profit on the mid-cap futures contracts is 97($222,432 − $216,500) = $575,404. The total value of the fund is, therefore, $51,235,000 − $495,840 + $575,404 = $51,314,564.

Had the transactions been executed by selling $20 million of large-cap stock and buying $20 million of mid-cap stock, the value of the large-cap stock would be $30,000,000(1.0247) = $30,741,000, and the value of the mid-cap stock would be $20,000,000(1.0288) = $20,576,000, for a total value of $30,741,000 + $20,576,000 = $51,317,000.

This amount produces a difference of $2,436 compared with making the allocation synthetically, an insignificant percentage of the original portfolio value. The difference comes from the fact that stocks do not always respond in the exact manner predicted by their betas and also that the number of futures contracts is rounded off.

---

**Example 6**

Q-Tech Advisors manages a portfolio consisting of $100 million, allocated 70 percent to stock at a beta of 1.05 and 30 percent to bonds at a modified duration of 5.5. As a tactical strategy, it would like to temporarily adjust the allocation to 60 percent stock and 40 percent bonds. Also, it would like to change the beta on the stock position from 1.05 to 1.00 and the modified duration from 5.5 to 5.0. It will use a stock index futures contract, which is priced at $280,000 and has a beta of 0.98, and a bond futures contract, which is priced at $125,000 and has an implied modified duration of 6.50.

A. Determine how many stock index and bond futures contracts it should use and whether to go long or short.

B. At the horizon date, the stock portfolio has fallen by 3 percent and the bonds have risen by 1 percent. The stock index futures price is $272,160, and the bond futures price is $126,500. Determine the market value of the portfolio assuming the transactions specified in Part A are done, and compare it to the market value of the portfolio had the transactions been done in the securities themselves.

### Solution to A:

To reduce the allocation from 70 percent stock ($70 million) and 30 percent bonds ($30 million) to 60 percent stock ($60 million) and 40 percent bonds ($40 million), Q-Tech must synthetically sell $10 million of stock and buy $10 million of bonds. First, assume that Q-Tech will sell $10 million of stock and leave the proceeds in cash. Doing so will require

$$N_{sf} = \left(\frac{0-1.05}{0.98}\right)\left(\frac{\$10,000,000}{\$280,000}\right) = -38.27$$

futures contracts. It should sell 38 contracts, which creates synthetic cash of $10 million. To buy $10 million of bonds, Q-Tech should buy

$$N_{bf} = \left(\frac{5.50-0.0}{6.50}\right)\left(\frac{\$10,000,000}{\$125,000}\right) = 67.69$$

futures contracts, which rounds to 68. This transaction allows Q-Tech to synthetically borrow $10 million (selling a stock futures contract is equivalent to borrowing cash) and buy $10 million of bonds. Because we have created synthetic cash and a synthetic loan, these amounts offset. Thus, at this point, having sold 38 stock index futures and bought 68 bond futures, Q-Tech has effectively sold $10 million of stock and bought $10 million of bonds. It has produced a synthetically re-allocated portfolio of $60 million of stock and $40 million of bonds.

Now it needs to adjust the beta on the $60 million of stock to its target of 1.00. The number of futures contracts would, therefore, be

$$N_{sf} = \left(\frac{1.00-1.05}{0.98}\right)\left(\frac{\$60,000,000}{\$280,000}\right) = -10.93$$

So it should sell an additional 11 contracts. In total, it should sell 38 + 11 = 49 contracts.

To adjust the modified duration from 5.50 to its target of 5.00 on the $40 million of bonds, the number of futures contracts is

$$N_{bf} = \left(\frac{5-5.50}{6.50}\right)\left(\frac{\$40,000,000}{\$125,000}\right) = -24.62$$

So it should sell 25 contracts. In total, therefore, it should buy 68 − 25 = 43 contracts.

### Solution to B:

The value of the stock will be $70,000,000(1 − 0.03) = $67,900,000.

The profit on the stock index futures will be −49($272,160 − $280,000) = $384,160.

The total value of the stock position is therefore $67,900,000 + $384,160 = $68,284,160.

The value of the bonds will be $30,000,000(1.01) = $30,300,000.

The profit on the bond futures will be 43($126,500 − $125,000) = $64,500.

The total value of the bond position is, therefore, $30,300,000 + $64,500 = $30,364,500.

Therefore, the overall position is worth $68,284,160 + $30,364,500 = $98,648,660.

Had the transactions been done in the securities themselves, the stock would be worth $60,000,000(1 − 0.03) = $58,200,000. The bonds would be worth $40,000,000(1.01) = $40,400,000. The overall value of the portfolio would be $58,200,000 + $40,400,000 = $98,600,000, which is a difference of only $48,660 or 0.05 percent of the original value of the portfolio.

So far, we have looked only at allocating funds among different asset classes. In the next section, we place ourselves in the position that funds are not available to invest in any asset classes, but market opportunities are attractive. Futures contracts enable an investor to place itself in the market without yet having the actual cash in place.

## 4.2 Pre-Investing in an Asset Class

In all the examples so far, the investor is already in the market and wants to either alter the position to a different asset allocation or get out of the market altogether. Now consider that the investor might not be in the market but wants to get into the market. The investor might not have the cash to invest at a time when opportunities are attractive. Futures contracts do not require a cash outlay but can be used to add exposure. We call this approach pre-investing.

An advisor to a mutual fund would like to pre-invest $10 million in cash that it will receive in three months. It would like to allocate this money to a position of 60 percent stock and 40 percent bonds. It can do this by taking long positions in stock index futures and bond futures. The trick is to establish the position at the appropriate beta and duration. This strategy is illustrated in Exhibit 9. We see that the result using futures is very close to what it would have been if the fund had actually had the money and invested it in stocks and bonds.

---

| Exhibit 9 | Pre-Investing in Asset Classes |
|---|---|

### Scenario (28 February)

Quantitative Mutual Funds Advisors (QMFA) uses modern analytical techniques to manage money for a number of mutual funds. QMFA is not necessarily an aggressive investor, but it does not like to be out of the market. QMFA has learned that it will receive an additional $10 million to invest. Although QMFA would like to receive the money now, the money is not available for three months. If it had the money now, QMFA would invest $6 million in stocks at an average beta of 1.08 and $4 million in bonds at a modified duration of 5.25. It believes the market outlook over the next three months is highly attractive. Therefore, QMFA would like to invest now, which it can do by trading stock and bond futures. An appropriate stock index futures contract is selling at $210,500 and has a beta of 0.97. An appropriate bond futures contract is selling for $115,750 and has an implied modified duration of 6.05. The current date is 28 February, and the money will be available on 31 May. The number of stock index futures contracts will be denoted as $N_{sf}$, and the number of bond futures contracts will be denoted as $N_{bf}$.

### Action

QMFA wants to take a position in $6 million of stock index futures at a beta of 1.08. It currently has no position; hence, its beta is zero. The required number of stock index futures contracts to obtain this position is

$$N_{sf} = \left(\frac{\beta_T - \beta_S}{\beta_f}\right)\left(\frac{S}{f}\right) = \left(\frac{1.08 - 0.0}{0.97}\right)\left(\frac{\$6,000,000}{\$210,500}\right) = 31.74$$

So QMFA buys 32 stock index futures contracts.

To gain exposure at a duration of 5.25 on $4 million of bonds, the number of bond futures contracts is

$$N_{bf} = \left(\frac{MDUR_T - MDUR_B}{MDUR_f}\right)\left(\frac{B}{f}\right) = \left(\frac{5.25 - 0.0}{6.05}\right)\left(\frac{\$4,000,000}{\$115,750}\right) = 29.99$$

Thus, QMFA buys 30 bond futures contracts.

| **Exhibit 9** | **Continued** |
|---|---|

## Scenario (31 May)

During this period, the stock increased by 2.2 percent and the bonds increased by 0.75 percent. The stock index futures price increased to $214,500, and the bond futures price increased to $116,734.

## Outcome and Analysis

The profit on the stock index futures contracts is 32($214,500 − $210,500) = $128,000. The profit on the bond futures contracts is 30($116,734 − $115,750) = $29,520. The total profit is, therefore, $128,000 + $29,520 = $157,520.

Had QMFA actually invested the money, the stock would have increased in value by $6,000,000(0.022) = $132,000, and the bonds would have increased in value by $4,000,000(0.0075) = $30,000, for a total increase in value of $132,000 + $30,000 = $162,000, which is relatively close to the futures gain of $157,520. The difference of $4,480 between this approach and the synthetic one is about 0.04 percent of the $10 million invested. This difference is due to the fact that stocks and bonds do not always respond in the manner predicted by their betas and durations and also that the number of futures contracts is rounded off.

---

In a transaction like the one just described, the fund is effectively borrowing against the cash it will receive in the future by pre-investing. Recall that

Long underlying + Short futures = Long risk-free bond

which means that

Long underlying = Long risk-free bond + Long futures

In this example, however, the investor does not have the long position in the risk-free bond. That would require cash. We can remove the long risk-free bond in the equation above by off-setting it with a loan in which we borrow the cash. Hence, adding a loan to both sides gives[31]

Long underlying + Loan = Long futures

An outright long position in futures is like a fully leveraged position in the underlying. So in this example, we have effectively borrowed against the cash we will receive in the future and invested in the underlying.

### Example 7

Total Asset Strategies (TAST) specializes in a variety of risk management strategies, one of which is to enable investors to take positions in markets in anticipation of future transactions in securities. One of its popular strategies is to have the client invest when it does not have the money but will be receiving it later. One client interested in this strategy will receive $6 million at a later date but wants to proceed and take a position of $3 million in stock and $3 million

---

**31** The right-hand side is a long risk-free bond and a loan of the same amount, which offset each other.

in bonds. The desired stock beta is 1.0, and the desired bond duration is 6.2. A stock index futures contract is priced at $195,000 and has a beta of 0.97. A bond futures contract is priced at $110,000 and has an implied modified duration of 6.0.

**A.** Find the number of stock and bond futures contracts TAST should trade and whether it should go long or short.

**B.** At expiration, the stock has gone down by 5 percent, and the stock index futures price is down to $185,737.50. The bonds are up 2 percent, and the bond futures price is up to $112,090. Determine the value of the portfolio and compare it with what it would have been had the transactions been made in the actual securities.

**Solution to A:**

The approximate number of stock index futures is

$$\left(\frac{1.00-0.0}{0.97}\right)\left(\frac{\$3,000,000}{\$195,000}\right) = 15.86$$

So TAST should buy 16 contracts. The number of bond futures is

$$\left(\frac{6.2-0.0}{6.0}\right)\left(\frac{\$3,000,000}{\$110,000}\right) = 28.18$$

So it should buy 28 contracts.

**Solution to B:**

The profit on the stock index futures is 16($185,737.50 − $195,000) = −$148,200.
    The profit on the bond futures is 28($112,090 − $110,000) = $58,520. The total profit is −$148,200 + $58,520 = −$89,680, a loss of $89,680. Suppose TAST had invested directly. The stock would have been worth $3,000,000(1 − 0.05) = $2,850,000, and the bonds would have been worth $3,000,000(1.02) = $3,060,000, for a total value of $2,850,000 + $3,060,000 = $5,910,000, or a loss of $90,000, which is about the same as the loss using only the futures.

When the cash is eventually received, the investor will close out the futures position and invest the cash. This transaction is equivalent to paying off this implicit loan. The investor will then be long the underlying.

We should remember that this position is certainly a speculative one. By taking a leveraged long position in the market, the investor is speculating that the market will perform well enough to cover the cost of borrowing. If this does not happen, the losses could be significant. But such is the nature of leveraged speculation with a specific horizon.

So far, all of the strategies we have examined have involved domestic transactions. We now take a look at how foreign currency derivatives can be used to handle common transactions faced in global commerce.

# 5   STRATEGIES AND APPLICATIONS FOR MANAGING FOREIGN CURRENCY RISK

The risk associated with changes in exchange rates between currencies directly affects many companies. Any company that engages in business with companies or customers in other countries is exposed to this risk. The volatility of exchange rates results in considerable uncertainty for companies that sell products in other countries as well as for those companies that buy products in other countries. Companies are affected not only by the exchange rate uncertainty itself but also by its effects on their ability to plan for the future. For example, consider a company with a foreign subsidiary. This subsidiary generates sales in the foreign currency that will eventually be converted back into its domestic currency. To implement a business plan that enables the company to establish a realistic target income, the company must not only predict its foreign sales, but it must also predict the exchange rate at which it will convert its foreign cash flows into domestic cash flows. The company may be an expert on whatever product it makes or service it provides and thus be in a good position to make reasonable forecasts of sales. But predicting foreign exchange rates with much confidence is extremely difficult, even for experts in the foreign exchange business. A company engaged in some other line of work can hardly expect to be able to predict foreign exchange rates very well. Hence, many such businesses choose to manage this kind of risk by locking in the exchange rate on future cash flows with the use of derivatives. This type of exchange rate risk is called **transaction exposure**.

In addition to the risk associated with foreign cash flows, exchange rate volatility also affects a company's accounting statements. When a company combines the balance sheets of foreign subsidiaries into a consolidated balance sheet for the entire company, the numbers from the balance sheets of foreign subsidiaries must be converted into its domestic currency at an appropriate exchange rate. Hence, exchange rate risk manifests itself in this arena as well. This type of exchange rate risk is called **translation exposure**.

Finally, we should note that exchange rate uncertainty can also affect a company by making its products or services either more or less competitive with those of comparable foreign companies. This type of risk can affect any type of company, even if it does not sell its goods or services in foreign markets. For example, suppose the U.S. dollar is exceptionally strong. This condition makes U.S. products and services more expensive to non-U.S. residents and will lead to a reduction in travel to the United States. Hence, the owner of a hotel in the Disney World area, even though her cash flow is entirely denominated in dollars, will suffer a loss of sales when the dollar is strong because fewer non-U.S. residents will travel to the United States, visit Disney World, and stay in her hotel. Likewise, foreign travel will be cheaper for U.S. citizens, and more of them will visit foreign countries instead of Disney World.[32] This type of risk is called **economic exposure**.

In this reading, we shall focus on managing the risk of transaction exposure. The management of translation exposure requires a greater focus on accounting than we can provide here. Managing economic exposure requires the forecasting of demand in light of competitive products and exchange rates, and we shall not address this risk.

The management of a single cash flow that will have to be converted from one currency to another is generally done using forward contracts. Futures contracts tend to be too standardized to meet the needs of most companies. Futures are primarily used by dealers to manage their foreign exchange portfolios.[33] Therefore, in the two examples here, we use forward contracts to manage the risk of a single foreign cash flow.

---

**32** Even U.S. citizens who would never travel abroad would not increase their trips to Disney World because of the more favorable exchange rate.

**33** In some cases, single cash flows are managed using currency options, which we cover in the reading on risk management applications of option strategies. A series of foreign cash flows is usually managed using currency swaps, which we cover in the reading on risk management applications of swap strategies.

## 5.1  Managing the Risk of a Foreign Currency Receipt

When due to receive cash flows denominated in a foreign currency, companies can be viewed as being long the currency. They will convert the currency to their domestic currency and, hence, will be selling the foreign currency to obtain the domestic currency. If the domestic currency increases in value while the company is waiting to receive the cash flow, the domestic currency will be more expensive, and the company will receive fewer units of the domestic currency for the given amount of foreign currency. Thus, being long the foreign currency, the company should consider selling the currency in the forward market by going short a currency forward contract.

Exhibit 10 illustrates the case of a company that anticipates the receipt of a future cash flow denominated in euros. By selling a forward contract on the amount of euros it expects to receive, the company locks in the exchange rate at which it will convert the euros. We assume the contract calls for actual delivery of the euros, as opposed to a cash settlement, so the company simply transfers the euros to the dealer, which sends the domestic currency to the company. If the transaction were structured to be settled in cash, the company would sell the euros on the market for the exchange rate at that time, $S_T$, and the forward contract would be cash settled for a payment of $-(S_T - F)$, where F is the rate agreed on at the start of the forward contract—in other words, the forward exchange rate. The net effect is that the company receives F, the forward rate for the euros.

| **Exhibit 10** | Managing the Risk of a Foreign Currency Receipt |
|---|---|

### Scenario (15 August)

H-Tech Hardware, a U.S. company, sells its products in many countries. It recently received an order for some computer hardware from a major European government. The sale is denominated in euros and is in the amount of €50 million. H-Tech will be paid in euros; hence, it bears exchange rate risk. The current date is 15 August, and the euros will be received on 3 December.

### Action

On 15 August, H-Tech decides to lock in the 3 December exchange rate by entering into a forward contract that obligates it to deliver €50 million and receive a rate of $0.877. H-Tech is effectively long the euro in its computer hardware sale, so a short position in the forward market is appropriate.

### Scenario (3 December)

The exchange rate on this day is $S_T$, but as we shall see, this value is irrelevant for H-Tech because it is hedged.

### Outcome and Analysis

The company receives its €50 million, delivers it to the dealer, and is paid $0.877 per euro for a total payment of €50,000,000($0.877) = $43,850,000. H-Tech thus pays the €50 million and receives $43.85 million, based on the rate locked in on 15 August.

## 5.2  Managing the Risk of a Foreign Currency Payment

In Exhibit 11, we see the opposite type of problem. A U.S. company is obligated to purchase a foreign currency at a later date. Because an increase in the exchange rate will hurt it, the U.S. company is effectively short the currency. Hence, to lock in the rate now, it needs to go long the forward contract. Regardless of the exchange rate at expiration, the company purchases the designated amount of currency at the forward rate agreed to in the contract now.

| Exhibit 11 | Managing the Risk of a Foreign Currency Payment |
| --- | --- |

### Scenario (2 March)

American Manufacturing Catalyst (AMC) is a U.S. company that occasionally makes steel and copper purchases from non-U.S. companies to meet unexpected demand that cannot be filled through its domestic suppliers. On 2 March, AMC determines that it will need to buy a large quantity of steel from a Japanese company on 1 April. It has entered into a contract with the Japanese company to pay ¥900 million for the steel. At a current exchange rate of $0.0083 per yen, the purchase will currently cost ¥900,000,000($0.0083) = $7,470,000. AMC faces the risk of the yen strengthening.

### Action

In its future steel purchase, AMC is effectively short yen, because it will need to purchase yen at a later date. Thus, a long forward contract is appropriate. AMC decides to lock in the exchange rate for 1 April by entering into a long forward contract on ¥900 million with a dealer. The forward rate is $0.008309. AMC will be obligated to purchase ¥900 million on 1 April and pay a rate of $0.008309.

### Scenario (1 April)

The exchange rate for yen is $S_T$. As we shall see, this value is irrelevant for AMC, because it is hedged.

### Outcome and Analysis

The company purchases ¥900 million from the dealer and pays $0.008309, for a total payment of ¥900,000,000($0.008309) = $7,478,100. This amount was known on 2 March. AMC gets the yen it needs and uses it to purchase the steel.

---

In Exhibit 10, a company agreed to accept a fixed amount of the foreign currency for the sale of its computer hardware. In Exhibit 11, a company agreed to pay a fixed amount of the foreign currency to acquire the steel. You may be wondering why in both cases the transaction was denominated in the foreign currency. In some cases, a company might be able to lock in the amount of currency in domestic units. It all depends on the relative bargaining power of the buyer and the seller and on how badly each wants to make the sale. Companies with the expertise to manage foreign exchange risk can use that expertise to offer contracts denominated in either currency to their counterparts on the other side of the transaction. For example, in the second case, suppose the Japanese company was willing to lock in the exchange rate using a forward contract with one of its derivatives dealers. Then the Japanese company could offer the U.S. company the contract in U.S. dollars. The ability to manage exchange rate risk and offer customers a price in either currency can be an attractive feature for a seller.

### Example 8

Royal Tech Ltd. is a U.K. technology company that has recently acquired a U.S. subsidiary. The subsidiary has an underfunded pension fund, and Royal Tech has absorbed the subsidiary's employees into its own pension fund, bringing the

U.S. subsidiary's defined-benefit plan up to an adequate level of funding. Soon Royal Tech will be making its first payments to retired employees in the United States. Royal Tech is obligated to pay about $1.5 million to these retirees. It can easily set aside in risk-free bonds the amount of pounds it will need to make the payment, but it is concerned about the foreign currency risk in making the U.S. dollar payment. To manage this risk, Royal Tech is considering using a forward contract that has a contract rate of £0.60 per dollar.

**A.** Determine how Royal Tech would eliminate this risk by identifying an appropriate forward transaction. Be sure to specify the notional principal and state whether to go long or short. What domestic transaction should it undertake?

**B.** At expiration of the forward contract, the spot exchange rate is $S_T$. Explain what happens.

### Solution to A:

Royal Tech will need to come up with $1,500,000 and is obligated to buy dollars at a later date. It is thus short dollars. To have $1,500,000 secured at the forward contract expiration, Royal Tech would need to go long a forward contract on the dollar. With the forward rate equal to £0.60, the contract will need a notional principal of £900,000. So Royal Tech must set aside funds so that it will have £900,000 available when the forward contract expires. When it delivers the £900,000, it will receive £900,000(1/£0.60) = $1,500,000, where 1/£0.60 ≈ $1.67 is the dollar-per-pound forward rate.

### Solution to B:

At expiration, it will not matter what the spot exchange rate is. Royal Tech will deliver £900,000 and receive $1,500,000.

## 5.3 Managing the Risk of a Foreign-Market Asset Portfolio

One of the dominant themes in the world of investments in the last 20 years has been the importance of diversifying internationally. The increasing globalization of commerce has created a greater willingness on the part of investors to think beyond domestic borders and add foreign securities to a portfolio.[34] Thus, more asset managers are holding or considering holding foreign stocks and bonds. An important consideration in making such a decision is the foreign currency risk. Should a manager accept this risk, hedge the foreign market risk and the foreign currency risk, or hedge only the foreign currency risk?

It is tempting to believe that the manager should accept the foreign market risk, using it to further diversify the portfolio, and hedge the foreign currency risk. In fact, many asset managers claim to do so. A closer look, however, reveals that it is virtually impossible to actually do this.

Consider a U.S. asset management firm that owns a portfolio currently invested in euro-denominated stock worth $S_0$, where $S_0$ is the current stock price in euros. The exchange rate is $FX_0$ dollars per euro. Therefore, the portfolio is currently worth $S_0(FX_0)$ in dollars. At a future time, t, the portfolio is worth $S_t$ in euros and the exchange rate is $FX_t$. So the portfolio would then be worth $S_t(FX_t)$. The firm is long both the stock and the euro.

---

**34** Ironically, the increasing globalization of commerce has increased the correlation among the securities markets of various countries. With this higher correlation, the benefits of international diversification are much smaller.

A forward contract on the euro would require the firm to deliver a certain number of euros and receive the forward rate, F. The number of euros to be delivered, however, would need to be specified in the contract. In this situation, the firm would end up delivering $S_t$ euros. This amount is unknown at the time the forward contract is initiated. Thus, it would not be possible to know how many euros the firm would need to deliver.

Some companies manage this problem by estimating an expected future value of the portfolio. They enter into a hedge based on that expectation and adjust the hedge to accommodate any changes in expectations. Other companies hedge a minimum portfolio value. They estimate that it is unlikely the portfolio value will fall below a certain level and then sell a forward contract for a size based on this minimum value.[35] This approach leaves the companies hedged for a minimum value, but any increase in the value of the portfolio beyond the minimum would not be hedged. Therefore, any such gains could be wiped out by losses in the value of the currency.

So, with the exception of one special and complex case we discuss below, it is not possible to leave the local equity market return exposed and hedge the currency risk.[36] If the local market return is hedged, then it would be possible to hedge the currency risk. The hedge of the local market return would lock in the amount of the foreign currency that would be converted at the hedge termination date. Of course, the company can hedge the local market return and leave the currency risk unhedged. Or it can hedge neither.[37]

In Exhibit 12, we examine the two possibilities that can be executed: hedging the local market risk and hedging both the local market risk *and* the foreign currency risk. We first use futures on the foreign equity portfolio as though no currency risk existed. This transaction attempts to lock in the future value of the portfolio. This locked-in return should be close to the foreign risk-free rate. If we also choose to hedge the currency risk, we then know that the future value of the portfolio will tell us the number of units of the foreign currency that we shall have available to convert to domestic currency at the hedge termination date. Then we would know the amount of notional principal to use in a forward contract to hedge the exchange rate risk.

| Exhibit 12 | Managing the Risk of a Foreign-Currency-Denominated Asset Portfolio |
|---|---|

## Scenario (31 December)

AZ Asset Management is a U.S. firm that invests money for wealthy individual investors. Concerned that it does not know how to manage foreign currency risk, so far AZ has invested only in U.S. markets. Recently, it began learning about managing currency risk and would like to begin investing in foreign markets with a small position worth €10 million. The proposed portfolio has a beta of 1.10. AZ is considering either hedging the European equity market return and leaving the currency risk unhedged, or hedging the currency risk as well as the European equity market return. If it purchases the €10 million portfolio, it will put this hedge in place on 31 December and plans to leave the position open until 31 December of the following year.

*(continued)*

**35** One way to assure a minimum value would be to use a put option. We shall take up this strategy in the reading on risk management applications of option strategies.

**36** The foreign equity market return is often referred to as the local market return, a term we shall use henceforth.

**37** In fact, some compelling arguments exist for hedging neither. The currency risk can be unrelated to the domestic market risk, thereby offering some further diversifying risk-reduction possibilities.

| Exhibit 12 | Continued |
|---|---|

For hedging the European equity market risk, it will use a stock index futures contract on a euro-denominated stock index. This contract is priced at €120,000 and has a beta of 0.95. If it hedges the currency risk, it will use a dollar-denominated forward contract on the euro. That contract has a price of $0.815 and can have any notional principal that the parties agree on at the start. The current spot exchange rate is $0.80. The foreign risk-free rate is 4 percent, which is stated as an annually compounded rate. The domestic risk-free rate is 6 percent.

## Action

*Hedging the equity market risk only*: To eliminate the risk on the portfolio of stock that has a beta of 1.10 would require

$$N_f = \left(\frac{0-1.10}{0.95}\right)\left(\frac{10,000,000}{120,000}\right) = -96.49$$

contracts. This amount would be rounded to 96, so AZ would sell 96 contracts.

*Hedging the equity market risk and the currency risk*: Again, AZ would sell 96 stock index futures contracts. It would enter into a forward contract to lock in the exchange rate on a certain amount of euros on 31 December. The question is, how many euros will it have? If the futures contract hedges the stock portfolio, it should earn the foreign risk-free rate. Thus, the portfolio should be worth €10,000,000(1.04) = €10,400,000. So, AZ expects to have €10,400,000 on the following 31 December and will convert this amount back to dollars. So the notional principal on the forward contract should be €10.4 million. Note that the starting portfolio value in dollars is €10,000,000($0.80) = $8,000,000.

## Scenario (31 December of the Following Year)

During the year, the European stock market went down 4.55 percent. Given the portfolio beta of 1.10, it declines by 4.55(1.10) = 5 percent. The portfolio is now worth €10,000,000(1 − 0.05) = €9,500,000. The exchange rate fell to $0.785, and the futures price fell to €110,600.

## Outcome and Analysis

*If nothing is hedged*: The portfolio is converted to dollars at $0.785 and is worth €9,500,000(0.785) = $7,457,500. This amount represents a loss of 6.8 percent over the initial value of $8,000,000.

*If only the European stock market is hedged*: The profit on the futures would be −96(€110,600 − €120,000) = €902,400. Adding this amount to the value of the portfolio gives a value of €9,500,000 + €902,400 = €10,402,400, which is an increase in value of 4.02 percent, or approximately the foreign risk-free rate, as it should be. This amount is converted to dollars to obtain €10,402,400($0.785) = $8,165,884, a gain of 2.07 percent.

*If the European stock market and the currency risk are both hedged*: AZ sold €10.4 million of euros in the forward market at $0.815. The contract will settle in cash and show a profit of €10,400,000($0.785 − $0.815) = $312,000. This leaves the overall portfolio value at $8,165,884 + $312,000 = $8,477,884, a gain of 5.97 percent, or approximately the domestic risk-free rate.

In this case, the foreign stock market went down *and* the foreign currency went down. Without the hedge, the loss was almost 7 percent. With the foreign

| Exhibit 12 | Continued |
|---|---|

stock market hedge, the loss turns into a gain of 2 percent. With the currency hedge added, the loss becomes a gain of almost 6 percent. Of course, different outcomes could occur. Gains from a stronger foreign stock market and a stronger currency would be lost if the company had made these same hedges.

Note, however, that once AZ hedges the foreign market return, it can expect to earn only the foreign risk-free rate. If it hedges the foreign market return and the exchange rate, it can expect to earn only its domestic risk-free rate. Therefore, neither strategy makes much sense for the long run. In the short run, however, this strategy can be a good tactic for investors who are already in foreign markets and who wish to temporarily take a more defensive position without liquidating the portfolio and converting it to cash.

## Example 9

FCA Managers (FCAM) is a U.S. asset management firm. Among its asset classes is a portfolio of Swiss stocks worth SF10 million, which has a beta of 1.00. The spot exchange rate is $0.75, the Swiss interest rate is 5 percent, and the U.S. interest rate is 6 percent. Both of these interest rates are compounded in the LIBOR manner: Rate × (Days/360). These rates are consistent with a six-month forward rate of $0.7537. FCAM is considering hedging the local market return on the portfolio and possibly hedging the exchange rate risk for a six-month period. A futures contract on the Swiss market is priced at SF300,000 and has a beta of 0.90.

**A.** What futures position should FCAM take to hedge the Swiss market return? What return could it expect?

**B.** Assuming that it hedges the Swiss market return, how could it hedge the exchange rate risk as well, and what return could it expect?

### Solution to A:

To hedge the Swiss local market return, the number of futures contracts is

$$N_f = \left(\frac{0-1.00}{0.90}\right)\left(\frac{SF10,000,000}{SF300,000}\right) = -37.04$$

So FCAM should sell 37 contracts. Because the portfolio is perfectly hedged, its return should be the Swiss risk-free rate of 5 percent.

### Solution to B:

If hedged, the Swiss portfolio should grow to a value of SF10,000,000[1 + 0.05(180/360)] = SF10,250,000.

FCAM could hedge this amount with a forward contract with this much notional principal. If the portfolio is hedged, it will convert to a value of SF10,250,000($0.7537) = $7,725,425.

In dollars, the portfolio was originally worth SF10,000,000($0.75) = 7,500,000.

Thus, the return is $\frac{\$7,725,425}{\$7,500,000} - 1 \approx 0.03$, which is the U.S. risk-free rate for six months.

We see that if only the foreign stock market return is hedged, the portfolio return is the foreign risk-free rate before converting to the domestic currency. If both the foreign stock market and the exchange rate risk are hedged, the return equals the domestic risk-free rate.

As a temporary and tactical strategy, hedging one or both risks can make sense. There are certainly periods when one might be particularly concerned about these risks and might wish to eliminate them. Executing this sort of strategy can be much easier than selling all of the foreign stocks and possibly converting the proceeds into domestic currency. But in the long run, a strategy of investing in foreign markets, hedging that risk, and hedging the exchange rate risk hardly makes much sense.

## 6    FUTURES OR FORWARDS?

As we have seen, numerous opportunities and strategies exist for managing risk using futures and forwards. We have largely ignored the issue of which instrument—futures or forwards—is better. Some types of hedges are almost always executed using futures, and some are almost always executed using forwards. Why the preference for one over the other? First, let us recall the primary differences between the two:

- Futures contracts are standardized, with all terms except for the price set by the futures exchange. Forward contracts are customized. The two parties set the terms according to their needs.

- Futures contracts are guaranteed by the clearinghouse against default. Forward contracts subject each party to the possibility of default by the other party.

- Futures contracts require margin deposits and the daily settlement of gains and losses. Forward contracts pay off the full value of the contract at expiration. Some participants in forward contracts agree prior to expiration to use margin deposits and occasional settlements to reduce the default risk.

- Futures contracts are regulated by federal authorities. Forward contracts are essentially unregulated.

- Futures contracts are conducted in a public arena, the futures exchange, and are reported to the exchanges and the regulatory authority. Forward contracts are conducted privately, and individual transactions are not generally reported to the public or regulators.

Risks that are associated with very specific dates, such as when interest rates are reset on a loan, usually require forward contracts. Thus, we used an FRA to lock in the rate on a loan. That rate is set on a specific day. A futures contract has specific expirations that may not correspond to the day on which the rate is reset. Although it is possible to use sophisticated models and software to compensate for this problem, typical borrowers do not usually possess the expertise to do so. It is much easier for them to use an FRA.

Oddly enough, however, the risk of most bond portfolios is managed using Treasury bond futures. Those portfolios have horizon dates for which the company is attempting to lock in values. But usually rates are not being reset on that date, and the hedge does not need to be perfect. Often there is flexibility with respect to the horizon date. Treasury bond futures work reasonably well for these investors. Likewise, the risk of equity portfolios tends to be managed with stock index futures. Even though the offsetting of risks is not precise, that is not a necessity. Equity and debt portfolio managers usually need only satisfactory protection against market declines. Nonetheless, in some cases equity and debt portfolio managers use over-the-counter instruments such as forward contracts. In fact, sometimes a portfolio manager will ask a derivatives dealer to write a forward contract on a specific portfolio. This approach is more costly than using futures and provides a better hedge, but, as noted, a perfect hedge is usually not needed. In practice, portfolio managers have traded off the costs of customized hedges with the costs of using standardized futures contracts and have found the latter to be preferable.[38]

Forward contracts are the preferred vehicle for the risk management of foreign currency. This preference partly reflects the deep liquidity in the forward market, which has been around longer than the futures market. Moreover, much of this trading is undertaken by corporations managing the risk of either the issuance of a bond or the inflows and outcomes of specific currency transactions, in which case the precision provided by customized transactions is preferred.

Nevertheless, one might wonder why certain contracts do not die out. Recall that most corporations do not use the Eurodollar futures market to hedge their floating-rate loans. Yet the Eurodollar futures contract is one of the most active of all futures contracts in the world. Where does this volume come from? It is from the dealers in swaps, options, and FRAs. When they enter into transactions with end users in which the underlying rate is LIBOR, they must manage the risk they have assumed, and they must do so very quickly. They cannot afford to leave their positions exposed for long. It is rarely possible for them to simply pick up the phone and find another customer to take the opposite side of the transaction. A corporate client with the exact opposite needs at the exact same time as some other end user would be rare. Therefore, dealers need to execute offsetting transactions very quickly. There is no better place to do this than in the Eurodollar futures markets, with its extremely deep liquidity. These dealer companies have sophisticated analysts and software and are able to manage the risk caused by such problems as the futures contract expiring on one day and the payoffs on the FRAs being set on another day. Thus, these risks can be more effectively measured and managed by dealers than by end users.

As we have emphasized, futures contracts require margin deposits and the daily settling of gains and losses. This process causes some administrative problems because money must be deposited into a futures account and cash flows must be managed on a daily basis. When futures brokers call for more money to cover losses, companies using futures contracts must send cash or very liquid securities. Although the brokers may be generating value on the other side of a hedge transaction, that value may not produce actual cash.[39] On the other hand, forward transactions, while not necessarily requiring margin deposits, generate concerns over whether the counterparty will be able to pay at expiration. Of course, those concerns lead some counterparties to require margins and periodic settlements.

Although forward contracts are essentially unregulated while futures contracts are heavily regulated, this factor is not usually a major consideration in deciding which type of contract to use. In some cases, however, regulation prevents use of a specific contract. For example, a country might prohibit foreign futures exchanges from offering their products in its markets. There would probably be no such prohibition on forward contracts.[40] In some cases, regulation prevents or delays usage of certain futures products, making it possible for innovative companies that can create forward

---

**38** Portfolio managers do use swaps on occasion, as we cover in the reading on risk management applications of swap strategies.

**39** Consider, for example, a company that sells futures contracts to hedge the value of a bond portfolio. Suppose interest rates fall, the bond portfolio rises, and the futures price also rises. Losses will be incurred on the futures contracts and additional margin deposits will be required. The bond portfolio has increased in value, but it may not be practical to liquidate the portfolio to generate the necessary cash.

**40** In some less developed but highly regulated countries, private financial transactions such as forward contracts can be prohibited.

products to offer them ahead of the comparable products of futures exchanges. The futures exchanges claim this is unfair by making it more difficult for them to compete with forward markets in providing risk management products.

We also noted that futures contracts are public transactions, whereas forward contracts are private transactions. This privacy characteristic can cause a company to prefer a forward transaction if it does not want others, such as traders on the futures exchange, to know its views.

## 7   FINAL COMMENTS

A few points are worth repeating. Because they can be somewhat unstable, betas and durations are difficult to measure, even under the best of circumstances. Even when no derivatives transactions are undertaken, the values believed to be the betas and durations may not truly turn out to reflect the sensitivities of stocks and bonds to the underlying sources of risk. Therefore, if derivatives transactions do not work out to provide the exact hedging results expected, users should not necessarily blame derivatives. If, however, speculative long (short) positions are added to an otherwise long position, risk should increase (decrease), although the exact amount of the increase (decrease) cannot be known for sure in advance.[41] Derivatives should not be maligned for their speculative use when there are valuable hedging uses.

We have mentioned that transaction costs are a major consideration in the use of derivatives, and this is clearly the case with futures and forwards. By some reports, transactions costs for stock index derivatives are approximately 95 percent lower than for stock indices.[42] Indeed, one of the major reasons that derivatives exist is that they provide a means of trading at lower transaction costs. To survive as risk management products, derivatives need to be much less expensive than the value of the underlying instruments. There are almost no situations in which transacting in the underlying securities would be preferable to using derivatives on a transaction-cost basis, when taking a position for a specified short horizon.

Transacting in futures and forwards also has a major advantage of being less disruptive to the portfolio and its managers. For example, the asset classes of many portfolios are managed by different persons or firms. If the manager of the overall portfolio wants to change the risk of certain asset classes or alter the allocations between asset classes, he can do so using derivatives. Instead of telling one manager that she must sell securities and another manager that he must buy securities, the portfolio manager can use derivatives to reduce the allocation to one class and increase the allocation to the other. The asset class managers need not even know that the overall asset allocation has been changed. They can concentrate on doing the best they can within their respective areas of responsibility.

In the matter of liquidity, however, futures and forwards do not always offer the advantages often attributed to them. They require less capital to trade than the underlying securities, but they are not immune to liquidity problems. Nowhere is this concern more evident than in using a futures contract that expires a long time from

---

**41** We use the expression "should increase (decrease)" to reflect the fact that some other factors could cause perverse results. We previously mentioned call features and credit risk of such assets as corporate and municipal bonds that could result in a bond price not moving in the same direction as a move in the general level of bond prices. A poorly diversified stock portfolio could move opposite to the market, thereby suggesting a negative beta that is really only diversifiable risk. We assume that these situations are rare or that their likelihood and consequences have been properly assessed by risk managers.

**42** These statements are based on trading all individual stocks that make up an index. Trading through exchange-traded funds would reduce some of these stock trading costs.

the present. The greatest liquidity in the futures markets is in the shortest expirations. Although there may be futures contracts available with long-term expirations, their liquidity is much lower. Many forward markets are very liquid, but others may not be. High liquidity should not automatically be assumed of all derivatives, although in general, derivatives are more liquid than the underlying securities.

Many organizations are not permitted to use futures or forwards. Futures and forwards are fully leveraged positions, because they essentially require no equity. Some companies might have a policy against fully leveraged positions but might permit options, which are not fully leveraged. Loss potential is much greater on purchased or sold futures or forwards, whereas losses are capped on purchased options. Some organizations, however, permit futures and forwards but prohibit options. Other organizations might prohibit credit-risky instruments, such as forwards and over-the-counter options, but permit credit-risk-free instruments, such as futures and exchange-listed options. These restrictions, although sometimes misguided, are realistic constraints that must be considered when deciding how to manage risk.

In conclusion, futures and forward contracts are both alike and different. On some occasions, one is preferred over the other. Both types of contracts have their niches. The most important point they have in common is that they have zero value at the start and offer linear payoffs, meaning that no one "invests" any money in either type of contract at the start, but the cost is paid for by the willingness to give up gains and incur losses resulting from movements in the underlying. Options, which require a cash investment at the start, allow a party to capture favorable movements in the underlying while avoiding unfavorable movements. This type of payoff is nonlinear. In some cases, options will be preferred to other types of derivatives.

## SUMMARY

OPTIONAL
SEGMENT

- A borrower can lock in the rate that will be set at a future date on a single-payment loan by entering into a long position in an FRA. The FRA obligates the borrower to make a fixed interest payment and receive a floating interest payment, thereby protecting the borrower if the loan rate is higher than the fixed rate in the FRA but also eliminating gains if the loan rate is lower than the fixed rate in the FRA.

- The duration of a bond futures contract is determined as the duration of the bond underlying the futures contract as of the futures expiration, based on the yield of the bond underlying the futures contract. The modified duration is obtained by dividing the duration by 1 plus the yield. The duration of a futures contract is implied by these factors and is called the implied (modified) duration.

- The implied yield of a futures contract is the yield implied by the futures price on the bond underlying the futures contract as of the futures expiration.

- The yield beta is the sensitivity of the yield on a bond portfolio relative to the implied yield on the futures contract.

- The number of bond futures contracts required to change the duration of a bond portfolio is based on the ratio of the market value of the bonds to the futures price multiplied by the difference between the target or desired modified duration and the actual modified duration, divided by the implied modified duration of the futures.

END OPTIONAL
SEGMENT

■ The actual adjusted duration of a bond portfolio may not equal the desired duration for a number of reasons, including that the yield beta may be inaccurate or unstable or the bonds could contain call features or default risk. In addition, duration is a measure of instantaneous risk and may not accurately capture the risk over a long horizon without frequent portfolio adjustments.

■ The number of equity futures contracts required to change the beta of an equity portfolio is based on the ratio of the market value of the stock to the futures price times the difference between the target or desired beta and the actual beta, divided by the beta of the futures.

■ A long position in stock is equivalent to a long position in futures and a long position in a risk-free bond; therefore, it is possible to synthetically create a long position in stock by buying futures on stock and a risk-free bond. This process is called equitizing cash and can be used to create a synthetic stock index fund.

■ A long position in cash is equivalent to a long position in stock and a short position in stock futures. Therefore, it is possible to synthetically create a long position in cash by buying stock and selling futures.

■ The allocation of a portfolio between equity and debt can be adjusted using stock index and bond futures. Buy futures to increase the allocation to an asset class, and sell futures to decrease the allocation to an asset class.

■ The allocation of a bond portfolio between cash and high-duration bonds can be adjusted by using bond futures. Sell futures to increase the allocation to cash, and buy futures to increase the allocation to long-term bonds.

■ The allocation of an equity portfolio among different equity sectors can be adjusted by using stock index futures. Sell futures on an index representing one sector to decrease the allocation to that sector, and buy futures on an index representing another sector to increase the allocation to that sector.

■ A portfolio manager can buy bond or stock index futures to take a position in an asset class without having cash to actually invest in the asset class. This type of strategy is sometimes used in anticipation of the receipt of a sum of cash at a later date, which will then be invested in the asset class and the futures position will be closed.

■ Transaction exposure is the risk associated with a foreign exchange rate on a specific business transaction such as a purchase or sale. Translation exposure is the risk associated with the conversion of foreign financial statements into domestic currency. Economic exposure is the risk associated with changes in the relative attractiveness of products and services offered for sale, arising out of the competitive effects of changes in exchange rates.

■ The risk of a future foreign currency receipt can be eliminated by selling a forward contract on the currency. This transaction locks in the rate at which the foreign currency will be converted to the domestic currency.

■ The risk of a future foreign currency payment can be eliminated by buying a forward contract on the currency. This transaction locks in the rate at which the domestic currency will be converted to the foreign currency.

■ It is not possible to invest in a foreign equity market and precisely hedge the currency risk only. To hedge the currency risk, one must know the exact amount of foreign currency that will be available at a future date. Without locking in the equity return, it is not possible to know how much foreign currency will be available.

■ It is possible to hedge the foreign equity market return and accept the exchange rate risk or hedge the foreign equity market return *and* hedge the exchange rate risk. By hedging the equity market return, one would know the proper amount of currency that would be available at a later date and could use a futures or forward contract to hedge the currency risk. The equity return, however, would equal the risk-free rate.

■ Forward contracts are usually preferred over futures contracts when the risk is related to an event on a specific date, such as an interest rate reset. Forward contracts on foreign currency are usually preferred over futures contracts, primarily because of the liquidity of the market. Futures contracts require margins and daily settlements but are guaranteed against credit losses and may be preferred when credit concerns are an issue. Either contract may be preferred or required if there are restrictions on the use of the other. Dealers use both instruments in managing their risk, occasionally preferring one instrument and sometimes preferring the other. Forward contracts are preferred if privacy is important.

■ Futures and forwards, as well as virtually all derivatives, have an advantage over transactions in the actual instruments by virtue of their significantly lower transaction costs. They also allow a portfolio manager to make changes in the risk of certain asset classes or the allocation among asset classes without disturbing the asset class or classes themselves. This feature allows the asset class managers to concentrate on their respective asset classes without being concerned about buying and selling to execute risk-altering changes or asset allocation changes.

■ Although futures and forwards tend to be more liquid than their underlying assets, they are not always highly liquid. Therefore, it cannot always be assumed that futures and forwards can solve liquidity problems.

# PRACTICE PROBLEMS FOR READING 36

1.  An investment management firm wishes to increase the beta for one of its portfolios under management from 0.95 to 1.20 for a three-month period. The portfolio has a market value of $175,000,000. The investment firm plans to use a futures contract priced at $105,790 in order to adjust the portfolio beta. The futures contract has a beta of 0.98.

    A.  Calculate the number of futures contracts that should be bought or sold to achieve an increase in the portfolio beta.

    B.  At the end of three months, the overall equity market is up 5.5 percent. The stock portfolio under management is up 5.1 percent. The futures contract is priced at $111,500. Calculate the value of the overall position and the effective beta of the portfolio.

2.  Consider an asset manager who wishes to create a fund with exposure to the Russell 2000 stock index. The initial amount to be invested is $300,000,000. The fund will be constructed using the Russell 2000 Index futures contract, priced at 498.30 with a $500 multiplier. The contract expires in three months. The underlying index has a dividend yield of 0.75 percent, and the risk-free rate is 2.35 percent per year.

    A.  Indicate how the money manager would go about constructing this synthetic index using futures.

    B.  Assume that at expiration, the Russell 2000 is at 594.65. Show how the synthetic position produces the same result as investment in the actual stock index.

3.  An investment management firm has a client who would like to temporarily reduce his exposure to equities by converting a $25 million equity position to cash for a period of four months. The client would like this reduction to take place without liquidating his equity position. The investment management firm plans to create a synthetic cash position using an equity futures contract. This futures contract is priced at 1170.10, has a multiplier of $250, and expires in four months. The dividend yield on the underlying index is 1.25 percent, and the risk-free rate is 2.75 percent.

    A.  Calculate the number of futures contracts required to create synthetic cash.

    B.  Determine the effective amount of money committed to this risk-free transaction and the effective number of units of the stock index that are converted to cash.

    C.  Assume that the stock index is at 1031 when the futures contract expires. Show how this strategy is equivalent to investing the risk-free asset, cash.

4.  Consider a portfolio with a 65 percent allocation to stocks and 35 percent to bonds. The portfolio has a market value of $200 million. The beta of the stock position is 1.15, and the modified duration of the bond position is 6.75. The portfolio manager wishes to increase the stock allocation to 85 percent and reduce the bond allocation to 15 percent for a period of six months. In addition to altering asset allocations, the manager would also like to increase the beta on the stock position to 1.20 and increase the modified duration of the bonds to 8.25. A stock index futures contract that expires in six months is priced at $157,500 and has a beta of 0.95. A bond futures contract that expires in six months is priced at $109,000 and has an implied modified duration of 5.25. The stock futures contract has a multiplier of one.

Practice Problems and Solutions: *Analysis of Derivatives for the Chartered Financial Analyst® Program*, by Don M. Chance, CFA. Copyright © 2003 by CFA Institute.

    **A.** Show how the portfolio manager can achieve his goals by using stock index and bond futures. Indicate the number of contracts and whether the manager should go long or short.

    **B.** After six months, the stock portfolio is up 5 percent and bonds are up 1.35 percent. The stock futures price is $164,005 and the bond futures price is $110,145. Compare the market value of the portfolio in which the allocation is adjusted using futures to the market value of the portfolio in which the allocation is adjusted by directly trading stocks and bonds.

**5.** A pension fund manager expects to receive a cash inflow of $50,000,000 in three months and wants to use futures contracts to take a $17,500,000 synthetic position in stocks and $32,500,000 in bonds today. The stock would have a beta of 1.15 and the bonds a modified duration of 7.65. A stock index futures contract with a beta of 0.93 is priced at $175,210. A bond futures contract with a modified duration of 5.65 is priced at $95,750.

    **A.** Calculate the number of stock and bond futures contracts the fund manager would have to trade in order to synthetically take the desired position in stocks and bonds today. Indicate whether the futures positions are long or short.

    **B.** When the futures contracts expire in three months, stocks have declined by 5.4 percent and bonds have declined by 3.06 percent. Stock index futures are priced at $167,559, and bond futures are priced at $93,586. Show that profits on the futures positions are essentially the same as the change in the value of stocks and bonds during the three-month period.

**6. A.** Consider a U.S. company, GateCorp, that exports products to the United Kingdom. GateCorp has just closed a sale worth £200,000,000. The amount will be received in two months. Because it will be paid in pounds, the U.S. company bears the exchange risk. In order to hedge this risk, GateCorp intends to use a forward contract that is priced at $1.4272 per pound. Indicate how the company would go about constructing the hedge. Explain what happens when the forward contract expires in two months.

    **B.** ABCorp is a U.S.-based company that frequently imports raw materials from Australia. It has just entered into a contract to purchase A$175,000,000 worth of raw wool, to be paid in one month. ABCorp fears that the Australian dollar will strengthen, thereby raising the U.S. dollar cost. A forward contract is available and is priced at $0.5249 per Australian dollar. Indicate how ABCorp would go about constructing a hedge. Explain what happens when the forward contract expires in one month.

# SOLUTIONS FOR READING 36

1. **A.** The number of futures contracts that must be bought is

$$N_f = \left( \frac{1.2 - 0.95}{0.98} \right) \left( \frac{\$175,000,000}{\$105,790} \right) = 421.99$$

Rounded off, this is 422 contracts.

**B.** The value of the stock portfolio is $\$175,000,000(1 + 0.051) = \$183,925,000$.

The profit on the long futures position is $422(\$111,500 - \$105,790) = \$2,409,620$.

The overall value of the position (stock plus long futures) is $\$183,925,000 + \$2,409,620 = \$186,334,620$.

The overall rate of return is $\left( \frac{\$186,334,620}{\$175,000,000} \right) - 1 = 0.0648$

The effective beta is $0.0648/0.055 = 1.18$, which is approximately equal to the target beta of 1.2.

2. **A.** The number of futures contracts that must be bought is

$$N_f = \frac{\$300,000,000(1.0235)^{0.25}}{\$500(498.30)} = 1,211.11$$

Rounded off, this is 1,211 contracts long.

Now invest the following amount in risk-free bonds, which pay 2.35 percent interest:

$$\frac{1,211(\$500)(498.30)}{(1.0235)^{0.25}} = \$299,973,626$$

This amount will grow to $\$299,973,626(1.0235)^{0.25} = \$301,720,650$. The number of synthetic units of stock is

$$\frac{1211(500)}{(1.0075)^{0.25}} = 604,369.98$$

which would grow to $604,369.98(1.0075)^{0.25} = 605,500$ with the reinvestment of dividends.

**B.** At expiration in three months, the payoff on the futures is $1,211(\$500)(594.65 - 498.30) = 605,500(594.65) - \$301,720,650$. In order to settle the futures contract, the money manager will owe $\$301,720,650$. This amount can be paid off with the proceeds from the investment in risk-free bonds, leaving the money manager with 605,500 units of the stock index, each worth 594.65. This transaction achieves the desired exposure to the stock index.

3. **A.** In order to create a synthetic cash position, the number of futures contracts to be sold is

$$N_f = \frac{\$25,000,000(1.0275)^{4/12}}{\$250(1170.10)} = 86.24$$

Rounded off, this is 86 contracts short.

**B.** The effective amount of stock committed to this transaction is actually

$$\frac{86(\$250)(1170.10)}{(1.0275)^{4/12}} = \$24,930,682$$

This amount invested at the risk-free rate should grow to $24,930,682(1.0275)^{4/12}$ = $25,157,150, resulting in the following number of shares:

$$\frac{86(\$250)}{(1.0125)^{4/12}} = 21,411.16$$

With reinvestment of dividends, this number would grow to $21,411.16(1.0125)^{4/12} = 21,500$ shares. The short position in futures is equivalent to selling $24,930,682 of stock.

**C.** In four months when the futures contract expires, the stock index is at 1031. The payoff of the futures contract is $-86(\$250)(1031 - 1170.10) =$ $-\$21,500(1031) + \$25,157,150 = \$2,990,650$.

Netting the futures payoff against the stock position produces $25,157,150, equivalent to investing $24,930,682 at 2.75 percent for four months. The short futures position has thus effectively converted equity to cash.

**4. A.** The current allocation is as follows: stocks, $0.65(200,000,000) =$ $130,000,000; bonds, $0.35(\$200,000,000) = \$70,000,000$. The new allocation desired is as follows: stocks, $0.85(\$200,000,000) = \$170,000,000$; bonds, $0.15(\$200,000,000) = \$30,000,000$. So, to achieve the new allocation, the manager must buy stock futures on $170,000,000 - $130,000,000 = $40,000,000. An equivalent amount of bond futures must be sold.

To synthetically sell $40 million in bonds and convert into cash, the manager must sell futures:

$$N_{bf} = \left(\frac{0.0 - 6.75}{5.25}\right)\left(\frac{\$40,000,000}{\$109,000}\right) = -471.82$$

He should sell 472 contracts and create synthetic cash.

To synthetically buy $40 million of stock with synthetic cash, the manager must buy futures:

$$N_{sf} = \left(\frac{1.15 - 0}{0.95}\right)\left(\frac{\$40,000,000}{\$157,500}\right) = 307.44$$

He should buy 307 contracts. Now the manager effectively has $170 million (85 percent) in stocks and $30 million (15 percent) in bonds.

The next step is to increase the beta on the $170 million in stock to 1.20 by purchasing futures. The number of futures contracts would, therefore, be

$$N_{sf} = \left(\frac{1.20 - 1.15}{0.95}\right)\left(\frac{\$170,000,000}{\$157,500}\right) = 56.81$$

An additional 57 stock futures contracts should be purchased. In total, 307 + 57 = 364 contracts are bought.

To increase the modified duration from 6.75 to 8.25 on the $30 million of bonds, the number of futures contracts is

$$N_{bf} = \left(\frac{8.25 - 6.75}{5.25}\right)\left(\frac{\$30,000,000}{\$109,000}\right) = 78.64$$

An additional 79 bond futures contracts should be purchased. In total, 472 − 79 = 393 contracts are sold.

**B.** The value of the stock will be $130,000,000(1 + 0.05) = $136,500,000. The profit on the stock index futures will be $364(\$164,005 - \$157,500) = \$2,367,820$.

The value of the bonds will be $70,000,000(1 + 0.0135) = $70,945,000. The profit on the bond futures will be −393($110,145 − $109,000) = −$449,985.

The total value of the position, therefore, is $136,500,000 + $2,367,820 + $70,945,000 − $449,985 = $209,362,835.

If the reallocation were carried out by trading bonds and stocks: The stock would be worth $170,000,000(1 + 0.05) = $178,500,000. The bonds would be worth $30,000,000(1 + 0.0135) = $30,405,000. The overall value of the portfolio would be $178,500,000 + $30,405,000 = $208,905,000.

The difference between the two approaches is $457,835, only 0.229 percent of the original value of the portfolio.

**5. A.** In order to gain effective exposure to stock and bonds today, the manager must use futures to synthetically buy $17,500,000 of stock and $32,500,000 of bonds.

To synthetically buy $17,500,000 in stock, the manager must buy futures:

$$N_{sf} = \left(\frac{1.15 - 0}{0.93}\right)\left(\frac{\$17,500,000}{\$175,210}\right) = 123.51$$

He should buy 124 contracts.

To synthetically buy $32,500,000 of bonds, the manager must buy futures:

$$N_{bf} = \left(\frac{7.65 - 0}{5.65}\right)\left(\frac{\$32,500,000}{\$95,750}\right) = 459.57$$

He should buy 460 contracts.

Now the manager effectively has invested $17,500,000 in stock and $32,500,000 in bonds.

**B.** The profit on the stock index futures will be 124($167,559 − $175,210) = −$948,724.

The profit on the bond futures will be 460($93,586 − $95,750) = −$995,440.

The total profit with futures = −$948,724 − $995,440 = −$1,944,164.

If bonds and stocks were purchased today, in three months:

The change in value of stock would be $17,500,000(−0.054) = −$945,000.

The change in value of bonds would be $32,500,000(−0.0306) = −$994,500.

The overall change in value of the portfolio would be −$945,000 − $994,500 = −$1,939,500.

The difference between the two approaches is $4,664, only 0.009 percent of the total expected cash inflow.

**6. A.** GateCorp will receive £200,000,000 in two months. To hedge the risk that the pound may weaken during this period, the firm should enter into a forward contract to deliver pounds and receive dollars two months from now at a price fixed now. Because it is effectively long the pound, GateCorp will take a short position on the pound in the forward market. GateCorp will thus enter into a two-month short forward contract to deliver £200,000,000 at a rate of $1.4272 per pound.

When the forward contract expires in two months, irrespective of the spot exchange rate, GateCorp will deliver £200,000,000 and receive ($1.4272/£1)(£200,000,000) = $285,440,000.

**B.** ABCorp will have to pay A$175,000,000 in one month. To hedge the risk that the Australian dollar may strengthen against the U.S. dollar during this period, it should enter into a forward contract to purchase Australian dollars one month from now at a price fixed today. Because it is effectively short the Australian dollar, ABCorp takes a long position in the forward market. ABCorp thus enters into a one-month long forward contract to purchase A$175,000,000 at a rate of US$0.5249 per Australian dollar.

When the forward contract expires in one month, irrespective of the spot exchange rate, ABCorp will pay ($0.5249/A$)(A$175,000,000) = $91,857,500 to purchase A$175,000,000. This amount is used to purchase the raw material needed.

| Index | | |
| --- | --- | --- |
| Japan (Tokyo) | | |
| Seoul | | |
| Taiwan (Taipei) | | |
| Mumbai | | -11.1% |
| Singapore | | -4.5% |
| Sydney | | -4.7% |
| Shanghai B | 2971.0 | 1.1% | -4.7% |
| Hong Kong | 4644.0 | 0.9% | -10.5% |
| Toronto | 316.8 | 0.7% | -6.9% |
| Stockholm | 22,700.9 | 0.5% | -4.2% |
| Mexico City | 13,524.8 | 0.1% | 4.1% |

# Risk Management Applications of Option Strategies

*by Don M. Chance, CFA*

## LEARNING OUTCOMES

| Mastery | The candidate should be able to: |
|---------|----------------------------------|
| ☐ | **a** compare the use of covered calls and protective puts to manage risk exposure to individual securities; |
| ☐ | **b** calculate and interpret the value at expiration, profit, maximum profit, maximum loss, breakeven underlying price at expiration, and general shape of the graph for the following option strategies: bull spread, bear spread, butterfly spread, collar, straddle, box spread; |
| ☐ | **c** calculate the effective annual rate for a given interest rate outcome when a borrower (lender) manages the risk of an anticipated loan using an interest rate call (put) option; |
| ☐ | **d** calculate the payoffs for a series of interest rate outcomes when a floating rate loan is combined with 1) an interest rate cap, 2) an interest rate floor, or 3) an interest rate collar; |
| ☐ | **e** explain why and how a dealer delta hedges an option position, why delta changes, and how the dealer adjusts to maintain the delta hedge; |
| ☐ | **f** interpret the gamma of a delta-hedged portfolio and explain how gamma changes as in-the-money and out-of-the-money options move toward expiration. |

# INTRODUCTION

1

In the reading on risk management applications of forward and futures strategies, we examined strategies that employ forward and futures contracts. Recall that forward and futures contracts have linear payoffs and do not require an initial outlay. Options, on the other hand, have nonlinear payoffs and require the payment of cash up front. By having nonlinear payoffs, options permit their users to benefit from movements in the underlying in one direction and to not be harmed by movements in the other direction. In many respects, they offer the best of all worlds, a chance to profit if expectations are realized with minimal harm if expectations turn out to be wrong. The price for this opportunity is the cash outlay required to establish the position. From the standpoint of the holder of the short position, options can lead to extremely large losses. Hence, sellers of options must be well compensated in the form of an adequate up-front premium and must skillfully manage the risk they assume.

In this reading we examine the most widely used option strategies. The reading is divided into three parts. In the first part, we look at option strategies that are typically used in equity investing, which include standard strategies involving single options and strategies that combine options with the underlying. In the second part, we look at the specific strategies that are commonly used in managing interest rate risk. In the third part, we examine option strategies that are used primarily by dealers and sophisticated traders to manage the risk of option positions.

Let us begin by reviewing the necessary notation. First recall that time 0 is the time at which the strategy is initiated and time T is the time the option expires, stated as a fraction of a year. Accordingly, the amount of time until expiration is simply $T - 0 = T$, which is (Days to expiration)/365. The other symbols are

$$c_0, c_T = \text{price of the call option at time 0 and time T}$$
$$p_0, p_T = \text{price of the put option at time 0 and time T}^1$$
$$X = \text{exercise price}$$
$$S_0, S_T = \text{price of the underlying at time 0 and time T}$$
$$V_0, V_T = \text{value of the position at time 0 and time T}$$
$$\Pi = \text{profit from the transaction: } V_T - V_0$$
$$r = \text{risk-free rate}$$

Some additional notation will be introduced when necessary.

Note that we are going to measure the profit from an option transaction, which is simply the final value of the transaction minus the initial value of the transaction. Profit does not take into account the time value of money or the risk. Although a focus on profit is not completely satisfactory from a theoretical point of view, it is nonetheless instructive, simple, and a common approach to examining options. Our primary objective here is to obtain a general picture of the manner in which option strategies perform. With that in mind, discussing profit offers probably the best trade-off in terms of gaining the necessary knowledge with a minimum of complexity.

In this reading, we assume that the option user has a view regarding potential movements of the underlying. In most cases that view is a prediction of the direction of the underlying, but in some cases it is a prediction of the volatility of the underlying. In all cases, we assume this view is specified over a horizon that corresponds to the option's life or that the option expiration can be tailored to the horizon date. Hence, for the most part, these options should be considered customized, over-the-counter options.[2] Every interest rate option is a customized option.

Because the option expiration corresponds to the horizon date for which a particular view is held, there is no reason to use American options. Accordingly, all options in this reading are European options. Moreover, we shall not consider terminating the strategy early. Putting an option in place and closing the position prior to expiration is certainly a legitimate strategy. It could reflect the arrival of new information over the holding period, but it requires an understanding of more complex issues, such

---

**1** Lower case indicates European options, and upper case indicates American options. In this reading, all options are European.

**2** If the options discussed were exchange-listed options, it would not significantly alter the material in this reading.

as valuation of the option and the rate at which the option loses its time value. Thus, we shall examine the outcome of a particular strategy over a range of possible values of the underlying only on the expiration day.

Section 2 of this reading focuses on option strategies that relate to equity investments. Section 3 concentrates on strategies using interest rate options. In Section 4, we focus on managing an option portfolio.

# OPTION STRATEGIES FOR EQUITY PORTFOLIOS

**2** OPTIONAL SEGMENT

Many typical illustrations of option strategies use individual stocks, but we shall use options on a stock index, the NASDAQ 100, referred to simply as the NASDAQ. We shall assume that in addition to buying and selling options on the NASDAQ, we can also buy the index, either through construction of the portfolio itself, through an index mutual fund, or an exchange-traded fund.[3] We shall simply refer to this instrument as a stock. We are given the following numerical data:

$S_0$ = 2000, value of the NASDAQ 100 when the strategy is initiated

$T$ = 0.0833, the time to expiration (one month = 1/12)

The options available will be the following:[4]

| Exercise Price | Call Price | Put Price |
|---|---|---|
| 1950 | 108.43 | 56.01 |
| 2000 | 81.75 | 79.25 |
| 2050 | 59.98 | 107.39 |

Let us start by examining an initial strategy that is the simplest of all: to buy or sell short the underlying. Panel A of Exhibit 1 illustrates the profit from the transaction of buying a share of stock. We see the obvious result that if you buy the stock and it goes up, you make a profit; if it goes down, you incur a loss. Panel B shows the case of selling short the stock. Recall that this strategy involves borrowing the shares from a broker, selling them at the current price, and then buying them back at a later date. In this case, if you sell short the stock and it goes down, you make a profit. Conversely, if it goes up, you incur a loss. Now we shall move on to strategies involving options, but we shall use the stock strategies again when we combine options with stock.

---

**3** Exchange-traded shares on the NASDAQ 100 are called NASDAQ 100 Trust Shares and QQQs, for their ticker symbol. They are commonly referred to as Qubes, trade on the AMEX, and are the most active exchange-traded fund and often the most actively traded of all securities. Options on the NASDAQ 100 are among the most actively traded as well.
**4** These values were obtained using the Black–Scholes–Merton model. By using this model, we know we are working with reasonable values that do not permit arbitrage opportunities.

| *Exhibit 1* | Simple Stock Strategies |
| --- | --- |

**A. Buy Stock**

Profit from Transaction ($)

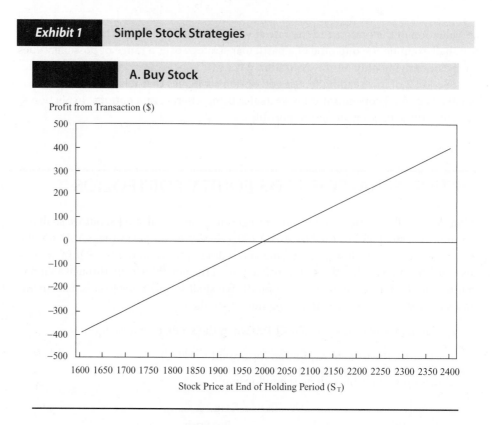

Stock Price at End of Holding Period ($S_T$)

**B. Sell Short Stock**

Profit from Transaction ($)

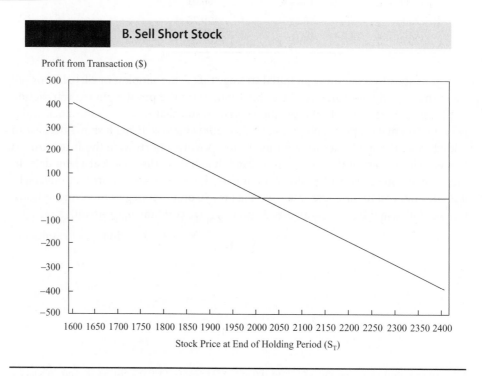

Stock Price at End of Holding Period ($S_T$)

In this section we examine option strategies in the context of their use in equity portfolios. Although these strategies are perfectly applicable for fixed-income portfolios, corporate borrowing scenarios, or even commodity risk management situations, they are generally more easily explained and understood in the context of investing in equities or equity indices.

To analyze an equity option strategy, we first assume that we establish the position at the current price. We then determine the value of the option at expiration for a specific value of the index at expiration. We calculate the profit as the value at expiration minus the current price. We then generate a graph to illustrate the value at expiration and profit for a range of index values at expiration. Although the underlying is a stock index, we shall just refer to it as the underlying to keep things as general as possible. We begin by examining the most fundamental option transactions, long and short positions in calls and puts.

## 2.1 Standard Long and Short Positions

### 2.1.1 *Calls*

Consider the purchase of a call option at the price $c_0$. The value at expiration, $c_T$, is $c_T = \max(0, S_T - X)$. Broken down into parts,

$$c_T = 0 \qquad \text{if } S_T \leq X$$
$$c_T = S_T - X \quad \text{if } S_T > X$$

The profit is obtained by subtracting the option premium, which is paid to purchase the option, from the option value at expiration, $\Pi = c_T - c_0$. Broken down into parts,

$$\Pi = -c_0 \qquad \text{if } S_T \leq X$$
$$\Pi = S_T - X - c_0 \quad \text{if } S_T > X$$

Now consider this example. We buy the call with the exercise price of 2000 for 81.75. Consider values of the index at expiration of 1900 and 2100. For $S_T = 1900$,

$$c_T = \max(0, 1900 - 2000) = 0$$
$$\Pi = 0 - 81.75 = -81.75$$

For $S_T = 2100$,

$$c_T = \max(0, 2100 - 2000) = 100$$
$$\Pi = 100 - 81.75 = 18.25$$

Exhibit 2 illustrates the value at expiration and profit when $S_T$, the underlying price at expiration, ranges from 1600 to 2400. We see that buying a call results in a limited loss of the premium, 81.75. For an index value at expiration greater than the exercise price of 2000, the value and profit move up one-for-one with the index value, and there is no upper limit.

| Exhibit 2 | Buy Call |
| --- | --- |

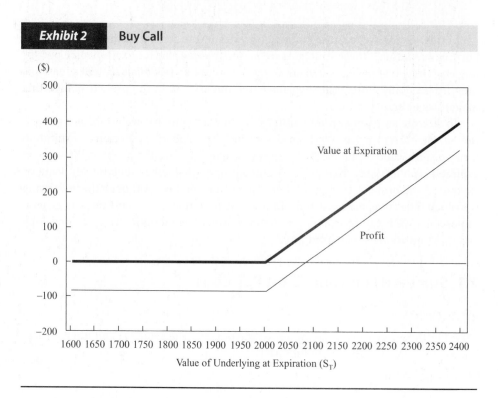

It is important to identify the breakeven index value at expiration. Recall that the formula for the profit is $\Pi = \max(0, S_T - X) - c_0$. We would like to know the value of $S_T$ for which $\Pi = 0$. We shall call that value $S_T^*$. It would be nice to be able to solve $\Pi = \max(0, S_T^* - X) - c_0 = 0$ for $S_T^*$, but that is not directly possible. Instead, we observe that there are two ranges of outcomes, one in which $\Pi = S_T^* - X - c_0$ for $S_T^* > X$, the case of the option expiring in-the-money, and the other in which $\Pi = -c_0$ for $S_T \leq X$, the case of the option expiring out-of-the-money. It is obvious from the equation and by observing Exhibit 2 that in the latter case, there is no possibility of breaking even. In the former case, we see that we can solve for $S_T^*$. Setting $\Pi = S_T^* - X - c_0 = 0$, we obtain $S_T^* = X + c_0$.

Thus, the breakeven is the exercise price plus the option premium. This result should be intuitive: The value of the underlying at expiration must exceed the exercise price by the amount of the premium to recover the cost of the premium. In this problem, the breakeven is $S_T^* = 2000 + 81.75 = 2081.75$. Observe in Exhibit 2 that the profit line crosses the axis at this value.

In summarizing the strategy, we have the following results for the option buyer:

$c_T = \max(0, S_T - X)$

Value at expiration = $c_T$

Profit: $\Pi = c_T - c_0$

Maximum profit = $\infty$

Maximum loss = $c_0$

Breakeven: $S_T^* = X + c_0$

Call options entice naive speculators, but it is important to consider the *likely* gains and losses more than the *potential* gains and losses. For example, in this case, the underlying must go up by about 4.1 percent in one month to cover the cost of the call. This increase equates to an annual rate of almost 50 percent and is an unreasonable expectation by almost any standard. If the underlying does not move at all, the loss is 100 percent of the premium.

For the seller of the call, the results are just the opposite. The sum of the positions of the seller and buyer is zero. Hence, we can take the value and profit results for the buyer and change the signs. The results for the maximum profit and maximum loss are changed accordingly, and the breakeven is the same. Hence, for the option seller,

$c_T = \max(0, S_T - X)$

Value at expiration $= -c_T$

Profit: $\Pi = -c_T + c_0$

Maximum profit $= c_0$

Maximum loss $= \infty$

Breakeven: $S_T^* = X + c_0$

Exhibit 3 shows the results for the seller of the call. Note that the value and profit have a fixed maximum. The worst case is an infinite loss. Just as there is no upper limit to the buyer's potential gain, there is no upper limit to how much the seller can lose.

| **Exhibit 3** | **Sell Call** |
| --- | --- |

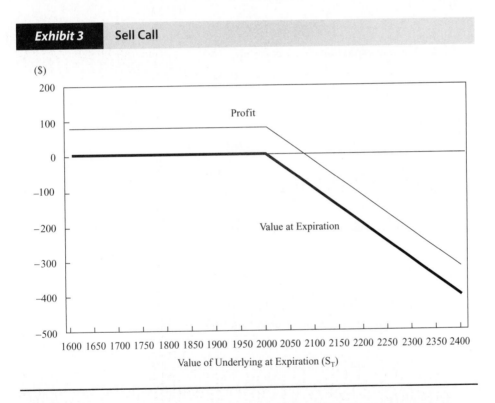

Call options are purchased by investors who are bullish. We now turn to put options, which are purchased by investors who are bearish.

**Example 1**

Consider a call option selling for $7 in which the exercise price is $100 and the price of the underlying is $98.

A.  Determine the value at expiration and the profit for a buyer under the following outcomes:

  i.  The price of the underlying at expiration is $102.

  ii.  The price of the underlying at expiration is $94.

**B.** Determine the value at expiration and the profit for a seller under the following outcomes:

    **i.** The price of the underlying at expiration is \$91.

    **ii.** The price of the underlying at expiration is \$101.

**C.** Determine the following:

    **i.** the maximum profit to the buyer (maximum loss to the seller).

    **ii.** the maximum loss to the buyer (maximum profit to the seller).

**D.** Determine the breakeven price of the underlying at expiration.

## Solutions:

**A.** Call buyer

    **i.** Value at expiration $= c_T = \max(0, S_T - X)$

$$= \max(0, 102 - 100) = 2$$
$$\Pi = c_T - c_0 = 2 - 7 = -5$$

    **ii.** Value at expiration $= c_T = \max(0, S_T - X)$

$$= \max(0, 94 - 100) = 0$$
$$\Pi = c_T - c_0 = 0 - 7 = -7$$

**B.** Call seller

    **i.** Value at expiration $= -c_T = -\max(0, S_T - X)$

$$= -\max(0, 91 - 100) = 0$$
$$\Pi = -c_T + c_0 = -0 + 7 = 7$$

    **ii.** Value at expiration $= -c_T = -\max(0, S_T - X)$

$$= -\max(0, 101 - 100) = -1$$
$$\Pi = -c_T + c_0 = -1 + 7 = 6$$

**C.** Maximum and minimum

    **i.** Maximum profit to buyer (loss to seller) $= \infty$

    **ii.** Maximum loss to buyer (profit to seller) $= c_0 = 7$

**D.** $S_T^* = X + c_0 = 100 + 7 = 107$

### 2.1.2 *Puts*

The value of a put at expiration is $p_T = \max(0, X - S_T)$. Broken down into parts,

$$p_T = X - S_T \quad \text{if } S_T < X$$
$$p_T = 0 \qquad\quad \text{if } S_T \geq X$$

The profit is obtained by subtracting the premium on the put from the value at expiration:

$$\Pi = p_T - p_0$$

Broken down into parts,

$$\Pi = X - S_T - p_0 \quad \text{if } S_T < X$$
$$\Pi = -p_0 \qquad\qquad \text{if } S_T \geq X$$

For our example and outcomes of $S_T = 1900$ and 2100, the results are as follows:

$S_T = 1900$:

$p_T = \max(0, 2000 - 1900) = 100$

$\Pi = 100 - 79.25 = 20.75$

$S_T = 2100$:

$p_T = \max(0, 2000 - 2100) = 0$

$\Pi = 0 - 79.25 = -79.25$

These results are shown in Exhibit 4. We see that the put has a maximum value and profit and a limited loss, the latter of which is the premium. The maximum value is obtained when the underlying goes to zero.[5] In that case, $p_T = X$. So the maximum profit is $X - p_0$. Here that will be $2000 - 79.25 = 1920.75$.

**Exhibit 4    Buy Put**

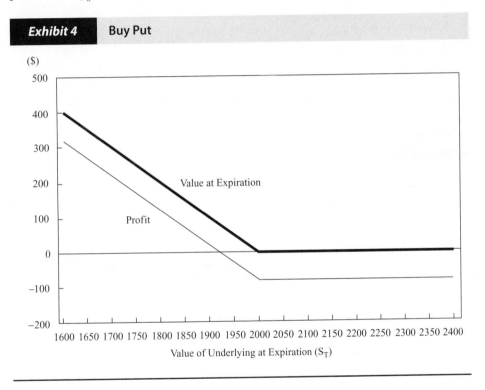

The breakeven is found by breaking up the profit equation into its parts, $\Pi = X - S_T - p_0$ for $S_T < X$ and $\Pi = -p_0$ for $S_T \geq X$. In the latter case, there is no possibility of breaking even. It refers to the range over which the entire premium is lost. In the former case, we denote the breakeven index value as $S_T^*$, set the equation to zero, and solve for $S_T^*$ to obtain $S_T^* = X - p_0$. In our example, the breakeven is $S_T^* = 2000 - 79.25 = 1920.75$.

In summary, for the strategy of buying a put we have

$p_T = \max(0, X - S_T)$

Value at expiration $= p_T$

Profit : $\Pi = p_T - p_0$

Maximum profit $= X - p_0$

Maximum loss $= p_0$

Breakeven : $S_T^* = X - p_0$

**5** The maximum value and profit are not visible on the graph because we do not show $S_T$ all the way down to zero.

Now consider the *likely* outcomes for the holder of the put. In this case, the underlying must move down by almost 4 percent in one month to cover the premium. One would hardly ever expect the underlying to move down at an annual rate of almost 50 percent. Moreover, if the underlying does not move downward at all (a likely outcome given the positive expected return on most assets), the loss is 100 percent of the premium.

For the sale of a put, we simply change the sign on the value at expiration and profit. The maximum profit for the buyer becomes the maximum loss for the seller and the maximum loss for the buyer becomes the maximum profit for the seller. The breakeven for the seller is the same as for the buyer. So, for the seller,

$$p_T = \max\left(0, X - S_T\right)$$

Value at expiration $= -p_T$

Profit : $\Pi = -p_T + p_0$

Maximum profit $= p_0$

Maximum loss $= X - p_0$

Breakeven : $S_T{}^* = X - p_0$

Exhibit 5 graphs the value at expiration and the profit for this transaction.

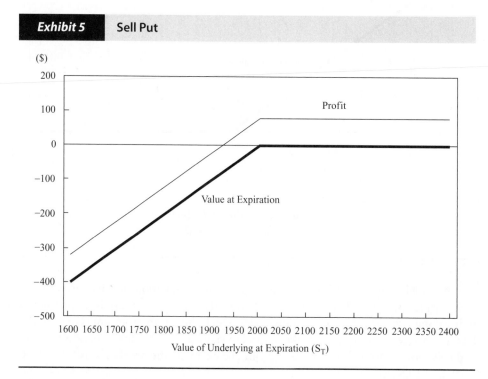

**Exhibit 5**    Sell Put

---

## Example 2

Consider a put option selling for $4 in which the exercise price is $60 and the price of the underlying is $62.

**A.** Determine the value at expiration and the profit for a buyer under the following outcomes:

   **i.** The price of the underlying at expiration is $62.

   **ii.** The price of the underlying at expiration is $55.

**B.** Determine the value at expiration and the profit for a seller under the following outcomes:

    **i.** The price of the underlying at expiration is $51.

    **ii.** The price of the underlying at expiration is $68.

**C.** Determine the following:

    **i.** the maximum profit to the buyer (maximum loss to the seller).

    **ii.** the maximum loss to the buyer (maximum profit to the seller).

**D.** Determine the breakeven price of the underlying at expiration.

## Solutions:

**A.** Put buyer

    **i.**
$$\text{Value at expiration} = p_T = \max\left(0, X - S_T\right)$$
$$= \max\left(0, 60 - 62\right) = 0$$
$$\Pi = p_T - p_0 = 0 - 4 = -4$$

    **ii.**
$$\text{Value at expiration} = p_T = \max\left(0, X - S_T\right)$$
$$= \max\left(0, 60 - 55\right) = 5$$
$$\Pi = p_T - p_0 = 5 - 4 = 1$$

**B.** Put seller

    **i.**
$$\text{Value at expiration} = -p_T = -\max\left(0, X - S_T\right)$$
$$= -\max\left(0, 60 - 51\right) = -9$$
$$\Pi = -p_T + p_0 = -9 + 4 = -5$$

    **ii.**
$$\text{Value at expiration} = -p_T = -\max\left(0, X - S_T\right)$$
$$= -\max\left(0, 60 - 68\right) = 0$$
$$\Pi = -p_T + p_0 = 0 + 4 = 4$$

**C.** Maximum and minimum

    **i.** Maximum profit to buyer $\left(\text{loss to seller}\right) = X - p_0 = 60 - 4 = 56$

    **ii.** Maximum loss to buyer $\left(\text{profit to seller}\right) = p_0 = 4$

**D.** $S_T^* = X - p_0 = 60 - 4 = 56$

It may be surprising to find that we have now covered all of the information we need to examine all of the other option strategies. We need to learn only a few basic facts. We must know the formula for the value at expiration of a call and a put. Then we need to know how to calculate the profit for the purchase of a call and a put, but that calculation is simple: the value at expiration minus the initial value. If we know these results, we can calculate the value at expiration of the option and the profit for any value of the underlying at expiration. If we can do that, we can graph the results for a range of possible values of the underlying at expiration. Because graphing can take a long time, however, it is probably helpful to learn the basic shapes of the value and profit graphs for calls and puts. Knowing the profit equation and the shapes of the graphs, it is easy to determine the maximum profit and maximum loss. The breakeven can be determined by setting the profit equation to zero for the case in which the profit equation contains $S_T$. Once we have these results for the long call and put, it is an easy matter to turn them around and obtain the results for the short call and put. Therefore, little if any memorization is required. From there, we can go on to strategies that combine an option with another option and combine options with the underlying.

**END OPTIONAL SEGMENT**

## 2.2 Risk Management Strategies with Options and the Underlying

In this section, we examine two of the most widely used option strategies, particularly for holders of the underlying. One way to reduce exposure without selling the underlying is to sell a call on the underlying; the other way is to buy a put.

### 2.2.1 Covered Calls

A **covered call** is a relatively conservative strategy, but it is also one of the most misunderstood strategies. A covered call is a position in which you own the underlying and sell a call. The value of the position at expiration is easily found as the value of the underlying plus the value of the short call:

$$V_T = S_T - \max(0, S_T - X)$$

Therefore,

$$V_T = S_T \qquad \text{if } S_T \leq X$$
$$V_T = S_T - (S_T - X) = X \quad \text{if } S_T > X$$

We obtain the profit for the covered call by computing the change in the value of the position, $V_T - V_0$. First recognize that $V_0$, the value of the position at the start of the contract, is the initial value of the underlying minus the call premium. We are long the underlying and short the call, so we must subtract the call premium that was received from the sale of the call. The initial investment in the position is what we pay for the underlying less what we receive for the call. Hence, $V_0 = S_0 - c_0$. The profit is thus

$$\Pi = S_T - \max(0, S_T - X) - (S_0 - c_0)$$
$$= S_T - S_0 - \max(0, S_T - X) + c_0$$

With the equation written in this manner, we see that the profit for the covered call is simply the profit from buying the underlying, $S_T - S_0$, plus the profit from selling the call, $-\max(0, S_T - X) + c_0$. Breaking it down into ranges,

$$\Pi = S_T - S_0 + c_0 \qquad \text{if } S_T \leq X$$
$$\Pi = S_T - S_0 - (S_T - X) + c_0 = X - S_0 + c_0 \quad \text{if } S_T > X$$

In our example, $S_0 = 2000$. In this section we shall use a call option with the exercise price of 2050. Thus $X = 2050$, and the premium, $c_0$, is 59.98. Let us now examine two outcomes: $S_T = 2100$ and $S_T = 1900$. The value at expiration when $S_T = 2100$ is $V_T = 2100 - (2100 - 2050) = 2050$, and when $S_T = 1900$, the value of the position is $V_T = 1900$.

In the first case, we hold the underlying worth 2100 but are short a call worth 50. Thus, the net value is 2050. In the second case, we hold the underlying worth 1900 and the option expires out-of-the-money.

In the first case, $S_T = 2100$, the profit is $\Pi = 2050 - 2000 + 59.98 = 109.98$. In the second case, $S_T = 1900$, the profit is $\Pi = 1900 - 2000 + 59.98 = -40.02$. These results are graphed for a range of values of $S_T$ in Exhibit 6. Note that for all values of ST greater than 2050, the value and profit are maximized. Thus, 2050 is the maximum value and 109.98 is the maximum profit.[6]

As evident in Exhibit 6 and the profit equations, the maximum loss would occur when $S_T$ is zero. Hence, the profit would be $S_T - S_0 + c_0$. The profit is $-S_0 + c_0$ when $S_T = 0$. This means that the maximum loss is $S_0 - c_0$. In this example, $-S_0 + c_0$ is $-2000 + 59.98 = -1940.02$. Intuitively, this would mean that you purchased the underlying for 2000 and sold the call for 59.98. The underlying value went to zero, resulting in a loss of 2000, but the call expired with no value, so the gain from the option is the option premium. The total loss is 1940.02.

| Exhibit 6 | Covered Call (Buy Underlying, Sell Call) |
| --- | --- |

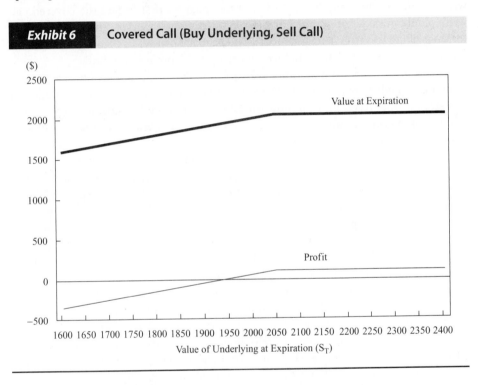

The breakeven underlying price is found by examining the profit equations and focusing on the equation that contains $S_T$. In equation form, $\Pi = S_T - S_0 + c_0$ when $S_T \leq X$. We let $S_T^*$ denote the breakeven value of $S_T$, set the equation to zero, and solve for $S_T^*$ to obtain $S_T^* = S_0 - c_0$. The breakeven and the maximum loss are identical. In this example, the breakeven is $S_T^* = 2000 - 59.98 = 1940.02$, which is seen in Exhibit 6.

To summarize the covered call, we have the following:

Value at expiration: $V_T = S_T - \max(0, S_T - X)$

Profit: $\Pi = V_T - S_0 + c_0$

Maximum profit $= X - S_0 + c_0$

Maximum loss $= S_0 - c_0$

Breakeven: $S_T^* = S_0 - c_0$

---

6 Note in Exhibit 6 that there is large gap between the value at expiration and profit, especially compared with the graphs of buying and selling calls and puts. This difference occurs because a covered call is mostly a position in the underlying asset. The initial value of the asset, $S_0$, accounts for most of the difference in the two lines. Note also that because of the put–call parity relationship, a covered call looks very similar to a short put.

Because of the importance and widespread use of covered calls, it is worthwhile to discuss this strategy briefly to dispel some misunderstandings. First of all, some investors who do not believe in using options fail to see that selling a call on a position in the underlying reduces the risk of that position. Options do not automatically increase risk. The option part of this strategy alone, viewed in isolation, seems an extremely risky strategy. We noted in Section 2.1.1 that selling a call without owning the stock exposes the investor to unlimited loss potential. But selling a covered call—adding a short call to a long position in a stock—reduces the overall risk. Thus, any investor who holds a stock cannot say he is too conservative to use options.

Following on that theme, however, one should also view selling a covered call as a strategy that reduces not only the risk but also the expected return compared with simply holding the underlying. Hence, one should not expect to make a lot of money writing calls on the underlying. It should be apparent that in fact the covered call writer could miss out on significant gains in a strong bull market. The compensation for this willingness to give up potential upside gains, however, is that in a bear market the losses on the underlying will be cushioned by the option premium.

It may be disconcerting to some investors to look at the profit profile of a covered call. The immediate response is to think that no one in their right mind would invest in a strategy that has significant downside risk but a limited upside. Just owning the underlying has significant downside risk, but at least there is an upside. But it is important to note that the visual depiction of the strategy, as in Exhibit 6, does not tell the whole story. It says nothing about the likelihood of certain outcomes occurring.

For example, consider the covered call example we looked at here. The underlying starts off at 2000. The maximum profit occurs when the option expires with the underlying at 2050 or above, an increase of 2.5 percent over the life of the option. We noted that this option has a one-month life. Thus, the underlying would have to increase at an approximate annual rate of at least 2.5%(12) = 30% for the covered call writer to forgo all of the upside gain. There are not many stocks, indices, or other assets in which an investor would expect the equivalent of an annual move of at least 30 percent. Such movements obviously do occur from time to time, but they are not common. Thus, covered call writers do not often give up large gains.

But suppose the underlying did move to 2050 or higher. As we previously showed, the value of the position would be 2050. Because the initial value of the position is 2000 − 59.98 = 1940.02, the rate of return would be 5.7 percent for one month. Hence, the maximum return is still outstanding by almost anyone's standards.[7]

Many investors believe that the initial value of a covered call should not include the value of the underlying if the underlying had been previously purchased. Suppose, for example, that this asset, currently worth 2000, had been bought several months ago at 1900. It is tempting to ignore the current value of the underlying; there is no current outlay. This view, however, misses the notion of opportunity cost. If an investor currently holding an asset chooses to write a call on it, she has made a conscious decision not to sell the asset. Hence, the current value of the asset should be viewed as an opportunity cost that is just as real as the cost to an investor buying the underlying at this time.

Sellers of covered calls must make a decision about the chosen exercise price. For example, one could sell the call with an exercise price of 1950 for 108.43, or sell the call with exercise price of 2000 for 81.75, or sell the call with exercise price of 2050 for 59.98. The higher the exercise price, the less one receives for the call but the more room for gain on the upside. There is no clear-cut solution to deciding which call is best; the choice depends on the risk preferences of the investor.

---

**7** Of course, we are not saying that the performance reflects a positive alpha. We are saying only that the upside performance given up reflects improbably high returns, and therefore the limits on the upside potential are not too restrictive.

Finally, we should note that anecdotal evidence suggests that writers of call options make small amounts of money, but make it often. The reason for this phenomenon is generally thought to be that buyers of calls tend to be overly optimistic, but that argument is fallacious. The real reason is that the expected profits come from rare but large payoffs. For example, consider the call with exercise price of 2000 and a premium of 81.75. As we learned in Section 2.1, the breakeven underlying price is 2081.75—a gain of about 4.1 percent in a one-month period, which would be an exceptional return for almost any asset. These prices were obtained using the Black–Scholes–Merton model, so they are fair prices. Yet the required underlying price movement to profit on the call is exceptional. Obviously someone buys calls, and naturally, someone must be on the other side of the transaction. Sellers of calls tend to be holders of the underlying or other calls, which reduces the enormous risk they would assume if they sold calls without any other position.[8] Hence, it is reasonable to expect that sellers of calls would make money often, because large underlying price movements occur only rarely. Following this line of reasoning, however, it would appear that sellers of calls can consistently take advantage of buyers of calls. That cannot possibly be the case. What happens is that buyers of calls make money less often than sellers, but when they do make money, the leverage inherent in call options amplifies their returns. Therefore, when call writers lose money, they tend to lose big, but most call writers own the underlying or are long other calls to offset the risk.

---

**Example 3**

Consider a bond selling for $98 per $100 face value. A call option selling for $8 has an exercise price of $105. Answer the following questions about a covered call.

**A.** Determine the value of the position at expiration and the profit under the following outcomes:

   **i.** The price of the bond at expiration is $110.

   **ii.** The price of the bond at expiration is $88.

**B.** Determine the following:

   **i.** The maximum profit.

   **ii.** The maximum loss.

**C.** Determine the breakeven bond price at expiration.

**Solutions:**

**A.** **i.** $V_T = S_T - \max(0, S_T - X) = 110 - \max(0, 110 - 105)$

$$= 110 - 110 + 105 = 105$$

$$\Pi = V_T - V_0 = 105 - (S_0 - c_0) = 105 - (98 - 8) = 15$$

   **ii.** $V_T = S_T - \max(0, S_T - X) = 88 - \max(0, 88 - 105)$

$$= 88 - 0 = 88$$

$$\Pi = V_T - V_0 = 88 - (S_0 - c_0) = 88 - (98 - 8) = -2$$

**B.** **i.** $\text{Maximum profit} = X - S_0 + c_0 = 105 - 98 + 8 = 15$

   **ii.** $\text{Maximum loss} = S_0 - c_0 = 98 - 8 = 90$

**C.** $S_T^* = S_0 - c_0 = 98 - 8 = 90$

---

**8** Sellers of calls who hold other calls are engaged in transactions called spreads. We discuss several types of spreads in Section 2.3.

Covered calls represent one widely used way to protect a position in the underlying. Another popular means of providing protection is to buy a put.

### 2.2.2 *Protective Puts*

Because selling a call provides some protection to the holder of the underlying against a fall in the price of the underlying, buying a put should also provide protection. A put, after all, is designed to pay off when the price of the underlying moves down. In some ways, buying a put to add to a long stock position is much better than selling a call. As we shall see here, it provides downside protection while retaining the upside potential, but it does so at the expense of requiring the payment of cash up front. In contrast, a covered call generates cash up front but removes some of the upside potential.

Holding an asset and a put on the asset is a strategy known as a **protective put**. The value at expiration and the profit of this strategy are found by combining the value and profit of the two strategies of buying the asset and buying the put. The value is $V_T = S_T + \max(0, X - S_T)$. Thus, the results can be expressed as

$$V_T = S_T + (X - S_T) = X \quad \text{if } S_T \leq X$$
$$V_T = S_T \qquad\qquad\qquad\quad \text{if } S_T > X$$

When the underlying price at expiration exceeds the exercise price, the put expires with no value. The position is then worth only the value of the underlying. When the underlying price at expiration is less than the exercise price, the put expires in-the-money and is worth $X - S_T$, while the underlying is worth $S_T$. The combined value of the two instruments is X. When the underlying is worth less than the exercise price at expiration, the put can be used to sell the underlying for the exercise price.

The initial value of the position is the initial price of the underlying, $S_0$, plus the premium on the put, $p_0$. Hence, the profit is $\Pi = S_T + \max(0, X - S_T) - (S_0 + p_0)$. The profit can be broken down as follows:

$$\Pi = X - (S_0 + p_0) \quad \text{if } S_T \leq X$$
$$\Pi = S_T - (S_0 + p_0) \quad \text{if } S_T > X$$

In this example, we are going to use the put with an exercise price of 1950. Its premium is 56.01. Recalling that the initial price of the underlying is 2000, the value at expiration and profit for the case of $S_T = 2100$ are

$$V_T = 2100$$
$$\Pi = 2100 - (2000 + 56.01) = 43.99$$

For the case of $S_T = 1900$, the value at expiration and profit are

$$V_T = 1950$$
$$\Pi = 1950 - (2000 + 56.01) = -106.01$$

The results for a range of outcomes are shown in Exhibit 7. Note how the protective put provides a limit on the downside with no limit on the upside.[9] Therefore, we can say that the upper limit is infinite. The lower limit is a loss of 106.01. In the worst possible case, we can sell the underlying for the exercise price, but the up-front cost of the underlying and put are 2056.01, for a maximum loss of 106.01.

---

[9] Note that the graph for a protective put looks like the graph for a call. This result is due to put–call parity.

| Exhibit 7 | Protective Put (Buy Underlying, Buy Put) |

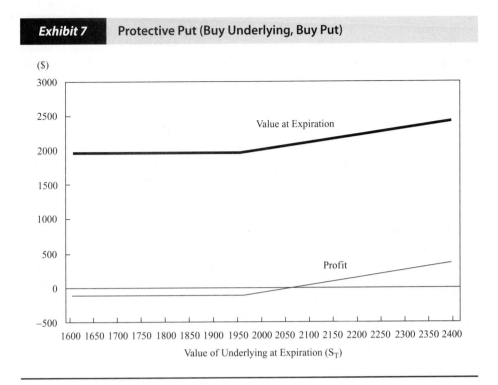

Now let us find the breakeven price of the underlying at expiration. Note that the two profit equations are $\Pi = S_T - (S_0 + p_0)$ if $S_T > X$ and $\Pi = X - (S_0 + p_0)$ if $S_T \leq X$. In the latter case, there is no value of the underlying that will allow us to break even. In the former case, $S_T > X$, we change the notation on $S_T$ to $S_T^*$ to denote the breakeven value, set this expression equal to zero, and solve for $S_T^*$:

$$S_T^* = S_0 + p_0$$

To break even, the underlying must be at least as high as the amount expended up front to establish the position. In this problem, this amount is $2000 + 56.01 = 2056.01$.

To summarize the protective put, we have the following:

Value at expiration: $V_T = S_T + \max(0, X - S_T)$

Profit: $\Pi = V_T - S_0 - p_0$

Maximum profit $= \infty$

Maximum lost $= S_0 + p_0 - X$

Breakeven: $S_T^* = S_0 + p_0$

A protective put can appear to be a great transaction with no drawbacks. It provides downside protection with upside potential, but let us take a closer look. First recall that this is a one-month transaction and keep in mind that the option has been priced by the Black–Scholes–Merton model and is, therefore, a fair price. The maximum loss of 106.01 is a loss of $106.01/2056.01 = 5.2\%$. The breakeven of 2056.01 requires an upward move of 2.8 percent, which is an annual rate of about 34 percent. From this angle, the protective put strategy does not look quite as good, but in fact, these figures simply confirm that protection against downside loss is expensive. When the protective put is fairly priced, the protection buyer must give up considerable upside potential that may not be particularly evident from just looking at a graph.

The purchase of a protective put also presents the buyer with some choices. In this example, the buyer bought the put with exercise price of 1950 for 56.01. Had he bought the put with exercise price of 2000, he would have paid 79.25. The put with exercise price of 2050 would have cost 107.39. The higher the price for which the investor wants to be able to sell the underlying, the more expensive the put will be.

The protective put is often viewed as a classic example of insurance. The investor holds a risky asset and wants protection against a loss in value. He then buys insurance in the form of the put, paying a premium to the seller of the insurance, the put writer. The exercise price of the put is like the insurance deductible because the magnitude of the exercise price reflects the risk assumed by the party holding the underlying. The higher the exercise price, the less risk assumed by the holder of the underlying and the more risk assumed by the put seller. The lower the exercise price, the more risk assumed by the holder of the underlying and the less risk assumed by the put seller. In insurance, the higher the deductible, the more risk assumed by the insured party and the less risk assumed by the insurer. Thus, a higher exercise price is analogous to a lower insurance deductible.

Like traditional insurance, this form of insurance provides coverage for a period of time. At the end of the period of time, the insurance expires and either pays off or not. The buyer of the insurance may or may not choose to renew the insurance by buying another put.

---

### Example 4

Consider a currency selling for $0.875. A put option selling for $0.075 has an exercise price of $0.90. Answer the following questions about a protective put.

**A.** Determine the value at expiration and the profit under the following outcomes:

   **i.** The price of the currency at expiration is $0.96.

   **ii.** The price of the currency at expiration is $0.75.

**B.** Determine the following:

   **i.** the maximum profit.

   **ii.** the maximum loss.

**C.** Determine the breakeven price of the currency at expiration.

**Solutions:**

**A.**  **i.**  $V_T = S_T + \max(0, X_T - S_T) = 0.96 + \max(0, 0.90 - 0.96) = 0.96$

        $\Pi = V_T - V_0 = 0.96 - (S_0 + p_0) = 0.96 - (0.875 + 0.075)$

          $= 0.01$

  **ii.**  $V_T = S_T + \max(0, X - S_T) = 0.75 + \max(0, 0.90 - 0.75) = 0.90$

        $\Pi = V_T - V_0 = 0.90 - (S_0 + p_0) = 0.90 - (0.875 + 0.075)$

          $= -0.05$

**B.**  **i.**  Maximum profit $= \infty$

  **ii.**  Maximum loss $= S_0 + p_0 - X = 0.875 + 0.075 - 0.90 = 0.05$

**C.**  $S_T^* = S_0 + p_0 = 0.875 + 0.075 = 0.95$

Finally, we note that a protective put can be modified in a number of ways. One in particular is to sell a call to generate premium income to pay for the purchase of the put. This strategy is known as a collar. We shall cover collars in detail in Section 2.4.1 when we look at combining puts and calls. For now, however, let us proceed with strategies that combine calls with calls and puts with puts. These strategies are called spreads.

## 2.3 Money Spreads

A spread is a strategy in which you buy one option and sell another option that is identical to the first in all respects except either exercise price or time to expiration. If the options differ by time to expiration, the spread is called a time spread. Time spreads are strategies designed to exploit differences in perceptions of volatility of the underlying. They are among the more specialized strategies, and we do not cover them here. Our focus is on money spreads, which are spreads in which the two options differ only by exercise price. The investor buys an option with a given expiration and exercise price and sells an option with the same expiration but a different exercise price. Of course, the options are on the same underlying asset. The term *spread* is used here because the payoff is based on the difference, or spread, between option exercise prices.

### 2.3.1 *Bull Spreads*

A **bull spread** is designed to make money when the market goes up. In this strategy we combine a long position in a call with one exercise price and a short position in a call with a higher exercise price. Let us use $X_1$ as the lower of the two exercise prices and $X_2$ as the higher. The European call prices would normally be denoted as $c(X_1)$ and $c(X_2)$, but we shall simplify this notation somewhat in this reading by using the symbols $c_1$ and $c_2$, respectively. The value of a call at expiration is $c_T = \max(0, S_T - X)$. So, the value of the spread at expiration is

$$V_T = \max\left(0, S_T - X_1\right) - \max\left(0, S_T - X_2\right)$$

Therefore,

$$
\begin{aligned}
V_T &= 0 - 0 = 0 & &\text{if } S_T \leq X_1 \\
V_T &= S_T - X_1 - 0 = S_T - X_1 & &\text{if } X_1 < S_T < X_2 \\
V_T &= S_T - X_1 - \left(S_T - X_2\right) = X_2 - X_1 & &\text{if } S_T \geq X_2
\end{aligned}
$$

The profit is obtained by subtracting the initial outlay for the spread from the above value of the spread at expiration. To determine the initial outlay, recall that a call option with a lower exercise price will be more expensive than a call option with a higher exercise price. Because we are buying the call with the lower exercise price and selling the call with the higher exercise price, the call we buy will cost more than the call we sell. Hence, the spread will require a net outlay of funds. This net outlay is the initial value of the position of $V_0 = c_1 - c_2$, which we call the net premium. The profit is $V_T - V_0$. Therefore,

$$\Pi = \max\left(0, S_T - X_1\right) - \max\left(0, S_T - X_2\right) - \left(c_1 - c_2\right)$$

In this manner, we see that the profit is the profit from the long call, $\max(0, S_T - X_1) - c_1$, plus the profit from the short call, $-\max(0, S_T - X_2) + c_2$. Broken down into ranges, the profit is

$$\Pi = -c_1 + c_2 \qquad \text{if } S_T \le X_1$$
$$\Pi = S_T - X_1 - c_1 + c_2 \quad \text{if } X_1 < S_T < X_2$$
$$\Pi = X_2 - X_1 - c_1 + c_2 \quad \text{if } S_T \ge X_2$$

If $S_T$ is below $X_1$, the strategy will lose a limited amount of money. The profit on the upside, if $S_T$ is at least $X_2$, is also limited. When both options expire out-of-the-money, the investor loses the net premium, $c_1 - c_2$.

In this example, we use exercise prices of 1950 and 2050. Thus $X_1 = 1950$, $c_1 = 108.43$, $X_2 = 2050$, and $c_2 = 59.98$. Let us examine the outcomes in which the asset price at expiration is 2100, 2000, and 1900. In one outcome, the underlying is above the upper exercise price at expiration, and in one, the underlying is below the lower exercise price at expiration. Let us also examine one case between the exercise prices with $S_T$ equal to 2000.

When $S_T = 2100$, the value at expiration is $V_T = 2050 - 1950 = 100$

When $S_T = 2000$, the value at expiration is $V_T = 2000 - 1950 = 50$

When $S_T = 1900$, the value at expiration is $V_T = 0$

To calculate the profit, we simply subtract the initial value for the call with exercise price $X_1$ and add the initial value for the call with exercise price $X_2$.

When $S_T = 2100$, the profit is $\Pi = 100 - 108.43 + 59.98 = 51.55$

When $S_T = 2000$, the profit is $\Pi = 50 - 108.43 + 59.98 = 1.55$

When $S_T = 1900$, the profit is $\Pi = -108.43 + 59.98 = -48.45$

When $S_T$ is greater than 2100, we would obtain the same outcome as when $S_T$ equals 2100. When $S_T$ is less than 1900, we would obtain the same outcome as when $S_T$ equals 1900.

Exhibit 8 depicts these results graphically. Note how the bull spread provides a limited gain as well as a limited loss. Of course, just purchasing a call provides a limited loss. But when selling the call in addition to buying the call, the investor gives up the upside in order to reduce the downside. In the bull spread, the investor sells gains from the call beyond the higher exercise price. Thus, a bull spread has some similarities to the covered call. With a covered call, the long position in the underlying "covers" the short position in the call. In a bull spread, the long position in the call with the lower exercise price "covers" the short position in the call with the higher exercise price. For both strategies, the short call can be viewed as giving up the gains beyond its exercise price. The upside gain can also be viewed as paying a premium of $c_1 - c_2$ to buy the underlying for $X_1$ and sell it for $X_2$. Accordingly, the maximum gain is $X_2 - X_1 - c_1 + c_2 = 2050 - 1950 - 108.43 + 59.98 = 51.55$, as computed above. This amount represents a maximum return of about 106 percent.[10] The maximum loss is the net premium, 48.45, which is a 100 percent loss.

---

**10** This calculation is based on the fact that the initial value of the position is $108.43 - 59.98 = 48.45$ and the maximum value is 100, which is a gain of 106.4 percent.

**Exhibit 8** | **Bull Spread (Buy Call with Exercise Price X₁, Sell Call with Exercise Price X₂)**

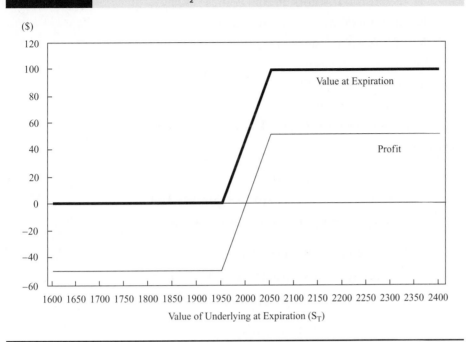

As can be seen from the graph and the profit equations, there is a breakeven asset price at expiration that falls between the two exercise prices. We let $S_T^*$ be the breakeven asset price at expiration and set the profit for the case of $X_1 < S_T < X_2$ to zero:

$$S_T^* = X_1 + c_1 - c_2$$

To achieve a profit of zero or more, the asset price at expiration must exceed the lower exercise price by at least the net premium paid for the options. The long option must expire in-the-money by enough to cover the net premium. In our example,

$$S_T^* = 1950 + 108.43 - 59.98 = 1,998.45$$

What this result means is that the underlying must not move down by more than 0.08 percent.

To summarize the bull spread, we have

Value at expiration: $V_T = \max(0, S_T - X_1) - \max(0, S_T - X_2)$

Profit: $\Pi = V_T - c_1 + c_2$

Maximum profit $= X_2 - X_1 - c_1 + c_2$

Maximum lost $= c_1 - c_2$

Breakeven: $S_T^* = X_1 - c_1 - c_2$

## Example 5

Consider two call options on a stock selling for $72. One call has an exercise price of $65 and is selling for $9. The other call has an exercise price of $75 and is selling for $4. Both calls expire at the same time. Answer the following questions about a bull spread:

**A.** Determine the value at expiration and the profit under the following outcomes:

   **i.** The price of the stock at expiration is \$78.

   **ii.** The price of the stock at expiration is \$69.

   **iii.** The price of the stock at expiration is \$62.

**B.** Determine the following:

   **i.** the maximum profit.

   **ii.** the maximum loss.

**C.** Determine the breakeven stock price at expiration.

**Solutions:**

**A.**  **i.** $V_T = \max(0, S_T - X_1) - \max(0, S_T - X_2)$

$$= \max(0, 78 - 65) - \max(0, 78 - 75) = 13 - 3 = 10$$

$$\Pi = V_T - V_0 = V_T - (c_1 - c_2) = 10 - (9 - 4) = 5$$

   **ii.** $V_T = \max(0, S_T - X_1) - \max(0, S_T - X_2)$

$$= \max(0, 69 - 65) - \max(0, 69 - 75) = 4 - 0 = 4$$

$$\Pi = V_T - V_0 = V_T - (c_1 - c_2) = 4 - (9 - 4) = -1$$

   **iii.** $V_T = \max(0, S_T - X_1) - \max(0, S_T - X_2)$

$$= \max(0, 62 - 65) - \max(0, 62 - 75) = 0 - 0 = 0$$

$$\Pi = V_T - V_0 = 0 - (c_1 - c_2) = 0 - (9 - 4) = 5$$

**B.**  **i.** Maximum profit $= X_2 - X_1 - (c_1 - c_2) = 75 - 65 - (9 - 4) = 5$

   **ii.** Maximum loss $= c_1 - c_2 = 9 - 4 = 5$

**C.** $S_T^* = X_1 + c_1 - c_2 = 65 + 9 - 4 = 70$

Bull spreads are used by investors who think the underlying price is going up. There are also bear spreads, which are used by investors who think the underlying price is going down.

### 2.3.2 *Bear Spreads*

If one uses the opposite strategy, selling a call with the lower exercise price and buying a call with the higher exercise price, the opposite results occur. The graph is completely reversed: The gain is on the downside and the loss is on the upside. This strategy is called a **bear spread**. The more intuitive way of executing a bear spread, however, is to use puts. Specifically, we would buy the put with the higher exercise price and sell the put with the lower exercise price.

The value of this position at expiration would be $V_T = \max(0, X_2 - S_T) - \max(0, X_1 - S_T)$. Broken down into ranges, we have the following relations:

$$V_T = X_2 - S_T - (X_1 - S_T) = X_2 - X_1 \quad \text{if } S_T \leq X_1$$
$$V_T = X_2 - S_T - 0 = X_2 - S_T \quad\quad\quad \text{if } X_1 < S_T < X_2$$
$$V_T = 0 - 0 = 0 \quad\quad\quad\quad\quad\quad\quad\quad \text{if } S_T \geq X_2$$

To obtain the profit, we subtract the initial outlay. Because we are buying the put with the higher exercise price and selling the put with the lower exercise price, the put we are buying is more expensive than the put we are selling. The initial value of the bear spread is $V_0 = p_2 - p_1$. The profit is, therefore, $V_T - V_0$, which is

$$\Pi = \max(0, X_2 - S_T) - \max(0, X_1 - S_T) - p_2 + p_1$$

We see that the profit is the profit from the long put, $\max(0, X_2 - S_T) - p_2$, plus the profit from the short put, $-\max(0, X_1 - S_T) + p_1$. Broken down into ranges, the profit is

$$\Pi = X_2 - X_1 - p_2 + p_1 \quad \text{if } S_T \leq X_1$$
$$\Pi = X_2 - S_T - p_2 + p_1 \quad \text{if } X_1 < S_T < X_2$$
$$\Pi = -p_2 + p_1 \qquad\qquad \text{if } S_T \geq X_2$$

In contrast to the profit in a bull spread, the bear spread profit occurs on the downside; the maximum profit occurs when $S_T \leq X_1$. This profit reflects the purchase of the underlying at $X_1$, which occurs when the short put is exercised, and the sale of the underlying at $X_2$, which occurs when the long put is exercised. The worst outcome occurs when $S_T > X_2$, in which case both puts expire out-of-the-money and the net premium is lost.

In the example, we again use options with exercise prices of 1950 and 2050. Their premiums are $p_1 - 56.01$ and $p_2 = 107.39$. We examine the three outcomes we did with the bull spread: $S_T$ is 1900, 2000, or 2100.

When $S_T = 1900$, the value at expiration is $V_T = 2050 - 1950 = 100$

When $S_T = 2000$, the value at expiration is $V_T = 2050 - 2000 = 50$

When $S_T = 2100$, the value at expiration is $V_T = 0$

The profit is obtained by taking the value at expiration, subtracting the premium of the put with the higher exercise price, and adding the premium of the put with the lower exercise price:

When $S_T = 1900$, the profit is $\Pi = 100 - 107.39 + 56.01 = 48.62$

When $S_T = 2000$, the profit is $\Pi = 50 - 107.39 + 56.01 = -1.38$

When $S_T = 2100$, the profit is $\Pi = -107.39 + 56.01 = -51.38$

When $S_T$ is less than 1900, the outcome is the same as when $S_T$ equals 1900. When $S_T$ is greater than 2100, the outcome is the same as when $S_T$ equals 2100.

The results are graphed in Exhibit 9. Note how this strategy is similar to a bull spread but with opposite outcomes. The gains are on the downside underlying moves and the losses are on the upside underlying. The maximum profit occurs when both puts expire in-the-money. You end up using the short put to buy the asset and the long put to sell the asset. The maximum profit is $X_2 - X_1 - p_2 + p_1$, which in this example is 100 − 107.39 + 56.01 = 48.62, a return of 94 percent.[11] The maximum loss of $p_2 - p_1$ occurs when both puts expire out-of-the-money, and in this case is 107.39 − 56.01 = 51.38, a loss of 100 percent.

---

11 The net premium is 107.39 − 56.01 = 51.38, so the maximum value of 100 is a return of about 94 percent.

| Exhibit 9 | Bear Spread (Buy Put with Exercise Price X$_2$, Sell Put with Exercise Price X$_1$) |
|---|---|

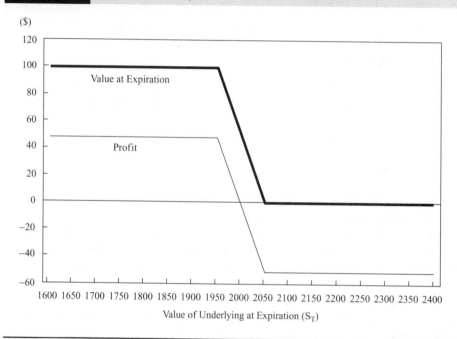

The breakeven asset price occurs between the two exercise prices. Let S$_T$* be the breakeven asset price at expiration, set the profit equation for the middle case to zero, and solve for S$_T$* to obtain S$_T$* = X$_2$ = p$_2$ + p$_1$. In this case, the breakeven is S$_T$* = 2050 − 107.39 + 56.01 = 1,998.62. The underlying need move down only as little as 0.07 percent to make a profit.

To summarize the bear spread, we have

Value at expiration: $V_T = \max(0, X_2 - S_T) - \max(0, X_1 - S_T)$

Profit: $\Pi = V_T - p_2 + p_1$

Maximum profit = $X_2 - X_1 - p_2 + p_1$

Maximum lost = $p_2 - p_1$

Breakeven: $S_T^* = X_2 - p_2 + p_1$

## Example 6

Consider two put options on a bond selling for $92 per $100 par. One put has an exercise price of $85 and is selling for $3. The other put has an exercise price of $95 and is selling for $11. Both puts expire at the same time. Answer the following questions about a bear spread:

**A.** Determine the value at expiration and the profit under the following outcomes:

   **i.** The price of the bond at expiration is $98.

   **ii.** The price of the bond at expiration is $91.

   **iii.** The price of the bond at expiration is $82.

**B.** Determine the following:

  **i.** the maximum profit.

  **ii.** the maximum loss.

**C.** Determine the breakeven bond price at expiration.

**Solutions:**

**A.**  **i.**  $V_T = \max(0, X_2 - S_T) - \max(0, X_1 - S_T)$

   $= \max(0, 95 - 98) - \max(0, 85 - 98) = 0 - 0 = 0$

   $\Pi = V_T - V_0 = V_T - (p_2 - p_1) = 0 - (11 - 3) = -8$

  **ii.**  $V_T = \max(0, X_2 - S_T) - \max(0, X_1 - S_T)$

   $= \max(0, 95 - 91) - \max(0, 85 - 91) = 4 - 0 = 4$

   $\Pi = V_T - V_0 = V_T - (p_2 - p_1) = 4 - (11 - 3) = -4$

  **iii.**  $V_T = \max(0, X_2 - S_T) - \max(0, X_1 - S_T)$

   $= \max(0, 95 - 82) - \max(0, 85 - 82) = 13 - 3 = 10$

   $\Pi = V_T - V_0 = 10 - (p_2 - p_1) = 10 - (11 - 3) = 2$

**B.**  **i.**  Maximum profit $= X_2 - X_1 - (p_2 - p_1) = 95 - 85 - (11 - 3) = 2$

  **ii.**  Maximum loss $= p_2 - p_1 = 11 - 3 = 8$

**C.**  $S_T^* = X_2 - p_2 + p_1 = 95 - 11 + 3 = 87$

---

The bear spread with calls involves selling the call with the lower exercise price and buying the one with the higher exercise price. Because the call with the lower exercise price will be more expensive, there will be a cash inflow at initiation of the position and hence a profit if the calls expire worthless.

Bull and bear spreads are but two types of spread strategies. We now take a look at another strategy, which combines bull and bear spreads.

### 2.3.3 *Butterfly Spreads*

In both the bull and bear spread, we used options with two different exercise prices. There is no limit to how many different options one can use in a strategy. As an example, the **butterfly spread** combines a bull and bear spread. Consider three different exercise prices, $X_1$, $X_2$, and $X_3$. Suppose we first construct a bull spread, buying the call with exercise price of $X_1$ and selling the call with exercise price of $X_2$. Recall that we could construct a bear spread using calls instead of puts. In that case, we would buy the call with the higher exercise price and sell the call with the lower exercise price. This bear spread is identical to the sale of a bull spread.

Suppose we sell a bull spread by buying the call with exercise price $X_3$ and selling the call with exercise price $X_2$. We have now combined a long bull spread and a short bull spread (or a bear spread). We own the calls with exercise price $X_1$ and $X_3$ and have sold two calls with exercise price $X_2$. Combining these results, we obtain a value at expiration of

$$V_T = \max(0, S_T - X_1) - 2\max(0, S_T - X_2) + \max(0, S_T - X_3)$$

This can be broken down into ranges of

$$V_T = 0 - 2(0) + 0 = 0 \qquad\qquad\qquad\qquad \text{if } S_T \leq X_1$$
$$V_T = S_T - X_1 - 2(0) + 0 = S_T - X_1 \qquad\qquad \text{if } X_1 < S_T < X_2$$
$$V_T = S_T - X_1 - 2(S_T - X_2) + 0 = -S_T + 2X_2 - X_1 \qquad \text{if } X_2 \leq S_T < X_3$$
$$V_T = S_T - X_1 - 2(S_T - X_2) + S_T - X_3 = 2X_2 - X_1 - X_3 \quad \text{if } S_T \geq X_3$$

If the exercise prices are equally spaced, $2X_2 - X_1 - X_3$ would equal zero.[12] In virtually all cases in practice, the exercise prices are indeed equally spaced, and we shall make that assumption. Therefore,

$$V_T = 2X_2 - X_1 - X_3 = 0 \quad \text{if } S_T \geq X_3$$

To obtain the profit, we must subtract the initial value of the position, which is $V_0 = c_1 - 2c_2 + c_3$. Is this value positive or negative? It turns out that it will always be positive. The bull spread we buy is more expensive than the bull spread we sell, because the lower exercise price on the bull spread we buy $(X_1)$ is lower than the lower exercise price on the bull spread we sell $(X_2)$. Because the underlying is more likely to move higher than $X_1$ than to move higher than $X_2$, the bull spread we buy is more expensive than the bull spread we sell.

The profit is thus $V_T - V_0$, which is

$$\Pi = \max(0, S_T - X_1) - 2\max(0, S_T - X_2) + \max(0, S_T - X_3) - c_1 + 2c_2 - c_3$$

Broken down into ranges,

$$\Pi = -c_1 + 2c_2 - c_3 \qquad\qquad\qquad \text{if } S_T \leq X_1$$
$$\Pi = S_T - X_1 - c_1 + 2c_2 - c_3 \qquad\qquad \text{if } X_1 < S_T < X_2$$
$$\Pi = -S_T + 2X_2 - X_1 - c_1 + 2c_2 - c_3 \quad \text{if } X_2 \leq S_T < X_3$$
$$\Pi = -c_1 + 2c_2 - c_3 \qquad\qquad\qquad \text{if } S_T \geq X_3$$

Note that in the lowest and highest ranges, the profit is negative; a loss. It is not immediately obvious what happens in the middle two ranges. Let us look at our example. In this example, we buy the calls with exercise prices of 1950 and 2050 and sell two calls with exercise price of 2000. So, $X_1 = 1950$, $X_2 = 2000$, and $X_3 = 2050$. Their premiums are $c_1 = 108.43$, $c_2 = 81.75$, and $c_3 = 59.98$. Let us examine the outcomes in which $S_T = 1900$, 1975, 2025, and 2100. These outcomes fit into each of the four relevant ranges.

When $S_T = 1900$, the value at expiration is $V_T = 0 - 2(0) + 0 = 0$

When $S_T = 1975$, the value at expiration is $V_T = 1975 - 1950 = 25$

When $S_T = 2025$, the value at expiration is $V_T$
$$= -2025 + 2(2000) - 1950 = 25$$

When $S_T = 2100$, the value at expiration is $V_T = 0$

Now, turning to the profit,

---

[12] For example, suppose the exercise prices are equally spaced with $X_1 = 30$, $X_2 = 40$, and $X_3 = 50$. Then $2X_2 - X_3 - X_1 = 2(40) - 50 - 30 = 0$.

When $S_T = 1900$, the profit will be $\Pi$

$$= 0 - 108.43 + 2(81.75) - 59.98 = -4.91$$

When $S_T = 1975$, the profit will be $\Pi$

$$= 25 - 108.43 + 2(81.75) - 59.98 = 20.09$$

When $S_T = 2025$, the profit will be $\Pi$

$$= 25 - 108.43 + 2(81.75) - 59.98 = 20.09$$

When $S_T = 2100$, the profit will be $\Pi$

$$= 0 - 108.43 + 2(81.75) - 59.98 = -4.91$$

Exhibit 10 depicts these results graphically. Note that the strategy is based on the expectation that the volatility of the underlying will be relatively low. The expectation must be that the underlying will trade near the middle exercise price. The maximum loss of 4.91 occurs if the underlying ends up below the lower strike, 1950, or above the upper strike, 2050. The maximum profit occurs if the underlying ends up precisely at the middle exercise price. This maximum profit is found by examining either of the middle two ranges with $S_T$ set equal to $X_2$:

$$\begin{aligned}
\Pi(\text{maximum}) &= S_T - X_1 - c_1 + 2c_2 - c_3 \\
&= X_2 - X_1 - c_1 + 2c_2 - c_3 && \text{if } S_T = X_2 \\
\Pi(\text{maximum}) &= -S_T + 2X_2 - X_1 - c_1 + 2c_2 - c_3 \\
&= X_2 - X_1 - c_1 + 2c_2 - c_3 && \text{if } S_T = X_2
\end{aligned}$$

In this case, the maximum profit is $\Pi$ (maximum) = 2000 − 1950 − 108.43 + 2(81.75) − 59.98 = 45.09, which is a return of 918 percent.[13]

| Exhibit 10 | Butterfly Spread (Buy Calls with Exercise Price $X_1$ and $X_3$, Sell Two Calls with Exercise Price $X_2$) |
|---|---|

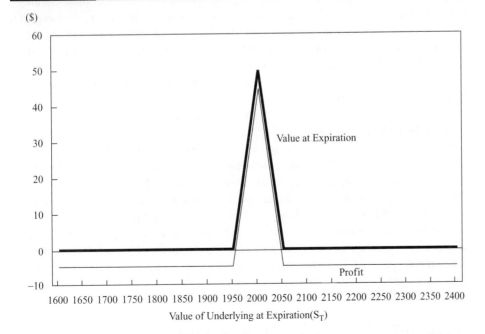

---

**13** This return is based on a maximum value of 2000 − 1950 = 50 versus the initial value of 4.91, a return of 918 percent.

There are two breakeven prices, and they lie within the two middle profit ranges. We find them as follows:

For $X_1 < S_T < X_2$:

$$\Pi = S_T^* - X_1 - c_1 + 2c_2 - c_3 = 0$$
$$S_T^* = X_1 + c_1 - 2c_2 + c_3$$

For $X_2 \leq S_T < X_3$:

$$\Pi = -S_T^* + 2X_2 - X_1 - c_1 + 2c_2 - c_3 = 0$$
$$S_T^* = 2X_2 - X_1 - c_1 + 2c_2 - c_3$$

In this example, therefore, the breakeven prices are

$$S_T^* = X_1 + c_1 - 2c_2 + c_3$$
$$= 1950 + 108.43 - 2(81.75) + 59.98 = 1954.91$$
$$S_T^* = 2X_2 - X_1 - c_1 + 2c_2 - c_3$$
$$= 2(2000) - 1950 - 108.43 + 2(81.75) - 59.98 = 2045.09$$

These movements represent a range of roughly ±2.3 percent from the starting value of 2000. Therefore, if the underlying stays within this range, the strategy will be profitable.

In summary, for the butterfly spread

Value at expiration: $V_T = \max(0, S_T - X_1) - 2\max(0, S_T - X_2) + \max(0, S_T - X_3)$

Profit: $\Pi = V_T - c_1 + 2c_2 - c_3$

Maximum profit = $X_2 - X_1 - c_1 + 2c_2 - c_3$

Maximum loss = $c_1 - 2c_2 + c_3$

Breakeven: $S_T^* = X_1 + c_1 - 2c_2 + c_3$ and $S_T^* = 2X_2 - X_1 - c_1 + 2c_2 - c_3$

As we noted, a butterfly spread is a strategy based on the expectation of low volatility in the underlying. Of course, for a butterfly spread to be an appropriate strategy, the user must believe that the underlying will be less volatile than the market expects. If the investor buys into the strategy and the market is more volatile than expected, the strategy is likely to result in a loss. If the investor expects the market to be more volatile than he believes the market expects, the appropriate strategy could be to sell the butterfly spread. Doing so would involve selling the calls with exercise prices of $X_1$ and $X_3$ and buying two calls with exercise prices of $X_2$.[14]

Alternatively, a butterfly spread can be executed using puts. Note that the initial value of the spread using calls is $V_0 = c_1 - 2c_2 + c_3$. Recall that from put–call parity, c = p + S – X/(1 + r)$^T$. If we use the appropriate subscripts and substitute $p_i$ + S – $X_i$/(1 + r)$^T$ for $c_i$ where i = 1, 2, and 3, we obtain $V_0 = p_1 - 2p_2 + p_3$. The positive signs on $p_1$ and $p_3$ and the negative sign on $2p_2$ mean that we could buy the puts with exercise prices $X_1$ and $X_3$ and sell two puts with exercise price of $X_2$ to obtain the same result. We would, in effect, be buying a bear spread with puts consisting of buying the put with exercise price of $X_3$ and selling the put with exercise price of $X_2$, and also selling a bear spread by selling the put with exercise price of $X_2$ and buying the put with exercise price of $X_1$. If the options are priced correctly, it does not really matter whether we use puts or calls.[15]

---

**14** A short butterfly spread is sometimes called a **sandwich spread**.

**15** If puts were underpriced, it would be better to buy the butterfly spread using puts. If calls were underpriced, it would be better to buy the butterfly spread using calls. Of course, other strategies could also be used to take advantage of any mispricing.

### Example 7

Consider three put options on a currency that is currently selling for $1.45. The exercise prices are $1.30, $1.40, and $1.50. The put prices are $0.08, $0.125, and $0.18, respectively. The puts all expire at the same time. Answer the following questions about a butterfly spread.

A. Determine the value at expiration and the profit under the following outcomes:

   i. The price of the currency at expiration is $1.26.

   ii. The price of the currency at expiration is $1.35.

   iii. The price of the currency at expiration is $1.47.

   iv. The price of the currency at expiration is $1.59.

B. Determine the following:

   i. the maximum profit.

   ii. the maximum loss.

C. Determine the breakeven currency price at expiration.

### Solutions:

A.  i. $V_T = \max(0, X_1 - S_T) - 2\max(0, X_2 - S_T) + \max(0, X_3 - S_T)$

$= \max(0, 1.30 - 1.26) - 2\max(0, 1.40 - 1.26) + \max(0, 1.50 - 1.26)$

$= 0.04 - 2(0.14) + 0.24 = 0.0$

$\Pi = V_T - V_0 = V_T - (p_1 - 2p_2 + p_3) = 0.0 - [0.08 - 2(0.125) + 0.18]$

$= -0.01$

   ii. $V_T = \max(0, X_1 - S_T) - 2\max(0, X_2 - S_T) + \max(0, X_3 - S_T)$

$= \max(0, 1.30 - 1.35) - 2\max(0, 1.40 - 1.35) + \max(0, 1.50 - 1.35)$

$= 0.0 - 2(0.05) + 0.15 = 0.05$

$\Pi = V_T - V_0 = V_T - (p_1 - 2p_2 + p_3)$

$= 0.05 - [0.08 - 2(0.125) + 0.18] = 0.04$

   iii. $V_T = \max(0, X_1 - S_T) - 2\max(0, X_2 - S_T) + \max(0, X_3 - S_T)$

$= \max(0, 1.30 - 1.47) - 2\max(0, 1.40 - 1.47) + \max(0, 1.50 - 1.47)$

$= 0.0 - 2(0) + 0.03 = 0.03$

$\Pi = V_T - V_0 = V_T - (p_1 - 2p_2 + p_3) = 0.03 - [0.08 - 2(0.125) + 0.18] = 0.02$

   iv. $V_T = \max(0, X_1 - S_T) - 2\max(0, X_2 - S_T) + \max(0, X_3 - S_T)$

$= \max(0, 1.30 - 1.59) - 2\max(0, 1.40 - 1.59) + \max(0, 1.50 - 1.59)$

$= 0.0 - 2(0) + 0.0 = 0.0$

$\Pi = V_T - V_0 = V_T - (p_1 - 2p_2 + p_3) = 0.0 - [0.08 - 2(0.125) + 0.18] = -0.01$

B.  i. Maximum profit $= X_2 - X_1 - (p_1 - 2p_2 + p_3) = 1.40 - 1.30$

$- [0.08 - 2(0.125) + 0.18] = 0.09$

> **ii.** Maximum loss $= p_1 - 2p_2 + p_3$
> $$= 0.08 - 2(0.125) + 0.18 = 0.01$$
>
> **C.** $S_T^* = X_1 + p_1 - 2p_2 + p_3 = 1.30 + 0.08 - 2(0.125) + 0.18 = 1.31$
> $$S_T^* = 2X_2 - X_1 - p_1 + 2p_2 - p_3 = 2(1.40) - 1.30 - 0.08$$
> $$+ 2(0.125) - 0.18 = 1.49$$

So far, we have restricted ourselves to the use of either calls or puts, but not both. We now look at strategies that involve positions in calls *and* puts.

## 2.4 Combinations of Calls and Puts

### 2.4.1 *Collars*

Recall that in Section 2.2 we examined the protective put. In that strategy, the holder of the underlying asset buys a put to provide protection against downside loss. Purchasing the put requires the payment of the put premium. One way to get around paying the put premium is to sell another option with a premium equal to the put premium, which can be done by selling a call with an exercise price above the current price of the underlying.

Although it is not necessary that the call premium offset the put premium, and the call premium can even be more than the put premium, the typical collar has the call and put premiums offset. When this offsetting occurs, no net premium is required up front. In effect, the holder of the asset gains protection below a certain level, the exercise price of the put, and pays for it by giving up gains above a certain level, the exercise price of the call. This strategy is called a **collar**. When the premiums offset, it is sometimes called a **zero-cost collar**. This term is a little misleading, however, as it suggests that there is no "cost" to this transaction. The cost takes the form of forgoing upside gains. The term "zero-cost" refers only to the fact that no cash is paid up front.

A collar is a modified version of a protective put and a covered call and requires different exercise prices for each. Let the put exercise price be $X_1$ and the call exercise price be $X_2$. With $X_1$ given, it is important to see that $X_2$ is not arbitrary. If we want the call premium to offset the put premium, the exercise price on the call must be set such that the price of the call equals the price of the put. We thus can select any exercise price of the put. Then the call exercise price is selected by determining which exercise price will produce a call premium equal to the put premium. Although the put can have any exercise price, typically the put exercise price is lower than the current value of the underlying. The call exercise price then must be above the current value of the underlying.[16]

So let $X_1$ be set. The put with this exercise price has a premium of $p_1$. We now need to set $X_2$ such that the premium on the call, $c_2$, equals the premium on the put, $p_1$. To do so, we need to use an option valuation model, such as Black–Scholes–Merton, to find the exercise price of the call that will make $c_2 = p_1$. Recall that the Black–Scholes–Merton formula is

---

[16] It can be proven in general that the call exercise price would have to be above the current value of the underlying. Intuitively, it can be shown through put–call parity that if the call and put exercise prices were equal to the current value of the underlying, the call would be worth more than the put. If we lower the put exercise price below the price of the underlying, the put price would decrease. Then the gap between the call and put prices would widen further. We would then need to raise the call exercise price above the current price of the underlying to make its premium come down.

$$c = S_0 N(d_1) - X e^{-r^c T} N(d_2)$$

where

$$d_1 = \frac{\ln(S_0/X) + (r^c + \sigma^2/2)T}{\sigma\sqrt{T}}$$

$$d_2 = d_1 - \sigma\sqrt{T}$$

and where $r^c$ is the continuously compounded risk-free rate and $N(d_1)$ and $N(d_2)$ are normal probabilities associated with the values $d_1$ and $d_2$. Ideally we would turn the equation around and solve for X in terms of c, but the equation is too complex to be able to isolate X on one side. So, we must solve for X by trial and error. We substitute in values of X until the option price equals c, where c is the call premium that we want to equal the put premium.

Consider the Nasdaq example. Suppose we use the put with exercise price of 1950. Its premium is 56.01. So now we need a call with a premium of 56.01. The call with exercise price of 2000 is worth 81.75. So to get a lower call premium, we need a call with an exercise price higher than 2000. By trial and error, we insert higher and higher exercise prices until the call premium falls to 56.01, which occurs at an exercise price of about 2060.[17] So now we have it. We buy the put with an exercise price of 1950 for 56.01 and sell the call with exercise price of 2060 for 56.01. This transaction requires no cash up front.

The value of the position at expiration is the sum of the value of the underlying asset, the value of the put, and the value of the short call:

$$V_T = S_T + \max(0, X_1 - S_T) - \max(0, S_T - X_2)$$

Broken down into ranges, we have

$$V_T = S_T + X_1 - S_T - 0 = X_1 \quad \text{if } S_T \leq X_1$$
$$V_T = S_T + 0 - 0 = S_T \quad \text{if } X_1 < S_T < X_2$$
$$V_T = S_T + 0 - (S_T - X_2) = X_2 \quad \text{if } S_T \geq X_2$$

The initial value of the position is simply the value of the underlying asset, $S_0$. The profit is $V_T - V_0$:

$$\Pi = S_T + \max(0, X_1 - S_T) - \max(0, S_T - X_2) - S_0$$

Broken down into ranges, we have

$$\Pi = X_1 - S_0 \quad \text{if } S_T \leq X_1$$
$$\Pi = S_T - S_0 \quad \text{if } X_1 < S_T < X_2$$
$$\Pi = X_2 - S_0 \quad \text{if } S_T \geq X_2$$

Using our example where $X_1 = 1950$, $p_1 = 56.01$, $X_2 = 2060$, $c_2 = 56.01$, and $S_0 = 2000$, we obtain the following values at expiration:

If $S_T = 1900$, $V_T = 1950$
If $S_T = 2000$, $V_T = 2000$
If $S_T = 2100$, $V_T = 2060$

The profit for $S_T = 1900$ is $\Pi = 1950 - 2000 = -50$.

---

**17** The other necessary information to obtain the exercise price of the call is that the volatility is 0.35, the risk-free rate is 0.02, and the dividend yield is 0.005. The actual call price at a stock price of 2060 is 56.18. At 2061, the call price is 55.82. Thus, the correct exercise price lies between 2060 and 2061; we simply round to 2060.

If $S_T = 2000$, $\Pi = 2000 - 2000 = 0$

If $S_T = 2100$, $\Pi = 2060 - 2000 = 60$

A graph of this strategy is shown in Exhibit 11. Note that the lines are flat over the range of $S_T$ up to the put exercise price of 1950 and in the range beyond the call exercise price of 2060. Below 1950, the put provides protection against loss. Above 2060, the short call forces a relinquishment of the gains, which are earned by the buyer of the call. In between these ranges, neither the put nor the call has value. The profit is strictly determined by the underlying and moves directly with the value of the underlying. The maximum profit is $X_2 - S_0$, which here is $2060 - 2000 = 60$, a return of 3 percent. The maximum loss is $S_0 - X_1$, which here is $2000 - 1950 = 50$, a loss of 2.5 percent. Keep in mind that these options have lives of one month, so those numbers represent one-month returns. The breakeven is simply the original underlying price of 2000.

In summary, for the collar

Value at expiration: $V_T = S_T + \max(0, X_1 - S_T) - \max(0, S_T - X_2)$

Profit: $\Pi = V_T - S_0$

Maximum profit $= X_2 - S_0$

Maximum loss $= S_0 - X_1$

Breakeven: $S_T^* = S_0$

| Exhibit 11 | Zero-Cost Collar (Buy Put with Exercise Price $X_1$, Sell Call with Exercise Price $X_2$, Put and Call Premiums Offset) |
|---|---|

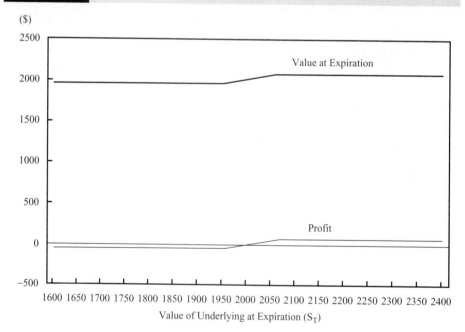

Collars are also known as range forwards and risk reversals.[18] Asset managers often use them to guard against losses without having to pay cash up front for the

---

**18** It is not clear why a collar is sometimes called a risk reversal. It is clear, however, why a collar is sometimes called a range forward. Like a forward contract, it requires no initial outlay other than for the underlying. Unlike a forward contract, which has a strictly linear payoff profile, the collar payoff breaks at the two exercise prices, thus creating a range.

protection. Clearly, however, they are virtually the same as bull spreads. The latter has a cap on the gain and a floor on the loss but does not involve actually holding the underlying. In Section 3 we shall encounter this strategy again in the form of an interest rate collar, which protects floating-rate borrowers against high interest rates.

---

**Example 8**

The holder of a stock worth $42 is considering placing a collar on it. A put with an exercise price of $40 costs $5.32. A call with the same premium would require an exercise price of $50.59.

A. Determine the value at expiration and the profit under the following outcomes:

    i. The price of the stock at expiration is $55.

    ii. The price of the stock at expiration is $48.

    iii. The price of the stock at expiration is $35.

B. Determine the following:

    i. the maximum profit.

    ii. the maximum loss.

C. Determine the breakeven stock price at expiration.

**Solutions:**

A.   i. $V_T = S_T + \max(0, X_1 - S_T) - \max(0, S_T - X_2)$

$$= 55 + \max(0, 40 - 55) - \max(0, 55 - 50.59)$$

$$= 55 + 0 - (55 - 50.59) = 50.59$$

$$\Pi = V_T - S_0 = 50.59 - 42 = 8.59$$

    ii. $V_T = S_T + \max(0, X_1 - S_T) - \max(0, S_T - X_2)$

$$= 48 + \max(0, 40 - 48) - \max(0, 48 - 50.59)$$

$$= 48 + 0 - 0 = 48$$

$$\Pi = V_T - S_0 = 48 - 42 = 6$$

    iii. $V_T = S_T + \max(0, X_1 - S_T) - \max(0, S_T - X_2)$

$$= 35 + \max(0, 40 - 35) - \max(0, 35 - 50.59)$$

$$= 35 + 5 - 0 = 40$$

$$\Pi = V_T - S_0 = 40 - 42 = -2$$

B.   i. Maximum profit $= X_2 - S_0 = 50.59 - 42 = 8.59$

    ii. Maximum loss $= S_0 - X_1 = 42 - 40 = 2$

C.  $S_T^* = S_0 = 42$

---

Collars are one of the many directional strategies, meaning that they perform based on the direction of the movement in the underlying. Of course, butterfly spreads perform based on the volatility of the underlying. Another strategy in which performance is based on the volatility of the underlying is the straddle.

### 2.4.2 *Straddle*

To justify the purchase of a call, an investor must be bullish. To justify the purchase of a put, an investor must be bearish. What should an investor do if he believes the market will be volatile but does not feel particularly strongly about the direction? We discussed earlier that a short butterfly spread is one strategy. It benefits from extreme movements, but its gains are limited. There are other, more complex strategies, such as time spreads, that can benefit from high volatility; however, one simple strategy, the **straddle**, also benefits from high volatility.

Suppose the investor buys both a call and a put with the same exercise price on the same underlying with the same expiration. This strategy enables the investor to profit from upside or downside moves. Its cost, however, can be quite heavy. In fact, a straddle is a wager on a large movement in the underlying.

The value of a straddle at expiration is the value of the call and the value of the put: $V_T = \max(0, S_T - X) + \max(0, X - S_T)$. Broken down into ranges,

$$V_T = X - S_T \ \text{ if } S_T < X$$
$$V_T = S_T - X \ \text{ if } S_T \geq X$$

The initial value of the straddle is simply $V_0 = c_0 + p_0$. The profit is $V_T - V_0$ or $\Pi = \max(0, S_T - X) + \max(0, X - S_T) - c_0 - p_0$. Broken down into ranges,

$$\Pi = X - S_T - c_0 - p_0 \ \text{ if } S_T < X$$
$$\Pi = S_T - X - c_0 - p_0 \ \text{ if } S_T \geq X$$

In our example, let $X = 2000$. Then $c_0 = 81.75$ and $p_0 = 79.25$.

If $S_T = 2100$, the value of the position at expiration is

$$V_T = 2100 - 2000 = 100$$

If $S_T = 1900$, the value of the position at expiration is

$$V_T = 2000 - 1900 = 100$$

If $S_T = 2100$, the profit is $\Pi = 100 - 81.75 - 79.25 = -61$

If $S_T = 1900$, the profit is $\Pi = 100 - 81.75 - 79.25 = -61$

Note the symmetry, whereby a move of 100 in either direction results in a change in value of 61. The put and call payoffs are obviously symmetric. It is also apparent that these outcomes are below breakeven.

Observe the results in Exhibit 12. Note that the value and profit are V-shaped, thereby benefiting from large moves in the underlying in either direction. Like the call option the straddle contains, the gain on the upside is unlimited. Like the put, the downside gain is not unlimited, but it is quite large. The underlying can go down no further than zero. Hence, on the downside the maximum profit is $X - c_0 - p_0$, which in this case is $2000 - 81.75 - 79.25 = 1839$. The maximum loss occurs if the underlying ends up precisely at the exercise price. In that case, neither the call nor the put expires with value and the premiums are lost on both. Therefore, the maximum loss is $c_0 + p_0$, which is $81.75 + 79.25 = 161$.

| Exhibit 12 | Straddle (Buy Call and Put with Exercise Price X) |
| --- | --- |

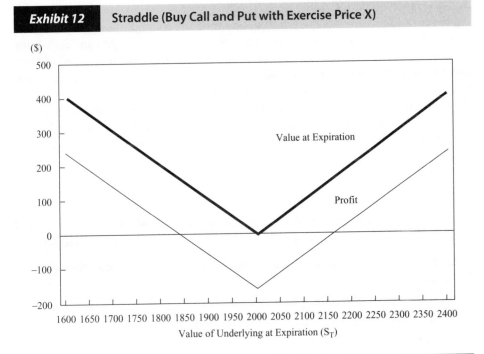

There are two breakevens. Using $S_T^*$ to denote the breakevens, we set each profit equation to zero and solve for $S_T^*$:

If $S_T \geq X$,

$$\Pi = S_T^* - X - c_0 - p_0 = 0$$

$$S_T^* = X + c_0 + p_0$$

If $S_T < X$,

$$\Pi = X - S_T^* - c_0 - p_0 = 0$$

$$S_T^* = X - c_0 - p_0$$

The breakevens thus equal the exercise price plus or minus the premiums. So in this case, the breakevens are $2000 \pm 161 = 2161$ and $1839$. A move of 161 is a percentage move of 8.1 percent over a one-month period. Hence, in this example, the purchase of a straddle is a bet that the underlying will move at nearly a 100 percent annual rate over a one-month period, quite a risky bet. An investor would make such a bet only when he felt that the underlying would be exceptionally volatile. An obvious time to use a straddle would be around major events such as earnings announcements. But because earnings announcements are known and anticipated events, the greater uncertainty surrounding them should already be reflected in the options' prices. Recall that the greater the volatility, the higher the prices of both puts and calls. Therefore, using a straddle in anticipation of an event that everyone knows is coming is not necessarily a good idea. Only when the investor believes the market will be more volatile than everyone else believes would a straddle be advised.

In summary, for a straddle

Value at expiration: $V_T = \max(0, S_T - X) + \max(0, X - S_T)$

Profit: $\Pi = V_T - (c_0 + p_0)$

Maximum profit $= \infty$

Maximum loss $= c_0 + p_0$

Breakeven: $S_T^* = X \pm (c_0 + p_0)$

As we have noted, a straddle would tend to be used by an investor who is expecting the market to be volatile but does not have strong feelings one way or the other on the direction. An investor who leans one way or the other might consider adding a call or a put to the straddle. Adding a call to a straddle is a strategy called a **strap**, and adding a put to a straddle is called a **strip**. It is even more difficult to make a gain from these strategies than it is for a straddle, but if the hoped-for move does occur, the gains are leveraged. Another variation of the straddle is a **strangle**, in which the put and call have different exercise prices. This strategy creates a graph similar to a straddle but with a flat section instead of a point on the bottom.

---

**Example 9**

Consider a stock worth $49. A call with an exercise price of $50 costs $6.25 and a put with an exercise price of $50 costs $5.875. An investor buys a straddle.

**A.** Determine the value at expiration and the profit under the following outcomes:

  **i.** The price of the stock at expiration is $61.

  **ii.** The price of the stock at expiration is $37.

**B.** Determine the following:

  **i.** the maximum profit.

  **ii.** the maximum loss.

**C.** Determine the breakeven stock price at expiration.

**Solutions:**

**A.** **i.** $V_T = \max(0, S_T - X) + \max(0, X - S_T)$

$\qquad = \max(0, 61 - 50) + \max(0, 50 - 61) = 11 - 0 = 11$

$\qquad \Pi = V_T - (c_0 + p_0) = 11 - (6.25 + 5.875) = -1.125$

   **ii.** $V_T = \max(0, S_T - X) + \max(0, X - S_T)$

$\qquad = \max(0, 37 - 50) + \max(0, 50 - 37) = 0 + 13 = 13$

$\qquad \Pi = V_T - S_0 = 13 - (6.25 + 5.875) = 0.875$

**B.** **i.** Maximum profit $= \infty$

   **ii.** Maximum loss $= c_0 + p_0 = 6.25 + 5.875 = 12.125$

**C.** $S_T^* = X \pm (c_0 + p_0) = 50 \pm (6.25 + 5.875) = 62.125, 37.875$

---

Now we turn to a strategy that combines more than one call and more than one put. It should not be surprising that we shall recognize this strategy as just a combination of something we have already learned.

### 2.4.3 *Box Spreads*

We can exploit an arbitrage opportunity with a neutral position many alternative ways: using put–call parity, using the binomial model, or using the Black–Scholes–Merton model. Exploiting put–call parity requires a position in the underlying. Using the binomial or Black–Scholes–Merton model requires that the model holds in the market. In addition, both models require a position in the underlying and an estimate of the volatility.

A **box spread** can also be used to exploit an arbitrage opportunity but it requires that neither the binomial nor Black–Scholes–Merton model holds, it needs no estimate of the volatility, and all of the transactions can be executed within the options market, making implementation of the strategy simpler, faster, and with lower transaction costs.

In basic terms, a box spread is a combination of a bull spread and a bear spread. Suppose we buy the call with exercise price $X_1$ and sell the call with exercise price $X_2$. This set of transactions is a bull spread. Then we buy the put with exercise price $X_2$ and sell the put with exercise price $X_1$. This is a bear spread. Intuitively, it should sound like a combination of a bull spread and a bear spread would leave the investor with a fairly neutral position, and indeed, that is the case.

The value of the box spread at expiration is

$$V_T = \max\left(0, S_T - X_1\right) - \max\left(0, S_T - X_2\right) + \max\left(0, X_2 - S_T\right)$$
$$- \max\left(0, X_1 - S_T\right)$$

Broken down into ranges, we have

$$V_T = 0 - 0 + X_2 - S_T - \left(X_1 - S_T\right) = X_2 - X_1 \quad \text{if } S_T \leq X_1$$
$$V_T = S_T - X_1 - 0 + X_2 - S_T - 0 = X_2 - X_1 \quad \text{if } X_1 < S_T < X_2$$
$$V_T = S_T - X_1 - \left(S_T - X_2\right) + 0 - 0 = X_2 - X_1 \quad \text{if } S_T \geq X_2$$

These outcomes are all the same. In each case, two of the four options expire in-the-money, and the other two expire out-of-the-money. In each case, the holder of the box spread ends up buying the underlying with one option, using either the long call at $X_1$ or the short put at $X_1$, and selling the underlying with another option, using either the long put at $X_2$ or the short call at $X_2$. The box spread thus results in buying the underlying at $X_1$ and selling it at $X_2$. This outcome is known at the start.

The initial value of the transaction is the value of the long call, short call, long put, and short put, $V_0 = c_1 - c_2 + p_2 - p_1$. The profit is, therefore, $\Pi = X_2 - X_1 - c_1 + c_2 - p_2 + p_1$.

In contrast to all of the other strategies, the outcome is simple. In all cases, we end up with the same result. Using the options with exercise prices of 1950 and 2050, which have premiums of $c_1 = 108.43$, $c_2 = 59.98$, $p_1 = 56.01$, and $p_2 = 107.39$, the value at expiration is always $2050 - 1950 = 100$ and the profit is always $\Pi = 100 - 108.43 + 59.98 - 107.39 + 56.01 = 0.17$. This value may seem remarkably low. We shall see why momentarily.

The initial value of the box spread is $c_1 - c_2 + p_2 - p_1$. The payoff at expiration is $X_2 - X_1$. Because the transaction is risk free, the present value of the payoff, discounted using the risk-free rate, should equal the initial outlay. Hence, we should have

$$\left(X_2 - X_1\right) / \left(1 + r\right)^T = c_1 - c_2 + p_2 - p_1$$

If the present value of the payoff exceeds the initial value, the box spread is underpriced and should be purchased.

In this example, the initial outlay is $V_0 = 108.43 - 59.98 + 107.39 - 56.01 = 99.83$. To obtain the present value of the payoff, we need an interest rate and time to expiration. The prices of these options were obtained using a time to expiration of one month and a risk-free rate of 2.02 percent. The present value of the payoff is

$$\left(X_2 - X_1\right) / \left(1 + r\right)^T = \left(2050 - 1950\right) / \left(1.0202\right)^{1/12} = 99.83$$

In other words, this box spread is correctly priced. This result should not be surprising, because we noted that we used the Black–Scholes–Merton model to price these options. The model should not allow arbitrage opportunities of any form.

Recall that the profit from this transaction is 0.17, a very low value. This profit reflects the fact that the box spread is purchased at 99.83 and matures to a value of 100, a profit of 0.17, which is a return of the risk-free rate for one month.[19] The reason the profit seems so low is that it is just the risk-free rate.

Let us assume that one of the long options, say the put with exercise price of 2050, is underpriced. Let its premium be 105 instead of 107.39. Then the net premium would be $108.43 - 59.98 + 105 - 56.01 = 97.44$. Again, the present value of the payoff is 99.83. Hence, the box spread would generate a gain in value clearly in excess of the risk-free rate. If some combination of the options was such that the net premium is more than the present value of the payoff, then the box spread would be overpriced. Then we should sell the $X_1$ call and $X_2$ put and buy the $X_2$ call and $X_1$ put. Doing so would generate an outlay at expiration with a present value less than the initial value.

So to summarize the box spread, we say that

Value at expiration: $V_T = X_2 - X_1$

Profit: $\Pi = X_2 - X_1 - (c_1 - c_2 + p_2 - p_1)$

Maximum profit = (same as profit)

Maximum loss = (no loss is possible, given fair option prices)

Breakeven: no breakeven; the transaction always earns the risk-free rate, given fair option prices.

---

### Example 10

Consider a box spread consisting of options with exercise prices of 75 and 85. The call prices are 16.02 and 12.28 for exercise prices of 75 and 85, respectively. The put prices are 9.72 and 15.18 for exercise prices of 75 and 85, respectively. The options expire in six months and the discrete risk-free rate is 5.13 percent.

**A.** Determine the value of the box spread and the profit for any value of the underlying at expiration.

**B.** Show that this box spread is priced such that an attractive opportunity is available.

### Solutions:

**A.** The box spread always has a value at expiration of $X_2 - X_1 = 85 - 75 = 10$

$$\Pi = V_T - (c_1 - c_2 + p_2 - p_1)$$
$$= 10 - (16.02 - 12.28 + 15.18 - 9.72) = 0.80$$

**B.** The box spread should be worth $(X_2 - X_1)/(1 + r)^T$, or

$$(85 - 75)/(1.0513)^{0.5} = 9.75$$

The cost of the box spread is $16.02 - 12.28 + 15.18 - 9.72 = 9.20$. The box spread is thus underpriced. At least one of the long options is priced too low or at least one of the short options is priced too high; we cannot tell which. Nonetheless, we can execute this box spread, buying the call with exercise price $X_1 = 75$ and put with exercise price $X_2 = 85$ and selling the call with exercise price $X_2 = 85$ and put with exercise price $X_1 = 75$. This would cost 9.20. The present value of the payoff is 9.75. Therefore, the box spread would generate an immediate increase in value of 0.55.

---

**19** That is, $99.83(1.0202)1/12 \approx 100$. Hence, the profit of 0.17 is about 2.02 percent, for one month.

We have now completed our discussion of equity option strategies. Although the strategies are applicable, with minor changes, to fixed-income securities, we shall not explore that area here. We shall, however, look at interest rate option strategies, which require some significant differences in presentation and understanding compared with equity option strategies.

## INTEREST RATE OPTION STRATEGIES

**3**

Consider a group of options in which the underlying is an interest rate and the exercise price is expressed in terms of a rate. Recall that this group of options consists of calls, which pay off if the option expires with the underlying interest rate above the exercise rate, and puts, which pay off if the option expires with the underlying interest rate below the exercise rate. Interest rate call and put options are usually purchased to protect against changes in interest rates. For dollar-based interest rate derivatives, the underlying is usually LIBOR but is always a specific rate, such as the rate on a 90- or 180-day underlying instrument. An interest rate option is based on a specific notional principal, which determines the payoff when the option is exercised. Traditionally, the payoff does not occur immediately upon exercise but is delayed by a period corresponding to the life of the underlying instrument from which the interest rate is taken, an issue we review below.

The payoff of an interest rate call option is

$$(\text{Notional principal}) \; \max\!\left(0, \text{Underlying rate at expiration} - \text{Exercise rate}\right)\!\left(\frac{\text{Days in underlying rate}}{360}\right)$$

where "days in underlying" refers to the maturity of the instrument from which the underlying rate is taken. In some cases, "days in underlying" may be the exact day count during a period. For example, if an interest rate option is used to hedge the interest paid over an m-day period, then "days in underlying" would be m. Even though LIBOR of 30, 60, 90, 180 days, etc., whichever is closest to m, might be used as the underlying rate, the actual day count would be m, the exact number of days. In such cases, the payment date is usually set at 30, 60, 90, 180, etc. days after the option expiration date. So, for example, 180-day LIBOR might be used as the underlying rate, and "days in underlying" could be 180 or perhaps 182, 183, etc. The most important point, however, is that the rate is determined on one day, the option expiration, and payment is made m days later. This practice is standard in floating-rate loans and thus is used with interest rate options, which are designed to manage the risk of floating-rate loans.

Likewise, the payoff of an interest rate put is

$$(\text{Notional principal}) \; \max\!\left(0, \text{Exercise rate} - \text{Underlying rate at expiration}\right)\!\left(\frac{\text{Days in underlying rate}}{360}\right)$$

Now let us take a look at some applications of interest rate options.

## 3.1 Using Interest Rate Calls with Borrowing

Let us examine an application of an interest rate call to establish a maximum interest rate for a loan to be taken out in the future. In brief, a company can buy an interest rate call that pays off from increases in the underlying interest rate beyond a chosen level. The call payoff then compensates for the higher interest rate the company has to pay on the loan.

Consider the case of a company called Global Computer Technology (GCT), which occasionally takes out short-term loans in U.S. dollars with the rate tied to LIBOR. Anticipating that it will take out a loan at a later date, GCT recognizes the potential for an interest rate increase by that time. In this example, today is 14 April, and GCT expects to borrow $40 million on 20 August at LIBOR plus 200 basis points. The loan will involve the receipt of the money on 20 August with full repayment of principal and interest 180 days later on 16 February. GCT would like protection against higher interest rates, so it purchases an interest rate call on 180-day LIBOR to expire on 20 August. GCT chooses an exercise rate of 5 percent. This option gives it the right to receive an interest payment of the difference between the 20 August LIBOR and 5 percent. If GCT exercises the option on 20 August, the payment will occur 180 days later on 16 February when the loan is paid off. The cost of the call is $100,000, which is paid on 14 April. LIBOR on 14 April is 5.5 percent.

The transaction is designed such that if LIBOR is above 5 percent on 20 August, GCT will benefit and be protected against increases in interest rates. To determine how the transaction works, we need to know the effective rate on the loan. Note that the sequence of events is as follows:

14 April ⟶ 20 August ⟶ 16 February
GCT buys call    Call expires; loan starts    Loan repaid and
                                              call payoff made

So cash is paid for the call on 14 April. Cash proceeds from the loan are received on 20 August. On 16 February, the loan is repaid and the call payoff (if any) is made.

To evaluate the effectiveness of the overall transaction, we need to determine how the call affects the loan. Therefore, we need to incorporate the payment of the call premium on 14 April into the cash flow on the loan. So, it would be appropriate to compound the call premium from 14 April to 20 August. In effect, we need to know what the call, purchased on 14 April, effectively costs on 20 August. We compound its premium for the 128 days from 14 April to 20 August at the rate at which GCT would have to borrow on 14 April. This rate would be LIBOR on 14 April plus 200 basis points, or 7.5 percent. The call premium thus effectively costs

$$\$100,000\left[1+0.075\left(\frac{128}{360}\right)\right] = \$102,667$$

on 20 August.[20] On that date, GCT takes out the loan, thereby receiving $40 million. We should, however, reduce this amount by $102,667, because GCT effectively receives less money because it must buy the call. So, the loan proceeds are effectively $40,000,000 − $102,667 = $39,897,333.

Next we must calculate the amount of interest paid on the loan and the amount of any call payoff. Let us assume that LIBOR on 20 August is 8 percent. In that case, the loan rate will be 10 percent. The interest on the loan will be

$$\$40,000,000(0.10)\left(\frac{180}{360}\right) = \$2,000,000$$

This amount, plus $40 million principal, is repaid on 16 February. With LIBOR assumed to be 8 percent on 20 August, the option payoff is

$$\$40,000,000\max\left(0,0.08-0.05\right)\left(\frac{180}{360}\right) = \$40,000,000(0.03)\left(\frac{180}{360}\right) = \$600,000$$

---

**20** The interpretation of this calculation is that GCT's cost of funds is 7.5 percent, making the option premium effectively $102,667 by the time the loan is taken out.

This amount is paid on 16 February. The effective interest paid on 16 February is thus $2,000,000 − $600,000 = $1,400,000. So, GCT effectively receives $39,897,333 on 20 August and pays back $40,000,000 plus $1,400,000 or $41,400,000 on 16 February. The effective annual rate is

$$\left(\frac{\$41,400,000}{\$39,897,333}\right)^{365/180} - 1 = 0.0779$$

Exhibit 13 presents a complete description of the transaction and the results for a range of possible LIBORs on 20 August. Exhibit 14 illustrates the effective loan rate compared with LIBOR on 20 August. We see that the strategy places an effective ceiling on the rate on the loan of about 7.79 percent while enabling GCT to benefit from decreases in LIBOR. Of course, a part of this maximum rate is the 200 basis point spread over LIBOR that GCT must pay.[21] In effect, the company's maximum rate without the spread is 5.79 percent. This reflects the exercise rate of 5 percent plus the effect of the option premium.

| Exhibit 13 | Outcomes for an Anticipated Loan Protected with an Interest Rate Call |
|---|---|

### Scenario (14 April)

Global Computer Technology (GCT) is a U.S. corporation that occasionally undertakes short-term borrowings in U.S. dollars with the rate tied to LIBOR. To facilitate its cash flow planning, it buys an interest rate call to put a ceiling on the rate it pays while enabling it to benefit if rates fall. A call gives GCT the right to receive the difference between LIBOR on the expiration date and the exercise rate it chooses when it purchases the option. The payoff of the call is determined on the expiration date, but the payment is not received until a certain number of days later, corresponding to the maturity of the underlying LIBOR. This feature matches the timing of the interest payment on the loan.

### Action

GCT determines that it will borrow $40 million at LIBOR plus 200 basis points on 20 August. The loan will be repaid with a single payment of principal and interest 180 days later on 16 February.

To protect against increases in LIBOR between 14 April and 20 August, GCT buys a call option on LIBOR with an exercise rate of 5 percent to expire on 20 August with the underlying being 180-day LIBOR. The call premium is $100,000. We summarize the information as follows:

| | |
|---|---|
| Loan amount | $40,000,000 |
| Underlying | 180-day LIBOR |
| Spread | 200 basis points over LIBOR |
| Current LIBOR | 5.5 percent |
| Expiration | 20 August (128 days later) |
| Exercise rate | 5 percent |
| Call premium | $100,000 |

*(continued)*

---

**21** It should be noted that the effective annual rate is actually more than 200 basis points. For example, if someone borrows $100 at 2 percent for 180 days, the amount repaid would be $100[1 + 0.02(180/360)] = $101. The effective annual rate would be ($101/$100)^{365/180} − 1 = 0.0204.

| **Exhibit 13** | **Continued** |
|---|---|

## Scenario (20 August)

LIBOR on 20 August is 8 percent.

## Outcome and Analysis

For any LIBOR, the call payoff at expiration is given below and will be received 180 days later:

$$\$40,000,000 \max\left(0, \text{LIBOR} - 0.05\right)\left(\frac{180}{360}\right)$$

For LIBOR of 8 percent, the payoff is

$$\$40,000,000 \max\left(0, 0.08 - 0.05\right)\left(\frac{180}{360}\right) = \$600,000$$

The premium compounded from 14 April to 20 August at the original LIBOR of 5.5 percent plus 200 basis points is

$$\$100,000\left[1 + \left(0.055 + 0.02\right)\left(\frac{128}{360}\right)\right] = \$102,667$$

So the call costs \$100,000 on 14 April, which is equivalent to \$102,667 on 20 August. The effective loan proceeds are \$40,000,000 − \$102,667 = \$39,897,333. The loan interest is

$$\$40,000,000\left(\text{LIBOR on 20 August} + 200 \text{ Basis points}\right)\left(\frac{180}{360}\right)$$

For LIBOR of 8 percent, the loan interest is

$$\$40,000,000\left(0.08 + 0.02\right)\left(\frac{180}{360}\right) = \$2,000,000$$

The call payoff was given above. The loan interest minus the call payoff is the effective interest. The effective rate on the loan is

$$\left(\frac{\$40,000,000 \text{ plus Effective interest}}{\$39,897,333}\right)^{365/180}$$

$$-1 = \left(\frac{\$40,000,000 + \$2,000,000 - \$600,000}{\$39,897,333}\right)^{365/180} - 1 = 0.0779$$

or 7.79 percent.

The results are shown below for a range of LIBORs on 20 August.

| LIBOR on 20 August | Loan Rate | Loan Interest Paid on 16 February | Call Payoff | Effective Interest | Effective Loan Rate |
|---|---|---|---|---|---|
| 0.010 | 0.030 | \$600,000 | \$0 | \$600,000 | 0.0360 |
| 0.015 | 0.035 | 700,000 | 0 | 700,000 | 0.0412 |
| 0.020 | 0.040 | 800,000 | 0 | 800,000 | 0.0464 |
| 0.025 | 0.045 | 900,000 | 0 | 900,000 | 0.0516 |
| 0.030 | 0.050 | 1,000,000 | 0 | 1,000,000 | 0.0568 |
| 0.035 | 0.055 | 1,100,000 | 0 | 1,100,000 | 0.0621 |

**Exhibit 13** *Continued*

| LIBOR on 20 August | Loan Rate | Loan Interest Paid on 16 February | Call Payoff | Effective Interest | Effective Loan Rate |
|---|---|---|---|---|---|
| 0.040 | 0.060 | 1,200,000 | 0 | 1,200,000 | 0.0673 |
| 0.045 | 0.065 | 1,300,000 | 0 | 1,300,000 | 0.0726 |
| 0.050 | 0.070 | 1,400,000 | 0 | 1,400,000 | 0.0779 |
| 0.055 | 0.075 | 1,500,000 | 100,000 | 1,400,000 | 0.0779 |
| 0.060 | 0.080 | 1,600,000 | 200,000 | 1,400,000 | 0.0779 |
| 0.065 | 0.085 | 1,700,000 | 300,000 | 1,400,000 | 0.0779 |
| 0.070 | 0.090 | 1,800,000 | 400,000 | 1,400,000 | 0.0779 |
| 0.075 | 0.095 | 1,900,000 | 500,000 | 1,400,000 | 0.0779 |
| 0.080 | 0.100 | 2,000,000 | 600,000 | 1,400,000 | 0.0779 |
| 0.085 | 0.105 | 2,100,000 | 700,000 | 1,400,000 | 0.0779 |
| 0.090 | 0.110 | 2,200,000 | 800,000 | 1,400,000 | 0.0779 |

**Exhibit 14** **The Effective Rate on an Anticipated Future Loan Protected with an Interest Rate Call Option**

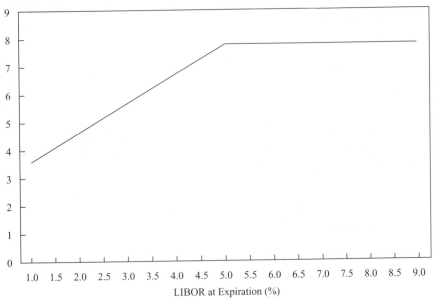

Effective Rate on Loan (%)

LIBOR at Expiration (%)

## Example 11

On 10 January, ResTex Ltd. determines that it will need to borrow $5 million on 15 February at 90-day LIBOR plus 300 basis points. The loan will be an add-on interest loan in which ResTex will receive $5 million and pay it back plus interest on 16 May. To manage the risk associated with the interest rate on 15 February,

ResTex buys an interest rate call that expires on 15 February and pays off on 16 May. The exercise rate is 5 percent, and the option premium is $10,000. The current 90-day LIBOR is 5.25 percent. Assume that this rate, plus 300 basis points, is the rate it would borrow at for any period of up to 90 days if the loan were taken out today. Interest is computed on the exact number of days divided by 360.

Determine the effective annual rate on the loan for each of the following outcomes:

1. 90-day LIBOR on 15 February is 6 percent.
2. 90-day LIBOR on 15 February is 4 percent.

### Solutions:

First we need to compound the premium from 10 January to 15 February, which is 36 days. This calculation tells us the effective cost of the call as of the time the loan is taken out:

$$\$10{,}000\left[1+\left(0.0525+0.03\right)\left(\frac{36}{360}\right)\right]=\$10{,}083$$

The loan proceeds will therefore be $5,000,000 − $10,083 = $4,989,917.

### Solution to 1:

LIBOR is 6 percent. The loan rate will be 9 percent.
The interest on the loan will be $5,000,000(0.06 + 0.03) (90/360) = $112,500.
The option payoff will be $5,000,000 max(0,0.06 − 0.05) (90/360) = $12,500.
Therefore, the effective interest will be $112,500 − $12,500 = $100,000.
The effective rate on the loan will be

$$\left(\frac{\$5{,}000{,}000+\$100{,}000}{\$4{,}989{,}917}\right)^{365/90}-1=0.0925$$

Of course, a little more than 300 basis points of this amount is the spread.

### Solution to 2:

LIBOR is 4 percent. The loan rate will be 7 percent.
The interest on the loan will be $5,000,000(0.04 + 0.03) (90/360) = $87,500.
The option payoff will be $5,000,000 max(0,0.04 − 0.05) (90/360) = $0.00.
The effective interest will, therefore, be $87,500.
The effective rate on the loan will be

$$\left(\frac{\$5{,}000{,}000+\$87{,}500}{\$4{,}989{,}917}\right)^{365/90}-1=0.0817$$

Of course, a little more than 300 basis points of this amount is the spread.

Whereas interest rate call options are appropriate for borrowers, lenders also face the risk of interest rates changing. As you may have guessed, they make use of interest rate puts.

## 3.2 Using Interest Rate Puts with Lending

Now consider an application of an interest rate put to establish a minimum interest rate for a commitment to give a loan in the future. A lender can buy a put that pays off if the interest rate falls below a chosen level. The put payoff then compensates the bank for the lower interest rate on the loan.

For example, consider Arbitrage Bank Inc. (ABInc) which makes loan commitments to corporations. It stands ready to make a loan at LIBOR at a future date. To protect itself against decreases in interest rates between the time of the commitment and the time the loan is taken out, it buys interest rate puts. These options pay off if LIBOR is below the exercise rate at expiration. If LIBOR is above the exercise rate at expiration, the option expires unexercised and the lender benefits from the higher rate on the loan.

In this example, ABInc makes a commitment on 15 March to lend $50 million at 90-day LIBOR plus 2.5 percent on 1 May, which is 47 days later. Current LIBOR is 7.25 percent. It buys a put with an exercise rate of 7 percent for $62,500. Assume that the opportunity cost of lending in the LIBOR market is LIBOR plus a spread of 2.5 percent. Therefore, the effective cost of the premium compounded to the option's expiration is[22]

$$\$62,500\left[1+\left(0.0725+0.025\right)\left(\frac{47}{360}\right)\right]=\$63,296$$

When it lends $50 million on 1 May, it effectively has an outlay of $50,000,000 + $63,296 = $50,063,296. The loan rate is set on 1 May and the interest, paid 90 days later on 30 July, is

$$\$50,000,000\left[\text{LIBOR on 1 May plus 250 Basis points}\left(\frac{90}{360}\right)\right]$$

The put payoff is

$$\$50,000,000\max\left(0,0.07-\text{LIBOR on 1 May}\right)\left(\frac{90}{360}\right)$$

The loan interest plus the put payoff make up the effective interest. The effective rate on the loan is

$$\left(\frac{\text{Principal plus Effective interest}}{\$50,063,296}\right)^{365/90}-1$$

Suppose LIBOR on 1 May is 6 percent. In that case, the loan rate will be 8.5 percent, and the interest on the loan will be

$$\$50,000,000\left[\left(0.06+0.025\right)\left(\frac{90}{360}\right)\right]=\$1,062,500$$

The put payoff is

$$\$50,000,000\max\left(0,0.07-0.06\right)\left(\frac{90}{360}\right)=\$125,000$$

This amount is paid on 30 July. The put cost of $62,500 on 15 March is equivalent to paying $63,296 on 1 May. Thus, on 1 May the bank effectively commits $50,000,000 + $63,296 = $50,063,296. The effective interest it receives is the loan interest of $1,062,500 plus the put payoff of $125,000, or $1,187,500. The effective annual rate is

$$\left(\frac{\$50,000,000+\$1,187,500}{\$50,063,296}\right)^{365/90}-1=0.0942$$

---

[22] The interpretation of this calculation is that the bank could have otherwise made a loan of $62,500, which would have paid back $63,296 on 1 May.

Exhibit 15 presents the results for a range of possible LIBORs at expiration, and Exhibit 16 graphs the effective loan rate against LIBOR on 1 May. Note how there is a minimum effective loan rate of 9.42 percent. Of this rate, 250 basis points is automatically built in as the loan spread.[23] The remaining amount reflects the exercise rate on the put of 7 percent minus the cost of the put premium.

| Exhibit 15 | Outcomes for an Anticipated Loan Protected with an Interest Rate Put |
|---|---|

### Scenario (15 March)

Arbitrage Bank Inc. (ABInc) is a U.S. bank that makes loan commitments to corporations. When ABInc makes these commitments, it recognizes the risk that LIBOR will fall by the date the loan is taken out. ABInc protects itself against interest rate decreases by purchasing interest rate puts, which give it the right to receive the difference between the exercise rate it chooses and LIBOR at expiration. LIBOR is currently 7.25 percent.

### Action

ABInc commits to lending $50 million to a company at 90-day LIBOR plus 250 basis points. The loan will be a single-payment loan, meaning that it will be made on 1 May and the principal and interest will be repaid 90 days later on 30 July.

To protect against decreases in LIBOR between 15 March and 1 May, ABInc buys a put option with an exercise rate of 7 percent to expire on 1 May with the underlying being 90-day LIBOR. The put premium is $62,500. We summarize the information as follows:

| | |
|---|---|
| Loan amount | $50,000,000 |
| Underlying | 90-day LIBOR |
| Spread | 250 basis points over LIBOR |
| Current LIBOR | 7.25 percent |
| Expiration | 1 May |
| Exercise rate | 7 percent |
| Put premium | $62,500 |

### Scenario (1 May)

LIBOR is now 6 percent.

### Outcome and Analysis

For any LIBOR, the payoff at expiration is given below and will be received 90 days later:

$$\$50,000,000 \max(0, 0.07 - \text{LIBOR})\left(\frac{90}{360}\right)$$

For LIBOR of 6 percent, the payoff is

$$\$50,000,000 \max(0, 0.07 - 0.060)\left(\frac{90}{360}\right) = \$125,000$$

---

**23** As in the case of the borrower, the spread is effectively more than 250 basis points when the effective annual rate is determined. For this 90-day loan, this effectively amounts to 256 basis points.

**Exhibit 15** *Continued*

The premium compounded from 15 March to 1 May at current LIBOR plus 250 basis points is

$$\$62,500\left[1+\left(0.0725+0.025\right)\left(\frac{47}{360}\right)\right]=\$63,296$$

So the put costs $62,500 on 15 March, which is equivalent to $63,296 on 1 May. The effective amount loaned is $50,000,000 + $63,296 = $50,063,296. For any LIBOR, the loan interest is

$$\$50,000,000\left[\text{LIBOR on 1 May plus 250 Basis points}\left(\frac{90}{360}\right)\right]$$

With LIBOR at 6 percent, the interest is

$$\$50,000,000\left[\left(0.06+0.025\right)\left(\frac{90}{360}\right)\right]=\$1,062,500$$

The loan interest plus the put payoff is the effective interest on the loan. The effective rate on the loan is

$$\left(\frac{\text{Principal plus Effective interest}}{\$50,063,296}\right)^{365/90}-1$$

$$=\left(\frac{\$50,000,000+\$1,062,500+\$125,000}{\$50,063,296}\right)^{365/90}-1=0.0942$$

or 9.42 percent. The results that follow are for a range of LIBORs on 1 May.

| LIBOR on 1 May | Loan Rate | Loan Interest Paid on 30 July | Put Payoff | Effective Interest | Effective Loan Rate |
|---|---|---|---|---|---|
| 0.030 | 0.055 | $687,500 | $500,000 | $1,187,500 | 0.0942 |
| 0.035 | 0.060 | 750,000 | 437,500 | 1,187,500 | 0.0942 |
| 0.040 | 0.065 | 812,500 | 375,000 | 1,187,500 | 0.0942 |
| 0.045 | 0.070 | 875,000 | 312,500 | 1,187,500 | 0.0942 |
| 0.050 | 0.075 | 937,500 | 250,000 | 1,187,500 | 0.0942 |
| 0.055 | 0.080 | 1,000,000 | 187,500 | 1,187,500 | 0.0942 |
| 0.060 | 0.085 | 1,062,500 | 125,000 | 1,187,500 | 0.0942 |
| 0.065 | 0.090 | 1,125,000 | 62,500 | 1,187,500 | 0.0942 |
| 0.070 | 0.095 | 1,187,500 | 0 | 1,187,500 | 0.0942 |
| 0.075 | 0.100 | 1,250,000 | 0 | 1,250,000 | 0.0997 |
| 0.080 | 0.105 | 1,312,500 | 0 | 1,312,500 | 0.1051 |
| 0.085 | 0.110 | 1,375,000 | 0 | 1,375,000 | 0.1106 |
| 0.090 | 0.115 | 1,437,500 | 0 | 1,437,500 | 0.1161 |
| 0.095 | 0.120 | 1,500,000 | 0 | 1,500,000 | 0.1216 |
| 0.100 | 0.125 | 1,562,500 | 0 | 1,562,500 | 0.1271 |

*(continued)*

| Exhibit 15 | Continued | | | | |
|---|---|---|---|---|---|

| LIBOR on 1 May | Loan Rate | Loan Interest Paid on 30 July | Put Payoff | Effective Interest | Effective Loan Rate |
|---|---|---|---|---|---|
| 0.105 | 0.130 | 1,625,000 | 0 | 1,625,000 | 0.1327 |
| 0.110 | 0.135 | 1,687,500 | 0 | 1,687,500 | 0.1382 |

| Exhibit 16 | The Effective Rate on an Anticipated Loan with an Interest Rate Put Option |
|---|---|

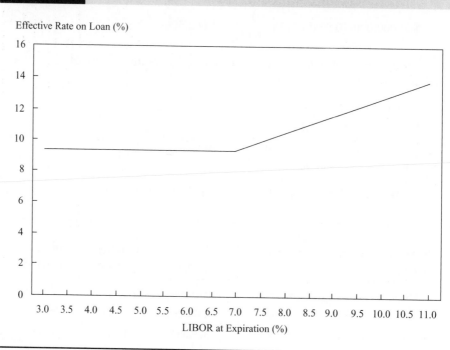

## Example 12

State Bank and Trust (SBT) is a lender in the floating-rate instrument market, but it has been hurt by recent interest rate decreases. SBT often makes loan commitments for its customers and then accepts the rate in effect on the day the loan is taken out. SBT has avoided floating-rate financing in the past. It takes out a certain amount of fixed-rate financing in advance to cover its loan commitments. One particularly large upcoming loan has it worried. This is a $100 million loan to be made in 65 days at 180-day LIBOR plus 100 basis points. The loan will be paid back 182 days after being taken out, and interest will be based on an exact day count and 360 days in a year. Current LIBOR is 7.125 percent, which is the rate it could borrow at now for any period less than 180 days. SBT considers the purchase of an interest rate put to protect it against an interest rate decrease over the next 65 days. The put will have an exercise price of 7 percent and a premium of $475,000.

Determine the effective annual rate on the loan for the following outcomes:

1. 180-day LIBOR at the option expiration is 9 percent.
2. 180-day LIBOR at the option expiration is 5 percent.

**Solutions:**

First we need to compound the premium for 65 days. This calculation tells us the effective cost of the put as of the time the loan is made:

$$\$475,000\left[1+\left(0.07125+0.01\right)\left(\frac{65}{360}\right)\right]=\$481,968$$

The outlay will effectively be $100,000,000 + $481,968 = $100,481,968.

**Solution to 1:**

LIBOR is 9 percent. The loan rate will be 10 percent.

The interest on the loan will be $100,000,000 (0.09 + 0.01)(182/360) = $5,055,556.

The option payoff will be $100,000,000 max (0,0.07 − 0.09)(182/360) = $0.0.

Because there is no option payoff, the effective interest will be $5,055,556. The effective rate on the loan will be

$$\left(\frac{\$100,000,000+\$5,055,556}{\$100,481,968}\right)^{365/182}-1=0.0934$$

Of course, a little more than 100 basis points of this amount is the spread.

**Solution to 2:**

LIBOR is 5 percent. The loan will be 6 percent. The interest on the loan will be $100,000,000 (0.05 + 0.01) (182/360) = $3,033,333.

The option payoff will be $100,000,000 max(0,0.07 − 0.05) (182/360) = $1,011,111.

The effective interest will, therefore, be $3,033,333 + $1,011,111 = $4,044,444. The effective rate on the loan will be

$$\left(\frac{\$100,000,000+\$4,044,444}{\$100,481,968}\right)^{365/182}-1=0.0724$$

Of course, a little more than 100 basis points of this amount is the spread.

Interest rate calls and puts can be combined into packages of multiple options, which are widely used to manage the risk of floating-rate loans.

## 3.3  Using an Interest Rate Cap with a Floating-Rate Loan

Many corporate loans are floating-rate loans. They require periodic interest payments in which the rate is reset on a regularly scheduled basis. Because there is more than one interest payment, there is effectively more than one distinct risk. If a borrower wanted to use an interest rate call to place a ceiling on the effective borrowing rate, it would require more than one call. In effect, it would require a distinct call option expiring on each interest rate reset date. A combination of interest rate call options designed to align with the rates on a loan is called a **cap**. The component options are called **caplets**. Each caplet is distinct in having its own expiration date, but typically the exercise rate on each caplet is the same.

To illustrate the use of a cap, consider a company called Measure Technology (MesTech), which borrows in the floating-rate loan market. It usually takes out a loan for several years at a spread over LIBOR, paying the interest semiannually and the full principal at the end. On 15 April, MesTech takes out a $10 million three-year loan at 100 basis points over 180-day LIBOR from a bank called SenBank. Current 180-day LIBOR is 9 percent, which sets the rate for the first six-month period at 10 percent. Interest payments will be on the 15th of October and April for three years. This means that the day counts for the six payments will be 183, 182, 183, 182, 183, and 182.

To protect against increases in interest rates, MesTech purchases an interest rate cap with an exercise rate of 8 percent. The component caplets expire on 15 October, the following 15 April, and so forth until the last caplet expires on a subsequent 15 October. The loan has six interest payments, but because the first rate is already set, there are only five risky payments so the cap will contain five caplets. The payoff of each caplet will be determined on its expiration date, but the caplet payoff, if any, will actually be made on the next payment date. This enables the caplet payoff to line up with the date on which the loan interest is paid. The cap premium, paid up front on 15 April, is $75,000.

In the example of a single interest rate call, we looked at a range of outcomes several hundred basis points around the exercise rate. In a cap, however, many more outcomes are possible. Ideally we would examine a range of outcomes for each caplet. In the example of a single cap, we looked at the exercise rate and 8 rates above and below for a total of 17 rates. For five distinct rate resets, this same procedure would require $5^{17}$ or more than 762 billion different possibilities. So, we shall just look at one possible combination of rates.

We shall examine a set of outcomes in which LIBOR is
8.50 percent on 15 October
7.25 percent on 15 April the following year
7.00 percent on the following 15 October
6.90 percent on the following 15 April
8.75 percent on the following 15 October
The loan interest is computed as

$$\$10,000,000\left(\text{LIBOR on previous reset date} + 100 \text{ Basis points}\right)$$
$$\times \left(\frac{\text{Days in settlement period}}{360}\right)$$

Thus, the first interest payment is

$$\$10,000,000(0.10)\left(\frac{183}{360}\right) = \$508,333$$

which is based on 183 days between 15 April and 15 October. This amount is certain, because the first interest rate has already been set. The remaining interest payments are based on the assumption we made above about the course of LIBOR over the life of the loan.

The results for these assumed rates are shown in the table at the end of Exhibit 17. Note several things about the effective interest, displayed in the last column. First, the initial interest payment is much higher than the other interest payments because the initial rate is somewhat higher than the remaining rates that prevailed over the life of the loan. Also, recall that the initial rate is already set, and it would make no sense to add a caplet to cover the initial rate, because the caplet would have to expire immediately in order to pay off on the first 15 October. If the caplet expired immediately, the amount MesTech would have to pay for it would be the amount of the caplet payoff, discounted for the deferral of the payoff. In other words, it would make no sense to have an option, or any derivative for that matter, that is purchased and expires immediately. Note also the variation in the effective interest payments, which occurs for two reasons. One is that, in contrast to previous examples, interest is computed over the exact number of days in the period. Thus, even if the rate were the same, the interest could vary by the effect of one or two days of interest. The other reason is that in some cases the caplets do expire with value, thereby reducing the effective interest paid.

| Exhibit 17 | Interest Rate Cap |
|---|---|

## Scenario (15 April)

Measure Technology (MesTech) is a corporation that borrows in the floating-rate instrument market. It typically takes out a loan for several years at a spread over LIBOR. MesTech pays the interest semiannually and the full principal at the end.

To protect against rising interest rates over the life of the loan, MesTech usually buys an interest rate cap in which the component caplets expire on the dates on which the loan rate is reset. The cap seller is a derivatives dealer.

## Action

MesTech takes out a $10 million three-year loan at 100 basis points over LIBOR. The payments will be made semiannually. The lender is SenBank. Current LIBOR is 9 percent, which means that the first rate will be at 10 percent. Interest will be based on 1/360 of the exact number of days in the six-month period. MesTech selects an exercise rate of 8 percent. The caplets will expire on 15 October, 15 April of the following year, and so on for three years, but the caplet payoffs will occur on the next payment date to correspond with the interest payment based on LIBOR that determines the cap payoff. The cap premium is $75,000. We thus have the following information:

| | |
|---|---|
| Loan amount | $10,000,000 |
| Underlying | 180-day LIBOR |
| Spread | 100 basis points over LIBOR |
| Current LIBOR | 9 percent |
| Interest based on | actual days/360 |
| Component caplets | five caplets expiring 15 October, 15 April, etc. |
| Exercise rate | 8 percent |
| Cap premium | $75,000 |

## Scenario (Various Dates throughout the Loan)

Shown below is one particular set of outcomes for LIBOR:
   8.50 percent on 15 October
   7.25 percent on 15 April the following year
   7.00 percent on the following 15 October
   6.90 percent on the following 15 April
   8.75 percent on the following 15 October

## Outcome and Analysis

The loan interest due is computed as

*(continued)*

| Exhibit 17 | Continued |
|---|---|

$$\$10,000,000\left(\text{LIBOR on previous reset date}+100\text{ Basis points}\right)$$
$$\times\left(\frac{\text{Days in settlement period}}{360}\right)$$

The caplet payoff is

$$\$10,000,000\max\left(0,\text{LIBOR on previous reset date}-0.08\right)$$
$$\times\left(\frac{\text{Days in settlement period}}{360}\right)$$

The previous reset date is the expiration date of the caplet. The effective interest is the interest due minus the caplet payoff.

The first caplet expires on the first 15 October and pays off the following April, because LIBOR on 15 October was 8.5 percent. The payoff is computed as

$$\$10,000,000\max\left(0,0.085-0.08\right)\left(\frac{182}{360}\right)$$
$$=\$10,000,000\left(0.005\right)\left(\frac{182}{360}\right)=\$25,278$$

which is based on 182 days between 15 October and 15 April. The following table shows the payments on the loan and cap:

| Date | LIBOR | Loan Rate | Days in Period | Interest Due | Caplet Payoffs | Effective Interest |
|---|---|---|---|---|---|---|
| 15 April | 0.0900 | 0.1000 | | | | |
| 15 October | 0.0850 | 0.0950 | 183 | $508,333 | | $508,333 |
| 15 April | 0.0725 | 0.0825 | 182 | 480,278 | $25,278 | 455,000 |
| 15 October | 0.0700 | 0.0800 | 183 | 419,375 | 0 | 419,375 |
| 15 April | 0.0690 | 0.0790 | 182 | 404,444 | 0 | 404,444 |
| 15 October | 0.0875 | 0.0975 | 183 | 401,583 | 0 | 401,583 |
| 15 April | | | 182 | 492,917 | 37,917 | 455,000 |

Note that on the following three dates, the caplets are out-of-the-money, because the LIBORs are all lower than 8 percent. On the final 15 October, however, LIBOR is 8.75 percent, which leads to a final caplet payoff of $37,917 on the following 15 April, at which time the loan principal is repaid.

We do not show the effective rate on the loan. Because the loan has multiple payments, the effective rate would be analogous to the internal rate of return on a capital investment project or the yield-to-maturity on a bond. This rate would have to be found with a financial calculator or spreadsheet, and we would have to account for the principal received up front and paid back at maturity, as well as the cap premium. It is sufficient for us to see that the cap protects the borrower any time the rate rises above the exercise rate and allows the borrower to benefit from rates lower than the exercise rate.

Finally, there is one circumstance under which this cap might contain a sixth caplet, one expiring on the date on which the loan is taken out. If the borrower purchased the cap in advance of taking out the loan, the first loan rate would not be set until the day the loan is actually taken out. The borrower would thus have an incentive to include a caplet that would protect the first rate setting.

**Example 13**

Healthy Biosystems (HBIO) is a typical floating-rate borrower, taking out loans at LIBOR plus a spread. On 15 January 2002, it takes out a loan of $25 million for one year with quarterly payments on 12 April, 14 July, 16 October, and the following 14 January. The underlying rate is 90-day LIBOR, and HBIO will pay a spread of 250 basis points. Interest is based on the exact number of days in the period. Current 90-day LIBOR is 6.5 percent. HBIO purchases an interest rate cap for $20,000 that has an exercise rate of 7 percent and has caplets expiring on the rate reset dates.

Determine the effective interest payments if LIBOR on the following dates is as given:

| | |
|---|---|
| 12 April | 7.250 percent |
| 14 July | 6.875 percent |
| 16 October | 7.125 percent |

**Solution:**

The interest due for each period is computed as $25,000,000(LIBOR on previous reset date + 0.0250)(Days in period/360). For example, the first interest payment is calculated as $25,000,000(0.065 + 0.025)(87/360) = $543,750, based on the fact that there are 87 days between 15 January and 12 April. Each caplet payoff is computed as $25,000,000 max(0,LIBOR on previous reset date − 0.07)(Days in period/360), where the "previous reset date" is the caplet expiration. Payment is deferred until the date on which the interest is paid at the given LIBOR. For example, the caplet expiring on 12 April is worth $25,000,000 max(0,0.0725 − 0.07)(93/360) = $16,145, which is paid on 14 July and is based on the fact that there are 93 days between 12 April and 14 July.

The effective interest is the actual interest minus the caplet payoff. The payments are shown in the table below:

| Date | LIBOR | Loan Rate | Days in Period | Interest Due | Caplet Payoff | Effective Interest |
|---|---|---|---|---|---|---|
| 15 January | 0.065 | 0.09 | | | | |
| 12 April | 0.0725 | 0.0975 | 87 | $543,750 | | $543,750 |
| 14 July | 0.06875 | 0.09375 | 93 | 629,688 | $16,146 | 613,542 |
| 16 October | 0.07125 | 0.09625 | 94 | 611,979 | 0 | 611,979 |
| 14 January | | | 90 | 601,563 | 7,813 | 593,750 |

Lenders who use floating-rate loans face the same risk as borrowers. As such they can make use of combinations of interest rate puts.

## 3.4 Using an Interest Rate Floor with a Floating-Rate Loan

Let us now consider the same problem from the point of view of the lender, which is SenBank in this example. It would be concerned about falling interest rates. It could, therefore, buy a combination of interest rate put options that expire on the various interest rate reset dates. This combination of puts is called a **floor**, and the component options are called **floorlets**. Specifically, let SenBank buy a floor with floorlets expiring on the interest rate reset dates and with an exercise rate of 8 percent. The premium is $72,500.[24] Exhibit 18 illustrates the results using the same outcomes we looked at when examining the interest rate cap. Note that the floorlet expires in-the-money on three dates when LIBOR is less than 8 percent, and out-of-the-money on two dates when LIBOR is greater than 8 percent. In those cases in which the floorlet expires in-the-money, the actual payoff does not occur until the next settlement period. This structure aligns the floorlet payoffs with the interest payments they are designed to protect. We see that the floor protects the lender against falling interest rates. Any time the rate is below 8 percent, the floor compensates the bank for any difference between the rate and 8 percent. When the rate is above 8 percent, the floorlets simply expire unused.

| Exhibit 18 | Interest Rate Floor |
| --- | --- |

### Scenario (15 April)

SenBank lends in the floating-rate instrument market. Often it uses floating-rate financing, thereby protecting itself against decreases in the floating rates on its loans. Sometimes, however, it finds it can get a better rate with fixed-rate financing, but it then leaves itself exposed to interest rate decreases on its floating-rate loans. Its loans are typically for several years at a spread over LIBOR with interest paid semiannually and the full principal paid at the end.

To protect against falling interest rates over the life of the loan, SenBank buys an interest rate floor in which the component floorlets expire on the dates on which the loan rate is reset. The floor seller is a derivatives dealer.

### Action

SenBank makes a $10 million three-year loan at 100 basis points over LIBOR to MesTech (see cap example). The payments will be made semiannually. Current LIBOR is 9 percent, which means that the first interest payment will be at 10 percent. Interest will be based on the exact number of days in the six-month period divided by 360. SenBank selects an exercise rate of 8 percent. The floorlets will expire on 15 October, 15 April of the following year, and so on for three years, but the floorlet payoffs will occur on the next payment date so as to correspond with the interest payment based on LIBOR that determines the floorlet payoff. The floor premium is $72,500. We thus have the following information:

| | |
| --- | --- |
| Loan amount | $10,000,000 |
| Underlying | 180-day LIBOR |
| Spread | 100 basis points over LIBOR |
| Current LIBOR | 9 percent |
| Interest based on | actual days/360 |
| Component floorlets | five floorlets expiring 15 October, 15 April, etc. |
| Exercise rate | 8 percent |
| Floor premium | $72,500 |

### Outcomes (Various Dates throughout the Loan)

Shown below is one particular set of outcomes for LIBOR:

8.50 percent on 15 October

---

[24] Note that the premiums for the cap and floor are not the same. This difference occurs because the premiums for a call and a put with the same exercise price are not the same, as can be seen by examining put–call parity.

**Exhibit 18**    *Continued*

7.25 percent on 15 April the following year
7.00 percent on the following 15 October
6.90 percent on the following 15 April
8.75 percent on the following 15 October

## Outcome and Analysis

The loan interest is computed as

$$\$10,000,000(\text{LIBOR on previous reset date} + 100 \text{ Basis points})$$
$$\times \left(\frac{\text{Days in settlement period}}{360}\right)$$

The floorlet payoff is

$$\$10,000,000 \max\left(0, 0.08 - \text{LIBOR on previous reset date}\right)$$
$$\times \left(\frac{\text{Days in settlement period}}{360}\right)$$

The effective interest is the interest due plus the floorlet payoff. The following table shows the payments on the loan and floor:

| Date | LIBOR | Loan Rate | Days in Period | Interest Due | Floorlet Payoffs | Effective Interest |
|------|-------|-----------|----------------|--------------|------------------|--------------------|
| 15 April | 0.0900 | 0.1000 | | | | |
| 15 October | 0.0850 | 0.0950 | 183 | $508,333 | | $508,333 |
| 15 April | 0.0725 | 0.0825 | 182 | 480,278 | $0 | 480,278 |
| 15 October | 0.0700 | 0.0800 | 183 | 419,375 | 38,125 | 457,500 |
| 15 April | 0.0690 | 0.0790 | 182 | 404,444 | 50,556 | 455,000 |
| 15 October | 0.0875 | 0.0975 | 183 | 401,583 | 55,917 | 457,500 |
| 15 April | | | 182 | 492,917 | 0 | 492,917 |

## Example 14

Capitalized Bank (CAPBANK) is a lender in the floating-rate loan market. It uses fixed-rate financing on its floating-rate loans and buys floors to hedge the rate. On 1 May 2002, it makes a loan of $40 million at 180-day LIBOR plus 150 basis points. Interest will be paid on 1 November, the following 5 May, the following 1 November, and the following 2 May, at which time the principal will be repaid. The exercise rate is 4.5 percent, the floorlets expire on the rate reset dates, and the premium will be $120,000. Interest will be calculated based on the actual number of days in the period over 360. The current 180-day LIBOR is 5 percent.

Determine the effective interest payments CAPBANK will receive if LIBOR on the following dates is as given:

| | |
|---|---|
| 1 November | 4.875 percent |
| 5 May | 4.25 percent |
| 1 November | 5.125 percent |

## Solution:

The interest due for each period is computed as $40,000,000(LIBOR on previous reset date + 0.0150)(Days in period/360). For example, the first interest payment is $40,000,000(0.05 + 0.0150)(184/360) = $1,328,889, based on the fact that there are 184 days between 1 May and 1 November. Each floorlet payoff is computed as $40,000,000 max(0,0.045 – LIBOR on previous reset date)(Days in period/360), where the "previous reset date" is the floorlet expiration. Payment is deferred until the date on which the interest is paid at the given LIBOR. For example, the floorlet expiring on 5 May is worth $40,000,000 max(0,0.045 – 0.0425)(180/360) = $50,000, which is paid on 1 November and is based on the fact that there are 180 days between 5 May and 1 November.

The effective interest is the actual interest plus the floorlet payoff. The payments are shown in the table below:

| Date | LIBOR | Loan Rate | Days in Period | Interest Due | Floorlet Payoff | Effective Interest |
|---|---|---|---|---|---|---|
| 1 May | 0.05 | 0.065 | | | | |
| 1 November | 0.04875 | 0.06375 | 184 | $1,328,889 | | $1,328,889 |
| 5 May | 0.0425 | 0.0575 | 185 | 1,310,417 | $0 | 1,310,417 |
| 1 November | 0.05125 | 0.06625 | 180 | 1,150,000 | 50,000 | 1,200,000 |
| 2 May | | | 182 | 1,339,722 | 0 | 1,339,722 |

When studying equity option strategies, we combined puts and calls into a single transaction called a collar. In a similar manner, we now combine caps and floors into a single transaction, also called a collar.

## 3.5 Using an Interest Rate Collar with a Floating-Rate Loan

As we showed above, borrowers are attracted to caps because they protect against rising interest rates. They do so, however, at the cost of having to pay a premium in cash up front. A collar combines a long position in a cap with a short position in a floor. The sale of the floor generates a premium that can be used to offset the premium on the cap. Although it is not necessary that the floor premium completely offset the cap premium, this arrangement is common.[25] The exercise rate on the floor is selected such that the floor premium is precisely the cap premium. As with equity options, this type of strategy is called a zero-cost collar. Recall, however, that this term is a bit misleading because it suggests that this transaction has no true "cost." The cost is simply not up front in cash. The sale of the floor results in the borrower giving up any gains from interest rates below the exercise rate on the floor. Therefore, the borrower pays for the cap by giving away some of the gains from the possibility of falling rates.

Recall that for equity investors, the collar typically entails ownership of the underlying asset and the purchase of a put, which is financed with the sale of a call. In contrast, an interest rate collar is more commonly seen from the borrower's point of view: a position as a borrower and the purchase of a cap, which is financed by the sale of a floor. It is quite possible, however, that a lender would want a collar. The lender is holding an asset, the loan, and wants protection against falling interest rates, which can be obtained by buying a floor, which itself can be financed by selling a cap. Most interest rate collars, however, are initiated by borrowers.

---

[25] It is even possible for the floor premium to be greater than the cap premium, thereby *generating cash* up front.

In the example we used previously, MesTech borrows $10 million at LIBOR plus 100 basis points. The cap exercise rate is 8 percent, and the premium is $75,000. We now change the numbers a little and let MesTech set the exercise rate at 8.625 percent. To sell a floor that will generate the same premium as the cap, the exercise rate is set at 7.5 percent. It is not necessary for us to know the amounts of the cap and floor premiums; it is sufficient to know that they offset.

Exhibit 19 shows the collar results for the same set of interest rate outcomes we have been previously using. Note that on the first 15 October, LIBOR is between the cap and floor exercise rates, so neither the caplet nor the floorlet expires in-the-money. On the following 15 April, 15 October, and the next 15 April, the rate is below the floor exercise rate, so MesTech has to pay up on the expiring floorlets. On the final 15 October, LIBOR is above the cap exercise rate, so MesTech gets paid on its cap.

| Exhibit 19 | Interest Rate Collar |
|---|---|

## Scenario (15 April)

Consider the Measure Technology (MesTech) scenario described in the cap and floor example in Exhibits 17 and 18. MesTech is a corporation that borrows in the floating-rate instrument market. It typically takes out a loan for several years at a spread over LIBOR. MesTech pays the interest semiannually and the full principal at the end.

To protect against rising interest rates over the life of the loan, MesTech usually buys an interest rate cap in which the component caplets expire on the dates on which the loan rate is reset. To pay for the cost of the interest rate cap, MesTech can sell a floor at an exercise rate lower than the cap exercise rate.

## Action

Consider the $10 million three-year loan at 100 basis points over LIBOR. The payments are made semiannually. Current LIBOR is 9 percent, which means that the first rate will be at 10 percent. Interest is based on the exact number of days in the six-month period divided by 360. MesTech selects an exercise rate of 8.625 percent for the cap. Generating a floor premium sufficient to offset the cap premium requires a floor exercise rate of 7.5 percent. The caplets and floorlets will expire on 15 October, 15 April of the following year, and so on for three years, but the payoffs will occur on the following payment date to correspond with the interest payment based on LIBOR that determines the caplet and floorlet payoffs. Thus, we have the following information:

| | |
|---|---|
| Loan amount | $10,000,000 |
| Underlying | 180-day LIBOR |
| Spread | 100 basis points over LIBOR |
| Current LIBOR | 9 percent |
| Interest based on | actual days/360 |
| Component options | five caplets and floorlets expiring 15 October, 15 April, etc. |
| Exercise rate | 8.625 percent on cap, 7.5 percent on floor |
| Premium | no net premium |

## Scenario (Various Dates throughout the Loan)

Shown below is one particular set of outcomes for LIBOR:

8.50 percent on 15 October
7.25 percent on 15 April the following year

(continued)

| Exhibit 19 | Continued |
|---|---|

7.00 percent on the following 15 October

6.90 percent on the following 15 April

8.75 percent on the following 15 October

## Outcome and Analysis

The loan interest is computed as

$$\$10,000,000(\text{LIBOR on previous reset date} + 100 \text{ Basis points})$$
$$\times \left(\frac{\text{Days in settlement period}}{360}\right)$$

The caplet payoff is

$$\$10,000,000 \max(0, \text{LIBOR on previous reset date} - 0.08625)$$
$$\times \left(\frac{\text{Days in settlement period}}{360}\right)$$

The floorlet payoff is

$$\Big(\$10,000,000 \max(0, 0.075 - \text{LIBOR on previous reset date})$$
$$\times \left(\frac{\text{Days in settlement period}}{360}\right)$$

The effective interest is the interest due minus the caplet payoff minus the floor-let payoff. Note that because the floorlet was sold, the floorlet payoff is either negative (so we would subtract a negative number, thereby adding an amount to obtain the total interest due) or zero.

The following table shows the payments on the loan and collar:

| Date | LIBOR | Loan Rate | Days in Period | Interest Due | Caplet Payoffs | Floorlet Payoffs | Effective Interest |
|---|---|---|---|---|---|---|---|
| 15 April | 0.0900 | 0.1000 | | | | | |
| 15 October | 0.0850 | 0.0950 | 183 | $508,333 | | | $508,333 |
| 15 April | 0.0725 | 0.0825 | 182 | 480,278 | $0 | $0 | 480,278 |
| 15 October | 0.0700 | 0.0800 | 183 | 419,375 | 0 | −12,708 | 432,083 |
| 15 April | 0.0690 | 0.0790 | 182 | 404,444 | 0 | −25,278 | 429,722 |
| 15 October | 0.0875 | 0.0975 | 183 | 401,583 | 0 | −30,500 | 432,083 |
| 15 April | | | 182 | 492,917 | 6,319 | 0 | 486,598 |

A collar establishes a range, the cap exercise rate minus the floor exercise rate, within which there is interest rate risk. The borrower will benefit from falling rates and be hurt by rising rates within that range. Any rate increases above the cap exercise rate will have no net effect, and any rate decreases below the floor exercise rate will have no net effect. The net cost of this position is zero, provided that the floor exercise rate is set such that the floor premium offsets the cap premium.[26] It is probably easy to see that collars are popular among borrowers.

---

**26** It is certainly possible that the floor exercise rate would be set first, and the cap exercise rate would then be set to have the cap premium offset the floor premium. This would likely be the case if a lender were doing the collar. We assume, however, the case of a borrower who wants protection above a certain level and then decides to give up gains below a particular level necessary to offset the cost of the protection.

**Example 15**

Exegesis Systems (EXSYS) is a floating-rate borrower that manages its interest rate risk with collars, purchasing a cap and selling a floor in which the cost of the cap and floor are equivalent. EXSYS takes out a $35 million one-year loan at 90-day LIBOR plus 200 basis points. It establishes a collar with a cap exercise rate of 7 percent and a floor exercise rate of 6 percent. Current 90-day LIBOR is 6.5 percent. The interest payments will be based on the exact day count over 360. The caplets and floorlets expire on the rate reset dates. The rates will be set on the current date (5 March), 4 June, 5 September, and 3 December, and the loan will be paid off on the following 3 March.

Determine the effective interest payments if LIBOR on the following dates is as given:

| | |
|---|---|
| 4 June | 7.25 percent |
| 5 September | 6.5 percent |
| 3 December | 5.875 percent |

## Solution:

The interest due for each period is computed as $35,000,000(LIBOR on previous reset date + 0.02)(Days in period/360). For example, the first interest payment is $35,000,000(0.065 + 0.02)(91/360) = $752,014, based on the fact that there are 91 days between 5 March and 4 June. Each caplet payoff is computed as $35,000,000 max(0,LIBOR on previous reset date − 0.07)(Days in period/360), where the "previous reset date" is the caplet expiration. Payment is deferred until the date on which the interest is paid at the given LIBOR. For example, the caplet expiring on 4 June is worth $35,000,000 max(0,0.0725 − 0.07)(93/360) = $22,604, which is paid on 5 September and is based on the fact that there are 93 days between 4 June and 5 September. Each floorlet payoff is computed as $35,000,000 max(0,0.06 − LIBOR on previous reset date)(Days in period/360). For example, the floorlet expiring on 3 December is worth $35,000,000 max(0,0.06 − 0.05875) (90/360) = $10,938, based on the fact that there are 90 days between 3 December and 3 March. The effective interest is the actual interest minus the caplet payoff plus the floorlet payoff. The payments are shown in the table below:

| Date | LIBOR | Loan Rate | Days in Period | Interest Due | Caplet Payoff | Floorlet Payoff | Effective Interest |
|---|---|---|---|---|---|---|---|
| 5 March | 0.065 | 0.085 | | | | | |
| 4 June | 0.0725 | 0.0925 | 91 | $752,014 | | | $752,014 |
| 5 September | 0.065 | 0.085 | 93 | 836,354 | $22,604 | $0 | 813,750 |
| 3 December | 0.05875 | 0.07875 | 89 | 735,486 | 0 | 0 | 735,486 |
| 3 March | | | 90 | 689,063 | 0 | −10,938 | 700,001 |

Of course, caps, floors, and collars are not the only forms of protection against interest rate risk. We have previously covered FRAs and interest rate futures. The most widely used protection, however, is the interest rate swap. We cover swap strategies in the reading on risk management applications of swap strategies.

In the final section of this reading, we examine the strategies used to manage the risk of an option portfolio.

# OPTION PORTFOLIO RISK MANAGEMENT STRATEGIES

**4**

So far we have looked at examples of how companies and investors use options. As we have described previously, many options are traded by dealers who make markets in these options, providing liquidity by first taking on risk and then hedging their positions in order to earn the bid–ask spread without taking the risk. In this section, we shall take a look at the strategies dealers use to hedge their positions.[27]

Let us assume that a customer contacts a dealer with an interest in purchasing a call option. The dealer, ready to take either side of the transaction, quotes an acceptable ask price and the customer buys the option. Recall from earlier in this reading that a short position in a call option is a very dangerous strategy, because the potential loss on an upside underlying move is open ended. The dealer would not want to hold a short call position for long. The ideal way to lay off the risk is to find someone else who would take the exact opposite position, but in most cases, the dealer will not be so lucky.[28] Another ideal possibility is for the dealer to lay off the risk using put–call parity. Recall that put–call parity says that $c = p + S - X/(1 + r)^T$. The dealer that has sold a call needs to buy a call to hedge the position. The put–call parity equation means that a long call is equivalent to a long put, a long position in the asset, and issuing a zero-coupon bond with a face value equal to the option exercise price and maturing on the option expiration date. Therefore, if the dealer could buy a put with the same exercise price and expiration, buy the asset, and sell a bond or take out a loan with face value equal to the exercise price and maturity equal to that of the option's expiration, it would have the position hedged. Other than buying an identical call, as described above, this hedge would be the best because it is static: No change to the position is required as time passes.

Unfortunately, neither of these transactions can be commonly employed. The necessary options may not be available or may not be favorably priced. As the next best alternative, dealers **delta hedge** their positions using an available and attractively priced instrument. The dealer is short the call and will need an offsetting position in another instrument. An obvious offsetting instrument would be a long position of a certain number of units of the underlying. The size of that long position will be related to the option's delta. Let us briefly review delta here. By definition,

$$\text{Delta} = \frac{\text{Change in option price}}{\text{Change in underlying price}}$$

Delta expresses how the option price changes relative to the price of the underlying. Technically, we should use an approximation sign ($\approx$) in the above equation, but for now we shall assume the approximation is exact. Let $\Delta S$ be the change in the underlying price and $\Delta c$ be the change in the option price. Then Delta = $\Delta c/\Delta S$. The delta usually lies between 0.0 and 1.0.[29] Delta will be 1.0 only at expiration and only if the option expires in-the-money. Delta will be 0.0 only at expiration and only if the option expires out-of-the-money. So most of the time, the delta will be between 0.0 and 1.0. Hence, 0.5 is often given as an "average" delta, but one must be careful because even before expiration the delta will tend to be higher than 0.5 if the option is in-the-money.

Now, let us assume that we construct a portfolio consisting of $N_s$ units of the underlying and $N_c$ call options. The value of the portfolio is, therefore,

$$V = N_s S + N_c c$$

---

[27] For over-the-counter options, these dealers are usually the financial institutions that make markets in these options. For exchange-traded options, these dealers are the traders at the options exchanges, who may trade for their own accounts or could represent firms.

[28] Even luckier would be the dealer's original customer who might stumble across a party who wanted to sell the call option. The two parties could then bypass the dealer and negotiate a transaction directly between each other, which would save each party half of the bid–ask spread.

[29] In the following text, we always make reference to the delta lying between 0.0 and 1.0, which is true for calls. For puts, the delta is between −1.0 and 0.0. It is common, however, to refer to a put delta of −1.0 as just 1.0, in effect using its absolute value and ignoring the negative. In all discussions in this reading, we shall refer to delta as ranging between 1.0 and 0.0, recalling that a put delta would range from −1.0 to 0.0.

The change in the value of the portfolio is

$$\Delta V = N_S \Delta S + N_c \Delta c$$

If we want to hedge the portfolio, then we want the change in V, given a change in S, to be zero. Dividing by $\Delta S$, we obtain

$$\frac{\Delta V}{\Delta S} = N_S \frac{\Delta S}{\Delta S} + N_c \frac{\Delta c}{\Delta S}$$

$$= N_S + N_c \frac{\Delta c}{\Delta S}$$

Setting this result equal to zero and solving for $N_c/N_S$, we obtain

$$\frac{N_c}{N_S} = -\frac{1}{\Delta c / \Delta S}$$

The ratio of calls to shares has to be the negative of 1 over the delta. Thus, if the dealer sells a given number of calls, say 100, it will need to own 100(Delta) shares.

How does delta hedging work? Let us say that we sell call options on 200 shares (this quantity is 2 standardized call contracts on an options exchange) and the delta is 0.5. We would, therefore, need to hold 200(0.5) = 100 shares. Say the underlying falls by $1. Then we lose $100 on our position in the underlying. If the delta is accurate, the option should decline by $0.50. By having 200 options, the loss in value of the options collectively is $100. Because we are short the options, the loss in value of the options is actually a gain. Hence, the loss on the underlying is offset by the gain on the options. If the dealer were long the option, it would need to sell short the shares.

This illustration may make delta hedging sound simple: Buy (sell) delta shares for each option short (long). But there are three complicating issues. One is that delta is only an approximation of the change in the call price for a change in the underlying. A second issue is that the delta changes if anything else changes. Two factors that change are the price of the underlying and time. When the price of the underlying changes, delta changes, which affects the number of options required to hedge the underlying. Delta also changes as time changes; because time changes continuously, delta also changes continuously. Although a dealer can establish a delta-hedged position, as soon as anything happens—the underlying price changes or time elapses—the position is no longer delta hedged. In some cases, the position may not be terribly out of line with a delta hedge, but the more the underlying changes, the further the position moves away from being delta hedged. The third issue is that the number of units of the underlying per option must be rounded off, which leads to a small amount of imprecision in the balancing of the two opposing positions.

In the following section, we examine how a dealer delta hedges an option position, carrying the analysis through several days with the additional feature that excess cash will be invested in bonds and any additional cash needed will be borrowed.

## 4.1 Delta Hedging an Option over Time

In the previous section, we showed how to set up a delta hedge. As we noted, a delta-hedged position will not remain delta hedged over time. The delta will change as the underlying changes and as time elapses. The dealer must account for these effects.

Let us first examine how actual option prices are sensitive to the underlying and what the delta tells us about that sensitivity. Consider a call option in which the underlying is worth 1210, the exercise price is 1200, the continuously compounded risk-free rate is 2.75 percent, the volatility of the underlying is 20 percent, and the expiration is 120 days. There are no dividends or cash flows on the underlying. Substituting these inputs into the Black–Scholes–Merton model, the option is worth 65.88. Recall from our study of the Black–Scholes–Merton model that delta is the term "$N(d_1)$" in the formula and represents a normal probability associated with the value $d_1$, which is provided as part of the Black–Scholes–Merton formula. In this example, the delta is 0.5826.[30]

Suppose that the underlying price instantaneously changes to 1200, a decline of 10. Using the delta, we would estimate that the option price would be

$$65.88 + (1200 - 1210)(0.5826) = 60.05$$

If, however, we plugged into the Black–Scholes–Merton model the same parameters but with a price of the underlying of 1200, we would obtain a new option price of 60.19—not much different from the previous result. But observe in Exhibit 20 what we obtain for various other values of the underlying. Two patterns become apparent: 1) The further away we move from the current price, the worse the delta-based approximation, and 2) the effects are asymmetric. A given move in one direction does not have the same effect on the option as the same move in the other direction. Specifically, for calls, the delta underestimates the effects of increases in the underlying and overestimates the effects of decreases in the underlying.[31] Because of this characteristic, the delta hedge will not be perfect. The larger the move in the underlying, the worse the hedge. Moreover, whenever the underlying price changes, the delta changes, which requires a rehedging or adjustment to the position. Observe in the last column of the table in Exhibit 20 we have recomputed the delta using the new price of the underlying. A dealer must adjust the position according to this new delta.

| Exhibit 20 | Delta and Option Price Sensitivity |
| --- | --- |

S = 1210
X = 1200
$r^c$ = 0.0275 (continuously compounded)
σ = 0.20
T = 0.328767 (based on 120 days/365)
No dividends
c = 65.88 (from the Black–Scholes–Merton model)

| New Price of Underlying | Delta-Estimated Call Price[a] | Actual Call Price[b] | Difference (Actual – Estimated) | New Delta |
| --- | --- | --- | --- | --- |
| 1180 | 48.40 | 49.69 | 1.29 | 0.4959 |
| 1190 | 54.22 | 54.79 | 0.57 | 0.5252 |
| 1200 | 60.05 | 60.19 | 0.14 | 0.5542 |
| 1210 | 65.88 | 65.88 | 0.00 | 0.5826 |
| 1220 | 71.70 | 71.84 | 0.14 | 0.6104 |
| 1230 | 77.53 | 78.08 | 0.55 | 0.6374 |
| 1240 | 83.35 | 84.59 | 1.24 | 0.6635 |

[a]Delta-estimated call price = Original call price + (New price of underlying – Original price of underlying)Delta.
[b]Actual call price obtained from Black–Scholes–Merton model using new price of underlying; all other inputs are the same.

---

30 All calculations were done on a computer for best precision.
31 For puts, delta underestimates the effects of price decreases and overestimates the effects of price increases.

Now let us consider the effect of time on the delta. Exhibit 21 shows the delta and the number of units of underlying required to hedge 1,000 short options when the option has 120 days, 119, etc. on down to 108. A critical assumption is that we are holding the underlying price constant. Of course, this constancy would not occur in practice, but to focus on understanding the effect of time on the delta, we must hold the underlying price constant. Observe that the delta changes slowly and the number of units of the underlying required changes gradually over this 12-day period. Another not-so-obvious effect is also present: When we round up, we have more units of the underlying than needed, which has a negative effect that hurts when the underlying goes down. When we round down, we have fewer units of the underlying than needed, which hurts when the underlying goes up.

| Exhibit 21 | The Effect of Time on the Delta |
| --- | --- |

S = 1210
X = 1200
$r^c$ = 0.0275 (continuously compounded)
σ = 0.20
T = 0.328767 (based on 120 days/365)
No dividends
c = 65.88 (from the Black–Scholes–Merton model)
Delta = 0.5826
Delta hedge 1,000 short options by holding 1,000(0.5826) = 582.6 units of the underlying.

| Time to Expiration (Days) | Delta | Number of Units of Underlying Required |
| --- | --- | --- |
| 120 | 0.5826 | 582.6 |
| 119 | 0.5825 | 582.5 |
| 118 | 0.5824 | 582.4 |
| 117 | 0.5823 | 582.3 |
| 116 | 0.5822 | 582.2 |
| 115 | 0.5821 | 582.1 |
| 114 | 0.5820 | 582.0 |
| 113 | 0.5819 | 581.9 |
| 112 | 0.5818 | 581.8 |
| 111 | 0.5817 | 581.7 |
| 110 | 0.5816 | 581.6 |
| 109 | 0.5815 | 581.5 |
| 108 | 0.5814 | 581.4 |

The combined effects of the underlying price changing and the time to expiration changing interact to present great challenges for delta hedgers. Let us set up a delta hedge and work through a few days of it. Recall that for the option we have been working with, the underlying price is $1,210, the option price is $65.88, and the delta is 0.5826. Suppose a customer comes to us and asks to buy calls on 1,000 shares. We need to buy a sufficient number of shares to offset the sale of the 1,000 calls. Because we are short 1,000 calls, and this number is fixed, we need 0.5826 shares per call or about 583 shares. So we buy 583 shares to balance the 1,000 short calls. The value of this portfolio is

$$583(\$1,210) - 1,000(\$65.88) = \$639,550$$

So, to initiate this delta hedge, we would need to invest $639,550. To determine if this hedge is effective, we should see this value grow at the risk-free rate. Because the Black–Scholes–Merton model uses continuously compounded interest, the formula for compounding a value at the risk-free rate for one day is $\exp(r^c/365)$, where $r^c$ is the continuously compounded risk-free rate. One day later, this value should be $639,550 $\exp(0.0275/365) = \$639,598$. This value becomes our benchmark.

Now, let us move forward one day and have the underlying go to $1,215. We need a new value of the call option, which now has one less day until expiration and is based on an underlying with a price of $1,215. The market would tell us the option price, but we do not have the luxury here of asking the market for the price. Instead, we have to appeal to a model that would tell us an appropriate price. Naturally, we turn to the Black–Scholes–Merton model. We recalculate the value of the call option using Black–Scholes–Merton, with the price of the underlying at $1,215 and the time to expiration at $119/365 = 0.3260$. The option value is $68.55, and the new delta is 0.5966. The portfolio is now worth

$$583(\$1,215) - 1,000(\$68.55) = \$639,795$$

This value differs from the benchmark by a small amount: $639,795 − $639,598 = $197. Although the hedge is not perfect, it is off by only about 0.03 percent.

Now, to move forward and still be delta hedged, we need to revise the position. The new delta is 0.5966. So now we need 1,000(0.5966) = 597 units of the underlying and must buy 14 units of the underlying. This purchase will cost 14($1,215) = $17,010. We obtain this money by borrowing it at the risk-free rate. So we issue bonds in the amount of $17,010. Now our position is 597 units of the underlying, 1,000 short calls, and a loan of $17,010. The value of this position is still

$$597(\$1,215) - 1,000(\$68.55) - \$17,010 = \$639,795$$

Of course, this is the same value we had before adjusting the position. We could not expect to generate or lose money just by rearranging our position. As we move forward to the next day, we should see this value grow by one day's interest to $639,795 $\exp(0.0275/365) = \$639,843$. This amount is the benchmark for the next day.

Suppose the next day the underlying goes to $1,198, the option goes to 58.54, and its delta goes to 0.5479. Our loan of $17,010 will grow to $17,010 $\exp(0.0275/365) =$ $17,011. The new value of the portfolio is

$$597(\$1,198) - 1,000(\$58.54) - \$17,011 = \$639,655$$

This amount differs from the benchmark by $639,655 − $639,843 = −$188, an error of about 0.03 percent.

With the new delta at 0.5479, we now need 548 shares. Because we have 597 shares, we now must sell 597 − 548 = 49 shares. Doing so would generate 49($1,198) = $58,702. Because the value of our debt was $17,011 and we now have $58,702 in cash, we can pay back the loan, leaving $58,702 − $17,011 = $41,691 to be invested at the risk-free rate. So now we have 548 units of the underlying, 1,000 short calls, and bonds of $41,691. The value of this position is

$$548(\$1,198) - 1,000(\$58.54) + \$41,691 = \$639,655$$

Of course, this is the same value we had before buying the underlying. Indeed, we cannot create or destroy any wealth by just rearranging the position.

Exhibit 22 illustrates the delta hedge, carrying it through one more day. After the third day, the value of the position should be $639,655 exp(0.0275/365) = $639,703. The actual value is $639,870, a difference of $639,870 − $639,703 = $167.

| Exhibit 22 | Delta Hedge of a Short Options Position |
| --- | --- |

S = $1,210
X = $1,200
$r^c$ = 0.0275 (continuously compounded)
$\sigma$ = 0.20
T = 0.328767 (based on 120 days/365)
No dividends
c = $65.88 (from the Black–Scholes–Merton model)
Delta = 0.5826
Units of option constant at 1,000
Units of underlying required = 1000 × Delta
Units of underlying purchased = (Units of underlying required one day) − (Units of underlying required previous day)
Bonds purchased = −S(Units of underlying purchased)
Bond balance = (Previous balance) exp($r^c$/365) + Bonds purchased
Value of portfolio = (Units of underlying)S + (Units of options)c + Bond balance

| Day | S | c | Delta | Options Sold | Units of Underlying Required | Units of Underlying Purchased | Value of Bonds Purchased | Bond Balance | Value of Portfolio |
| --- | --- | --- | --- | --- | --- | --- | --- | --- | --- |
| 0 | $1,210 | $65.88 | 0.5826 | 1,000 | 583 | 583 | $0 | $0 | $639,550 |
| 1 | 1,215 | 68.55 | 0.5965 | 1,000 | 597 | 14 | −17,010 | −17,010 | 639,795 |
| 2 | 1,198 | 58.54 | 0.5479 | 1,000 | 548 | −49 | 58,702 | 41,691 | 639,655 |
| 3 | 1,192 | 55.04 | 0.5300 | 1,000 | 530 | −18 | 21,456 | 63,150 | 639,870 |

As we can see, the delta hedge is not perfect, but it is pretty good. After three days, we are off by $167, only about 0.03 percent of the benchmark.

In our example and the discussions here, we have noted that the dealer would typically hold a position in the underlying to delta-hedge a position in the option. Trading in the underlying would not, however, always be the preferred hedge vehicle. In fact, we have stated quite strongly that trading in derivatives is often easier and more cost-effective than trading in the underlying. As noted previously, ideally a short position in a particular option would be hedged by holding a long position in that same option, but such a hedge requires that the dealer find another customer or dealer who wants to sell that same option. It is possible, however, that the dealer might be able to more easily buy a different option on the same underlying and use that option as the hedging instrument.

For example, suppose one option has a delta of $\Delta_1$ and the other has a delta of $\Delta_2$. These two options are on the same underlying but are not identical. They differ by exercise price, expiration, or both. Using $c_1$ and $c_2$ to represent their prices and $N_1$ and $N_2$ to represent the quantity of each option in a portfolio that hedges the value of one of the options, the value of the position is

$$V = N_1 c_1 + N_2 c_2$$

Dividing by $\Delta S$, we obtain

$$\frac{\Delta V}{\Delta S} = N_1 \frac{\Delta c_1}{\Delta S} + N_2 \frac{\Delta c_2}{\Delta S}$$

To delta hedge, we set this amount to zero and solve for $N_1/N_2$ to obtain

$$\frac{N_1}{N_2} = -\frac{\Delta c_2}{\Delta c_1}$$

The negative sign simply means that a long position in one option will require a short position in the other. The desired quantity of Option 1 relative to the quantity of Option 2 is the ratio of the delta of Option 2 to the delta of Option 1. As in the standard delta-hedge example, however, these deltas will change and will require monitoring and modification of the position.[32]

---

### Example 16

DynaTrade is an options trading company that makes markets in a variety of derivative instruments. DynaTrade has just sold 500 call options on a stock currently priced at $125.75. Suppose the trade date is 18 November. The call has an exercise price of $125, 60 days until expiration, a price of $10.89, and a delta of 0.5649. DynaTrade will delta-hedge this transaction by purchasing an appropriate number of shares. Any additional transactions required to adjust the delta hedge will be executed by borrowing or lending at the continuously compounded risk-free rate of 4 percent.

DynaTrade has begun delta hedging the option. Two days later, 20 November, the following information applies:

| | |
|---|---|
| Stock price | $122.75 |
| Option price | $9.09 |
| Delta | 0.5176 |
| Number of options | 500 |
| Number of shares | 328 |
| Bond balance | −$6,072 |
| Market value | $29,645 |

**A.** At the end of 19 November, the delta was 0.6564. Based on this number, show how 328 shares of stock is used to delta hedge 500 call options.

**B.** Show the allocation of the $29,645 market value of DynaTrade's total position among stock, options, and bonds on 20 November.

**C.** Show what transactions must be done to adjust the portfolio to be delta hedged for the following day (21 November).

**D.** On 21 November, the stock is worth $120.50 and the call is worth $7.88. Calculate the market value of the delta-hedged portfolio and compare it with a benchmark, based on the market value on 20 November.

---

[32] Because the position is long one option and short another, whenever the options differ by exercise price, expiration, or both, the position has the characteristics of a spread. In fact, it is commonly called a **ratio spread**.

### Solution to A:

If the stock moves up (down) $1, the 328 shares should change by $328. The 500 calls should change by 500(0.6564) = $328.20, rounded off to $328. The calls are short, so any change in the value of the stock position is an opposite change in the value of the options.

### Solution to B:

Stock worth 328($122.75) = $40,262

Options worth −500($9.09) = −$4,545

Bonds worth −$6,072

   Total of $29,645

### Solution to C:

The new required number of shares is 500(0.5176) = 258.80. Round this number to 259. So we need to have 259 shares instead of 328 shares and must sell 69 shares, generating 69($122.75) = $8,470. We invest this amount in risk-free bonds. We had a bond balance of −$6,072, so the proceeds from the sale will pay off all of this debt, leaving a balance of $8,470 −$6,072 = $2,398 going into the next day. The composition of the portfolio would then be as follows:

Shares worth 259($122.75) = $31,792

Options worth −500($9.09) = −$4,545

Bonds worth $2,398

   Total of $29,645

### Solution to D:

The benchmark is $29,645 exp(0.04/365) = $29,648. Also, the value of the bond one day later will be $2,398 exp(0.04/365) = $2,398. (This is less than a half-dollar's interest, so it essentially leaves the balance unchanged.) Now we have

Shares worth 259($120.50) = $31,210

Options worth −500($7.88) = −$3,940

Bonds worth $2,398

   Total of $29,668

This is about $20 more than the benchmark.

As previously noted, the delta is a fairly good approximation of the change in the option price for a very small and rapid change in the price of the underlying. But the underlying does not always change in such a convenient manner, and this possibility introduces a risk into the process of delta hedging.

Note Exhibit 23, a graph of the actual option price and the delta-estimated option price from the perspective of day 0 in Exhibit 20. At the underlying price of $1,210, the option price is $65.88. The curved line shows the exact option price, calculated with the Black–Scholes–Merton model, for a range of underlying prices. The heavy line shows the option price estimated using the delta as we did in Exhibit 20. In that exhibit, we did not stray too far from the current underlying price. In Exhibit 23, we let the underlying move a little further. Note that the further we move from the current price of the underlying of $1,210, the further the heavy line deviates from the solid line. As noted earlier, the actual call price moves up more than the delta approximation and moves down less than the delta approximation. This effect occurs because the option price is convex with respect to the underlying price. This convexity, which is quite similar to the convexity of a bond price with respect to its yield, means that a first-order price sensitivity measure like delta, or its duration analog for bonds, is accurate only if the underlying moves by a small amount. With duration, a second-order measure called convexity reflects the extent of the deviation of the actual pricing curve from the approximation curve. With options, the second-order measure is called **gamma**.

| **Exhibit 23** | **Actual Option Price and Delta-Estimated Option Price** |
| --- | --- |

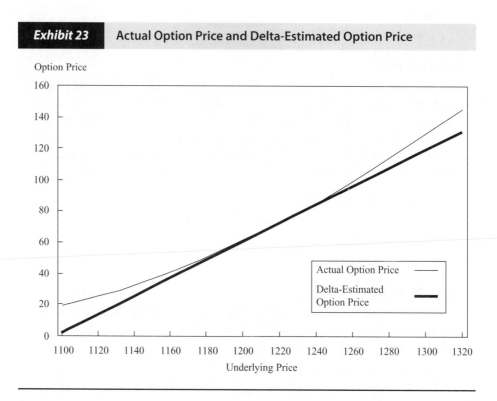

## 4.2 Gamma and the Risk of Delta

A gamma is a measure of several effects. It reflects the deviation of the exact option price change from the price change as approximated by the delta. It also measures the sensitivity of delta to a change in the underlying. In effect, it is the delta of the delta. Specifically,

$$\text{Gamma} = \frac{\text{Change in delta}}{\text{Change in underlying price}}$$

Like delta, gamma is actually an approximation, but we shall treat it as exact. Although a formula exists for gamma, we need to understand only the concept.

If a delta-hedged position were risk free, its gamma would be zero. The larger the gamma, the more the delta-hedged position deviates from being risk free. Because gamma reflects movements in the delta, let us first think about how delta moves. Focusing on call options, recall that the delta is between 0.0 and 1.0. At expiration, the delta is 1.0 if the option expires in-the-money and 0.0 if it expires out-of-the-money. During its life, the delta will tend to be above 0.5 if the option is in-the-money and below 0.5 if the option is out-of-the-money. As expiration approaches, the deltas of in-the-money options will move toward 1.0 and the deltas of out-of-the-money options will move toward 0.0.[33] They will, however, move slowly in their respective directions. The largest moves occur near expiration, when the deltas of at-the-money options move quickly toward 1.0 or 0.0. These rapid movements are the ones that cause the most problems for delta hedgers. Options that are deep in-the-money or deep out-of-the-money tend to have their deltas move closer to 1.0 or 0.0 well before expiration. Their movements are slow and pose fewer problems for delta hedgers. Thus, it is the rapid movements in delta that concern delta hedgers. These rapid movements are more likely to occur on options that are at-the-money and/or near expiration. Under these conditions, the gammas tend to be largest and delta hedges are hardest to maintain.

When gammas are large, some delta hedgers choose to also gamma hedge. This somewhat advanced strategy requires adding a position in another option, combining the underlying and the two options in such a manner that the delta is zero and the gamma is zero. Because it is a somewhat advanced and specialized topic, we do not cover the details of how this is done.

The delta is not the only important factor that changes in the course of managing an option position. The volatility of the underlying can also change.

## 4.3 Vega and Volatility Risk

The sensitivity of the option price to the volatility is called the vega and is defined as

$$\text{Vega} = \frac{\text{Change in option price}}{\text{Change in volatility}}$$

As with delta and gamma, the relationship above is an approximation, but we shall treat it as exact. An option price is very sensitive to the volatility of the underlying. Moreover, the volatility is the only unobservable variable required to value an option. Hence, volatility is the most critical variable. When we examined option-pricing models, we studied the Black–Scholes–Merton and binomial models. In neither of these models is the volatility allowed to change. Yet no one believes that volatility is constant; on some days the stock market is clearly more volatile than on other days. This risk of changing volatility can greatly affect a dealer's position in options. A delta-hedged position with a zero or insignificant gamma can greatly change in value if the volatility changes. If, for example, the dealer holds the underlying and sells options to delta hedge, an increase in volatility will raise the value of the options, generating a potentially large loss for the dealer.

Measuring the sensitivity of the option price to the volatility is difficult. The vega from the Black–Scholes–Merton or binomial models is a somewhat artificial construction. It represents how much the model price changes if one changes the volatility by a small amount. But in fact, the model itself is based on the assumption that volatility does not change. Forcing the volatility to change in a model that does not acknowledge that volatility can change has unclear implications.[34] It is clear, however, that an option price is more sensitive to the volatility when it is at-the-money.

---

**33** The deltas of options that are very slightly in-the-money will temporarily move down as expiration approaches. Exhibit 21 illustrates this effect. But they will eventually move up toward 1.0.

**34** If this point seems confusing, consider this analogy. In the famous Einstein equation $E = mc^2$, E is energy, m is mass, and c is the constant representing the speed of light. For a given mass, we could change c, which would change E. The equation allows this change, but in fact the speed of light is constant at 186,000 miles per second. So far as scientists know, it is a universal constant and can never change. In the case of option valuation, the model assumes that volatility of a given stock is like a universal constant. We can change it, however, and the equation would give us a new option price. But are we allowed to do so? Unlike the speed of light, volatility does indeed change, even though our model says that it does not. What happens when we change volatility in our model? We do not know.

Dealers try to measure the vega, monitor it, and in some cases hedge it by taking on a position in another option, using that option's vega to offset the vega on the original option. Managing vega risk, however, cannot be done independently of managing delta and gamma risk. Thus, the dealer is required to jointly monitor and manage the risk associated with the delta, gamma, and vega. We should be aware of the concepts behind managing these risks.

## 5    FINAL COMMENTS

In the reading on risk management applications of forward and futures strategies, we examined forward and futures strategies. These types of contracts provide gains from movements of the underlying in one direction but result in losses from movements of the underlying in the other direction. The advantage of a willingness to incur losses is that no cash is paid at the start. Options offer the advantage of having one-directional effects: The buyer of an option gains from a movement in one direction and loses only the premium from movements in the other direction. The cost of this advantage is that options require the payment of cash at the start. Some market participants choose forwards and futures because they do not have to pay cash at the start. They can justify taking positions without having to come up with the cash to do so. Others, however, prefer the flexibility to benefit when their predictions are right and suffer only a limited loss when wrong. The trade-off between the willingness to pay cash at the start versus incurring losses, given one's risk preferences, is the deciding factor in whether to use options or forwards/futures.

All option strategies are essentially rooted in the transactions of buying a call or a put. Understanding a short position in either type of option means understanding the corresponding long position in the option. All remaining strategies are just combinations of options, the underlying, and risk-free bonds. We looked at a number of option strategies associated with equities, which can apply about equally to index options or options on individual stocks. The applicability of these strategies to bonds is also fairly straightforward. The options must expire before the bonds mature, but the general concepts associated with equity option strategies apply similarly to bond option strategies.

Likewise, strategies that apply to equity options apply in nearly the same manner to interest rate options. Nonetheless, significant differences exist between interest rate options and equity or bond options. If nothing else, the notion of bullishness is quite opposite. Bullish (bearish) equity investors buy calls (puts). In interest rate markets, bullish (bearish) investors buy puts (calls) on interest rates, because being bullish (bearish) on interest rates means that one thinks rates are going down (up). Interest rate options pay off as though they were interest payments. Equity or bond options pay off as though the holder were selling or buying stocks or bonds. Finally, interest rate options are very often combined into portfolios in the form of caps and floors for the purpose of hedging floating-rate loans. Standard option strategies such as straddles and spreads are just as applicable to interest rate options.

Despite some subtle differences between the option strategies examined in this reading and comparable strategies using options on futures, the differences are relatively minor and do not warrant separate coverage here. If you have a good grasp of the basics of the option strategies presented in this reading, you can easily adapt those strategies to ones in which the underlying is a futures contract.

In the reading on risk management applications of swap strategies, we take up strategies using swaps. As we have so often mentioned, interest rate swaps are the most widely used financial derivative. They are less widely used with currencies and equities than are forwards, futures, and options. Nonetheless, there are many applications of swaps to currencies and equities, and we shall certainly look at them. To examine swaps, however, we must return to the types of instruments with two-directional payoffs and no cash payments at the start. Indeed, swaps are a lot like forward contracts, which themselves are a lot like futures.

## SUMMARY

- The profit from buying a call is the value at expiration, $\max(0, S_T - X)$, minus $c_0$, the option premium. The maximum profit is infinite, and the maximum loss is the option premium. The breakeven underlying price at expiration is the exercise price plus the option premium. When one sells a call, these results are reversed.

- The profit from buying a put is the value at expiration, $\max(0, X - S_T)$, minus $p_0$, the option premium. The maximum profit is the exercise price minus the option premium, and the maximum loss is the option premium. The breakeven underlying price at expiration is the exercise price minus the option premium. When one sells a put, these results are reversed.

- The profit from a covered call—the purchase of the underlying and sale of a call—is the value at expiration, $S_T - \max(0, S_T - X)$, minus $S_0 - c_0$, the cost of the underlying minus the option premium. The maximum profit is the exercise price minus the original underlying price plus the option premium, and the maximum loss is the cost of the underlying less the option premium. The breakeven underlying price at expiration is the original price of the underlying minus the option premium.

- The profit from a protective put—the purchase of the underlying and a put—is the value at expiration, $S_T + \max(0, X - S_T)$, minus the cost of the underlying plus the option premium, $S_0 + p_0$. The maximum profit is infinite, and the maximum loss is the cost of the underlying plus the option premium minus the exercise price. The breakeven underlying price at expiration is the original price of the underlying plus the option premium.

- The profit from a bull spread—the purchase of a call at one exercise price and the sale of a call with the same expiration but a higher exercise price—is the value at expiration, $\max(0, S_T - X_1) - \max(0, S_T - X_2)$, minus the net premium, $c_1 - c_2$, which is the premium of the long option minus the premium of the short option. The maximum profit is $X_2 - X_1$ minus the net premium, and the maximum loss is the net premium. The breakeven underlying price at expiration is the lower exercise price plus the net premium.

- The profit from a bear spread—the purchase of a put at one exercise price and the sale of a put with the same expiration but a lower exercise price—is the value at expiration, $\max(0, X_2 - S_T) - \max(0, X_1 - S_T)$, minus the net premium, $p_2 - p_1$, which is the premium of the long option minus the premium of the short option. The maximum profit is $X_2 - X_1$ minus the net premium, and the maximum loss is the net premium. The breakeven underlying price at expiration is the higher exercise price minus the net premium.

- The profit from a butterfly spread—the purchase of a call at one exercise price, $X_1$, sale of two calls at a higher exercise price, $X_2$, and the purchase of a call at a higher exercise price, $X_3$—is the value at expiration, $\max(0, S_T - X_1) - 2\max(0, S_T - X_2), + \max(0, S_T - X_3)$, minus the net premium, $c_1 - 2c_2 + c_3$. The maximum profit is $X_2 - X_1$ minus the net premium, and the maximum loss is

OPTIONAL SEGMENT

END OPTIONAL SEGMENT

the net premium. The breakeven underlying prices at expiration are $2X_2 - X_1$ minus the net premium and $X_1$ plus the net premium. A butterfly spread can also be constructed by trading the corresponding put options.

- The profit from a collar—the holding of the underlying, the purchase of a put at one exercise price, $X_1$, and the sale of a call with the same expiration and a higher exercise price, $X_2$, and in which the premium on the put equals the premium on the call—is the value at expiration, $S_T + \max(0, X_1 - S_T) - \max(0, S_T - X_2)$, minus $S_0$, the original price of the underlying. The maximum profit is $X_2 - S_0$, and the maximum loss is $S_0 - X_1$. The breakeven underlying price at expiration is the initial price of the underlying.

- The profit from a straddle—a long position in a call and a put with the same exercise price and expiration—is the value at expiration, $\max(0, S_T - X) + \max(0, X - S_T)$, minus the premiums on the call and put, $c_0 + p_0$. The maximum profit is infinite, and the maximum loss is the sum of the premiums on the call and put, $c_0 + p_0$. The breakeven prices at expiration are the exercise price plus and minus the premiums on the call and put.

- A box spread is a combination of a bull spread using calls and a bear spread using puts, with one call and put at an exercise price of $X_1$ and another call and put at an exercise price of $X_2$. The profit is the value at expiration, $X_2 - X_1$, minus the net premiums, $c_1 - c_2 + p_2 - p_1$. The transaction is risk free, and the net premium paid should be the present value of this risk-free payoff.

- A long position in an interest rate call can be used to place a ceiling on the rate on an anticipated loan from the perspective of the borrower. The call provides a payoff if the interest rate at expiration exceeds the exercise rate, thereby compensating the borrower when the rate is higher than the exercise rate. The effective interest paid on the loan is the actual interest paid minus the call payoff. The call premium must be taken into account by compounding it to the date on which the loan is taken out and deducting it from the initial proceeds received from the loan.

- A long position in an interest rate put can be used to lock in the rate on an anticipated loan from the perspective of the lender. The put provides a payoff if the interest rate at expiration is less than the exercise rate, thereby compensating the lender when the rate is lower than the exercise rate. The effective interest paid on the loan is the actual interest received plus the put payoff. The put premium must be taken into account by compounding it to the date on which the loan is taken out and adding it to initial proceeds paid out on the loan.

- An interest rate cap can be used to place an upper limit on the interest paid on a floating-rate loan from the perspective of the borrower. A cap is a series of interest rate calls, each of which is referred to as a caplet. Each caplet provides a payoff if the interest rate on the loan reset date exceeds the exercise rate, thereby compensating the borrower when the rate is higher than the exercise rate. The effective interest paid is the actual interest paid minus the caplet payoff. The premium is paid at the start and is the sum of the premiums on the component caplets.

- An interest rate floor can be used to place a lower limit on the interest received on a floating-rate loan from the perspective of the lender. A floor is a series of interest rate puts, each of which is called a floorlet. Each floorlet provides a payoff if the interest rate at the loan reset date is less than the exercise rate, thereby compensating the lender when the rate is lower than the exercise rate. The effective interest received is the actual interest plus the floorlet payoff. The premium is paid at the start and is the sum of the premiums on the component floorlets.

- An interest rate collar, which consists of a long interest rate cap at one exercise rate and a short interest rate floor at a lower exercise rate, can be used to place an upper limit on the interest paid on a floating-rate loan. The floor, however, places a lower limit on the interest paid on the floating-rate loan. Typically the floor exercise rate is set such that the premium on the floor equals the premium on the cap, so that no cash outlay is required to initiate the transaction. The effective interest is the actual interest paid minus any payoff from the long caplet plus any payoff from the short floorlet.

- Dealers offer to take positions in options and typically hedge their positions by establishing delta-neutral combinations of options and the underlying or other options. These positions require that the sensitivity of the option position with respect to the underlying be offset by a quantity of the underlying or another option. The delta will change, moving toward 1.0 for in-the-money calls (−1.0 for puts) and 0.0 for out-of-the-money options as expiration approaches. Any change in the underlying price will also change the delta. These changes in the delta necessitate buying and selling options or the underlying to maintain the delta-hedged position. Any additional funds required to buy the underlying or other options are obtained by issuing risk-free bonds. Any additional funds released from selling the underlying or other options are invested in risk-free bonds.

- The delta of an option changes as the underlying changes and as time elapses. The delta will change more rapidly with large movements in the underlying and when the option is approximately at-the-money and near expiration. These large changes in the delta will prevent a delta-hedged position from being truly risk free. Dealers usually monitor their gammas and in some cases hedge their gammas by adding other options to their positions such that the gammas offset.

- The sensitivity of an option to volatility is called the vega. An option's volatility can change, resulting in a potentially large change in the value of the option. Dealers monitor and sometimes hedge their vegas so that this risk does not impact a delta-hedged portfolio.

# PRACTICE PROBLEMS FOR READING 37

1. You are bullish about an underlying that is currently trading at a price of $80. You choose to go long one call option on the underlying with an exercise price of $75 and selling at $10, and go short one call option on the underlying with an exercise price of $85 and selling at $2. Both the calls expire in three months.

   A. What is the term commonly used for the position that you have taken?

   B. Determine the value at expiration and the profit for your strategy under the following outcomes:

      i. The price of the underlying at expiration is $89.

      ii. The price of the underlying at expiration is $78.

      iii. The price of the underlying at expiration is $70.

   C. Determine the following:

      i. the maximum profit.

      ii. the maximum loss.

   D. Determine the breakeven underlying price at expiration of the call options.

   E. Verify that your answer to Part D above is correct.

2. You expect a currency to depreciate with respect to the U.S. dollar. The currency is currently trading at a price of $0.75. You decide to go long one put option on the currency with an exercise price of $0.85 and selling at $0.15, and go short one put option on the currency with an exercise price of $0.70 and selling at $0.03. Both the puts expire in three months.

   A. What is the term commonly used for the position that you have taken?

   B. Determine the value at expiration and the profit for your strategy under the following outcomes:

      i. The price of the currency at expiration is $0.87.

      ii. The price of the currency at expiration is $0.78.

      iii. The price of the currency at expiration is $0.68.

   C. Determine the following:

      i. the maximum profit.

      ii. the maximum loss.

   D. Determine the breakeven underlying price at the expiration of the put options.

   E. Verify that your answer to Part D above is correct.

3. A stock is currently trading at a price of $114. You construct a butterfly spread using calls of three different strike prices on this stock, with the calls expiring at the same time. You go long one call with an exercise price of $110 and selling at $8, go short two calls with an exercise price of $115 and selling at $5, and go long one call with an exercise price of $120 and selling at $3.

   A. Determine the value at expiration and the profit for your strategy under the following outcomes:

      i. The price of the stock at the expiration of the calls is $106.

      ii. The price of the stock at the expiration of the calls is $110.

      iii. The price of the stock at the expiration of the calls is $115.

Practice Problems and Solutions: *Analysis of Derivatives for the Chartered Financial Analyst® Program*, by Don M. Chance, CFA. Copyright © 2003 by AIMR.

iv. The price of the stock at the expiration of the calls is $120.

v. The price of the stock at the expiration of the calls is $123.

B. Determine the following:

i. the maximum profit.

ii. the maximum loss.

iii. the stock price at which you would realize the maximum profit.

iv. the stock price at which you would incur the maximum loss.

C. Determine the breakeven underlying price at expiration of the call options.

4. A stock is currently trading at a price of $114. You construct a butterfly spread using puts of three different strike prices on this stock, with the puts expiring at the same time. You go long one put with an exercise price of $110 and selling at $3.50, go short two puts with an exercise price of $115 and selling at $6, and go long one put with an exercise price of $120 and selling at $9.

A. Determine the value at expiration and the profit for your strategy under the following outcomes:

i. The price of the stock at the expiration of the puts is $106.

ii. The price of the stock at the expiration of the puts is $110.

iii. The price of the stock at the expiration of the puts is $115.

iv. The price of the stock at the expiration of the puts is $120.

v. The price of the stock at the expiration of the puts is $123.

B. Determine the following:

i. the maximum profit.

ii. the maximum loss.

iii. the stock price at which you would realize the maximum profit.

iv. the stock price at which you would incur the maximum loss.

C. Determine the breakeven underlying price at expiration of the put options.

D. Verify that your answer to Part C above is correct.

5. A stock is currently trading at a price of $80. You decide to place a collar on this stock. You purchase a put option on the stock, with an exercise price of $75 and a premium of $3.50. You simultaneously sell a call option on the stock with the same maturity and the same premium as the put option. This call option has an exercise price of $90.

A. Determine the value at expiration and the profit for your strategy under the following outcomes:

i. The price of the stock at expiration of the options is $92.

ii. The price of the stock at expiration of the options is $90.

iii. The price of the stock at expiration of the options is $82.

iv. The price of the stock at expiration of the options is $75.

v. The price of the stock at expiration of the options is $70.

B. Determine the following:

i. the maximum profit.

ii. the maximum loss.

iii. the stock price at which you would realize the maximum profit.

iv. the stock price at which you would incur the maximum loss.

C. Determine the breakeven underlying price at expiration of the put options.

6.  You believe that the market will be volatile in the near future, but you do not feel particularly strongly about the direction of the movement. With this expectation, you decide to buy both a call and a put with the same exercise price and the same expiration on the same underlying stock trading at $28. You buy one call option and one put option on this stock, both with an exercise price of $25. The premium on the call is $4 and the premium on the put is $1.

    A.  What is the term commonly used for the position that you have taken?

    B.  Determine the value at expiration and the profit for your strategy under the following outcomes:

        i.   The price of the stock at expiration is $35.

        ii.  The price of the stock at expiration is $29.

        iii. The price of the stock at expiration is $25.

        iv.  The price of the stock at expiration is $20.

        v.   The price of the stock at expiration is $15.

    C.  Determine the following:

        i.   the maximum profit.

        ii.  the maximum loss.

    D.  Determine the breakeven stock price at expiration of the options.

# The following information relates to Questions 7 - 12[1]

Stanley Singh, CFA is the risk manager at SS Asset Management. Singh works with individual clients to manage their investment portfolios. One client, Sherman Hopewell, is worried about how short-term market fluctuations over the next three months might impact his equity position in Walnut Corporation. While Hopewell is concerned about short-term downside price movements, he wants to remain invested in Walnut shares as he remains positive about its long-term performance. Hopewell has asked Singh to recommend an option strategy that will keep him invested in Walnut shares while protecting against a short-term price decline. Singh gathers the information in Exhibit 1 to explore various strategies to address Hopewell's concerns.

Another client, Nigel French, is a trader who does not currently own shares of Walnut Corporation. French has told Singh that he believes that Walnut shares will experience a modest move in price after the upcoming quarterly earnings release in two weeks. However, French tells Singh he is unsure which direction the stock will move. French asks Singh to recommend an option strategy that would allow him to profit should the share price move in either direction.

A third client, Wanda Tills, does not currently owns Walnut shares and has asked Singh to explain the profit potential of three strategies using options in Walnut: a bull call spread, a straddle and a butterfly spread. In addition, Tills asks Singh to explain the gamma of a call option. In response, Singh prepares a memo to be shared with Tills that provides a discussion of gamma and presents his analysis on three option strategies:

**Strategy 1:**  A straddle position at the $67.50 strike option

**Strategy 2:**  A bull call spread using the $65 and $70 strike options

**Strategy 3:**  A butterfly spread using the $65, $67.50, and $70 strike call options

---

1  This item set was developed by Don Taylor, CFA (West Chester, PA, USA)

| Exhibit 1 | Walnut Corporation Current Stock Price: $67.79 Walnut Corporation European Options | | | |
|---|---|---|---|---|
| **Exercise Price** | **Market Call Price** | **Call Delta** | **Market Put Price** | **Put Delta** |
| $ 55.00 | $ 12.83 | 4.7 | $ 0.24 | −16.7 |
| $ 65.00 | $ 3.65 | 12.0 | $ 1.34 | −16.9 |
| $ 67.50 | $ 1.99 | 16.5 | $ 2.26 | −15.3 |
| $ 70.00 | $ 0.91 | 22.2 | $ 3.70 | −12.9 |
| $ 80.00 | $ 0.03 | 35.8 | $ 12.95 | −5.0 |

*Note*: Each option has 106 days remaining until expiration.

7. The option strategy Singh is *most likely* to recommend to Hopewell is a:
   A. collar.
   B. covered call.
   C. protective put.

8. The option strategy that Singh is *most likely* to recommend to French is a:
   A. straddle.
   B. butterfly.
   C. box spread.

9. Based upon Exhibit 1, Strategy 1 is profitable when the share price at expiration is *closest* to:
   A. $63.24.
   B. $65.24.
   C. $69.49.

10. Based upon Exhibit 1, the maximum profit, on a per share basis, from investing in Strategy 2, is *closest* to:
    A. $2.26.
    B. $2.74.
    C. $5.00.

11. Based upon Exhibit 1, and assuming the market price of Walnut's shares at expiration is $66, the profit or loss, on a per share basis, from investing in Strategy 3, is *closest* to:
    A. −$1.57.
    B. $0.42.
    C. $1.00.

12. Based on the data in Exhibit 1, Singh would advise Tills that the call option with the *largest* gamma would have a strike price *closest* to:
    A. $55.
    B. $67.50.
    C. $80.

## SOLUTIONS FOR READING 37

1. **A.** This position is commonly called a bull spread.

   **B.** Let $X_1$ be the lower of the two strike prices and $X_2$ be the higher of the two strike prices.

   **i.** $V_T = \max(0, S_T - X_1) - \max(0, S_T - X_2)$
   $$= \max(0, 89 - 75) - \max(0, 89 - 85) = 14 - 4 = 10$$
   $$\Pi = V_T - V_0 = V_T - (c_1 - c_2) = 10 - (10 - 2) = 2$$

   **ii.** $V_T = \max(0, S_T - X_1) - \max(0, S_T - X_2)$
   $$= \max(0, 78 - 75) - \max(0, 70 - 85) = 3 - 0 = 3$$
   $$\Pi = V_T - V_0 = V_T - (c_1 - c_2) = 3 - (10 - 2) = -5$$

   **iii.** $V_T = \max(0, S_T - X_1) - \max(0, S_T - X_2)$
   $$= \max(0, 70 - 75) - \max(0, 70 - 85) = 0 - 0 = 0$$
   $$\Pi = V_T - V_0 = V_T - (c_1 - c_2) = 0 - (10 - 2) = -8$$

   **C.** **i.** Maximum profit $= X_2 - X_1 - (c_1 - c_2) = 85 - 75 - (10 - 2) = 2$

   **ii.** Maximum loss $= c_1 - c_2 = 10 - 2 = 8$

   **D.** $S_T^* = X_1 + (c_1 - c_2) = 75 + (10 - 2) = 83$

   **E.** $V_T = \max(0, S_T - X_1) - \max(0, S_T - X_2)$
   $$= \max(0, 83 - 75) - \max(0, 83 - 85) = 8 - 0 = 8$$
   $$\Pi = V_T - V_0 = V_T - (c_1 - c_2) = 8 - (10 - 2) = 0$$

   Therefore, the profit or loss if the price of the underlying increases to 83 at expiration is indeed zero.

2. **A.** This position is commonly called a bear spread.

   **B.** Let $X_1$ be the lower of the two strike prices and $X_2$ be the higher of the two strike prices.

   **i.** $V_T = \max(0, X_2 - S_T) - \max(0, X_1 - S_T)$
   $$= \max(0, 0.85 - 0.87) - \max(0, 0.70 - 0.87) = 0 - 0 = 0$$
   $$\Pi = V_T - V_0 = V_T - (p_2 - p_1) = 0 - (0.15 - 0.03) = -0.12$$

   **ii.** $V_T = \max(0, X_2 - S_T) - \max(0, X_1 - S_T)$
   $$= \max(0, 0.85 - 0.78) - \max(0, 0.70 - 0.78) = 0.07 - 0 = 0.07$$
   $$\Pi = V_T - V_0 = V_T - (p_2 - p_1) = 0.07 - (0.15 - 0.03) = -0.05$$

   **iii.** $V_T = \max(0, X_2 - S_T) - \max(0, X_1 - S_T)$
   $$= \max(0, 0.85 - 0.68) - \max(0, 0.70 - 0.68) = 0.17 - 0.02 = 0.15$$
   $$\Pi = V_T - V_0 = V_T - (p_2 - p_1) = 0.15 - (0.15 - 0.03) = 0.03$$

   **C.** **i.** Maximum profit $= X_2 - X_1 - (p_2 - p_1) = 0.85 - 0.70 - (0.15 - 0.03) = 0.03$

   **ii.** Maximum loss $= p_2 - p_1 = 0.15 - 0.03 = 0.12$

**D.**  Breakeven point $= X_2 - (p_2 - p_1) = 0.85 - (0.15 - 0.03) = 0.73$

**E.**  $V_T = \max(0, X_2 - S_T) - \max(0, X_1 - S_T)$

$\qquad = \max(0, 0.85 - 0.73) - \max(0, 0.70 - 0.73) = 0.12 - 0 = 0.12$

$\qquad \Pi = V_T - V_0 = V_T - (p_2 - p_1) = 0.12 - (0.15 - 0.03) = 0$

Therefore, the profit or loss if the price of the currency decreases to $0.73 at expiration of the puts is indeed zero.

**3. A.**  Let $X_1$ be 110, $X_2$ be 115, and $X_3$ be 120.

$V_0 = c_1 - 2c_2 + c_3 = 8 - 2(5) + 3 = 1$

**i.**  $V_T = \max(0, S_T - X_1) - 2\max(0, S_T - X_2) + \max(0, S_T - X_3)$

$\quad V_T = \max(0, 106 - 110) - 2\max(0, 106 - 115)$

$\qquad + \max(0, 106 - 120) = 0$

$\quad \Pi = V_T - V_0 = 0 - 1 = -1$

**ii.**  $V_T = \max(0, S_T - X_1) - 2\max(0, S_T - X_2) + \max(0, S_T - X_3)$

$\quad V_T = \max(0, 110 - 110) - 2\max(0, 110 - 115)$

$\qquad + \max(0, 110 - 120) = 0$

$\quad \Pi = V_T - V_0 = 0 - 1 = -1$

**iii.**  $V_T = \max(0, S_T - X_1) - 2\max(0, S_T - X_2) + \max(0, S_T - X_3)$

$\quad V_T = \max(0, 115 - 110) - 2\max(0, 115 - 115)$

$\qquad + \max(0, 115 - 120) = 5$

$\quad \Pi = V_T - V_0 = 5 - 1 = 4$

**iv.**  $V_T = \max(0, S_T - X_1) - 2\max(0, S_T - X_2) + \max(0, S_T - X_3)$

$\quad V_T = \max(0, 120 - 110) - 2\max(0, 120 - 115)$

$\qquad + \max(0, 120 - 120) = 10 - 10 + 0 = 0$

$\quad \Pi = V_T - V_0 = 0 - 1 = -1$

**v.**  $V_T = \max(0, S_T - X_1) - 2\max(0, S_T - X_2) + \max(0, S_T - X_3)$

$\quad V_T = \max(0, 123 - 110) - 2\max(0, 123 - 115)$

$\qquad + \max(0, 123 - 120) = 13 - 16 + 3 = 0$

$\quad \Pi = V_T - V_0 = 0 - 1 = -1$

**B.**  **i.**  Maximum profit $= X_2 - X_1 - (c_1 - 2c_2 + c_3) = 115 - 110 - 1 = 4$

**ii.**  Maximum loss $= c_1 - 2c_2 + c_3 = 1$

**iii.**  The maximum profit would be realized if the price of the stock at expiration of the options is at the exercise price of $115.

**iv.**  The maximum loss would be incurred if the price of the stock is at or below the exercise price of $110, or if the price of the stock is at or above the exercise price of $120.

**C.**  Breakeven: $S_T^* = X_1 + (c_1 - 2c_2 + c_3)$ and $S_T^* = 2X_2 - X_1 - (c_1 - 2c_2 + c_3)$. So, $S_T^* = 110 + 1 = 111$ and $S_T^* = 2(115) - 110 - 1 = 119$

**4. A.** Let $X_1$ be 110, $X_2$ be 115, and $X_3$ be 120.

$$V_0 = p_1 - 2p_2 + p_3 = 3.50 - 2(6) + 9 = 0.50$$

**i.** $V_T = \max(0, X_1 - S_T) - 2\max(0, X_2 - S_T) + \max(0, X_3 - S_T)$

$V_T = \max(0, 110 - 106) - 2\max(0, 115 - 106)$
$\qquad + \max(0, 120 - 106) = 4 - 2(9) + 14 = 0$

$\Pi = V_T - V_0 = 0 - 0.50 = -0.50$

**ii.** $V_T = \max(0, X_1 - S_T) - 2\max(0, X_2 - S_T) + \max(0, X_3 - S_T)$

$V_T = \max(0, 110 - 110) - 2\max(0, 115 - 110)$
$\qquad + \max(0, 120 - 110) = 0 - 2(5) + 10 = 0$

$\Pi = V_T - V_0 = 0 - 0.50 = -0.50$

**iii.** $V_T = \max(0, X_1 - S_T) - 2\max(0, X_2 - S_T) + \max(0, X_3 - S_T)$

$V_T = \max(0, 110 - 115) - 2\max(0, 115 - 115)$
$\qquad + \max(0, 120 - 115) = 0 - 2(0) + 5 = 5$

$\Pi = V_T - V_0 = 5 - 0.50 = 4.50$

**iv.** $V_T = \max(0, X_1 - S_T) - 2\max(0, X_2 - S_T) + \max(0, X_3 - S_T)$

$V_T = \max(0, 110 - 120) - 2\max(0, 115 - 120)$
$\qquad + \max(0, 120 - 120) = 0$

$\Pi = V_T - V_0 = 0 - 0.50 = -0.50$

**v.** $V_T = \max(0, X_1 - S_T) - 2\max(0, X_2 - S_T) + \max(0, X_3 - S_T)$

$V_T = \max(0, 110 - 123) - 2\max(0, 115 - 123)$
$\qquad + \max(0, 120 - 123) = 0$

$\Pi = V_T - V_0 = 0 - 0.50 = -0.50$

**B. i.** Maximum profit $= X_2 - X_1 - (p_1 - 2p_2 + p_3) = 115 - 110 - 0.50 = 4.50$

**ii.** Maximum loss $= p_1 - 2p_2 + p_3 = 0.50$

**iii.** The maximum profit would be realized if the expiration price of the stock is at the exercise price of \$115.

**iv.** The maximum loss would be incurred if the expiration price of the stock is at or below the exercise price of \$110, or if the expiration price of the stock is at or above the exercise price of \$120.

**C.** Breakeven: $S_T{}^* = X_1 + (p_1 - 2p_2 + p_3)$ and $S_T{}^* = 2X_2 - X_1 - (p_1 - 2p_2 + p_3)$. So, $S_T{}^* = 110 + 0.50 = 110.50$ and $S_T{}^* = 2(115) - 110 - 0.50 = 119.50$

**D.** For $S_T = 110.50$:

$V_T = \max(0, X_1 - S_T) - 2\max(0, X_2 - S_T) + \max(0, X_3 - S_T)$

$V_T = \max(0, 110 - 110.50) - 2\max(0, 115 - 110.50) + \max(0, 120 - 110.50)$

$\qquad = -2(4.50) + 9.50 = 0.50$

$\Pi = V_T - V_0 = 0.50 - 0.50 = 0$

For $S_T = 119.50$:

$V_T = \max(0, X_1 - S_T) - 2\max(0, X_2 - S_T) + \max(0, X_3 - S_T)$

$V_T = \max(0, 110 - 119.50) - 2\max(0, 115 - 119.50) + \max(0, 120 - 119.50) = 0.50$

$\Pi = V_T - V_0 = 0.50 - 0.50 = 0$

Therefore, we see that the profit or loss at the breakeven points computed in Part D above is indeed zero.

5. **A.** **i.** $V_T = S_T + \max(0, X_1 - S_T) - \max(0, S_T - X_2)$

$= 92 + \max(0, 75 - 92) - \max(0, 92 - 90) = 92 + 0 - 2 = 90$

$\Pi = V_T - S_0 = 90 - 80 = 10$

**ii.** $V_T = S_T + \max(0, X_1 - S_T) - \max(0, S_T - X_2)$

$= 90 + \max(0, 75 - 90) - \max(0, 90 - 90) = 90 + 0 - 0 = 90$

$\Pi = V_T - S_0 = 90 - 80 = 10$

**iii.** $V_T = S_T + \max(0, X_1 - S_T) - \max(0, S_T - X_2)$

$= 82 + \max(0, 75 - 82) - \max(0, 82 - 90) = 82 + 0 - 0 = 82$

$\Pi = V_T - S_0 = 82 - 80 = 2$

**iv.** $V_T = S_T + \max(0, X_1 - S_T) - \max(0, S_T - X_2)$

$= 75 + \max(0, 75 - 75) - \max(0, 75 - 90) = 75 + 0 - 0 = 75$

$\Pi = V_T - S_0 = 75 - 80 = -5$

**v.** $V_T = S_T + \max(0, X_1 - S_T) - \max(0, S_T - X_2)$

$= 70 + \max(0, 75 - 70) - \max(0, 70 - 90) = 70 + 5 - 0 = 75$

$\Pi = V_T - S_0 = 75 - 80 = -5$

**B.** **i.** Maximum profit $= X_2 - S_0 = 90 - 80 = 10$

**ii.** Maximum loss $= -(X_1 - S_0) = -(75 - 80) = 5$

**iii.** The maximum profit would be realized if the price of the stock at the expiration of options is at or above the exercise price of \$90.

**iv.** The maximum loss would be incurred if the price of the stock at the expiration of options were at or below the exercise price of \$75.

**C.** Breakeven: $S_T^* = S_0 = 80$

6. **A.** This position is commonly called a straddle.

**B.** **i.** $V_T = \max(0, S_T - X) + \max(0, X - S_T)$

$= \max(0, 35 - 25) + \max(0, 25 - 35) = 10 + 0 = 10$

$\Pi = V_T - (c_0 + p_0) = 10 - (4 + 1) = 5$

**ii.** $V_T = \max(0, S_T - X) + \max(0, X - S_T)$

$= \max(0, 29 - 25) + \max(0, 25 - 29) = 4 + 0 = 4$

$\Pi = V_T - (c_0 + p_0) = 4 - (4 + 1) = -1$

**iii.** $V_T = \max(0, S_T - X) + \max(0, X - S_T)$

$= \max(0, 25 - 25) + \max(0, 25 - 25) = 0 + 0 = 0$

$\Pi = V_T - (c_0 + p_0) = 0 - (4 + 1) = -5$

**iv.** $V_T = \max(0, S_T - X) + \max(0, X - S_T)$

$= \max(0, 20 - 25) + \max(0, 25 - 20) = 0 + 5 = 5$

$\Pi = V_T - (c_0 + p_0) = 5 - (4 + 1) = 0$

**v.** $V_T = \max(0, S_T - X) + \max(0, X - S_T)$

$= \max(0, 15 - 25) + \max(0, 25 - 15) = 0 + 10 = 10$

$\Pi = V_T - (c_0 + p_0) = 10 - (4 + 1) = 5$

    **C. i.** Maximum profit $= \infty$

      **ii.** Maximum loss $= c_0 + p_0 = 4 + 1 = 5$

    **D.** $S_T^* = X \pm (c_0 + p_0) = 25 \pm (4+1) = 30, 20$

7. C is correct. A protective put accomplishes Hopewell's goal of short-term price protection. A protective put provides downside protection while retaining the upside potential. While Hopewell is concerned about the downside in the short-term, he wants to remain invested in Walnut shares, as he is positive about the stock in the long-term.

8. A is correct. The straddle strategy is a strategy based upon the expectation of high volatility in the underlying stock. The straddle strategy consists of simultaneously buying a call option and a put option at the same strike price. Singh could recommend that French buy a straddle using near at-the-money options ($67.50 strike). This allows French to profit should Walnut stock price experience a modest move in either direction after the earnings release.

9. A is correct. The straddle strategy consists of simultaneously buying a call option and buying a put option at the same strike price. The market price for the $67.50 call option is $1.99, and the market price for the $67.50 put option is $2.26, for an initial net cost of $4.25 per share. Thus, this straddle position requires a move greater than $4.25 in either direction from the strike price of $67.50 to become profitable. So, the straddle becomes profitable at $67.50 − $4.26 = $63.24 or lower, or $67.50 + $4.26 = $71.76 or higher. At $63.24, the profit on the straddle is positive.

10. A is correct. The bull call strategy consists of buying the lower strike option, and selling the higher strike option. The purchase of the $65 strike call option costs $3.65 per share, and selling the $70 strike call option generates an inflow of $0.91 per share, for an initial net cost of $2.74 per share. At expiration, the maximum profit occurs when the stock price is $70 or higher, which yields a $5.00 per share payoff ($70 - 65). After deduction of the $2.74 per share cost required to initiate the bull call spread, the profit is $2.26 ($5.00 − $2.74).

11. B is correct. The butterfly strategy consists of buying a call option with a low strike price ($65), selling 2 call options with a higher strike price ($67.50), and buying another call option with an even higher strike price ($70). The market price for the $65 call option is $3.65 per share, the market price for the $70 call option is $0.91 per share, and selling the two call options generates an inflow of $3.98 per share (market price of $1.99 per share × 2 contracts). Thus, the initial net cost of the butterfly position is $3.65 + $0.91 − $3.98 = $0.58 per share. If Walnut shares are $66 at expiration, the $67.50 strike option and $70 strike option are both out-of-the-money and therefore worthless. The $65 call option is in the money by $1.00 per share, and after deducting the cost of $0.58 per share to initiate the butterfly position, the net profit is $0.42 per share.

12. B is correct. The $67.50 call option is approximately at-the-money, as Walnut share price is currently $67.76. A gamma measures i) the deviation of the exact option price changes from the price change approximated by the delta and ii) the sensitivity of delta to a change in the underlying. The largest moves for gamma occur when options are trading at-the-money or near expiration, when the deltas of at-the-money options move quickly toward 1.0 or 0.0. Under these conditions, the gammas tend to be largest and delta hedges are hardest to maintain.

# 38

# Risk Management Applications of Swap Strategies

*by Don M. Chance, CFA*

## LEARNING OUTCOMES

| Mastery | The candidate should be able to: |
|---|---|
| ☐ | **a** demonstrate how an interest rate swap can be used to convert a floating-rate (fixed-rate) loan to a fixed-rate (floating-rate) loan; |
| ☐ | **b** calculate and interpret the duration of an interest rate swap; |
| ☐ | **c** explain the effect of an interest rate swap on an entity's cash flow risk; |
| ☐ | **d** determine the notional principal value needed on an interest rate swap to achieve a desired level of duration in a fixed-income portfolio; |
| ☐ | **e** explain how a company can generate savings by issuing a loan or bond in its own currency and using a currency swap to convert the obligation into another currency; |
| ☐ | **f** demonstrate how a firm can use a currency swap to convert a series of foreign cash receipts into domestic cash receipts; |
| ☐ | **g** explain how equity swaps can be used to diversify a concentrated equity portfolio, provide international diversification to a domestic portfolio, and alter portfolio allocations to stocks and bonds; |
| ☐ | **h** demonstrate the use of an interest rate swaption 1) to change the payment pattern of an anticipated future loan and 2) to terminate a swap. |

# INTRODUCTION

1

This reading is the final in a series of three in which we examine strategies and applications of various derivative instruments. We now turn to swaps. Recall that a swap is a transaction in which two parties agree to exchange a series of cash flows over a specific period of time. At least one set of cash flows must be variable—that is, not known at the beginning of the transaction and determined over the life of the swap by the course of an underlying source of uncertainty. The other set of cash flows can be fixed or variable. Typically, no net exchange of money occurs between the two parties at the start of the contract.[1]

Because at least one set of swap payments is random, it must be driven by an underlying source of uncertainty. This observation provides a means for classifying swaps. The four types of swaps are interest rate, currency, equity, and commodity swaps. Interest rate swaps typically involve one side paying at a floating interest rate and the other paying at a fixed interest rate. In some cases both sides pay at a floating rate, but the floating rates are different. Currency swaps are essentially interest rate swaps in which one set of payments is in one currency and the other is in another currency. The payments are in the form of interest payments; either set of payments can be fixed or floating, or both can be fixed or floating. With currency swaps, a source of uncertainty is the exchange rate so the payments can be fixed and still have uncertain value. In equity swaps, at least one set of payments is determined by the course of a stock price or stock index. In commodity swaps at least one set of payments is determined by the course of a commodity price, such as the price of oil or gold. In this reading we focus exclusively on financial derivatives and, hence, do not cover commodity swaps.

Swaps can be viewed as combinations of forward contracts. A forward contract is an agreement between two parties in which one party agrees to buy from another an underlying asset at a future date at a price agreed on at the start. This agreed-upon price is a fixed payment, but the value received for the asset at the future date is a variable payment because it is subject to risk. A swap extends this notion of an exchange of variable and fixed payments to more than one payment. Hence, a swap is like a series of forward contracts.[2] We also saw that a swap is like a combination of options. We showed that pricing a swap involves determining the terms that the two parties agree to at the start, which usually involves the amount of any fixed payment. Because no net flow of money changes hands at the start, a swap is a transaction that starts off with zero market value. Pricing the swap is done by finding the terms that result in equivalence of the present values of the two streams of payments.

After a swap begins, market conditions change and the present values of the two streams of payments are no longer equivalent. The swap then has a nonzero market value. To one party, the swap has a positive market value; to the other, its market value is negative. The process of valuation involves determining this market value. For the most part, valuation and pricing is a process that requires only the determination of present values using current interest rates and, as necessary, stock prices or exchange rates.

We also examined the swaption, an instrument that combines swaps and options. Specifically, a swaption is an option to enter into a swap. There are two kinds of swaptions: those to make a fixed payment, called payer swaptions, and those to receive a fixed payment, called receiver swaptions. Like options, swaptions require the payment of a premium at the start and grant the right, but not the obligation, to enter into a swap.[3]

In this reading, we shall examine ways in which swaps can be used to achieve risk management objectives. We already examined certain risk management strategies when we discussed swaps in the reading on risk management applications of option

---

**1** Currency swaps can be structured to have an exchange of the notional principals in the two currencies at the start, but because these amounts are equivalent after adjusting for the exchange rate, no *net* exchange of money takes place. At expiration of the swap, the two parties reverse the original exchange, which does result in a net flow of money if the exchange rate has changed, as will probably be the case. A few swaps, called *off-market swaps*, involve an exchange of money at the start, but they are the exception, not the rule.
**2** There are some technical distinctions between a series of forward contracts and a swap, but the essential elements of equivalence are there.
**3** Forward swaps, on the other hand, are obligations to enter into a swap.

strategies. Here, we go into more detail on these strategies and, of course, introduce quite a few more. We shall also discuss how swaptions are used to achieve risk management objectives.

## STRATEGIES AND APPLICATIONS FOR MANAGING INTEREST RATE RISK

**2**

In previous readings, we examined the use of forwards, futures, and options to manage interest rate risk. The interest rate swap, however, is unquestionably the most widely used instrument to manage interest rate risk.[4] In the readings on risk management applications of forward, futures, and options strategies, we examined two primary forms of interest rate risk. One is the risk associated with borrowing and lending in short-term markets. This risk itself has two dimensions: the risk of rates changing from the time a loan is anticipated until it is actually taken out, and the risk associated with changes in interest rates once the loan is taken out. Swaps are not normally used to manage the risk of an anticipated loan; rather, they are designed to manage the risk on a series of cash flows on loans already taken out or in the process of being taken out.[5]

The other form of interest rate risk that concerns us is the risk associated with managing a portfolio of bonds. As we saw in the reading on risk management applications of forward and futures strategies, managing this risk generally involves controlling the portfolio duration. Although futures are commonly used to make duration changes, swaps can also be used, and we shall see how in this reading.

In this section, we look at one more situation in which swaps can be used to manage interest rate risk. This situation involves the use of a relatively new financial instrument called a **structured note**, which is a variation of a floating-rate note that has some type of unusual characteristic. We cover structured notes in Section 2.3.

### 2.1 Using Interest Rate Swaps to Convert a Floating-Rate Loan to a Fixed-Rate Loan (and Vice Versa)

Because much of the funding banks receive is at a floating rate, most banks prefer to make floating-rate loans. By lending at a floating rate, banks pass on the interest rate risk to borrowers. Borrowers can use forwards, futures, and options to manage their exposure to rising interest rates, but swaps are the preferred instrument for managing this risk.[6] A typical situation involves a corporation agreeing to borrow at a floating rate even though it would prefer to borrow at a fixed rate. The corporation will use a swap to convert its floating-rate loan to a fixed-rate loan.

---

**4** The Bank for International Settlements, in its June 2002 survey of derivative positions of global banks published on 8 November 2002, indicates that swaps make up more than 75 percent of the total notional principal of all interest rate derivative contracts (see www.bis.org).

**5** It is technically possible to use a swap to manage the risk faced in anticipation of taking out a loan, but it would not be easy and would require a great deal of analytical skill to match the volatility of the swap to the volatility of the gain or loss in value associated with changes in interest rates prior to the date on which a loan is taken out. Other instruments are better suited for managing this type of risk.

**6** It is not clear why swaps are preferred over other instruments to manage the exposure to rising interest rates, but one possible reason is that when swaps were first invented, they were marketed as equivalent to a pair of loans. By being long one loan and short another, a corporation could alter its exposure without having to respond to claims that it was using such instruments as futures or options, which might be against corporate policy. In other words, while swaps are derivatives, their equivalence to a pair of loans meant that no policy existed to prevent their use. Moreover, because of the netting of payments and no exchange of notional principal, interest rate swaps were loans with considerably less credit risk than ordinary loans. Hence, the corporate world easily and widely embraced them.

Internet Book Publishers (IBP) is a corporation that typically borrows at a floating rate from a lender called Prime Lending Bank (PLB). In this case, it takes out a one-year $25 million loan at 90-day LIBOR plus 300 basis points. The payments will be made at specific dates about 91 days apart. The rate is initially set today, the day the loan is taken out, and is reset on each payment date: On the first payment date, the rate is reset for the second interest period. With four loan payments, the first rate is already set, but IBP is exposed to risk on the other three reset dates. Interest is calculated based on the actual day count since the last payment date, divided by 360. The loan begins on 2 March and the interest payment dates are 2 June, 2 September, 1 December, and the following 1 March.

IBP manages this interest rate risk by using a swap. It contacts a swap dealer, Swaps Provider Inc. (SPI), which is the derivatives subsidiary of a major investment banking firm. Under the terms of the swap, SPI will make payment to IBP at a rate of LIBOR, and IBP will pay SPI a fixed rate of 6.27 percent, with payments to be made on the dates on which the loan interest payments are made.

The dealer prices the fixed rate on a swap into the swap such that the present values of the two payment streams are equal. The floating rates on the swap will be set today and on the first, second, and third loan interest payment dates, thereby corresponding to the dates on which the loan interest rate is reset. The notional principal on the swap is $25 million, the face value of the loan. The swap interest payments are structured so that the actual day count is used, as is done on the loan.

So, IBP borrows $25 million at a floating rate and arranges for the swap, which involves no cash flows at the origination date. The flow of money on each loan/swap payment date is illustrated in Exhibit 1. We see that IBP makes its loan payments at LIBOR plus 0.03.[7] The actual calculation of the loan interest is as follows:

$$(\$25 \text{ million})(\text{LIBOR} + 0.03)(\text{Days}/360)$$

---

**Exhibit 1**     **Converting a Floating-Rate Loan to a Fixed-Rate Loan Using an Interest Rate Swap**

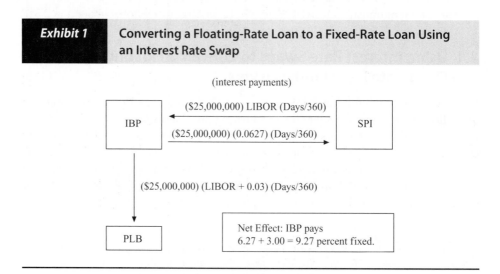

---

The swap payments are calculated in the same way but are based on either LIBOR or the fixed rate of 6.27 percent. The interest owed on the loan based on LIBOR is thus offset by the interest received on the swap payment based on LIBOR.[8] Consequently,

---

[7] Remember that when we refer to the payment at a rate of LIBOR, that rate was established at the previous settlement date or at the beginning of the swap if this is the first settlement period.

[8] Of course in practice, the swap payments are netted and only a single payment flows from one party to the other. Netting reduces the credit risk but does not prevent the LIBOR component of the net swap payment from offsetting the floating loan interest payment, which is the objective of the swap.

IBP does not *appear to be exposed* to the uncertainty of changing LIBOR, but we shall see that it is indeed exposed. The net effect is that IBP pays interest at the swap fixed rate of 6.27 percent plus the 3 percent spread on the loan for a total of 9.27 percent.

IBP's swap transaction appears to remove its exposure to LIBOR. Indeed, having done this transaction, most corporations would consider themselves hedged against rising interest rates, which is usually the justification corporations give for doing swap transactions. It is important to note, however, that IBP is also speculating on rising interest rates. If rates fall, IBP will not be able to take advantage, as it is locked in to a synthetic fixed-rate loan at 9.27 percent. There can be a substantial opportunity cost to taking this position and being wrong. To understand this point, let us reintroduce the concept of duration.

We need to measure the sensitivity of the market value of the overall position compared to what it would have been had the loan been left in place as a floating-rate loan. For that we turn to duration, a measure of sensitivity to interest rates. If a default-free bond is a floating-rate bond, its duration is nearly zero because interest sensitivity reflects how much the market value of an asset changes for a given change in interest rates. A floating-rate bond is designed with the idea that its market value will not drift far from par. Because the coupon will catch up with the market rate periodically, only during the period between interest payment dates can the market value stray from par value. Moreover, during this period, it would take a substantial interest rate change to have much effect on the market value of the floating-rate bond. Without showing the details, we shall simply state the result that a floating-rate bond's duration is approximately the amount of time remaining until the next coupon payment. For a bond with quarterly payments, the maximum duration is 0.25 years and the minimum duration is zero. Consequently, the average duration is about 0.125 years. From the perspective of the *issuer* rather than the holder, the duration of the position is −0.125.

The duration of IBP's floating-rate loan position in this example is an average of −0.125, which is fairly low compared with most financial instruments. Therefore, the market value of the loan is not very interest-rate sensitive. If interest rates fall, the loan rate will fall in three months, and IBP will not have much of a loss from the market value of the loan. If interest rates rise, IBP will not have much of a gain from the market value of the loan.

Now let us discuss the duration of a swap. Remember that entering a pay-fixed, receive-floating swap is similar to issuing a fixed-rate bond and using the proceeds to buy a floating-rate bond. The duration of a swap is thus equivalent to the duration of a long position in a floating-rate bond and a short position in a fixed-rate bond. The duration of the long position in the floating-rate bond would, again, be about 0.125. What would be the duration of the short position in the fixed-rate bond? A one-year fixed-rate bond with quarterly payments would probably have a duration of between 0.6 and 1.0. Let us assume this duration is about 0.75 (nine months) or 75 percent of the maturity, an assumption we shall make from here out. So the duration of the swap would be roughly 0.125 − 0.75 = −0.625.

Combining the swap with the loan means that the duration of IBP's overall position will be −0.125 − 0.625 = −0.75. The swap was designed to convert the floating-rate loan to a fixed-rate loan. Hence, the position should be equivalent to that of taking out a fixed-rate loan. As we assumed for a one-year fixed-rate bond with quarterly payments, the duration would be 0.75. The duration of a borrower's position in a fixed-rate loan would be −0.75, the same as the duration of borrowing with the floating-rate loan and engaging in the swap. The negative duration means that a fixed-rate borrower will be helped by rising rates and a falling market value.[9]

---

**9** Remember from the reading on risk management applications of forward and futures strategies that the percentage change in the market value of an asset or portfolio is −1 times the duration times the change in yield over 1 plus the yield. So, if the duration is negative, the double minus results in the position benefiting from rising interest rates.

Although the duration of the one-year fixed-rate loan is not large, at least relative to that of bonds and longer-term loans, it is nonetheless six times that of the floating-rate loan. Consequently, the sensitivity of the market value of the overall position is six times what it would have been had the loan been left in place as a floating-rate loan. From this angle, it is hard to see how such a transaction could be called a hedge because declining rates and increasing market values will hurt the fixed-rate borrower. The actual risk increases sixfold with this transaction![10]

So, can this transaction be viewed as a hedge? If not, why is it so widely used? From a cash flow perspective, the transaction does indeed function as a hedge. IBP knows that its interest payments will all be $25,000,000(0.0927)(Days/360). Except for the slight variation in days per quarter, this amount is fixed and can be easily built into plans and budgets. So from a planning and accounting perspective, the transaction serves well as a hedge. From a market value perspective, however, it is tremendously speculative. But does market value matter? Indeed it does. From the perspective of finance theory, maximizing the market value of shareholders' equity is the objective of a corporation. Moreover, under recently enacted accounting rules, companies must mark derivative and asset positions to market values, which has improved transparency.

So, in summary, using a swap to convert a floating-rate loan to a fixed-rate loan is a common transaction, one ostensibly structured as a hedge. Such a transaction, despite stabilizing a company's cash outflows, however, increases the risk of the company's market value. Whether this issue is of concern to most companies is not clear. This situation remains one of the most widely encountered scenarios and the one for which interest rate swaps are most commonly employed.

### Example 1

Consider a bank that holds a $5 million loan at a fixed rate of 6 percent for three years, with quarterly payments. The bank had originally funded this loan at a fixed rate, but because of changing interest rate expectations, it has now decided to fund it at a floating rate. Although it cannot change the terms of the loan to the borrower, it can effectively convert the loan to a floating-rate loan by using a swap. The fixed rate on three-year swaps with quarterly payments at LIBOR is 7 percent. We assume the number of days in each quarter to be 90 and the number of days in a year to be 360.

**A.** Explain how the bank could convert the fixed-rate loan to a floating-rate loan using a swap.

**B.** Explain why the effective floating rate on the loan will be less than LIBOR.

### Solution to A:

The interest payments it will receive on the loan are $5,000,000(0.06)(90/360) = $75,000. The bank could do a swap to pay a fixed rate of 7 percent and receive a floating rate of LIBOR. Its fixed payment would be $5,000,000(0.07)(90/360) = $87,500. The floating payment it would receive is $5,000,000L(90/360), where L is LIBOR established at the previous reset date. The overall cash flow is thus $5,000,000(L − 0.01)(90/360), LIBOR minus 100 basis points.

### Solution to B:

The bank will effectively receive less than LIBOR because when the loan was initiated, the rate was 6 percent. Then when the swap was executed, the rate was 7 percent. This increase in interest rates hurts the fixed-rate lender. The

---

**10** In the example here, the company is a corporation. A bank might have assets that would be interest sensitive and could be used to balance the duration. A corporation's primary assets have varying, inconsistent, and difficult-to-measure degrees of interest sensitivity.

bank cannot implicitly change the loan from fixed rate to floating rate without paying the price of this increase in interest rates. It pays this price by accepting a lower rate than LIBOR when the loan is effectively converted to floating. Another factor that could contribute to this rate being lower than LIBOR is that the borrower's credit risk at the time the loan was established is different from the bank's credit risk as reflected in the swap fixed rate, established in the LIBOR market when the swap is initiated.

Equipped with our introductory treatment of the duration of a swap, we are now in a position to move on to understanding how to use swaps to manage the risk of a longer-term position that is also exposed to interest rate risk.

## 2.2 Using Swaps to Adjust the Duration of a Fixed-Income Portfolio

We saw in the previous section that the duration of a swap is the net of the durations of the equivalent positions in fixed- and floating-rate bonds. Thus, the position of the pay-fixed party in a pay-fixed, receive-floating swap has the duration of a floating-rate bond minus the duration of a fixed-rate bond, where the floating- and fixed-rate bonds have cash flows equivalent to the corresponding cash flows of the swap.[11] The pay-fixed, receive-floating swap has a negative duration, because the duration of a fixed-rate bond is positive and larger than the duration of a floating-rate bond, which is near zero. Moreover, the negative duration of this position makes sense in that the position would be expected to benefit from rising interest rates.

Consider the following transaction. Quality Asset Management (QAM) controls a $500 million fixed-income portfolio that has a duration of 6.75. It is considering reducing the portfolio duration to 3.50 by using interest rate swaps. QAM has determined that the interest sensitivity of the bond portfolio is adequately captured by its relationship with LIBOR; hence, a swap using LIBOR as the underlying rate would be appropriate. But first there are several questions to ask:

- Should the swap involve paying fixed, receiving floating or paying floating, receiving fixed?
- What should be the terms of the swap (maturity, payment frequency)?
- What should be the notional principal?

As for whether the swap should involve paying fixed or receiving fixed, the value of the bond portfolio is inversely related to interest rates. To reduce the duration, it would be necessary to hold a position that moves directly with interest rates. To do this we must add a negative-duration position. Hence, the swap should be a pay-fixed swap to receive floating.

The terms of the swap will affect the need to renew it as well as its duration and the notional principal required. It would probably be best for the swap to have a maturity at least as long as the period during which the duration adjustment applies. Otherwise, the swap would expire before the bond matures, and QAM would have to initiate another swap. The maturity and payment frequency of the swap affect the duration. Continuing with the assumption (for convenience) that the duration of the fixed-rate bond is approximated as 75 percent of its maturity, we find, for example,

---

11 Recall, however, that an interest rate swap does not involve a notional principal payment up front or at expiration. But because a swap is equivalent to being long a fixed- (or floating-) rate bond and short a floating- (or fixed-) rate bond, the principals on the bonds offset, leaving their cash flows identical to that of a swap.

that a one-year swap with semi-annual payments would have a duration of $0.25 - 0.75 = -0.50$. A one-year swap with quarterly payments would have a duration of $0.125 - 0.75 = -0.625$. A two-year swap with semiannual payments would have a duration of $0.25 - 1.50 = -1.25$. A two-year swap with quarterly payments would have a duration of $0.125 - 1.50 = -1.375$.

These different durations affect the notional principal required, which leads us to the third question. Prior to the duration adjustment, the portfolio consists of $500 million at a duration of 6.75. QAM then adds a position in a swap with a notional principal of NP and a modified duration of $MDUR_S$. The swap will have zero market value.[12] The bonds and the swap will then combine to make up a portfolio with a market value of $500 million and a duration of 3.50. This relationship can be expressed as follows:

$$\$500,000,000(6.75) + NP(MDUR_S) = \$500,000,000(3.50)$$

The solution for NP is

$$NP = \$500,000,000\left(\frac{3.50 - 6.75}{MDUR_S}\right)$$

The duration of the swap is determined once QAM decides which swap to use. Suppose it uses a one-year swap with semiannual payments. Then, as shown above, the duration would be $-0.50$. The amount of notional principal required would, therefore, be

$$NP = \$500,000,000\left(\frac{3.50 - 6.75}{-0.50}\right) = \$3,250,000,000$$

In other words, this portfolio adjustment would require a swap with a notional principal of more than $3 billion! This would be a very large swap, probably too large to execute. Consider the use of a five-year swap with semiannual payments. Its duration would be $0.25 - 3.75 = -3.50$. Then the notional principal would be

$$NP = \$500,000,000\left(\frac{3.50 - 6.75}{-3.50}\right) = \$464,290,000$$

With this longer duration, the notional principal would be about $464 million, a much more reasonable amount, although still a fairly large swap.

So, in general, the notional principal of a swap necessary to change the duration of a bond portfolio worth B from $MDUR_B$ to a target duration, $MDUR_T$, is

$$NP = B\left(\frac{MDUR_T - MDUR_B}{MDUR_S}\right)$$

---

**Example 2**

A $250 million bond portfolio has a duration of 5.50. The portfolio manager wants to reduce the duration to 4.50 by using a swap. Consider the possibility of using a one-year swap with monthly payments or a two-year swap with semiannual payments.

**A.** Determine the durations of the two swaps under the assumption of paying fixed and receiving floating. Assume that the duration of a fixed-rate bond is 75 percent of its maturity.

---

**12** Recall that the market value of a swap is zero at the start. This market value can obviously vary over time from zero, and such deviations should be taken into account, but to start, the market value will be zero.

**B.** Choose the swap with the longer absolute duration and determine the notional principal of the swap necessary to change the duration as desired. Explain your results.

### Solution to A:

The duration of a one-year pay-fixed, receive-floating swap with monthly payments is the duration of a one-year floating-rate bond with monthly payments minus the duration of a one-year fixed-rate bond with monthly payments. The duration of the former is about one-half of the length of the payment interval. That is 1/24 of a year, or 0.042. Because the duration of the one-year fixed-rate bond is 0.75 (75 percent of one year), the duration of the swap is 0.042 − 0.75 = −0.708.

The duration of a two-year swap with semiannual payments is the duration of a two-year floating-rate bond with semiannual payments minus the duration of a two-year fixed-rate bond. The duration of the former is about one-quarter of a year, or 0.25. The duration of the latter is 1.50 (75 percent of two years). The duration of the swap is thus 0.25 − 1.50 = −1.25.

### Solution to B:

The longer (more negative) duration swap is the two-year swap with semiannual payments. The current duration of the $250 million portfolio is 5.50 and the target duration is 4.50. Thus, the required notional principal is

$$NP = B\left(\frac{MDUR_T - MDUR_B}{MDUR_S}\right)$$

$$= \$250,000,000\left(\frac{4.50 - 5.50}{-1.25}\right) = \$200,000,000$$

So, to lower the duration requires the addition of an instrument with a duration lower than that of the portfolio. The duration of a receive-floating, pay-fixed swap is negative and, therefore, lower than that of the existing portfolio.

## 2.3 Using Swaps to Create and Manage the Risk of Structured Notes

Structured notes are short- or intermediate-term floating-rate securities that have some type of unusual feature that distinguishes them from ordinary floating-rate notes. This unusual feature can be in the form of leverage, which results in the interest rate on the note moving at a multiple of market rates, or can be an inverse feature, meaning that the interest rate on the note moves opposite to market rates. Structured notes are designed to be sold to specific investors, who are often motivated by constraints that restrict their ability to hold derivatives or use leverage. For example, many insurance companies and pension funds are attracted to structured notes, because the instruments qualify as fixed-income securities but have features that are similar to options, swaps, and margin transactions. Issuers typically create the notes, sell them to these investors, and then manage the risk, earning a profit by replicating the opposite position at a cost lower than what they could sell the notes for.

In this section, we shall use the notation FP as the principal/face value of the note, $c_i$ as the fixed interest rate on a bond, and FS as the fixed interest rate on the swap.

### 2.3.1 *Using Swaps to Create and Manage the Risk of Leveraged Floating-Rate Notes*

Kappa Alpha Traders (KAT) engages in a variety of arbitrage-related transactions designed to make small risk-free or low-risk profits. One such transaction involves the issuance of structured notes, which it sells to insurance companies. KAT plans to issue a leveraged structured note with a principal of FP that pays an interest rate of 1.5 times LIBOR. This type of instrument is usually called a **leveraged floating-rate note**, or **leveraged floater**. The reference to *leverage* is to the fact that the coupon is a multiple of a specific market rate of interest such as LIBOR. The note will be purchased by an insurance company called LifeCo. KAT will use the proceeds to buy a fixed-rate bond that pays an interest rate of ci. It will then combine the position with a plain vanilla swap with dealer Omega Swaps. Exhibit 2 illustrates how this works.

| Exhibit 2 | Proceeds from a Leveraged Floater Used to Buy a Fixed-Rate Bond, with Risk Managed with a Plain Vanilla Swap |
|---|---|

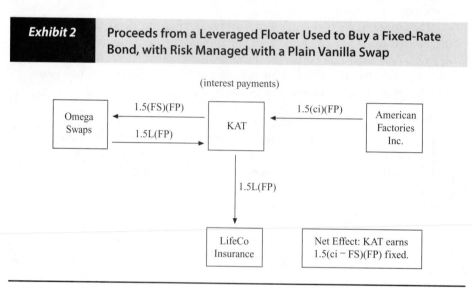

KAT issues the leveraged floater, selling it to LifeCo Insurance with the intent of financing it with a fixed-rate bond and swapping the fixed rate for a floating rate to match the leveraged floater. The periodic interest payment on the leveraged floater will be 1.5L, where L is LIBOR, times FP.[13] It then takes the proceeds and buys a fixed-rate bond issued by a company called American Factories Inc. This bond will have face value of 1.5(FP) and pay a coupon of ci. KAT is then in a position of receiving a fixed coupon of ci on principal of 1.5(FP) and paying a floating coupon of 1.5L on a principal of FP. It then enters into a swap with dealer Omega Swaps on notional principal of 1.5FP. KAT will pay a fixed rate of FS and receive a floating rate of LIBOR (L). Note the net effect: KAT's obligation on the leveraged floater of 1.5L(FP) is matched by its receipt on the swap. KAT receives 1.5(ci)(FP) on the fixed-rate bond and pays out 1.5(FS)(FP) on the swap, netting 1.5(FP)(ci − FS). Is this amount an inflow or outflow? It depends. If the interest rate on American Factories' debt reflects greater credit risk than that implied by the fixed rate on the swap, then KAT receives a net payment. Generally that would be the case. Thus, KAT identifies an attractively priced fixed-rate note and captures its return over the swap rate, offsetting the floating rate on the swap with the structured note. Of course, KAT is assuming some credit risk, the risk of default by American Factories, as well as the risk of default by Omega Swaps. On the other hand, KAT put up no capital to engage in this transaction. The cost of the American Factories bond was financed by issuing the structured note.

---

**13** These payments could be made semiannually, in which case they would be half of 1.5L(FP).

**Example 3**

A company issues a floating-rate note that pays a rate of twice LIBOR on notional principal FP. It uses the proceeds to buy a bond paying a rate of ci. It also enters into a swap with a fixed rate of FS to manage the risk of the LIBOR payment on the leveraged floater.

**A.** Demonstrate how the company can engage in these transactions, leaving it with a net cash flow of 2(FP)(ci − FS).

**B.** Explain under what condition the amount (ci − FS) is positive.

**Solution to A:**

The company has issued a leveraged floater at a rate of 2L on notional principal FP. Then it should purchase a bond with face value of 2(FP) and coupon ci. It enters into a swap to pay a fixed rate of FS and receive a floating rate of L on notional principal 2(FP). The net cash flows are as follows:

| | |
|---|---|
| From leveraged floater | −2L(FP) |
| From bond | +(ci)2(FP) |
| Floating side of swap | +(L)2(FP) |
| Fixed side of swap | −(FS)2(FP) |
| Total | 2FP(ci − FS) |

**Solution to B:**

The difference between the bond coupon rate, ci, and the swap fixed rate, FS, will be positive if the bond has greater credit risk than is implied by the fixed rate in the swap, which is based on the LIBOR term structure and reflects the borrowing rate of London banks. Thus, the gain of 2(ci − FS)(FP) is likely to reflect a credit risk premium.

### 2.3.2 *Using Swaps to Create and Manage the Risk of Inverse Floaters*

Another type of structured note is the **inverse floater**. Consider a company called Vega Analytics that, like KAT, engages in a variety of arbitrage trades using structured notes. Vega wants to issue an inverse floater paying a rate of b minus LIBOR, b − L, on notional principal FP. Vega sets the value of b in negotiation with the buyer of the note, taking into account a number of factors. The rate on the note moves inversely with LIBOR, but if LIBOR is at the level b, the rate on the note goes to zero. If LIBOR rises above b, the rate on the note is negative! We shall address this point later in this section.

The pattern will be the same as the pattern used for the leveraged floater: Finance the structured note by a fixed-rate note and then swap the fixed rate for a floating rate to match the structured note. Exhibit 3 shows how Vega issues the note to a company called Metrics Finance and uses the proceeds to purchase a fixed-rate note issued by a company called Telltale Systems, Inc., which pays a rate of (ci)(FP). Vega then enters into an interest rate swap with notional principal FP with a counterparty called Denman Dealer Holdings. In this swap, Vega receives a fixed rate of FS and pays L. Observe that the net effect is that Vega's overall cash flow is FP[ − (b − L) + ci + FS − L] = FP(FS + ci − b).

| Exhibit 3 | Proceeds from an Inverse Floater Used to Buy a Fixed-Rate Bond, with Risk Managed with a Plain Vanilla Swap |
|---|---|

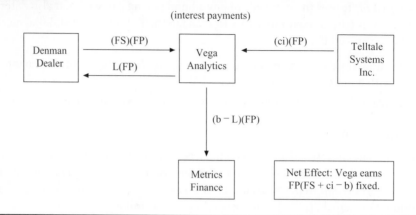

(interest payments)

Clearly if b is set below FS + ci, then the overall cash flow is positive. Vega can potentially do this because of the credit risk it assumes. Vega sets b but cannot set FS, and ci is based on both the level of market interest rates and the credit risk of Telltale. The lower Vega sets b, the larger its cash flow from the overall transactions. But one major consideration forces Vega to limit how low it sets b: The lower it sets b, the less attractive the note will be to potential investors.

Remember that the inverse floater pays b − L. When L reaches the level of b, the interest rate on the inverse floater is zero. If L rises above b, then the interest rate on the inverse floater becomes negative. A negative interest rate would imply that the lender (Metrics) pays interest to the borrower (Vega). Most lenders would find this result unacceptable, but the lower b is set, the more likely this outcome will occur. Thus, Vega will want to set b at a reasonably high level but below FS + ci.

Regardless of where Vega sets b, the possibility remains that L will exceed b. Metrics may have Vega guarantee that the interest rate on the floater will go no lower than 0 percent. To manage the risk associated with this guarantee, Vega will buy an interest rate cap. Let us see how all of this works with a numerical example.

Suppose the swap fixed rate, FS, is 6 percent, and ci, the rate on Telltale's note, is 7 percent. Vega sets b at 12 percent and guarantees to Metrics that the interest rate will go no lower than zero. Then the inverse floater pays 12 percent − L. As long as LIBOR is below 12 percent, Vega's cash flow is 6 + 7 − 12 = 1 percent. Suppose L is 14 percent. Then Vega's cash flows are

+7 percent from the Telltale note

0 percent to Metrics

+6 percent from Denman

14 percent to Denman

Net: outflow of 1 percent

Vega's net cash flow is negative. To avoid this problem, Vega would buy an interest rate cap in which the underlying is LIBOR and the exercise rate is b. The cap would have a notional principal of FP and consist of individual caplets expiring on the dates on which the inverse floater rates are set. Thus, on a payment date, when L exceeds b, the inverse floater does not pay interest, but the caplet expires in-the-money and pays L − b. Then the cash flows would be

+7 percent from the Telltale note

0 percent to Metrics

+6 percent from Denman

14 percent to Denman

(14% − 12%) = 2 percent from the caplet

Net: inflow of 1 percent

Thus, Vega has restored its guaranteed cash inflow of 1 percent.

Of course, the premium on the cap would be an additional cost that Vega would pass on in the form of a lower rate paid to Metrics on the inverse floater. In other words, for Metrics to not have to worry about ever having a negative interest rate, it would have to accept a lower overall rate. Thus, b would be set a little lower.

## Example 4

A company issues an inverse floating-rate note with a face value of $30 million and a coupon rate of 14 percent minus LIBOR. It uses the proceeds to buy a bond with a coupon rate of 8 percent.

**A.** Explain how the company would manage the risk of this position using a swap with a fixed rate of 7 percent, and calculate the overall cash flow given that LIBOR is less than 14 percent.

**B.** Explain what would happen if LIBOR exceeds 14 percent. What could the company do to offset this problem?

## Solution to A:

The company would enter into a swap in which it pays LIBOR and receives a fixed rate of 7 percent on notional principal of $30 million. The overall cash flows are as follows:

| | |
|---|---|
| From the inverse floater | − (0.14 − L)$30,000,000 |
| From the bond it buys | + (0.08)$30,000,000 |
| From the swap | |
|     Fixed payment | + (0.07)$30,000,000 |
|     Floating payment | − (L)$30,000,000 |
| Overall total | + (0.01)$30,000,000 |

## Solution to B:

If LIBOR is more than 14 percent, then the inverse floater payment of (0.14 − L) would be negative. The lender would then have to pay interest to the borrower. For this reason, in most cases, an inverse floater has a floor at zero. In such a case, the total cash flow to this company would be (0 + 0.08 + 0.07 − L)$30,000,000. There would be zero total cash flow at L = 15 percent. But at an L higher than 15 percent, the otherwise positive cash flow to the lender becomes negative.

To offset this effect, the lender would typically buy an interest rate cap with an exercise rate of 14 percent. The cap would have caplets that expire on the interest rate reset dates of the swap/loan and have a notional principal of $30 million. Then when L > 0.14, the caplet would pay off L − 0.14 times the $30 million. This payoff would make up the difference. The price paid for the cap would be an additional cost.

Interest rate swaps are special cases of currency swaps—cases in which the payments are made in different currencies. We now take a look at ways in which currency swaps are used.

# 3 STRATEGIES AND APPLICATIONS FOR MANAGING EXCHANGE RATE RISK

Currency swaps are designed for the purpose of managing exchange rate risk. They also play a role in managing interest rate risk, but only in cases in which exchange rate risk is present. In this section, we look at three situations in which exchange rate risk can be managed using currency swaps.

## 3.1 Converting a Loan in One Currency into a Loan in Another Currency

Royal Technology Ltd. (ROTECH) is a British high-tech company that is currently planning an expansion of about £30 million into Europe. To implement this expansion, it requires funding in euros. The current exchange rate is €1.62/£, so the expansion will cost €48.6 million. ROTECH could issue a euro-denominated bond, but it is not as well known in the euro market as it is in the United Kingdom where, although not a top credit, its debt is rated investment grade. As an alternative, ROTECH could issue a pound-denominated bond and convert it to a euro-denominated bond using a currency swap. Exhibit 4 illustrates how it could do this.

The transaction begins on 1 June. ROTECH will borrow for three years. It issues a bond for £30 million, receiving the proceeds from its bondholders. The bond carries an interest rate of 5 percent and will require annual interest payments each 1 June. ROTECH then enters into a currency swap with a dealer called Starling Bank (SB). It pays SB £30 million and receives from SB €48.6 million. The terms of the swap call for ROTECH to pay interest to SB at a rate of 3.25 percent in euros and receive interest from SB at a rate of 4.5 percent in pounds. With the exchange of principals up front, ROTECH then has the euros it needs to proceed with its expansion. Panel A of Exhibit 4 illustrates the flow of funds at the start of the transaction.

The interest payments and swap payments, illustrated in Panel B, occur each year on 1 June. The interest payments on the pound-denominated bond will be £30,000,000(0.05) = £1,500,000. The interest due to ROTECH from SB is £30,000,000(0.045) = £1,350,000. The interest ROTECH owes SB is €48,600,000(0.0325) = €1,579,500. The net effect is that ROTECH pays interest in euros. The interest received from the dealer, however, does not completely offset the interest it owes on its bond. ROTECH cannot borrow in pounds at the swap market fixed rate, because its credit rating is not as good as the rating implied in the LIBOR market term structure.[14] The net effect is that ROTECH will pay additional interest of (0.05 − 0.045)£30,000,000 = £150,000.

Panel C of Exhibit 4 shows the cash flows that occur at the end of the life of the swap and the maturity date of the bond. ROTECH receives the principal of £30 million from SB and pays it to its bondholders, discharging its liability. It then pays €48.6 million to SB to make the final principal payment on the swap.

---

[14] Remember that swap fixed rates are determined in the LIBOR market. This market consists of high-quality London banks, which borrow at an excellent rate. Hence, it is unlikely that ROTECH can borrow at as favorable a rate as these London banks.

| **Exhibit 4** | Issuing a Pound-Denominated Bond and Using a Currency Swap to Convert to a Euro-Denominated Bond |

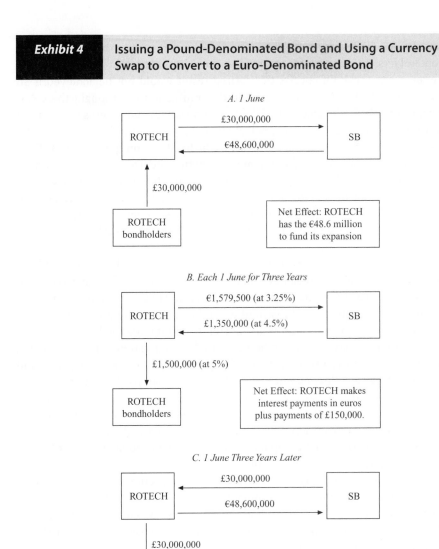

*A. 1 June*

ROTECH → £30,000,000 → SB

ROTECH ← €48,600,000 ← SB

ROTECH bondholders → £30,000,000 → ROTECH

Net Effect: ROTECH has the €48.6 million to fund its expansion

*B. Each 1 June for Three Years*

ROTECH → €1,579,500 (at 3.25%) → SB

ROTECH ← £1,350,000 (at 4.5%) ← SB

ROTECH → £1,500,000 (at 5%) → ROTECH bondholders

Net Effect: ROTECH makes interest payments in euros plus payments of £150,000.

*C. 1 June Three Years Later*

ROTECH ← £30,000,000 ← SB

ROTECH → €48,600,000 → SB

ROTECH → £30,000,000 → ROTECH bondholders

Net Effect: ROTECH pays off its bondholders and terminates its swap.

This type of transaction is an extremely common use of currency swaps. The advantage of borrowing this way rather than directly in another currency lies in the fact that the borrower can issue a bond or loan in the currency in which it is better known as a creditor. Then, by engaging in a swap with a bank with which it is familiar and probably already doing business, it can borrow in the foreign currency indirectly. For example, in this case, SB is probably a large multinational bank and is well known in foreign markets. But SB also has a longstanding banking relationship with ROTECH. Consequently, SB can operate in foreign exchange markets, using its advantage, and pass that advantage on to ROTECH.[15]

Another reason this transaction is attractive for borrowers like ROTECH is that the company can lower its borrowing cost by assuming some credit risk. If ROTECH had issued debt in euros directly, it would face no credit risk.[16] By engaging in the swap, however, ROTECH assumes the credit risk that SB will default on its swap payments.

---

**15** SB accepts the foreign exchange in the swap from ROTECH and almost surely passes on that risk by hedging its position with some other type of foreign exchange transaction.

**16** Of course, ROTECH's bondholders would face the credit risk that ROTECH could default.

If SB defaults, ROTECH would still have to make its interest and principal payments to its bondholders. In exchange for accepting this risk, it is likely that ROTECH would get a better overall deal. Of course, the desired result would not be achieved if SB defaults. But ROTECH would not engage in the transaction if it thought there was much chance of default. Therefore, ROTECH acknowledges and accepts some credit risk in return for expecting a better overall rate than if it issues euro-denominated debt.

Because it cannot borrow at the same rate as the fixed rate on the swap, ROTECH must pay £150,000 more in interest annually. Recall that the fixed rate on the swap is the rate that would be paid if a London bank issued a par bond. ROTECH, like most companies, would not be able to borrow at a rate that attractive. The £150,000 in interest that ROTECH pays can be viewed as a credit risk premium, which it would have to pay regardless of whether it borrowed directly in the euro market or indirectly through a swap.

In this transaction, the interest payments were made at a fixed rate. As we previously learned, a currency swap can be structured to have both sides pay fixed, both pay floating, or one pay fixed and the other floating. If ROTECH wanted to issue debt in euros at a floating rate, it could issue the bond at a fixed rate and structure the swap so that the dealer pays it pounds at a fixed rate and it pays the dealer euros at a floating rate. Alternatively, it could issue the pound-denominated bond at a floating rate and structure the swap so that the dealer pays it pounds at a floating rate and ROTECH pays euros at a floating rate.[17] A currency swap party's choice to pay a fixed or floating rate depends on its views about the direction of interest rate movements. Companies typically choose floating rates when they think interest rates are likely to fall. They choose fixed rates when they think interest rates are likely to rise.

It should also be noted that companies often choose a particular type of financing (fixed or floating) and then change their minds later by executing another swap. For example, suppose ROTECH proceeds with this transaction as we illustrated it: paying a fixed rate on its pound-denominated bonds, receiving a fixed rate on the pound payments on its swap, and paying a fixed rate on its euro payments on the swap. Suppose that part of the way through the life of the swap, ROTECH thinks that euro interest rates are going down. If it wants to take action based on this view, it could enter into a plain vanilla interest rate swap in euros with SB or some other dealer. It would promise to pay the counterparty interest in euros at a floating rate and receive interest in euros at a fixed rate. This transaction would shift the euro interest obligation to floating.

Exhibit 5 illustrates this example. Of course, this transaction is speculative, based as it is on a perception of likely interest rate movements. Moreover, the fixed payments would not offset due to different interest rates.

---

**17** It would not matter how ROTECH structured the payments on the pound-denominated bond. Either type of payment would be passed through with the currency swap, which would be structured to match that type of payment.

| Exhibit 5 | Reversing a Prior Swap to Change from a Fixed-Rate to an Overall Floating-Rate Status |
|---|---|

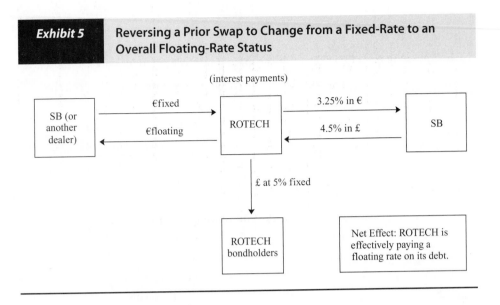

One important way in which currency swaps differ from interest rate swaps is that currency swaps involve the payment of notional principal. However, not all currency swaps involve the payment of notional principal. In transactions such as the ROTECH swap with SB described here, the payment of notional principal is important. The notional principal payment is required, because it offsets the principal on the bond that ROTECH issued in pounds. In the next section, we look at a currency swap in which the notional principal is not paid.

## Example 5

A Japanese company issues a bond with face value of ¥1.2 billion and a coupon rate of 5.25 percent. It decides to use a swap to convert this bond into a euro-denominated bond. The current exchange rate is ¥120/€. The fixed rate on euro-denominated swaps is 6 percent, and the fixed rate on yen-denominated swaps is 5 percent. All payments will be made annually, so there is no adjustment such as Days/360.

**A.** Describe the terms of the swap and identify the cash flows at the start.

**B.** Identify all interest cash flows at each interest payment date.

**C.** Identify all principal cash flows at the maturity of the bond.

### Solution to A:

The company will enter into a swap with notional principal of ¥1,200,000,000/(¥120/€1) = €10,000,000. The swap will involve an exchange of notional principals at the beginning and end. The annual cash flows will involve paying euros and receiving yen. The following cash flows occur at the start:

| | |
|---|---|
| From issuance of yen bond | + ¥1,200,000,000 |
| From swap | − ¥1,200,000,000 |
| | + €10,000,000 |
| Net | + €10,000,000 |

### Solution to B:

The following cash flows occur at the annual interest payment dates:

| | |
|---|---|
| Interest payments on bond | $(¥1,200,000,000)(0.0525) = -¥63,000,000$ |
| Swap payments | |
| Yen | $+ (¥1,200,000,000)(0.05) = +¥60,000,000$ |
| Euro | $- (€10,000,000)(0.06) = -€600,000$ |
| Net | $-¥3,000,000 - €600,000$ |

### Solution to C:

The following cash flows occur at the end of the life of the swap:

| | |
|---|---|
| Principal repayment on bond | $-¥1,200,000,000$ |
| Swap principal payments | |
| Yen | $+¥1,200,000,000$ |
| Euro | $-€10,000,000$ |
| Net | $-€10,000,000$ |

## 3.2 Converting Foreign Cash Receipts into Domestic Currency

Companies with foreign subsidiaries regularly generate cash in foreign currencies. Some companies repatriate that cash back into their domestic currency on a regular basis. If these cash flows are predictable in quantity, the rate at which they are converted can be locked in using a currency swap.

Colorama Software (COLS) is a U.S. company that writes software for digital imaging. So far it has expanded internationally only into the Japanese market, where it generates a net cash flow of about ¥1.2 billion a year. It converts this cash flow into U.S. dollars four times a year, with conversions taking place on the last day of March, June, September, and December. The amounts converted are equal to ¥300 million at each conversion.

COLS would like to lock in its conversion rate for several years, but it does not feel confident in predicting the amount it will convert beyond one year. Thus, it feels it can commit to only a one-year transaction to lock in the conversion rate. It engages in a currency swap with a dealer bank called U.S. Multinational Bank (USMULT) in which COLS will make fixed payments in Japanese yen and receive fixed payments in U.S. dollars. The current spot exchange rate is ¥132/$, which is $0.00757576/¥, or $0.757576 per 100 yen.

The fixed rate on plain vanilla swaps in Japan is 6 percent, and the fixed rate on plain vanilla swaps in the United States is 6.8 percent. To create a swap that will involve the exchange of ¥300 million per quarter into U.S. dollars would require a Japanese notional principal of ¥300,000,000/(0.06/4) = ¥20,000,000,000, which is equivalent to a U.S. dollar notional principal of ¥20,000,000,000/¥132 = $151,515,152.[18]

Thus, COLS engages in a swap for ¥20 billion in which it will pay 6 percent on a quarterly basis, or 1.5 percent per quarter in Japanese yen, and receive 6.8 percent on a quarterly basis, or 1.7 percent on $151,515,152. There is no initial or final exchange of notional principals. The cash flows in the swap are illustrated in Exhibit 6.

---

**18** A currency swap at 6 percent with quarterly payments and a notional principal of ¥20 billion would require payments of $(¥20,000,000,000)(0.06/4) = ¥300,000,000$ per quarter.

| Exhibit 6 | Converting a Series of Foreign Cash Flows into Domestic Currency Using a Currency Swap |

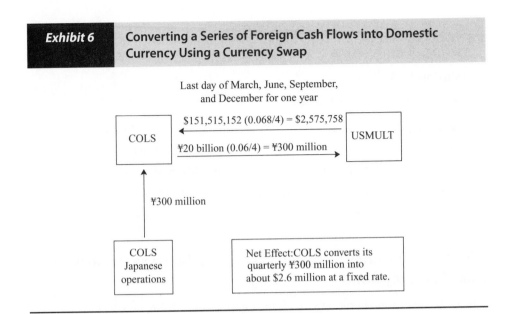

COLS pays USMULT ¥20,000,000,000(0.06/4) = ¥300,000,000 quarterly on the swap. This amount corresponds to the cash flow it generates on its Japanese operations. It then receives 6.8 percent on a dollar notional principal of $151,515,152 for a total of $151,515,152(0.068/4) = $2,575,758. So the swap effectively locks in the conversion of its quarterly yen cash flows for one year.

COLS does face some risk in this transaction. Besides the credit risk of the swap counterparty defaulting, COLS faces the risk that its operations will not generate at least ¥300 million. Of course, COLS' operations could generate more than ¥300 million, but that would mean only that some of its cash flows would not convert at a locked-in rate. If its operations do not generate at least ¥300 million, COLS still must pay ¥300 million to the swap counterparty.

Currency swaps can be used for purposes other than managing conversion risks. These swaps are also used by dealers to create synthetic strategies that allow them to offer new instruments or hedge existing instruments. In the next section, we look at how currency swaps can be used to synthesize an instrument called a dual-currency bond.

## Example 6

A Canadian corporation with a French subsidiary generates cash flows of €10 million a year. It wants to use a currency swap to lock in the rate at which it converts to Canadian dollars. The current exchange rate is C$0.825/€. The fixed rate on a currency swap in euros is 4 percent, and the fixed rate on a currency swap in Canadian dollars is 5 percent.

**A.** Determine the notional principals in euros and Canadian dollars for a swap with annual payments that will achieve the corporation's objective.

**B.** Determine the overall periodic cash flow from the subsidiary operations and the swap.

### Solution to A:

With the euro fixed rate at 4 percent, the euro notional principal should be

$$\frac{€10,000,000}{0.04} = €250,000,000$$

The equivalent Canadian dollar notional principal would be €250,000,000 × C$0.825 = C$206,250,000.

**Solution to B:**

The cash flows will be as follows:

| | |
|---|---|
| From subsidiary operations | €10,000,000 |
| Swap euro payment | −0.04(€250,000,000) = −€10,000,000 |
| Swap Canadian dollar payment | 0.05(C$206,250,000) = C$10,312,500 |

The net effect is that the €10 million converts to C$10,312,500.

## 3.3 Using Currency Swaps to Create and Manage the Risk of a Dual-Currency Bond

A financial innovation in recent years is the dual-currency bond, on which the interest is paid in one currency and the principal is paid in another. Such a bond can be useful to a multinational company that might generate sufficient cash in a foreign currency to pay interest but not enough to pay the principal, which it thus might want to pay in its home currency. Dual-currency bonds can be shown to be equivalent to issuing an ordinary bond in one currency and combining it with a currency swap that has no principal payments. Consider the following transactions:

- Issue a bond in dollars.

- Engage in a currency swap with no principal payments. The swap will require the company to pay interest in the foreign currency and receive interest in dollars.

Because the company issued the bond in dollars, it will make interest payments in dollars. The currency swap, however, will result in the company receiving interest in dollars to offset the interest paid on the dollar-denominated bond and making interest payments on the currency swap in the foreign currency.[19] Effectively, the company will make interest payments in the foreign currency. At the maturity date of the bond and swap, the company will pay off the dollar-denominated bond, and there will be no payments on the swap.

Of course, this example illustrates the synthetic creation of a dual-currency bond. Alternatively, a company can create the dual-currency bond directly by issuing a bond in which it promises to pay the principal in one currency and the interest in another. Then, it might consider offsetting the dual-currency bond by synthetically creating the opposite position. The company is short a dual-currency bond. A synthetic dual-currency bond can be created through the purchase of a domestic bond and a currency swap. If the synthetic dual-currency bond is cheaper than the actual dual-currency bond, the company can profit by offsetting the short position in the actual bond by a long position in the synthetic bond. Let us see how this strategy can be implemented using a trading firm that finds an opportunity to earn an arbitrage profit doing so.

Trans Mutual Arbitrage (TMARB) is such a firm. It has a major client, Omega Construction (OGCONS), that would like to purchase a five-year dual-currency bond. The bond will have a face value of $10 million and an equivalent face value in euros of €12.5 million.[20] The bond will pay interest in euros at a rate of 4.5 percent.

---

19 It does not matter if the dollar bond has fixed- or floating-rate interest. The currency swap would be structured to have the same type of interest to offset.

20 The current exchange rate must, therefore, be $0.80/€.

TMARB sees an opportunity to issue the bond, take the proceeds, and buy a 5.25 percent (coupon rate) U.S. dollar-denominated bond issued by an insurance company called Kappa Insurance Co. (KINSCO). TMARB will also engage in a currency swap with dealer American Trading Bank (ATB) in which TMARB will receive interest payments in euros at a rate of 4.5 percent on notional principal of €12.5 million and pay interest at a rate of 5.0 percent on notional principal of $10 million.[21] The swap does not involve the payment of notional principals. The swap and bond begin on 15 May and involve annual payments every 15 May for five years.

Exhibit 7 illustrates the structure of this swap. In Panel A, we see the initial cash flows. TMARB receives $10 million from OGCONS for the issuance of the dual-currency bond. It then takes the $10 million and buys a $10 million dollar-denominated bond issued by KINSCO. There are no initial cash flows on the currency swap.

Panel B shows the annual cash flows, which occur on 15 May for five years. TMARB pays interest of €12,500,000(0.045) = €562,500 to OGCONS on the dual-currency bond. It receives interest of an equivalent amount from ATB on the currency swap. It pays interest of $10,000,000(0.5) = $500,000 on the currency swap and receives interest of $10,000,000 × 0.0525 = $525,000 from KINSCO on the dollar-denominated bond. TMARB's euro interest payments are fully covered, and it nets a gain from its dollar interest payments. This opportunity resulted because TMARB found a synthetic way to issue a bond at 5.00 percent and buy one paying 5.25 percent. Of course, TMARB will be accepting some credit risk, from both the swap dealer and KINSCO, and its gain may reflect only this credit risk.

Panel C provides the final payments. TMARB pays off OGCONS its $10 million obligation on the dual-currency bond and receives $10 million from KINSCO on the dollar-denominated bond. There are no payments on the swap.

The end result is that TMARB issued a dual-currency bond and offset it with an ordinary dollar-denominated bond and a currency swap with no principal payments. TMARB earned a profit, which may be compensation for the credit risk taken.

---

21 We have made the fixed rate on the bond the same as the euro fixed rate on the swap for convenience. In practice, there probably would be a spread between the two rates, but the size of the spread would be fixed.

| Exhibit 7 | Issuing a Dual-Currency Bond and Managing the Risk with an Ordinary Bond and a Currency Swap |
|---|---|

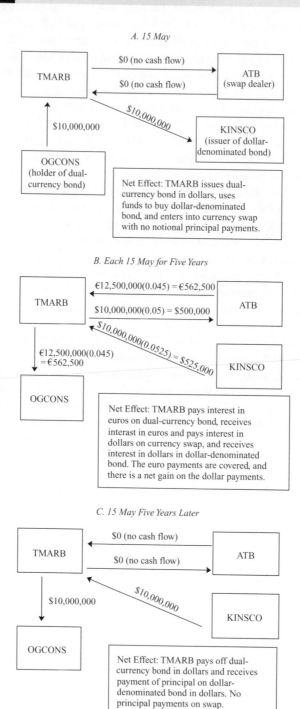

A. 15 May

$0 (no cash flow)
$0 (no cash flow)
TMARB
ATB (swap dealer)
$10,000,000
$10,000,000
KINSCO (issuer of dollar-denominated bond)
OGCONS (holder of dual-currency bond)

Net Effect: TMARB issues dual-currency bond in dollars, uses funds to buy dollar-denominated bond, and enters into currency swap with no notional principal payments.

B. Each 15 May for Five Years

€12,500,000(0.045) = €562,500
$10,000,000(0.05) = $500,000
TMARB
ATB
$10,000,000(0.0525) = $525,000
€12,500,000(0.045) = €562,500
KINSCO
OGCONS

Net Effect: TMARB pays interest in euros on dual-currency bond, receives interast in euros and pays interest in dollars on currency swap, and receives interest in dollars in dollar-denominated bond. The euro payments are covered, and there is a net gain on the dollar payments.

C. 15 May Five Years Later

$0 (no cash flow)
$0 (no cash flow)
TMARB
ATB
$10,000,000
$10,000,000
KINSCO
OGCONS

Net Effect: TMARB pays off dual-currency bond in dollars and receives payment of principal on dollar-denominated bond in dollars. No principal payments on swap.

## Example 7

From the perspective of the issuer, construct a synthetic dual-currency bond in which the principal is paid in U.S. dollars and the interest is paid in Swiss francs. The face value will be $20 million, and the interest rate will be 5 percent in Swiss francs. The exchange rate is $0.80/SF. Assume that the appropriate interest rate for a $20 million bond in dollars is 5.5 percent. The appropriate fixed rates on a currency swap are 5.5 percent in dollars and 5.0 percent in Swiss francs.

**Solution:**

Issue a $20 million bond in dollars, paying interest at 5.5 percent. Enter into a currency swap on $20 million, equivalent to SF25 million. The currency swap will involve the receipt of dollar interest at 5.5 percent and payment of Swiss franc interest at 5.0 percent. You will receive $20 million at the start and pay back $20 million at maturity. The annual cash flows will be as follows:

| | | |
|---|---|---|
| On dollar bond issued: | − 0.055($20,000,000) = | − $1,100,000 |
| On swap: | | |
| Dollars | + 0.055($20,000,000) = | + $1,100,000 |
| Swiss francs | − 0.05(SF25,000,000) = | − SF1,250,000 |
| Net | | − SF1,250,000 |

In the next section, we look at swap strategies in the management of equity market risk.

# STRATEGIES AND APPLICATIONS FOR MANAGING EQUITY MARKET RISK

**4**

Equity portfolio managers often want to realign the risk of their portfolios. Swaps can be used for this purpose. In the reading on risk management applications of forward and futures strategies, we covered equity swaps, which are swaps in which at least one set of payments is tied to the price of a stock or stock index. Equity swaps are ideal for use by equity managers to make changes to portfolios by synthetically buying and selling stock without making any trades in the actual stock. Of course, equity swaps have a defined expiration date and thus achieve their results only temporarily. To continue managing equity market risk, a swap would need to be renewed periodically and would be subject to whatever new conditions exist in the market on the renewal date.

## 4.1 Diversifying a Concentrated Portfolio

Diversification is one of the most important principles of sound investing. Some portfolios, however, are not very diversified. A failure to diversify can be due to investor ignorance or inattention, or it can arise through no fault of the investor. For example, a single large donation to a charitable organization can result in a high degree of concentration of an endowment portfolio. The recipient could be constrained or at least feel constrained from selling the stock. Equity swaps can be used to achieve diversification without selling the stock, as we shall see in the following example.

Commonwealth Foundation (CWF) is a charitable organization with an endowment of $50 million invested in diversified stock. Recently, Samuel Zykes, a wealthy member of the community, died and left CWF a large donation of stock in a company he founded called Zykes Technology (ZYKT). The stock is currently worth $30 million. The overall endowment value is now at $80 million, but the portfolio is highly undiversified, with more than a third of its value concentrated in one stock. CWF has considered selling the stock, but its development director believes that the Zykes family will possibly give more money to the foundation at a later date. If CWF sells the stock, the Zykes family may get the impression that the foundation does not want or appreciate the gift. Therefore, the foundation has concluded that it must hold onto the stock. The prospects for very limited growth in the portfolio through other sources, combined with the desire to attract further donations from the Zykes family, lead CWF to conclude that it cannot diversify the portfolio by traditional means anytime soon.

CWF's bank suggests that it consult with a swap dealer called Capital Swaps (CAPS). CAPS recommends an equity swap in which CWF would pay CAPS the return on the $30 million of ZYKT stock, while CAPS would pay CWF the return on $30 million of the S&P 500 Index, considered by all parties to be an acceptable proxy for a diversified portfolio. The payments will be made quarterly. CAPS mentions that technically the transaction would need an ending date. Anticipating the possibility of another transaction of this sort pending further donations by the Zykes family in about five years, the parties agree to set the maturity date of the swap at five years. The transaction entails no exchange of notional principal at the start or at the end of the life of the swap. Thus, CWF will maintain possession of the stock, including the voting rights. Exhibit 8 illustrates the structure of the transaction.

| Exhibit 8 | Diversifying a Concentrated Portfolio |
|---|---|

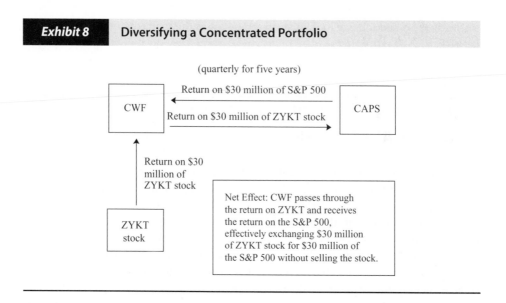

So, CWF passes through the return on $30 million of ZYKT stock and receives the return on the S&P 500. Both parties, however, must keep in mind a number of considerations. One is that a cash flow problem could arise for CWF, which must make cash payments each quarter equal to the return on the ZYKT stock. Though CWF will receive cash payments equal to the return on the S&P 500, CWF will have a net cash outflow if ZYKT outperforms the S&P 500. In fact, it is quite possible that in some quarters, ZYKT will have a positive total return, necessitating a cash obligation, and the S&P 500 will have a negative total return. In that case, the cash payment that CAPS would ordinarily make to CWF for the S&P 500 return would actually be reversed: CWF would owe CAPS for the S&P 500. In short, CWF would owe on both legs of the swap. This possibility could pose a significant cash flow problem and might necessitate the actual sale of some ZYKT stock. The position would then be imbalanced because CWF would own less than $30 million of ZYKT stock but still owe payments on $30 million of ZYKT stock. Cash flow management can be a major difficulty in equity swaps.

> ### Example 8
>
> The manager of a charitable foundation's $50 million stock portfolio is concerned about the portfolio's heavy concentration in one stock, Noble Petroleum (NBP). Specifically, the fund has $20 million of this stock as a result of a recent donation to the fund. She is considering using an equity swap to reduce the exposure to NBP and allow the fund to invest indirectly in the Wilshire 5000 Index. The stock is currently selling for $20 a share, and the fund owns 1 million shares. The manager is not quite ready to reduce all of the fund's exposure to NBP, so she decides to synthetically sell off one-quarter of the position. Explain how she would do this and identify some problems she might encounter.
>
> ### Solution:
>
> To reduce her exposure on one quarter of her NBP holdings, the manager would have the fund enter into a swap to sell the total return on $5 million of NBP stock, which is 250,000 shares. The fund will receive from the swap dealer the return on $5 million invested in the Wilshire 5000.
>
> The swap may result in cash flow problems, however, because the fund must pay out the return on 250,000 shares of NBP stock but does not want to sell that stock. If the return received on $5 million invested in the Wilshire 5000 is significantly less than the return the fund pays, or if the return on the Wilshire is negative, the fund could have insufficient cash to make its payment. Then it might be forced to sell the stock, something it was trying to avoid in the first place.

Continuing with the example of ZYKT stock, what is the position of the dealer CAPS? It agrees to accept the return on ZYKT stock and pay the return on the S&P 500. This means it is long ZYKT and short the S&P 500. It is likely to hedge its position by buying the equivalent of the S&P 500 through either an index fund or an exchange-traded fund, and selling short ZYKT stock.[22] In fact, its short sale of the ZYKT stock is analogous to CWF selling the stock. CAPS effectively sells the stock for CWF. Also, CAPS is not likely to be able to sell all of the ZYKT stock at one time so it will probably do so over a period of a few days. CAPS may also have a cash flow problem on occasion. If it owes more on the S&P 500 payment than is due it on the ZYKT payment, CAPS may have to liquidate some S&P 500 stock.[23]

In addition, to make a profit CAPS would probably either not pay quite the full return on the S&P 500 stock or require that CWF pay slightly more than the full return on the ZYKT stock.

We see that equity swaps can be used to diversify a concentrated portfolio. Next we turn to a situation in which equity swaps can be used to achieve diversification on an international scale.

## 4.2  Achieving International Diversification

The benefits of international diversification are well documented. The correlations between foreign markets and domestic markets generally lead to greater diversification and more efficient investing. Nonetheless, many investors have not taken the step of diversifying their portfolios across international boundaries. Here we shall take a look at a situation in which equity swaps can facilitate the transition from domestic to global diversification.

---

22  Instead of buying or selling short stock, it could use any of a variety of derivative strategies in which it would benefit from a decrease in the price of ZYKT relative to the S&P 500.

23  To make matters worse, if the S&P goes up and ZYKT goes down, it will owe both sets of payments.

In this example, Underscore Retirement Management (USRM) is responsible for a $500 million fund of retirement accounts in the United States. It has never diversified internationally, investing all of its funds in U.S. stock. Representing U.S. large-, medium- and small-cap stocks, the Russell 3000 Index is the portfolio's benchmark. USRM has decided that it needs to add non-U.S. stocks to its portfolio. It would like to start by selling 10 percent of its U.S. stock and putting the funds in non-U.S. stock. Its advisor, American Global Bank (AGB), has suggested that an equity swap would be a better way to do this than to transact in the stock directly. AGB often deals in non-U.S. stock and has subsidiaries and correspondent relationships in many countries to facilitate the transactions. It is capable of transacting in all stock at lower costs than its clients, and can pass on those savings through derivative transactions.

AGB suggests an equity swap with quarterly payments in which USRM would pay it the return on $50 million of the Russell 3000 Index. USRM would presumably generate this return from the portfolio it holds. AGB would, in turn, pay USRM the return on $50 million invested in the Morgan Stanley Capital International (MSCI) EAFE Index, which provides broad coverage of equity markets in Europe, Australasia, and the Far East. This transaction would result in USRM giving up some diversified domestic stock performance and receiving diversified international stock performance. Exhibit 9 illustrates the structure of the transaction.

---

**Exhibit 9**     **Achieving International Diversification**

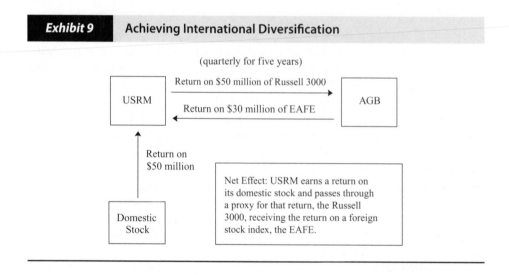

---

USRM must also consider a number of additional factors. The points made in Section 4.1 regarding the possibility of negative cash flow are highly relevant here as well, and we shall not repeat them. In addition, USRM's domestic stock holding generates a return that will not match perfectly the return on the Russell 3000. This difference in returns, in which the performance of an index does not match the performance of a portfolio that is similar to the index, is called the tracking error. In an extreme case, the domestic stock may go down while the Russell index goes up, which could pose a serious cash flow problem for USRM. USRM may be able to quantify this problem and find that it can effectively manage it. Otherwise, this concern could be an important one for USRM to weigh against the benefits of doing this transaction, which are primarily the savings in transaction costs on the domestic side and on the foreign side. In addition, AGB has currency risk and market risk and passes on to USRM its costs of hedging that risk.

**Example 9**

A Canadian trust fund holds a portfolio of C$300 million of Canadian domestic stock. The manager would like to sell off C$100 million and invest the funds in a pan-European portfolio. The manager arranges to do so using an equity swap in which the domestic stock is represented by the Toronto 300 Composite and the European portfolio is represented by the Dow Jones Euro STOXX 50, an index of leading stocks in the eurozone. Explain how to structure such a swap, and describe how tracking error could potentially interfere with the success of the transaction.

**Solution:**

The swap would specify the following transactions on a periodic basis for a specific number of years:

- receive return on DJ Euro STOXX 50,
- pay return on Toronto 300.

Tracking error here is the failure of the derivative cash flow to match precisely the cash flow from the underlying portfolio. In this case, tracking error means that the return actually earned on the domestic portfolio is not likely to perfectly match the Toronto 300 return. These returns are supposed to offset, but they are not likely to do so, certainly not with perfection. The return received on the DJ Euro STOXX 50 does not give rise to tracking error concerns. The index will simply represent the return on the investment in European stocks. If an actual investment in European stocks were made, it would likely differ from this return.

---

We see in this example that a company can use an equity swap to change its asset allocation. Indeed, an asset allocation change is the major use of equity swaps. In the next section, we shall see a company use equity swaps, combined with a similar swap based on a fixed-income instrument, to implement an asset allocation change. This fixed-income swap will be a slightly new and different instrument from what we have already seen.

## 4.3 Changing an Asset Allocation between Stocks and Bonds

Consider an investment management firm called Tactical Money Management (TMM). It is interested in changing the asset allocation on a $200 million segment of its portfolio. This money is invested 75 percent in domestic stock and 25 percent in U.S. government and corporate bonds. Within the stock sector, the funds are invested 60 percent in large cap, 30 percent in mid cap, and 10 percent in small cap. Within the bond sector, the funds are invested 80 percent in U.S. government and 20 percent in investment-grade corporate bonds. TMM would like to change the overall allocation to 90 percent stock and 10 percent bonds. Within each class, TMM would also like to make some changes. Specifically, TMM would like to change the stock allocation to 65 percent large cap and 25 percent mid cap, leaving the small-cap allocation at 10 percent. It would like to change the bond allocation to 75 percent U.S. government and 25 percent investment-grade corporate. TMM knows that these changes would entail a considerable amount of trading in stocks and bonds. Below we show the current position, the desired new position, and the necessary transactions to get from the current position to the new position:

| Stock | Current ($150 Million, 75%) | New ($180 Million, 90%) | Transaction |
|---|---|---|---|
| Large cap | $90 million (60%) | $117 million (65%) | Buy $27 million |
| Mid cap | $45 million (30%) | $45 million (25%) | None |
| Small cap | $15 million (10%) | $18 million (10%) | Buy $3 million |

| Bonds | Current ($50 Million, 25%) | New ($20 Million, 10%) | Transaction |
|---|---|---|---|
| Government | $40 million (80%) | $15 million (75%) | Sell $25 million |
| Corporate | $10 million (20%) | $5 million (25%) | Sell $5 million |

TMM decides it can execute a series of swaps that would enable it to change its position temporarily, but more easily and less expensively than by executing the transactions in stock and bonds. It engages a dealer, Dynamic Derivatives Inc. (DYDINC), to perform the swaps. The return on the large-cap sector is represented by the return on $27 million invested in the S&P 500 (SP500) Index. Note that the mid-cap exposure of $45 million does not change, so we do not need to incorporate a mid-cap index into the swap. The return on the small-cap sector is represented by the return on $3 million invested in the S&P Small Cap 600 Index (SPSC). The return on the government bond sector is represented by the return on $25 million invested in the Lehman Long Treasury Bond index (LLTB), and the return on the corporate bond sector is represented by the return on $5 million invested in the Merrill Lynch Corporate Bond index (MLCB). Note that for the overall fixed-income sector, TMM will be reducing its exposure.

TMM must decide the frequency of payments and the length of the swap. Equity swap payments tend to be set at quarterly intervals. Fixed-income payments in the form of coupon interest tend to occur semiannually. TMM could arrange for quarterly equity swap payments and semiannual fixed-income swap payments. It decides, however, to structure the swap to have all payments occur on the same dates six months apart. The length of the swap should correspond to the period during which the firm wants this new allocation to hold. TMM decides on one year. Should it wish to extend this period, TMM would need to renegotiate the swap at expiration. Likewise, TMM could decide to unwind the position prior to one year, which it could do by executing a new swap with opposite payments for the remainder of the life of the original swap.

The equity swaps in this example involve receiving payments tied to the SP500 and the SPSC and making either fixed payments or floating payments tied to LIBOR. Let us start by assuming that the equity swap payments will be paired with LIBOR-based floating payments. For the fixed-income payments, however, TMM needs a slightly different type of swap—specifically, a fixed-income swap. This instrument is exactly like an equity swap, but instead of the payment being tied to a stock or stock index, it is tied to a bond or bond index. This type of swap is not the same as an interest rate swap, which involves payments tied to a floating rate such as LIBOR. Fixed-income swaps, like equity swaps, require the payment of the total return on a bond or bond index against some other index, such as LIBOR. They are very similar to equity swaps in many respects: The total return is not known until the end of the settlement period, and because the capital gain can be negative, it is possible for the overall payment to be negative. In contrast to equity swaps, however, fixed-income swaps are more dominated by the fixed payment of interest. For equities, the dividends are small, not fixed, and do not tend to dominate capital gains. Other than the amounts paid, however, fixed-income swaps are conceptually the same as equity swaps.[24]

---

24 Fixed-income swaps, when referred to as total return swaps, are a form of a credit derivative.

The swaps are initially structured as follows:

*Equity swaps*

    Receive return on SP500 on $27 million

        Pay LIBOR on $27 million

    Receive return on SPSC on $3 million

        Pay LIBOR on $3 million

*Fixed-income swaps*

    Receive LIBOR on $25 million

        Pay return on LLTB on $25 million

    Receive LIBOR on $5 million

        Pay return on MLCB on $5 million

Note that the overall position involves no LIBOR payments. TMM pays LIBOR on $27 million and on $3 million from its equity swaps, and it receives LIBOR on $25 million and on $5 million from the fixed-income swaps. Therefore, the LIBOR payments can be eliminated. Furthermore, the equity and fixed-income swaps can be combined into a single swap with the following payments:

    Receive return on SP500 on $27 million

    Receive return on SPSC on $3 million

        Pay return on LLTB on $25 million

        Pay return on MLCB on $5 million

This combined equity/fixed-income swap is a single transaction that accomplishes TMM's objective. Exhibit 10 illustrates the overall transaction.

| **Exhibit 10** | **Changing an Asset Allocation** |
| --- | --- |

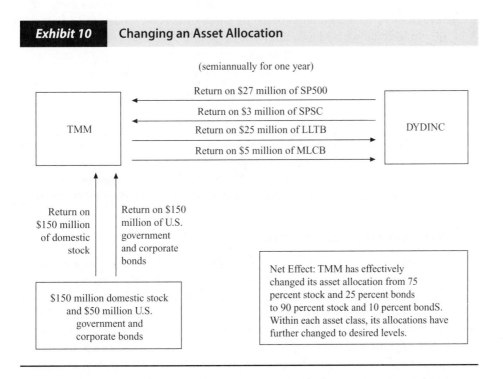

Of course, this transaction will not completely achieve TMM's goals. The performance of the various sectors of its equity and fixed-income portfolios are not likely to match perfectly the indices on which the swap payments are based. This problem is what we referred to previously as tracking error. In addition, TMM could encounter a cash flow problem if its fixed-income payments exceed its equity receipts and its portfolio does not generate enough cash to fund its net obligation. The actual stock and bond portfolio will generate cash only from dividends and interest. The capital gains on the stock and bond portfolio will not be received in cash unless a portion of the portfolio is liquidated. But avoiding liquidation of the portfolio is the very reason that TMM wants to use swaps.[25]

---

**Example 10**

A $30 million investment account of a bank trust fund is allocated one-third to stocks and two-thirds to bonds. The portfolio manager wants to change the overall allocation to 50 percent stock and 50 percent bonds, and the allocation within the stock fund from 70 percent domestic stock and 30 percent foreign stock to 60 percent domestic and 40 percent foreign. The bond allocation will remain entirely invested in domestic corporate issues. Explain how an equity swap could be used to implement this adjustment. You do not need to refer to specific stock indices.

**Solution:**

Currently the allocation is $10 million stock and $20 million bonds. Within the stock category, the current allocation is $7 million domestic and $3 million foreign. The desired allocation is $15 million stock and $15 million bonds. Thus, the allocation must change by moving $5 million into stock and out of bonds. The desired stock allocation is $9 million domestic and $6 million foreign. The desired bond allocation is $15 million, all domestic corporate.

To make the change with a swap, the manager must enter into a swap to receive the return on $5 million based on a domestic equity index and pay the return on $5 million based on a domestic corporate bond index. The $5 million return based on a domestic equity index should be allocated such that $2 million is based on domestic stock and $3 million is based on foreign stock.

---

So far we have seen that an equity swap can be used to reduce or increase exposure to a stock or stock index. One type of investor that is highly exposed to the performance of a single stock is a corporate insider. In the following section, we examine a swap strategy that has been increasingly used in recent years to reduce such exposure.

## 4.4 Reducing Insider Exposure

Michael Spelling is the founder and sole owner of a U.S.-based company called Spelling Software and Technology (SPST). After founding the company about 10 years ago, Spelling took it public 2 years ago and retains significant ownership in the form of 10,200,000 shares, currently valued at $35 a share, for a total value of $357 million, which represents about 10 percent of the company. Spelling wants to retain this degree of control of the company, so he does not wish to sell any of his shares. He is concerned, however, that his personal wealth is nearly 100 percent exposed to the fortunes of a single company.

---

**25** Even worse would be if its fixed-income payments were positive and its equity receipts were negative.

A swap dealer called Swap Solutions Inc. (SSI) approaches Spelling about a strategy that it has been using lately with much success. This transaction involves an equity swap whereby Spelling would pay the dealer the return on some of his shares in SPST and receive a diversified portfolio return. Spelling finds the idea intriguing and begins thinking about how he would like to structure the arrangement. He decides to initially base the transaction on 500,000 shares of stock, about 4.9 percent of his ownership. If he is satisfied with how the strategy works, he may later increase his commitment to the swap. At $35 a share, this transaction has an exposure of $17.5 million. Specifically, Spelling will pay the total return on 500,000 shares of SPST stock and receive a diversified portfolio return on $17.5 million. He decides to split the diversified return into 80 percent stock and 20 percent bonds. The former will be represented by the return on $14.0 million invested in the Russell 3000, and the latter will be represented by the return on $3.5 million invested in the Lehman Brothers Government Bond Index (LGB). The payments will occur quarterly for two years, at which time Spelling will re-evaluate his position and may choose to extend the swap, terminate it, or change the allocation or other terms.

Exhibit 11 illustrates the structure of the swap. Spelling achieves his objectives, but he must consider some important issues in addition to the cash flow problem we have already mentioned. One is that under U.S. law, this transaction is considered an insider sale and must be reported to the regulatory authorities. Thus, there is some additional paperwork. Shareholders and potential investors may consider the sale a signal of bad prospects for the company. U.S. tax laws also require that the synthetic sale of securities through equity swaps forces a termination of the holding period on the stock. Hence, this transaction has no tax advantages. Spelling will also want to consider the fact that he has sold off some of his exposure but retains control. Shareholders will surely resent the fact that Spelling controls 500,000 votes but does not have any exposure to this stock.[26] Of course, he still retains exposure to 9.7 million shares.

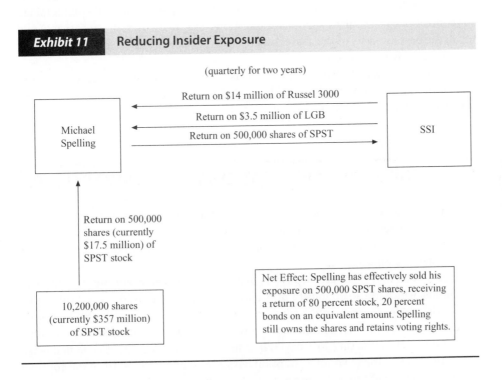

| Exhibit 11 | Reducing Insider Exposure |
| --- | --- |

(quarterly for two years)

Return on $14 million of Russel 3000

Return on $3.5 million of LGB

Return on 500,000 shares of SPST

Michael Spelling

SSI

Return on 500,000 shares (currently $17.5 million) of SPST stock

10,200,000 shares (currently $357 million) of SPST stock

Net Effect: Spelling has effectively sold his exposure on 500,000 SPST shares, receiving a return of 80 percent stock, 20 percent bonds on an equivalent amount. Spelling still owns the shares and retains voting rights.

---

**26** An interesting question in this regard is whether the shareholders would actually know that the executive had done such a transaction. Careful research is required to identify that executives have made these transactions.

**Example 11**

The CEO of a corporation owns 100 million shares of his company's stock, which is currently priced at €30 a share. Given the tremendous exposure of his personal wealth to this one company, he has decided to sell 10 percent of his position and invest the funds in a floating interest rate instrument. A derivatives dealer suggests that he do so using an equity swap. Explain how to structure such a swap.

**Solution:**

The swap is structured so that the executive pays the return on 10 million shares, which is 10 percent of his holdings, of the company's stock and receives the return based on a floating interest rate, such as LIBOR, on a notional principal of €300 million.

Equity swaps of this sort can be a significant concern for financial analysts. Their possible use makes it difficult to determine if executives have the full exposure represented by the number of shares they own.

Equity swaps involving executives can also have significant agency cost implications. A company incurs agency costs when an executive does not act on behalf of shareholders. Consider the extreme case of an executive who owns more than 50 percent of a company but who reduces her equity exposure to zero with equity swaps. The executive retains full control of the company, although she has eliminated her equity exposure. This action could entail significant costs to outside shareholders, as the executive does not bear any of the costs of actions or expenditures that increase her personal welfare at the expense of the company. Of course, executives are unlikely to sell off all of their exposure, but the elimination of any exposure on shares still retained for control purposes raises significant questions about whether an executive would act in the best interests of the shareholders. The executive's incentive to perform well would certainly be reduced.

In Sections 2, 3, and 4, we examined the use of interest rate swaps, currency swaps, and equity swaps for managing risk. In the following section, we examine strategies involving the use of swaptions to manage risk.

# 5    STRATEGIES AND APPLICATIONS USING SWAPTIONS

A swaption is an option to enter into a swap. Although there are swaptions to enter into equity, currency, and commodity swaps, we will focus exclusively on swaptions to enter into interest rate swaps, which is by far the largest swaptions market. Let us briefly review swaptions.

First, recall that there are two types of swaptions, payer swaptions and receiver swaptions, which are analogous to puts and calls. A payer swaption is an option that allows the holder to enter into a swap as the fixed-rate payer, floating-rate receiver. A receiver swaption is an option that allows the holder to enter into a swap as the fixed-rate receiver, floating-rate payer. In both cases, the fixed rate is specified when the option starts. The buyer of a swaption pays a premium at the start of the contract and receives the right to enter into a swap. The counterparty is the seller of the swaption. The seller receives the premium at the start and grants the right to enter into the swap at the specified fixed rate to the buyer of the swaption. A swaption can be

European style or American style, meaning that it can be exercised only at expiration (European) or at any time prior to expiration (American). We shall illustrate applications of both.

A swaption is based on an underlying swap. The underlying swap has a specific set of terms: the notional principal, the underlying interest rate, the time it expires, the specific dates on which the payments will be made, and how the interest is calculated. *All* of the terms of the underlying swap must be specified. Although an ordinary option on an asset has an exercise *price*, a swaption is more like an interest rate option in that it has an exercise *rate*. The exercise rate is the fixed rate at which the holder can enter into the swap as either a fixed-rate payer or fixed-rate receiver. When a swaption expires, the holder decides whether to exercise it based on the relationship of the then-current market rate on the underlying swap to the exercise rate on the swaption. A swaption can be exercised either by actually entering into the swap or by having the seller pay the buyer an equivalent amount of cash. The method used is determined by the parties when the contract is created.

For example, suppose the underlying swap is a three-year swap with semiannual payments with LIBOR as the underlying floating rate. Consider a payer swaption, which allows entry into this swap as the fixed-rate payer, with an exercise rate of 7 percent. At expiration, let us say that three-year, semiannual-pay LIBOR swaps have a fixed rate of 7.25 percent. If the holder exercises the swaption, it enters a swap, agreeing to pay a fixed rate of 7 percent and receive a floating rate of LIBOR. If the holder has another position for which it might want to maintain the swap, it might simply hold the swap in place. If the holder does not want to maintain the swap, it can enter into a swap in the market, specifying the opposite set of payments—it can pay LIBOR and receive the market fixed rate of 7.25 percent. If this swap is done with a different counterparty than the swaption seller, then the two sets of LIBOR payments are made but are equivalent in amount. Then the payer swaption holder finds itself with a stream of cash flows consisting of 7 percent payments and 7.25 percent receipts, for a net overall position of an annuity of 0.25 percent, split into 0.125 percent twice a year, for three years. If this swap at the market rate of 7.25 percent is done with the swaption seller, the two parties are likely to agree to offset the LIBOR payments and have the swaption seller pay the holder the stream of payments of 0.125 percent twice a year. If the parties settle the contract in cash, the swaption seller pays the swaption holder the present value of a series of six semiannual payments of 0.125 percent.

A swaption can also be viewed as an option on a coupon bond. Specifically, a payer swaption with exercise rate x in which the underlying is a swap with notional principal P and maturity of N years at the swaption expiration is equivalent to an at-the-money put option in which the underlying is an N-year bond at expiration with a coupon of x percent. Likewise, a receiver swaption is analogous to an at-the-money call option on a bond. These identities will be useful in understanding swaption strategies.

## 5.1 Using an Interest Rate Swaption in Anticipation of a Future Borrowing

We have illustrated extensively the use of swaps to convert fixed-rate loans to floating-rate loans and vice versa. We now consider a situation in which a company anticipates taking out a loan at a future date. The company expects that the bank will require the loan to be at a floating rate, but the company would prefer a fixed rate. It will use a swap to convert the payment pattern of the loan. A swaption will give it the flexibility to enter into the swap at an attractive rate.

In this section, we will use the notation FS(1,3) for the fixed rate on a swap established at time 1 and ending at time 3.

Benelux Chemicals (BCHEM) is a Brussels-based industrial company that often takes out floating-rate loans. In the course of planning, BCHEM finds that it must borrow €10 million in one year at the floating rate of Euribor, the rate on euros in Frankfurt, from the Antwerp National Bank (ANB). The loan will require semiannual payments for two years. BCHEM knows that it will swap the loan into a fixed-rate loan, using the going rate for two-year Euribor-based swaps at the time the loan is taken out. BCHEM is concerned that interest rates will rise before it takes out the loan. DTD, a Rotterdam derivatives dealer, approaches BCHEM with the idea of doing a European-style swaption. Specifically, for a cash payment up front of €127,500, BCHEM can obtain the right to enter into the swap in one year as a fixed-rate payer at a rate of 7 percent. BCHEM decides to go ahead with the deal; that is, it buys a 7 percent payer swaption.

Exhibit 12 illustrates this transaction. In Panel A, BCHEM pays DTD €127,500 in cash and receives the payer swaption. In Panel B, we examine what happens starting when the swaption expires one year later. Note first that regardless of the outcome of the swaption, BCHEM will make floating interest payments of Euribor (180/360)€10 million on its loan.[27] In Part (i) of Panel B, we assume that at expiration of the swaption, the rate in the market on the underlying swap, FS(1,3), is greater than the swaption exercise rate of 7 percent. In this case, the swaption is worth exercising.[28] BCHEM enters into the swap with DTD, thereby making payments of 0.07(180/360)€10 million and receiving payments of Euribor (180/360)€10 million.[29] Both streams of floating payments at Euribor are made, but the payment from DTD exactly offsets the payment to ANB. BCHEM is left paying 7 percent fixed.

---

[27] Again, recall that being a floating rate, Euribor is set at the beginning of the settlement period, and the payment is made at the end of that period.

[28] To review, remember that at the swaption expiration in one year, which we denote as time 1, the underlying swap is a two-year swap. If the fixed rate on a two-year swap is higher than the rate at which the swaption holder can pay to enter a two-year swap, the swaption is in-the-money. Its value at that point is the present value of a stream of payments equal to the difference between the market fixed rate and the exercise rate on the swaption.

[29] The swap payments would, of course, be netted, but that fact does not affect the point we are making here.

| **Exhibit 12** | **Using a Swaption in Anticipation of a Future Borrowing** |

*A. Today*

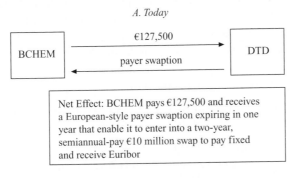

Net Effect: BCHEM pays €127,500 and receives a European-style payer swaption expiring in one year that enable it to enter into a two-year, semiannual-pay €10 million swap to pay fixed and receive Euribor

*B. Starting One Year Later, Semiannually for Two Years*
(i) Rate on swap in market FS(1,3) > 7 percent, swaption exercised

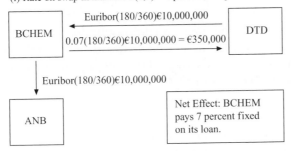

Net Effect: BCHEM pays 7 percent fixed on its loan.

(ii) Rate on swap in market FS(1,3) ≤ 7 percent, swaption not exercised

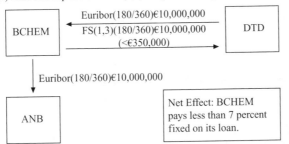

Net Effect: BCHEM pays less than 7 percent fixed on its loan.

In Part (ii) of Panel B, at expiration of the swaption, the rate in the market on the underlying swap, FS(1,3), is less than or equal to the swaption exercise rate of 7 percent. The swaption, therefore, expires out-of-the-money. BCHEM still enters into a swap with DTD but does so at the market rate of FS(1,3), which is less than 7 percent and the payments are less than €350,000. Of course, both sets of Euribor payments must be made on the loan.

Thus, BCHEM obtained the advantage of flexibility, the right to pay a fixed rate of 7 percent or less. Of course, this right does not come without a cost. BCHEM had to pay a premium of €127,500 for that right. Therefore, when the loan was taken out one year after the swaption was purchased, the €10 million received was effectively reduced by the €127,500 paid one year earlier plus one year's interest. Whether this premium would be worth paying depends on whether the swaption is correctly priced.[30] Whether this premium was worth it after the fact depends on how far the market rate ended above 7 percent at the time the loan was taken out.

---

30 The basic idea behind swaption pricing is that a model would be used to obtain a fair price for the swaption, to which the market price of €127,500 would be compared.

## Example 12

A company plans to take out a $10 million floating-rate loan in two years. The loan will be for five years with annual payments at the rate of LIBOR. The company anticipates using a swap to convert the loan into a fixed-rate loan. It would like to purchase a swaption to give it the flexibility to enter into the swap at an attractive rate. The company can use a payer or a receiver swaption. Assume that the exercise rate would be 6.5 percent.

**A.** Identify what type of swaption would achieve this goal and whether the company should buy or sell the swaption.

**B.** Calculate the company's annual cash flows beginning two years from now for two cases: The fixed rate on a swap two years from now to terminate five years later, FS(2,7), is 1) greater or 2) not greater than the exercise rate. Assume the company takes out the $10 million floating-rate loan as planned.

**C.** Suppose that when the company takes out the loan, it has changed its mind and prefers a floating-rate loan. Now assume that the swaption expires in-the-money. What would the company do, given that it now no longer wants to convert to a fixed-rate loan?

### Solution to A:

The company wants the option to enter into the swap as a fixed-rate payer, so the company would buy a payer swaption.

### Solution to B:

The outcomes based on the swap rate at swaption expiration, denoted as FS(2,7), are as follows:

FS(2,7) > 6.5 percent
Exercise the swaption, entering into a swap. The annual cash flows will be as follows:

Pay 0.065($10 million) = $650,000 on swap
Receive L($10 million) on swap
Pay L($10 million) on loan
Net, pay $650,000

FS(2,7) ≤ 6.5 percent
Do not exercise swaption; enter into swap at market rate. The annual cash flows will be as follows:

Pay FS(2,7)($10 million) on swap
Receive L($10 million) on swap
Pay L($10 million) on loan
Net, pay FS(2,7)($10 million)
(Note: This is less than $650,000)

### Solution to C:

In this situation, the company has changed its mind about converting the floating-rate loan to a fixed-rate loan. If the swaption expires out-of-the-money, the company will simply take out the floating-rate loan. If the swaption expires in-the-money, it has value and the company should not fail to exercise it. But exercising the swaption will initiate a swap to pay fixed and receive floating, which would leave the company in the net position of paying a fixed rate of 6.5 percent when it wants a floating-rate loan. The company would exercise the swaption and then enter into the opposite swap in the market, receiving a fixed rate of FS(2,7) and paying L. The net effect is that the company will pay 6.5 percent, receive FS(2,7), which is more than 6.5 percent, and pay L. So in effect it will pay a floating-rate loan of less than LIBOR.

In this example, we showed how a swaption is used to create a swap. Similarly, a swaption can be used to terminate a swap.

## 5.2  Using an Interest Rate Swaption to Terminate a Swap

When a company enters a swap, it knows it may need to terminate the swap before the expiration day. It can do so by either entering an offsetting swap or buying a swaption.

As with any over-the-counter option, the holder of a swap can terminate the swap by entering into an identical swap from the opposite perspective at whatever rate exists in the market. Consider, for example, a Japanese company that enters into a five-year ¥800 million notional principal swap in which it pays a fixed rate and receives a floating rate; that is, it enters a pay-fixed swap. Two years later, the company wants to terminate the swap. It can do so by entering into a new swap with a notional principal of ¥800 million, a remaining life of three years, and with the company paying the floating rate and receiving the fixed rate. If it engages in this swap with a different counterparty than the counterparty of the original swap, then both swaps would remain in place, but the floating payments would be equivalent. The net effect would be that the company would make a stream of fixed payments at one rate and receive a stream of fixed payments at another rate. The rate that is greater depends on the course of interest rates since the time the original swap was put into place. If the new swap is done with the same counterparty as in the original swap, the two parties would likely agree to offset and eliminate both swaps. Then one party would be paying the other a lump sum of the present value of the difference between the two streams of fixed payments. If the company offsets the swap with a new swap in this manner, it must accept the conditions in the market at the time it offsets the swap.

The second way of terminating a swap is for a company to buy a swaption before it wants to offset the swap. Suppose that when this Japanese company enters into a pay-fixed, receive-floating swap, it also purchases a receiver swaption that allows it to enter into an ¥800 million swap to receive fixed and pay floating with the same terms as the original swap. The swaption exercise rate is 8 percent. The company must pay cash up front for the swaption, but it then has the right to enter into a new swap to receive a fixed rate of 8 percent and pay the floating rate. We assume for maximum flexibility that the swaption is structured as an American-style option, allowing the company to exercise it at any time. We also assume that the swaption counterparty is the counterparty to the swap, so that if the swaption is exercised, the payments can be canceled and replaced by a lump sum payment.

Consider this example. Internet Marketing Solutions (IMS) takes out a $20 million one-year loan with quarterly floating payments at LIBOR from a lender called Financial Solutions (FINSOLS). Fearing an increase in interest rates, IMS engages in a pay-fixed, receive-floating swap that converts the loan into a fixed-rate loan at 8 percent. IMS believes, however, that the interest rate outlook could change, and it would like the flexibility to terminate the swap, thereby returning to the status of a floating-rate payer. To give it this flexibility, IMS purchases an American-style receiver swaption for $515,000. The swaption allows it to enter into a receive-fixed, pay-floating swap at a fixed rate of 8 percent at the swaption expiration. The swap and swaption counterparty is Wheatstone Dealer (WHD).

Exhibit 13 illustrates this transaction. In Panel A, IMS takes out the loan from FINSOLS, receiving $20 million. It engages in the swap with WHD, thereby committing to pay fixed and receive LIBOR. There are no cash flows at the start of the swap contract, but IMS pays WHD $515,000 for the swaption. Now let us move to the expiration of the swaption, at which time we shall assume that IMS is no longer concerned about rising interest rates and would like to return to the status of a floating-rate borrower. In Panel B(i), at the expiration of the swaption, the market swap rate is greater than or equal to 8 percent. This panel shows the cash flows if the loan plus swap (note that the loan is floating rate) is converted to a fixed rate using the market fixed rate because the swaption is out-of-the-money. IMS makes interest payments of LIBOR(90/360)$20 million to FINSOLS. IMS makes a swap payment of 8 percent, which is $400,000, to WHD, which pays LIBOR.[31] Thus, to offset the effect of the pay-fixed swap, IMS is better off entering a new swap rather than exercising its swaption. IMS then enters into a swap to receive the market fixed rate, FS, which is greater than or equal to 8 percent, and pay LIBOR. IMS is, in effect, paying a floating rate less than LIBOR (or equal to LIBOR if the market swap rate is exactly 8 percent).[32]

In Panel B(ii), the market swap rate is less than 8 percent and the loan is converted back to a floating-rate loan by exercising the swaption. IMS makes loan interest payments at LIBOR to FINSOLS and swap payment of 8 percent or $400,000 to WHD, which pays LIBOR. Exercise of the swaption results in IMS entering into a swap to receive a fixed rate of 8 percent and pay a floating rate of LIBOR. The swap and swaption would probably be structured to offset and terminate both swaps. At the end of the transaction, the loan is paid off and there are no payments on the swap or swaption. If IMS wants to continue as a fixed-rate payer, the swaption would still be exercised if it is in-the-money but not if it is out-of-the-money.

---

**31** In practice, the two parties would net the difference and have one party pay the other.
**32** In practice, IMS might choose to not enter into the swap at the market fixed rate and just carry the old swap to reduce the cost of the loan.

| Exhibit 13 | Using an American-Style Swaption to Terminate a Swap |
|---|---|

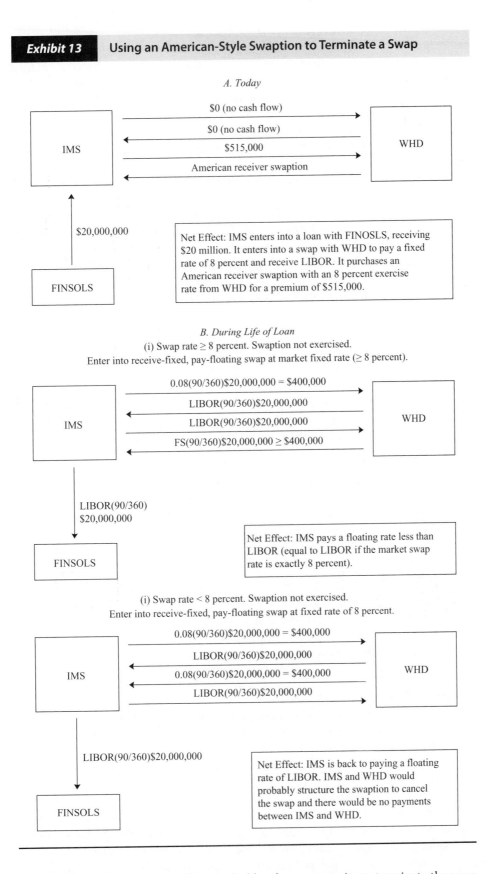

*A. Today*

$0 (no cash flow)

$0 (no cash flow)

$515,000

American receiver swaption

IMS    WHD

$20,000,000

FINSOLS

Net Effect: IMS enters into a loan with FINOSLS, receiving $20 million. It enters into a swap with WHD to pay a fixed rate of 8 percent and receive LIBOR. It purchases an American receiver swaption with an 8 percent exercise rate from WHD for a premium of $515,000.

*B. During Life of Loan*
(i) Swap rate ≥ 8 percent. Swaption not exercised.
Enter into receive-fixed, pay-floating swap at market fixed rate (≥ 8 percent).

0.08(90/360)$20,000,000 = $400,000

LIBOR(90/360)$20,000,000

LIBOR(90/360)$20,000,000

FS(90/360)$20,000,000 ≥ $400,000

IMS    WHD

LIBOR(90/360)
$20,000,000

FINSOLS

Net Effect: IMS pays a floating rate less than LIBOR (equal to LIBOR if the market swap rate is exactly 8 percent).

(i) Swap rate < 8 percent. Swaption not exercised.
Enter into receive-fixed, pay-floating swap at fixed rate of 8 percent.

0.08(90/360)$20,000,000 = $400,000

LIBOR(90/360)$20,000,000

0.08(90/360)$20,000,000 = $400,000

LIBOR(90/360)$20,000,000

IMS    WHD

LIBOR(90/360)$20,000,000

FINSOLS

Net Effect: IMS is back to paying a floating rate of LIBOR. IMS and WHD would probably structure the swaption to cancel the swap and there would be no payments between IMS and WHD.

We see that the swaption offers the holder the opportunity to terminate the swap at the exercise rate or better. Because the swaption is American style, a variety of complex issues are involved in the exercise decision, but let us focus on the moneyness and the holder's view of market conditions. If a borrower feels that rates will fall, it would then want to convert its pay-fixed position to a pay-floating position. If the market rate is more than the exercise rate, the borrower can do so by entering into a swap at the market rate. It can then receive more than the exercise rate, which more than offsets the rate it pays on the swap. The borrower would then effectively be paying less than LIBOR. If the rate in the market is less than the exercise rate, the borrower can exercise the swaption, thereby receiving the exercise rate to offset the rate it pays on the swap. Alternatively, it can choose to continue paying a floating rate but can still exercise the swaption if doing so is optimal.

As we previously described, swaptions are equivalent to options on bonds. A payer swaption is equivalent to a put option on a bond, and a receiver swaption is equivalent to a call option on a bond. The interest rate swaptions market is a very liquid one, and many companies use swaptions as substitutes for options on bonds. Any strategy that one might apply with options on bonds can be applied with swaptions. We shall not go over the myriad of such strategies, as they have been covered extensively in other literature. We shall, however, look at a particular one, in which a swaption can be used to substitute for a callable bond.

## Example 13

A company is engaged in a two-year swap with quarterly payments. It is paying 6 percent fixed and receiving LIBOR. It would like the flexibility to terminate the swap at any time prior to the end of the two-year period.

**A.** Identify the type of swaption that would achieve this objective.

**B.** Consider a time t during this two-year life of the swaption in which it is being considered for exercise. Use a 7 percent exercise rate. The fixed rate in the market on a swap that would offset the existing swap is denoted as $FS(t,2)$. Examine the payoffs of the swaption based on whether $FS(t,2)$ is 1) equal to or above 7 percent or 2) below 7 percent.

### Solution to A:

Because the company is paying a fixed rate and receiving a floating rate, it should enter into a swap to receive a fixed rate and pay a floating rate. It thus would want a receiver swaption. For maximum flexibility, it should structure the transaction as an American-style swaption.

### Solution to B:

$FS(t,2) \geq 7$ percent

The swaption is out-of-the-money and is not exercised. To terminate the existing swap, one would enter into a swap at the market rate. This swap would involve receiving the market rate $FS(t,2)$, which is at least 7 percent, and paying LIBOR. The LIBOR payments offset, and the net effect is a net positive cash flow of $FS(t,2) - 6$ percent.

$FS(t,2) < 7$ percent

Exercise the swaption, entering into a swap to receive 7 percent and pay LIBOR. The other swap involves paying 6 percent and receiving LIBOR. The LIBORs offset, leaving a net positive cash flow of $7 - 6 = 1$ percent.

Note: It is not necessary that the net cash flow be positive. The positive net cash flow here is a result of choosing a 7 percent exercise rate, but a lower exercise rate could be chosen. The higher the exercise rate, the more expensive the receiver swaption.

## 5.3 Synthetically Removing (Adding) a Call Feature in Callable (Noncallable) Debt

A callable bond is a bond in which the issuer has the right to retire it early. The issuer has considerable flexibility to take advantage of declining interest rates. This feature is like a call option on the bond. As interest rates fall, bond prices rise. By calling the bond, the issuer essentially buys back the bond at predetermined terms, making it equivalent to exercising a call option to buy the bond. The issuer pays for this right by paying a higher coupon rate on the bond.

In some cases, the issuer of a callable bond may find that it no longer expects interest rates to fall sufficiently over the remaining life of the bond to justify calling the bond. Then it would feel that it is not likely to use the call feature, but it is still paying the higher coupon rate for the call feature. A swaption can be used to effectively sell the embedded call. This strategy involves synthetically removing the call from callable debt by selling a receiver swaption.[33] A receiver swaption (receive fixed) becomes more valuable as rates decline, thus balancing the short call. In effect, the call feature is sold for cash. Recall that a receiver swaption is like a call option on a bond. Because the issuer of the callable bond holds a call on the bond, it would need to sell a call to offset the call embedded in the debt. It can effectively do so by selling a receiver swaption. This swaption will not cancel the bond's call feature. Both options will be in force, but both options should behave identically. If the call feature is worth exercising, so should the swaption. Let us see how this strategy works.

### 5.3.1 *Synthetically Removing the Call from Callable Debt*

Several years ago, Chemical Industries (CHEMIND) issued a callable $20 million face value bond that pays a fixed rate of 8 percent interest semiannually. The bond now has five years until maturity. CHEMIND does not believe it is likely to call the bond for the next two years and would like to effectively eliminate the call feature during that time. To simplify the problem somewhat, we shall assume that the bond would be called only in exactly two years and not any time sooner. Thus, CHEMIND can manage this problem by selling a European swaption that would expire in two years.[34] Because the bond would have a three-year life when it is called, the swap underlying the swaption would be a three-year swap. It would also be a swap to receive fixed and pay floating, with payment dates aligned with the interest payment dates on the bond.

Let us suppose that the 8 percent rate CHEMIND is paying on the bond includes a credit spread of 2.5 percent, which should be viewed as a credit premium paid over the LIBOR par rate. CHEMIND is paying 2.5 percent for the credit risk it poses for the holder of the bond. On the receiver swaption it wants to sell, CHEMIND must set the exercise rate at $8 - 2.5 = 5.5$ percent. Note that the credit spread is not part of the exercise rate. The swaption can be used to manage only the risk of interest rate changes driven by the term structure and not credit. We are assuming no change in CHEMIND's credit risk. Hence, it will continue to pay the credit spread in the rate on the new bond that it issues if it calls the old bond.

The swaption dealer, Top Swaps (TSWAPS), prices the swaption at $425,000. The strategy is illustrated in Exhibit 14.

---

**33** This strategy is sometimes referred to as *monetizing* a call.
**34** CHEMIND might prefer an American swaption to give it the flexibility to exercise at any time, but we simplify the problem a little and use a European swaption.

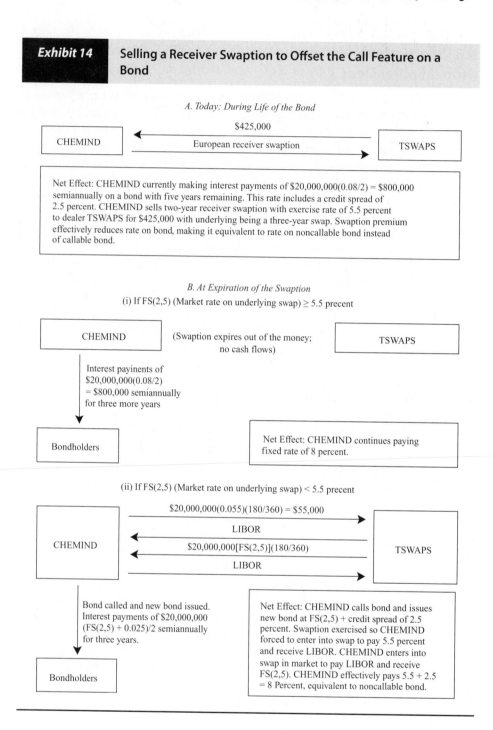

**Exhibit 14**    Selling a Receiver Swaption to Offset the Call Feature on a Bond

*A. Today; During Life of the Bond*

$425,000

CHEMIND ← European receiver swaption → TSWAPS

Net Effect: CHEMIND currently making interest payments of $20,000,000(0.08/2) = $800,000 semiannually on a bond with five years remaining. This rate includes a credit spread of 2.5 percent. CHEMIND sells two-year receiver swaption with exercise rate of 5.5 percent to dealer TSWAPS for $425,000 with underlying being a three-year swap. Swaption premium effectively reduces rate on bond, making it equivalent to rate on noncallable bond instead of callable bond.

*B. At Expiration of the Swaption*
(i) If FS(2,5) (Market rate on underlying swap) ≥ 5.5 precent

CHEMIND        (Swaption expires out of the money;        TSWAPS
                        no cash flows)

Interest payments of
$20,000,000(0.08/2)
= $800,000 semiannually
for three more years

Bondholders            Net Effect: CHEMIND continues paying fixed rate of 8 percent.

(ii) If FS(2,5) (Market rate on underlying swap) < 5.5 precent

$20,000,000(0.055)(180/360) = $55,000

LIBOR

CHEMIND        $20,000,000[FS(2,5)](180/360)        TSWAPS

LIBOR

Bond called and new bond issued. Interest payments of $20,000,000 (FS(2,5) + 0.025)/2 semiannually for three years.

Bondholders

Net Effect: CHEMIND calls bond and issues new bond at FS(2,5) + credit spread of 2.5 percent. Swaption exercised so CHEMIND forced to enter into swap to pay 5.5 percent and receive LIBOR. CHEMIND enters into swap in market to pay LIBOR and receive FS(2,5). CHEMIND effectively pays 5.5 + 2.5 = 8 Percent, equivalent to noncallable bond.

Panel A shows that CHEMIND receives $425,000 from selling the receiver swaption to dealer TSWAPS. This cash effectively reduces its remaining interest payments on the bond. In Panel B, we see what happens at the swaption expiration in two years. Remember that the swaption is identical to a call option on the bond, so if the swaption is exercised, the call on the bond will be exercised at the same time. Let FS(2,5) be the fixed rate at the swaption expiration on a three-year swap. We first assume that FS(2,5) is greater than or equal to the exercise rate on the swaption of 5.5 percent. Because interest rates have not fallen below 5.5 percent, it is unprofitable to exercise the swaption or call the bond. CHEMIND continues making interest payments of 8 percent on $20 million, which is $800,000 semiannually for three more years. Panel B(i) illustrates this outcome.

In Panel B(ii), we let FS(2,5) be less than 5.5 percent. Then the swaption will be exercised and the bond will be called. To fund the bond call, a new bond will be issued at a rate of FS(2,5) plus the credit spread of 2.5 percent, which we assume has not changed. The swaption is exercised, so CHEMIND is obligated to enter into a swap to pay 5.5 percent and receive LIBOR. Now, however, CHEMIND is receiving LIBOR and making fixed payments to its bondholders and to TSWAPS. It can reverse the LIBOR flow by entering into a swap at the market rate of FS(2,5). In other words, it enters into a new swap to receive FS(2,5) and pay LIBOR. Note from the figure that it receives LIBOR and pays LIBOR. These two flows would likely be canceled. CHEMIND makes fixed swap payments at a rate of 5.5 percent and receives fixed swap payments at a rate of FS(2,5), which is 250 basis points (the credit spread) less than the rate on the new fixed rate bond it has issued. These payments at the rate FS(2,5) offset all but the credit spread portion of the interest payments on its loan. CHEMIND then effectively pays a fixed rate of 5.5 percent, the swaption exercise rate, plus 2.5 percent, the credit spread. So, CHEMIND ends up paying 8 percent, the same as the rate on the original debt. The swaption has effectively converted the callable bond into a noncallable bond by removing the call feature from the bond. It hopes that this outcome, in which the bond is called and the swaption is exercised, does not occur, or it will regret having removed the call feature. Nonetheless, it received cash up front for the swaption and is paying a lower effective interest rate as it would had the bond been noncallable in the first place, so it must accept this risk.

### 5.3.2 *Synthetically Adding a Call to Noncallable Debt*

If a swaption can undo a call feature, it can also add a call feature. Market Solutions, Inc. (MSI) has a $40 million noncallable bond outstanding at a rate of 9 percent paid semiannually with three more years remaining. Anticipating the possibility of declining interest rates in about one year, MSI wishes this bond were callable. It can synthetically add the call feature by purchasing a receiver swaption. A receiver swaption is equivalent to a call option on a bond because the option to receive a fixed rate increases in value as rates decline. By purchasing the receiver swaption, it has in effect purchased an option on the bond.

To structure the receiver swaption properly, MSI notes that the interest rate it is paying on the bond includes a credit spread of 3 percent over the par bond rate from the LIBOR term structure. It should set the exercise rate on the swaption at 9 − 3 = 6 percent. The swaption will be on a two-year swap with payment dates coinciding with the interest payment dates on the bond. The notional principal will be the $40 million face value on the bond. To simplify the problem, we assume a European swaption, meaning that the only time MSI will consider exercising the swaption or calling the bond will be in exactly one year, with the bond having two years to maturity at that time. The swaption will cost $625,000, and the counterparty dealer will be Swap Shop (SWSHP). Exhibit 15 illustrates the transaction.

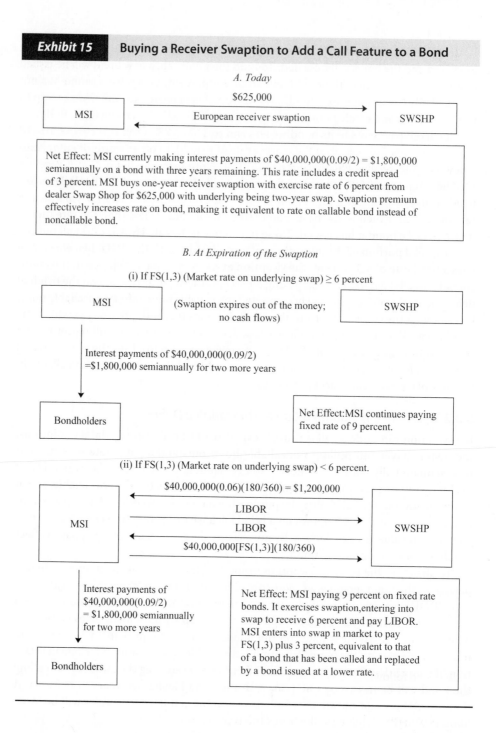

**Exhibit 15   Buying a Receiver Swaption to Add a Call Feature to a Bond**

*A. Today*

MSI — $625,000 → SWSHP
MSI ← European receiver swaption — SWSHP

Net Effect: MSI currently making interest payments of $40,000,000(0.09/2) = $1,800,000 semiannually on a bond with three years remaining. This rate includes a credit spread of 3 percent. MSI buys one-year receiver swaption with exercise rate of 6 percent from dealer Swap Shop for $625,000 with underlying being two-year swap. Swaption premium effectively increases rate on bond, making it equivalent to rate on callable bond instead of noncallable bond.

*B. At Expiration of the Swaption*

(i) If FS(1,3) (Market rate on underlying swap) ≥ 6 percent

MSI       (Swaption expires out of the money;       SWSHP
              no cash flows)

Interest payments of $40,000,000(0.09/2)
=$1,800,000 semiannually for two more years

Bondholders

Net Effect:MSI continues paying fixed rate of 9 percent.

(ii) If FS(1,3) (Market rate on underlying swap) < 6 percent.

$40,000,000(0.06)(180/360) = $1,200,000
LIBOR
LIBOR
$40,000,000[FS(1,3)](180/360)

MSI                                              SWSHP

Interest payments of
$40,000,000(0.09/2)
= $1,800,000 semiannually
for two more years

Bondholders

Net Effect: MSI paying 9 percent on fixed rate bonds. It exercises swaption,entering into swap to receive 6 percent and pay LIBOR. MSI enters into swap in market to pay FS(1,3) plus 3 percent, equivalent to that of a bond that has been called and replaced by a bond issued at a lower rate.

In Panel A, we see MSI paying $625,000 for the swaption. This cost effectively raises the interest rate MSI pays on the bond to that of a callable bond. Panel B(i) illustrates the case in which the fixed rate on the underlying swap, FS(1,3), is greater than or equal to the exercise rate on the swaption at the swaption expiration. Remember that if market conditions are such that the swaption would be exercised, then the bond would be called. In this case, however, interest rates are not low enough to justify exercise of the swaption or calling of the bond. MSI will continue making its 9 percent interest payments on the bond.

In Panel B(ii), we let FS(1,3) be less than 6 percent. Then MSI will exercise the swaption, thereby entering into a swap to pay LIBOR and receive 6 percent. Note, however, that it is receiving a fixed rate of 6 percent, paying a fixed rate of 9 percent, and paying LIBOR. Here, this transaction is not equivalent to it having called the bond, because MSI makes floating payments. To offset the floating payments, it enters into a new swap in the market at the market rate of FS(1,3). Specifically, it pays FS(1,3) and receives LIBOR. The two streams of LIBOR payments would offset and would probably be canceled, leaving an inflow of 6 percent and an outflow of FS(1,3) on the swaps and an outflow of 9 percent on the bond. The net effect would be an outflow of FS(1,3) plus 3 percent. Because FS(1,3) is below 6 percent, the overall rate paid is below 9 percent, thereby making this position similar to that of a bond that has been called, with a new bond issued in its place at a lower rate.

So we see that a swaption can be used to replicate the call feature on a callable bond. A swaption can synthetically add a call feature when it does not exist or offset a call feature that does exist. The cash paid or received from the swaption occurs all at once, but if allocated appropriately over time, it would be equivalent to the additional amount of interest that a borrower pays for the call feature. Of course, there are some tricky elements to making this strategy work. We have ignored taxes and transaction costs, which can affect exercise and call decisions. Also, when the swaption is held by another party, there is no guarantee that exercise will occur at the optimal time.

---

**Example 14**

A German company issues a five-year noncallable bond with a face value of €40 million. The bond pays a coupon annually of 10 percent, of which 3 percent is estimated to be a credit premium.

**A.** The company would like to make the bond callable in exactly two years. Design a strategy using a European swaption that will achieve this goal. When the swaption expires, the fixed rate on the underlying swap will be denoted as FS(2,5). Evaluate what happens when this rate is at least the exercise rate and also when it is less than the exercise rate.

**B.** Reconsider the bond described above and assume it was actually issued as a callable bond with a 10 percent coupon. Construct a swaption strategy that will synthetically remove the call feature. As in Part A, let the swaption expire in two years and evaluate the outcomes.

**Solution to A:**

To synthetically add the call feature to this bond, the company should purchase a receiver swaption. The exercise rate should be the coupon rate on the bond minus the credit premium: 10 − 3 = 7 percent. At the swaption expiration, we have the following outcomes:

FS(2,5) ≥ 7 percent
The swaption will not be exercised, and the bond will not be called. The company continues to pay 10 percent on its bond.

FS(2,5) < 7 percent
The swaption is exercised.

Enter into swap
Receive 7 percent
Pay LIBOR

Enter into a new swap at the market rate.

Receive LIBOR
Pay FS(2,5)
Company continues to pay 10 percent on its bond
Net effect: Pay FS(2,5) + 10% − 7% = Pay FS(2,5) + 3% < 10%

The company has thus effectively issued a new bond at a lower rate. The option premium, however, effectively raised the coupon rate on the old bond to that of a callable bond.

**Solution to B:**

To synthetically remove the call feature on this bond, the company should sell a receiver swaption. The exercise rate should be the coupon rate on the bond minus the credit premium: $10 - 3 = 7$ percent. At the swaption expiration, we have the following outcomes:

FS(2,5) ≥ 7 percent
The swaption will not be exercised. The company continues to pay 10 percent on its bond.

FS(2,5) < 7 percent
　The swaption is exercised.

　　Enter into swap
　　Receive LIBOR
　　Pay 7 percent

　Enter into a new swap at the market rate.

　　Receive FS(2,5)
　　Pay LIBOR
　　Bond called. Issue new bond at FS(2,5) + 3%

　Net effect: Pay FS(2,5) + 3% + 7% − FS(2,5) = 10%

Therefore, if the company sells the receiver swaption, the bond's call option is offset and effectively removed. The option premium, received up front, effectively reduces the coupon rate on the outstanding bond to make it equivalent to that of a noncallable bond.

---

Finally, you may be wondering why a receiver swaption was used in these strategies. Why not a payer swaption? Remember that a call feature on a bond is a call option. To add or offset a call feature, we need to use an instrument equivalent to a call option. A receiver swaption is equivalent to a call option. A payer swaption is equivalent to a put option. Payer swaptions would be useful in situations involving put features. Putable bonds do exist but are not particularly common. A putable bond allows the bondholder to sell the bond back, usually at par, to the issuer. Therefore, the option, which is a put, is held by the bondholder and sold by the bond issuer. If a bond is putable, the coupon rate on the bond would be lower. If the issuer of the bond wanted to synthetically add a put to an otherwise nonputable bond, it would sell a payer swaption. The premium received would effectively lower the coupon rate on the bond. If the issuer of a putable bond wanted to eliminate the put, it would buy a payer swaption. This would give it the right to exercise the swaption, which is a put on the bond, at the same time as the put feature would be exercised by the holder of the bond. Again, we note that put features are not common, and we shall not pursue this strategy here.

## 5.4 A Note on Forward Swaps

There are also forward contracts on swaps. Called forward swaps, these instruments are commitments to enter into swaps. They do not require a cash payment at the start but force the parties to enter into a swap at a later date at terms, including the fixed rate, set at the start. Although we shall not examine forward swap strategies, note that the same strategies examined in this section can all be used with forward swaps.

## CONCLUSIONS

**6**

In the previous readings we saw how to use forwards, futures, options, and swaps in strategies. These instruments are designed to manage risk. Managing risk involves the buying and selling of risk, perhaps to increase the overall level of one's risk or perhaps to offset an existing risk. As we have seen, these instruments are highly leveraged. As you can imagine, proper use of derivatives requires a significant amount of expertise. More importantly, however, monitoring and control are essential ingredients for the proper use of derivatives. Managing risk is the primary justification for the use of derivatives.

## SUMMARY

- A floating-rate loan can be converted to a fixed-rate loan by entering into an interest rate swap to pay a fixed rate and receive a floating rate. The floating cash flows offset, leaving the borrower with a net fixed payment. Likewise, a fixed-rate loan can be converted to a floating-rate loan by entering into an interest rate swap to pay a floating rate and receive a fixed rate. The fixed cash flows offset, leaving the party paying a floating rate.

- To obtain the duration of an interest rate swap, consider the difference between the duration of a fixed-rate bond and the duration of a floating-rate bond. The latter is close to zero, leaving the duration of an interest rate swap close to that of a fixed-rate bond. If the party pays a fixed rate and receives a floating rate, the duration of the position is that of the equivalent floating-rate bond minus that of the equivalent fixed-rate bond.

- When a floating-rate loan is converted to a fixed-rate loan, the resulting duration is that of a fixed-rate loan. The duration of a fixed-rate loan is normally much higher than that of a floating-rate loan, which has a duration relatively close to zero. Compared with a floating-rate loan, however, a fixed-rate loan has stable cash flows, which reduce cash flow risk, but has a much greater duration, which increases market value risk.

- The notional principal on an interest rate swap added to a position to adjust its overall duration is determined by the existing duration of the portfolio, the duration of the swap, the desired duration, and the market value of the portfolio. A swap can be used to change the duration of the position without changing the market value.

- An interest rate swap can be used to manage the risk related to a structured note with a coupon at a multiple of a floating rate by adjusting the notional principal on the swap to reflect the coupon multiple for the structured note. The swap should be a receive-floating, pay-fixed swap.

- An interest rate swap can be used to manage the risk of the issuance of an inverse floating-rate note by paying the floating rate to the swap dealer. When interest rates rise (fall), the inverse floater payments decrease (increase), and this effect is passed on to the dealer, which in turn pays a fixed rate.

- A loan in one currency can be converted into a loan in another currency by entering into a currency swap in which it pays interest in one currency and receives interest in the currency in which it makes its loan interest payments. This strategy leaves the borrower paying interest in a different currency than the one in which the loan interest is paid. To offset the principal payment, the currency swap should provide for payment of the notional principal as well.

- Converting a loan in one currency into a loan in another using a currency swap can offer savings because a borrower can normally issue debt at a more attractive rate in its own currency. By entering into a swap with a dealer that can operate more efficiently in global markets, the borrower can effectively convert its domestic debt into foreign debt. In addition, by engaging in the currency swap rather than borrowing in the desired currency in the first place, the borrower takes on a small amount of credit risk that can generate savings if no default takes place.

- The party to a currency swap would make the payments be fixed or floating depending on whether a loan paired with the currency swap is made at a fixed or floating rate and whether the party wants to make payments at a fixed or floating rate. This decision is usually made based on the expected direction of interest rates.

- A series of foreign cash receipts can be combined with a currency swap with no notional principal payments to convert the receipts into domestic currency cash flows. The foreign interest payments on the currency swap must equal the amounts of the foreign cash flows.

- In a dual-currency bond, the interest is paid in one currency and the principal is paid in another. A borrower issuing a dual-currency bond can use the proceeds to buy a bond denominated in the currency of the principal repayment on the dual-currency bond. It can then enter into a currency swap with no notional principal payment, enabling it to fund the interest payments from the dual-currency bond in one currency and make interest payments in another currency.

- An equity swap can be used to provide diversification to a concentrated portfolio by having the party pay the return on the stock that makes up too large a portion of the portfolio and receive the return on a diversified market proxy.

- An equity swap can add international diversification to a domestic portfolio by having the party pay the return on a domestic market benchmark and receive the return on an international market benchmark.

- An equity swap can be used to change the allocation between stock and bond asset classes by having the party pay the return on the asset class in which it wants to reduce its exposure and receive the return on the asset class in which it wants to increase its exposure.

- A corporate insider can use an equity swap to reduce exposure to his company by paying the return on the company's stock and receiving the return on a diversified portfolio benchmark or a fixed- or floating-rate interest payment.

- There can be important implications if corporate insiders use equity swaps. Insiders can reduce their exposure without giving up their voting rights, which can lead to significant agency costs. Although it is clearly necessary for investors and analysts to gauge the exposure of corporate insiders, equity swaps can make this task more difficult.

- Equity swaps pose some difficulties not faced in interest rate and currency swaps. In particular, equity swaps can generate significant cash flow problems, resulting from the fact that equity returns can be negative, meaning that one party can be required to make both sides of payments. In addition, equity swaps can involve tracking error, in which the swap returns, which are pegged to an index, do not match the returns on the actual equity portfolio that is combined with the swap.

■ A party would use an interest rate swaption if it anticipates taking out a loan at a future date and entering into a swap to convert the loan from floating rate to fixed rate or vice versa. The swaption gives the party the right to enter into the swap at a specific fixed rate or better. The cost of this flexibility is the swaption premium paid up front.

■ An interest rate swaption can be used to provide a means of terminating a swap at a favorable rate. A party engaged in a swap can use a swap with the opposite cash flows to effectively terminate the position. By purchasing a swaption, the party can enter into this swap at a specific rate, established in advance, or take a better rate as given in the market.

■ An interest rate receiver swaption is equivalent to a call option on a bond. A party that has issued a callable bond and believes it will not call the bond can sell an interest rate receiver swaption to offset the call feature. The swaption premium received at the start offsets the higher coupon paid for the call feature on the bond. If interest rates fall enough to trigger the bond being called, the swaption will also be exercised. The party must enter into the underlying swap and can enter into an opposite swap at the market rate. The net effect is that the party ends up paying the same rate it would have paid if it had not called the bond.

■ A party that has issued a noncallable bond can synthetically add a call feature by purchasing an interest rate receiver swaption. The premium paid for the swaption effectively raises the coupon rate on the bond. If rates fall sufficiently, the receiver swaption is exercised and the party enters into the underlying swap. The party then enters into a swap in the market at the market rate. The net effect is that the party pays a lower fixed rate, as though the bond had been called.

# PRACTICE PROBLEMS FOR READING 38

1. A company has issued floating-rate notes with a maturity of one year, an interest rate of LIBOR plus 125 basis points, and total face value of $50 million. The company now believes that interest rates will rise and wishes to protect itself by entering into an interest rate swap. A dealer provides a quote on a swap in which the company will pay a fixed rate 6.5 percent and receive LIBOR. Interest is paid quarterly, and the current LIBOR is 5 percent. Indicate how the company can use a swap to convert the debt to a fixed rate. Calculate the overall net payment (including the loan) by the company. Assume that all payments will be made on the basis of 90/360.

2. Assume that you manage a $100 million bond portfolio with a duration of 1.5 years. You wish to increase the duration of the bond portfolio to 3.5 years by using a swap. Assume the duration of a fixed-rate bond is 75 percent of its maturity.

   A. Discuss whether the swap you enter into should involve paying fixed, receiving floating or paying floating, receiving fixed.

   B. Would you prefer a four-year swap with quarterly payments or a three-year swap with semiannual payments?

   C. Determine the notional principal of the swap you would prefer.

3. A company issues a leveraged floating-rate note with a face value of $5,000,000 that pays a coupon of 2.5 times LIBOR. The company plans to generate a profit by selling the notes, using the proceeds to purchase a bond with a fixed coupon rate of 7 percent a year, and hedging the risk by entering into an appropriate swap. A swap dealer provides a quote with a fixed rate of 6 percent and a floating rate of LIBOR. Discuss whether the company should enter into a swap involving paying fixed, receiving floating or paying floating, receiving fixed. Calculate the amount of the arbitrage profit the company can earn by entering into the appropriate swap. In your answer, indicate the cash flows generated at each step. Also explain what additional risk the company is taking on by doing the swap.

4. A U.S. company needs to raise €100,000,000. It plans to raise this money by issuing dollar-denominated bonds and using a currency swap to convert the dollars to euros. The company expects interest rates in both the United States and the eurozone to fall.

   A. Should the swap be structured with interest paid at a fixed or a floating rate?

   B. Should the swap be structured with interest received at a fixed or a floating rate?

5. A company based in the United Kingdom has a German subsidiary. The subsidiary generates €15,000,000 a year, received in equivalent semiannual installments of €7,500,000. The British company wishes to convert the euro cash flows to pounds twice a year. It plans to engage in a currency swap in order to lock in the exchange rate at which it can convert the euros to pounds. The current exchange rate is €1.5/£. The fixed rate on a plain vanilla currency swap in pounds is 7.5 percent per year, and the fixed rate on a plain vanilla currency swap in euros is 6.5 percent per year.

   A. Determine the notional principals in euros and pounds for a swap with semiannual payments that will help achieve the objective.

   B. Determine the semiannual cash flows from this swap.

Practice Problems and Solutions: 1–9 taken from *Analysis of Derivatives for the Chartered Financial Analyst Program,* by Don M. Chance, CFA. Copyright © 2003 by AIMR. All other problems and solutions copyright © CFA Institute.

6. A portfolio has a total market value of $105,000,000. The portfolio is allocated as follows: $65,000,000 is invested in a broadly diversified portfolio of domestic stocks, and $40,000,000 is invested in the stock of the JK Corporation. The portfolio manager wishes to reduce exposure to JK stock by $30,000,000. The manager plans to achieve this objective by entering into a three-year equity swap using the S&P 500. Assume that settlement is made at the end of each year. Also assume that after one year the return on JK stock is 4 percent and the return on the S&P 500 market index is −3 percent.

   A. Explain the structure of the equity swap.

   B. Calculate the net cash flow for the swap at the end of one year.

7. The LKS Company is a U.S.-based mutual fund company that manages a global portfolio 80 percent invested in domestic stocks and 20 percent invested in international stocks. The international component mimics the MSCI EAFE index. The total market value of the portfolio is $750,000,000. The fund manager wishes to reduce the allocation to domestic stocks to 70 percent and increase the international allocation to 30 percent. The manager plans to achieve this objective by entering into a two-year equity swap using the Russell 3000 and the EAFE index. Assume that settlement is made at the end of the first year. Also assume that after one year, the return on the Russell 3000 market index is 5 percent and the return on the EAFE index is 6 percent.

   A. Explain the structure of the equity swap.

   B. Calculate the net cash flow for the swap at the end of one year.

8. A diversified portfolio with a market value of $800,000,000 currently has the following allocations:

   | Equity | 80 percent | $640,000,000 |
   |--------|------------|--------------|
   | Bonds | 20 percent | $160,000,000 |

   The equity portion of the portfolio is allocated as follows:

   | U.S. large-cap stocks | 70 percent | $448,000,000 |
   |-----------------------|------------|--------------|
   | International stocks | 30 percent | $192,000,000 |

   The bond portion of the portfolio is allocated as follows:

   | U.S. government bonds | 80 percent | $128,000,000 |
   |-----------------------|------------|--------------|
   | U.S corporate bonds | 20 percent | $32,000,000 |

   The portfolio manager wishes to change the overall allocation of the portfolio to 75 percent equity and 25 percent bonds. Within the equity category, the new allocation is to be 75 percent U.S. large cap and 25 percent international stocks. In the bond category, the new allocation is to be 75 percent U.S. government bonds and 25 percent U.S. corporate bonds. The manager wants to use four-year swaps to achieve the desired allocations, with settlements at the end of each year. Assume that the counterparty payments or receipts are tied to LIBOR. Use generic stock or bond indices where appropriate. Indicate how the manager can use swaps to achieve the desired allocations. Construct the most efficient overall swap, in which all equivalent but opposite LIBOR payments are consolidated.

9. A company plans to borrow $20,000,000 in two years. The loan will be for three years and pay a floating interest rate of LIBOR with interest payments made every quarter. The company expects interest rates to rise in future years and thus is certain to swap the loan into a fixed-rate loan. In order to ensure that it can lock in an attractive rate, the company plans to purchase a payer swaption expiring in two years, with an exercise rate of 5 percent a year. The cost of

the swaption is $250,000, and the settlement dates coincide with the interest payment dates for the original loan. Assume LIBOR at the beginning of the settlement period is 6.5 percent a year.

**A.** Calculate the net cash flows on the first settlement date if FS(2,5) is above the exercise rate.

**B.** Calculate the net cash flows on the first settlement date if FS(2,5) is below the exercise rate.

## The following information relates to Questions 10–15 and is based on the readings on Risk Management Applications of Derivatives[1]

Catherine Gide is the risk management director of the Millau Corporation, a large, diversified, French multinational corporation with subsidiaries in Japan, the United States, and Switzerland. One of Gide's primary responsibilities is to manage Millau's currency exposure. She has the flexibility to take tactical positions in foreign exchange markets if these positions are justified by her research. Gide and her assistant, Albert Darc, are meeting to discuss how best to deal with Millau's currency exposure over the next 12 months.

Specifically, Gide is concerned about the following:

**1.** Millau has just sold a Japanese subsidiary for 65 billion yen (JPY65,000,000,000). Because of an impending tax law change, Gide wishes to wait six months before repatriating these funds. Gide plans to invest the sale proceeds in six-month Japanese government securities and hedge the currency risk by using forward contracts. Gide's research indicates that the yen will depreciate against the euro (EUR) over the next six months. Darc has gathered the exchange rate and interest rate information given in Exhibit 1. The day-count convention is 30/360.

**2.** Millau has a contract to deliver computerized machine tools to a U.S. buyer in three months. A payment of 50 million U.S. dollars (USD50,000,000) is due from the buyer at that time. Gide is concerned about the dollar weakening relative to the euro. She plans to use options to hedge this currency exposure. Specifically, Gide expects the U.S. dollar to weaken to 1.2250USD/EUR in the next three months. Euro options quotations are given in Exhibit 2. All options are European-style and expire in three months.

**3.** Darc says to Gide:

> "I believe the volatility of the USD/EUR exchange rate will soon increase by more than the market expects. We may be able to profit from this volatility increase by buying an equal number of at-the-money call and put options on the euro at the same strike price and expiration date."

**4.** Millau needs 100 million Swiss francs (CHF100,000,000) for a period of one year. Millau can issue at par a 2.8 percent one-year euro-denominated note with semiannual coupons and swap the proceeds into Swiss francs. The euro swap fixed rate is 2.3 percent and the Swiss franc swap fixed rate is 0.8 percent.

Darc tells Gide that he expects interest rates in both the euro currency zone and Switzerland to rise in the near future. Exchange rate and interest rate information is given in Exhibit 1.

---

**1** Question 12 relies on the reading "Currency Risk Management."

| Exhibit 1 | Exchange Rate and Interest Rate Information |
|---|---|

| Currency Exchange Rates | Spot | 3-Month Forward | 6-Month Forward | 1-Year Forward |
|---|---|---|---|---|
| U.S. dollars per euro (USD/EUR) | 1.1930 | 1.1970 | 1.2030 | 1.2140 |
| Japanese yen per euro (JPY/EUR) | 133.83 | 133.14 | 132.46 | 131.13 |
| Swiss francs per euro (CHF/EUR) | 1.5540 | 1.5490 | 1.5440 | 1.5340 |

| Annualized Risk-Free Interest Rates (%) | 1 Month | 3 Month | 6 Month | 1 Year |
|---|---|---|---|---|
| Euro area | 2.110 | 2.120 | 2.130 | 2.150 |
| United States | 3.340 | 3.560 | 3.770 | 3.990 |
| Japan | 0.040 | 0.056 | 0.066 | 0.090 |
| Switzerland | 0.730 | 0.750 | 0.760 | 0.780 |

| Exhibit 2 | Euro Options Quotations (Options Expire in 3 Months) |
|---|---|

| Strike (USD/EUR) | Calls on Euro (USD/EUR) | Puts on Euro (USD/EUR) |
|---|---|---|
| 1.1800 | 0.0275 | 0.0125 |
| 1.1900 | 0.0216 | 0.0161 |
| 1.2000 | 0.0169 | 0.0211 |
| 1.2100 | 0.0127 | 0.0278 |

10. If Gide uses a six-month forward currency contract to convert the yen received from the sale of the Japanese subsidiary into euros, the total amount Millau will receive is *closest* to:

    A. EUR490,714,000.

    B. EUR490,876,000.

    C. EUR491,038,000.

11. If Gide uses a six-month forward currency contract to convert the yen received from the sale of the Japanese subsidiary into euros, the annualized return in euros that Millau will realize is *closest* to:

    A. 0.066%.

    B. 2.130%.

    C. 2.196%.

12. Based on Gide's expectation for the USD/EUR rate in concern #2, Gide's *most* appropriate action with regard to the USD50,000,000 due in three months is to:

    A. remain unhedged.

    B. buy euro calls with a strike price of 1.1800USD/EUR.

    C. buy euro puts with a strike price of 1.2100USD/EUR and sell euro calls with a strike price of 1.1800USD/EUR.

**13.** Darc's statement to Gide (in concern #3) about the option strategy to use in order to profit from a volatility increase of the euro/U.S. dollar exchange rate is:

A. correct.

B. incorrect, because he is describing a strategy that benefits only from a weakening euro.

C. incorrect, because he is describing a strategy that benefits from low volatility in the exchange rate.

**14.** If Millau issues euro-denominated debt and enters into a fixed-rate currency swap (in concern #4), which of the following *best* describes transactions between Millau and the swap counterparty in six months? Millau pays the swap counterparty:

A. EUR740,026 and receives CHF400,000.

B. CHF400,000 and receives EUR740,026.

C. CHF800,000 and receives EUR900,901.

**15.** Based on Darc's interest rate expectations for the euro currency zone and Switzerland, Gide's *best* choice is to structure the currency swap so that Millau pays interest at a:

A. fixed rate and receives it at a fixed rate.

B. fixed rate and receives it at a floating rate.

C. floating rate and receives it at a floating rate.

# The following information relates to Questions 16–21 and is based on the readings on Risk Management Applications of Derivatives

Hadley Elbridge, managing director for Humber Wealth Managers, LLC, is concerned about the risk level of a client's equity portfolio. The client, Pat Cassidy, has 60 percent of this portfolio invested in two equity positions: Hop Industries and Sure Securities. Cassidy refuses to sell his shares in either company, but has agreed to use option strategies to manage these concentrated equity positions. Elbridge recommends either a collar strategy or a protective put strategy on the Hop position, and a covered call strategy on the Sure position. The options available to construct the positions are shown in Exhibit 1.

| Exhibit 1 | Equity Positions and Options Available | | | |
|-----------|--------|-------------|--------|--------------|
| **Stock** | **Shares** | **Stock Price** | **Options** | **Option Price** |
| Hop | 375,000 | $26.20 | September 25.00 put | $0.80 |
| | | | September 27.50 call | $0.65 |
| Sure | 300,000 | $34.00 | September 32.50 put | $0.85 |
| | | | September 35.00 call | $1.20 |

Cassidy makes the following comments:

Comment #1   "The Hop protective put position provides a maximum per share loss of $2.00 and a breakeven underlying price at expiration of $27.00."

Comment #2   "The Sure covered call position provides a maximum per share gain of $2.20 and a breakeven underlying price at expiration of $32.80."

Comment #3  "The general shape of a profit-and-loss graph for the protective put closely resembles the general shape of the graph for another common option position."

Elbridge also investigates whether a privately negotiated equity swap could be used to reduce the risk of the Hop and Sure holdings. A swap dealer offers Elbridge the following:

- The dealer will receive the return on 250,000 shares of Hop and 200,000 shares of Sure from Cassidy.
- The dealer will pay Cassidy the return on an equivalent dollar amount on the Russell 3000 Index.

The dealer demonstrates the quarterly cash flows of this transaction under the assumptions that Hop is up 2 percent, Sure is up 4 percent, and the Russell 3000 is up 5 percent for the quarter.

The remaining 40 percent of Cassidy's equity portfolio is invested in a diversified portfolio of equities valued at $13,350,000. Elbridge believes this portfolio is too risky, so he recommends lowering the beta of this portfolio from its current level of 1.20 to a target beta of 0.80. To accomplish this, he will use a two-month futures contract with a price (including multiplier) of $275,000 and a beta of 0.97.

16. Disregarding the initial cost of the Hop collar strategy, the value per share of the strategy at expiration with the stock at $26.90 is:
   A. $26.05.
   B. $26.20.
   C. $26.90.

17. Cassidy's Comments #1 and #2 about the Hop protective put and Sure covered call positions, respectively, are:

|    | Protective Put | Covered Call |
|----|----------------|--------------|
| A. | Correct | Correct |
| B. | Correct | Incorrect |
| C. | Incorrect | Incorrect |

18. The general shape of the profit-and-loss graph in Cassidy's Comment #3 is *most* similar to the general shape of the profit-and-loss graph for:
   A. buying a call.
   B. selling a call.
   C. buying a put.

19. If an options dealer takes the other side of the Sure option position, the dealer's initial option delta and hedging transaction, respectively, will be:

|    | Dealer's Initial Option Delta | Dealer's Hedging Transaction |
|----|-------------------------------|------------------------------|
| A. | Negative | Buy the underlying |
| B. | Positive | Buy the underlying |
| C. | Positive | Sell the underlying |

20. What is the payoff to Cassidy in the equity swap example?
   A. –$269,500.
   B. $264,500.
   C. $269,500.

21. To achieve the target beta on Cassidy's diversified stock portfolio, Elbridge would sell the following number of futures contracts (rounded to the nearest whole contract):

**A.** 13.

**B.** 20.

**C.** 27.

# Questions 22 through 27 relate to the Westfield Tool Company.[2]

The Westfield Machine Tool and Die Company (WMTC) is a U.S.-based manufacturer of cutting tools that operates production plants in the United States and Spain. WMTC's CEO has received an economic report forecasting that interest rates in the future will likely increase worldwide. He has asked WMTC's CFO, Yolanda Lopez, to examine ways by which different kinds of swaps could be used as a means of reducing the company's interest rate and currency risks.

Lopez has identified the following areas where swaps might be an attractive tool for managing risk:

- WMTC's employee pension plan portfolio
- WMTC's existing five-year bank loan
- Foreign exchange risk associated with cash flows repatriated from the operations in Spain
- New debt issue associated with upcoming expansion projects

Information regarding WMTC's pension plan portfolio is shown in Exhibit 1. Within the WMTC pension plan portfolio, the allocation within equities is heavily weighted towards the company's own stock. WMTC would like to retain these shares for corporate control purposes.

| Exhibit 1 | Pension Plan Portfolio of Westfield Machine Tool Company (in millions of US dollars) |
|---|---|
| **Equities** | |
| Diversified Equities | $200 |
| WMTC Common Stock | $400 |
| Equities Total | $600 |
| **Fixed Income (Bonds)*** | |
| Treasuries | $200 |
| Corporates | $300 |
| Fixed Income Total | $500 |
| Bond Portfolio Duration | 6 years |
| Total Portfolio Value | $1,100 |

*All bonds are fixed rate, and pay interest semiannually and on the same date.

Lopez recommends the allocation to WMTC equity be reduced to 20% of the overall equity portfolio. Lopez determines that WTMC can achieve this reallocation objective by executing an equity swap that would enable it to alter the allocation more easily and less expensively than by executing transactions in the underlying securities. Furthermore, using the equity swap would allow WMTC to retain the company shares held in the WMTC pension portfolio.

---

**2** This item set was developed by Samuel Penkar, CFA (Houston, TX, U.S.A.).

Lopez also recommends that WMTC reduce the duration of the bond portfolio by 50%. She states that, in order to achieve this duration target, WMTC should use a 6-year interest rate swap with semiannual payments. Lopez estimates the duration of the swap's fixed payments to be 75% of the swap maturity.

Lopez is also concerned about WMTC's five-year variable rate loan given the forecast of rising interest rates. Additionally, Lopez would like to use a currency swap to lock in the exchange rate when WMTC repatriates Euro cash flows from Spain into U.S. dollars over the next two years. Additional pertinent facts regarding WMTC's existing debt obligation and cash flows from Spain are provided in Exhibit 2.

| Exhibit 2 | Relevant Debt and Cash Flow Information |
|---|---|
| **Debt:** | Five-year variable rate loan. Principal amount: $10,000,000. Rate: LIBOR + 200 basis points, paid semiannually, reset every six months. Loan rate was reset today at a LIBOR of 5%. |
| **Cash Flows:** | Estimated €12 million annually to be repatriated to U.S. from operations in Spain, in equal semiannual installments. Current spot exchange rate: 1.4 USD/EUR |

To hedge the interest rate risk on the five-year variable rate loan, Lopez recommends that WMTC enter into a contract with Swap Traders International (STI), who offers an interest rate swap with a notional principal of $10 million that provides a fixed rate of 6% in exchange for LIBOR, with semiannual payments.

To hedge the currency risk associated with the cash flows to be repatriated from its operations in Spain. Lopez recommends that WMTC enter into a currency swap with semiannual payments, where the fixed swap rate in Euros is 4.5%, and the fixed swap rate in U.S. dollars is 5.00%.

WMTC also has some major expansion plans for its Spanish operations. In two years, Lopez expects that WMTC will need to raise €50 million. Lopez expects that WMTC will raise the funds using a floating interest rate loan at the prevailing LIBOR rate in 2 years with annual interest payments. Lopez is considering hedging the interest rate risk relating to the future borrowing, so she contacts STI, who offers a swaption expiring in 2 years with LIBOR as the underlying floating rate and an exercise rate of 6%.

22. Lopez will *most likely* achieve the pension plan's equity reallocation objective by entering into an equity swap whereby WMTC receives a return on:

    A. $320 million of the S&P 500 index and pays a return on $320 million of WMTC common stock.

    B. $280 million of the S&P 500 index and pays a return on $280 million of WMTC common stock.

    C. $280 million of WMTC common stock and pays a return on $280 million of the S&P 500 index.

23. To achieve the target duration for the pension plan's bond portfolio, WMTC should enter into an interest rate swap with a modified duration that is:

    A. negative, requiring WTMC to make fixed rate payments and receive floating rate payments.

    B. negative, requiring WTMC to make floating rate payments and receive fixed rate payments.

    C. positive, requiring WTMC to make fixed rate payments and receive floating rate payments.

**24.** WMTC can achieve the bond portfolio duration target by using an interest rate swap with a notional principal *closest* to:

**A.** $343 million.

**B.** $353 million.

**C.** $375 million.

**25.** If WMTC hedges the interest rate risk on the five-year variable rate loan by using the interest rate swap recommended by Lopez, the net interest payment at the first settlement date in six months would be *closest* to:

**A.** $300,000.

**B.** $400,000.

**C.** $800,000.

**26.** If WMTC hedges the currency risk relating to the cash flows from its Spanish operations using the currency swap recommended by Lopez, WMTC would generate semiannual cash inflows from the swap *closest* to:

**A.** $4.8 million.

**B.** $8.4 million.

**C.** $9.3 million.

**27.** If Lopez decides to use a swaption with STI to hedge the interest rate risk relating to the expansion loan, then Lopez should:

**A.** sell a payer swaption.

**B.** buy a payer swaption.

**C.** buy a receiver swaption.

# SOLUTIONS FOR READING 38

1. The company can enter into a swap to pay a fixed rate of 6.5 percent and receive a floating rate. The first floating payment will be at 5 percent.

   Interest payment on the floating rate note = $50,000,000(0.05 + 0.0125)(90/360) = $781,250

   Swap fixed payment = $50,000,000(0.065)(90/360) = $812,500
   Swap floating receipts = $50,000,000(0.05)(90/360) = $625,000

   The overall cash payment made by the company is $812,500 + $781,250 − $625,000 = $968,750.

2. **A.** The value of the bond portfolio is inversely related to interest rates. To increase the duration, it would be necessary to hold a position that moves inversely with the interest rates. Hence the swap should be pay floating, receive fixed.

   **B.** Duration of a four-year pay-floating, receive-fixed swap with quarterly payments = (0.75)(4) − 0.125 = 2.875

   Duration of a three-year pay-floating, receive-fixed swap with semiannual payments = (0.75)(3) − 0.25 = 2.0

   Because the objective is to increase the duration of the bond portfolio, the four-year pay-floating, receive-fixed swap is the better choice.

   **C.** The notional principal is

   $$NP = B\left(\frac{MDUR_T - MDUR_B}{MDUR_S}\right)$$

   $$NP = \$100,000,000\left(\frac{3.5 - 1.5}{2.875}\right) = \$69,565,217$$

3. Because the company has a floating-rate obligation on the floating-rate note, it should enter into a swap involving receiving a floating rate. Accordingly, the appropriate swap to hedge the risk and earn a profit would be a pay-fixed, receive-floating swap. Let LIBOR be L. Cash flows generated at each step are as follows:

   **A.** Issue leveraged floating-rate notes and pay coupon =
   L(2.5)($5,000,000) = $12,500,000L

   **B.** Buy bonds with a face value = (2.5)($5,000,000) = $12,500,000
   Receive a coupon = (0.07)($12,500,000) = $875,000

   **C.** Enter into a pay-fixed, receive-floating swap:
   Pay = (0.06)(2.5)($5,000,000) = $750,000
   Receive = L(2.5)($5,000,000) = $12,500,000L

   **D.** Net cash flow = −$12,500,000L + $875,000 − $750,000 + $12,500,000L = $125,000

   In addition to the risk of default by the bond issuer, the company is taking the credit risk of the dealer by entering into a swap. The profit of $125,000 may be compensation for taking on this additional risk.

4. **A.** The U.S. company would pay the interest rate in euros. Because it expects that the interest rate in the eurozone will fall in the future, it should choose a swap with a floating rate on the interest paid in euros to let the interest rate on its debt float down.

   **B.** The U.S. company would receive the interest rate in dollars. Because it expects that the interest rate in the United States will fall in the future, it should choose a swap with a fixed rate on the interest received in dollars to prevent the interest rate it receives from going down.

5. **A.** The semiannual cash flow that must be converted into pounds is €15,000,000/2 = €7,500,000. In order to create a swap to convert €7,500,000, the equivalent notional principals are:

   - Euro notional principal = €7,500,000/(0.065/2) = €230,769,231
   - Pound notional principal = €230,769,231/€1.5/£ = £153,846,154

   **B.** The cash flows from the swap will now be:

   - Company makes swap payment = €230,769,231(0.065/2) = €7,500,000
   - Company receives swap payment = £153,846,154(0.075/2) = £5,769,231

   The company has effectively converted euro cash receipts to pounds.

6. **A.** The portfolio manager can reduce exposure to JK stock by entering into an equity swap in which the manager:

   - pays or sells the return on $30,000,000 of JK stock.
   - receives or buys the return on $30,000,000 worth of the S&P 500.

   **B.** On the equity swap, at the end of each year, the manager will:

   $$\text{Pay } (0.04)(\$30,000,000) = \$1,200,000$$
   $$\text{Receive } (-0.03)(\$30,000,000) = -\$900,000$$
   $$(\text{Note: Receiving a negative value means paying.})$$
   $$\text{Net cash flow} = -\$1,200,000 - \$900,000 = -\$2,100,000$$

   Notice here that because the return on the index is significantly lower than the return on the stock, the swap has created a large cash flow problem.

7. **A.** The manager needs to reduce the allocation to domestic stocks by 10 percent and increase the allocation to international stocks by 10 percent. So the manager needs to reduce the allocation to domestic stocks by (0.10)($750,000,000) = $75,000,000 and increase the allocation to international stocks by $75,000,000. This can be done by entering into an equity swap in which the manager:

   - pays or sells the return on the Russell 3000 on notional principal of $75,000,000.

   - receives or buys the return on the MSCI EAFE index on notional principal of $75,000,000.

   **B.** On the equity swap, at the end of the first year, the manager will:

   $$\text{Pay } (0.05)(\$75,000,000) = \$3,750,000$$
   $$\text{Receive } (0.06)(\$75,000,000) = \$4,500,000$$

   $$\text{Net cash flow} = -\$3,750,000 + \$4,500,000 = \$750,000$$

8. The following are the current allocations, the desired new allocations, and the transactions needed to go from the current positions to the new positions.

| Stock | Current ($640 Million, 80%) | New ($600 Million, 75%) | Transaction |
|---|---|---|---|
| Large cap | $448 million (70%) | $450 million (75%) | Buy $2 million |
| International | $192 million (30%) | $150 million (25%) | Sell $42 million |

| Bonds | Current ($160 Million, 20%) | New ($200 Million, 25%) | Transaction |
|---|---|---|---|
| Government | $128 million (80%) | $150 million (75%) | Buy $22 million |
| Corporate | $ 32 million (20%) | $ 50 million (25%) | Buy $18 million |

The following swap transactions would achieve the desired allocations:

*Equity Swaps*

Receive return on U.S. large-cap index on $2,000,000
Pay LIBOR on $2,000,000
Pay return on international stock index on $42,000,000
Receive LIBOR on $42,000,000

*Fixed-Income Swaps*

Receive return on U.S. government bond index on $22,000,000
Pay LIBOR on $22,000,000
Receive return on U.S. corporate bond index on $18,000,000
Pay LIBOR on $18,000,000

The overall position involves no LIBOR payments or receipts. The portfolio receives LIBOR on $42 million on equity swaps. It pays LIBOR on $2 million on equity swaps, and $22 million and $18 million on fixed-income swaps, for a total payment of LIBOR on $42 million. Thus, overall, there are no LIBOR payments or receipts.

**9. A.** If FS(2,5) is above the exercise rate, it will be worth exercising the swaption to enter a three-year swap to pay a fixed rate of 5 percent and receive LIBOR of 6.5 percent.

Swap payments on first quarterly settlement date:

Pay $20,000,000(90/360)(0.05) = $250,000
Receive $20,000,000(90/360)(0.065) = $325,000
Loan payment = $20,000,000(90/360)(0.065) = $325,000

Net cash flow = –$250,000

**B.** If FS(2,5) is below the exercise rate, it will not be worth exercising the swaption. However, the company can enter a three-year swap to pay a fixed rate of 4 percent, for example, and receive LIBOR of 6.5 percent.

Swap payments on first quarterly settlement date:

Pay $20,000,000(90/360)(0.04) = $200,000
Receive $20,000,000(90/360)(0.065) = $325,000
Loan payment = $20,000,000(90/360)(0.065) = $325,000

Net cash flow = –$200,000

**10.** B is correct. Gide will invest the 65 billion yen for six months at 0.066% (refer to Exhibit 1). She will convert the yen to euros using the 6-month forward rate of 132.46. Solve 65,000,000,000 × [1 + (0.00066 × (180/360))]/132.46 = 490,876,114.

**11.** B is correct. Assuming that interest parity holds, if Gide uses a six-month forward to convert the yen, she should expect to earn the six-month euro rate of 2.13% as shown in Exhibit 1. As a check, you can convert 65 billion yen to euros at the spot exchange rate. Then, calculate the return associated with this number and the answer in the previous question. Converting at the spot gives 65,000,000,000/133.83 = 485,690,802. According to the previous question she actually ended up with 490,876,114. The return is (490,876,114 − 485,690,802)/485,690,802 = 0.01067616. Annualizing this six-month HPR provides the answer of 2.13%.

**12.** B is correct. If Gide remains unhedged and her expectation of a future exchange rate of 1.225 USD/EUR comes true, the $50,000,000 will convert to €40,816,327. If she buys a call on the euro (the right to buy euros with dollars) with a strike of 1.18, her effective conversion rate will be (1.18 (the strike) + 0.0275 (the call premium)) = 1.2075. Converting the dollars to euros results in $50,000,000/1.2075 = €41,407,867. This exceeds the expected amount of euros under the unhedged option. Answer C does not provide a hedge against a weaker dollar.

**13.** A is correct. Darc's statement in concern #3 describes buying a straddle. A long straddle is one way to profit from an increase in volatility as the increase in volatility will, ceteris paribus, increase the values of both the put and the call.

**14.** B is correct. In order to raise 100 million Swiss francs, Millau needs to issue bonds totaling 100,000,000 SF/1.554 = €64,350,064. To convert the euros into Swiss francs, Millau could enter into a currency swap. In a currency swap, notional amounts are exchanged at initiation. In this case, Millau will pay €64,350,064 and receive 100 million in Swiss francs. Subsequent payments do not net as they are denominated in different currencies. Remembering to adjust the given swap rates for semi-annual payments, in six months Millau will pay (0.008/2) × 100,000,000 = 400,000 Swiss francs and receive 64,350,064 × (0.023/2) = 740,026 euros.

**15.** B is correct. Darc expects interest rates in the euro zone and in Switzerland to increase. Given such an expectation, the best swap would be to pay fixed and receive floating. If the expected increases come about, the amount paid remains fixed while the amount received increases.

**16.** C is correct. If the stock price at expiration of the options is $26.90, the put will expire worthless, the call will expire worthless, and the value of the strategy will reflect solely the value of the stock.

**17.** A is correct. The protective put combines a long stock position with a long put position. The stock price of $26.20 plus the cost of the put, $0.80, provides the breakeven point for the combination, which is $27.00. If the stock price declines below $25.00, the value of the put at expiration will increase dollar-for-dollar with the stock decline. Thus, Cassidy effectively locks in a sales price of at least $25.00. At that $25.00 stock price, Cassidy loses $1.20 per share on his stock as well as the $0.80 put premium. Thus, his maximum loss is $2.00. Regarding the Sure covered call, if the Sure stock price increases above $35.00, the value of the call at expiration will increase dollar-for-dollar with increases in the share price. As Cassidy is short the call, this represents a dollar-for-dollar loss to him. Thus, the maximum gain of the covered call is the difference between today's stock price and the strike ($1.00) plus the premium received ($1.20) equals $2.20. If the stock price falls, the $1.20 premium offsets, in part, the loss. At $32.80, the $1.20 premium exactly offsets the loss on the stock. Thus, $32.80 is the breakeven point for the strategy.

**18.** A is correct. A protective put combines a long stock position with a long put. The put effectively "clips" the downside risk of the stock while allowing upside potential. A long call also exhibits a truncated downside and upside potential.

**19.** C is correct. Initially, the dealer will be long the call. Long calls have positive deltas. If stock prices fall, the value of the call will decrease, harming the dealer. To hedge the risk of a price decline, the dealer will sell the underlying.

**20.** B is correct. Multiply 250,000 shares times the price per share of Hop: $250,000 \times \$26.20 = \$6,550,000$. Multiply 200,000 shares times the price per share of Sure: $200,000 \times \$34.00 = \$6,800,000$. The total notional value of the swap is the sum of these two amounts: $\$6,550,000 + \$6,800,000 = \$13,350,000$. If Hop is up 2%, Sure is up 4%, and the Russell 3000 is up 5%, the swap cash flows will be $0.02 \times \$6,550,000$ plus $0.04 \times \$6,800,000$ equals $\$403,000$ from Eldridge to the dealer and $0.05 \times \$13,350,000 = \$667,500$ from the dealer to Eldridge. Only the net payment, $\$264,500$ from the dealer to Cassidy, is actually paid.

**21.** B is correct. The target beta is 0.80 and the dollar value of the portfolio is $\$13,350,000$. Multiply $0.80 \times \$13,350,000 = \$10,680,000$. This is the desired result. Currently, the beta of the portfolio is 1.20. Multiplying the current beta by the portfolio value generates a value of $\$16,020,000$ ($1.20 \times \$13,350,000$). The short futures position must reduce the beta-times-dollar amount by $\$5,340,000$ ($\$16,020,000 - \$10,680,000$). Given that the beta of the futures contract is 0.97, the dollar amount of futures contracts needed is $\$5,505,155$ ($\$5,340,000/0.97$). Divide this number by the per contract value of the futures contract to calculate the needed number of contracts: $\$5,505,155/\$275,000 = 20.018$ contracts. Round to 20 contracts.

**22.** B is correct. 20% of the $600 million equity portfolio is $120 million, and 80% is $480 million. WMTC needs to reduce its WMTC equity holding from it current value of $400 million to $120 million, a decrease of $280 million. This result implies an increase of $320 million in diversified equities. Hence, WMTC needs to pay a return on $280 million of WMTC equity and receive a return on $280 million of the S&P 500 index, which is a proxy for diversified equities.

**23.** A is correct. To achieve the lower target duration using an interest rate swap, Lopez needs to use an interest rate swap that has a negative modified duration, which requires a pay fixed, receive floating swap. The pay-fixed, receive-floating swap has a negative duration, because the duration of a fixed-rate bond is positive and larger than the duration of a floating-rate bond, which is near zero.

**24.** B is correct. Lopez would like to reduce the duration of the bond portfolio by 50% from 6 years to 3 years. The notional principal of the swap is calculated as:

$$[\$500,000,000 \times (6)] + [\text{notional principal} \times (MDUR_s)] = [\$500,000,000 \times (3)]$$

Solving for notional principal:

$$\text{Notional Principal} = \$500,000,000 \times (3 - 6 / MDUR_s)$$

To estimate the modified duration of the swap ($MDUR_s$), note that the swap's floating-rate payments are semiannual payments, which implies an average duration of 0.25 years. So, given Lopez's estimate of the duration of the swap's fixed payments to be 75% of the swap maturity, the modified duration of the swap ($MDUR_s$) is −4.25 years, calculated as:

$$0.25 - (0.75 \times 6) = -4.25 \text{ years};$$

Solving for notional principal:

Notional principal = $500,000,000 \times [(3 - 6)/-4.25] = \$352,941,177$, or $353 million.

**25.** B is correct. WMTC would enter the interest rate swap as the pay-fixed, receive-floating party, and the net interest payment would be $400,000. This net interest payment is calculated as:

First, the loan interest payment that WMTC owes on the loan would be calculated as:

LIBOR of 5% + 200 basis points = 7%

$10,000,000 \times (0.07/2) = \$350,000$.

On the swap, the company pays a fixed rate of 6%: $10,000,000 (0.06/2) = $300,000, and receives a floating payment equal to LIBOR: $10,000,000 (0.05/2) = $250,000.

So, the net interest payment would be: $250,000 − $350,000 − $300,000 = −$400,000, implying a net payment of $400,000.

**26.** C is correct. The notional principals for the swap, based upon the prevailing given rates, are calculated as:

WMTC receives €6 million from Spanish operations semiannually.

To make a swap payment equal to €6 million at the given 4.5% Euro fixed rate, the Euro notional principal would need to be €266,666,667, calculated as:

€6 million/(0.045/2) = €266,666,667.

Consequently, at the given spot rate of 1.4 USD/EUR, the Euro notional principal would be $373,333,333. The given fixed rate in the U.S. is 5%.

So, WMTC would make a swap payment in Euros equal to €266,666,666 × 0.0225 = €6 million and receive a swap payment in U.S. dollars of $373,333,333 × 0.025 = $9,333,333, or approximately $9.3 million.

**27.** B is correct. The buyer of a payer swaption holds the right to become the pay-fixed, receive-floating party in an interest rate swap. This arrangement would allow WMTC to hedge unknown LIBOR in two years when WMTC will need to borrow to fund the expansion.

# Glossary

**10-year moving average price/earnings** A price-to-earnings ratio in which the numerator (in a U.S. context) is defined as the real S&P 500 price index and the denominator as the moving average of the preceding 10 years of real reported earnings on the S&P 500.

**AUM fee** A fee based on assets under management; an ad valorem fee.

**Absolute-return vehicles** Investments that have no direct benchmark portfolios.

**Accounting risk** The risk associated with accounting standards that vary from country to country or with any uncertainty about how certain transactions should be recorded.

**Accreting swap** A swap where the notional amount increases over the life of the swap.

**Accumulated benefit obligation (ABO)** The present value of pension benefits, assuming the pension plan terminated immediately such that it had to provide retirement income to all beneficiaries for their years of service up to that date.

**Accumulated service** Years of service of a pension plan participant as of a specified date.

**Active management** An approach to investing in which the portfolio manager seeks to outperform a given benchmark portfolio.

**Active return** The portfolio's return in excess of the return on the portfolio's benchmark.

**Active risk** A synonym for tracking risk.

**Active-lives** The portion of a pension fund's liabilities associated with active workers.

**Active/immunization combination** A portfolio with two component portfolios: an immunized portfolio which provides an assured return over the planning horizon and a second portfolio that uses an active high-return/high-risk strategy.

**Active/passive combination** Allocation of the core component of a portfolio to a passive strategy and the balance to an active component.

**Actual extreme events** A type of scenario analysis used in stress testing. It involves evaluating how a portfolio would have performed given movements in interest rates, exchange rates, stock prices, or commodity prices at magnitudes such as occurred during past extreme market events (e.g., the stock market crash of October 1987).

**Ad valorem fees** Fees that are calculated by multiplying a percentage by the value of assets managed; also called assets under management (AUM) fees.

**Adaptive markets hypothesis** (also AMH) A hypothesis that applies principles of evolution—such as competition, adaptation, and natural selection—to financial markets in an attempt to reconcile efficient market theories with behavioral alternatives.

**Adverse selection risk** The risk associated with information asymmetry; in the context of trading, the risk of trading with a more informed trader.

**Algorithmic trading** Automated electronic trading subject to quantitative rules and user-specified benchmarks and constraints.

**Allocation/selection interaction return** A measure of the joint effect of weights assigned to both sectors and individual securities; the difference between the weight of the portfolio in a given sector and the portfolio's benchmark for that sector, times the difference between the portfolio's and the benchmark's returns in that sector, summed across all sectors.

**Alpha** Excess risk-adjusted return.

**Alpha and beta separation** An approach to portfolio construction that views investing to earn alpha and investing to establish systematic risk exposures as tasks that can and should be pursued separately.

**Alpha research** Research related to capturing excess risk-adjusted returns by a particular strategy; a way investment research is organized in some investment management firms.

**Alternative investments** Groups of investments with risk and return characteristics that differ markedly from those of traditional stock and bond investments.

**Amortizing swap** A swap where the notional amount declines over the life of the swap.

**Anchoring and adjustment** An information-processing bias in which the use of a psychological heuristic influences the way people estimate probabilities.

**Anchoring and adjustment bias** An information-processing bias in which the use of a psychological heuristic influences the way people estimate probabilities.

**Anchoring trap** The tendency of the mind to give disproportionate weight to the first information it receives on a topic.

**Angel investor** An accredited individual investing chiefly in seed and early-stage companies.

**Anomalies** Apparent deviations from market efficiency.

**Ask price** (or ask, offer price, offer) The price at which a dealer will sell a specified quantity of a security.

**Ask size** The quantity associated with the ask price.

**Asset allocation reviews** A periodic review of the appropriateness of a portfolio's asset allocation.

**Asset covariance matrix** The covariance matrix for the asset classes or markets under consideration.

**Asset swap** A swap, typically involving a bond, in which fixed bond payments are swapped for payments based on a floating rate.

**Asset-only (AO) approach** In the context of determining a strategic asset allocation, an approach that focuses on the characteristics of the assets without explicitly modeling the liabilities.

**Asset/liability management** The management of financial risks created by the interaction of assets and liabilities.

**Asset/liability management (ALM) approach** In the context of determining a strategic asset allocation, an asset/liability management approach involves explicitly modeling liabilities and adopting the allocation of assets that is optimal in relationship to funding liabilities.

**Assurity of completion** In the context of trading, confidence that trades will settle without problems under all market conditions.

**Assurity of the contract**   In the context of trading, confidence that the parties to trades will be held to fulfilling their obligations.

**Asynchronism**   A discrepancy in the dating of observations that occurs because stale (out-of-date) data may be used in the absence of current data.

**Automated trading**   Any form of trading that is not manual, including trading based on algorithms.

**Availability bias**   An information-processing bias in which people take a heuristic approach to estimating the probability of an outcome based on how easily the outcome comes to mind.

**Average effective spread**   A measure of the liquidity of a security's market. The mean effective spread (sometimes dollar weighted) over all transactions in the stock in the period under study.

**Back office**   Administrative functions at an investment firm such as those pertaining to transaction processing, record keeping, and regulatory compliance.

**Back-to-back transaction**   A transaction where a dealer enters into offsetting transactions with different parties, effectively serving as a go-between.

**Backtesting**   A method for gaining information about a model using past data. As used in reference to VAR, it is the process of comparing the number of violations of VAR thresholds over a time period with the figure implied by the user-selected probability level.

**Backwardation**   A condition in the futures markets in which the benefits of holding an asset exceed the costs, leaving the futures price less than the spot price.

**Balance of payments**   An accounting of all cash flows between residents and nonresidents of a country.

**Bancassurance**   The sale of insurance by banks.

**Barbell portfolio**   A portfolio made up of short and long maturities relative to the investment horizon date and interim coupon payments.

**Base-rate neglect**   A type of representativeness bias in which the base rate or probability of the categorization is not adequately considered.

**Basis**   The difference between the cash price and the futures price.

**Basis point value (BPV)**   Also called *present value of a basis point* or *price value of a basis point* (PVBP), the change in the bond price for a 1 basis point change in yield.

**Basis risk**   The risk that the basis will change in an unpredictable way.

**Batch auction markets**   Auction markets where multilateral trading occurs at a single price at a prespecified point in time.

**Bayes' formula**   A mathematical rule explaining how existing probability beliefs should be changed given new information; it is essentially an application of conditional probabilities.

**Bear spread**   An option strategy that involves selling a put with a lower exercise price and buying a put with a higher exercise price. It can also be executed with calls.

**Behavioral finance**   An approach to finance based on the observation that psychological variables affect and often distort individuals' investment decision making.

**Behavioral finance macro**   A focus on market level behavior that considers market anomalies that distinguish markets from the efficient markets of traditional finance.

**Behavioral finance micro**   A focus on individual level behavior that examines the behavioral biases that distinguish individual investors from the rational decision makers of traditional finance.

**Best efforts order**   A type of order that gives the trader's agent discretion to execute the order only when the agent judges market conditions to be favorable.

**Beta**   A measure of the sensitivity of a given investment or portfolio to movements in the overall market.

**Beta research**   Research related to systematic (market) risk and return; a way investment research is organized in some investment management firms.

**Bid**   (or bid price) The price at which a dealer will buy a specified quantity of a security.

**Bid price**   The price at which a dealer will buy a specified quantity of a security.

**Bid size**   The quantity associated with the bid price.

**Bid–ask spread**   The difference between the current bid price and the current ask price of a security.

**Binary credit options**   Options that provide payoffs contingent on the occurrence of a specified negative credit event.

**Block order**   An order to sell or buy in a quantity that is large relative to the liquidity ordinarily available from dealers in the security or in other markets.

**Bond-yield-plus-risk-premium method**   An approach to estimating the required return on equity which specifies that required return as a bond yield plus a risk premium.

**Bottom-up**   Focusing on company-specific fundamentals or factors such as revenues, earnings, cash flow, or new product development.

**Bounded rationality**   The notion that people have informational and cognitive limitations when making decisions and do not necessarily optimize when arriving at their decisions.

**Box spread**   An option strategy that combines a bull spread and a bear spread having two different exercise prices, which produces a risk-free payoff of the difference in the exercise prices.

**Broad market indexes**   An index that is intended to measure the performance of an entire asset class. For example, the S&P 500 Index, Wilshire 5000, and Russell 3000 indexes for U.S. common stocks.

**Broker**   An agent of a trader in executing trades.

**Brokered markets**   Markets in which transactions are largely effected through a search-brokerage mechanism away from public markets.

**Bubbles**   Episodes in which asset market prices move to extremely high levels in relation to estimated intrinsic value.

**Buffering**   With respect to style index construction, rules for maintaining the style assignment of a stock consistent with a previous assignment when the stock has not clearly moved to a new style.

**Build-up approach**   Synonym for the risk premium approach.

**Bull spread**   An option strategy that involves buying a call with a lower exercise price and selling a call with a higher exercise price. It can also be executed with puts.

**Bullet portfolio**   A portfolio made up of maturities that are very close to the investment horizon.

**Business cycle**   Fluctuations in GDP in relation to long-term trend growth, usually lasting 9–11 years.

**Business risk**   The equity risk that comes from the nature of the firm's operating activities.

**Butterfly spread**   An option strategy that combines two bull or bear spreads and has three exercise prices.

**Buy side**   Investment management companies and other investors that use the services of brokerages.

**Buy-side traders** Professional traders that are employed by investment managers and institutional investors.

**Calendar rebalancing** Rebalancing a portfolio to target weights on a periodic basis; for example, monthly, quarterly, semi-annually, or annually.

**Calendar-and-percentage-of-portfolio rebalancing** Monitoring a portfolio at regular frequencies, such as quarterly. Rebalancing decisions are then made based upon percentage-of-portfolio principles.

**Calmar ratio** The compound annualized rate of return over a specified time period divided by the absolute value of maximum drawdown over the same time period.

**Cap** A combination of interest rate call options designed to hedge a borrower against rate increases on a floating-rate loan.

**Cap rate** With respect to options, the exercise interest rate for a cap.

**Capital adequacy ratio** A measure of the adequacy of capital in relation to assets.

**Capital allocation line** A graph line that describes the combinations of expected return and standard deviation of return available to an investor from combining an optimal portfolio of risky assets with a risk-free asset.

**Capital flows forecasting approach** An exchange rate forecasting approach that focuses on expected capital flows, particularly long-term flows such as equity investment and foreign direct investment.

**Capital market expectations** (CME) Expectations concerning the risk and return prospects of asset classes.

**Caplet** Each component call option in a cap.

**Carried interest** A private equity fund manager's incentive fee; the share of the private equity fund's profits that the fund manager is due once the fund has returned the outside investors' capital.

**Carry** Another term for owning an asset, typically used to refer to commodities. (See also *carry market*).

**Carry market** A situation where the forward price is such that the return on a cash-and-carry is the risk-free rate.

**Cash balance plan** A defined-benefit plan whose benefits are displayed in individual recordkeeping accounts.

**Cash flow at risk** A variation of VAR that measures the risk to a company's cash flow, instead of its market value; the minimum cash flow loss expected to be exceeded with a given probability over a specified time period.

**Cash flow matching** An asset/liability management approach that provides the future funding of a liability stream from the coupon and matured principal payments of the portfolio. A type of dedication strategy.

**Cell-matching technique** (stratified sampling) A portfolio construction technique used in indexing that divides the benchmark index into cells related to the risk factors affecting the index and samples from index securities belonging to those cells.

**Certainty equivalent** The maximum sum of money a person would pay to participate or the minimum sum of money a person would accept to not participate in an opportunity.

**Chain-linking** A process for combining periodic returns to produce an overall time-weighted rate of return.

**Cheapest-to-deliver** A bond in which the amount received for delivering the bond is largest compared with the amount paid in the market for the bond.

**Civil law** A legal system derived from Roman law, in which judges apply general, abstract rules or concepts to particular cases. In civil systems, law is developed primarily through legislative statutes or executive action.

**Claw-back provision** With respect to the compensation of private equity fund managers, a provision that specifies that money from the fund manager be returned to investors if, at the end of a fund's life, investors have not received back their capital contributions and contractual share of profits.

**Closed-book markets** Markets in which a trader does not have real-time access to all quotes in a security.

**Closeout netting** In a bankruptcy, a process by which multiple obligations between two counterparties are consolidated into a single overall value owed by one of the counterparties to the other.

**Cobb-Douglas model** A production function (model for economic output) based on factors of labor and capital that exhibits constant returns to scale.

**Cobb-Douglas production function** A production function (model for economic output) based on factors of labor and capital that exhibits constant returns to scale.

**Cognitive dissonance** The mental discomfort that occurs when new information conflicts with previously held beliefs or cognitions.

**Cognitive errors** Behavioral biases resulting from faulty reasoning; cognitive errors stem from basic statistical, information processing, or memory errors.

**Collar** An option strategy involving the purchase of a put and sale of a call in which the holder of an asset gains protection below a certain level, the exercise price of the put, and pays for it by giving up gains above a certain level, the exercise price of the call. Collars also can be used to provide protection against rising interest rates on a floating-rate loan by giving up gains from lower interest rates.

**Collateral return** (or collateral yield) The component of the return on a commodity futures contract that comes from the assumption that the full value of the underlying futures contract is invested to earn the risk-free interest rate.

**Collateralized debt obligation** A securitized pool of fixed-income assets.

**Combination matching** (or horizon matching) A cash flow matching technique; a portfolio is duration-matched with a set of liabilities with the added constraint that it also be cash-flow matched in the first few years, usually the first five years.

**Commingled real estate funds (CREFs)** Professionally managed vehicles for substantial commingled (i.e., pooled) investment in real estate properties.

**Commitment period** The period of time over which committed funds are advanced to a private equity fund.

**Commodities** Articles of commerce such as agricultural goods, metals, and petroleum; tangible assets that are typically relatively homogeneous in nature.

**Commodity spread** Offsetting long and short positions in closely related commodities. (See also *crack spread* and *crush spread*).

**Commodity trading advisors** Registered advisors to managed futures funds.

**Common law** A legal system which draws abstract rules from specific cases. In common law systems, law is developed primarily through decisions of the courts.

**Community property regime** A marital property regime under which each spouse has an indivisible one-half interest in property received during marriage.

**Completeness fund** A portfolio that, when added to active managers' positions, establishes an overall portfolio with approximately the same risk exposures as the investor's overall equity benchmark.

**Confidence band** With reference to a quality control chart for performance evaluation, a range in which the manager's value-added returns are anticipated to fall a specified percentage of the time.

**Confidence interval** An interval that has a given probability of containing the parameter it is intended to estimate.

**Confirmation bias** A belief perseverance bias in which people tend to look for and notice what confirms their beliefs, to ignore or undervalue what contradicts their beliefs, and to misinterpret information as support for their beliefs.

**Confirming evidence trap** The bias that leads individuals to give greater weight to information that supports an existing or preferred point of view than to evidence that contradicts it.

**Conjunction fallacy** An inappropriate combining of probabilities of independent events to support a belief. In fact, the probability of two independent events occurring in conjunction is never greater than the probability of either event occurring alone; the probability of two independent events occurring together is equal to the multiplication of the probabilities of the independent events.

**Conservatism bias** A belief perseverance bias in which people maintain their prior views or forecasts by inadequately incorporating new information.

**Consistent growth** A growth investment substyle that focuses on companies with consistent growth having a long history of unit-sales growth, superior profitability, and predictable earnings.

**Constant returns to scale** A characteristic of a production function such that a given percentage increase in capital stock and labor input results in an equal percentage increase in output.

**Contango** A condition in the futures markets in which the costs of holding an asset exceed the benefits, leaving the futures price more than the spot price.

**Contingent immunization** A fixed-income strategy in which immunization serves as a fall-back strategy if the actively managed portfolio does not grow at a certain rate.

**Continuous auction markets** Auction markets where orders can be executed at any time during the trading day.

**Contrarian** A value investment substyle focusing on stocks that have been beset by problems.

**Controlled foreign corporation** A company located outside a taxpayer's home country and in which the taxpayer has a controlling interest as defined under the home country law.

**Convenience yield** The nonmonetary return offered by an asset when the asset is in short supply, often associated with assets with seasonal production processes.

**Conversion factor** An adjustment used to facilitate delivery on bond futures contracts in which any of a number of bonds with different characteristics are eligible for delivery.

**Convexity** A measure of how interest rate sensitivity changes with a change in interest rates.

**Convexity adjustment** An estimate of the change in price that is not explained by duration.

**Cooling degree-day** The greater of i) 65 degrees Fahrenheit minus the average daily temperature, and ii) zero.

**Core capital** The amount of capital required to fund spending to maintain a given lifestyle, fund goals, and provide adequate reserves for unexpected commitments.

**Core-plus** A fixed-income mandate that permits the portfolio manager to add instruments with relatively high return potential to core holdings of investment-grade debt.

**Core–satellite** A way of thinking about allocating money that seeks to define each investment's place in the portfolio in relation to specific investment goals or roles.

**Core-satellite portfolio** A portfolio in which certain investments (often indexed or semiactive) are viewed as the core and the balance are viewed as satellite investments fulfilling specific roles.

**Corner portfolio** Adjacent corner portfolios define a segment of the minimum-variance frontier within which portfolios hold identical assets and the rate of change of asset weights in moving from one portfolio to another is constant.

**Corner portfolio theorem** In a sign-constrained mean–variance optimization, the result that the asset weights of any minimum-variance portfolio are a positive linear combination of the corresponding weights in the two adjacent corner portfolios that bracket it in terms of expected return (or standard deviation of return).

**Corporate governance** The system of internal controls and procedures used to define and protect the rights and responsibilities of various stakeholders.

**Corporate venturing** Investments by companies in promising young companies in the same or a related industry.

**Country beta** A measure of the sensitivity of a specified variable (e.g., yield) to a change in the comparable variable in another country.

**Covered call** An option strategy involving the holding of an asset and sale of a call on the asset.

**Crack spread** The difference between the price of crude oil futures and that of equivalent amounts of heating oil and gasoline.

**Credit VAR** A variation of VAR related to credit risk; it reflects the minimum loss due to credit exposure with a given probability during a period of time.

**Credit default swap** A swap used to transfer credit risk to another party. A protection buyer pays the protection seller in return for the right to receive a payment from the seller in the event of a specified credit event.

**Credit derivative** A contract in which one party has the right to claim a payment from another party in the event that a specific credit event occurs over the life of the contract.

**Credit event** An event affecting the credit risk of a security or counterparty.

**Credit forwards** A type of credit derivative with payoffs based on bond values or credit spreads.

**Credit method** When the residence country reduces its taxpayers' domestic tax liability by the amount of taxes paid to a foreign country that exercises source jurisdiction.

**Credit protection seller** With respect to a credit derivative, the party that accepts the credit risk of the underlying financial asset.

**Credit risk** (or default risk) The risk of loss caused by a counterparty's or debtor's failure to make a timely payment or by the change in value of a financial instrument based on changes in default risk.

**Credit spread forward** A forward contract used to transfer credit risk to another party; a forward contract on a yield spread.

**Credit spread option** An option based on the yield spread between two securities that is used to transfer credit risk.

**Credit spread risk** The risk that the spread between the rate for a risky bond and the rate for a default risk-free bond may vary after the purchase of the risky bond.

**Credited rates** Rates of interest credited to a policyholder's reserve account.

**Cross hedging** With respect to hedging bond investments using futures, hedging when the bond to be hedged is not identical to the bond underlying the futures contract. With respect to currency hedging, a hedging technique that uses two currencies other than the home currency.

**Cross-default provision** A provision stipulating that if a borrower defaults on any outstanding credit obligations, the borrower is considered to be in default on all obligations.

**Crush spread** The difference between the price of a quantity of soybeans and that of the soybean meal and oil that can be produced by those soybeans.

**Currency return** The percentage change in the spot exchange rate stated in terms of home currency per unit of foreign currency.

**Currency risk** The risk associated with the uncertainty about the exchange rate at which proceeds in the foreign currency can be converted into the investor's home currency.

**Currency swap** A swap in which the parties make payments based on the difference in debt payments in different currencies.

**Currency-hedged instruments** Investment in nondomestic assets in which currency exposures are neutralized.

**Current credit risk** (or jump-to-default risk) The risk of credit-related events happening in the immediate future; it relates to the risk that a payment currently due will not be paid.

**Cushion spread** The difference between the minimum acceptable return and the higher possible immunized rate.

**Custom security-based benchmark** A custom benchmark created by weighting a manager's research universe using the manager's unique weighting approach.

**Cyclical stocks** The shares of companies whose earnings have above-average sensitivity to the business cycle.

**Day traders** Traders that rapidly buy and sell stocks in the hope that the stocks will continue to rise or fall in value for the seconds or minutes they are prepared to hold a position. Day traders hold a position open somewhat longer than a scalper but closing all positions at the end of the day.

**Dealer** (or market maker) A business entity that is ready to buy an asset for inventory or sell an asset from inventory to provide the other side of an order.

**Decision price** (also called arrival price or strike price) The prevailing price when the decision to trade is made.

**Decision risk** The risk of changing strategies at the point of maximum loss.

**Deduction method** When the residence country allows taxpayers to reduce their taxable income by the amount of taxes paid to foreign governments in respect of foreign-source income.

**Deemed dispositions** Tax treatment that assumes property is sold. It is sometimes seen as an alternative to estate or inheritance tax.

**Deemed distribution** When shareholders of a controlled foreign corporation are taxed as if the earnings were distributed to shareholders, even though no distribution has been made.

**Default risk** The risk of loss if an issuer or counterparty does not fulfill its contractual obligations.

**Default risk premium** Compensation for the possibility that the issue of a debt instrument will fail to make a promised payment at the contracted time and in the contracted amount.

**Default swap** A contract in which the swap buyer pays a regular premium; in exchange, if a default in a specified bond occurs, the swap seller pays the buyer the loss due to the default.

**Defaultable debt** Debt with some meaningful amount of credit risk.

**Deferred swap** A swap with terms specified today, but for which swap payments begin at a later date than for an ordinary swap.

**Defined-benefit plan** A pension plan that specifies the plan sponsor's obligations in terms of the benefit to plan participants.

**Defined-contribution plan** A pension plan that specifies the sponsor's obligations in terms of contributions to the pension fund rather than benefits to plan participants.

**Deflation** A decrease in the general level of prices; an increase in the purchasing power of a unit of currency.

**Delay costs** (or slippage) Implicit trading costs that arise from the inability to complete desired trades immediately due to order size or market liquidity.

**Delivery option** The feature of a futures contract giving the short the right to make decisions about what, when, and where to deliver.

**Delta** The relationship between the option price and the underlying price, which reflects the sensitivity of the price of the option to changes in the price of the underlying.

**Delta hedge** An option strategy in which a position in an asset is converted to a risk-free position with a position in a specific number of options. The number of options per unit of the underlying changes through time, and the position must be revised to maintain the hedge.

**Delta-normal method** A measure of VAR equivalent to the analytical method but that refers to the use of delta to estimate the option's price sensitivity.

**Demand deposit** A deposit that can be drawn upon without prior notice, such as a checking account.

**Demutualizing** The process of converting an insurance company from mutual form to stock.

**Descriptive statistics** Methods for effectively summarizing data to describe important aspects of a dataset.

**Diff swap** A swap in which payments are based on the difference in floating interest rates on a given notional amount denominated in a single currency.

**Differential returns** Returns that deviate from a manager's benchmark.

**Diffusion index** An index that measures how many indicators are pointing up and how many are pointing down.

**Direct commodity investment** Commodity investment that involves cash market purchase of physical commodities or exposure to changes in spot market values via derivatives, such as futures.

**Direct market access** Platforms sponsored by brokers that permit buy-side traders to directly access equities, fixed income, futures, and foreign exchange markets, clearing via the broker.

**Direct quotation** Quotation in terms of domestic currency/ foreign currency.

**Discounted cash flow models** (DCF models) Valuation models that express the idea that an asset's value is the present value of its (expected) cash flows.

**Discretionary trust** A trust structure in which the trustee determines whether and how much to distribute in the sole discretion of the trustee.

**Disintermediation** To withdraw funds from financial intermediaries for placement with other financial intermediaries offering a higher return or yield. Or, to withdraw funds from a financial intermediary for the purposes of direct investment, such as withdrawing from a mutual fund to make direct stock investments.

**Disposition effect**   As a result of loss aversion, an emotional bias whereby investors are reluctant to dispose of losers. This results in an inefficient and gradual adjustment to deterioration in fundamental value.

**Distressed debt arbitrage**   A distressed securities investment discipline that involves purchasing the traded bonds of bankrupt companies and selling the common equity short.

**Distressed securities**   Securities of companies that are in financial distress or near bankruptcy; the name given to various investment disciplines employing securities of companies in distress.

**Diversification effect**   In reference to VAR across several portfolios (for example, across an entire firm), this effect equals the difference between the sum of the individual VARs and total VAR.

**Dividend recapitalization**   A method by which a buyout fund can realize the value of a holding; involves the issuance of debt by the holding to finance a special dividend to owners.

**Dollar duration**   A measure of the change in portfolio value for a 100 bps change in market yields.

**Double inflection utility function**   A utility function that changes based on levels of wealth.

**Downgrade risk**   The risk that one of the major rating agencies will lower its rating for an issuer, based on its specified rating criteria.

**Downside deviation**   A measure of volatility using only rate of return data points below the investor's minimum acceptable return.

**Downside risk**   Risk of loss or negative return.

**Due diligence**   Investigation and analysis in support of an investment action or recommendation, such as the scrutiny of operations and management and the verification of material facts.

**Duration**   A measure of the approximate sensitivity of a security to a change in interest rates (i.e., a measure of interest rate risk).

**Dynamic approach**   With respect to strategic asset allocation, an approach that accounts for links between optimal decisions at different points in time.

**ESG risk**   The risk to a company's market valuation resulting from environmental, social, and governance factors.

**Earnings at risk (EAR)**   A variation of VAR that reflects the risk of a company's earnings instead of its market value.

**Earnings momentum**   A growth investment substyle that focuses on companies with earnings momentum (high quarterly year-over-year earnings growth).

**Econometrics**   The application of quantitative modeling and analysis grounded in economic theory to the analysis of economic data.

**Economic exposure**   The risk associated with changes in the relative attractiveness of products and services offered for sale, arising out of the competitive effects of changes in exchange rates.

**Economic indicators**   Economic statistics provided by government and established private organizations that contain information on an economy's recent past activity or its current or future position in the business cycle.

**Economic surplus**   The market value of assets minus the present value of liabilities.

**Effective duration**   Duration adjusted to account for embedded options.

**Effective spread**   Two times the distance between the actual execution price and the midpoint of the market quote at the time an order is entered; a measure of execution costs that captures the effects of price improvement and market impact.

**Efficient frontier**   The graph of the set of portfolios that maximize expected return for their level of risk (standard deviation of return); the part of the minimum-variance frontier beginning with the global minimum-variance portfolio and continuing above it.

**Electronic communications networks (ECNs)**   Computer-based auctions that operate continuously within the day using a specified set of rules to execute orders.

**Emerging market debt**   The sovereign debt of nondeveloped countries.

**Emotional biases**   Behavioral biases resulting from reasoning influenced by feelings; emotional biases stem from impulse or intuition.

**Endogenous variable**   A variable whose values are determined within the system.

**Endowment bias**   An emotional bias in which people value an asset more when they hold rights to it than when they do not.

**Endowments**   Long-term funds generally owned by operating nonprofit institutions such as universities and colleges, museums, hospitals, and other organizations involved in charitable activities.

**Enhanced derivatives products companies**   (or special purpose vehicles) A type of subsidiary separate from an entity's other activities and not liable for the parent's debts. They are often used by derivatives dealers to control exposure to ratings downgrades.

**Enterprise risk management**   An overall assessment of a company's risk position. A centralized approach to risk management sometimes called firmwide risk management.

**Equal probability rebalancing**   Rebalancing in which the manager specifies a corridor for each asset class as a common multiple of the standard deviation of the asset class's returns. Rebalancing to the target proportions occurs when any asset class weight moves outside its corridor.

**Equal weighted**   In an equal-weighted index, each stock in the index is weighted equally.

**Equitized**   Given equity market systematic risk exposure.

**Equity $q$**   The ratio of a company's equity market capitalization divided by net worth measured at replacement cost.

**Equity risk premium**   Compensation for the additional risk of equity compared with debt.

**Equity-indexed annuity**   A type of life annuity that provides a guarantee of a minimum fixed payment plus some participation in stock market gains, if any.

**Estate**   All of the property a person owns or controls; may consist of financial assets, tangible personal assets, immovable property, or intellectual property.

**Estate planning**   The process of preparing for the disposition of one's estate (e.g., the transfer of property) upon death and during one's lifetime.

**Eurozone**   The region of countries using the euro as a currency.

**Ex post alpha**   (or Jensen's alpha) The average return achieved in a portfolio in excess of what would have been predicted by CAPM given the portfolio's risk level; an after-the-fact measure of excess risk-adjusted return.

**Excess capital**   An investor's capital over and above that which is necessary to fund their lifestyle and reserves.

**Excess currency return**   The expected currency return in excess of the forward premium or discount.

**Exchange**   A regulated venue for the trading of investment instruments.

**Exchange fund**   A fund into which several investors place their different share holdings in exchange for shares in the diversified fund itself.

**Execution uncertainty**   Uncertainty pertaining to the timing of execution, or if execution will even occur at all.

**Exemption method**   When the residence country imposes no tax on foreign-source income by providing taxpayers with an exemption, in effect having only one jurisdiction impose tax.

**Exogenous shocks**   Events from outside the economic system that affect its course. These could be short-lived political events, changes in government policy, or natural disasters, for example.

**Exogenous variable**   A variable whose values are determined outside the system.

**Externality**   Those consequences of a transaction (or process) that do not fall on the parties to the transaction (or process).

**Factor covariance matrix**   The covariance matrix of factors.

**Factor push**   A simple stress test that involves pushing prices and risk factors of an underlying model in the most disadvantageous way to estimate the impact of factor extremes on the portfolio's value.

**Factor sensitivities**   (also called factor betas or factor loadings) In a multifactor model, the responsiveness of the dependent variable to factor movements.

**Factor-model-based benchmark**   A benchmark that is created by relating one or more systematic sources of returns (factors or exposures) to returns of the benchmark.

**Fallen angels**   Debt that has crossed the threshold from investment grade to high yield.

**Fed model**   An equity valuation model that relates the earnings yield on the S&P 500 to the yield to maturity on 10-year U.S. Treasury bonds.

**Federal funds rate**   The interest rate on overnight loans of reserves (deposits) between U.S. Federal Reserve System member banks.

**Fee cap**   A limit on the total fee paid regardless of performance.

**Fiduciary**   A person or entity standing in a special relation of trust and responsibility with respect to other parties.

**Financial capital**   As used in the text, an individual investor's investable wealth; total wealth minus human capital. Consists of assets that can be traded such as cash, stocks, bonds, and real estate.

**Financial equilibrium models**   Models describing relationships between expected return and risk in which supply and demand are in balance.

**Financial risk**   Risks derived from events in the external financial markets, such as changes in equity prices, interest rates, or currency exchange rates.

**Fiscal policy**   Government activity concerning taxation and governmental spending.

**Fixed annuity**   A type of life annuity in which periodic payments are fixed in amount.

**Fixed trust**   A trust structure in which distributions to beneficiaries are prescribed in the trust document to occur at certain times or in certain amounts.

**Fixed-rate payer**   The party to an interest rate swap that is obligated to make periodic payments at a fixed rate.

**Flexible-premium variable life**   (or variable universal life) A type of life insurance policy that combines the flexibility of universal life with the investment choice flexibility of variable life.

**Floating supply of shares**   (or free float) The number of shares outstanding that are actually available to investors.

**Floating-rate payer**   The party to an interest rate swap that is obligated to make periodic payments based on a benchmark floating rate.

**Floor**   A combination of interest rate options designed to provide protection against interest rate decreases.

**Floor broker**   An agent of the broker who, for certain exchanges, physically represents the trade on the exchange floor.

**Floorlet**   Each component put option in a floor.

**Forced heirship rules**   Legal ownership principles whereby children have the right to a fixed share of a parent's estate.

**Formal tools**   Established research methods amenable to precise definition and independent replication of results.

**Forward curve**   The set of forward or futures prices with different expiration dates on a given date for a given asset.

**Forward discount**   (or forward premium) The forward rate less the spot rate, divided by the spot rate; called the forward discount if negative, and forward premium if positive.

**Forward hedging**   Hedging that involves the use of a forward contract between the foreign asset's currency and the home currency.

**Forward strip**   Another name for the *forward curve*.

**Foundations**   Typically, grant-making institutions funded by gifts and investment assets.

**Fourth market**   A term occasionally used for direct trading of securities between institutional investors; the fourth market would include trading on electronic crossing networks.

**Framing**   An information-processing bias in which a person answers a question differently based on the way in which it is asked (framed).

**Framing bias**   An information-processing bias in which a person answers a question differently based on the way in which it is asked (framed).

**Front office**   The revenue generating functions at an investment firm such as those pertaining to trading and sales.

**Front-run**   To trade ahead of the initiator, exploiting privileged information about the initiator's trading intentions.

**Full replication**   When every issue in an index is represented in the portfolio, and each portfolio position has approximately the same weight in the fund as in the index.

**Fully funded plan**   A pension plan in which the ratio of the value of plan assets to the present value of plan liabilities is 100 percent or greater.

**Functional duration**   (or multifunctional duration) The key rate duration.

**Fund of funds**   A fund that invests in a number of underlying funds.

**Fundamental law of active management**   The relation that the information ratio of a portfolio manager is approximately equal to the information coefficient multiplied by the square root of the investment discipline's breadth (the number of independent, active investment decisions made each year).

**Funded status**   The relationship between the value of a plan's assets and the present value of its liabilities.

**Funding ratio**   A measure of the relative size of pension assets compared to the present value of pension liabilities. Calculated by dividing the value of pension assets by the present value of pension liabilities. Also referred to as the funded ratio or funded status.

**Funding risk**   The risk that liabilities funding long asset positions cannot be rolled over at reasonable cost.

**Futures contract**   An enforceable contract between a buyer (seller) and an established exchange or its clearinghouse in which the buyer (seller) agrees to take (make) delivery of something at a specified price at the end of a designated period of time.

**Futures price**   The price at which the parties to a futures contract agree to exchange the underlying.

**Gain-to-loss ratio**   The ratio of positive returns to negative returns over a specified period of time.

**Gamblers' fallacy**   A misunderstanding of probabilities in which people wrongly project reversal to a long-term mean.

**Gamma**   A numerical measure of the sensitivity of delta to a change in the underlying's value.

**Global custodian**   An entity that effects trade settlement, safekeeping of assets, and the allocation of trades to individual custody accounts.

**Global investable market**   A practical proxy for the world market portfolio consisting of traditional and alternative asset classes with sufficient capacity to absorb meaningful investment.

**Global minimum-variance (GMV) portfolio**   The portfolio on the minimum-variance frontier with smallest variance of return.

**Gold standard currency system**   A currency regime under which currency could be freely converted into gold at established rates.

**Gordon (constant) growth model**   A version of the dividend discount model for common share value that assumes a constant growth rate in dividends.

**Government structural policies**   Government policies that affect the limits of economic growth and incentives within the private sector.

**Grinold–Kroner model**   An expression for the expected return on a share as the sum of an expected income return, an expected nominal earnings growth return, and an expected repricing return.

**Growth in total factor productivity**   A component of trend growth in GDP that results from increased efficiency in using capital inputs; also known as technical progress.

**Guaranteed investment contract**   A debt instrument issued by insurers, usually in large denominations, that pays a guaranteed, generally fixed interest rate for a specified time period.

**H-model**   A variant of the two-stage dividend discount model in which growth begins at a high rate and declines linearly throughout the supernormal growth period until it reaches a normal growth rate that holds in perpetuity.

**Hague Conference on Private International Law**   An intergovernmental organization working toward the convergence of private international law. Its 69 members consist of countries and regional economic integration organizations.

**Halo effect**   An emotional bias that extends a favorable evaluation of some characteristics to other characteristics.

**Heating degree-day**   The greater of i) the average daily temperature minus 65 degree Fahrenheit, and ii) zero.

**Hedge funds**   A historically loosely regulated, pooled investment vehicle that may implement various investment strategies.

**Hedge ratio**   The relationship of the quantity of an asset being hedged to the quantity of the derivative used for hedging.

**Hedged return**   The foreign asset return in local currency terms plus the forward discount (premium).

**Hedging**   A general strategy usually thought of as reducing, if not eliminating, risk.

**Herding**   When a group of investors trade on the same side of the market in the same securities, or when investors ignore their own private information and act as other investors do.

**High yield**   A value investment substyle that focuses on stocks offering high dividend yield with prospects of maintaining or increasing the dividend.

**High-water mark**   A specified net asset value level that a fund must exceed before performance fees are paid to the hedge fund manager.

**High-yield investing**   A distressed securities investment discipline that involves investment in high-yield bonds perceived to be undervalued.

**Hindsight bias**   A bias with selective perception and retention aspects in which people may see past events as having been predictable and reasonable to expect.

**Historical simulation method**   The application of historical price changes to the current portfolio.

**Holdings-based style analysis**   An approach to style analysis that categorizes individual securities by their characteristics and aggregates results to reach a conclusion about the overall style of the portfolio at a given point in time.

**Home bias**   An anomaly by which portfolios exhibit a strong bias in favor of domestic securities in the context of global portfolios.

**Human capital**   (or net employment capital) An implied asset; the present value of expected future labor income.

**Hybrid markets**   Combinations of market types, which offer elements of batch auction markets and continuous auction markets, as well as quote-driven markets.

**Hypothetical events**   A type of scenario analysis used in stress testing that involves the evaluation of performance given events that have never happened in the markets or market outcomes to which we attach a small probability.

**Illiquidity premium**   Compensation for the risk of loss relative to an investment's fair value if an investment needs to be converted to cash quickly.

**Illusion of control**   A bias in which people tend to believe that they can control or influence outcomes when, in fact, they cannot. Illusion of knowledge and self-attribution biases contribute to the overconfidence bias.

**Illusion of control bias**   A bias in which people tend to believe that they can control or influence outcomes when, in fact, they cannot. Illusion of knowledge and self-attribution biases contribute to the overconfidence bias.

**Immunization**   An asset/liability management approach that structures investments in bonds to match (offset) liabilities' weighted-average duration; a type of dedication strategy.

**Immunized time horizon**   The time horizon over which a portfolio's value is immunized; equal to the portfolio duration.

**Implementation shortfall**   The difference between the money return on a notional or paper portfolio and the actual portfolio return.

**Implementation shortfall strategy**   (or arrival price strategy) A strategy that attempts to minimize trading costs as measured by the implementation shortfall method.

**Implied yield**   A measure of the yield on the underlying bond of a futures contract implied by pricing it as though the underlying will be delivered at the futures expiration.

**Incremental VAR**   A measure of the incremental effect of an asset on the VAR of a portfolio by measuring the difference between the portfolio's VAR while including a specified asset and the portfolio's VAR with that asset eliminated.

**Indexing**   A common passive approach to investing that involves holding a portfolio of securities designed to replicate the returns on a specified index of securities.

**Indifference curve analysis** A decision-making approach whereby curves of consumption bundles, among which the decision-maker is indifferent, are constructed to identify and choose the curve within budget constraints that generates the highest utility.

**Indirect commodity investment** Commodity investment that involves the acquisition of indirect claims on commodities, such as equity in companies specializing in commodity production.

**Inferential statistics** Methods for making estimates or forecasts about a larger group from a smaller group actually observed.

**Inflation** An increase in the general level of prices; a decrease in the purchasing power of a unit of currency.

**Inflation hedge** An asset whose returns are sufficient on average to preserve purchasing power during periods of inflation.

**Inflation premium** Compensation for expected inflation.

**Information coefficient** The correlation between forecast and actual returns.

**Information ratio** The mean excess return of the account over the benchmark (i.e., mean active return) relative to the variability of that excess return (i.e., tracking risk); a measure of risk-adjusted performance.

**Information-motivated traders** Traders that seek to trade on information that has limited value if not quickly acted upon.

**Infrastructure funds** Funds that make private investment in public infrastructure projects in return for rights to specified revenue streams over a contracted period.

**Initial public offering** The initial issuance of common stock registered for public trading by a formerly private corporation.

**Input uncertainty** Uncertainty concerning whether the inputs are correct.

**Inside ask** (or market ask) The lowest available ask price.

**Inside bid** (or market bid) The highest available bid price.

**Inside bid–ask spread** (also called market bid–ask spread, inside spread, or market spread) Market ask price minus market bid price.

**Inside quote** (or market quote) Combination of the highest available bid price with the lowest available ask price.

**Inside spread** (also called market bid–ask spread, inside bid–ask spread, or market spread) Market ask price minus market bid price.

**Institutional investors** Corporations or other legal entities that ultimately serve as financial intermediaries between individuals and investment markets.

**Interest rate management effect** With respect to fixed-income attribution analysis, a return component reflecting how well a manager predicts interest rate changes.

**Interest rate parity** A formula that expresses the equivalence or parity of spot and forward rates, after adjusting for differences in the interest rates.

**Interest rate risk** Risk related to changes in the level of interest rates.

**Interest rate swap** A contract between two parties (counterparties) to exchange periodic interest payments based on a specified notional amount of principal.

**Interest spread** With respect to banks, the average yield on earning assets minus the average percent cost of interest-bearing liabilities.

**Internal rate of return** The growth rate that will link the ending value of the account to its beginning value plus all intermediate cash flows; money-weighted rate of return is a synonym.

**Intestate** Having made no valid will; a decedent without a valid will or with a will that does not dispose of their property is considered to have died intestate.

**Inventory cycle** A cycle measured in terms of fluctuations in inventories, typically lasting 2–4 years.

**Inverse floater** A floating-rate note or bond in which the coupon is adjusted to move opposite to a benchmark interest rate.

**Investment skill** The ability to outperform an appropriate benchmark consistently over time.

**Investment style** A natural grouping of investment disciplines that has some predictive power in explaining the future dispersion in returns across portfolios.

**Investment style indexes** Indices that represent specific portions of an asset category. For example, subgroups within the U.S. common stock asset category such as large-capitalization growth stocks.

**Investor's benchmark** The benchmark an investor uses to evaluate performance of a given portfolio or asset class.

**Irrevocable trust** A trust arrangement wherein the settlor has no ability to revoke the trust relationship.

**J factor risk** The risk associated with a judge's track record in adjudicating bankruptcies and restructuring.

**Joint ownership with right of survivorship** Jointly owned; assets held in joint ownership with right of survivorship automatically transfer to the surviving joint owner or owners outside the probate process.

**Justified P/E** The price-to-earnings ratio that is fair, warranted, or justified on the basis of forecasted fundamentals.

**Key rate duration** A method of measuring the interest rate sensitivities of a fixed-income instrument or portfolio to shifts in key points along the yield curve.

**Lagging economic indicators** A set of economic variables whose values correlate with recent past economic activity.

**Leading economic indicators** A set of economic variables whose values vary with the business cycle but at a fairly consistent time interval before a turn in the business cycle.

**Legal/contract risk** The possibility of loss arising from the legal system's failure to enforce a contract in which an enterprise has a financial stake; for example, if a contract is voided through litigation.

**Leverage-adjusted duration gap** A leverage-adjusted measure of the difference between the durations of assets and liabilities which measures a bank's overall interest rate exposure.

**Leveraged floating-rate note** (leveraged floater) A floating-rate note or bond in which the coupon is adjusted at a multiple of a benchmark interest rate.

**Liability** As used in the text, a financial obligation.

**Life annuity** An annuity that guarantees a monthly income to the annuitant for life.

**Lifetime gratuitous transfer** A lifetime gift made during the lifetime of the donor; also known as *inter vivos* transfers.

**Limit order** An instruction to execute an order when the best price available is at least as good as the limit price specified in the order.

**Linear programming** Optimization in which the objective function and constraints are linear.

**Liquidity** The ability to trade without delay at relatively low cost and in relatively large quantities.

**Liquidity risk** Any risk of economic loss because of the need to sell relatively less liquid assets to meet liquidity requirements; the risk that a financial instrument cannot be purchased or sold without a significant concession in price because of the market's potential inability to efficiently accommodate the desired trading size.

**Liquidity-motivated traders**   Traders that are motivated to trade based upon reasons other than an information advantage. For example, to release cash proceeds to facilitate the purchase of another security, adjust market exposure, or fund cash needs.

**Lock-up period**   A minimum initial holding period for investments during which no part of the investment can be withdrawn.

**Locked up**   Said of investments that cannot be traded at all for some time.

**Logical participation strategies**   Protocols for breaking up an order for execution over time. Typically used by institutional traders to participate in overall market volumes without being unduly visible.

**Longevity risk**   The risk of outliving one's financial resources.

**Loss-aversion bias**   A bias in which people tend to strongly prefer avoiding losses as opposed to achieving gains.

**Low P/E**   A value investment substyle that focuses on shares selling at low prices relative to current or normal earnings.

**M²**   A measure of what a portfolio would have returned if it had taken on the same total risk as the market index.

**Macaulay duration**   The percentage change in price for a percentage change in yield. The term, named for one of the economists who first derived it, is used to distinguish the calculation from modified duration. (See also *modified duration*).

**Macro attribution**   Performance attribution analysis conducted on the fund sponsor level.

**Macro expectations**   Expectations concerning classes of assets.

**Managed futures**   Pooled investment vehicles, frequently structured as limited partnerships, that invest in futures and options on futures and other instruments.

**Manager continuation policies**   Policies adopted to guide the manager evaluations conducted by fund sponsors. The goal of manager continuation policies is to reduce the costs of manager turnover while systematically acting on indications of future poor performance.

**Manager monitoring**   A formal, documented procedure that assists fund sponsors in consistently collecting information relevant to evaluating the state of their managers' operations; used to identify warning signs of adverse changes in existing managers' organizations.

**Manager review**   A detailed examination of a manager that currently exists within a plan sponsor's program. The manager review closely resembles the manager selection process, in both the information considered and the comprehensiveness of the analysis. The staff should review all phases of the manager's operations, just as if the manager were being initially hired.

**Market ask**   The lowest available ask price.

**Market bid**   The best available bid; highest price any buyer is currently willing to pay.

**Market bid–ask spread**   (also called inside bid–ask spread, inside spread, or market spread) Market ask price minus market bid price.

**Market fragmentation**   A condition whereby a market contains no dominant group of sellers (or buyers) that are large enough to unduly influence the market.

**Market impact**   (or price impact) The effect of the trade on transaction prices.

**Market integration**   The degree to which there are no impediments or barriers to capital mobility across markets.

**Market microstructure**   The market structures and processes that affect how the manager's interest in buying or selling an asset is translated into executed trades (represented by trade prices and volumes).

**Market model**   A regression equation that specifies a linear relationship between the return on a security (or portfolio) and the return on a broad market index.

**Market on close order**   A market order to be executed at the closing of the market.

**Market on open order**   A market order to be executed at the opening of the market.

**Market order**   An instruction to execute an order as soon as possible in the public markets at the best price available.

**Market oriented**   With reference to equity investing, an intermediate grouping for investment disciplines that cannot be clearly categorized as value or growth.

**Market quote**   (or inside quote) Combination of the highest available bid price with the lowest available ask price.

**Market risk**   The risk associated with interest rates, exchange rates, and equity prices.

**Market segmentation**   The degree to which there are some meaningful impediments to capital movement across markets.

**Market spread**   (also called market bid–ask spread, inside spread, or Inside bid–ask spread) Market ask price minus market bid price.

**Market-adjusted implementation shortfall**   The difference between the money return on a notional or paper portfolio and the actual portfolio return, adjusted using beta to remove the effect of the return on the market.

**Market-not-held order**   A variation of the market order designed to give the agent greater discretion than a simple market order would allow. "Not held" means that the floor broker is not required to trade at any specific price or in any specific time interval.

**Marking to market**   A procedure used primarily in futures markets in which the parties to a contract settle the amount owed daily. Also known as the *daily settlement*.

**Mass affluent**   An industry term for a segment of the private wealth marketplace that is not sufficiently wealthy to command certain individualized services.

**Matrix prices**   Prices determined by comparisons to other securities of similar credit risk and maturity; the result of matrix pricing.

**Matrix pricing**   An approach for estimating the prices of thinly traded securities based on the prices of securities with similar attributions, such as similar credit rating, maturity, or economic sector.

**Maturity premium**   Compensation for the increased sensitivity of the market value of debt to a change in market interest rates as maturity is extended.

**Maturity variance**   A measure of how much a given immunized portfolio differs from the ideal immunized portfolio consisting of a single pure discount instrument with maturity equal to the time horizon.

**Maximum loss optimization**   A stress test in which we would try to optimize mathematically the risk variable that would produce the maximum loss.

**Mega-cap buy-out funds**   A class of buyout funds that take public companies private.

**Mental accounting bias**   An information-processing bias in which people treat one sum of money differently from another equal-sized sum based on which mental account the money is assigned to.

**Micro attribution**   Performance attribution analysis carried out on the investment manager level.

**Micro expectations**   Expectations concerning individual assets.

**Middle-market buy-out funds**   A class of buyout funds that purchase private companies whose revenues and profits are too small to access capital from the public equity markets.

**Midquote**   The halfway point between the market bid and ask prices.

**Minimum-variance frontier**   The graph of the set of portfolios with smallest variances of return for their levels of expected return.

**Missed trade opportunity costs**   Unrealized profit/loss arising from the failure to execute a trade in a timely manner.

**Model risk**   The risk that a model is incorrect or misapplied; in investments, it often refers to valuation models.

**Model uncertainty**   Uncertainty concerning whether a selected model is correct.

**Modified duration**   An adjustment of the duration for the level of the yield. Contrast with *Macaulay duration*.

**Monetary policy**   Government activity concerning interest rates and the money supply.

**Money markets**   Markets for fixed-income securities with maturities of one year or less.

**Money-weighted rate of return**   Same as the internal rate of return; the growth rate that will link the ending value of the account to its beginning value plus all intermediate cash flows.

**Mortality risk**   The risk of loss of human capital in the event of premature death.

**Multifactor model**   A model that explains a variable in terms of the values of a set of factors.

**Multifactor model technique**   With respect to construction of an indexed portfolio, a technique that attempts to match the primary risk exposures of the indexed portfolio to those of the index.

**Multiperiod Sharpe ratio**   A Sharpe ratio based on the investment's multiperiod wealth in excess of the wealth generated by the risk-free investment.

**Mutuals**   With respect to insurance companies, companies that are owned by their policyholders, who share in the company's surplus earnings.

**Natural liquidity**   An extensive pool of investors who are aware of and have a potential interest in buying and/or selling a security.

**Net employment capital**   See human capital.

**Net interest margin**   With respect to banks, net interest income (interest income minus interest expense) divided by average earning assets.

**Net interest spread**   With respect to the operations of insurers, the difference between interest earned and interest credited to policyholders.

**Net worth**   The difference between the market value of assets and liabilities.

**Net worth tax or net wealth tax**   A tax based on a person's assets, less liabilities.

**Nominal default-free bonds**   Conventional bonds that have no (or minimal) default risk.

**Nominal gross domestic product**   (nominal GDP) A money measure of the goods and services produced within a country's borders.

**Nominal risk-free interest rate**   The sum of the real risk-free interest rate and the inflation premium.

**Nominal spread**   The spread of a bond or portfolio above the yield of a Treasury of equal maturity.

**Nonfinancial risk**   Risks that arise from sources other than the external financial markets, such as changes in accounting rules, legal environment, or tax rates.

**Nonparametric**   Involving minimal probability-distribution assumptions.

**Nonstationarity**   A property of a data series that reflects more than one set of underlying statistical properties.

**Normal portfolio**   A portfolio with exposure to sources of systematic risk that are typical for a manager, using the manager's past portfolios as a guide.

**Notional amount**   The dollar amount used as a scale factor in calculating payments for a forward contract, futures contract, or swap.

**Notional principal amount**   The amount specified in a swap that forms the basis for calculating payment streams.

**Objective function**   A quantitative expression of the objective or goal of a process.

**Open market operations**   The purchase or sale by a central bank of government securities, which are settled using reserves, to influence interest rates and the supply of credit by banks.

**Open outcry auction market**   Public auction where representatives of buyers and sellers meet at a specified location and place verbal bids and offers.

**Operational risk**   The risk of loss from failures in a company's systems and procedures (for example, due to computer failures or human failures) or events completely outside of the control of organizations (which would include "acts of God" and terrorist actions).

**Opportunistic participation strategies**   Passive trading combined with the opportunistic seizing of liquidity.

**Optimization**   With respect to portfolio construction, a procedure for determining the best portfolios according to some criterion.

**Optimizer**   A heuristic, formula, algorithm, or program that uses risk, return, correlation, or other variables to determine the most appropriate asset allocation or asset mix for a portfolio.

**Option-adjusted spread (OAS)**   The current spread over the benchmark yield minus that component of the spread that is attributable to any embedded optionality in the instrument.

**Options on futures**   (futures options) Options on a designated futures contract.

**Options on physicals**   With respect to options, exchange-traded option contracts that have cash instruments rather than futures contracts on cash instruments as the underlying.

**Order-driven markets**   Markets in which transaction prices are established by public limit orders to buy or sell a security at specified prices.

**Ordinary life insurance**   (also whole life insurance) A type of life insurance policy that involves coverage for the whole of the insured's life.

**Orphan equities investing**   A distressed securities investment discipline that involves investment in orphan equities that are perceived to be undervalued.

**Orphan equity**   Investment in the newly issued equity of a company emerging from reorganization.

**Output gap**   The difference between the value of GDP estimated as if the economy were on its trend growth path (potential output) and the actual value of GDP.

**Overall trade balance**   The sum of the current account (reflecting exports and imports) and the financial account (consisting of portfolio flows).

**Overconfidence bias**  A bias in which people demonstrate unwarranted faith in their own intuitive reasoning, judgments, and/or cognitive abilities.

**Overconfidence trap**  The tendency of individuals to overestimate the accuracy of their forecasts.

**Pairs trade**  (or pairs arbitrage) A basic long–short trade in which an investor is long and short equal currency amounts of two common stocks in a single industry.

**Panel method**  A method of capital market expectations setting that involves using the viewpoints of a panel of experts.

**Partial correlation**  In multivariate problems, the correlation between two variables after controlling for the effects of the other variables in the system.

**Partial fill**  Execution of a purchase or sale for fewer shares than was stipulated in the order.

**Participate (do not initiate) order**  A variant of the market-not-held order. The broker is deliberately low-key and waits for and responds to the initiatives of more active traders.

**Passive management**  A buy-and-hold approach to investing in which an investor does not make portfolio changes based upon short-term expectations of changing market or security performance.

**Passive traders**  Traders that seek liquidity in their rebalancing transactions, but are much more concerned with the cost of trading.

**Payer swaption**  A swaption that allows the holder to enter into a swap as the fixed-rate payer and floating-rate receiver.

**Payment netting**  A means of settling payments in which the amount owed by the first party to the second is netted with the amount owed by the second party to the first; only the net difference is paid.

**Pension funds**  Funds consisting of assets set aside to support a promise of retirement income.

**Pension surplus**  Pension assets at market value minus the present value of pension liabilities.

**Percentage-of-portfolio rebalancing**  Rebalancing is triggered based on set thresholds stated as a percentage of the portfolio's value.

**Percentage-of-volume strategy**  A logical participation strategy in which trading takes place in proportion to overall market volume (typically at a rate of 5–20 percent) until the order is completed.

**Perfect markets**  Markets without any frictional costs.

**Performance appraisal**  The evaluation of portfolio performance; a quantitative assessment of a manager's investment skill.

**Performance attribution**  A comparison of an account's performance with that of a designated benchmark and the identification and quantification of sources of differential returns.

**Performance evaluation**  The measurement and assessment of the outcomes of investment management decisions.

**Performance measurement**  A component of performance evaluation; the relatively simple procedure of calculating an asset's or portfolio's rate of return.

**Performance netting risk**  For entities that fund more than one strategy and have asymmetric incentive fee arrangements with the portfolio managers, the potential for loss in cases where the net performance of the group of managers generates insufficient fee revenue to fully cover contractual payout obligations to all portfolio managers with positive performance.

**Performance-based fee**  Fees specified by a combination of a base fee plus an incentive fee for performance in excess of a benchmark's.

**Periodic auction markets**  Auction markets where multilateral trading occurs at a single price at a prespecified point in time.

**Permanent income hypothesis**  The hypothesis that consumers' spending behavior is largely determined by their long-run income expectations.

**Plan sponsor**  An enterprise or organization—such as a business, labor union, municipal or state government, or not-for-profit organization—that sets up a pension plan.

**Pledging requirement**  With respect to banks, a required collateral use of assets.

**Point estimate**  A single-valued estimate of a quantity, as opposed to an estimate in terms of a range of values.

**Policy portfolio**  A synonym of strategic asset allocation; the portfolio resulting from strategic asset allocation considered as a process.

**Policyholder reserves**  With respect to an insurance company, an amount representing the estimated payments to policyholders, as determined by actuaries, based on the types and terms of the various insurance policies issued by the company.

**Political risk**  (or geopolitical risk) The risk of war, government collapse, political instability, expropriation, confiscation, or adverse changes in taxation.

**Portable**  Moveable. With reference to a pension plan, one in which a plan participant can move his or her share of plan assets to a new plan, subject to certain rules, vesting schedules, and possible tax penalties and payments.

**Portable alpha**  A strategy involving the combining of multiple positions (e.g., long and short positions) so as to separate the alpha (unsystematic risk) from beta (systematic risk) in an investment.

**Portfolio segmentation**  The creation of subportfolios according to the product mix for individual segments or lines of business.

**Portfolio trade**  (also known as program trade or basket trade) A trade in which a number of securities are traded as a single unit.

**Position a trade**  To take the other side of a trade, acting as a principal with capital at risk.

**Post-trade transparency**  Degree to which completed trades are quickly and accurately reported to the public.

**Potential output**  The value of GDP if the economy were on its trend growth path.

**Preferred return**  With respect to the compensation of private equity fund managers, a hurdle rate.

**Premium**  Regarding life insurance, the asset paid by the policy holder to an insurer who, in turn, has a contractual obligation to pay death benefit proceeds to the beneficiary named in the policy.

**Prepackaged bankruptcy**  A bankruptcy in which the debtor seeks agreement from creditors on the terms of a reorganization before the reorganization filing.

**Prepaid swap**  A contract calling for payment today and delivery of the asset or commodity at multiple specified times in the future.

**Present value distribution of cash flows**  A list showing what proportion of a portfolio's duration is attributable to each future cash flow.

**Present value of a basis point (PVBP)**  The change in the bond price for a 1 basis point change in yield. Also called *basis point value* (BPV).

**Pretrade transparency**   Ability of individuals to quickly, easily, and inexpensively obtain accurate information about quotes and trades.

**Price discovery**   Adjustment of transaction prices to balance supply and demand.

**Price improvement**   Execution at a price that is better than the price quoted at the time of order placement.

**Price risk**   The risk of fluctuations in market price.

**Price uncertainty**   Uncertainty about the price at which an order will execute.

**Price value of a basis point**   (also PVBP) The change in the bond price for a 1 basis point change in yield. Also called *basis point value* (BPV).

**Price weighted**   With respect to index construction, an index in which each security in the index is weighted according to its absolute share price.

**Priced risk**   Risk for which investors demand compensation.

**Primary risk factors**   With respect to valuation, the major influences on pricing.

**Prime brokerage**   A suite of services that is often specified to include support in accounting and reporting, leveraged trade execution, financing, securities lending (related to short-selling activities), and start-up advice (for new entities).

**Principal trade**   A trade with a broker in which the broker commits capital to facilitate the prompt execution of the trader's order to buy or sell.

**Private equity**   Ownership interests in non-publicly-traded companies.

**Private equity funds**   Pooled investment vehicles investing in generally highly illiquid assets; includes venture capital funds and buyout funds.

**Private exchange**   A method for handling undiversified positions with built-in capital gains in which shares that are a component of an index are exchanged for shares of an index mutual fund in a privately arranged transaction with the fund.

**Private placement memorandum**   A document used to raise venture capital financing when funds are raised through an agent.

**Probate**   The legal process to confirm the validity of a will so that executors, heirs, and other interested parties can rely on its authenticity.

**Profit-sharing plans**   A defined-contribution plan in which contributions are based, at least in part, on the plan sponsor's profits.

**Projected benefit obligation (PBO)**   A measure of a pension plan's liability that reflects accumulated service in the same manner as the ABO but also projects future variables, such as compensation increases.

**Prospect theory**   An alternative to expected utility theory, it assigns value to gains and losses (changes in wealth) rather than to final wealth, and probabilities are replaced by decision weights. In prospect theory, the shape of a decision maker's value function is assumed to differ between the domain of gains and the domain of losses.

**Protective put**   An option strategy in which a long position in an asset is combined with a long position in a put.

**Proxy hedging**   Hedging that involves the use of a forward contract between the home currency and a currency that is highly correlated with the foreign asset's currency.

**Prudence trap**   The tendency to temper forecasts so that they do not appear extreme; the tendency to be overly cautious in forecasting.

**Public good**   A good that is not divisible and not excludable (a consumer cannot be denied it).

**Purchasing power parity**   The theory that movements in an exchange rate should offset any difference in the inflation rates between two countries.

**Pure sector allocation return**   A component of attribution analysis that relates relative returns to the manager's sector-weighting decisions. Calculated as the difference between the allocation (weight) of the portfolio to a given sector and the portfolio's benchmark weight for that sector, multiplied by the difference between the sector benchmark's return and the overall portfolio's benchmark return, summed across all sectors.

**Quality control charts**   A graphical means of presenting performance appraisal data; charts illustrating the performance of an actively managed account versus a selected benchmark.

**Quality option**   (or swap option) With respect to Treasury futures, the option of which acceptable Treasury issue to deliver.

**Quantitative easing**   A policy measure in which a central bank buys financial assets to inject a predetermined quantity of money in the financial system.

**Quote-driven markets**   (or dealer markets) Markets that rely on dealers to establish firm prices at which securities can be bought and sold.

**Quoted depth**   The number of shares available for purchase or sale at the quoted bid and ask prices.

**Rate duration**   A fixed-income instrument's or portfolio's sensitivity to a change in key maturity, holding constant all other points along the yield curve.

**Ratio spread**   An option strategy in which a long position in a certain number of options is offset by a short position in a certain number of other options on the same underlying, resulting in a risk-free position.

**Rational economic man**   A self-interested, risk-averse individual who has the ability to make judgments using all available information in order to maximize his/her expected utility.

**Re-base**   With reference to index construction, to change the time period used as the base of the index.

**Real estate**   Interests in land or structures attached to land.

**Real estate investment trusts (REITs)**   Publicly traded equities representing pools of money invested in real estate properties and/or real estate debt.

**Real option**   An option involving decisions related to tangible assets or processes.

**Real risk-free interest rate**   The single-period interest rate for a completely risk-free security if no inflation were expected.

**Rebalancing ratio**   A quantity involved in reestablishing the dollar duration of a portfolio to a desired level, equal to the original dollar duration divided by the new dollar duration.

**Recallability trap**   The tendency of forecasts to be overly influenced by events that have left a strong impression on a person's memory.

**Receiver swaption**   A swaption that allows the holder to enter into a swap as the fixed-rate receiver and floating-rate payer.

**Recession**   A broad-based economic downturn, conventionally defined as two successive quarterly declines in GDP.

**Reference entity**   An entity, such as a bond issuer, specified in a derivatives contract.

**Regime**   A distinct governing set of relationships.

**Regret**   The feeling that an opportunity has been missed; typically an expression of *hindsight bias*.

**Regret-aversion bias**   An emotional bias in which people tend to avoid making decisions that will result in action out of fear that the decision will turn out poorly.

**Regulatory risk**   The risk associated with the uncertainty of how a transaction will be regulated or with the potential for regulations to change.

**Reinvestment risk**   The risk of reinvesting coupon income or principal at a rate less than the original coupon or purchase rate.

**Relative economic strength forecasting approach**   An exchange rate forecasting approach that suggests that a strong pace of economic growth in a country creates attractive investment opportunities, increasing the demand for the country's currency and causing it to appreciate.

**Relative strength indicators**   A price momentum indicator that involves comparing a stock's performance during a specific period either to its own past performance or to the performance of some group of stocks.

**Remaindermen**   Beneficiaries of a trust; having a claim on the residue.

**Representativeness bias**   A belief perseverance bias in which people tend to classify new information based on past experiences and classifications.

**Repurchase agreement**   A contract involving the sale of securities such as Treasury instruments coupled with an agreement to repurchase the same securities at a later date.

**Repurchase yield**   The negative of the expected percent change in number of shares outstanding, in the Grinold–Kroner model.

**Resampled efficient frontier**   The set of resampled efficient portfolios.

**Resampled efficient portfolio**   An efficient portfolio based on simulation.

**Residence jurisdiction**   A framework used by a country to determine the basis for taxing income, based on residency.

**Residence–residence conflict**   When two countries claim residence of the same individual, subjecting the individual's income to taxation by both countries.

**Residence–source conflict**   When tax jurisdiction is claimed by an individual's country of residence and the country where some of their assets are sourced; the most common source of double taxation.

**Residue**   With respect to trusts, the funds remaining in a trust when the last income beneficiary dies.

**Retired-lives**   The portion of a pension fund's liabilities associated with retired workers.

**Returns-based benchmarks**   Benchmarks that are constructed using 1) a series of a manager's account returns and 2) the series of returns on several investment style indexes over the same period. These return series are then submitted to an allocation algorithm that solves for the combination of investment style indexes that most closely tracks the account's returns.

**Returns-based style analysis**   An approach to style analysis that focuses on characteristics of the overall portfolio as revealed by a portfolio's realized returns.

**Reverse optimization**   A technique for reverse engineering the expected returns implicit in a diversified market portfolio.

**Revocable trust**   A trust arrangement wherein the settlor (who originally transfers assets to fund the trust) retains the right to rescind the trust relationship and regain title to the trust assets.

**Risk budgeting**   The establishment of objectives for individuals, groups, or divisions of an organization that takes into account the allocation of an acceptable level of risk.

**Risk exposure**   A source of risk. Also, the state of being exposed or vulnerable to a risk.

**Risk premium approach**   An approach to forecasting the return of a risky asset that views its expected return as the sum of the risk-free rate of interest and one or more risk premiums.

**Risk profile**   A detailed tabulation of the index's risk exposures.

**Risk tolerance**   The capacity to accept risk; the level of risk an investor (or organization) is willing and able to bear.

**Risk tolerance function**   An assessment of an investor's tolerance to risk over various levels of portfolio outcomes.

**Roll return**   (or roll yield) The component of the return on a commodity futures contract that comes from rolling long futures positions forward through time.

**Rolling return**   The moving average of the holding-period returns for a specified period (e.g., a calendar year) that matches the investor's time horizon.

**Sample estimator**   A formula for assigning a unique value (a point estimate) to a population parameter.

**Sample-size neglect**   A type of representativeness bias in which financial market participants incorrectly assume that small sample sizes are representative of populations (or "real" data).

**Sandwich spread**   An option strategy that is equivalent to a short butterfly spread.

**Satisfice**   A combination of "satisfy" and "suffice" describing decisions, actions, and outcomes that may not be optimal, but are adequate.

**Savings–investment imbalances forecasting approach**   An exchange rate forecasting approach that explains currency movements in terms of the effects of domestic savings–investment imbalances on the exchange rate.

**Scenario analysis**   A risk management technique involving the examination of the performance of a portfolio under specified situations. Closely related to *stress testing*.

**Secondary offering**   An offering after the initial public offering of securities.

**Sector/quality effect**   In a fixed-income attribution analysis, a measure of a manager's ability to select the "right" issuing sector and quality group.

**Security selection effect**   In a fixed-income attribution analysis, the residual of the security's total return after other effects are accounted for; a measure of the return due to ability in security selection.

**Segmentation**   With respect to the management of insurance company portfolios, the notional subdivision of the overall portfolio into sub-portfolios each of which is associated with a specified group of insurance contracts.

**Self-attribution bias**   A bias in which people take personal credit for successes and attribute failures to external factors outside the individual's control.

**Self-control bias**   A bias in which people fail to act in pursuit of their long-term, overarching goals because of a lack of self-discipline.

**Sell side**   Broker/dealers that sell securities and make recommendations for various customers, such as investment managers and institutional investors.

**Semiactive management**   (also called enhanced indexing or risk-controlled active management) A variant of active management. In a semiactive portfolio, the manager seeks to outperform a given benchmark with tightly controlled risk relative to the benchmark.

**Semivariance**   A measure of downside risk. The average of squared deviations that fall below the mean.

**Separate property regime**   A marital property regime under which each spouse is able to own and control property as an individual.

**Settlement date**   (payment date) The designated date at which the parties to a trade must transact.

**Settlement netting risk**   The risk that a liquidator of a counterparty in default could challenge a netting arrangement so that profitable transactions are realized for the benefit of creditors.

**Settlement risk**   When settling a contract, the risk that one party could be in the process of paying the counterparty while the counterparty is declaring bankruptcy.

**Settlor (or grantor)**   An entity that transfers assets to a trustee, to be held and managed for the benefit of the trust beneficiaries.

**Shari'a**   The law of Islam. In addition to the law of the land, some follow guidance provided by Shari'a or Islamic law.

**Sharpe ratio**   (or reward-to-variability) A measure of risk-adjusted performance that compares excess returns to the total risk of the account, where total risk is measured by the account's standard deviation of returns.

**Shortfall risk**   The risk that portfolio value will fall below some minimum acceptable level during a stated time horizon; the risk of not achieving a specified return target.

**Shrinkage estimation**   Estimation that involves taking a weighted average of a historical estimate of a parameter and some other parameter estimate, where the weights reflect the analyst's relative belief in the estimates.

**Shrinkage estimator**   The formula used in shrinkage estimation of a parameter.

**Sign-constrained optimization**   An optimization that constrains asset class weights to be nonnegative and to sum to 1.

**Smart routing**   The use of algorithms to intelligently route an order to the most liquid venue.

**Smoothing rule**   With respect to spending rates, a rule that averages asset values over a period of time in order to dampen the spending rate's response to asset value fluctuation.

**Social proof**   A bias in which individuals tend to follow the beliefs of a group.

**Socially responsible investing**   (ethical investing) An approach to investing that integrates ethical values and societal concerns with investment decisions.

**Soft dollars**   (also called soft dollar arrangements or soft commissions) The use of commissions to buy services other than execution services.

**Sole ownership**   Owned by one person; assets held in sole ownership are typically considered part of a decedent's estate. The transfer of their ownership is dictated by the decedent's will through the probate process.

**Solow residual**   A measure of the growth in total factor productivity that is based on an economic growth model developed by economist Robert M. Solow.

**Sortino ratio**   A performance appraisal ratio that replaces standard deviation in the Sharpe ratio with downside deviation.

**Source jurisdiction**   A framework used by a country to determine the basis for taxing income or transfers. A country that taxes income as a source within its borders imposes source jurisdiction.

**Source–source conflict**   When two countries claim source jurisdiction of the same asset; both countries may claim that the income is derived from their jurisdiction.

**Sovereign risk**   A form of credit risk in which the borrower is the government of a sovereign nation.

**Spot return**   (or price return) The component of the return on a commodity futures contract that comes from changes in the underlying spot prices via the cost-of-carry model.

**Spread duration**   The sensitivity of a non-Treasury security's price to a widening or narrowing of the spread over Treasuries.

**Spread risk**   Risk related to changes in the spread between Treasuries and non-Treasuries.

**Stack and roll**   A hedging strategy in which an existing stack hedge with maturing futures contracts is replaced by a new stack hedge with longer dated futures contracts.

**Stack hedge**   Hedging a stream of obligations by entering futures contracts with a *single* maturity, with the number of contracts selected so that changes in the *present value* of the future obligations are offset by changes in the value of this "stack" of futures contracts.

**Stale price bias**   Bias that arises from using prices that are stale because of infrequent trading.

**Static approach**   With respect to strategic asset allocation, an approach that does not account for links between optimal decisions in future time periods.

**Static spread**   (or zero-volatility spread) The constant spread above the Treasury spot curve that equates the calculated price of the security to the market price.

**Stationary**   A series of data for which the parameters that describe a return-generating process are stable.

**Status quo bias**   An emotional bias in which people do nothing (i.e., maintain the "status quo") instead of making a change.

**Status quo trap**   The tendency for forecasts to perpetuate recent observations—that is, to predict no change from the recent past.

**Sterling ratio**   The compound annualized rate of return over a specified time period divided by the average yearly maximum drawdown over the same time period less an arbitrary 10 percent.

**Stock companies**   With respect to insurance companies, companies that have issued common equity shares.

**Stock index futures**   Futures contracts on a specified stock index.

**Straddle**   An option strategy involving the purchase of a put and a call with the same exercise price. A straddle is based on the expectation of high volatility of the underlying.

**Straight-through processing**   Systems that simplify transaction processing through the minimization of manual and/or duplicative intervention in the process from trade placement to settlement.

**Strangle**   A variation of a straddle in which the put and call have different exercise prices.

**Strap**   An option strategy involving the purchase of two calls and one put.

**Strategic asset allocation**   1) The process of allocating money to IPS-permissible asset classes that integrates the investor's return objectives, risk tolerance, and investment constraints with long-run capital market expectations. 2) The result of the above process, also known as the policy portfolio.

**Stratified sampling**   (or representative sampling) A sampling method that guarantees that subpopulations of interest are represented in the sample.

**Strike spread**   A spread used to determine the strike price for the payoff of a credit option.

**Strip**   An option strategy involving the purchase of two puts and one call.

**Strip hedge**   Hedging a stream of obligations by offsetting each individual obligation with a futures contract matching the maturity and quantity of the obligation.

**Structural level of unemployment**   The level of unemployment resulting from scarcity of a factor of production.

**Structured note**   A variation of a floating-rate note that has some type of unusual characteristic such as a leverage factor or in which the rate moves opposite to interest rates.

**Style drift**   Inconsistency in style.

**Style index**   A securities index intended to reflect the average returns to a given style.

**Stylized scenario**   A type of analysis often used in stress testing. It involves simulating the movement in at least one interest rate, exchange rate, stock price, or commodity price relevant to the portfolio.

**Sunshine trades**   Public display of a transaction (usually high-volume) in advance of the actual order.

**Surplus**   The difference between the value of assets and the present value of liabilities. With respect to an insurance company, the net difference between the total assets and total liabilities (equivalent to policyholders' surplus for a mutual insurance company and stockholders' equity for a stock company).

**Surplus efficient frontier**   The graph of the set of portfolios that maximize expected surplus for given levels of standard deviation of surplus.

**Survey method**   A method of capital market expectations setting that involves surveying experts.

**Survival probability**   The probability an individual survives in a given year; used to determine expected cash flow required in retirement.

**Survivorship bias**   Bias that arises in a data series when managers with poor track records exit the business and are dropped from the database whereas managers with good records remain; when a data series as of a given date reflects only entities that have survived to that date.

**Swap**   A contract calling for the exchange of payments over time. Often one payment is fixed in advance and the other is floating, based upon the realization of a price or interest rate.

**Swap rate**   The interest rate applicable to the pay-fixed-rate side of an interest rate swap.

**Swap spread**   The difference between the fixed rate on an interest rate swap and the rate on a Treasury note with equivalent maturity; it reflects the general level of credit risk in the market.

**Swap tenor**   The lifetime of a swap.

**Swap term**   Another name for *swap tenor*.

**Swaption**   An option to enter into a swap.

**Symmetric cash flow matching**   A cash flow matching technique that allows cash flows occurring both before and after the liability date to be used to meet a liability; allows for the short-term borrowing of funds to satisfy a liability prior to the liability due date.

**Tactical asset allocation**   Asset allocation that involves making short-term adjustments to asset class weights based on short-term predictions of relative performance among asset classes.

**Tactical rebalancing**   A variation of calendar rebalancing that specifies less frequent rebalancing when markets appear to be trending and more frequent rebalancing when they are characterized by reversals.

**Tail value at risk**   (or conditional tail expectation) The VAR plus the expected loss in excess of VAR, when such excess loss occurs.

**Target covariance matrix**   A component of shrinkage estimation; allows the analyst to model factors that are believed to influence the data over periods longer than observed in the historical sample.

**Target semivariance**   The average squared deviation below a target value.

**Target value**   The value that the portfolio manager seeks to ensure; the value that the life insurance company has guaranteed the policyholder.

**Tax avoidance**   Developing strategies that minimize tax, while conforming to both the spirit and the letter of the tax codes of jurisdictions with taxing authority.

**Tax efficiency**   The proportion of the expected pretax total return that will be retained after taxes.

**Tax evasion**   The practice of circumventing tax obligations by illegal means such as misreporting or not reporting relevant information to tax authorities.

**Tax premium**   Compensation for the effect of taxes on the after-tax return of an asset.

**Tax risk**   The uncertainty associated with tax laws.

**Taylor rule**   A rule linking a central bank's target short-term interest rate to the rate of growth of the economy and inflation.

**Term life insurance**   A type of life insurance policy that provides coverage for a specified length of time and accumulates little or no cash values.

**Territorial tax system**   A framework used by a country to determine the basis for taxing income or transfers. A country that taxes income as a source within its borders imposes source jurisdiction.

**Testamentary gratuitous transfer**   The bequeathing or transfer of assets upon one's death. From a recipient's perspective, it is called an inheritance.

**Testator**   A person who makes a will.

**Theta**   The change in price of an option associated with a one-day reduction in its time to expiration; the rate at which an option's time value decays.

**Tick**   The smallest possible price movement of a security.

**Time deposit**   A deposit requiring advance notice prior to a withdrawal.

**Time to expiration**   The time remaining in the life of a derivative, typically expressed in years.

**Time-series estimators**   Estimators that are based on lagged values of the variable being forecast; often consist of lagged values of other selected variables.

**Time-weighted average price (TWAP) strategy**   A logical participation strategy that assumes a flat volume profile and trades in proportion to time.

**Time-weighted rate of return**   The compound rate of growth over a stated evaluation period of one unit of money initially invested in the account.

**Timing option**   With respect to certain futures contracts, the option that results from the ability of the short position to decide when in the delivery month actual delivery will take place.

**Tobin's *q*** An asset-based valuation measure that is equal to the ratio of the market value of debt and equity to the replacement cost of total assets.

**Top-down** Proceeding from the macroeconomy, to the economic sector level, to the industry level, to the firm level.

**Total factor productivity (TFP)** A variable which accounts for that part of $Y$ not directly accounted for by the levels of the production factors ($K$ and $L$).

**Total future liability** With respect to defined-benefit pension plans, the present value of accumulated and projected future service benefits, including the effects of projected future compensation increases.

**Total rate of return** A measure of the increase in the investor's wealth due to both investment income (for example, dividends and interest) and capital gains (both realized and unrealized).

**Total return** The rate of return taking into account capital appreciation/depreciation and income. Often qualified as follows: **Nominal** returns are unadjusted for inflation; **real** returns are adjusted for inflation; **pretax** returns are returns before taxes; **post-tax** returns are returns after taxes are paid on investment income and realized capital gains.

**Total return analysis** Analysis of the expected effect of a trade on the portfolio's total return, given an interest rate forecast.

**Total return swap** A swap in which one party agrees to pay the total return on a security. Often used as a credit derivative, in which the underlying is a bond.

**Tracking risk** (also called tracking error, tracking error volatility, or active risk) The condition in which the performance of a portfolio does not match the performance of an index that serves as the portfolio's benchmark.

**Trade blotter** A device for entering and tracking trade executions and orders to trade.

**Trade settlement** Completion of a trade wherein purchased financial instruments are transferred to the buyer and the buyer transfers money to the seller.

**Trading activity** In fixed-income attribution analysis, the effect of sales and purchases of bonds over a given period; the total portfolio return minus the other components determining the management effect in an attribution analysis.

**Transaction exposure** The risk associated with a foreign exchange rate on a specific business transaction such as a purchase or sale.

**Translation exposure** The risk associated with the conversion of foreign financial statements into domestic currency.

**Transparency** Availability of timely and accurate market and trade information.

**Treasury spot curve** The term structure of Treasury zero coupon bonds.

**Twist** With respect to the yield curve, a movement in contrary directions of interest rates at two maturities; a nonparallel movement in the yield curve.

**Type I error** With respect to manager selection, keeping (or hiring) managers with zero value-added. (Rejecting the null hypothesis when it is correct).

**Type II error** With respect to manager selection, firing (or not hiring) managers with positive value-added. (Not rejecting the null hypothesis when it is incorrect).

**Unconstrained optimization** Optimization that places no constraints on asset class weights except that they sum to 1. May produce negative asset weights, which implies borrowing or shorting of assets.

**Underfunded plan** A pension plan in which the ratio of the value of plan assets to the present value of plan liabilities is less than 100 percent.

**Underlying** An asset that trades in a market in which buyers and sellers meet, decide on a price, and the seller then delivers the asset to the buyer and receives payment. The underlying is the asset or other derivative on which a particular derivative is based. The market for the underlying is also referred to as the spot market.

**Underwriting (profitability) cycle** A cycle affecting the profitability of insurance companies' underwriting operations.

**Unhedged return** A foreign asset return stated in terms of the investor's home currency.

**Unit-linked life insurance** (or variable life insurance) A type of ordinary life insurance in which death benefits and cash values are linked to the investment performance of a policyholder-selected pool of investments held in a so-called separate account.

**Universal life insurance** A type of life insurance policy that provides for premium flexibility, an adjustable face amount of death benefits, and current market interest rates on the savings element.

**Unrelated business income** With respect to the U.S. tax code, income that is not substantially related to a foundation's charitable purposes.

**Unstructured modeling** Modeling without a theory on the underlying structure.

**Uptick rules** Trading rules that specify that a short sale must not be on a downtick relative to the last trade at a different price.

**Urgency of the trade** The importance of certainty of execution.

**Utility** The level of relative satisfaction received from the consumption of goods and services.

**Utility theory** Theory whereby people maximize the present value of utility subject to a present value budget constraint.

**Valuation reserve** With respect to insurance companies, an allowance, created by a charge against earnings, to provide for losses in the value of the assets.

**Value** The amount for which one can sell something, or the amount one must pay to acquire something.

**Value at risk (VAR)** A probability-based measure of loss potential for a company, a fund, a portfolio, a transaction, or a strategy over a specified period of time.

**Value weighted** (or market-capitalization weighted) With respect to index construction, an index in which each security in the index is weighted according to its market capitalization.

**Value-motivated traders** Traders that act on value judgments based on careful, sometimes painstaking research. They trade only when the price moves into their value range.

**Variable annuity** A life annuity in which the periodic payment varies depending on stock prices.

**Variable life insurance** (or unit-linked life insurance) A type of ordinary life insurance in which death benefits and cash values are linked to the investment performance of a policyholder-selected pool of investments held in a so-called separate account.

**Variable prepaid forward** A monetization strategy that involves the combination of a collar with a loan against the value of the underlying shares. When the loan comes due, shares are sold to pay off the loan and part of any appreciation is shared with the lender.

**Variable universal life** (or flexible-premium variable life) A type of life insurance policy that combines the flexibility of universal life with the investment choice flexibility of variable life.

**Vega** A measure of the sensitivity of an option's price to changes in the underlying's volatility.

**Venture capital** The equity financing of new or growing private companies.

**Venture capital firms** Firms representing dedicated pools of capital for providing equity or equity-linked financing to privately held companies.

**Venture capital fund** A pooled investment vehicle for venture capital investing.

**Venture capital trusts** An exchange-traded, closed-end vehicle for venture capital investing.

**Venture capitalists** Specialists who seek to identify companies that have good business opportunities but need financial, managerial, and strategic support.

**Vested** With respect to pension benefits or assets, said of an unconditional ownership interest.

**Vintage year** With reference to a private equity fund, the year it closed.

**Vintage year effects** The effects on returns shared by private equity funds closed in the same year.

**Volatility** Represented by the Greek letter sigma ($\sigma$), the standard deviation of price outcomes associated with an underlying asset.

**Volatility clustering** The tendency for large (small) swings in prices to be followed by large (small) swings of random direction.

**Volume-weighted average price** (or VWAP) The average price at which a security is traded during the day, where each trade price is weighted by the fraction of the day's volume associated with the trade.

**Volume-weighted average price (VWAP) strategy** A logical participation strategy that involves breaking up an order over time according to a prespecified volume profile.

**Wealth relative** The ending value of one unit of money invested at specified rates of return.

**Weather derivative** A derivative contract with a payment based on a weather-related measurement, such as heating or cooling degree days.

**Whole life insurance** (also ordinary life insurance) A type of life insurance policy that involves coverage for the whole of the insured's life.

**Wild card option** A provision allowing a short futures contract holder to delay delivery of the underlying.

**Will** (or testament) A document associated with estate planning that outlines the rights others will have over one's property after death.

**Within-sector selection return** In attribution analysis, a measure of the impact of a manager's security selection decisions relative to the holdings of the sector benchmark.

**Worst-case scenario analysis** A stress test in which we examine the worst case that we actually expect to occur.

**Yardeni model** An equity valuation model, more complex than the Fed model, that incorporates the expected growth rate in earnings.

**Yield beta** A measure of the sensitivity of a bond's yield to a general measure of bond yields in the market that is used to refine the hedge ratio.

**Yield curve** The relationship between yield and time to maturity.

**Yield curve risk** Risk related to changes in the shape of the yield curve.

**Yield to worst** The yield on a callable bond that assumes a bond is called at the earliest opportunity.

**Zero-cost collar** A transaction in which a position in the underlying is protected by buying a put and selling a call with the premium from the sale of the call offsetting the premium from the purchase of the put. It can also be used to protect a floating-rate borrower against interest rate increases with the premium on a long cap offsetting the premium on a short floor.

**Zero-premium collar** A hedging strategy involving the simultaneous purchase of puts and sale of call options on a stock. The puts are struck below and the calls are struck above the underlying's market price.

# Index